THE LIBRARY

OF

CHARLES E. FEINBERG

DETROIT

PART I

AUTOGRAPHS AND MANUSCRIPTS

Publ

Tuesday · April 2 at

Wednesday · A

{SALE
CATALOGUE PR

PARKE-BERNET

980 Madison

CATALOGUE No. 1191

FIRST EDITIONS

OF

AMERICAN AUTHORS

AND

OTHER MISCELLANEOUS WORKS

COLLECTED BY

J. Chester Chamberlain

OF NEW YORK

PART TWO

ALDRICH	EVERETT	PARKMAN
BANCROFT	FISKE	PRESCOTT
BRET HARTE	HALLECK	STEDMAN
COOPER	HOWELLS	STODDARD
CURTIS	MITCHELL	TAYLOR
DRAKE	MOTLEY	WHITMAN

AND IMPORTANT DUPLICATES OF

BRYANT	HOLMES	LOWELL
ON	IRVING	POE
HORNE	LONGFELLOW	THOREAU
	WHITTIER	

NOVEMBER 4 AND 5, 1909

Y AFTERNOON, · · · Lots 1–197
Y EVENING, · · · " 198–393
AFTERNOON, · · · " 394–596
EVENING, · · · " 597–788

SALES BEGIN AT 2.30 AND 8.15 O'CLOCK

Anderson Auction Company

12 East 46th Street
New York

TELEPHONE, MURRAY HILL 190

SALE NUMBER 4251

EXHIBITION DAILY FROM APRIL 11
WEEKDAYS 9 TO 6 · SUNDAY 2 TO 5

Manuscripts, Autograph Letters
First Editions and Portraits of

WALT WHITMAN

Formerly the Property of the Late
DR. RICHARD MAURICE BUCKE
London, Ontario, Canada

Purchased at Public Sale in London, England, by
THE ULYSSES BOOKSHOP, LTD.

Or by Private Treaty by
DR. JACOB SCHWARTZ
London, England

To be Dispersed at Public Sale
April 15 and 16, at 8:15 p.m.

By Order of Dr. Jacob Schwartz
Individually and as President of the
Ulysses Bookshop, Ltd., London, England

FOREWORD BY CHRISTOPHER MORLEY

AMERICAN ART ASSOCIATION
ANDERSON GALLERIES · INC

30 EAST 57TH STREET · NEW YORK

1936

No. 887

CATALOGUE OF

LIBRARY OF ASSOCIATION

AND THE

UTOGRAPH COLLECTION

OF

mund Clarence Stedman

PART III

S AND MANUSCRIPTS OF EDMUND CLARENCE
DGAR ALLAN POE, WITH THE MANUSCRIPT
OF A PART OF "MARGINALIA," JAMES WHITCOMB
RILEY, WM. SHARP, PERCY BYSSHE SHELLEY, R. H.
STODDARD, ALGERNON CHARLES SWINBURNE,
BAYARD TAYLOR, WM. WATSON, WALT
WHITMAN, J. G. WHITTIER,

MANUSCRIPT OF THOMSON'S "CITY OF DREADFUL NIGHT,"
AND MANY OTHER IMPORTANT SINGLE ITEMS.

TO BE SOLD

JANUARY 24 AND 25, 1911

TUESDAY AFTERNOON,	· · ·	Lots 2159–2509
TUESDAY EVENING,	· · ·	" 2510–2814
WEDNESDAY AFTERNOON,	· · ·	" 2815–3113
WEDNESDAY EVENING,	· · ·	" 3114–3372

SALES BEGIN AT 2.30 AND 8.15 O'CLOCK

The Anderson Auction Company

12 East 46th Street
New York

TELEPHONE, BRYANT 271

Valuable Library of

Thomas B. Harned, Esq.

One of the Literary Executors of Walt Whitman,

INCLUDING

Much Autographic and other material relating to Walt Whitman

AND

Fine and Special Editions of the most noted English, American
and French Authors, many in Fine Bindings

WORKS ON THE FINE ARTS

AND MISCELLANEOUS LITERATURE

TO BE SOLD

TUESDAY AFTERNOON, MAY 8th, 1917

AT 2.30 O'CLOCK.

WHITMAN

AT

AUCTION

1899-1972

Overleaf—The Robert J. Hammershlag copy which sold at American Art Association Anderson Galleries on 18 January 1935 for $1850 and again in the Frank Capra Sale at Parke-Bernet Galleries on 27 April 1949 for $1600. See p. 402.

Walt Whitman
August 9 1884

Leaves

of

Grass.

———•———

Brooklyn, New York:
1855.

WHITMAN

AT

AUCTION

1899-1972

Compiled by
Gloria A. Francis
Artem Lozynsky

Introduction by
Charles E. Feinberg

 A Bruccoli Clark Book

Gale Research Company, Book Tower, Detroit

First Printing

Book design and layout by Margaret Swanson Clark

Photography by Earle A. Williamson,
John Henderson Studios

Library of Congress Cataloging in Publication Data

Main entry under title:

Whitman at auction, 1899-1972.

    "A Bruccoli Clark book."
    Includes index.
    1. Whitman, Walt, 1819-1892--Bibliography--Catalogs.
2. Catalogs, Booksellers'. 3. Libraries, Private.
I. Francis, Gloria A. II. Lozynsky, Artem, 1941-
Z8971.5.W49 ₍PS3231₎   016.811'3   77-16647
ISBN 0-8103-0921-1

To. F. F. and H. F., J. L. and S. L.

CONTENTS

"It is truly remarkable that no one,
as far as I know, has had the idea
of summoning authors from their graves
and having them attend an auction of
their immortal works."

—Soren Kierkegaard.

FOREWORD

After the auctioneer brings the hammer down on the last lot, and the successful bidders assess their purchases and leave the auction room, there remains as a matter of record the auction catalogue. Originally compiled as a vehicle for a commercial enterprise, the auction catalogue eventually becomes a tool for reference and research. It can help establish provenance of unique items such as manuscripts, letters and association copies; it can prove the mere existence of a certain item that arrived at the auction room and subsequently dropped from view; and it can provide elusive bibliographical information not readily found elsewhere. Bringing together in one compilation the auction catalogues of significant sales of the works of a particular author not only presents a picture of the author's "collectibility"—his reputation among collectors as it waxes or wanes throughout the years—but also provides, in a single unit, hitherto scattered resource materials important to the study of the author.

Whitman at Auction, 1899-1972 reproduces pages from forty-three auction catalogues containing substantial and representative Whitman material recorded in *American Book Prices Current* and *Book-Auction Records*. Selections were made from over 470 catalogues examined. Whenever possible, we have reproduced all Whitman items from those catalogues most important in the history of Whitman collecting; other catalogues have been excerpted to avoid needless repetition and omit irrelevant material.

Two distinct but interwoven strands form the pattern of this volume. Included are the auction catalogues of Whitman's disciples and friends, who acquired their collections first-hand from the poet himself, and the bibliophiles and scholars who acquired them on the open market, either through book dealers or auction houses. Representative of the first group are Whitman's literary executors, Dr. Richard Maurice Bucke and Thomas B. Harned; his contemporary biographers, John Burroughs and Col. Thomas Donaldson; and such friends as John H. Johnston and Dr. Isaac Hull Platt.[1] The second group includes such well-known collectors as George M. Williamson, H. Buxton Forman, William F. Gable, Jerome Kern and A. Edward Newton.

---

[1]Whitman's third literary executor, Horace L. Traubel, gave away his Whitman material; accordingly, we see his property recorded in the catalogues of his friends such as Thomas Bird Mosher.

The autograph collection of Col. Thomas Donaldson, which was put on the block in 1899, was the first substantial Whitman material sold at auction. The catalogue was compiled by the auctioneer, Stan. V. Henkels, who had deemed it necessary only a year previous to identify Whitman for his clientele as "a wild, pathetic and nonsensical poet." Henkels's descriptions of the manuscripts were meager; however, he waxed eloquent over two Tennyson letters to Whitman. The prices fetched correlated with the length of the descriptions—the Tennyson letters brought $21.00 and $23.00, while Whitman manuscripts ranged from $3.50 to $11.00.

Among the early collectors of American first editions who recognized Walt Whitman as a major literary figure were George M. Williamson and Jacob Chester Chamberlain. Auctions of their collections took place in 1904, 1908, and 1909. The 30-31 January 1908 sale of the Williamson collection included two copies of the first issue, first edition of *Leaves of Grass*—one in the original pink wrappers, the other in the original green cloth. The two copies fetched $95.00 and $90.00, acceptable prices in comparison to the $12.75, $13.50, $18.50, and $26.00 recorded in previous auctions. The high spot of the Chamberlain sale was lot 668, Whitman's own copy of *Two Rivulets* with his holograph corrections and revisions. This brought $137.50.

In 1917 the library of Thomas B. Harned was put up for sale, again under the hammer of Stan. V. Henkels. Forty-nine items of Whitmaniana fetched a total of $496.50. Two years later Henkels handled Dr. Isaac Hull Platt's collection, describing it as "the most important collection of manuscripts, books and relics of Walt Whitman ever offered for public sale." (He forgot his Donaldson sale of 1899!) Henkels at this point, along with the more astute collectors of American literature, was at last recognizing the importance of Walt Whitman. Only one lot from the Platt sale is reproduced in this volume, since a subsequent auction—that of William W. Cohen—includes all the major items.

The 1920s saw the sale of the collections of H. Buxton Forman, Carolyn Wells Houghton (the Whitman bibliographer), William F. Gable, Jerome Kern, and William H. Cohen. H. Buxton Forman was the noted editor of Keats and Shelley and a great admirer of Whitman. His endorsement of Whitman had an important influence on furthering Whitman's literary reputation among British authors and critics. Of the ninety-four Whitman items in the Forman sales, the compilers have selected a sampling of lots containing Forman's customary bibliographic notes.

On 18 October 1923, one year after the publication of *A Concise Bibliography of the Works of Walt Whitman* by Carolyn Wells and Alfred F. Goldsmith, Carolyn Wells Houghton put up for auction at Anderson Galleries duplicates and selections from her library, her reason being that the "library has utterly outgrown its bookcases." A high spot of this sale was one of two known copies of *Letters Written by Walt Whitman to his Mother from 1866 to 1872*, which was knocked down at $500. Further Whitman material from the Houghton collection reached auction in 1942 after her death. The collection of Alfred F. Goldsmith was auctioned at the Swann Auction Galleries in 1947.

In the same year as the Houghton sale came the first of eight auctions of the outstanding collection of English and American authors formed by William F. Gable. The collection was sold by the order of his executor, "that his books, manuscripts and letters that meant so much to William F. Gable should go to other loving hands." The sales took place from 5-6 November 1923 to 16 April 1925 and included 259 Whitman lots. Many of the Whitman volumes were enhanced by manuscript fragments or inserted letters, which was characteristic of Gable's bibliophilic taste.

John Burroughs's Whitman material reached the auction market in 1927 and 1931 through sales of the property of Dr. Clara Barrus, Burroughs's biographer and literary executor. The sale of 25 November 1927 saw the highest price paid for a Whitman manuscript to that time—$1,900 for the fourteen-page introduction to the London edition of *Leaves of Grass* (lot 136).

The sale of the library of Jerome Kern in January 1929 realized phenomenal prices. His copy of the 1855 *Leaves of Grass* brought $3,400, a staggering figure. However, one month later at the William W. Cohen sale, another copy topped this price by $50. About forty years would pass before a comparable figure would be reached once more. Of particular note in the Cohen sale is lot 501, nine autograph letters and one telegram from Whitman to James R. Osgood & Co. concerning the suppression of *Leaves of Grass*. This series of letters appeared originally at auction at Bangs and Company, New York, in 1898 and brought $23. The successful bid at the Cohen sale was $1,100.

The monumental sales of Whitman material occurred in the thirties when the entire collection (with a few exceptions) of Dr. Richard Maurice Bucke was purchased at the Sotheby auction of 13 May 1935 by Dr. Jacob Schwartz of the Ulysses Bookshop, removed to New York, and offered again at auction on 15-16 April 1936 in the American Art Association / Anderson Galleries. Dr. Schwartz increased the number of lots offered to the bidders by separating items grouped together at Sotheby's. Descriptions were expanded. Newly-made bindings, hand-drawn title-pages, and typed transcriptions were provided for the manuscripts. The total amount realized at the Sotheby sale was £1,655 / 15 (roughly $8,060.00). The American Art Association sale totalled $13,489.50. If one compares individual items in both sales it is obvious that the return on Dr. Schwartz's investment was disappointing. Six Whitman letters to Sergeant Thomas P. Sawyer brought £48 ($233) in the Sotheby sale (lot 57) and $355 at American Art (lot 166); Whitman's holograph account of the adjournment of the House of Representatives of the 37th Congress brought £20 ($97) as lot 57A at Sotheby's and $50 as lot 164 at American Art; Whitman letters to Bethuel Smith brought £11 ($53) as lots 58/59 at Sotheby's and $35 as lot 168 at American Art.

In addition to the second Barrus sale and the Bucke sales in the thirties, two other outstanding Whitman auctions took place, one of which was at the Rains Galleries on 25-26 March 1936. Sixty-seven lots at that sale brought a total of $7,255, with the highest-priced lot being number 245, Whitman's holograph will of 15 May 1873, which fetched $3,100. This document originally sold at the first Barrus auction in 1927 for $1,300. It seems incredible when one looks at the Rains sale and the Bucke sale, one month later, that there could be such a disparity in the hammer prices—even taking into account the unknown variables that might affect any auction. The other outstanding Whitman auction of the period was the 13-14 January 1937 sale at the American Art Association Anderson Galleries. The Whitman portion of the catalogue followed closely the format of the Bucke sale, but included fuller notes, quotations from manuscripts, and specific references to the 1902 edition of Whitman's *Writings* to help identify the manuscripts. It was a thorough and admirable job of descriptive cataloguing and a far cry from the terse and often inadequate descriptions of the 1899 Donaldson sale, the first sale reproduced in this volume. When eleven of the items returned to the Parke-Bernet Galleries in 1946 to be auctioned by order of the widow of William W. Cohen, the descriptions were used without any change.

After the major sales of the 1930s, the comprehensiveness and quality of the Whitman material at auction dropped off sharply. Significant sales in the next three decades were sporadic and characterized primarily by a scant number of lots. This presented a great challenge to collectors. Instead of picking up basketsful of plums, they had to scour the trees.

There were approximately seventy-five auctions in the 1940s which included Whitman material, but all except a handful offered only one or two items of any interest to the buying public. The three-part A. Edward Newton sale in 1941 contained only seventeen Whitman lots, of which the compilers have selected only one—a Whitman holograph concerning the unauthorized publication of *Leaves of Grass* by Richard Worthington. The Howard J. Sachs sale at Parke-Bernet Galleries on 1 February 1944 included two Whitman lots, exciting because they reveal Whitman's relationship with two of his contemporary British authors, Bram Stoker and Oscar Wilde. Lot 119, the first issue of the 1855 *Leaves of Grass* inscribed to John Boyle O'Reilly with a holograph note by Oscar Wilde, did not meet Parke-Bernet's estimate of between $2,000 and $3,000, and was knocked down for only $1,050. Thomas Bird Mosher's material was auctioned off in two sales at the Parke-Bernet Galleries on 10-11 May and 11 October 1948. Excerpts from the first sale have been included in this volume.

The 1950s and 1960s show a steady decline in the number of auctions containing significant Whitman material: down by twenty-five sales in the fifties and thirty-five in the sixties from the peak years of the thirties; with much of the manuscript material reappearing from previous sales. This, of course, furnished an opportunity for younger collectors—or those whose interest in Whitman was newly developing or whose pocketbooks could now afford the strain—to put together a Whitman collection of some depth. The highlight of the two decades was the appearance of what is considered to be the only surviving page of manuscript from *Leaves of Grass*, which was put up for sale at the Parke-Bernet Galleries on 12 May 1953. John H. Johnston's collection, especially rich in materials associated with Whitman's disciples, came to auction at Swann Galleries in 1957 through his daughter, Bertha Johnston.

Whitman at auction concludes with the sale at Sotheby's on 17-18 July 1972 of the property of Mrs. Madeleine Buxton Holmes, granddaughter of H. Buxton Forman. The Whitman material was somehow not included in the Forman sales of 1920 and remained in the family until 1972, unknown to Whitman scholars. The appearance of the letters and manuscripts caused a stir among the institutional and private collectors. It had been many years since such exciting Whitman manuscripts had come on the market. The bidding was spirited, but all fifteen lots were knocked down to the House of El Dieff for the total price of £9555 ($23,218.65). The material is now in the Berg Collection of the New York Public Library.

As a final observation on the Walt Whitman auction market, it is apparent that less and less original material will reach the block, since private collectors of the stature of Charles E. Feinberg generally choose to place their collections in an institution rather than to disperse them at public sale. The years to come, then, will bring very little action in the Whitman market.

The compilers wish to thank Charles E. Feinberg, whose knowledge of Whitman was so readily and generously made available; C. E. Frazer Clark, Jr.; Mary Brown, The American Antiquarian Society; Charles W. Mann, Jr., Pennsylvania State University Library; Joel Myerson, University of South Carolina; the staff of the Henry Ford Museum Library, Dearborn, Michigan; and the Burton Historical Collection of the Detroit Public Library.

> How all times mischoose the objects of their adulation and reward,
> And how the same inexorable price must still be paid for the same great purchase.

> Walt Whitman, "Beginners."

INTRODUCTION

Walt Whitman, discussing George Williamson's request for the manuscript of *November Boughs*, said to Horace Traubel that "the whole mania for collecting things strikes me as evidence of a disease—sometimes of a disease in an acute form." While every collector has his reasons for collecting, it is hard to disagree with Whitman's diagnosis. I have never felt my collecting to be just a mania for owning things, but my intense interest in an individual author has put me in determined pursuit of every fragment of Whitman's autograph. Acquisition is the first law of a good collector and I don't think this ever changes. What does change is what you learn to do with your collection. In the end, the use made of your collection is what matters.

My feelings about my collecting changed when I found that scholars were interested in what I was accumulating. Today, we are involved in vast areas of literary research and scholarly re-evaluation of our literary heritage which have necessarily widened the importance of collecting first editions, manuscripts, and letters. This scholarly interest has changed the attitude of many collectors. Collectors still cherish the capture of a rare prize and feel all the pride and physical pleasure of ownership they have always felt. But now there is a sense of added responsibility, an obligation to make new information available to scholarship.

Many of today's collectors, particularly collectors who have built single-author, subject, or special-area collections, feel a responsibility to keep intact any collection so fruitfully brought together that it represents more in its sum than in its parts. Where the past generation of collectors, like George M. Williamson, Dr. R. M. Bucke, Stephen H. Wakeman, Charles B. Foote, Jerome Kern, Thomas Streeter, and others consigned their monumental collections to auction to be broken up for the benefit of other buyers, many of today's collectors seek to have their collections preserved at a single institution, because only an institution can assume the responsibility of keeping them intact for future generations.

The collector's tendency as he gains experience is to specialize—to choose a period, a subject matter, or the life of a man. This serves scholarship better. Anyone who has done research for a biography of someone long dead knows how many libraries and archives, scattered in many cities, one has to visit—just for the published material. And when one has to find manuscripts and letters, it's a blessing to find the material concentrated in a few places.

The collector has his satisfaction and sport in bringing the material together. I have. I have had excitement and pleasure and education: the friendships I have enjoyed; the cooperation of dealers in this country and abroad; and the chase of acquiring Whitman manuscript notes, fragments, trial lines of poems and prose, manuscripts of every conceivable size—from one page to hundreds of pages—letters and drafts of letters, slips for diary entries, tiny homemade notebooks used for hospital notes, labels for sending out various pieces of writing and photographs, marginalia on articles, galley proofs and page proofs, instructions to printers, lists of names and addresses, checks, old envelopes. All this is essential to a determined collector.

In my acquisitions I have discovered and recovered, as is possible in no other way, a great many of Whitman's rejected thoughts, his discarded phrases, his cancelled passages and stillborn paragraphs. Many of the manuscripts reveal Whitman's mind at work, correcting, rejecting, and substituting. All these furnish a clue to his taste and the process of his thought. The poet who wrote nine versions of "Out of the Cradle Endlessly Rocking" provides a convincing demonstration of his creative intelligence at work. He also proves that he was not a careless poet.

All this material was generated by Whitman—and for only one reason have I brought it together again. It was all written and handled by Whitman, and this makes it important. Following this reasoning, I have also collected the books from Whitman's library, particularly with his signature on the title page, and other books inscribed by him.

I have shared my collection with scholars by allowing publication of the Whitman manuscripts and letters in my possession. The final repository for my Walt Whitman collection is our National Library, The Library of Congress.

I

Wherever bookmen get together they talk about the market drying up— that books, manuscripts, and letters are being presented to institutions, and that collections are no longer being formed because material is no longer available. Occasionally entire collections are still being placed on the auction block—the Streeter Collection is a good example. High market prices have brought out many minor collections and individual items, but sales are certainly not as frequent nor as important as they used to be. The sale of a collection of Whitman letters at the Rains Galleries of New York, 25-26 March 1936 tells its own story. All these letters were written to William Sloane Kennedy and were included in the sale that was advertised as "a fine collection of letters and manuscripts by Walt Whitman together with his will dated May 15, 1873." The collection was dispersed as follows: one letter is now in the Huntington Public Library, Huntington, Long Island, New York; one letter is at Ohio Wesleyan University, Delaware, Ohio; two of the letters are in the C. Waller Barrett Collection at the University of Virginia, Charlottesville, Virginia; four letters are at Rutgers University, New Brunswick, New Jersey; four letters are in the Trent Collection, Duke University, Durham, North Carolina; and ten letters are in the Feinberg Collection at The Library of Congress. We have no knowledge of the whereabouts of the remaining seven letters. (I would appreciate hearing from anyone having a letter from Whitman to W. S. Kennedy in his private or institutional library collection.) But of the thirty-one letters available for purchase in 1936, at least twenty-four are now in permanent collections at institutional libraries.

II

It is natural to remember and write a few words about the Walt Whitman items that I was successful in buying at different auction sales, and yet I will always remember a sale where I lost the chance to buy an item. The fault was mine. In the Howard J. Sachs sale (1 February 1944) there was listed a first edition of *Leaves of Grass* (1855) signed in 1877 by John Boyle O'Reilly, Irish patriot and American poet-journalist. Walt Whitman inscribed it, "The days in Boston on my visit—April 12th-19th—1881—the good times with you dear Boyle & my other dear new friends—the affectionate kindnesses—talks, etc. Walt Whitman." Whitman had written that when he was in Boston for the publication by James R. Osgood of *Leaves of Grass* (1881-1882), the suppressed edition; and Oscar Wilde, who signed this copy while visiting Boston in 1882 after seeing Whitman in Camden, New Jersey, in January, had added his inscription below Whitman's: "The spirit who living blamelessly yet dared to kiss the smitten mouth of his own century. Oscar Wilde." I was not in New York at the sale and had given my bid to my dealer, David Kirschenbaum of Carnegie Books, with a limit of $1,000. Gabriel Wells, a New York dealer acting for an anonymous bidder, bought the book for $1,050. I phoned Mr. Wells immediately after I had the news from my dealer, and Wells asked $3,000, which was beyond me. To this day I am sorry I lost the book, and I have never found out to whom.

The library of the late Thomas Bird Mosher (Parke-Bernet, 10-11 May 1948) was of interest to me. I had never met him, but his publications were familiar to me. His facsimile of the first edition of *Leaves of Grass* was an early possession of mine. I also knew of his friendship with Horace Traubel, one of Walt Whitman's literary executors. Mrs. Anne Montgomerie Traubel had shown me some of Mosher's printings of Whitman titles and had told me of the Whitman items that her husband, Horace, had given Mosher. The sale catalogue verified what she had told me. I went to New York with mixed emotions. Though money at that time was tight, I should have bought much more than I did. Item 471, Whitman's "Whispers of Heavenly Death" was the star attraction among the Whitman items—a fine association items with a poem entirely in Whitman's hand, including his revisions. It brought some spirited bidding, and I added it to my collection. After another item, we came to what I felt was a particularly important lot. It was a scarce Whitman title, *Memoranda During the War*, described in the catalogue as "unbound unstitched sheets." Whitman had given it to Traubel, who in turn gave it to Thomas Mosher. I had seen a letter from Traubel referring to this item as proof sheets. To verify that these were indeed proof sheets, I had measured the sheets before the sale and had found them larger than the published pages. I instructed Dave Kirschenbaum to buy. I very rarely ask him to bid without a limit, but I did so on this occasion. The bid opened at twenty-five dollars. We bid fifty, and there were no further bids. Another Whitman collector, a stockbroker coming uptown to the sale from Wall Street, had been delayed in traffic and arrived late. After the sale, he remarked to me, "Do you know what you stole?" I nodded yes. I left this sale very satisfied with our afternoon's results.

I have been chided for having an obsession about letters of literary interest, possibly because I have acquired every Whitman letter that I could, except during periods when I had little or no money. I know now that I made mistakes. One of the greatest of the mistakes was in not buying items, even when I had no money. If you pass up the purchase of a first edition, there is always the possibility of another copy becoming available next year or in ten years or even twenty. But my experience has proven that if you do not buy a letter or a manuscript you want at the time that it is available, you will not likely get another chance in your lifetime.

Most book dealers and collectors remember the first sale in May 1948 of the library of Thomas Bird Mosher. But few remember the sale of the final portion of his library later in October of the same year, included in the sale with libraries of other collectors. There was only one

Whitman lot listed in the catalogue, item 590, appraised at $75. It was catalogued as a collection of material relating to Walt Whitman or of Whitman interest, and was in a box the size of a shirt box. I looked at it without too much interest, as it looked like a number of leftovers from the earlier sale. I bought it for very little and, among other things, acquired Mosher's manuscript introduction to the facsimile edition of *Leaves of Grass* (1919), many letters written to him on the publishing of other Whitman titles, and a few water-soaked pieces of a Whitman letter draft. I put the pieces of the letter together, but some were missing. I did not have the exact date—that part of the letter was missing—and I had no way of knowing to whom it was addressed. In the body of the letter there was a name "Al," and I knew from the draft of the letter itself that it was written to a soldier, because of the war and hospital experiences mentioned.

For many years I searched for Whitman letters written to this "Al." I looked for Alfreds, Alberts, and Allens. I checked Whitman's writings on the Civil War, checked his hospital notebooks, but never found the right soldier. Years later at the University of Nebraska, a professor told me of a friend who knew someone who had a letter from Whitman to a grandfather who had been a Civil War soldier. He promised to get me the name of his friend. After waiting a few months, I got the name of the individual who supposedly had the letter. I wrote and, after waiting six months, I wrote again—no reply. One day I picked up the telephone and talked with the person I had written to. There had been illness and death in the family and no opportunity to answer my letters. Yes, they had a Whitman letter, and the grandfather to whom the letter had been written was named Alfred. I told my story of the pieces of the draft I had and said I would send it on to them to see if it corresponded to the one they had. In a short time I had the answer. I had found the Civil War soldier to whom Whitman had written, and I acquired not only the letter for which I had the draft, but also several other Whitman letters, written to the parents of the soldier while he was in the Washington hospital where Whitman had visited him and to the young man himself after he had moved out West. What I had bought for a song at the second Mosher sale led to an interesting collecting experience.

IV

I had bought some desirable Whitman items from Arthur Pforzheimer, the book dealer upstairs on East 56th Street. The items came from the Dr. Jacob Schwartz Sale of the Dr. R. M. Bucke Collection. I happened to be in New York when the inventory of the Pforzheimer book business was being sold at the Kende Galleries by the order of the estate. One item in the sale was a page of Whitman manuscript numbered "2." The page had been presented to Ernest Crosby by John H. Johnston, a Fifth Avenue jeweler and friend of Walt Whitman's. Some of Whitman's friends to whom he had presented complete manuscripts had no compunction about breaking up the manuscript and distributing a page or two at various times to people they wanted to please.

The page I acquired proved to be a part of an article titled "How I Get Around and Take Notes at Sixty," which was published in the first issue of *The Critic* (29 January 1881). I immediately got in touch with the surviving children of John H. Johnston, who at that time were living in Brooklyn, and found that they still had pages "9" and "10" of the same article. By acquiring these two pages I had reunited three pages of what I knew to be an eleven-page manuscript. Then came the fun of trying to locate the missing pages. I found page "1" at the Library of Congress and page "7" at Yale University, where it had been acquired from the Henry Goldsmith Collection. Several years ago, while visiting the University of Texas, I found pages "4" and "5" in the De Golyer Collection. I learned that Mr. De Golyer had acquired his two pages from a dealer in London, and that these two pages had been presented to Sir Henry Irving by Johnston.

Then an unusual event occurred which shows how curious collecting can be. When I found page "1" of the Whitman manuscript at The Library of Congress, I had naturally assumed it would be there forever. The collecting world was very surprised to learn in 1963 that this item, and various other literary and historical documents, had been only provisionally deposited at The Library of Congress by the American Academy of Arts and Letters and would be auctioned at Sotheby's in London. I bought this page and added it to those already in my collection—with which it has ultimately returned to The Library of Congress. I am still looking for pages "3," "6," "8," and "11" of the Whitman manuscript Johnston so cavalierly broke up.

V

In 1953, I was called by an old friend, Arthur Swann of Parke-Bernet, and asked whether Whitman had ever made a statement regarding the original manuscript of *Leaves of Grass*. I referred him to the unimpeachable source which credited Whitman with saying that the original manuscript had been used accidentally to start a fire at the printer's. Sometime later Parke-Bernet announced a sale of "Choice Whitman Material Including the Only Known Manuscript Page from *Leaves of Grass*."

I asked several well-known Whitman scholars to examine the page and received various opinions. The age of the paper was right. One imaginative scholar gave me his version as to how it survived the fire. One wasn't certain of the manuscript's authenticity because of the cancellation of a word. And so on. Finally I went to New York the day prior to the sale and examined the page for myself. There were a number of educated guesses as to what price it would bring. Arthur Swann in answer to a question as to what would happen to the value if other pages were found, cited his experience with the Gutenberg Bible pages. He was positive that whatever price the Whitman page would bring would be a base price if any other pages were found in the future. A competing collector told me that his expert knew of a dozen such pages at Duke University and that he would not be bidding on the item. The opening bid was $500. There was a short spurt of bids—each bid raising the price by $100—then my successful bid of $1,500, a price I considered very low. After the excitement had died down, Dave Kirschenbaum and I were approached by a dealer who offered $5000 for the page. When I asked him for an explanation, he answered that his instructions were not to bid, but to make the offer if I bought the page because my purchase would authenticate it. My erstwhile competitor came up to tell me he thought I had made a mistake: but I knew he had blundered, because I was familiar with the holdings of the Trent-Bucke Collection at Duke University and knew that this page was different. The reason I was so positive about the authenticity of the manuscript was that Whitman drew a line down the face of the page, which meant it had been set in type. He must have had an idea for a poem while the Rome Brothers were setting his manuscript, because on the verso of the page he had listed several columns of words and definitions. The words were used in "Song of the Broad-Axe," published in the second edition of *Leaves of Grass* (1856). Of the thirty-three words that Whitman listed in the first column, he used four in a single line. Of twenty-six words in the third column, he used only one. Up to the present time, this page remains the only known portion of the original manuscript of the 1855 *Leaves of Grass*.

VI

Every collector who attends an auction can tell a number of stories about various experiences, about acquisitions, and about the items he didn't buy. I remember particularly the sale of the autograph collection of Dr. Max Thorek (15-16 November 1960). His collection included a six-page Whitman manuscript published in *Specimen Days* (1882) with the title, "In Memory of Thomas Paine." There were also several Whitman letters and a postcard. Meeting one of my friends who collected both Whitman and Paine, I told him I hoped he would buy the Whitman-Paine items. He stated he was only interested in other items and had no interest in competing for these. The Whitman lots came as they usually do at the end of the sale, and I sat patiently until item 626, the Whitman manuscript, came up. It was appraised at $1,000. Dave Kirschenbaum sat on my left, and my collector friend, on my right, sat on the aisle. The bidding started at $500, jumped quickly to $1,000, and then to $1,100, $1,200, and up to $1,700. It seemed to stop for a while, then started all over again. We looked around but couldn't see where the competitive bidding was coming from. The $2,100 bid was ours. It was already over the limit I had set, but I got stubborn and kept going. Finally it was knocked down to us at $2,900. Later I was told that my friend, sitting on the aisle, had been signalling his own bids to his dealer. But the afternoon was not over for me. In the Thorek Collection had been a Whitman manuscript poem, "The Dismantled Ship," which I felt was a forgery, and it had been withdrawn. But the collection also included Whitman letters, postcard, and an envelope addressed by Whitman. For the first time, I saw my name in an auction catalogue as having a letter for which the envelope was being sold. I bought the next two items (627 and 628, both autograph letters), and then started bidding for item 629, a Whitman postcard. At that time Whitman postcards were selling for about $50, but the bidding quickly passed the $50 price. We bid $100 and, in $25 jumps, were at $200 when I gave my signal that that was enough. The next bid of $225 bought the postcard. I couldn't imagine why I had been outbid for the card. Was there something written on it that I had missed? We were outside the auction room after the sale when I heard about my friend's competitive bidding. This information didn't help my disposition when the dealer who had bought the Whitman postcard approached me and introduced himself. I asked him why the card was so important to him. He answered that I could have the card at cost—he just wanted to bring to my attention that there were other dealers in the world besides the one who always represented me. I said it was a costly introduction and foolishly turned down his offer of the card. I have since apologized and we have become friendly. At the time, it had been a bruising afternoon. But I did take home some prizes, and a few years later bought the card from another dealer.

VII

Many years ago I was writing a paper having to do with the doctors that took care of Walt Whitman and how he constantly made records of his illnesses. One such record Whitman had made on a piece of rumpled paper, the top part of which was torn off. He had written about his health during the summer of 1872 and his paralytic stroke in January of 1873. Whitman, who never threw away a piece of paper he could write on, used the blank side to draft a letter. Because the top part of the paper was torn off, there was no way of knowing to whom the letter was written. Part of what we had, read: ". . . to give you a moment's diversion from the weighty stream of official and political cares, I take the liberty of sending (same mail as this) some reminiscences I have written about the war. In Nos. of the N. Y. Weekly Graphic, and thinking you of all men can best return to them in the vein in which they are composed. I am not sure whether you will remember me—or my occasional salute to you in Washington.

"I am laid up here with tedious paralysis, but think I shall get well and return to Washington."

Because of the dates on the back of the paper and those articles in the *New York Weekly Graphic* ("Tis But Ten Years Since," 29 January-7 March 1874), we can date this letter as sometime in February or early March 1874, and from the contents we know it is to an important person in Washington.

At another time, I acquired a letter written to Walt Whitman:

March 6th, 1874

Dear Sir:
    The President desires me to acknowledge the receipt of your very kind letter of the 27th, ultimo, also the numbers of the N. Y. Weekly Graphic, containing your reminiscences of the war.
    He wishes to assure you of his appreciation of the polite attention, and his best wishes for your speedy recovery.

Very resptly, Yours
Levi P. Luckey
Secretary

Mr. Walt Whitman
Camden, New Jersey

I started to search the National Archives. I was almost certain that Whitman had written President Grant and that the torn scrap I had was part of an early draft. But no luck. There is a letter from Whitman to President Grant, dated 22 June 1874, in the National Archives but not the letter Whitman wrote to him in February 1874. Nor is there a listing of the letter in *Walt Whitman's Correspondence: A Checklist* by Edwin H. Miller and Rosalind S. Miller (New York: The New York Public Library, 1957). William White wrote a paper on it in 1960; and Edwin Miller published the draft in the *Walt Whitman Correspondence*, II (New York: New York University Press, 1961). I thought that was the end of it.

But I was wrong. Auction houses perform a valuable service in attracting private collections for sale which often are unknown to scholars until the sale catalogue appears. This was true of the 3 December 1963 Parke-Bernet sale of a collection of historical documents, mostly for Abraham Lincoln and President Grant, which had been in the hands of the Rev. Dr. J. Laurence Plumley, the grandson of a former secretary of President Grant. Included in the sale was the letter Whitman had written to the President. I look forward to most auction sales offering Whitman autograph items with a degree of excitement, but this sale was something special. It would tie up a loose end.

VIII

One learns by mistakes and one learns by experiences—experiences which are good and bad. You've got to make up your mind before the auction how badly you want an item. Regardless of what the appraisals give you as an indication of an item's worth, you, in your own mind, have to decide just what you can afford. The only regrets I have are for the items I could have bought and didn't, or the items I bid on and didn't bid high enough. The ones I didn't get, the ones that got away—these are my lasting regrets.

Collecting has brought me welcomes and honors. Books have brought me a full life, but I've had the most fun chasing things at auctions.

Charles E. Feinberg

WHITMAN

AT

AUCTION

1899-1972

Catalogue No. 832

THE COLLECTION

OF

AUTOGRAPHS

OF THE LATE

Col. THOMAS DONALDSON

OF PHILADELPHIA

Expert Agent of the Indian Bureau, Washington, D. C.

EMBRACING

WASHINGTON'S AUTOGRAPH MILITARY ORDER BOOK

ORIGINAL THIRTEENTH AMENDMENT TO THE CONSTITUTION
OF THE UNITED STATES

RARE SPECIMENS OF AUTOGRAPH LETTERS OF GENERALS IN
THE REVOLUTION AND CIVIL WARS, STATESMEN,
CROWNED HEADS AND AUTHORS

HISTORICAL DOCUMENTS AND ORIGINAL MANUSCRIPTS

RELICS OF

WASHINGTON, LINCOLN, JACKSON, SHERIDAN,
GRANT, GARFIELD, SHERMAN AND
WALT WHITMAN, ETC.

TO BE SOLD

On Thursday, October 26th, 1899,

COMMENCING AT 10.30 O'CLOCK AND 2 O'CLOCK

———————

CATALOGUE COMPILED AND SALE
CONDUCTED BY
STAN. V. HENKELS.

AT THE BOOK AUCTION ROOMS OF
DAVIS & HARVEY,
1112 Walnut Street, Philadelphia, Pa.

WHITMANIANA.

Appertaining to Walt Whitman, the Poet.

565 Whitman to Tennyson. Autograph Draft of Walt Whitman's letter to Lord Alfred Tennyson. 2 pp. 4to (in pencil). Signed in ink. Dated, Aug. 9, 1878.

"The last letter I sent you was Sep. 14. '76 (nearly two years ago) to which I have received no response I also sent my Two Vols, New edition—having rec'd your subscription of 5£ (with an intimation from Robert Buchanan that no books' were expected in return—but I prefer'd to send," etc.

566 Whitman to Tennyson. Autograph Draft of his Letter to Lord Alfred Tennyson. 5 pp. 8vo. Not signed. Dated, April 27, 1872.

A curious medley.

567 Tennyson to Whitman. Autograph Letter, Signed. 4 pp. 8vo. From Lord Alfred Tennyson, Poet Laurate to Walt Whitman. July, 1874. With addressed envelope.

"I am grieved to hear that you have been so unwell & can only trust that your physician is a true prophet, & that you will recover & be as well as ever, I have myself known a case of ———— in a young lady living near me, She lost her mind & no one who saw her believed she could live; but under the superintendence of a good doctor she is perfectly recovered & looks plumper and fresher than ever she did before.

"This is the first letter I have written for weeks & I am afraid I write rather obscurely for my hands and arms have been crippled with rheumatism (I hope it is not gout) & I am not yet perfectly recovered

"I am beholden to you for your Democratic Vistas & if I did not answer and acknowledge them I regret to have done so; but if you knew how great the mass of my correspondence is & Lord knows I dislike letterwriting, I doubt not you would forgive me easily.

"When I next hear of or from you may the news be that you are fully re-established in your old vigour of mind and body."

568 Tennyson to Whitman. *a. l. s.* 2 pp. 8vo. From Lord Alfred Tennyson, to Walt Whitman. Aug. 11, 1875. With addressed envelope.

"My dear Walt Whitman

"(Somehow the Mr does not come well before Walt Whitman) I am glad to hear from you again & to learn that at any rate you are no worse than when you last wrote, & that though your health be shattered your good spirits flourish up like a plant from broken ground, glad also that you find something to approve of in a work so utterly unlike your own as my Queen Mary.

"I am this morning starting with my wife & Sons on a tour to the Continent. She has been very unwell for two years obliged always to lie down & incapable of any work in consequence of overwork,—the case of so many in this age, Yours among others & we are now going into a land of fuller sunshine in hopes that it may benefit her.

"I am in an extreme hurry, packing up & after these few words must bid you goodbye, not without expressing my hope however that you will ultimately recover all your pristine vigor I shall be charmed to receive your book."

569 Whitman to Tennyson. Autograph Draft, unsigned, of a Letter from Walt Whitman to Lord Alfred Tennyson. May 24, 1874. 4to.

569½ Tennyson. Two Addressed and Stamped Envelopes from Tennyson to Whitman.

570 Leggett, Elisa S. *a. l. s.* 8 pp. 8vo. Detroit, June 22, 1881. To Walt Whitman.

Giving an interesting account of "Sojourners," "Truth," "The Old Negro Woman and Slave."

571 Leggett, Elisa S. *a. l. s.* 6 pp. 8vo. Detroit, Dec. 19, 1882. To Walt Whitman.

572 Whitman Walt. Etched Portrait, with Autograph. 8vo. 8 copies.

573 Whitman, Walt. Original Manuscript of an Article. Entitled, "Carlyle, from American Points of View." 36 pp. 8vo.

   Sent to the North American Review, May 20, 1882, but was rejected.

574 Whitman, Walt. Autograph Manuscript of an Article, on Abraham Lincoln.

575 Whitman, Walt. Autograph Manuscript of an Article, on Aaron Burr.

576 Whitman, Walt. Autograph Manuscript of an Article, on George Sand.

577 Whitman, Walt. Original Manuscript. Signed. Folio. "The Dead Tenor." With proof of same, in print.

578 Whitman, Walt. Original Manuscript. Signed. "Interpolation Sounds." Folio.

579 Whitman, Walt. Original Manuscript, signed. Folio. "After the Supper and Talk."

580 Whitman, Walt. Original Manuscript. Entitled, "Yon Lingering Sparse Leaves of Me." Three copies, in various stages of correction, two signed, 4to; and corrected printed proof.

581 Whitman, Walt. Original Manuscript. "Fancies at Navesink," in various stages of correction. With corrected printed proof.

582 Whitman, Walt. Menu of a Dinner given to, May 31, 1889. With portrait and autograph.   2 copies.

583 Whitman, Walt. Autograph Memoranda Book which he carried in his coat pocket.

584 Whitman, Walt. Original Manuscript. "Recollections of Lafayette's Visit to America, in 1824."

585 Whitman, Walt. Original Manuscript on "Old Age," "Millionaires," etc.

586 Whitman, Walt. Original Manuscript. "Pictures." About 23 pp. 4to.

587 Whitman, Walt. His Article on Ralph W. Emerson. Partly written and partly printed. With his autograph postal card, signed, offering it to the Philadelphia "Sunday Press," April 28, 1882; which paper refused it.

588 Whitman, Walt. Original Manuscript. "The Soul's Procession." 12 pp. 8vo.

589 Whitman, Walt. Original Manuscript. "Hancock and the Scout." 3 pp. 4to.

590 Whitman, Walt. Original Manuscript (in pencil). His Seventieth Birthday Poem. Signed. Folio.

591 Whitman, Walt. Process Portrait, with autograph. 8vo.

592 Whitman, Walt. Original Manuscript. Leaves from his war diary. 21 pp.

593 Whitman, Walt. Rough draft of old poems, proof sheets, etc. Interesting lot.

594 Whitman, Walt. "November Boughs." Proof sheets. 140 pp, complete. So inscribed by, in his autograph on paper wrapper.

595 Whitman, Walt. "November Boughs." First proof sheets (wanting pp. 126 to 130). So inscribed in his autograph on outside of cover.

596 Whitman, Walt. Autograph notes and data, gathered on his Western trip.

597 Whitman, Walt. Original Manuscript. "Autumn Nights."

598 Whitman, Walt. His pass, to go within and return from the fortifications, at Alexandria, March 25, 1864.

599 Whitman, Walt. His portrait, with autograph, on the same sheet with the portrait of Abraham Lincoln. 6 copies.

600 Whitman, Walt. Leaves of Grass. Portrait. 12mo, cloth. Thayer & Eldridge, Boston, 1860–61

601 Whitman, Walt, Leaves of Grass. Portrait. Autograph on title. 12mo, half sheep. Camden, 1876
In paper wrapper, endorsed with title of book and price in ink.

602 Whitman, Walt. Leaves of Grass. Two Portraits and Autograph on title. 12mo, cloth, top edges gilt, uncut. Camden, 1882

603 Whitman, Walt. Leaves of Grass; including Sands at Seventy—1st Annex; Good-Bye, My Fancy—2d Annex; A Backward glance o'er Travel'd Roads and Portrait. 12mo, paper, uncut. Philadelphia, 1891–2

604 Whitman, Walt. Specimen Days and Collect. 12mo, cloth. Philadelphia, 1882–3

605 Whitman, Walt. Complete Poems and Prose of. 1885–1888. Authenticated and Personal Book (handled by W. W.) Portraits from life, and autograph. 8vo, boards, uncut.

606 Whitman, Walt. Good-Bye, My Fancy. Second Annex to Leaves of Grass. With autograph. 8vo, uncut. Philadelphia, 1891

607 Whitman, Walt. November Boughs. With portrait and autograph. 8vo, cloth, top edge gilt, uncut.
Philadelphia, 1888

608 ——— Another copy.

609 Whitman, Walt. Two Rivulets; including Democratic Vistas, Centennial Songs, and Passage to India. Without photograph. 12mo, half sheep.   Camden, 1876

610 Whitman, Walt. As a Strong Bird on Pinions Free, and other Poems. 12mo, cloth, uncut. 2 copies.
Washington, 1872

611 Whitman, Walt. Passage to India. With Page of Original Manuscript. 12mo, paper, uncut. Washington, 1871

612 ——— Another copy.

613 Whitman, Walt. Drum-Taps. 12mo, cloth.
New York, 1865

614 Whitman, Walt. Leaves of Grass, with Sands at Seventy, and A Backward Glance O'er Travel'd Roads. Photograph and autograph. 12mo, morocco tucks, gilt edge.

Special edition. Only three hundred copies printed.

615 Whitman, Walt. Of that Blithe Throat of Thine. A Poem. With autograph. 8vo.

616 Goshek, Jos. German Literature. With manuscript notes throughout, in pencil, by Walt Whitman. 12mo, cloth. (Imperfect.)   Philadelphia, 1854

617 Voltaire, M. D. A Philosophical Dictionary. With Autograph on Title and Directions to the Binder in Walt. Whitman's Writing. 8vo, sheep. (Broken.)
Boston, 1836

618 Whitman, Walt. Autograph Poem, signed. "By the Bivouac's Fitful Flame." Beautifully illustrated, in water colors, by the celebrated artist, Julian Scott. With portrait, from life, of Whitman sleeping. Framed and glazed.

"By the bivouac's fitful flame
 A procession winding around me. Solemn and
         sweet and slow—But first I note
 The Tents of the sleeping army—the fields
         and woods dim outline,
 The darkness, lit by spots of Kindled fire—the silence;
 Like a phantom far or near an occasional figure moving
 The Shrubs and trees (as I lift my eyes they seem to be
         Stealthily watching me—)
 While wind in procession thought—O tender & wondrous thoughts
 Of Life & death—of home & the past & loved—and of those
         that are far away;
 A Solemn & slow procession there as I sit on the ground
 By the bivouac's fitful flame

         "WALT WHITMAN."

619   Whitman, Walt.   Autograph Poem, signed.   " Bivouac on a Mountain Side."   Beautifully illustrated in water colors by the celebrated artist, Julian Scott.

> " I see before me now a traveling army halting ;
> Below, a fertile valley spread with barns, and the or'
>   chards of summer
> Behind the terraced sides of a mountain, abrupt in
>   places rising high.
> Broken with rocks with tall cedars, with tall shapes
>   dingily seen ;
> The numerous camp fires scattered near & far—some
>   away up on the mountain
> The Shadowy forms of men & horses, looming large
>   sized flickering,
> And over all the sky—the Sky ; far far out of
>   reach, studded with the eternal Stars—
>
>   " WALT WHITMAN."

The artist has drawn around the poem a sketch of a mountain army encampment, in all its realistic and weird beauty in the light of the camp fire.

————   ————   ————

WALT WHITMAN'S INKSTAND AND PEN.

641   Inkstand and Pen, used by Walt Whitman, the " Good, Gray Poet," for 15 years.

Certificate of the late Colonel Donaldson, certifying that he secured it personally.

————   ————   ————

WALT WHITMAN'S BIBLE.

654   Holy Bible. Containing the Old and New Testaments. 16mo, morocco, gilt edges.   Cambridge, 1879

Presented by the " Good Gray Poet " to Thomas Donaldson. Has inscribed on the title : " Thomas Donaldson with everlasting life wishes fr'm Walt Whitman April 1890."

Sale No. 274

CATALOGUE

OF

LITERARY MANUSCRIPTS

AND

AUTOGRAPH LETTERS

GATHERED BY

George M. Williamson

TO BE SOLD AT AUCTION

TUESDAY EVENING, MARCH 1, 1904

BY

The Anderson Auction Company

5 WEST 29TH STREET, NEW YORK

SALE BEGINS AT 7.30 O'CLOCK

N. B.—Bids are always understood to be at so much per volume or piece

87 WHITMAN (WALT). A. L. S. 1 page, 4to. Washington, June 9, 1865. An interesting reminiscence of the period when Whitman was visiting, and nursing, the sick and wounded of the Civil War. " . . . I go to the hospitals daily and nightly—as I find a greater proportion of sad cases than ever—and for some reason or other there are few or no visitors. I enjoy my visits with a sad but profound joy and satisfaction—especially at night, when the light is nearly turned off, and I am soothing some suffering one."

12.50

88 —— A. L. S. 1 page, 8vo. Camden, N. J., April 12 [no year]. "I am entirely satisfied with your letter [as with Buchanan's and Rossetti's action in London]." . . . "When you see any thing *notable* or pungent about me or my affairs send it to me as I neither see or hear much here."

5.00

89 —— A. L. S. 2 pages, 4to. Camden, N. J., May 5 [1876 ?]. "This is one of my comfortable days . . . still get out a little most every day as formely—*my book-business* and a little writing and reading give me three hours or so occupation (lazily) every day when I am not too ill—and then the baby, my brother's 6mo's infant boy, very fine and bright (of course) is an unfailing delight and diversion to me—the young one knows me *so well*, and is never so happy as when I am tending him . . . Don't know what vile paragraph in the *Graphic* you allude to in your letter."

8.50

90 —— Corrected proof of Whitman's poem, "The Voice of the Rain." Originally this was called "A Rain Enigma," but the poet altered the title to the above. An additional line has been written by Whitman and one or two other slight alterations made. [The additional line—it is interesting to note—forms an essential part of the poem. It occurs after the passage, "I descend to lave the drouths, atomies, dust layers of the globe, to complete which line Whitman has added in this proof, " *And all that in them without me were seeds only, latent, unborn* ".]

4.50

91 —— Original manuscript of his poem "Old Age's Ship and Crafty Death's," written on one 4to page, 13 lines, in ink, and signed. Commencing:

> " From east and west across the horizons's edge,
> Two mighty masterful vessels sailers steal upon us."

21.00

At the end is written, in Whitman's autograph, instructions to the printer to follow the copy and punctuation strictly.

92 **WHITMAN (WALT.)** The original manuscript of his poem "The Patrol at Barnegat." This famous poem—one of Whitman's most vigorously descriptive, if not his best in this form of composition— is written on a quarto sheet, headed "First Draught—May, 1870," in a clear and distinct handwriting, and signed. A few corrections are interlined in pencil. It is almost superfluous to quote such well-known lines, but the beauty, the form, and the vigor appeal so strongly to all admirers of poetical composition and specially to admirers of Whitman, that we cannot refrain from giving the open-ing lines:

36.00

> "Wild, wild the storm, and the sea high running,
> Steady the roar of the gale with incessant undertone muttering:
> Shouts of demoniac laughter fitfully piercing and pealing,
> Waves, air, and midnight, their savagest trinity lashing."

93 —— Original manuscript of his poem "A Twilight Song." Written on one 4to page, 27 lines, and signed. (The copy has been through the printer's hands and is naturally somewhat soiled.) Written wholly in pencil. Commencing:

14.00

> "As I sit in the twilight late alone by the flickering oak flame,
> Musing on long past war scenes—of the countless buried unknown soldiers."

Ending with

> Recording for many a future year
> "Your mystic roll entire of unknown names or North or South,
> Embalmed with love in this twilight song."

94 —— The original first draft of Whitman's poem—almost the last he wrote—"Sail out for Good, Eidolon Yacht." Written in his auto-graph, signed, and dated Camden, N. J., July 25, 1890. At the end the poet has written "rough crude outlines." Written on a quarto sheet in pencil, with his interlineations and corrections. The chief interest in this poem lies in its personal relation, for there is no doubt that Whitman was thinking of his own end in writing it, for in the line which reads: "I will not call it our concluding voyage," he has written above the word "our," the word "my." An impor-tant and deeply pathetic relic.

12.00

first draught — May 1880   Walt Whitman

The Patrol at Barnegat

By Walt Whitman

Wild, wild the storm, and the sea high-running,
Steady the roar of the gale with incessant under-
tone muttering
Shouts of demoniac laughter fitfully piercing and
pealing,
Waves, air, and midnight, their savagest trinity
lashing,
Out in the shadows there, the milk-white combs ca-
reering,
On beachy slush and sand, spirts of snow fierce-
slanting
As, through the murk, the easterly death-wind
breasting,
Through cutting swirl and spray, watchful and
firm advancing,
(That in the distance! is that a wreck? is the
red signal flaring?)
Slush and sand of the beach, tireless till daylight
wending,
A group of dim, wierd forms, snow-drift and
night confronting,
Steadily, slowly, the hoarse roar never remitting,
Along the beach, by those milk-white combs ca-
reering,
That savage trinity warily watching

Sale No. 626

The George M. Williamson Collection

CATALOGUE

OF THE

EXTREMELY CHOICE COLLECTION

OF

FIRST EDITIONS OF ENGLISH AND AMERICAN AUTHORS

AND

ASSOCIATION BOOKS

FORMED BY

GEORGE M. WILLIAMSON

OF GRAND-VIEW-ON-HUDSON

TO BE SOLD

THURSDAY AFTERNOON, JANUARY 30, 1908, Lots 1– 294
THURSDAY EVENING,   JANUARY 30, 1908, '' 295– 590
FRIDAY AFTERNOON,   JANUARY 31, 1908, '' 591– 885
FRIDAY EVENING,   JANUARY 31, 1908, '' 886–1180

BY

The Anderson Auction Company

5 WEST 29TH STREET
NEW YORK

SALES BEGIN IN THE AFTERNOON AT 2.30 ; IN THE EVENING AT 8

TELEPHONE: 3150 MADISON

1103. [WHITMAN (WALT).] The New World for Nov. 20, 1841 (Vol. III, No. 21, containing poem, "*Each has his Grief*," and prose sketch, "*The Child's Champion*," by Whitman). Folio sewn as issued. N. Y. 1841

1104. —— Franklin Evans: or, The Inebriate. A Tale of the Times. By Walter Whitman. Small folio, sewn (water-stained, edges frayed and two tears running about an inch into the text from back). N. Y. 1842

The New World, Extra Series, No. 34.
THE AUTHOR'S FIRST SEPARATE PUBLICATION. VERY RARE.

1105. [——] Voices from the Press: A Collection of Sketches, Essays and Poems by Practical Printers. Edited by J. J. Brenton. 8vo, original cloth (back and corners slightly worn). N. Y. 1850

First Edition, with contributions by Walt Whitman, Samuel Woodworth, Bayard Taylor and others.

IN THE ORIGINAL WRAPPERS.

1106. —— Leaves of Grass. *Portrait.* Thin 4to (corner of back wrapper missing and front and inner margin of title neatly repaired). Brooklyn, N. Y., 1855

THE EXTREMELY RARE FIRST ISSUE OF THE FIRST EDITION, IN THE ORIGINAL PINK PAPER COVERS AS ISSUED, with the portrait in the first state of the plate on India paper, and wanting the 4 preliminary leaves of "Press Notices."

In this first issue the front cover is lettered in bold black type and not in the rustic type as occurs in the cloth copies. Enclosed in half morocco solander case.

1107. —— Another copy of the Same. *Portrait.* Thin 4to, original green cloth gilt, gilt edges. Brooklyn, N. Y., 1855

THE RARE FIRST ISSUE OF THE FIRST EDITION without the preliminary leaves of "*Press Notices.*" With a number (5) of newspaper notices and Emerson's letter, being THE ONLY SEPARATE ISSUE OF THE SAME (on single sheets) inserted. This copy has printed slip "London: Wm. Harsell, 492 Oxford-Street," pasted on title. VERY FINE COPY.

1108. —— Another edition of the Same. (32 Poems. To which is added "Leaves-Droppings," an Appendix containing the Emerson Correspondence, Press Notices, etc.) *Portrait.* 16mo, original green cloth. Brooklyn, N. Y., 1856

THE RARE SECOND EDITION, CONTAINING MANY POEMS NOW FIRST PUBLISHED. In this issue the prose preface is first given in poetic form—divided into the four poems, "*By Blue Ontario's Shore,*" "*Song of the Answerer,*" "*To a foil'd European Revolutionaire,*" and "*Song of Prudence.*" Choice copy, unusually free from fox stains.

1109. —— Another edition of the same. (154 poems.) *Portrait.* 12mo, original bevelled salmon-colored cloth (slight erasure at lower margin of titles.)

Bost.: Thayer & Eldridge, 1860–61
GENUINE FIRST BOSTON EDITION, containing within tinted border.

1110. —— Another edition of the same. (154 poems.)
Bost. 1860-61

THE SPURIOUS REPRINT, with the tinted border around portrait.

1111. —— Another edition of the same (including Drum-Taps, sequel to same, and Songs before Parting). 12mo, original half morocco (slightly rubbed). N. Y. 1867

RARE EDITION, in which the poems are re-arranged, and many are published for the first time.

1112 —— Another edition of the same (including poems now first published). 12mo, original green paper wrappers, TOTALLY UNCUT (back a little worn). Wash. (D.C.)1871

VERY RARE IN WRAPPERS.

1113. —— Another edition of the same [including "Passage to India," with separate title and pagination]. 12mo, original cloth, uncut. Wash., D. C., 1872

Edition not mentioned in Foley. Scarce.

PRESENTATION COPY.

1114. —— Another edition of the Same. Author's Edition. With portrait, and Intercalations. 12mo, original half calf, gilt edges. Camden, N. J., 1876

PRESENTATION COPY with inscription in author's autograph: "John Swinton, from his friend the author." Also author's autograph on title. This copy has a new title-page without printer's name on verso, also additions (printed slips inserted) to preface at p. vi. and at pp. 207, 247, 359 and 369.

PRESENTATION COPY FROM BURROUGHS.

1115. —— Another copy of the Same. (288 Poems.) Portrait. 12mo, original half sheep. Camden, N. J., 1876

Author's Edition. With autograph post-card from the author inserted.

PRESENTATION COPY FROM JOHN BURROUGHS, WITH INSCRIPTION and enveloped addressed in his autograph.

1116 —— Another copy of the same (288 poems). 12mo, original half sheep. Camden, N. J., 1876

Author's Edition. WITH THE AUTOGRAPH ON TITLE, AND AUTOGRAPH POST-CARD signed "W. W." inserted.

1117. —— Another copy of the same (288 poems). Portrait. 12mo, original half sheep. Camden, N. J., 1876

Author's Edition. WITH AUTHOR'S AUTOGRAPH SIGNATURE ON TITLE and autograph post-card from him inserted.

PRESENTATION COPY.

1118. —— Another copy of the same (288 poems). Engraved portrait. 12mo, original half sheep (rubbed and joints loose). Camden, N. J., 1876

Author's Edition, with autograph on title, and presentation inscription "H. R. Haweis from the Author," in his autograph.

1119. —— Another edition of the same (293 poems). Portrait. 12mo, original cloth. Bost. 1881-82

Fine copy of the SCARCE SUPPRESSED BOSTON EDITION, with autograph post-card from the author inserted.

1120. —— Another copy of the same, in cloth (slightly faded).

With autograph of John Russell Young on fly-leaf.

1121. —— Another edition of the same (293 poems). 12mo, original cloth, gilt top, uncut.   Camden, N. J., 1882

Author's Edition, with his autograph signature on title. Reprinted without alteration, except in imprint, from the plates of the suppressed Boston Edition.

1122. —— Another edition of the same.   Preface (only) to the Original Edn., 1855. 8vo, original paper covers, uncut.   VERY SCARCE.   Lond.: Trübner, 1881

FINE COPY.

1123. —— Another edition of the same. *Portrait.* Small 8vo, original cloth, gilt top, other edges uncut.
                              Phil.: McKay, 1884

WITH AUTHOR'S SIGNATURE ON TITLE.

1124. —— Another copy of the same (293 Poems). *Portrait inserted.* Small 8vo, cloth (name on title and covers a little soiled).   Phil.: McKay, 1884

From the plates of the suppressed Boston Edition.

1125. —— Another edition of the Same. With Sands at Seventy and A Backward Glance O'er Travel'd Roads. *Portraits.* 16mo, original limp black morocco, gilt edges.
                              [Phil.: May 31, 1889]

A Special edition issued on the author's seventieth birthday *"celebrating* (the event) *by a special, complete final utterance in one handy volume of L. of G.''* WITH AUTOGRAPH SIGNATURE OF THE AUTHOR on title. VERY SCARCE.
Edition limited to 300 copies.

1126. —— Another. copy of the Same edition, WITH AUTHOR'S AUTOGRAPH ON TITLE. Bound in limp black morocco, pocket book style, with flap.

Edition 300 copies.

PRESENTATION COPY.

1127. —— Another edition of the Same, including Sands at Seventy, Good Bye My Fancy, A Backward Glance O'er Travel'd Roads, *and a portrait from Life.* Post 8vo, in the original gray wrappers and label, uncut as issued.
                              Phil.: McKay, 1891-'2

EARLIEST ISSUE OF THIS IMPORTANT EDITION, giving the text as finally arranged and revised by the author and about which he says: *"I wish to say that I prefer and recommend this present edition for future printing if there should be any; a copy and fac-simile indeed of these 438 pages.''*
PRESENTATION COPY FROM THE AUTHOR, with inscription in the autograph of Horace Traubel. RARE IN WRAPPERS. VERY FINE COPY.

1128. —— Another edition of the same, including Sands at Seventy, Good-Bye My Fancy, Old Age Echoes, and A Backward Glance o'er Travel'd Roads. *Portraits.* Post 8vo, cloth gilt, gilt tops, uncut.   Bost. 1897

1129. —— Another edition of the same (selected). With a Prefatory Note by Harry Roberts. (Vol. I. of the Vagabond's Library.) 16mo, cloth. Lond. 1904

1130. —— Drum-Taps. FIRST EDN. 12mo, original cloth. N. Y. 1865
First issue before addition of the "Sequel."

1131. —— Another copy of the same.

1132. —— Another edition of the same (with Sequel "When Lilacs Last in the Dooryard Bloom'd" now first added). FIRST EDN. 12mo, original cloth. Wash. 1865–66

1133. —— Another copy of the same.

1134. —— Another copy of the same.

1135. [——] The Good Gray Poet [Walt Whitman]. A Vindication [by W. D. O'Connor]. FIRST EDN. 8vo, original wrappers, uncut. N. Y. 1866
Very scarce. The McKee copy, with bookplate engraved by E. D. French.

THE AUTHOR'S FIRST BOOK.

1136. —— BURROUGHS (JOHN). Notes on Walt Whitman as Poet and Person. 12mo, original cloth, uncut. THE AUTHOR'S FIRST BOOK. VERY SCARCE. N. Y. 1867

1137. —— Another copy of the Same. Second edn. 12mo, original cloth, uncut. N. Y. 1871
With MSS. note of fly-leaf IN THE AUTHOR'S AUTOGRAPH. "This edition of the notes was made by inserting notes on page five and the supplementary notes into bound copies of the first edition.—John Burroughs."

PROOF SHEETS.

1138. —— Poems. Selected and Edited by William Michael Rossetti. PROOF SHEETS CORRECTED IN THE AUTOGRAPH OF THE EDITOR, ALSO MSS. OF THE INTRODUCTION, DEDICATION AND CONTENTS, ALL IN HIS AUTOGRAPH. 12mo, bound in half morocco. Lond. 1868

1139. —— Poems. Selected and Edited by Wm. M. Rossetti. Portrait. 16mo, original blue cloth. Lond.: J. C. Hotten, 1868
In this edition the poems of Whitman were first introduced to the English public and by whom, it is strange to say, he was greeted with more true appreciation and encouragement than ever he was in the land whose life and destinies he sang so bravely.

1140. —— The Radical, for May, 1870. (With "A Woman's Estimate of Walt Whitman. Letters to W. M. Rossetti.") 8vo, paper, uncut. Bost. 1870

PRESENTATION COPY.

1141. —— Democratic Vistas. FIRST EDN. 12mo, sewn, TOTALLY UNCUT. Wash., D. C., 1871
PRESENTATION COPY, WITH INSCRIPTION IN THE AUTHOR'S AUTOGRAPH: "M. B. Brady from his friend, Walt. Whitman." The McKee copy, with bookplate engraved by French.

1142. —— Another copy of the Same. FIRST EDN. 12mo, original green paper covers, TOTALLY UNCUT.
Rare in wrappers. Wash., D. C., 1871

WITH AUTOGRAPH LETTER.

1143. —— After All, Not to Create Only. Recited by Walt Whitman * * * New York, Sept. 7, 1891. FIRST EDN. 12mo, original bevelled cloth. Bost. 1871
FINE COPY OF THE FIRST EDITION. With A. N. S. of the author inserted: *"Can you use this poemet in your cluster? It would probably do to go out just as well during the week immediately preceding Christmas. The price is $11 (ten for the little piece and one for printing the slip,"* etc.

1144. —— Another copy of the same. FIRST EDN. 12mo, limp cloth. Bost. 1871
With autograph of Jeany L. Gilder in pencil on title.

1145. —— Passage to India. FIRST EDN. 12mo, original green paper covers, TOTALLY UNCUT. Wash., D. C., 1871
Rare in wrappers.

PRESENTATION COPY.

1146. —— As a Strong Bird on Pinions Free, and other Poems. 12mo, original cloth. Washington, D. C., 1872
Presentation copy, with inscription in the Author's autograph: *"From Walt Whitman, 1887."* FINE COPY.

1147. —— Another copy of the same. FIRST EDN. Narrow post 8vo, original cloth, uncut. Wash. 1872

PRESENTATION COPY.

1148. —— Memorandum During the War. 12mo, original cloth. Author's Publication. Camden, N. J., 1875-'76
ONE OF THE RAREST OF WHITMAN'S WRITINGS PRIVATELY PRINTED FOR DISTRIBUTION TO FRIENDS.
"REMEMBRANCE." PRESENTATION COPY OF THE FIRST EDITION TO JOHN SWINTON, WITH INSCRIPTION IN AUTHOR'S AUTOGRAPH on a sheet (containing brief biographical notes regarding the author) specially printed for presentation copies of this book. Also an extra portrait inserted. Fine copy.

PRESENTATION COPY.

1149. —— Two Rivulets, including Democratic Vistas, Centennial Songs, and Passage to India. *Photo-portrait inscribed by the author.* 12mo, original half calf gilt, gilt edges.
Camden, N. J., 1876
Author's Edition. PRESENTATION COPY WITH INSCRIPTION IN AUTHOR'S AUTOGRAPH: *"John Swinton, from his friend the Author."* M. S. alteration on p. 60 in the autograph of the author.

PRESENTATION COPY.

1150. —— Another copy of the Same. 12mo, original half sheep (rubbed). Camden, N. J., 1876
Author's Edition, with original photo-portrait inscribed by the author: *"Walt Whitman, born May 31, 1819,"* and presentation inscription in his autograph: *"H. R. Haweis, from the Author."*

16

1151. ——Another copy of the Same. 12mo, original half sheep. Camden, N. J., 1876

Author's Edition, with two portraits (one an original photograph, N. Y., 1872). Checque made out in the author's autograph and A. L. S. of H. L. Traubel (relating to this copy) inserted.

1152. —— Another copy of the Same. 12mo, original half sheep (lacks photo-portrait). Camden, N. J., 1876

Author's Edition. PRESENTATION COPY from Horace Traubel, with autograph inscription.

WALT WHITMAN'S BIBLE.

1153. —— The Holy Bible, containing the Old and New Testaments. 24mo, morocco, gilt edges. Cambridge, 1879

WALT WHITMAN'S BIBLE, PERSONALLY HANDLED BY THE POET AND PRESENTED TO HIS FRIEND THOMAS DONALDSON.

Although hailed by Ingersoll as ''knowing all creeds but believing in none,'' it is well known that Walt Whitman knew the Bible almost by heart and about which he has written, ''No true bard will ever contravene the Bible. If the time ever comes when iconoclasm does its extremest against the books of the Bible in its present form, the collection must still survive in another and dominate just as much as hitherto, through its divine and primal structure, . . . here are the fountain heads of song.''

The copy is inscribed across the title in Whitman's autograph thus:

''Thomas Donaldson, with everlasting life wishes from Walt Whitman, Apl., 1890.'' AN ITEM OF THE HIGHEST INTEREST.

CORRECTED BY THE AUTHOR.

1154. —— Poetry to-day in America (as published in the North American Review for Feb'y, 1881). 8vo, sewn, pp. 197-210. Boston

PROOF SHEETS CORRECTED AND ANNOTATED THROUGHOUT IN THE AUTOGRAPH OF THE AUTHOR.

1155. —— Essays from ''The Critic.'' By John Burroughs, Walt Whitman, E. C. Stedman, and others. FIRST EDN. 12mo, original cloth. Bost. 1882

1156. —— Specimen Days and Collect. FIRST EDN. 12mo, original cloth. Phil. 1882-'83

With autograph of the author on fly-leaf ''Oct. 11, 1890.'' In this edition are contained all of the author's prose writings to date which he wished to have handed down to posterity. FINE COPY.

1157. —— Complete Poems and Prose: Leaves of Grass, Specimen Days, and Collect, November Boughs, with Sands at Seventy. Portraits from Life. Royal 8vo, original half cloth and boards, with label, totally uncut. Phil. [1888-'9]

Authenticated and Personal Book (handled by W. W.) WITH AUTOGRAPH OF THE POET ON TITLE. Edition 600 copies. Fine copy. Scarce.

1158. —— November Boughs. 12mo. Phil. 1888

FIRST PROOF SHEETS (title and pp. 140). The entire work lacking pp. 19-20, 22, 44-45, 126-130, laid loose in cloth covers, with label IN THE AUTHOR'S AUTOGRAPH AND A FEW M.S. CORRECTIONS.

Presented to the owner by the author.

1159. —— November Boughs. FIRST EDN. 8vo, original flexible cloth, totally uncut. Phil. 1888

With M.S. in ink and pencil and proof sheet, corrected (of "Italian Music in Dakota—[The Seventeenth, the Finest Regimental Band I ever Heard]."), in the author's autograph and original photo-portrait inserted. Also A. N. S. from H. L. Traubel accompanying the above when presented.

1160. —— Another copy of the Same. FIRST EDN. Royal 8vo, original cloth, uncut. Phil. 1888

LARGE PAPER? With slip of paper bearing Author's Autograph inserted.

1161. —— Good-Bye My Fancy. 2d Annex to Leaves of Grass. Large 8vo, sewn, uncut. Phil. 1891

PRESENTATION COPY, WITH INSCRIPTION IN AUTHOR'S AUTOGRAPH across title: "Geo. M. Williamson from the author Sept. 7, 1891." With slip of paper also bearing author's presentation inscription and original photo-portrait laid in.

1162. —— Good-Bye, My Fancy. 2d Annex to Leaves of Grass. Portrait. 8vo, original green cloth, gilt top, uncut. Phil.: McKay, 1891

Fine copy of the Large Paper edition?

1163. [——] At the Graveside of Walt Whitman: Harleigh, Camden, New Jersey, March 30; and Sprigs of Lilac. Edited by H. L. Traubel (with Discourses, Poems, etc., by John Burroughs, R. G. Ingersoll, and others). Royal 8vo, original wrappers, uncut. n. p., 1892

Edition 750 copies. No. 333. Signed and numbered by the Editor, and presentation inscription by him to owner.

1164. —— Another copy of the same. No. 199.

1165. —— In Re Walt Whitman. Edited by his Literary Executors, Horace L. Traubel, R. M. Bucke and Thos. B. Harned. Royal 8vo, cloth, gilt top, uncut. Phil. 1893

No. 330 of 1,000 copies.

1166. [——] Conversations with Walt Whitman. By Sadakichi. FIRST EDN. 12mo, original paper covers, uncut. N. Y. 1895

1167. [——] Little Journeys to the Homes of American Authors. Walt Whitman. By Elbert Hubbard. 16mo, wrappers. N. Y. 1896

1168. [——] Calamus. A Series of Letters written during the years 1868–80 by Walt Whitman to a Young Friend [Peter Doyle]. Edited, with an Introduction, by R. M. Bucke. *Portrait.* Square 12mo, original half cloth and boards, with label. Bost. 1897

LARGE PAPER COPY OF THE FIRST EDITION. No. 14 of only 25 copies so issued for sale, and signed by the editor.

1169. —— The Wound Dresser. A Series of Letters, written from the Hospitals in Washington during the War of the Rebellion. Edited by R. M. Bucke. *Portrait.* 12mo, original cloth, gilt top, uncut. Bost. 1898

First impression of the First Edition. Only about 25 copies so issued.

1170. —— Notes and Fragments left by Walt Whitman, and now edited by R. M Bucke, one of his Literary Executors. Imp. 8vo, cloth. [Lond., Ontario]: Printed for private distribution only, 1899.

No. 24 of only 225 copies printed from type and signed by the editor.

A volume of scattered fragments revealing the poet as he really was, his spiritual genesis and mental evolution, and forming a record of the early ideas and impulses of which grew his matured works.

1171. —— The same. Another copy. This one is No. 23.

1172. —— Catalogue of a Collection of Books, Letters and Manuscripts written by Walt Whitman. In the Library of Geo. M. Williamson. *Portrait in duplicate and facsimile.* 4to, cloth, uncut. N. Y.: Dodd, Mead, 1903

No. 3 OF ONLY 25 COPIES ON JAPAN PAPER.

1173. —— Lafayette in Brooklyn. Introduction by John Burroughs. FIRST EDN. *Portrait and facsimile.* 8vo, boards and label, uncut. N. Y. 1905

No. 51 of 235 copies on American hand-made paper.

Sale No. 777

FIRST EDITIONS

OF

AMERICAN AUTHORS

AND

OTHER MISCELLANEOUS WORKS

COLLECTED BY

J. Chester Chamberlain

OF NEW YORK

PART TWO

ALDRICH	EVERETT	PARKMAN
BANCROFT	FISKE	PRESCOTT
BRET HARTE	HALLECK	STEDMAN
COOPER	HOWELLS	STODDARD
CURTIS	MITCHELL	TAYLOR
DRAKE	MOTLEY	WHITMAN

AND IMPORTANT DUPLICATES OF

BRYANT	HOLMES	LOWELL
EMERSON	IRVING	POE
HAWTHORNE	LONGFELLOW	THOREAU
	WHITTIER	

NOVEMBER 4 AND 5, 1909

THURSDAY AFTERNOON,	- -	LOTS 1–197
THURSDAY EVENING,	- - -	" 198–393
FRIDAY AFTERNOON,	- - - -	" 394–596
FRIDAY EVENING,	- - - -	" 597–788

SALES BEGIN AT 2.30 AND 8.15 O'CLOCK

The Anderson Auction Company

12 EAST 46TH STREET

NEW YORK

TELEPHONE, MURRAY HILL 120

Works of Walt Whitman.

660. FRANKLIN EVANS. Folio, sewed, pp. 33. (The New World.) Extra Series, Vol. 2, No. 10, Nov., 1842. Extracted from the bound volume. *15*

> * THE VERY RARE ORIGINAL ISSUE OF WALT WHITMAN'S FIRST BOOK. Very few copies have been offered at auction, the last apparently being the one sold in these rooms in October, 1906, for $43. This is the exact form in which it first was issued, as a supplement to the periodical. Laid in is a leaf of the "New World" of December 3, advertising "Franklin Evans." [Also see Dickens' American Notes, No. 772.]

661. THE AMERICAN REVIEW, May and June, 1845. *Portrait of J. Q. Adams.* Two pieces, 8vo, original numbers. New York: Wiley and Putnam, 1845

> * Contains "The Boy-Lover" and "Death of Wind-Foot" by Whitman.

662. LEAVES OF GRASS. *Portrait* (with tinted border). 12mo, original cloth (somewhat worn, and soiled in places). Boston: Thayer and Eldridge [1860-1] *6*

> * GENUINE FIRST ISSUE OF THE BOSTON EDITION. Many of the Poems (154) comprising this issue appear here for the first time in book form. AUTOGRAPH PRESENTATION COPY FROM THE AUTHOR, WITH INSCRIPTION: "R. J. HINTON, WITH ESTEEM OF WALT WHITMAN." Pasted in is an envelope with "Whispers of Heavenly Death" written on in Whitman's hand.

663. LEAVES OF GRASS. The same. 12mo, original plain wrappers (soiled and worn), uncut (lacks portrait, another having been inserted (and title). *5 25*

> [Boston: Thayer and Eldridge, 1860-1]
> * RARE, IN WRAPPERS. AUTOGRAPH PRESENTATION COPY FROM THE AUTHOR, WITH INSCRIPTION:—"MERRILL G. WHEELOCK. WITH BEST REGARDS OF WALT WHITMAN," on the outside wrapper.

664. DEMOCRATIC VISTAS. 8vo, original printed wrappers, uncut, pp. 84. *13*

> Washington [Smith and McDougal], 1871
> * PRESENTATION COPY FROM THE AUTHOR AND WITH MS. CORRECTION IN HIS AUTOGRAPH:—"MRS. BOTTA [ANNE LYNCH], FROM THE AUTHOR," and with "*When the hundredth year,*" on page 60, altered in WHITMAN'S AUTOGRAPH to "*Long ere the second centennial.*"

665. PASSAGE TO INDIA. 8vo, original printed wrappers, uncut (back worn), pp. 120. *6 75*

> Washington [Smith and McDougal], 1871
> * AUTOGRAPH PRESENTATION COPY FROM THE AUTHOR, WITH INSCRIPTION:—"RICHARD J. HINTON, FROM HIS FRIEND, WALT WHITMAN."

666. LEAVES OF GRASS. 12mo, original cloth (worn). *8 25*

> Washington: [Smith and McDougal], 1872
> * This edition includes the "Passage to India." AUTOGRAPH PRESENTATION FROM THE AUTHOR: "*R. J. Hinton from Walt Whitman, with his love, Washington, April, 1872.*"

667. AS A STRONG BIRD ON PINIONS FREE.
12mo, original cloth, uncut.   With the Advertisements, pp. 8.
Washington: [S. W. Green, printer], 1872

*FINE COPY. AUTOGRAPH PRESENTATION COPY FROM THE AUTHOR: "*Dr. R. M. Bucke, from Walt Whitman.*" With bookplate of Dr. Bucke, who was Whitman's biographer.

1 75

137 50

668. TWO RIVULETS, Including Democratic Vistas, Centennial Songs, *and* Passage to India.   Post 8vo, contemporary half calf gilt, ONLY 100 COPIES ISSUED.   Text followed by Whitman's "Leaf of Advertisement."

Author's Edition.   Camden, New Jersey, 1876

*A COPY OF REMARKABLE INTEREST, BEING WALT WHITMAN'S OWN COPY (for which he helped set the type in the Camden printing office) PREPARED BY HIM FOR ANOTHER EDITION, with many corrections, erasures and additions in his hand and with a cabinet photograph inserted which he has signed and on which he has written the date of his birth, May 31, 1819. No revised edition of Two Rivulets has been issued, though many of the separate poems have appeared in later editions.

So NUMEROUS ARE HIS ALTERATIONS AND ADDITIONS that it is impossible to mention more than a few, and as some of them apparently have never been printed, their importance will readily be recognized. The original title-page commences with a two-line verse, but Whitman has added another couplet:

(Thou, Reader, rambling hither,
My living hand I hereby clasp in thine.)

In addition he has scored through the words *"Centennial Songs"* and written above *"Memoranda of the War"* (See Reproduction). In the preface he has scored on both margins the passage beginning *"Then I meant Leaves of Grass, as published, to be the Poem of Identity, etc."*, evidently for the purpose of emphasizing the statement. A passage in the Preface (page 13) wherein he writes of recognizing the still higher fact *"The Eternal Soul of Man"* is emphasized in the same manner. Other passages throughout the volume are similarly marked, with some word added or struck out, indicating his latest beliefs or aspirations; very few are changed—the alterations being more in the nature of confirmation or emphasis.

One of the best-known of Whitman's poems is the famous Centennial Song: *"After all, not to create only,"* and it is apparent that the author had been intently considering this. The first verse is lightly pencilled through, whether or not for the purpose of omission it is difficult to tell, and at the top of the page he has written the following additional verse [part of which appears in later editions]:

"Labor's religious temples these!
Ah, little recks the laborer
How near his work is holding him to God,
The Laborer of Time, Space, All."

In the third verse Whitman has struck out all the lines after the words *"She comes"* and in the same way later has scored through the lines *"And I can hear what may-be you do not,"* etc., ending with *"journey'd considerable,"* apparently indicating Whitman's extreme dissatisfaction with this poem. Other lines are scored over to be omitted from later editions, some of which have been retained.

On the reverse of the title of *"As a Strong Bird on Pinions Free"* Whitman has written several lines evidently intended as notes for an introduction. Many words are rewritten, making incoherent commencement, though the sense is plain enough: *"All my poems merging and finishing in the meditations of Passage to*

(Thou, Reader, rambling hither
My living hand I hereby clasp
in thine.)

For the Eternal Ocean I send,
These ripples, passing surges, streams of Death and Life.

TWO

RIVULETS

Including DEMOCRATIC VISTAS, *Memoranda* ~~CONFIDENTIAL~~ *of the War* ~~Notes~~, and PASSAGE TO INDIA.

AUTHOR'S EDITION.
CAMDEN, NEW JERSEY.
1876.

[No. 668]

India as the embouchure and finish and final explanation of all that have gone before, and the final" (not concluded).

"Memoranda During the War" he has left practically untouched, but one alteration having been made. That is in the account of the assassination of Lincoln, referring to the play ("Our American Cousin") he writes of it as a *"singularly written composition,"* "written" he has changed to "witless."

On *"Ashes of Soldiers"* he has pencilled *"Written March 1870,"* and on President Lincoln's Burial Hymn, *"When Lilacs last in the Dooryard bloomed,"* he has pencilled *"Written May 1866."*

The commencement of *"A Carol of Harvest for 1867"* evidently did not satisfy him, for it has been struck out and then marked *"stet"* (for the printer to leave as written). Another verse is written in ink at the top of the page, and another version of the same verse pencilled on a slip of paper that he has pasted in, with one or two notes on the leaf opposite referring to the same. First, apparently, the title had been thought over, and as alternative titles he has written

"A Harvest Carol," and
"A Western Harvest Song the year following Peace."

A line *"As at thy Portals Death"* has also been written as a suggestion, but altered to

*"No more the Wars and Deaths
I lately (or erewhile) chanted."*

The verse as written in ink, and presumably as his final thought is as follows:

"A song no more of the War!
A song of the teeming harvest following close
A song of the serried regiments changed by magic
A song of the good green grass."

These additions and alterations are fundamental data in the study of Whitman's writings; no criticism can be of permanent value without their being taken into consideration. Future essayists of the "Good Gray Poet" should study this volume with all Whitman's alterations and corrections in forming an estimate of his position in the literature of America.

Whitman presented this copy to Sidney Morse, the sculptor, and later it passed into the possession of E. T. Billings, the Boston artist.

[See Reproduction.]

669. **NOVEMBER BOUGHS.** *Portrait.* 8vo, original cloth, gilt top, uncut. Philadelphia: David McKay, 1888
* Autograph presentation copy from the author: " *Walt Whitman to Julian Scott of Plainfield, N. J., July 24, 1891.*"

No. 887

CATALOGUE OF

THE LIBRARY OF ASSOCIATION

AND THE

AUTOGRAPH COLLECTION

OF

Edmund Clarence Stedman

PART III

TO BE SOLD

JANUARY 24 AND 25, 1911

TUESDAY AFTERNOON, - - LOTS 2159–2509
TUESDAY EVENING, - - - " 2510–2814
WEDNESDAY AFTERNOON, - - 2815–3113
WEDNESDAY EVENING, - - - " 3114–3372

SALES BEGIN AT **2.30** AND **8.15** O'CLOCK

The Anderson Auction Company

12 EAST 46TH STREET
NEW YORK

3230. —— FIRST ROUGH DRAFT OF WHITMAN'S "*Song of the Universal*," delivered at Tuft's College, Mass., June 17, 1874. Written on five leaves, ENTIRELY IN HIS AUTOGRAPH.

35—

* An interesting manuscript, dated March 31, 1874, outlining the ideas Whitman wished to convey. One or two verses are practically the same as in the finished copy, others give merely the germ of the idea, a line used as a suggestion, or a few words indicating the thought in his mind. In one place he

WHITMAN (WALT)—*Continued.*

had evidently meant to make a reference to Christ, Buddha, Socrates and Confucius, for he has written these names and beneath them the following three lines:

> "*All the ? saviours of the earth*
> *The few the mighty known, the countless*
> *unknown mightier yet.*"

This verse was apparently abandoned, and replaced with that commencing:

> "*The measur'd faiths of other lands—the grandeurs of*
> *the past,*
> *Are not for Thee—but grandeurs of thine own.*"

3231. WHITMAN (WALT). A SECOND DRAFT of the Poem, written on eleven leaves, WITH MANY CORRECTIONS AND INTERLINEATIONS. Entirely in Whitman's autograph.

50'

    *Another stage in the composition containing many lines not finally accepted. One verse that he had completed is entirely abandoned in the final version. It reads:

> "*Heard you that earnest babble everywhere*
> *Printed in books, accepted in men's minds ? The bad is*
> *universal*
> '*Tis false—'tis seeming only*
> *The good alone is universal.*"

3232. —— The THIRD DRAFT of the Poem, written on four quarto leaves, WITH MANY INTERLINEATIONS. ENTIRELY IN HIS AUTOGRAPH.

46'

    *In the first three drafts there was evidently some idea—perhaps rather indefinite—of plans of God in the Universal scheme of Good and Bad. In this third draft they mostly appear for the last time, the final version abandoning any reference to them. One verse in this commences:

> "*Forth from their masks, no matter what,*
> *In plans of God,*" etc.

This was changed to:

> "*Forth from their masks, no matter what,*
> *From the huge festering trunk, from craft and guile and*
> *tears,*" etc.

The last verse in the second draft commences:

> "*Give me, O God, to sing that hymn to thee.*"

This was changed in this third version to:

> "*Give me O Heaven to sing that thought.*"

In the final version, however, he has adopted the words:

> "*O God to sing that thought.*"

87⁵⁰ **3233.** —— The FINALLY COMPLETED VERSION of the poem, written on five quarto leaves, ENTIRELY IN HIS AUTOGRAPH, and endorsed by Whitman on the back "*Song of the Universal (printer's copy), Camden, N. J., June 1874.* With a printed galley proof of the poem.

No. 385—1911

The Powers Collection

OF

ASSOCIATION COPIES AND FIRST EDITIONS OF THE WORKS

OF

Samuel L. Clemens (s)

(Mark Twain)

AND OTHER WELL-KNOWN

19th Century American and English Authors

TO BE SOLD AT AUCTION

Tuesday, Wednesday, Thursday and Friday, April 4th, 5th, 6th and 7th, 1911

Commencing at 2:30 P. M.

BY

The Merwin-Clayton Sales Company

20-24 East 20th Street
New York

CATALOGUE OF A
REMARKABLE COLLECTION OF

ASSOCIATION COPIES AND FIRST EDITIONS

FORMED BY THE

Rev. L. M. Powers

OF HAVERHILL, MASS.

INCLUDING UNUSUALLY COMPLETE AND INTERESTING
COLLECTIONS OF THE WORKS OF

S. L. CLEMENS, JOHN ADDINGTON SYMONDS, JOHN BURROUGHS,
WILLIAM MORRIS, LAFCADIO HEARN, WALT WHITMAN, EDWARD
ROWLAND SILL, H. D. THOREAU, MATTHEW ARNOLD,
AMBROSE BIERCE, JOAQUIN MILLER, GEORGE BERNARD
SHAW, JOHN HAY, RICHARD JEFFRIES, O. HENRY,
JAMES THOMSON, BRET HARTE, SIDNEY
LANIER, JAMES WHITCOMB RILEY,
HAMLIN GARLAND, ERNEST H.
CROSBY, BLISS CARMAN, JOHN
FISKE, C. F. BROWNE,
AND OTHERS

TO BE SOLD AT AUCTION

Tuesday, Wednesday, Thursday and Friday
April 4th, 5th, 6th and 7th, 1911

COMMENCING AT 2:30 P. M.

BY

The Merwin-Clayton Sales Company

20-24 EAST 20TH STREET, NEW YORK

MAIL ORDERS CAREFULLY EXECUTED

TELEPHONE, GRAMERCY 567

28

1265. WHITMAN (WALT). Brother Jonathan. Vol. 1
6.50 (Nos. 2-17, with many Extra Numbers and Supplements).
4to, half calf. N. Y.: 1842.
> With No. 5 containing the poem "Ambition" by Walter Whitman. Probably Whitman's first appearance in print. Laid in is a photo of Walt Whitman's Vault.

1266. —— Democratic Review. Vol. XI. (1842). 8vo,
5.50 half roan. N. Y.: 1842.
> Contains "The Angel of Tears" by Whitman, pp. 282-284.

1267. —— Franklin Evans; or, The Inebriate. A Tale of
the Times. THE RARE FIRST EDITION. Bound in a volume of
32 - "The New World" for 1842. Imp. 8vo, half sheep (worn).
N. Y.: 1842.
> One of the rarest of Whitman First Editions. Issued as an extra number of "The New World." Whitman said of "Franklin Evans": *'I doubt if there is a copy in existence. I have none and have not had one for years.'* Inserted is a 1p. L. S. from Dr. R. M. Bucke (one of Whitman's literary executors) referring to the above work, in which he says among other things, that he had "hunted and advertised for 'Franklin Evans' for over twenty years, and at last got a copy of it."

1268. —— Brother Jonathan for March 11, 1843. 4to,
6 0 folded as issued, uncut. N. Y.: 1843.
> Contains a poem *"Death of the Nature-Lover,"* by Whitman, of which the Editor says in a note: *"The following wants but a half hour's polish to make of it an effusion of very uncommon beauty."*

1269. —— The Columbian Lady's and Gentleman's Mag-
.75 azine. Edited by John Inman. Vols. 1 and 2. *Steel engravings and colored costume plates.* 2 vols. in 1. 8vo, half roan.
N. Y.: 1844.
> Contains: "Dumb Kate," "Eris," "The Little Sleighers," "The Child and the Profligate" by Whitman, besides several contributions by Poe, Bryant, Paulding and others.

1270. —— The American Review. For June 1845. 8vo,
.20 wrappers. N. Y.: 1845.
> Contains: "The Death of Wind-Foot," by Whitman.

1271. —— The United States and Democratic Review for
.15 July and August, 1845. 8vo, wrappers. N. Y.: 1845.
> Contains: "Revenge and Requital" by Whitman.

1272. —— The Union Magazine. Edited by Mrs. Kirkland.
.60 *Numerous steel engravings and colored costume plates.* Vols.
2 and 3 in one volume. Very fine copy. N. Y.: 1848.
> Contains: "The Shadow and the Light of a Young Man's Soul," by Whitman, also contributions by Poe, Bryant, Simms, Street, and others.

1273. —— Voices from the Press: A Collection of Sketches,
Essays, and Poems, by Practical Printers. Edited by James
19 - J. Brenton. FIRST EDITION. 8vo, cloth. N. Y.: 1850.
> Contains: "The Tomb Blossoms" by Whitman, also original contributions by Willis, Bayard Taylor and others.
> Laid in is a delightfully characteristic one page A. L. S. by Whitman, written in pencil and signed in full. The letter is to S. H. M(orse) the Sculptor, and after referring to several works that are going through the press, says: *"Your bust of me still holds out fully in my estimation—I consider it (to me at any rate) the best and most characteristic—really artistic and satisfactory rendering of any-so tho't by me."*

1274. —— Leaves of Grass. *Portrait.* Royal 8vo, original
48 - cloth. (title and portrait loose). Brooklyn: 1855.
> FIRST EDITION. VERY RARE. Laid in is an advertisement relating to the book. The author himself worked as compositor on the above.
> The original issue of this great book stands in the first class of American book rarities.

10.75 1275. —— Leaves of Grass. (SECOND EDITION). *Portrait.*
16mo, cloth (a little shaken). Brooklyn, N. Y.: 1856.

This issue contains 32 poems, including 11 out of the 12 originally published. Also with the "Leaves-Droppings," which contains the famous letter from Emerson to Whitman, regarding the book. Whitman's reply, extracts from London and other reviews, etc.

5.50 1276. —— Leaves of Grass. *Tinted portrait of the author.*
12mo, orange colored cloth (a trifle shaken, but good clean copy). Bost.: Thayer and Eldridge, (1860-61).

The genuine First issue of this edition, with both cloth and portrait in the right state.

.75 1277. —— Leaves of Grass. *Engraved portrait.* Thick 12mo, cloth. Bost.: Thayer and Eldridge, (1860-61).

With imprints of George C. Rand and Avery and Bost. Stereotype Foundry on verso of title.

5— 1278. —— Drum-Taps. FIRST EDITION. 12mo, cloth. 72pp. N. Y.: 1865.

THE RARE FIRST ISSUE, WITHOUT "When Lilacs Last in the Door-Yard Bloomed," etc. "Owing to the Death of President Lincoln, the author delayed the publication of this volume, of which some copies were bound at the time, until a few weeks later when he added 'When Lilacs Last in the Door-Yard Bloomed.' 'O, Captain, My Captain,' and a few other poems." Foley.

3— 1279. —— Drum-Taps. FIRST EDITION. 12mo, cloth. N. Y.: 1865.

Second issue of the First Edition, containing the Sequel to Drum-Taps. printed in Washington, shortly after the death of President Lincoln, and including "When Lilacs Last in the Door-Yard Bloomed" and other pieces. Moncure D. Conway's copy, with his autograph on fly-leaf.

9.25 1280. —— [O'Connor (W. D.)]. The Good Gray Poet, A Vindication. FIRST EDITION. 8vo. half seude calf. with the original wrappers bound in. N. Y.: 1866.

Issued anonymously, and very scarce, especially in this state. Inserted is a 3pp. A. L. S. from the author to Mr. Dwight introducing Miss Fanny Malone Raymond, and referring to her literary ability.

4.25 1281. —— Leaves of Grass. 12mo, half morocco. N. Y.: 1867.

First issue of this edition, not containing "Drum-Taps" and sequel to "Drum-Taps," as in the following lot. Contains some poems here first published.

1282. —— Leaves of Grass. 12mo, half morocco. N. Y.: 1867.

11.50 Second issue of this edition, containing "Drum-Taps" and sequel to "Drum-Taps."
PRESENTATION COPY FROM THE AUTHOR TO THOMAS NAST, with inscription: "Thomas Nast from Walt Whitman. March, 1869."

2.25 1283. —— Poems by Walt Whitman. Selected and Edited by William Michael Rosetti. FIRST EDITION. *Portrait.* 16mo, cloth. Lond.: 1868.

Scarce. This edition contains a Preface of 64 pages by Whitman.

.80 1284. —— After All, Not to Create Only. FIRST EDITION. 12mo, limp cloth. Bost.: 1871.

1285. —— Leaves of Grass. Post 8vo, newly bound in half olive levant, gilt top, uncut. Washington: 1871.
45— The rare first Washington issue, with "Passage to India" bound in at the end.
Laid in is a manuscript poem by the author. "*With Husky, Haughty Lips, O! Sea,*" and MS. prose notes on four sheets.

1286. —— Passage to India. 12mo, full morocco, with the original green wrappers bound in.   Wash.: 1871.

3.25

FIRST EDITION contains "*President Lincoln's Burial Hymn.*" Fine copy. Scarce.

1287. —— As a Strong Bird on Pinions Free. And other Poems. FIRST EDITION. Small 8vo, cloth, uncut.
Wash.: 1872.

1.60

Laid in is a mounted reproduction of a bas relief of a Whitman (bust).

1288. —— Buchanan (Robert). The Fleshly School of Poetry and other Phenomena of the Day. 12mo, half undressed calf and boards, with the original pink printed wrappers bound in.   Lond.: Strahan and Co., 1872.

10.50

First Edition. Fine, clean copy of Buchanan's caustic attack upon Rossetti, Swinburne and other poets of the "Fleshly School." The last two pages of Notes are devoted to the highly eulogistic criticisms of Walt Whitman.

1289. —— Leaves of Grass. Post 8vo, green cloth, uncut.
Wash.: 1872.

15.—

VERY RARE. Laid in is an L. S. from Dr. R. M. Bucke referring to Whitman's works. Of this edition he says: "*I undertake to say you have not 'Leaves of Grass' (including 'Passage to India') 1872, green cloth. I never saw but one copy and that Mr. Whitman had and gave me.*"
This copy is in green cloth, and contains "Passage to India." A fine copy.

1290. —— Leaves of Grass. Post, 8vo. cloth, top uncut.
Wash.: 1872.

3.50

A different issue from the preceding, although bearing the same date. Contains also "Passage to India" with the title in different type from the greeen cloth edition.
Inserted is a slip in Whitman's autograph, in pencil, "*The item however of Buchanan's send'g W. W. $100 is wrong, entirely. No such sum nor any sum was ever so sent.*"

1291. ——Memoranda During the War. *Photo portrait.* 12mo, half brown morocco.
Camden: Author's Publication, 1875-76.
A very fine copy of the First Edition.

3.75

1292. —— Memoranda During the War. (lacks portrait). 12mo, cloth.   Camden: Author's Publication, 1875-76.

17.50

FIRST EDITION. PRESENTATION COPY, inscribed: "*To John R. Johnston, Jr., from his friend the Author.*" One of the rarest of Whitman items. Whitman's unpublished Diary shows that about a dozen copies were given away.

1293. —— Leaves of Grass. AUTHOR'S EDITION. 12mo, half sheep.   Camden: 1876.

1.10

Of this edition. which was issued and sold by Whitman himself. only 100 copies were printed. With autograph of the author on title-page. Contains the leaf of advertisement of this volume and "Two Rivulets." The title-page calls for "portraits from life," but this copy does not appear to have contained any.

1294. —— Two Rivulets. Including Democratic Vistas, Centennial Songs, and Passage to India. AUTHOR'S EDITION. 12mo, original half sheep.   Camden: 1876.

1.50

The Centennial edition of which only 100 copies were printed and sold by the author. Contains a fine original photograph portrait of Whitman. autographed, and the leaf of advertisement of Whitman's writings.

6.20 1295. —— The Radical Review. Edited by Benj. R. Tucker. Vol. 1. Thick 8vo, half morocco. New Bedford. 1877-78.

Contains an article on Walt Whitman by Joseph B. Marvin (pp.: 224-259), also four articles by Sidney H. Morse, the Sculptor. each autographed, and a 2pp. A. L. S. from S. H. Morse. There is also laid in a 1p. A. L. S. from Elizabeth Keller. Whitman's nurse.

.50 1296. —— Progress. A Mirror for Men and Women. Vol. 1, Nos. 1-15. Folio, half roan.

Contains the poem: *"Thou who hast Slept All Night upon the Storm."* by Whitman. With a photo. portrait (a little faded and torn through center) mounted, with his autograph, dated Sept. '87.

.70 1297. —— Leaves of Grass. *Portrait.* 12mo. cloth.
Bost.: 1860-61 (1879).

The spurious re-issue of the 1860-61 edition. bound in maroon cloth. and with plain portrait.

.25 1298. —— Man's Moral Nature. An Essay. By Richard Maurice Bucke (one of Whitman's literary executors). 12mo, cloth uncut. N. Y.: 1879.

"I dedicate this book to the man who inspired it—to the man . . . who has the most exalted moral nature, to Walt Whitman."

.75 1299. —— Leaves of Grass. 12mo. cloth. Bost: 1881-82.
The suppressed Boston edition.

.55 1300. —— Leaves of Grass. 12mo. cloth (names on title).
Phila.: 1882.

First Philadelphia edition with Rees. Welsh and Co.'s imprint. Printed from the plates of the suppressed Boston edition. Laid in is a bill against Walt Whitman for "repairing chimney at house on Mickle Street." Camden. 1886, on the back of which Whitman has written. "Kellenbeck's Bill. Dec. '86, $2.75. Paid."

.50 1301. —— The Poet's Tribute to Garfield. A collection of many Memorial Poems. *With portrait and biography.* 12mo, cloth. Cambridge: 1882.

Contains contributions from Walt Whitman, Longfellow, Aldrich Holmes, Joaquin Miller, and others. Laid in is the Memorial Broadside from the Mayor of Lowell, Mass., to the Pupils of the Public Schools.

.60 1302. —— Specimen Days and Collect. FIRST EDITION. (without portrait.) 12mo, cloth.
Phila.: Rees Welsh and Co.: 1882-83.

Laid in is an autograph Postal Caard from Will Carleton to Walt Whitman, on which he writes: *"Book received safely and much enjoyed."*

.50 1303. —— Leaves of Grass. 12mo, cloth. Phila.: 1883.

.40 1304. —— Specimen Days and Collect. *Portrait from photo.* 8vo, cloth, uncut and unopened. Glasgow: 1883.
A scarce edition.

.10 1305. —— The North American Review. November, 1885. 8vo, original wrappers, uncut. N. Y.: 1885.

Contains an article by Whitman on "Slang in America," also "Abraham Lincoln in Illinois," by E. B. Washburne.

.25 1306. —— Transactions of the Buffalo Historical Society. Vol. III. Red Jacket. *Portrait frontispiece.* 8vo, wrappers. Buffalo: 1885.

Contains a poem on Red Jacket by Whitman.

.25 1307. —— Poems of Walt Whitman (from 'Leaves of Grass'), with Introduction by Ernest Rhys. 18mo, limp morocco. Lond.: n. d. (1886).

1308. —— The Poet as a Craftsman. By W. Sloane Kennedy. 8vo, wrappers. Phila.: 1886.

"Privately published and set in type by the author's own hands; only a small number were issued and these were in a few months suppressed by the author."

1309. —— Anne Gilchrist, her Life and Writings. Edited by Herbert Harlakenden Gilchrist. With a Prefatory Notice by William Michael Rossetti. *Portrait and illustrations.* 8vo, cloth, uncut. N. Y.: 1887.

CHARLES WARREN STODDARD'S COPY, WITH HIS AUTOGRAPH.

1310. —— Specimen Days in America. Newly revised by the author, with fresh Preface and additional Notes. 12mo, cloth, paper label, uncut and unopened. Lond.: 1887.

1311. —— Complete Poems and Prose by Walt Whitman. 1855-1888. Authenticated and Personal Book (handled by W. W.). *Portraits from Life.* Royal 8vo, boards, cloth back paper label, uncut. (Phila.: 1888).

No. 20 of 600 copies printed. WITH AUTOGRAPH OF WALT WHITMAN, under which he has written in blue pencil, "For Melville Phillips. Camden. Jan. 29, 1890."

1312. —— November Boughs. FIRST EDITION. *Portrait.* 8vo, cloth *totally uncut.* Phila.: 1888.

Laid in is a ragged portion of a note sheet, on which is written in Whitman's autograph: "Walt Whitman, May 23, 1887. S(idney) H. M(orse) is here (Camden, N. J.) Sculping. W. W. ——." This copy is bound entirely different from the regular published edition, and in all probability this is one which was bound up by some Camden binder (or Whitman himself) from the original sheets furnished him by the publisher

1313. —— Camden's Compliment to Walt Whitman. May 31, 1889. Notes. Addresses, Letters, Telegrams. Edited by Horace L. Traubel. FIRST EDITION. *Frontispiece of the Clay model by Sidney H. Morse.* 8vo, cloth, uncut. Phila.: 1889.

With a one page A. L. S. from the Editor inserted.

1314. —— Gems from Walt Whitman. Selected by Elizabeth Porter Gould. FIRST EDITION. Oblong 18mo, cloth. Phila.: 1889.

With Autograph inscription on fly-leaf, signed E. P. G., consisting of "Lines sent to the dinner (5 P. M.) given in honor of Walt Whitman's seventieth birthday at Camden, N. J., May 31. 1889." There are four stanzas of four lines each. There is also an autograph poem written on the back fly-leaf, "To Walt Whitman," and signed in full. Evidently the author's own copy as annotations and quotations, comments and memos, throughout indicate.

1315. —— Leaves of Grass. With Sands at Seventy and a Backward Glance O'er Travel'd Roads. *Portraits.* 16mo, original limp black morocco, gilt edges. (Phila.: May 31, 1889).

A special edition issued on the author's seventieth birthday, "celebrating (the event) by a special complete final utterance in one handy volume of L. of G." WITH AUTOGRAPH SIGNATURE OF THE AUTHOR ON TITLE. Edition limited to 300 copies.

1316. —— An Oration on Walt Whitman. By Col. Robert G. Ingersoll. FIRST EDITION. 16mo, original wrappers. Lond.: 1890.

1317. —— Good-Bye my Fancy. 2d Annex to Leaves of Grass. FIRST EDITION. *Portrait frontispiece.* 8vo, cloth, gilt top. Phila.: 1891.

Laid in is a self-addressed envelope to Walt Whitman, Solicitor's Office, Treasury, Washington, D. C.

1318. —— At the Graveside of Walt Whitman: Harleigh, Camden, New Jersey, March 30th; and Sprigs of Lilac. Edited by Horace L. Traubel (with Discourses, Poems, etc., by John Burroughs, R. G. Ingersoll, and others.) Royal 8vo, original wrappers, uncut. N. Y.: 1892.

5.50

Number 66 of only 750 copies issued, numbered and signed by the Editor. From the McKee collection, with presentation inscription from the Editor.

1319. —— Autobiographia; or, The Story of a Life. Selected from his Prose Writings, and Edited by Arthur Stedman. *Frontispiece of Whitman's house in Camden.* FIRST EDITION. 12mo, cloth. N. Y.: 1892.

30

Owing to the failure of the publishers, very few copies were put on the market.

1320. —— Complete Prose Works. 8vo, cloth, uncut. Phila.: 1892.

.75

Inserted is a 3pp. A. L. S. from David McKay (Whitman's Publisher) to Mr. Powers relating to Whitman's works. Also laid in is a Programme of the Third Annual Meeting of the Walt Whitman Fellowship.

1321. —— Liberty in Literature. Testimonial to Walt Whitman by Robert G. Ingersoll. FIRST EDITION. *Vignette.* 12mo, wrappers. N. Y.: 1892.

2.60

1322. —— Selected Poems. Edited by Arthur Stedman. *Portrait.* 12mo, cloth. N. Y.: 1892.

1—

Cabinet photograph of Whitman laid in.

1323. —— Three Tales. The Ghost. The Brazen Android. The Carpenter. By William Douglas O'Connor. FIRST EDITION. . 12mo, cloth. Bost.: 1892.

.25

The Preface is by Whitman.

1324. —— In Re Walt Whitman: Edited by his Literary Executors, Horace L. Traubel, Richard Maurice Bucke, Thomas B. Harned. Royal 8vo, cloth, uncut. Phila.: 1893.

.40

Only 1,000 copies printed. One or two of the articles are signed by the authors.

1325. —— Walt Whitman. The Poet of Democracy. By William Gay. FIRST EDITION. 12mo, original printed wrappers. Melbourne: 1893.

.50

Rare.

1326. —— Memories of Walt Whitman. By Richard Bucke. FIRST EDITION. 8vo, stitched, 12pp. Phila.: 1894.

.50

"Walt Whitman Fellowship Papers: No. 6."

1327. —— Leaves of Grass, including Sands at Seventy. 1st Annex, Good-Bye my Fancy. 2d Annex. A Backward Glance O'er Travel'd Roads, and *Portrait from Life.* 8vo, cloth, uncut. Phila.: 1894.

.50

Inserted is a self-addressed envelope to Walt Whitman. Attorney-General's Office, Washington, D. C., postmarked Brooklyn, Oct. 30 (1860's as indicated by stamp). On the end of the envelope, Whitman has written, *"From Dear Mother."*

1328. —— Conversations with Walt Whitman. By Sadakichi. Written in 1894. FIRST EDITION. 12mo, wrappers, uncut. N. Y.: 1895.

.25

Out of print and very scarce.

1329. —— Reminiscences of Walt Whitman with extracts from his Letters and Remarks upon his Writings. By William Sloane Kennedy. FIRST EDITION. 12mo, cloth. Paisley: 1896.

.70

Inserted is an A. L. S. FROM THE AUTHOR to Mr. Powers, requesting the loan of the (Washington) '71 edition of "Leaves of Grass" for Bibliographical purposes.

1330. —— Calamus. A Series of Letters written during the years 1868-80 by Walt Whitman to a Young Friend (Peter Doyle). Edited, with an Introduction by Richard Maurice Bucke, M. D. (one of Whitman's Literary Executors). *Portraits.* Square 12mo, boards, uncut. Bost.: 1897.
ONE OF 35 COPIES PRINTED ON LARGE PAPER. This No. 8 Signed by R. M. Bucke.

1331. —— Leaves of Grass, including Sands at Seventy, Good Bye My Fancy, Old Age Echoes, and A Backward Glance O'er Travel'd Roads. *Fine frontispiece portrait.* Post 8vo, cloth, gilt top, uncut. Bost.: 1897.
First issue of this edition, copyrighted by the Literary Executors of Walt Whitman. Inserted is a 1p., 4to, A. L. S. from Small, Maynard and Co., relating to the '71 Edition, and speaking of a possible further edition, when the copyright expires in 1899.

1332. —— Poetical Sermons, including the Ballad of Plymouth Church. By William E. Davenport. FIRST EDITION. 16mo, cloth, gilt top, uncut. N. Y.: 1897.
Written in imitation of the style of Whitman.

1333. —— Johnston (John) Diary Notes of a Visit to Walt Whitman and some of his Friends in 1890. *With a series of original protographs.* 12mo, cloth, uncut and unopened.
Manchester: 1898.
Laid in is a 6pp. A. L. S. from Elizabeth Keller, who was Walt Whitman's nurse during his last illness.

1334. —— Selections from the Prose and Poetry of Walt Whitman. Edited with an Introduction by Oscar Lovell Triggs. *Portrait.* 12mo, cloth, gilt top, uncut.
Bost.: 1898.

1335. —— Walt Whitman at Home. By Himself. *Portrait and facsimiles.* 12mo. stitched, printed wrappers. Critic Pamphlet No. 2. N. Y.: 1898.

1336. —— Another copy.

1337. —— The Wound Dresser. A series of letters written from the Hosptials in Washington during the War of the Rebellion. Edited by Richard Maurice Bucke. FIRST EDITION. *Portrait.* 12mo, cloth, gilt top, uncut. Bost.: 1898.
ONLY 60 COPIES PRINTED ON ALTON MILLS PAPER, this No. 14.. Signed by R. M. Bucke.

1338. —— Notes and Fragments left by Walt Whitman and now edited by Dr. R. M. Bucke. Royal 8vo, cloth.
Lond.: (Ontario), 1899.
PRIVATELY PRINTED. Only 225 copies issued, each signed by Dr. Bucke.

1339. —— Walt Whitman. Two Addresses by William Mackintire Salter. 12mo, boards, paper label. Phila.: 1899.
Laid in is a Programme and Extract from the Constitution of the Boston Branch of the "Walt Whitman Fellowship."

1340. —— Walt Whitman's Poetry. A Study and a Selection. By Edmond Holmes. FIRST EDITION. Small 4to, decorated cloth, uncut and unopened. Fine copy. Lond.: 1902.

1341. —— Whitman's Ideal Democracy and other Writings by Helena Born. With a Biography by the Editor, Helen Tufts. *Portrait.* Small 4to, boards, uncut. Bost.: 1902.
Inserted is a 1 p. A. L. S. from Helen M. Tufts relating to the book, and referring also to the assassination of Pres. McKinley.

1342. —— An American Primer. *With facsimiles of the Original Manuscript.* Edited by Horace Traubel. *Portrait.* FIRST EDITION. 8vo, boards, uncut. Bost.: 1904.
Only 500 copies printed. Not in his collected works.

1343. —— Song of Myself. *Portrait.* 4to, half undressed calf, gilt top, uncut. East Aurora: 1904.
Inscribed by Elbert Hubbard, *"Remember the week-day to keep it holy. Elbert Hubbard."* Also laid in is an Autograph postal card from Mr. Hubbard, signed Roycroft.

1344. —— Walt Whitman's Diary in Canada. With Extracts from other of his Diaries and Literary Note Books. Edited by William Sloane Kennedy. FIRST EDITION. *Portrait.* 8vo, boards, uncut. Bost.: 1904.
Only 500 copies printed. Not in his collected works.

1345. —— Walt Whitman: Seer. A Brief Study. By Henry Wallace. FIRST EDITION. 12mo, wrappers.
Lond.: 1904.

1346. —— The Book of Heavenly Death. Compiled from Leaves of Grass by Horace Traubel. FIRST EDITION. *Portrait.* Small 4to, boards, uncut. Portland: Mosher, 1905.
Only 500 copies printed.

1347. —— Lafayette in Brooklyn. With an Introduction by John Burroughs. FIRST EDITION. *Portraits and facsimiles.* 8vo, boards, uncut. N. Y.: 1905.
With a 2 pp. A. L. S. from John Burroughs inserted. *"I have a plan by and by to make a book on Whitman . . . I find it very difficult to make a satisfactory statement about Whitman, he is so baffling; his horizon lines recede as I advance."*

1348. —— Lafayette in Brooklyn. With an Introduction by John Burroughs. FIRST EDITION. *Portrait and facsimile.* 8vo, boards, uncut. N. Y.: 1905.
Inscribed by the author:
"After sixty years I have little doubt that Whitman's was the finest head this age or country has seen. John Burroughs."

1349. —— Walt Whitman and Leaves of Grass. An Introduction. By W. H. Trimble. FIRST EDITION. 12mo, wrappers.
Lond.: 1905.

1350. —— Whitman, the Poet-Liberator of Woman. By Mabel MacCoy Irwin. *Frontispiece portrait from the "Lear" Photo.* FIRST EDITION. 16mo, gray cloth, gilt top, uncut.
N. Y.: Published by the author, 1905.
Only 500 copies printed, each one numbered and signed by the author.

1351. —— A Little Book of Nature Thoughts. Selected by Anne Montgomerie Traubel. Narrow 18mo, paper covers, uncut. Portland: Mosher, 1906.

1352. —— Memories of President Lincoln and other Lyrics of the War. 12mo, boards, paper labels, uncut and unopened. Portland: Mosher, 1906.

1353. —— Fair Play. Jan., 1908. 12mo, wrappers.
N. Y.: 1908.
Contains Walt Whitman and his Disciples: A Voice from the Nile by James Thomson, etc., etc.

1354. —— The Wisdom of Walt Whitman. Selected and Edited, with Introduction by Laurens Maynard. Square 18mo, limp leather, gilt edges. N. Y.: 1908.

1355. —— Walt Whitman: The Last Phase. By Elizabeth Leavitt Keller (his nurse during his last illness). As issued in Putnam's Magazine for June, 1909.

Laid in is a Postal Card from the author referring to the article, together with a 3 pp. A. L. S. from her, referring to her literary work about Whitman and her close association with him as nurse.

1.35

1356. —— Anne Gilchrist and Walt Whitman. By Elizabeth Porter Gould. *Fine portraits of Whitman, Burroughs, Anne Gilchrist, etc.* Square 12mo, cloth, uncut.

Phila.: n. d.

45

1357. —— The Broadway Annual. Vol. 1. Thick 8vo, half morocco. Lond.: n. d.

Contains an article of Walt Whitman by Robert Buchanan, pp. 188-195.

50

1358. —— Poems by Walt Whitman. "The Penny Poets." 12mo, wrappers. Lond.: n. d.

1—

1359. —— Walt Whitman. By Richard Maurice Bucke. To which is added, English Critics on Walt Whitman. Edited by Edward Dowden. *Etched frontispiece portrait and other portraits and views.* 12mo, cloth, uncut.

Paisley: Gardner, n. d.

Laid in is a L. S. by the author referring to "Washington Editions" spurious and real, and commenting on Edward Carpenter.

4.50

1360. —— Autograph check drawn by him and signed. November 12, 1887. Also a fine cabinet portrait, and a lock of his hair. The whole neatly mounted and framed in oak. This was procured from Elizabeth Keller (Whitman's nurse in his last illness) as intimated in a postal from her accompanying the frame.

10—

1361. —— Excerpts. Comprising: What Edward Carpenter says about Walt Whitman in his latest Book;—"My Boys and Girls" by Whitman;—Reminiscences of Walt Whitman, by J. T. Trowbridge. 3 pieces.

45

1362. —— Magazine excerpts by and on Walt Whitman. "Death in the School-Room"; Portraits of Walt Whitman (Bucke); Walt Whitman (Anon.); "Have We a National Literature?" (Whitman); "A Memorandum at a Venture" (Whitman); "Personalism" (Whitman); "Old-Age Echoes" (Whitman); "Some Personal and Old-Age Memoranda" ((Whitman); "Slang in America' (Whitman), etc. 13 pieces.

1.30

1363. —— Walt Whitman Fellowship Papers. 1894-1898, not quite consecutive. 76 pieces.

Comprises articles by Richard Le Gallienne, Laurens Maynard, Kelley Miller, Richard M. Bucke, Thomas B. Harned, Hamlin Garland, Daniel G. Brinton, and others.

6.66

No. 915

UNPUBLISHED
AUTOGRAPH LETTERS

AND

BOOKS OF
ENGLISH AND AMERICAN AUTHORS
WITH ASSOCIATION INTEREST

FROM THE ESTATE OF

Ferdinand Freiligrath
1810–1876
GERMAN LYRIC AND PATRIOTIC POET

———

TO BE SOLD

WEDNESDAY AFTERNOON, OCTOBER 25, 1911

AT **2.30** O'CLOCK

———

The Anderson Auction Company
MADISON AVENUE AT FORTIETH STREET
NEW YORK

———

298. WHITMAN (WALT). Leaves of Grass. 12mo, half roan. N. Y. 1867

*First editions of some of the poems. The whole work is here re-arranged. AUTOGRAPH PRESENTATION COPY FROM THE AUTHOR, with inscription "*F. Freiligrath, from the author.*" Inserted at p. 22 is a portrait of Whitman (copy of the one issued with the first edition of "Leaves of Grass"), on the reverse of which Whitman has written "*W. W.—born 1819 this picture taken 1854.*"

Accompanying the volume is an A. L. S., from the author, 1 p. 8vo, Washington, Jan. 26, 1869. To Mr. Freiligrath: "*I have sent you to-day by ocean mail, a copy of my latest printed Leaves of Grass. . . . I shall be well pleased to hear from you,*" etc.

AN EXTRAORDINARY COLLECTION

OF

AUTOGRAPH LETTERS

AND

HISTORICAL DOCUMENTS

Relating to Colonial and Revolutionary Times and the Civil War,
Fine Letters of Poets, Authors, Composers, Statesmen,
Presidents, Signers of the Declaration, Members of
the Old Congress, Officers in the Continental
and United States Navy

ALSO

A Large Collection of Original Autograph Manuscripts, Letters
and Corrected Proofs of Walt Whitman, and many Letters
of Eminent English and American Authors to him

TO BE SOLD

Tuesday Afternoon and Evening, November 7th, 1911,

AT 2.30 AND 8 O'CLOCK P. M.

Catalogue Compiled and Sale
Conducted by
STAN. V. HENKELS

At the Book Auction Rooms of
SAMUEL T. FREEMAN & CO.
1519-21 Chestnut St., Phila.

TENNYSON'S LETTER TO WHITMAN.

663 **Tennyson, Alfred, Lord.** Poet Laureate. A. L. S. **3** pages, 8vo. Aldworth, Haslemere, Surrey, Aug. 24, 1878. To Walt Whitman, with stamped addressed envelope and autograph draft of Whitman's answer.

An interesting friendly letter from the great English poet to the good gray poet. Tennyson in addressing the envelope neglected to write the name of the town (i. e., Camden), so he corrected the error by writing his apology for the neglect on the back of the envelope.

" My dear Walt Whitman. I am not overfond of letter-writing— rather hate it indeed—and am so overburdened with correspondence that I neglect half of it,—nevertheless let me hope that I answered your last of September 14, '76—and that it miscarried. I am very glad to hear that you are so improved in health, that you move about the fields and woods freely and have enjoyment of your life. As to myself I am pretty well for my time of life—sixty-nine on the sixth of this month— but somewhat troubled about my eyes—for I am not only the shortest- sighted man in England—but have a great black island floating in each eye, and these blacknesses increase with increasing years, however my oculist assures me that I shall not go blind, and bids me as much as possible spare my eyes, neither reading nor writing too much. My wife is still an invalid and forced to be on the sofa all day but still I trust somewhat stronger than when I last wrote you. My younger son Lionel (whom you enquired about) was married to the daughter of F. Locker the author of London Lyrics in Feby. The wedding was celebrated in our old grand historical Abbey of Westminster, there was a great attendance of literati, &c., of all which I read an account in one of your New York papers—every third word a lie ! Trubner wrote this morning, stating that you wished to see a parody of your- self, which appears among other parodies of modern authors in a paper called " The London." I have it not or I would send it you. Good bye, good friend, I think I have answered all your questions. Yours ever. A. Tennyson."

CATALOGUE

OF

THE LIBRARY

OF

ALGERNON CHARLES SWINBURNE, ESQ.

Deceased

(SOLD BY ORDER OF THE EXECUTORS OF THE LATE W. T. WATTS-DUNTON, ESQ.)

COMPRISING

FIRST EDITIONS OF EMINENT ENGLISH AUTHORS,

including BROWNING, COLERIDGE, LAMB, ARNOLD, ROSSETTI, SHELLEY,
SWINBURNE, THACKERAY, ETC.;

KELMSCOTT PRESS PUBLICATIONS

(including CHAUCER'S WORKS);

SCARCE FRENCH LITERATURE;

HISTORICAL & TOPOGRAPHICAL WORKS; ILLUSTRATED BOOKS;

ETC.

MANY PRESENTATION COPIES,

WITH AUTOGRAPH INSCRIPTIONS OF SWINBURNE, V. HUGO, ROSSETTI, ETC.

———————

WHICH WILL BE SOLD BY AUCTION

BY MESSRS.

SOTHEBY, WILKINSON & HODGE,

Auctioneers of Literary Property & Works illustrative of the Fine Arts,

AT THEIR HOUSE, No. 13, WELLINGTON STREET, STRAND, W.C.

On MONDAY, 19th of JUNE, 1916, and Two following Days,

AT ONE O'CLOCK PRECISELY.

May be Viewed Two Days prior.   Catalogues may be had.

Dryden Press: J. Davy & Sons, 8 9, Frith-street, Soho-square, W.

847   Whitman (Walt) Drum Taps, FIRST EDITION, *original cloth*
                            New York, 1865

848   Whitman (W.) Leaves of Grass, 1867 ; Drum Taps, 1865 ;
      in 1 vol. *half bound, m. e. presentation copy to Swinburne
      with autograph inscription :* " *Algernon Charles Swinburne
      from Walt Whitman* "   *New York,* 1865-7

849   Whitman (W.) Poems, selected and edited by Wm. Michael
      Rossetti, FIRST EDITION, *portrait, original cloth*   1868

850   Whitman (W.) After All, not to create only, recited by Walt
      Whitman on Invitation of Managers American Institute on
      opening their 40th Annual Exhibition, New York, noon,
      September 7, 1871, *presentation copy with autograph in-
      scription on half-title :* " *To Alg. Chs. Swinburne from the
      author* "   *Boston,* 1871

851   Whitman (W.) Democratic Vistas, FIRST EDITION, *original
      wrappers, uncut, presentation copy with autograph inscrip-
      tion :* " *Alg. Chs. Swinburne, from Walt Whitman, Nov.
      1871* "   *Washington, D. C.* 1871

852   Whitman (W.) Leaves of Grass, *portrait inserted, uncut, pre-
      sentation copy from the author, with autograph inscription :*
      " *To Alg. Chs. Swinburne from Walt Whitman, Washing-
      ton, U.S. November, 1871* "   *ib.* 1871

853   Whitman (W.) Leaves of Grass, *presentation copy from the
      author with autograph inscription :* " *Algernon Charles
      Swinburne from the author with thanks and love,* " *and por-
      trait and photograph of the author inserted, one with his
      autograph signature*   *Boston,* 1881-2

854   Whitman (W.) As a Strong Bird on Pinions Free, and other
      Poems, *original cloth, with the advertisements*
                            Washington, 1872

855   Whitman. Gems from Walt Whitman, selected by Elizabeth
      Porter Gould, *presentation copy with inscription :* " *For Mr.
      Algernon C. Swinburne with the compliments of Elizabeth
      Porter Gould, Boston, Massachusetts, U.S.A.* "
               oblong. Philadelphia, 1889

856   Whitman (W.) Gems from : selected by Elizabeth Porter Gould,
      *presentation copy to Swinburne, with autograph inscription
      of E. P. Gould, and MS. poem sent to the dinner given in
      honour of Walt Whitman's seventieth birthday*
               oblong. Philadelphia, 1889

Valuable Library of
Thomas B. Harned, Esq.

One of the Literary Executors of Walt Whitman,

INCLUDING

Much Autographic and other material relating to Walt Whitman

AND

Fine and Special Editions of the most noted English, American and French Authors, many in Fine Bindings

WORKS ON THE FINE ARTS

AND MISCELLANEOUS LITERATURE

TO BE SOLD

TUESDAY AFTERNOON, MAY 8th, 1917

AT 2.30 O'CLOCK.

———

STAN. V. HENKELS
AUCTION COMMISSION MERCHANT
1904 Walnut St., Phila., Pa.

CATALOGUE

WHITMANIANA.

THE EARLIEST KNOWN LETTERS OF
WALT WHITMAN.

Ohio —

1   **Whitman, Walt.** The Good Gray Poet. A. L. S. *69.00* / *Brownback*
"Walter Whitman" 4to. New York, June 14 (1842). To
N. Hale, Jr., with address.

*One of the very few letters in existence signed " Walter Whit-
man," and this and the following are the two earliest known
letters of the poet in existence. They were presented to Thos.
B. Harned by Dr. Edward Everett Hale, in 1889. This
letter refers to his early literary work.*

"I took the liberty two or three weeks since, of forwarding you a
MS. tale, 'The Angel of Tears,'' intended for the ' Boston Miscellany.''
Be so kind, if you accept it, to forward a note, informing me thereof,
to this place (your agency in New York) and if you decline, please
return the MS.

My Stories, I believe, have been pretty popular, and extracted liberally. Several of them in the Democratic Review have received
public favor, instance " Death in the School-Room, &c., &c.

Walter Whitman."

2   **Whitman, Walt.** A. L. S. "Walter Whitman" 4to. *32.00* / *Rose*
(New York), June 1, 1842. To the Editor of the Boston
Miscellany, with address.

" The undersigned takes the liberty of offering you the accompanying MS. for your 'Miscellany.' The price is $8. The undersigned
would be glad to furnish you an article for each number, if it would be
agreeable to you.

Please forward an answer to the address given herewith, stating
whether you accept or decline.   Walter Whitman."

EARLIEST KNOWN MANUSCRIPT OF
WALT WHITMAN.

3   **Whitman, Walt** Earliest known Autograph Manuscript,
8 pages, folio, entitled "A Visit to the Opera with some

Gossip about the Singers and Music. By Mose Velsor, of Brooklyn.''

One of the most interesting of Whitman items, and signed by him under his nom de plume "Mose Velsor," this being his mother's maiden name. The article is not quite complete; it seems to lack a few pages, as it is numbered from 1 to 7 and then 10, and the lower half of the last page is missing.

8.00 Brownback

4   **Whitman, Walt.** Original Antograph Manuscript. "A Word about Tennyson," written on five sheets of paper of different size, as was his custom of latter days.

6.00 S. Weiss

VERY EARLY MANUSCRIPT OF WALT WHITMAN.

5   **Whitman, Walt.** Original Autograph Manuscript of a Poem, 5 pages, 4to.

An exceedingly interesting manuscript.

10.00 "

> " Power, passion, vehement joys,
>   driven as by winds and waves,
> With open voice here is a newer
>   Song I vaunt you once for
>   all,
> Thrilling to life's maturity,''
>   &c.   &c.   &c.

6   **Whitman, Walt.** Original Autograph Manuscript, a Portion of his Will, 4to.

6.00 "

" My house and lot 328 Mickle Street Camden New Jersey, and all my money in bank, and all other estate and property in books or any property whatever, I give and bequeath and devise to my brother Edward L. Whitman," &c.

7   Whitman, Walt.   A. L. S. 4to, no date.

" Tom here are some scraps and MS. for your friend at a venture, gather'd up from the heap, if they will do.   (You put on the right address)   Best respects & love to the Madame.''

8.00 Madigan

Ohio
13.00

8   **Whitman, Walt.** A. L. S. 4to.   July 7, no year.   To Thos. B. Harned, with addressed envelope.

In reference to his portrait for November Boughs.

" Tom I wish you would say to Frank the pictures of Elias Hicks and my own bust are entirely satisfactory & I want to see what I can do to print them, so as each to illustrate in the *Nov. Boughs*, one of each * * * I am having a bad day, had about a bad night. As you said, Bennett of New York has sent the check to me *back*."

9   **Whitman. Walt.** A. L. S. 4to. Camden, April 19, 1888. To Thos. B. Harned, with addressed envelope. *A characteristic letter.*

10.00 Ohio

"Billy Thompson of Gloucester, has just been here to invite me down to baked shad dinner at his place, Tuesday next, abt 2. Wishes me to invite you in his name & my own. You come here say ½ past 12 & we will drive down in my rig. Be back by dark," &c.

10   **Whitman, Walt.** A. L. S. 4to. Camden, Jan. 8, 1889. To Thos. B. Harned, with addressed envelope.

7.00 Madigan

"Tom, if you have it and you can, I wish you w'd fill my bottle again with that Sherry.

Love & respects to Mr H. by no means forgetting Anna, Tommy & little Herbert."

This is written on the back of a letter to him from Wm. F. Cornell.

11   **Whitman, Walt.** A. L. S. on Card. May 10, 1889.
"Tom if you will fill the brown bottle with Sherry for me & the small white bottle with Cognac. My dear friend O'Connor is dead."

3.25 "

12   **Whitman, Walt.** A. L. S. on Card. Camden, June 9, 1889. To Thos. B. Harned, with addressed envelope.

3.50 "

"Have had such a good time with the Champagne you sent me, must at least thank for it. I drank the whole bottle (except a little swig I insisted on Ed taking for going for it) had it in a big white mug half fill'd with broken ice, it has done me good already (for I was sort of 'under the weather' the last 30 hours."

13   **Whitman, Walt.** A. N. S. on Postal Card. Camden, Nov. 27, no year. To Thos. B. Harned.

1.50 order

"Yes I shall be very glad to take dinner with you on Thursday, at 1. If I see Morse I will ask him to come along."

14   **Whitman, Walt.** A. L. S. on Card. Camden, Dec. 28, 1880.

1.25 "

"I shall be glad to supply you with a set (Two Volumes) of my books. There is only one kind of binding."

15   **Whitman, Walt.** A. L. S. with initials, Nov. 7, no year, on the front of an envelope to Mr. and Mrs. Harned.

25 Cullen

"I send the two tickets for the lecture. Also a little book for Anne. Also a Programme of Donnelly's 'Cipher' Book, curious to look over. Also your Sunday Tribune w'h I pilfered last night," &c.

16   **Whitman, Walt.** Invitation, signed. "At Home on Thursday Evening, April 15, 1887."

25 "

EARLY STORIES BY WALT WHITMAN.

17 **The United States Magazine and Democratic Review.** 9.00
New Series, Vol. IX. *Roberta*

8vo, sheep. New York, 1841

*In this volume will be found the earliest appearance in print of the Writings of Walt Whitman, viz.: At page 177 we find "*DEATH IN THE SCHOOL ROOM.*" In his letter catalogued as Lot 1 in this Sale, and which is one of his earliest known letters, he makes mention that he had published this story in the Democratic Review, and that it was received with popular favor. At page 476 will be found "*WILD FRANK'S RETURN*," and at page 560 "*BERVANCE; OR FATHER AND SON.*" These three stories are unknown to most lovers of the Works of the Good Grey Poet, and were instrumental in establishing his reputation as an Author of uncommon ability. The volume is very rare and was presented to Thos. B. Harned by Judge C. G. Garrison of Camden and so inscribed.*

WHITMAN'S ONLY NOVEL.

10.00
*Drake
lot y=
(yyc per price)*

18 **The New World.** Edited by Park Benjamin. Odd numbers running from Oct., 1842, to April, 1843.

Imperial 8vo. 11 pieces. New York

*In the Nov., 1842, Number will be found the first appearance in print of Walt Whitman's Only Novel, "*FRANKLIN EVANS; OR, THE INEBRIATE. A TALE OF THE TIMES.*" Mr. Thos. B. Harned, who was one of Whitman's literary executors, informs me that after an exhaustive research he has only been able to find two other copies of this number in existence. The Magazine was a very erratic publication, which was issued with supplemental numbers and extras in such a manner that we doubt whether the editor himself could tell how to put them together for binding. In the Nov., 1842, Number, Extra Series, will be found the First American Edition of Dickens' American Notes, and in the February Number, 1843, Extra Series, is the First American Edition of Borrow's Bible in Spain.*

FIRST EDITION OF LEAVES OF GRASS.

31.00
G. Weiss

19 **Whitman, Walt.** Leaves of Grass, with portrait.

Imperial 8vo, original green cloth, with title in gold on sides and back.
Brooklyn, New York, 1855

A good clean copy of the very rare First Edition.   Loose in the covers.

SECOND EDITION OF LEAVES OF GRASS.

20   Whitman, Walt.   Leaves of Grass, with portrait.
12mo, original green cloth.   Brooklyn, New York, 1856
Excessively rare; loose in binding.

*5.00
Fenster*

21   **Whitman, Walt.**   Two Rivulets, including Democratic
Vistas, Centennial Songs, and Passage to India.
12mo, half kid.   Camden, 1876
   "This book was in Walt Whitman's room in Camden, N. J., where
he died, and it came into my possession as his literary Executor.
                              Thos. B. Harned, April 15, 1917."

*1.00
Cullen*

22   Whitman, Walt.   November Boughs.
8vo, cloth, uncut.   Philadelphia, 1888
   *First Edition, and so inscribed by Thos. B. Harned, Whit-
man's Literary Executor.*

*4.25
Dav*

23   **Whitman, Walt.**   Notes and Fragments, Left by Walt
Whitman, and now edited by Dr. Richard Maurice Bucke,
one of his Literary Executors.
Imperial 8vo, cloth, uncut.   Printed for Private Distribution only, 1899
Mr. Harned says:

   "I bought the few remaining copies of this book and it is entirely
out of print and very scarce.   The New York Sun said it would be
worth its weight in gold."

1.75 "

24   **Whitman, Walt.** Complete Poems and Prose of. 1855–
1888.   Portrait on title and engraved portrait.
Royal 8vo, boards, cloth back, uncut.   1888
   *Authenticated and Personal Book, handled by W. W.; por-
traits from life; autographed by Walt Whitman. Of this
Mr. Harned, his Literary Executor, says is "An important
Edition, very scare, authographed, much sought after," and
this is written on the fly-leaf.*

6.00 "

PAUMANOK EDITION OF WHITMAN'S WORKS.

25   **Whitman, Walt.**   The Complete Writings of. Issued
under the editorial supervision of his Literary Executors,
Richard Maurice Bucke, Thomas B. Harned and Horace
L. Traubel.   With additional bibliographical and critical
material prepared by Oscar Lovell Triggs.   *With colored
frontispieces and other illustrations on Japan paper.*

10 vols. 8vo, full green crushed levant, gilt tooling on back and sides, broad dentelle borders, leather doublé and fly-leaves, top edges gilt, uncut. Putnam : New York, 1902 *9.50 Stonestreet*

Paumanok Edition. No. 1 of 300 sets. This copy belonged to Thomas B. Harned, one of Whitman's Literary Executors, who has written about this edition on the fly-leaf of volume one.

25A Book from Whitman's Library. The Century Guild Hobby Horse. *Illustrated.*

2 vols. 4to, half vellum. London, n. d. *2.00 Sinn*

" This work was presented to Walt Whitman at the time of its publication by an English friend, and he presented it to me in 1887. Thos. B. Harned, Literary Executor of Walt Whitman."

The work is very scarce, and contains much rare literary and artistic material, including an etching of the Burial of Stephen by Wm. Strange; The Entombment by Ford. Maddox Brown; woodcuts by Arthur Burgess; Original Poems and Essays by Arthur Galton, W. M. Rossetti, Oscar Wilde, Arthur H. Mackmurde, Christina G. Rosetti, Jno. Ruskin, and others.

26 Young, Jno. R. Around the World with General Grant. *Illustrated.* *2.00 Bigby*

2 vols. Royal 8vo, half calf, gilt, marbled edges. New York, n. d.
On the fly-leaf is inscribed by the author :

" To Walt Whitman with the affectionate reverence of many years.
John Russell Young."

27 Symonds, John Addington. Wine, Women and Song. Mediaeval Latin Students Songs. Now first translated into English Verse, with an Essay. *15.00 Arnold*

12mo, vellum, uncut. London : Chatto & Windus, 1884

The very rare First Edition. Presented to Walt Whitman by the Author, and presented by Walt Whitman to Thos. B. Harned, Aug. 17, 1788, and so inscribed by Harned on the fly-leaf. *n.g* *all written by Harned*

FROM DR. DANIEL LONGAKER,

WALT WHITMAN'S PHYSICIAN.

28 Whitman, Walt. Autograph Manuscript, 1 page, 4to, entitled " A Crude Notion." *9.00 Plainfield*

" My great corpus is like an old wooden log. Possibly (even probably) that slow vital almost impalpable byplay of automatic stimulus belonging to living fibre has by gradual habit of years and years, in me (and especially of the last three years) got quite diverted into

> *mental play, and vitality & attention,* instead of attending to its normal play in stomachic, & muscular & peristaltic use. Does this acc't for Stomachic non-action, non-stimulus? Or what is there in this, if any thing?"

29   **Whitman, Walt.** Autograph memorandum, by himself, of the Condition of his health, and the action of the medicine administered by his Physician (Dr. Longaker) dating from March 20, to April 14, 1891, written on Backs of letters from friends and publishers and on the inside of addressed envelopes cut open.   20 pieces

lot
14.00
Plainfield

> *An interesting memento of the good old poet. In these notes he tells when he took his medicine, and notes in a particular manner its action. Of course it would not do for us to quote them, as they are of a peculiar nature and were intended for his physician only.*

30   **Whitman, Walt.** Facsimile of his letter to Dr. J. Johnston, Bolton, England, of June 1, 1891, and Feb. 6, 1892. facsimiled at the Poet's request and with an A. L. S. of Dr. J. Johnston to Dr. D. Longaker dated Bolton, April 14, 1891, asking for information as to Whitman's health, and requesting a Diagnosis of his disease.   As a lot.

1.00
Roberts

31   Whitman, Walt.   2 A. L. S. and 1 L. S. 4to.   Dated March 9th, 21st and 27th, from R. M. Bucke to Dr. D. Longaker, concurring with Mr. Horace Traubel, in selecting Dr. Longaker to be Walt Whitman's physician, and asking Dr. Longaker to give all the attention to the case possible.   3 pieces

lot
1.00
Plainfield

In one of these letters Mr. Bucke says:

> "His danger at present (I think) is heart failure, but with care he may go on many years.   Mentally Mr. W. is failing a good deal. Makes slips now that would have been impossible for *him* a very few years ago, for instance : I have a post card from him dated 23d inst. He says : 'Dr. Yorkman came yesterday, I like him.'   A *name* was something that he *never* went wrong in.   I am very much pleased that he likes you and feel satisfied that you will get on well with him." This is a pathetic episode in the life of the Poet, as he calls Dr. Longaker "Dr. Yorkman" in writing to Mr. Bucke, and shows the dissolution of a great mind.

32   **Whitman, Walt.**   Fellowship Papers.   Second, Third and Fourth Years, not quite consecutive.   1894–98.
          36 pieces

lot
8.00
Roberts

33   **Advertising Notices** of the Publication of Walt Whitman's Works.   5 pieces

lot
1.00
Plainfield

50

34 **Whitman, Walt.** Complete Poems and Prose of. 1855–1888. Authenticated and Personal Book (handled by W. W.) Portrait from Life. Autographed.

Royal 8vo, half green cloth, uncut.

Autograph presentation copy from the author, and so inscribed on fly-leaf. "Dan'l Longaker, from the Author, June 16, 1890." No. 56 of 600 copies published.

8.00 Roberts

35 **Whitman, Walt.** Leaves of Grass.

12mo, rough paper wrappers, uncut.　　　Philadelphia, 1891–2

3.00 Plainfield

36 **Whitman, Walt.** Leaves of Grass, with Sands at Seventy and A Backward Glance o'er Travel'd Roads, with six portraits, one a Photograph from Life.

12mo, limp morocco, gilt edges.

Special Edition. Autographed, with Portrait from Life. Only 300 copies printed.

9.00 "

9.00 Roberts

37 **Another Copy.**

38 **Whitman, Walt.** Leaves of Grass. Portrait.

12mo, cloth.　　　Boston, 1860–61

The Third Edition.

2.75 Plainfield

39 **Another Copy.**

2.00 Bacon

40 **Whitman, Walt.** Leaves of Grass and Two Rivulets, with Photographic Portrait from Life in the latter.

2 vols. 12mo, half leather.　　　Author's Edition : Camden, New Jersey, 1876

The Leaves of Grass is Autographed on the Title and The Two Rivulets is Autographed on the Portrait. This is the Centennial Edition, and the Author has written on a piece of paper inserted on the inside of Cover of Leaves of Grass:

"Centennial Ed'n—Two Vols *Leaves of Grass & Two Rivulets,* bound in half leather & Italian Card. Containing Autograph Portraits (Three from life) Personal Memoranda of the War 'Democratic Vistas' &c &c."

2.25 Plainfield

41 **Whitman, Walt.** As a Strong Bird on Pinions Free, and other Poems.

12mo, cloth, uncut.　　　Washington, 1872

A very few copies published.

10.00 Ohio

42 **Whitman, Walt.** Calmus. A Series of Letters written during the years 1868–1880, by Walt Whitman to a Young Friend (Peter Doyle). Edited, with an Introduction, by Richard M. Bucke, M. D., one of Whitman's Literary Executors. Portrait.

12mo, cloth.　　　Boston, 1897

3.25 Plainfield

Lots 43–48 omitted

LIBRARY

OF THE LATE

DR. ISAAC HULL PLATT

OF PHILADELPHIA

AND FROM OTHER SOURCES

CONTAINING

The most important Collection of Manuscripts, Books and
Relics of

WALT WHITMAN

ever offered at Public Sale, including his Gold Watch, and
Portrait by Littlefield

Rare and Scarce American History

EMBRACING

State, County and Town History, Western Travel, and
Explorations, Early Guide Books, Early Maps,
Indian History, Franklin and other Early American
Imprints, Almanacs, Confederate Publications, Revo-
lutionary History, War with Mexico, and Scarce
Pamphlets

TO BE SOLD

MONDAY AFTERNOON, DEC. 22d, 1919

AT 2.30 O'CLOCK.

STAN. V. HENKELS

AUCTION COMMISSION MERCHANT

For the Sale of Books, Autographs, Paintings and Engravings

1304 WALNUT STREET

PHILADELPHIA, PA.

Assistant—STAN. V. HENKELS, Jr.

CATALOGUE

Whitmaniana.

ORIGINAL MANUSCRIPT OF WHITMAN'S PROUD
MUSIC OF THE SEA-STORM.

1   WHITMAN, WALT. The Original Autograph Manuscript of his noted Poem, entitled "Proud Music of the Sea-Storm." 17 cantos on 9 folio pages.

Whitman's poem was printed from this manuscript, and after proving was materially altered in several instances. This manuscript was presented to Dr. Isaac Hull Platt by T. H. Rome, and is accompanied by a letter of presentation, dated Brooklyn, Jan. 20, 1896, from Mr. Rome, in which he says:

"Whitman's poem 'Proud Music of the Sea Storm,' was printed from the MS. now in your possession, in 1874 or '75 not for private distribution but for revision before publication. It was carefully put in type, proved and compared with the original—a literal copy being made. A proof was then sent to Washington. It was returned in due time with Walt's corrections. Whatever discrepancy there may be between the MS. and the published form is thus explained. After correcting his proof, two or three copies were struck off and mailed to him. Your remarks on Whitman before the Ethical Society put me in the notion of sending you a bit of his handwork. The genuineness of the poem is beyond the shadow of a doubt."

This is really the neatest manuscript from the hand of the "Good Gray Poet" I ever saw. It is written in his well-known plain hand on nine folio pages, with only a few inter-lineations or corrections, and the fact of this being written on foolscap, every page the same size, will go far to make this a most desirable specimen. You know he generally wrote on scraps of paper of all kinds and sizes, but in the manuscript of this poem (which went far to place him among the great poets of his age), he seems to have taken particular pains to write it in a more uniform and neater manner than was his wont.

60.00

Lepington

SALE NUMBER 1480
ON PUBLIC EXHIBITION FROM MONDAY, MARCH EIGHTH

THE LIBRARY
OF THE LATE
H. BUXTON FORMAN
[PART I]

ORDER OF SALE

MONDAY AFTERNOON,   MARCH 15, LOTS   1– 200
MONDAY EVENING,   MARCH 15, LOTS 201– 400
TUESDAY AFTERNOON,   MARCH 16, LOTS 401– 600
TUESDAY EVENING,   MARCH 16, LOTS 601– 800
WEDNESDAY AFTERNOON, MARCH 17, LOTS 801–1000

THE ANDERSON GALLERIES
[MITCHELL KENNERLEY, PRESIDENT]
PARK AVENUE AND FIFTY-NINTH STREET, NEW YORK
1920

932. WHITMAN (WALT). Leaves of Grass. 12mo, half mo- *30—*
rocco.   New York, 1867

THE VERY SCARCE FOURTH EDITION. Autograph presentation copy from
R. Maurice Bucke to Mr. Forman. On the fly-leaf Mr. Forman has
written: "Forty years ago, when Maurice Bucke gave me this book he
& I were both outside students of Walt Whitman; and the collation of
this edition with that of 1855 was one of his earliest bits of Whitman
work. Most of the variations are in the writing of his brother Julius,
who noted them under his instructions."
The variations referred to are on interleaves in the first part of the
book.

933. WHITMAN (WALT). Notes on Walt Whitman as Poet
and Person. By John Burroughs. 12mo, original cloth, uncut.
                                            New York, 1867

FIRST EDITION. Autograph presentation copy from Moncure D. Conway to John Stuart Mill. The author has signed the Preface, and on the
last page has written "The End."

———— ———— ————

942. WHITMAN (WALT). Leaves of Grass. 12mo, cloth, uncut top.   Washington, 1872

On the fly-leaf Mr. Forman has written: "This edition of 'Leaves of
Grass' purporting to be printed in New York, was in reality printed in
London,—one of the many meaningless swindles of the late John Hotten." On the back of an envelope laid in, he has noted two variations
between this spurious and the genuine edition.

———— ———— ————

950. WHITMAN (WALT). Specimen Days & Collect. 12mo, *57⁵⁰*
full red levant morocco, gilt edges, by Tout. Original covers bound
in.   Philadelphia: David McKay, 1882-'83

With a tinted phototype portrait inserted, AUTOGRAPHED IN BLUE PEN-
CIL BY WHITMAN. On pp. 315-316 Whitman has deleted "Two Letters"
in indelible pencil, and had originally torn from this volume pp. 317 to
the end. These have been neatly replaced. On p. 339 he had written
"out all to 374."
THIS IS THE COPY PREPARED BY WALT WHITMAN AND SENT TO ERNEST
RHYS FOR PUBLICATION IN ENGLAND. The addressed portion of the wrapper in which the volume was sent to Mr. Rhys, with Whitman's signature thereon, has been mounted and inserted.
A 2pp. note by Mr. Forman relating to this volume and its association
interest appears on one of the fly-leaves.

———— ———— ————   *22—*

953. WHITMAN (WALT). Poems by Walt Whitman. Selected and Edited by William Michael Rossetti. *Portrait.* A new
edition. 12mo, cloth, gilt top, uncut.   London, 1886

Autograph presentation copy from Rossetti to Forman.

958. WHITMAN (WALT). Good-Bye My Fancy. 2d Annex to Leaves of Grass. *Phototype portrait.* 8vo, full red levant morocco, gilt top, uncut, by Tout. Philadelphia: David McKay, 1891

> A SPECIAL UNCUT COPY OF THE FIRST EDITION. Inserted is the addressed portion of the wrapper in which the volume was sent to Mr. Forman, with autograph of Whitman thereon. The portrait is also AUTOGRAPHED.
>
> On the fly-leaf Mr. Forman has written: " 'Good Bye My Fancy' was issued in red cloth boards, with much margin cut off. I obtained this uncut copy direct from Walt at the time of publication. . . . The inscription under the portrait is written by him: it does not appear in ordinary copies."
>
> THE PRESENT COPY IS SO LARGE AS TO BE PRACTICALLY A LARGE PAPER COPY.

959. WHITMAN (WALT). Leaves of Grass. Including Sands at Seventy. 1st Annex, Good-Bye My Fancy. 2d Annex, A Backward Glance o'er Travel'd Roads, and *Portrait from Life.* 8vo, original wrappers, paper label, uncut.

Philadelphia: David McKay, 1891-'92

> Autograph presentation copy to Mr. Forman, with inscription on fly-leaf: "To H. Buxton Forman, Jan. 7, 1892. Sent by Walt Whitman from his sick bed. H. L. T. Canada."
>
> Laid in is an Autograph Post Card from Whitman to Forman: [Sept. 27, 1891.]
>
> "I send copy of the complete works (for Maurice) & copies unbound of the little 'Good-Bye,' with more. Others will follow, especially a new fuller version of L. of G. now in press—I am physically an almost complete wreck (right arm & mentally & fair spirits left). Respects and love to you & yrs. Walt Whitman."
>
> There is also laid in, a post card from Traubel, in which he says: "Whitman in fatal condition. We watch him day by day with grave concern." [Jan. 8, 1892.]

WALT WHITMAN'S HOSPITAL NOTE BOOK

963. WHITMAN (WALT). Autograph Note Book kept by Walt Whitman during his services in the Civil War. 28 leaves, 2½ by 4 inches, with a cover of yellow paper.

435

> A MOST IMPORTANT RELIC OF WHITMAN AND THE CIVIL WAR. On the front cover is inscribed by Whitman: "Hospital Note Book. Walt Whitman." During the war his brother was wounded on the battlefield, which led to the poet's volunteering as an army nurse, which work he continued from 1862 to 1865, at Washington and in Virginia. His experiences are vividly recorded in "Drum-Taps" and "Memoranda during the War."
>
> The book contains many names, with direction for finding the soldiers in the various wards, a list of men shot for desertion; with pitiful notes regarding them, and occasionally a note such as follows: "*Ward F. get from the 1st Mass. Cavalry man as good and vivid account as possible of a cavalry fight—he tells me of full regiment charging.*"
>
> Overwork in the hospitals brought on a serious illness from which Whitman never fully recovered.

SELECTIONS FROM

THE LIBRARY OF
MR. EUSTACE CONWAY

OF NEW YORK

INCLUDING BOOKS AND MANUSCRIPTS
FORMERLY BELONGING TO THE LATE

MONCURE D. CONWAY

TO BE SOLD
MONDAY AFTERNOON, JUNE SEVENTH
AT TWO-THIRTY

THE ANDERSON GALLERIES
[MITCHELL KENNERLEY, PRESIDENT]
PARK AVENUE AND FIFTY-NINTH STREET, NEW YORK
1920

**WITH COPY IN WHITMAN'S HANDWRITING OF EMERSON'S
FAMOUS LETTER ABOUT "LEAVES OF GRASS"**

247. WHITMAN (WALT). Leaves of Grass. *Engraved frontispiece portrait.* Small folio, original stamped cloth, with the title in gilt and gilt borders on both covers.   Brooklyn, 1855

690

THE EXTREMELY RARE FIRST ISSUE OF THE FIRST EDITION. With contemporary autograph of the Author on title. Inserted is an A. L. S. of Whitman, to Moncure D. Conway dated Washington, July 21, 1870, of a very interesting nature.

"*I send herewith a verbatim copy of Emerson's note as requested. . . . . Am still employed in the Attorney General's office. A new edition of my book will be printed this fall, with another small volume in prose. You shall have early copies, may-be in sheets.*"

There is also inserted the verbatim copy of Emerson's note referred to above. As is well known, Whitman used the letter he received from Emerson, which was highly commendatory, to advertise "Leaves of Grass." This caused Emerson much annoyance, and he afterwards said that he would have qualified his praise had he known that the letter would be published.

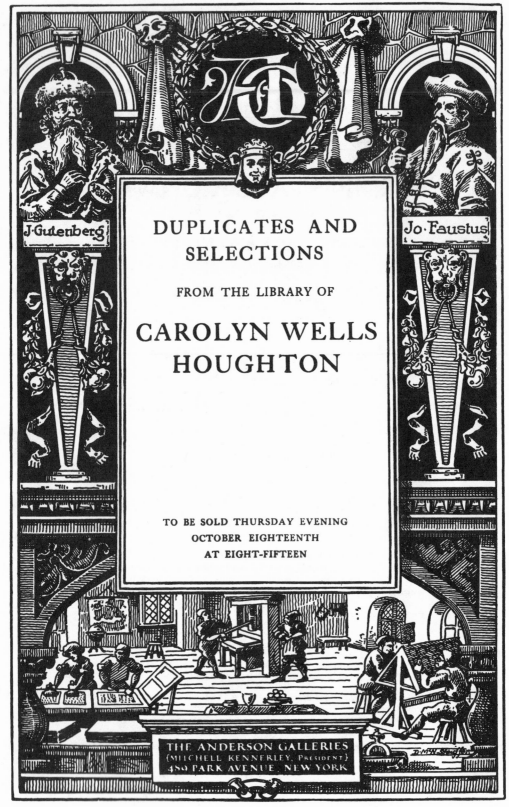

J. Gutenberg

Jo. Faustus

DUPLICATES AND SELECTIONS

FROM THE LIBRARY OF

CAROLYN WELLS HOUGHTON

TO BE SOLD THURSDAY EVENING
OCTOBER EIGHTEENTH
AT EIGHT-FIFTEEN

THE ANDERSON GALLERIES
(MITCHELL KENNERLEY, President)
489 PARK AVENUE, NEW YORK

TELEPHONE PLAZA 9356

SALE NUMBER 1760
ON PUBLIC EXHIBITION FROM WEDNESDAY, OCTOBER TENTH

DUPLICATES AND SELECTIONS

FROM THE LIBRARY OF

CAROLYN WELLS HOUGHTON

"CAROLYN WELLS"

OF NEW YORK CITY

AN EXTENSIVE AND VALUABLE COLLECTION OF WALT
WHITMAN FIRST EDITIONS AND AUTOGRAPHIC
MATERIAL, TOGETHER WITH THE FAREWELL
LINES OF WHITMAN'S MOTHER; FIRST
EDITIONS OF MODERN AUTHORS
ASSOCIATION COPIES AND
MINIATURE BOOKS

TO BE SOLD BY HER ORDER
THURSDAY EVENING, OCTOBER EIGHTEENTH
AT EIGHT-FIFTEEN O'CLOCK

THE ANDERSON GALLERIES

[MITCHELL KENNERLEY, President]

PARK AVENUE AND FIFTY-NINTH STREET, NEW YORK

1923

Friday Sept 19 '79
on the Plains (western
edge of Kansas, on to Colorado) — plains — plains — plains
The Dug-outs
antelope
the Prairie-Dog
^ emigrant wagons
Camped for the night
The vast, stretching plains
hundreds of miles area
the buffalo grass
the yellow, wild flowers.
the rare, clear, pure,
cool, rarefied air
(over 3000 ft above
sea level)
the Dry rivers

AUTOGRAPH NOTES OF WHITMAN'S WESTERN TRIP
[NUMBER 271]

AN INTRODUCTION

By A. Edward Newton

HERE in the midst of this awful heat comes a request, a command rather, from Carolyn Wells, that I write a brief introduction to the Sale Catalogue of a portion of her library. "Dear A. Edward," she says, "you must write a few lines and send 'em to Mitchell Kennerley for my catalogue; you got me into this mess, it's up to you to get me out. When this letter reaches you I shall be on the briny."

What am I to do? I can't "wireless" the lady where to go; she is probably ill by this time and thinks she is there already. I know what she means by the "mess." Several years ago we were in my library and I was showing her with pride a small blunder in a book which greatly enhanced its value. "And this mistake by that stupid printer adds eighty dollars to the value of that book?" she inquired.

"It does," I replied.

"Well, I call this game the Idiot's Delight," was her rejoinder.

"All right," I said, "you qualify."

"Tell me where to begin," she said.

It's great fun to bandy words with Carolyn Wells, but when she decides to do a thing she does it with an amount of intelligence that might lead you to believe that she is exhausting herself, but not so; she is only drawing upon her surplus energy. Now I believed at the time, and I still do, that anyone who wants to get the greatest sport out of collecting rare books cannot do better than to buy "Americana," for whatever happens to democracy, (and I am the last man that would wish to save it) I believe that the continent is safe.

That reminds me of a story. An old lady went into a broker's office to make an investment. The broker was very conservative and would not commit himself as to the value of several gilt edge securities she considered buying. Finally she said, "Well, then, it's your opinion that I should buy Government bonds; you regard them as absolutely safe, I suppose." "Well," said the broker, cautiously, "I would hardly say that, but they will be the last things to go."

Now, next to bonds on the continent, I believe in books about it. I haven't any myself and don't want any, for the reason that they don't interest me; my passion is English literature.

"What do you fancy?" I inquired of Carolyn.

"Something American," she said.

"In that case," I replied, "you could not do better than Walt Whitman. As a singer,—God, no! not as a singer, but as a yelper of the brotherhood of man, he is destined to take an important place."

"Comics are more in my line," said she, "but I believe you are right, I'll take on Whitman."

And the next thing I knew people were telling me about Carolyn Wells's Whitman collection, and after a year or two I heard that she had the finest lot of Whitman that had ever been put together. Then someone told me that she was doing a bibliography, and I asked her about it.

"Bibliography, no," she said, "check list, yes. Great fun."

Then I heard that her Whitman collection was to be sold; then I heard that it wasn't. Then that she was selling some rare duplicates and some other choice items because she had gone off on another tangent. It may be so, I do not know; very likely it is. But in whatever direction she has gone, people will know that she has passed that way.

Coming back to Whitman. I firmly believe that the first edition of the "Leaves of Grass" will reach a higher figure than any other important book published in the nineteenth century,—and I do not forget that valuable Shelleys and Keats were published in that century. I may not be around at the time. If I am not, let some kindly disposed soul go west; "Change cars at Paoli"; take a motor, and visit the Washington Memorial Chapel at Valley Forge (that's where these "Democratic Vistas" start), and after visiting the Chapel, which is one of the loveliest shrines in America, search out my modest tombstone in the leaves of grass nearby, sit down upon it, and whisper to me: "You were right about that Whitman item." I shall be listening eagerly for the latest prices of rare books.

A. EDWARD NEWTON

"Oak Knoll"
Daylesford, Pennsylvania
July 10th, 1923

"The price of growth is always to outgrow," is an old quotation that is quite as applicable to a library as to a human being. And when a library outgrows its shelves, something must be done.

It has also been written: "A house without a library is like a body without a soul."

This is true enough; but when the soul outgrows the body, again, -- something must be done.

So, as my library has utterly outgrown its bookcases, even though forced to that bête noire of all book lovers, double rows of books on the shelves! -- I am convinced that something must be done.

I am somewhat in the position of the farmer with an enormous harvest of apples. When asked how he disposed of them, he said: "Oh, I gave away all I could, and sold the rest."

Following his wise decision, I have concluded to part with (that's the proper phrase, I believe) my duplicates.

Duplicates, to a collector, are of great interest and value, but, ethically, they should pass into the hands of other collectors; -- so, here are mine, at your service.

Arthur Amwell Houghton

64

236 **WHITMAN (WALT).** Leaves of Grass. *Engraved portrait on plain paper* (a little foxed). Small folio, original green cloth, title in gilt on back, with gilt floral ornaments; title in gilt on both covers, with blind-tooled floral ornaments, gilt borders, gilt edges. Brooklyn, 1855

160

FIRST ISSUE OF THE FIRST EDITION.

237 —— Leaves of Grass. *Portrait.* 12mo, crushed red morocco, gilt line panel on sides, gilt edges (somewhat foxed). Brooklyn, 1856

18

THE VERY RARE SECOND EDITION. The Fowler and Wells leaf of advertisement usually found at the end is missing.

238 —— Leaves of Grass Imprints. 16mo, original wrappers. In a brocaded silk cover. Boston, 1860

40

EXTREMELY RARE. This is a reprint of criticisms of the First and Second Editions. Pages 7, 30, and 38 contain articles written by Walt Whitman anonymously to various papers. Dr. Bucke is the authority for this statement.
A letter from Emerson to Whitman is reprinted in full on verso of title-page.

239 —— Leaves of Grass. *Engraved portrait with buff background.* 12mo, red polished calf, gilt back, gilt top, by Riviere. Boston: Thayer and Eldridge, [1860-61]

16

The Genuine ''Thayer and Eldridge'' Edition, with the correct title-page, bearing imprint of Rand and Avery on verso.

240 [——] The Good Gray Poet. A Vindication. [By William Douglas O'Connor.] 8vo, original wrappers, uncut. New York: Bruce and Huntington, 1866

29

VERY RARE.

241 —— Democratic Vistas. 12mo, original wrappers, uncut. Washington, 1871

7

FIRST EDITION. FINE COPY.

242 —— Leaves of Grass. 12mo, dark red morocco, title on side, with inlaid Grasses at bottom, gilt top. In a cloth case. Washington, 1871

10

243 —— Passage to India. 12mo, original wrappers (worn, and some few pp. slightly stained at tops), uncut. Washington, 1871

10

FIRST EDITION. VERY SCARCE.

244 —— As a Strong Bird on Pinions Free. And other Poems. 12mo, original cloth. Washington, 1872

12

FIRST EDITION.

15 244A —— Another copy. 12mo, cloth. Washington, 1872

FIRST EDITION. Inscribed by Whitman in pencil: *"Hank Wright from his friend the author. July 30, '87."*

3⁵⁰ 245 —— Leaves of Grass. 12mo, original green cloth, uncut (a little shabby). Washington, 1872

H. Buxton Forman considered this one of Hotten's pirated editions, although there is nothing about the book to indicate this.

246 —— Leaves of Grass. 8vo, cloth, gilt top, uncut.
3⁵⁰ London: David Bogue, 1881

THE FIRST LONDON EDITION WITH WHITMAN'S OWN TITLES TO THE POEMS.

10 247 —— Leaves of Grass. 12mo, cloth.
Boston: James R. Osgood and Co., 1881-2

THE SUPPRESSED BOSTON EDITION, of which only a few copies were circulated, with the error "Third Edition" on the title-page. VERY RARE.

248 —— Specimen Days and Collect. *Photographic portrait.* 8vo,
3 cloth, uncut. Glasgow, 1883

THE SCARCE SCOTCH EDITION.

249 —— Specimen Days and Collect. 12mo, cloth.
Philadelphia, 1882-3
4 FIRST EDITION.

249A —— Walt Whitman. By Richard Maurice Bucke, M.D. *Etched portrait.* 12mo, cloth, uncut. Philadelphia, 1883
11 FIRST EDITION. Inscribed: *"Mrs. Constance M. Pott, Respects and regards of W. D. O'Connor. Washington, D. C., July 1883."*

249B —— Leaves of Grass. *Portrait.* 8vo, cloth.
3 Glasgow: Wilson & McCormick, 1884

249C —— Poems. Selected and arranged by William Michael Rossetti. *Portrait.* 12mo, buckram, uncut. London, 1886
5⁰ New Edition.

250 —— Photograph (a little faded), size 9¼ by 7½ inches. Auto-
6 graphed by Whitman, and dated Sept., 1887.

251 —— Complete Poems and Prose of Walt Whitman. 1855 . . .
1888. Authenticated & Personal Book (handled by W. W.)
18 *Portraits from Life . . . Autograph.* Royal 8vo, half calf
(rubbed). N. p., n. d. [Philadelphia, 1888]

One of 600 copies. WITH AUTOGRAPH OF WHITMAN on the half-title.

251A —— Another copy. 8vo, half cloth and boards, uncut.

[Philadelphia, 1888|

19

ONE OF 600 COPIES, AUTOGRAPHED BY THE AUTHOR. Inscribed on fly-leaf in Whitman's hand: *"Mrs. Martha Fels. March 14, '91."*

252 —— November Boughs. 8vo, green cloth, uncut.

Philadelphia, 1888

3

FIRST EDITION, and one of a specially bound small lot for Whitman for presentation purposes. According to Horace Traubel, none of the copies in green cloth was sold. Inscribed: *"A first edition. Thomas B. Harned, Literary Executor of Walt Whitman."* Printed on Large Paper.

253 —— Another Edition. 8vo, maroon cloth, gilt top, uncut.

Paisley and London, 1889

1

This edition appears to be the American sheets with the Gardner imprint.

254 —— Grashalme. In Auswahl ubersetzt von Karl Knortz und T. W. Rolleston. 12mo, original wrappers, uncut. Zurich, 1889

2

Laid in is a slip reading *"With the compliments of the translators."*

254A [——] Thomson (James). Selections from Original Contributions to "Cope's Tobacco Plant." *Portrait and facsimile.* 12mo, wrappers, uncut. Liverpool, 1889

1

SCARCE. Contains an Essay on Whitman on p. 50. With the Buxton Forman bookplate.

255 —— Good-Bye My Fancy. 2d Annex to Leaves of Grass. *Phototype portrait.* 8vo, green cloth, gilt top, uncut.

Philadelphia, 1891

7

FIRST EDITION. Bound the same as "November Boughs," and also probably specially bound in green for the author's presentation copies, as was that volume. Printed on Large Paper.

256 —— Traubel (Horace L.). At the Graveside of Walt Whitman: Harleigh, Camden, New Jersey, March 30, and Sprigs of Lilac. Royal 8vo, gray wrappers, uncut. N. p., 1892

4

One of 750 copies on Large Paper, autographed by Traubel.

257 —— In re Walt Whitman: Edited by his Literary Executors, Horace L. Traubel, Richard Maurice Bucke, Thomas B. Harned. Royal 8vo, cloth, gilt top, uncut. Philadelphia, 1893

2

FIRST EDITION. One of 1000 copies.

258 —— The Wound Dresser. A Series of Letters Written from the Hospitals in Washington during the War of the Rebellion. Edited by Richard Maurice Bucke. *Portrait.* 12mo, cloth, gilt top, uncut. Boston, 1898

5—

FIRST EDITION, second issue.

259 —— Notes and Fragments: Left by Walt Whitman and now edited by Dr. Richard Maurice Bucke, one of his Literary Executors. Imp. 8vo, cloth. Printed for Private Distribution only, 1899

15—

One of 225 copies, signed by the Editor.

260 —— Thomson (James). Walt Whitman, the Man and the Poet. With an Introduction by Bertram Dobell. 12mo, white buckram, uncut. London, 1900

2—

FIRST EDITION ON LARGE PAPER.

ONE OF ONLY TWO COPIES AVAILABLE

261 **WHITMAN (WALT).** Letters written by Walt Whitman to his Mother, from 1866 to 1872. Together with certain Papers prepared from material now first utilized. Edited by Thomas B. Harned, one of Whitman's Literary Executors. 8vo, original wrappers, uncut. New York: Putnam, 1902

500—

OF EXCESSIVE RARITY. ONLY FIVE COPIES WERE PRINTED, OF WHICH TWO ARE IN THE LIBRARY OF CONGRESS. One copy was retained by the publishers, which was lost by them, leaving only this and one other copy available.

262 [——] Rivers (W. C.). Walt Whitman's Anomaly. *Portrait.* 12mo, wrappers. London, 1913

SCARCE.

263 —— Wall's Etched Monthly for Feb., 1921. *Illustrated and etched throughout.* 4to, wrappers. New York, 1921

Contains an etched portrait of Whitman, also an etched reproduction of a fragment of a MS. by him.

264 —— Anne Gilchrist and Walt Whitman. By Elizabeth Porter Gould. *Portrait.* Phila., n.d.; A Life of Walt Whitman. By Henry Bryan Binns. *Illustrated.* London, [1905]; 2 vols., 12mo and 8vo, cloth.

FIRST EDITIONS.

265 —— BROADSIDE: Fancies at Navesink. Tall narrow folio, linen-backed, in cloth covers. N. p., n. d.

VERY SCARCE. In this Broadside the stanza headings differ from those in the book form printing. Only a few copies were made for Whitman's personal friends.

266 —— Leaves of Grass. Boston, 1860-61; The same. Phila., n. d.; The same. Phila., [1900]; Specimen Days in America, London, 1887; Democratic Vistas, London, 1888. 5 vols., mainly 12mo, cloth.

267 —— Walt Whitman. By William Clarke. *Portrait*. London, 1892; A "Canterbury" Whitman. By Richard Le Gallienne. Portland, 1913; Three Selections from Leaves of Grass. Portland, 1912; Memories of President Lincoln, Portland, 1904. 4 vols., 16mo, cloth and wrappers.

267A —— Poems. 12mo, wrappers.
London: "Review of Reviews" Office, n. d.

No. 27 of "The Masterpiece Library," containing: Songs of Myself, Songs of Sex, Songs of the War, Songs of Death, Songs Democratic.

268 —— Walt Whitman Fellowship Papers. First Year, 14 Papers (a few duplicates); Second Year, 1-9, with 3 duplicates; Third Year, 1-4; Fourth Year, No. 9; Eighth Year, No. 2, and a Programme of the Fellowship for May 31, 1895. 33 pieces, 8vo, sewn and single sheets.

These include papers by Richard M. Bucke, John Burroughs, Daniel G. Brinton, Hamlin Garland, Horace L. Traubel, Thomas B. Harned, and others.

269 —— AUTOGRAPH MANUSCRIPT, SIGNED, of "The Prairie States." Written on 1 p., oblong 4to, one stanza of six lines.

A REMARKABLY FINE SPECIMEN, totally unlike most of Whitman's short MSS., which were usually written on scraps of paper of various sorts.

MANUSCRIPT HOSPITAL NOTES

270 **WHITMAN (WALT).** Autograph Notes made by Walt Whitman, of interviews with wounded men, jottings of scenes, etc., gathered possibly while he was searching for his brother George, who had been wounded. Written on 10 sheets of paper of various sizes, in Whitman's well-known fashion. In an octavo cloth portfolio.

A MOST INTERESTING COLLECTION. One of the notes reads: *"The sights seen in the Hospitals of Washington by a Soldiers' Missionary (an amateur without pay) not confining his visits to the sick of that State (New York) afford a most significant illustration of the current times and events of our country."* Other notes read: *"The badly wounded are generally in good*

spirits, the sick, those low with fever etc., are disheartened and out of sorts."
*"I saw the bloody holocaust of the Wilderness and Manassas; I saw the
wounded and the dead, and never forget them. Ever since have they been
with me—they have fused ever since in my poems."* There are also interesting accounts of soldiers interviewed.

AUTOGRAPH NOTES OF WHITMAN'S WESTERN TRIP

271 **WHITMAN (WALT).** Autograph Notes of a trip West made
by Whitman, in 1879, written on 10 small scraps of paper. In
paper folder, *with portrait.*

These comprise jottings made by him, as: *"Friday Sept. 19, '79. On the
Plains (Western edge of Kansas, on to Colorado)—plains—plains—plains.
The Dug-outs. The Prairie dog. Antelope. Emigrant wagons. Camped for
the night";* etc. *"Glints and flashes. The swift-passing sights and flashes
(as swiftly while the cars were rushing by)—the bits, names, incidents told
me, passing the localities."*
*"I did not go through to San Francisco, though I hope to do so one of these
days. Indeed I have a good deal of travel laid out; among the rest Tennessee and Alabama";* etc., etc.

[SEE FRONTISPIECE]

272 —— A. L. s., 1 p., 8vo. Camden, Nov. 13, no year. To John
Lucas. *With portrait.* Framed library panel.

A fine piece, introducing a young friend, in the hope that he may find a
place of employment for his friend.

273 —— A. L. s., written in pencil. 1 p., 8vo. Camden, July 21,
1885. [Written to Johnston, Whitman's jeweller, friend, and
benefactor.]

*"The watch (a beauty), the knives & forks & the china ware all reach'd
me safely this afternoon—thanks, thanks, & best love. . . . Am just going
out for my evening sail on the Delaware. God bless you & yours."*

274 —— A. L. s., written in blue pencil. 1 p., 8vo. Camden, Aug.
19, '85. Probably written to Herbert Gilchrist.

*"Glad to hear your mother is getting along, & better—give my respects
and best wishes to her. . . . I got out a little yesterday for the first time,
but find myself weaker and lamer than ever";* etc.

275 —— Original draft of a letter to The Century Co. relative to
"Hospital Notes." 1 p., 8vo, unsigned. July 26, '86.

*"I send you the Hospital article at last. I have preferred to give human
cases, with their emotional accompaniments, sketched in on the spot, to any
statistics . . . the price of the article if you want it is $150";* etc.

276 —— A. N. s. on postal card. Undated [Aug. 8, 1887]. To Erastus Brainerd. Asking for 8 copies of the Philadelphia Daily
News.

277 —— A. L. s., 1 p., 4to. Camden, Aug. 29, '89.

> *"Yrs. of yesterday rec'd with picture suggesting piece (illustration in text). Will this do: I shall want proof (wh—don't forget)—the price is $25."*

278 —— Copyright certificate of "Leaves of Grass. As a Strong Bird on Pinions Free and other Poems." 1 p., 4to. Washington, 1892. (Worn in folds.)

279 —— A. L., written in indelible pencil, and signed with initials. Undated. Refers to his health and increasing lameness.

> *"I am writing this up in my big den—the floor all around horribly litter-rary—but a cheery wood fire in the little stove—& I comfortable in my great capacious rattan arm-chair—which I may will to Al. if he cares for it."*

280 —— Autograph Notes of "The Problem of the Blacks." 1 p., small 4to.

> *"The South will yet come up—the blacks must either filter through in time or gradually eliminate & disappear, which is most likely, though that termination is far off, or else so develope in mental and moral qualities, and in all the attributes of a leading and dominant race (which I do not think likely)"; etc.*

281 —— Early Manuscript Notes, written on 2 pp., 4to and small 4to, in Whitman's well-known style. An envelope accompanying these bears the following inscription: "This is an early lot of MSS. of the N. Y. Days Newspaper work—probably about 1855-8 —surely not later than 1860."

282 —— Portion of a letter, written from Washington, May 14, 1863. Small oblong 4to. Unsigned. Relative to his work in the Hospitals in Washington, among the sick, wounded and dying men.

283 —— Facsimile of the Earliest known letter of Walt. Whitman. Written to Nathan Hale Jr., Boston. Referring to a MS. Tale: "The Angel of Years." A signed note by T. B. Harned, one of Whitman's Literary Executors, is written at the foot of the letter. The original letter was written in June 1842.

THE FAREWELL LINES OF WHITMAN'S MOTHER

284 [WHITMAN.] AUTOGRAPH MESSAGE OF MRS. WHITMAN, WRITTEN ON HER DEATH BED, 1 p., small 4to.

127⁵⁰

> AN INTENSELY INTERESTING PIECE, EXHIBITING HER WARM LOVE FOR HER CHILDREN, AND EXPRESSING HER PROFOUND SATISFACTION AND HAPPINESS IN HER LIFE SPENT WITH THEM:
> *"farewell my beloved sons farewell i have lived beyond all comfort in this world dont mourn for me my beloved sons and daughters farewell my dear beloved Walter."*

THIS IS BELIEVED TO BE THE ONLY SPECIMEN OF MRS. WHITMAN'S AUTO-
GRAPH EVER OFFERED.
Accompanying it, is an envelope, on which Whitman has written: *"Mother's
last lines."*

Mother's last lines

285 —— Bronze Medal of Whitman, by R. Tait Mackenzie, executed
for The Franklin Inn Club.

286 —— Burroughs (John). Typewritten letter, signed 1 p., 8vo.
Roxbury, N. Y., Oct. 5, 1920. A most interesting letter to Carolyn
Wells, in relation to the Humor of Walt Whitman.

287 —— A Collection of Portraits of Whitman, various processes and
at various ages, nearly all dissimilar. 28 pieces, besides a number
of woodcuts.

288 —— Daguerreotype Portrait of Walt Whitman. In original case,
rebacked. Modern.

One of three copies made by George Barlow, an old photographer who has
made photographs for 60 years.

289 —— Etched Portrait, in sepia. Signed. Framed, and one other
Portrait of Whitman. Framed. 2 pieces.

290 —— Etched Portrait, by Bernhardt Wall. Signed Proof, with
an impression of the cancelled plate. 2 pieces.

291 —— Line Portrait on Japan Vellum. Proof, signed by T. Johnson. Framed.

292 —— Music. As I watch'd the Ploughman Ploughing and other
Chants of Freedom. [Portals; Twilight; A Clear Midnight.]
4to, wrappers. In a cloth protecting case. A tinted lithograph
portrait of Whitman is laid in, published in "Our Poet's Corner,"
1895.

293 —— Sheet Music: Ethiopia Saluting the Colours; O Captain!
My Captain!; By the Bivouac's Fitful Flame. Words by Whitman. 3 pieces.

294 —— Proof Lithograph Portrait, by S. J. Woolf. Signed. Un-
framed.

THE RENOWNED COLLECTION OF THE LATE

WILLIAM F. GABLE

OF ALTOONA, PENNSYLVANIA

FIRST EDITIONS, AUTOGRAPH MANUSCRIPTS AND LETTERS OF ENGLISH AND AMERICAN AUTHORS

PART ONE

SOLD BY ORDER OF THE ADMINISTRATOR

ROBERT B. GABLE

AMERICAN ART ASSOCIATION, INC.

30 EAST 57TH STREET   ↗   NEW YORK CITY

Telephone: PLAZA 1270

Nov. 5 & 6, 1923

861. WHITMAN (WALT). The New World. Volume III, No. 21. November 20, 1841; containing the poem, "Each has his Grief," signed, "W. W.," and the original tale, "The Child's Champion. By Walter Whitman." Folio, stitched.   New York, 1841

  Believed to be the first of Whitman's writings published under his own name. VERY RARE and in perfect state of preservation.

862. WHITMAN (WALT). Brother Jonathan. Vol. I, No. 5. January 29, 1842, containing, "Ambition—A Poem, by Walter Whitman." Royal 4to, original wrappers, uncut. New York, 1842

3

FINE COPY of one of the earliest appearances of Whitman's work under his own name. EXCEEDINGLY RARE.

863. WHITMAN (WALT). Franklin Evans; or the Inebriate. A Tale of the Times. By Walter Whitman. Small folio, stitched. New-York, 1842

17 50

The Author's first separate publication and EXTREMELY RARE. Was published as the Extra to the *New World*, New York, November, 1842, Number 34. Printed in pamphlet form with no covers, and never printed as a separate bound book.

FINE CLEAN COPY IN PRACTICALLY PERFECT CONDITION, with only a former owner's name in ink at top of first page and a few insignificant spots or tears.

EXCEPTIONALLY FINE EARLY WHITMAN MANUSCRIPT

864. [WHITMAN (WALT).] ORIGINAL AUTOGRAPH MANUSCRIPT of his article, "A Visit to the Opera, with some Gossip about the Singers, and Music. By Mose Velsor of Brooklyn." Manuscript of about FOURTEEN HUNDRED WORDS, written in ink on one side of 8 folio leaves, lacking pp. 8 and 9 and the last part of p. 10. Each leaf hinged to larger sheet. Enclosed in half morocco slip-case, with inner protecting wrapper.

100

OF UNUSUAL INTEREST TO THE WHITMAN COLLECTOR (although incomplete), being one of his early articles written for the daily or weekly press and signed with a pseudonym, thus showing that it was written before his name had become known in the literary world.

He describes a visit to the Opera at the old Academy of Music in Fourteenth Street, New York and speaks with feeling and understanding of the music and the artists. The manuscript begins,—

Come reader, would you not like to go with us to the Italian Opera?—We will suppose you are some good fellow of a man—or woman either, it makes no difference— whose days are mostly spent in work; so the Opera will be altogether new to you.—

Here we are, up Broadway, turning round the corner to our right hand, down East 14th street—us two—part of quite an animated crowd.—

Continuing, he mentions the boys selling the librettos, and answers the question of "What then is the Opera?" by saying,—*For the information of you, our unsophisticated companion, we will say that it is a composition, of the same nature as a play in the theatre, all the dialogue [sic] of the characters being sung, or melodiously recited by note, to the accompaniment of a band of instruments, the orchestra.—By acknowledged consent, the music of the Italian composers and singers is at the head of the rest;—Germans, French, English, all bow down to the Italian style.—*

Here follows a rather detailed description of a grand opera; then, a description of the New York Academy of Music, its façade, the arrival of the carriages with their richly dressed occupants, the interior of this famous old play-house and of the audience which is gathering to enjoy the opera; ending with the words,—*Those who have been in the habit of going only to the other theatres or places of amusement, will be struck with the quietness and blandness that pervades the whole place, like an atmosphere—no hubbub—no "hi-hi's."—*

This is followed by a delightful description of the orchestra, with an appreciation of the beauty and the rendition of the music, the *finale* with its *grand crash of all the instruments together*, which he says would probably not be appreciated by his guest, *but*, continuing,—*which we privately confess in your ear is one of the greatest treats we obtain from a visit to the opera.—*

Then comes an eulogy on "Italian Music and Method," of which he says,—*That is the only large, fresh, free, magnificent method—and under its auspices alone will there ever be great and perfect American singers, male and female.*

At the foot of p.7 is the beginning of a paragraph headed, *Long study and practice needed to make a singer*, only a few lines of which are here included, the balance of this part of the manuscript being wanting.

On the last page Whitman names some of the great Italian singers,—*Bettini, Mario, Tiberini, Brignoli and Steffani*; adding,—*There are no better, probably in Europe or America, than the two last named.—*

This page ends with,—*Au revoir. So friendly reader, we have filled our column, more or less, with a visit, us two, to the Italian Opera, with you, and with random,* . . . the balance of the sheet being wanting.

THIS IS WITHOUT DOUBT ONE OF THE FINEST AND MOST DESIRABLE WHITMAN MANUSCRIPTS WHICH HAS EVER APPEARED IN THE AUCTION MARKET.

865. WHITMAN (WALT). Excerpt from the magazine *The Rover*, Vol. 3, No. 5, April 1844. 8vo, paper wrappers.   New York, 1844

> Contains an article by Whitman entitled "My Boys and Girls," and with his name printed as "Walter Whitman." He contributed this article at the time he was working as a compositor on *The New World*.

866. WHITMAN (WALT). The Democratic Review, Vol. XVII, Nos. 85 and 89, July and August, November, 1845. *Portraits*. 2 vols. 8vo, original wrappers.   New York, 1845

> The Number for July and August contains "Revenge and Requital. A Tale of a Murderer Escaped" by Whitman; the number for November contains "A Dialogue" by Whitman. In both articles his name is printed as *Walter Whitman*. There are included in the above, articles by J. G. Whittier, Walter Savage Landor, and others.

867. [WHITMAN (WALT).] Voices from the Press; a Collection of Sketches, Essays, and Poems, by practical Printers. Edited by James J. Brenton. 8vo, original cloth.   New York, 1850

> FINE COPY. Contains *The Tomb Blossoms* by Walter Whitman, also poems by Bayard Taylor, Samuel Woodworth, N. Parker Willis and others.
> Laid in is a card in the autograph of Whitman, reading,—*431 Stevens Street Camden Jan: 18 Walt Whitman will be in from 2 till 3½ this afternoon, & will be most happy to see Mr. Wilde & Mr. Stoddart*. An interesting note, regarding what was evidently a meeting between the American poet and the English æsthetic writer.

868. WHITMAN (WALT). ORIGINAL AUTOGRAPH MANUSCRIPT of Preface to "Leaves of Grass." Manuscript of about 340 words, written on one side of 3 12mo leaves, the whole originally written in ink, but with corrections, revisions and deletions in lead pencil.   [1855?]

> APPARENTLY UNPUBLISHED. It is entitled "Inscription to precede Leaves of Grass, when finished."
> The above manuscript, ENTIRELY IN WHITMAN'S AUTOGRAPH, is the PREFACE to the book which made the great American poet and democrat famous. The manuscript *Preface* reads in part,—
>
> > *While the schools and the teachers are teaching*
> > *Others, often their kind, . . .*
> > *Some obedience to look to the protection of the laws,*
> > *Some, to assert a sovereign and God over all, to rely on,*
> > *Some, enjoining to build outside forts and embankments;*
> > *Solitary, I here, I to enjoin for you, whoever you are to*
> > > *build inside invisible forts,*
> > *Counseling every man and woman to become the fortress,*
> > > *the lord and sovereign, of himself or herself,*
> > *To grow through infinite time*
> > > *finally to be supreme God himself or herself,*
> > *Acknowledging none greater, now or after death, than*
> > > *himself or herself.*
>
> Laid in is a pamphlet of the Toronto Theosophical Society,—Calendar 1914–15, which contains a 9-line poem of Whitman, which begins,—"Listen! I will be honest with you," etc.

869. [WHITMAN (WALT).] Leaves of Grass. *Frontispiece portrait*. 16mo, original dark green cloth, blind-stamped on sides, title in gilt on front and in blind on back cover; gilt lettered and ornamented back strip, with quotation from Emerson's letter also in gilt.   Brooklyn, New York, 1856

> SECOND EDITION. IN IMMACULATE CONDITION, and with the leaf of Fowler & Wells advertisements at the end. The Whitman Bibliography by Wells and Goldsmith says that the book "is quite a rarity and is seldom found in good condition."
> Laid in is an AUTOGRAPH NOTE SIGNED IN FULL BY WHITMAN, 1p. 8vo. Attorney General's Office, Washington, March 12, 1868. To C. B. Tillinghast, saying,—*I publish Leaves of Grass myself—& send it by mail, post paid, on receipt of the price, $3*.

870. [WHITMAN (WALT).] Leaves of Grass. *Frontispiece portrait on plain paper.* Imperial 8vo, original green cloth, blind-stamped sides with rustic lettered title in gilt and triple gilt border on both front and back covers, gilt floral sprays and gilt lettered title on backbone, marbled end-papers, gilt edges. Enclosed in linen slip-case, with inner protecting wrapper.

275-

Brooklyn, New York, 1855

BEAUTIFUL COPY OF FIRST ISSUE OF THE FIRST EDITION AND THAT MOST DESIRED BY COLLECTORS. In the green cloth binding with the rustic title, the gilt lines and marbled end-papers. Later issues lacked the gilt lines on the cover, had plain end-papers and plain edges and the frontispiece portrait on India paper. The later issues also contained some press notices of the book.

Laid in is a note in the AUTOGRAPH OF WHITMAN, 1p. 4to, containing 123 words, relating to his *Leaves of Grass*, in which he says that the same thoughts and themes which Wordsworth treats in his *Intimations of Immortality*, Bryant in his *Thanatopsis* and his *Flood of Years*, and Whittier in many of his poems is also treated in *Leaves of Grass*, adding,—*But how different the treatment! Instead of the gloom and hopelessness and spirit of wailing reproach, or bowed-down submission as to some grim destiny, which is the basis & background of those fine poems, Instead of life and Nature growing stale—instead of Death coming like a blight and end-all*—Here the poet stops without telling us what his treatment of the theme might be.

SUPERB COPY. BOTH THE LEAVES AND BINDING IN IMMACULATE CONDITION, AND MADE STILL MORE DESIRABLE by the autograph note relating to the same which is inserted.

[See Reproduction of Title-page]

Leaves

of

Grass.

————◆————

Brooklyn, New York:
1855.
[No. 870]

76

871. WHITMAN (WALT). Autograph Letter Signed, 4pp. 4to, Brooklyn, Saturday Afternoon, July 20, 1857. To "Dear Friend." 90

A REMARKABLE LETTER which brings out Whitman's characteristics at their best. Speaks of many of his friends and contemporaries; among whom he mentions Mr. Arnold, Mrs. Hatch, Andrew Jackson Davis (clairvoyant and spiritualist), Rev. Mr. Porter, Mrs. Walton, Messrs. Fowler & Wells, Ralph Waldo Emerson.

In speaking of the sewing machine, which was then in its infancy, he says,— *Mrs. Price and Helen had been out all day with the sewing machine, at Mr. Beecher's— either Henry Ward's, or his father's. They had done a great day's work—as much, one of the Beecher ladies said, as a sempstress could have got through with in six months.— Mrs. P. and Helen had engagements for a fortnight ahead, to go out among families and take the sewing machine.—What a revolution this little piece of furniture is producing.— Isn't it quite an encouragement . . .*

In this epistle is possibly disclosed Whitman's profoundest religious beliefs, which—as will be seen by perusing the two following paragraphs—show broad and democratic tendencies:

I got into quite a talk with Mr. Arnold about Mrs. Hatch.—He says the pervading thought of her speeches is that first exists the spirituality of any thing, and that gives existence of things, the earth, plants, animals, men, women.—But that Andrew Jackson Davis puts matter as the subject of his homilies, and the primary source of all results— I suppose the soul among the rest.—Both are quite determined in their theories.— Perhaps when they know much more, both of them will be much less determined.—

A minister, Rev. Mr. Porter, was introduced to me this morning,—a Dutch Reformed minister, and editor of the "Christian Intelligencer," N. Y.—Would you believe it,— he had been reading "Leaves of Grass," and wanted more?—He said he hoped I retained the true Reformed faith which I must have inherited from my mother's Dutch ancestry.— I not only assured him of my retaining faith in that sect, but that I had perfect faith in all sects, and was not inclined to reject one single one—but believed each to be about as

[No. 871]

[Continued

77

far advanced as it could be, considering what had preceded it—and moreover that every one was the needed representative of its truth—or of something needed as much as truth . . .

He then states that Messrs. Fowler & Wells are retarding the publication of the Third Edition of his book, *Leaves of Grass.* In the last paragraph speaks of his mother with filial respect and ends the communication thus,—*Before I come to Philadelphia, I shall send you or Hector a line.—Wishing Peace & Friendship . . .*

[See Reproduction]

872. [WHITMAN (WALT).] Leaves of Grass Imprints. American and European Criticisms on "Leaves of Grass." 16mo, stitched.

15⁻

Boston: Thayer and Eldridge, 1860

EXCESSIVELY RARE on account of its size and frail makeup. FINE CLEAN COPY but lacks the wrappers.

Laid in is an AUTOGRAPH LETTER SIGNED BY WHITMAN, 1p. 8vo. 431 Stevens Street, Camden, New Jersey, Jan. 11 '83. To E. S. Marsh, Brandon, Vermont, relating to the Centennial or 1876 edition of *Leaves of Grass* and *Two Rivulets,* saying that he has some copies and adding,—*Should you wish them send me p o order & I will forward them by mail*—[Signed] *Walt Whitman.* With addressed envelope also in Whitman's autograph bearing his stenciled stamp in lower corner.

873. [WHITMAN (WALT).] Leaves of Grass. *Frontispiece portrait with buff tinted background.* 12mo, light brown embossed cloth, with title and ornamental designs stamped in blind on sides, and title and butterfly in gilt on back strip, light greenish gray end-papers.

20⁻

Boston: Thayer and Eldridge, 1860–61

THE GENUINE THAYER AND ELDRIDGE EDITION, with the inscription,—"Electrotyped at the Boston Stereotype Foundry. Printed by George C. Rand & Avery," below the copyright notice on verso of title, and with the embossed and heavily blind-stamped covers. EXCEPTIONALLY FINE, WELL-PRESERVED COPY.

Laid in is an AUTOGRAPH POSTAL CARD SIGNED BY WHITMAN. London, Ontario, Canada, July 25, no year. To Mr. F. B. Sanborn, Concord, Mass. Acknowledging an invitation from Mr. Sanborn and saying,—*Should be delighted to accept it and be with you all—but I start to-morrow morning on a three weeks' trip over the Lakes, the St. Lawrence & up the Saguenay—I have been pretty ill but am now better & the doctor thinks the trip will do me good . . .*

874. WHITMAN (WALT). ORIGINAL AUTOGRAPH MANUSCRIPT of his sketch, "Boston and Walt Whitman." Manuscript of 135 words, written in indelible pencil on 1p. of a 4to sheet, with typewritten transcript. Enclosed in half morocco slip-case, gilt lettered, with inner folding wrapper.

25⁻

A DESIRABLE WHITMAN MANUSCRIPT, RELATING TO "LEAVES OF GRASS," AND THOROUGHLY CHARACTERISTIC OF THE WRITER. It reads in part:

The Bostonians—perhaps to make up for their absurd official set-down on "Leaves of Grass" some years since, have now started—or at any rate have furnished the area of —a "Walt Whitman Society"—described in the circular as having for its object to endow the old poet with a weekly pension, and to cultivate generally his poetical and patriotic lessons and writings. But Whitman . . . peremptorily declines the pension effort and is willing his poems should take their chances with other candidates for public appreciation . . .

875. [WHITMAN (WALT).] Leaves of Grass. *Frontispiece portrait on plain paper.* 12mo, reddish brown pebbled cloth, title and ornaments blind-stamped on sides, title lettered in gilt on back strip, with author's name and ornament stamped in blind.

7⁵⁰

Boston: Thayer and Eldridge, 1860–61 [New York: Richard Worthington, *circa* 1879]

[*Continued*

THE SPURIOUS ISSUE of the 1860–61 Thayer and Eldridge Edition. Identical with the original issue, excepting that it lacks the inscription below the copyright on the verso of the title and is bound in a different colored cloth. This copy contains no advertisements at the end.

Laid in is an AUTOGRAPH POSTCARD SIGNED BY WHITMAN. Camden, New Jersey, June 14, '87. To Mr. Cox, Photographer, Cor: Broadway & 12th Street, New York City. Acknowledging receipt of a note in which the photographer had apparently asked him to autograph photographs for sale, and saying,—*I have no objection to either of your plans—Will sign autographically & coöperate—Send on the proofs, specimens, all of them. Walt Whitman.*

876. WHITMAN (WALT). ORIGINAL AUTOGRAPH MANUSCRIPT of "Facts in the Matter of Worthington illegally publishing 'Leaves of Grass.'" SIGNED. Manuscript of about 400 words, written in ink on one side of 3 4to leaves.

85—

EXCEEDINGLY IMPORTANT MANUSCRIPT, being in his autograph and relating entirely to his work, *Leaves of Grass*. It commences:

Leavitt the auctioneer in New York City in the latter part of 1879 sold to a Mr. Williams (bookseller still in the trade in N. Y.) the electrotype plates (456 pages) of the Boston 1860-'61 edition of my book "Leaves of Grass"—plates originally made by Thayer & Eldridge a firm of your Boston booksellers, under agreement with me to make & publish the book for five years from then date, 1860-61—An edition was printed and sold—but the Secession War came on—Thayer & Eldridge failed—& these plates, becoming the property of Mr. Wentworth a creditor of T. & E. were stored away & locked up for many years in Boston—eventually (as said above) sent on by Wentworth to N. Y. & sold at auction to Williams, who makes them over to Worthington . . .

The point is that Worthington has for the last eight or nine years been making issuing & selling against my express prohibition & to my great loss & injury—& putting into the market by his traveling salesmen & "drummers"—a printed book of mine, from the plates the right to issue which ran out twenty years ago & over.

[Signed in full]   *Walt Whitman*
328 Mickle Street
Camden New Jersey

877. WHITMAN (WALT). ORIGINAL AUTOGRAPH CIVIL WAR MANUSCRIPT written at Falmouth, December, 1862, and marked "*Proofs. Walt Whitman.*" Manuscript of about 700 words, written in ink (with the exception of one page, in pencil) on 4½pp. 8vo, one page of which is on "Sanitary Commission" paper.

150—

In all probability part of the ORIGINAL MANUSCRIPT OF THE RAREST OF WHITMAN'S WORKS, *Memoranda during the War*, first published at Camden, New Jersey, 1875–1876, although the title-page reads,—"Walt Whitman's Memoranda of the War written on the spot in 1863–1865."

Very interesting RARE MANUSCRIPT OF CIVIL WAR INTEREST, written while Whitman was a volunteer army nurse, from which the following are excerpts:

The following brief of visits as a volunteer during the last two years (from December '62 to October '64) among the soldiers, the Army Hospitals at Washington & Camp Hospitals in the field is made for a few friends interested in the wounded & sick & who have faithfully aided me in ministering to them. The items are merely transferred from discarded & well worn little note books. I merely transfer from the now discarded little note-books a sheet of paper folded . . . carried in the pocket at the time to assist the memory . . .

Dec. 22d to 31st—Am among the brigade & division hospital somewhat. Few at home realise what they are. They are our tents; The wounded lie right on the ground, on a blanket & lucky if that is spread on a heap of pine twigs . . . No cots, not even a mattress [sic] between them and the ground .|. . I go around from one of the sufferers to another. I do not see that I can do any good, but I cannot leave them. Once in a while some youngster holds on to me convulsively & of course, I do what I can for him & if needed . . . stop for hours . . .

From the celebrated Donaldson collection. Mr. Donaldson was an intimate friend of Walt Whitman.

878. WHITMAN (WALT). Walt Whitman's Drum-Taps. 12mo, original brown cloth, title on gilt ground in circle on front cover and in blind on back, thin paper fly-leaves, plain edges.   New-York, 1865

65⁻

EXCEPTIONALLY FINE COPY OF THE VERY RARE FIRST ISSUE OF THE FIRST EDITION, WITHOUT the additional poem on the Death of Lincoln. ONLY A FEW COPIES WERE ISSUED IN THIS FORM; the publication being held up at Lincoln's death and the poem, *When Lilacs last in the Door Yard Bloom'd*, with a separate title-page and pagination, added to the balance of the edition. The Second Issue, which contained *The Sequel to Drum-Taps*, as well as the above, had the fly-leaves of heavier paper and sprinkled edges.

In addition to the rarity of this little volume, making it doubly precious, it is an AUTHOR'S PRESENTATION COPY, with full-page inscription in Whitman's autograph, —*To my friend, Mrs. Johnston. Accept a copy of my little book, Drum Taps. Many of the pieces were written in Camp, or on the field, or in the Army Hospitals, under strange & sad surroundings.* [Signed] *Walt Whitman Camden, N. J. Nov. 9, 1873.*

Also on fly-leaf is an autograph note signed by Horace Traubel. Altoona, June 28th, '10, regarding the Johnstons and their friendship with Whitman.

879. WHITMAN (WALT). [O'CONNOR (WILLIAM DOUGLAS).] The Good Gray Poet A Vindication. 8vo, stitched, uncut, wrappers and title-page lacking. [Washington, 1866;] ORIGINAL AUTOGRAPH MANUSCRIPT, "Memoranda," relating to Whitman, by W. D. O'CONNOR, 13pp. 8vo; MANUSCRIPT, EXTRACT from Preface to first Edition of Leaves of Grass, 3pp. 8vo, in the same hand; [ALSO] Autograph Letter Signed by MR. O'CONNOR, 10pp. 8vo. Washington, D. C. December 5, 1866. To Moncure D. Conway, Esq. Together, 4 pieces, laid in morocco folder.

30⁻

FIRST EDITION OF THIS RARE PAMPHLET.

The manuscripts and letter, all of which are in the autograph of Mr. O'Connor, are exceedingly interesting Whitman material.

The *Memoranda* begins with a short biography of Whitman, tells of his preferences in literature, of his own writings and especially of *Leaves of Grass*. In reference to this last work, Mr. O'Connor writes,—*Let me say one thing in this connection. It is generally supposed that his book is the offspring of his reading of Emerson and that he is in some sort a pupil of that noble thinker . . . Up to the time of the publication of his first edition, he had never to his own knowledge read one line of Emerson's writings. It is since that time that he has read them . . .*

In his letter to Mr. Conway, Mr. O'Connor speaks of having read Mr. Conway's article on Walt Whitman published in *Every Saturday*. Says he is sending him a package of half a dozen copies of the new edition [Drum-Taps]—*one for you, the others for distribution, as you suggest, to persons who will be likely to review the book with some justice and intelligence, if any such there be . . . I also send you a masterly critique and notice by John Burroughs, which recently came out in our New York "Galaxy"—the first article, I might almost say, that reveals real critical power and insight, and a proper reverence, upon the subject of Walt Whitman's poetry.* Continuing, he asks if there is any possibility of finding an English publisher for Whitman's works. The last four pages of the letter are concerned with *Leaves of Grass*, which he characterizes as unparalleled *modernness . . . No faded sunset of the antique, but the fresh morning of the modern world, is in it from first to last. After that, the next thing is its national character.—Time fails me to say all I might on this subject.*

880. WHITMAN (WALT). BURROUGHS (JOHN). Notes on Walt Whitman, as Poet and Person. 12mo, original cloth.   New York, 1867

45⁻

FIRST EDITION. RARE. AUTOGRAPH PRESENTATION COPY FROM THE AUTHOR, with inscription, in ink, on fly-leaf,—*To Mrs. Sara A. Booth from her friend John Burroughs Feb. 28th 1881.* At a later date the book was sent to John Burroughs with the query, in ink, on the inside of the front cover,—*How large an edition was published?* and beneath is his autograph answer, also in ink,—*About 250 copies John Burroughs Jany. 18, 1910.*

Laid in is an original photograph of Walt Whitman, WITH AUTOGRAPH SIGNATURE, dated 1874.

881. [WHITMAN (WALT).] Leaves of Grass. 12mo, half black morocco, sides of brown paper in imitation of pebbled cloth, title and "Ed'n. 1867" lettered in gilt on back strip, canary-colored end-papers, sprinkled edges.   *17*50

New York [Wm. E. Chapin & Co., Printers] 1867

VERY RARE ISSUE of the Fourth Edition, containing,—*Leaves of Grass, Drum-Taps, Sequel to Drum-Taps* and *Songs Before Parting*. This edition was published in four different forms, all issued the same year, the present one with the four parts being the SCARCEST.

Laid in is an AUTOGRAPH NOTE SIGNED BY WHITMAN, 1p. oblong 8vo. Camden, New Jersey, no date, evidently originally attached to some proof sheets and addressed to his printers or publishers, reading,—*If convenient pull two sets of proofs (slips like these) & send me, address'd as below. I will keep them in my hands & of course will prevent any publication or extract until after issued by the magazine.*

882. WHITMAN (WALT). Poems by Walt Whitman. Selected and edited by William Michael Rossetti. *Frontispiece portrait of Whitman.* 16mo, original blue cloth, uncut.   *12*50

London, 1868

FIRST ISSUE OF THIS ENGLISH EDITION. Without the price mark 7/6 on back strip which appears on the Second Issue. FINE COPY OF A VERY RARE EDITION.

Laid in is an AUTOGRAPH CARD SIGNED by Walt Whitman. Camden, April 28 [1882]. To the Editor of the Philadelphia *Press*, offering him an article for publication. On the reverse of the card is an autograph note signed by Thomas Donaldson. Philadelphia, April 30/82, stating that he was in the office of this newspaper when this card was received and that the publication of the same was declined by the editors.

883. [WHITMAN (WALT).] Democratic Vistas. Memoranda. Narrow 8vo, green wrappers, uncut and unopened, edges stained.   Washington, D. C., 1871

FIRST EDITION. AUTOGRAPH PRESENTATION COPY, with inscription,—*M. B. Brady, from his friend, Walt Whitman.*

Laid in is an autograph letter signed by Horace Traubel, 2pp. 8vo. Phila., Feb. 20, '08. To Mr. Gable, stating that the wrappers on this volume are not the original ones, and mentioning the exceptional beauty of the autograph signature on the fly-leaf. He also adds,—*You remember that Sumner was very fond of this book—spoke of it as a classic. He did not extend his admiration to Walt's poems . . .*

Although, according to the above statement, the wrappers are not the original ones, from the appearance of the volume it is probable that it was presented to Whitman's friend before any wrappers were attached, as there is no indication that the pamphlet has ever had the lighter green printed wrappers, with advertisements, which are found on the regular copies.

From the Thomas T. McKee collection, with bookplate.

884. WHITMAN (WALT). After All, not to Create Only. 12mo, sheets, uncut and unopened.   Boston: Roberts Brothers, 1871

FIRST EDITION IN BOOK FORM. VERY RARE IN SHEETS UNCUT. FINE CLEAN COPY.

Laid in is a canceled check, written and signed by Walt Whitman. Camden, N. J. May 25, 1889. National State Bank of Camden, for $7.65. Payable to Billstein & Son; also two autograph letters, signed by Horace Traubel, to Mr. Gable regarding Whitman and his writings. In the first (2pp. 4to), dated Phila., Feb. 27, '08, speaking of the desire to procure First Editions, he says,—*Walt used to laugh at our scramble for these books . . . Why wasn't the latest edn good enough for us . . .* In the second letter (1p. 4to), which is undated, he speaks of Whitman's first book, *Franklin Evans*, saying that Whitman always protested against their hunting for a copy, and adds,—*I don't see that it has any value except as a curio. Perhaps it gives us a look in upon the evolution of W. from commonplace to Leaves of Grass,* and quotes Whitman as saying to him,—

"*Why don't you let the dead alone. Why do you fellows go rooting in graveyards?*"

885. WHITMAN (WALT). After All, Not to Create Only. Recited by Walt Whitman . . . New York, Sept. 7, 1871. 12mo, original maroon beveled cloth.   *10*

Boston, 1871

FINE COPY OF THE FIRST EDITION. With autograph note signed in full by the author inserted,—*Can you use this poemet in your cluster? It would probably do to go out just as well during the week immediately preceding Christmas—The price is $11 (ten for the little piece & one for printing the slips)—*

886. [WHITMAN (WALT).] Passage to India. Leaves of Grass. Narrow 8vo, original light green printed wrappers, with advertisement on back wrapper, uncut and unopened. Washington, D. C., 1871

17^{50}

> EXCEPTIONALLY FINE COPY OF THE RARE FIRST ISSUE, ENTIRELY UNCUT AND UNOPENED.
> Laid in is an autograph post card signed by Whitman. Camden, June 9, '91. To J. M. Stoddart, editor of Lippincott's Magazine, relating to a manuscript which Whitman sent to him.

887. [WHITMAN (WALT).] BURROUGHS (JOHN). Notes on Walt Whitman, As Poet and Person. Second Edition. 12mo, original cloth, uncut. New York, 1871

10^-

> With autograph note signed by the author on fly-leaf, reading,—*This edition of the Notes was made by inserting notes on page five & the Supplementary Notes into bound Copies of the first edition* [Signed] *John Burroughs.*
> Laid in is an autograph letter signed by John Burroughs, 1p. 8vo. West Park N. Y. Mch 31, 1893. To Mr. Stoddard, the editor, referring to Burroughs' essay on Whitman, which had been sent for publication, saying,—*Could you not print the paper in your May or June number?* . . .
> Also laid in is a halftone portrait of John Burroughs.

888. [WHITMAN (WALT).] As a Strong Bird on Pinions Free. And other Poems. Narrow 8vo, original dark green cloth, gilt lettered title on front cover, uncut. Washington, D. C., 1872

6^-

> FIRST EDITION. With facsimile autograph signature of Walt Whitman at end of the poem, *Souvenirs of Democracy,* and "Leaves of Grass" printed in small type at head of title, tear in one leaf repaired; otherwise, a FINE COPY.
> Laid in is an autograph note signed by Walt Whitman. Attorney General's Office, Washington, no date. To the Superintendent of the Printing Office.

889. [WHITMAN (WALT).] Leaves of Grass. 8vo, original smooth dark green cloth, gilt lettered title on back strip, uncut, binding somewhat worn.
Washington [Electrotyped by Smith & McDougal, New York] 1872

15^-

> FIRST ISSUE OF THIS EDITION, including,—*Passage to India* with extra title-page and separate pagination; but without *After All, not to Create Only,* which was included in the later issues of this edition.
> AUTOGRAPH PRESENTATION COPY from the author, with inscription,—*R. J. Hinton, from Walt Whitman with his love. Washington, April, 1872.*
> The J. C. Chamberlain copy, with bookplate.

890. WHITMAN (WALT). Autograph Letter Signed, 2pp. 4to, Camden, Sept. 2, 1873. To "Dear John Burroughs". With addressed envelope. Laid in is an *etched portrait of Whitman,* 8vo, signed in pencil by the artist,—*Bernhardt Wall.*

25^-

> FINE WHITMAN LETTER TO HIS OLD FRIEND, JOHN BURROUGHS.
> Written in a familiar tone regarding the naturalist's proposed house, and suggesting that Mr. Burroughs talk with his brother, George Whitman, of whom he writes,—*My brother George is just finishing a nice house here he has built to suit himself—he is a natural carpenter* . . . He then solicits the work of constructing Burroughs' house for his brother's partner, Mr. Smith, whom he recommends highly, and adds:
> *John I think—"the Birds of the Poets," you best article, in many respects—it has a jaunty air, in a perfectly natural way—flits and hops & soars & sings around—in a birdish way itself.*
> *I shall still remain here for the present—or rather remain here indefinitely—I have put in a substitute at my desk in Washington. Love to 'Sula. Direct to me here until further notice.*

891. WHITMAN (WALT). Harper's New Monthly Magazine for February, 1874, *5—*
containing "Song of the Redwood-Tree" by Walt Whitman; [ALSO] Same
for March, 1874, containing "Prayer of Columbus" by Walt Whitman.
Together, 2 numbers, original wrappers, uncut.   New York, 1874
  The original appearance of these two famous poems by Whitman. A present to
his fr.end, Ida Johnston, WITH AUTOGRAPH INSCRIPTION ON EACH COVER; that for
February reading,—*Ida Johnston, Camden, from Walt Whitman* (written in ink);
and that for March,—*Ida Johnston from W. W.* (in blue pencil).

892. [WHITMAN (WALT).] Two Rivulets. Including Democratic Vistas, Centennial   *47 50*
Songs, and Passage to India. *Original photograph autographed, as frontis-*
piece. 12mo, half light calf, gilt back, colored leather labels, yellow cloth,
yellow cloth sides, gilt edges.   Camden, New Jersey, 1876
  AUTHOR'S EDITION. SPECIAL LIMITED ISSUE OF 100 COPIES ONLY. With the
extra labels on the back and the yellow cloth in place of board sides, uniform with
the special issue of *Leaves of Grass* listed above. The photograph is autographed,—
Walt Whitman born May 31 1819.
  AUTOGRAPH PRESENTATION COPY, with inscription,—*E. C. Stedman from the*
author with his friendship & thanks. With Mr. Stedman's bookplate.
  Laid in is an autograph letter signed by Mr. Stedman, 4pp. 12mo. 137 West
78th Street, April 7th, 1895. To Mr. Fred M. Hopkins, referring to Stedman's
Library of American Literature and thanking Mr. Hopkins for his good criticisms
on the same. From the E. C. Stedman collection, with bookplate.

893. [WHITMAN (WALT).] HAYNE (PAUL H). Autograph Letter Signed, 4pp. 12mo,   *5—*
Copse Hill, Georgia, March 19, 1876, to A. H. Dooley, Esq., Terre Haute,
Indiana, with addressed envelope.
  A VERY CAUSTIC CRITIQUE OF WALT WHITMAN, whom he characterizes as that
colossal Humbug. He also quotes a criticism made by Fawcett:—*Walt Whitman is*
nothing more than a kind of high-flown Cataloguist of everything in general and nothing
in particular . . . His trick is to be gigantic in everything. He is a colossal Poseur . . .

894. [WHITMAN (WALT).] Leaves of Grass. Author's Edition, With Portraits and   *55—*
Intercalations. *2 portraits.* 12mo, half fawn calf, gilt-tooled back, with gilt
lettered title on brown label and three dark green leather strips lettered,—
"Centennial Ed'n. 1876," "Walt Whitman," "Portraits" respectively, on
back strip, burned orange cloth sides, pale green embossed end-papers, gilt
edges, with binder's label of JAS. ARNOLD, Philadelphia.
                                          Camden, New Jersey, 1876
  AUTHOR'S EDITION, WITH AUTOGRAPH SIGNATURE ON TITLE. ONE OF A VERY
FEW COPIES WITH THE WORDS,—"With Portraits and Intercalations" at the bottom
of the title-page, and without the printer's name on verso. The "Intercalations"
consist of an Index slip at the end of the Contents on p.vi and additions on small
printed slips inserted at pp.207, 249, 359 and 369, also the title of the poem, "The
Wound Dresser," at p.285. The Index slip and this last mentioned title slip are not
listed in *A Concise Bibliography of Whitman* by Carolyn Wells and Alfred F. Goldsmith.
  AUTOGRAPH PRESENTATION COPY, WITH INSCRIPTION,—*John Swinton from his*
friend the author.
  VERY FINE COPY OF AN EXCESSIVELY RARE ISSUE.

895. WHITMAN (WALT). Autograph Letter Signed, 2pp. 8vo, 431 Stevens Street,   *15—*
Camden, New Jersey, September 8, 1876. To Professor Edward Dowden,
Dublin, Ireland. With addressed envelope.
  REFERS TO HIS WRITINGS, and gives the names and addresses of a number of
people in Great Britain to whom he has sent books. The letter reads in part:
  I send you by mail to-day, same address as this note, 1 copy "Leaves of Grass" and two
copies "Two Rivulets"—Also the set, Two Vols. for . . . Per-a-B-Grosart "My Second
Batch" of the new edition (600 copies each Vol.) is at last now ready, & I promptly
supply orders henceforward. I have many things to say to you, my dear friend. I am
sitting here by the open window, writing this, 'most sundown—feeling pretty well for
me, as things go—Often think of you & yours, & the friends in Ireland . . .

896. WHITMAN (WALT). Autograph Letter Signed, 2pp. small 4to, 431 Stevens St., Camden, N. Jersey, May 5, 1876—p.m. To [Mr. Smith].

12 50

FINE SPECIMEN, in bold and legible handwriting, reading in part,—

I adopted your suggestion of 3 or 4 weeks since—with result as follows—wrote to Wm Swinton—no answer
to E. C. Stedman, sent an order at once enc'g: $30
" J. Q. A. Ward, Kind answer, will order presently
" Dr. Seeger, answer, order 1 set & money enc.
" Joaquin Miller, ordered a copy sent & sent the money
" Mr. Jardine, answered a few days ago
I did not write either to G. A. Townsend or to W. C. Church—have not sent the set to J. Russell Young, nor yours, as in your last requested,—but will do so forthwith—recd the slip from Cincinnati Com. (Conway's letter) you sent—Lont know what "vile" paragraph in the Graphic you allude to in your letter of April 7—Best remembrances to Mrs. Smith—Are you coming on to the Exposition opening next Wednesday?

897. WHITMAN (WALT). Autograph Letter Signed in full, 1p. 8vo, Camden, New Jersey, Nov. 20, 1877. To Edward D. Bellows; [ALSO] *Two portraits*, one a photograph half-length, 8vo, the other an engraved three-quarter length portrait, by Hollyer and signed by the latter in pencil. Accompanying this interesting trio, is the stamped addressed letter. Together, 4 pieces, matted as one in a black frame and glazed.

16

VERY INTERESTING LETTER wherein Whitman makes mention of "Leaves of Grass," "Two Rivulets" with John Burroughs' Notes, also O'Connor's pamphlet, "Good Gray Poet."

898. WHITMAN (WALT). Autograph Letter Signed in full, 1p. 12mo, Camden, New Jersey, October 18, 1884. To William Cullen Bryant; [ALSO] *Photographic bust portrait* of Whitman taken in his declining years. 12mo. Together, 2 pieces, matted as one in a gray frame and glazed.

11

A letter of acknowledgment which follows: *Thanks for your kind letter about the Red Jacket bit. Best wishes to you, wife, children & (unknown) friends there. Walt Whitman.* In the upper left hand corner of letter the newspaper clipping of the poem "Red Jacket" is placed.

899. WHITMAN (WALT). Autograph Letter Signed, 1p. 8vo, 431 Stevens Street, Camden, New Jersey, May 8, 1881. To Mr. James R. Osgood, Boston.

22 50

VERY INTERESTING LETTER to his publisher ABOUT THE PUBLICATION OF THE FAMOUS BOSTON SUPPRESSED EDITION of *Leaves of Grass*, which reads in part:

I write in answer to the note on the other side from my dear friend O'Reilly—My plan is to have all my poems down to date, comprised in one 12mo volume, under the name "Leaves of Grass"—I think it will have to be in brevier (or bourgeois) solid—and I want as fine a (plain) specimen in type, paper, ink, binding, &c. as bookmaking can produce,—not for luxury however, but solid wear, use, reading, (to carry in the pocket, valise &c.)—a book of about 400 pages to sell at $3— . . .
Fair warning on one point—the old pieces, the sexuality-ones, about which the original row was started & kept up so long, are all retained, & must go in the same as ever—

The above letter is written on the reverse of a letter from John Boyle O'Reilly ("The Pilot Editorial Rooms" letter head) to Whitman, reading:

Dear Mr. Whitman, Hope you got safe home. James R. Osgood wants to see the material for your complete book. Can you let him have a look at it, or write him & tell him about it? Always faithfully yours. [Signed[*John Boyle O'Reilly.*

900. [WHITMAN (WALT).] Leaves of Grass. *Portrait.* 12mo, original dull yellow cloth, author's name in gilt on front cover; title, author's name, butterfly and publisher's name in gilt on back strip.

17 50

Boston: James R. Osgood and Company, 1881-2

FINE COPY OF THE SCARCE SUPPRESSED BOSTON EDITION. With AUTOGRAPH

[Continued

POSTCARD INITIALED by the author, inserted. Dated Camden, New Jersey, June 11, no year. To John Swinton, New York City.

Laid in is an autograph letter signed by Horace Traubel (one of Whitman's literary executors), 2pp. 12mo. Philadelphia, April 30, '08. To Mr. Gable, in which he speaks of this suppressed edition, saying,—*The Boston persecution was a blessing in disguise.—It not only sold more books for Walt.—It likewise created a discussion that continued for years and must have had a powerful effect in hastening the more general recognition of Leaves of Grass.*

901. WHITMAN (WALT). Autograph Letter Signed, 2pp. 8vo, 431 Stevens Street, Camden, N. J., April 28, 82. To "Dear friend."

25—

AN IMPORTANT LETTER, evidently written to an English friend. Refers to his own ill health, the death of Ralph Waldo Emerson (whose praise of *Leaves of Grass* first brought it into public favor); speaks of the Massachusetts authorities' request that Whitman expurgate *Leaves of Grass* (now considered his principal work, the publication of which was the cause of his dismissal by the Department of the Interior from a government position at Washington), which he refuses to do, an excerpt of which letter follows:

A new deal in the fortunes of Leaves of Grass—the District Attorney at Boston has threatened Osgood with indictment "under the statutes against obscene literature," specifies a long list of pieces lines &c.—Osgood is frightened asks me to change & expurgate—I refuse peremptorily—he throws up the book & will not publish it any more—wants me to take the plates, wh. I shall try to do & publish it as before (in some respects shall like it just as well)—can you help me? Can you loan me $100?—

Mention is also made of the following Whitman publications,—*A Memorandum at a Venture*, containing his theory of sexual matters, and *Children of Adam*.

902. WHITMAN (WALT). Original Profile Photograph of Walt Whitman. With autograph signature,—*Walt Whitman December 1883.* 8¾ by 5½ inches. Enclosed in white envelope, upon which is written IN WHITMAN'S AUTOGRAPH,—*Profile Photo: Walt Whitman For Mr. Whittier.* This again enclosed in manilla envelope, upon which is inscribed ALSO IN WHITMAN'S AUTOGRAPH,—*Thos. Donaldson from Walt Whitman with love & thanks.* Date on each envelope written by Mr. Donaldson.

20—

A UNIQUE AND VALUABLE WHITMAN MEMENTO. Below Whitman's signature on the photograph is the following note in the autograph of and signed by Thomas Donaldson (Whitman's friend and author of the work, *Walt Whitman the Man*),—

There was an abolition or Anti Slavery anniversary advertised at Philadelphia for Dec. 4–1883. John G. Whittier was to be present. He did not come. Mr. Whitman mounted this photograph himself—and brought it to the meeting. He came to our house to dinner and handed it to me saying "It was for Mr. Whittier. As he did not come I have brought it to you." 132 N. 40 St Phil Pa Dec 4–1883. [Signed] *Thomas Donaldson.*

This note explains the inscriptions on the two envelopes, the first one being the original one marked for Whittier, and the other, the one in which it was later presented to Mr. Donaldson. In addition to Whitman's inscriptions on this latter, is the record in Mr. Donaldson's autograph,—*Rec'd Oct. 16–|1889;* and on the former he has written the original date, *Dec 4–|83,* and the words, *Abolitionist Meeting.*

903. WHITMAN (WALT). Specimen Days & Collect. 12mo, original yellow cloth, author's facsimile signature in gilt on front cover; title, butterfly and publisher's name in gilt on back strip.

5—

Philadelphia: Rees Welsh & Co., 1882–'83

FIRST EDITION. FINE COPY.

Laid in is an autograph card signed by Walt Whitman. Camden, New Jersey, June 2, '84. To Henry Tyrrell, New York City, thanking him for a note and other things received. With autograph addressed envelope, bearing Whitman's stenciled stamp in lower corner.

904. WHITMAN (WALT). Specimen Days & Collect. *Frontispiece portrait.* 8vo, original dull yellow cloth, with author's facsimile signature in gilt on front cover; title, author's name and publisher's name in gilt on back strip, uncut, slightly shaken. Glasgow, Wilson & McCormick, 1883

9 ⁓

> FIRST ISSUE of this edition, with the publisher's name on the back strip.
> Laid in is an exceedingly interesting autograph post card signed by Whitman. Camden, New Jersey, Sept: 23, '90. To J. H. Johnston, New York City, relating to Robert Ingersoll, of whom he says,—*I too think with pride (& something more if there is anything more) of having Ingersoll go on permanent record on L of G.—have no sharper regret than the passing away unrecorded of that Reisser speech in Phila: I don't believe either Ing: or any of you realize how inimitable & perfect it was. . . .*

905. WHITMAN (WALT). [ROBERTSON (JOHN).] The Round Table Series IV. Walt Whitman Poet and Democrat. 8vo, original decorated vellum wrappers, uncut and unopened, with outer cloth protecting wrapper.
Edinburgh, 1884

15 ⁓

> SCARCE, only 100 copies having been privately printed, of which this is, No. 34, initialed by the publisher. Laid in is a excerpt from *Town Topics* containing an article on Walt Whitman.
> The Frank Maier copy, with bookplate.

906. WHITMAN (WALT). SYMONDS (JOHN ADDINGTON). Walt Whitman a Study. *Frontispiece portrait and 4 illustrations.* 8vo, original green cloth, gilt top, uncut and unopened. London, 1893

> FIRST EDITION. IMMACULATE COPY.
> Laid in is an autograph post card initialed by Walt Whitman. Camden, New Jersey [March 27, 1884] To J. H. Johnston, New York City, acknowledging receipt of a letter and some money from his friend.
> Also laid in is a photolithograph of Walt Whitman, with facsimile signature. No. 13 of 30 numbered copies from the original photograph, autographed by *Alfred F. Goldsmith 1919*, the collaborator with Carolyn Wells of the latest Whitman Bibliography.

907. WHITMAN (WALT). Specimen Days in America. Newly revised by the Author, with fresh Preface and additional Note. 12mo, original gilt decorated cloth, gilt top, uncut, with outer protecting wrapper. London, 1887

12 50

> FINE COPY OF THE FIRST ISSUE OF THIS EDITION. PRESENTATION COPY FROM THE AUTHOR, with autograph letter signed, inserted, 1p. 4to. Camden, New Jersey, June 20, '87, reading in part,—*Please accept a copy of my little book "Specimen Days" London ed'n, which I send for the young folks. Walt Whitman. . . . I have been ill. (I suppose Pearsall Smith was the cause of your sending it* [some chocolate mentioned above] *to me.)*
> From the Frank Maier collection, with bookplate.

908. WHITMAN (WALT). Complete Poems & Prose of Walt Whitman 1855 . . . 1888. Authenticated & Personal Book (handled by W. W.) . . . Portraits from Life . . . Autograph. *Portrait on title and other full-page portraits.* Royal 4to, half black calf, gilt, gilt top, uncut, BY OLDACH.
[Philadelphia: Ferguson Bros. & Co.] 1888

14 ⁓

> Edition limited to 600 copies, of which this is, No. 41. With facsimile autograph signature of the author, *Walt Whitman,* on the half-title of *Leaves of Grass.*
> Laid in is an interesting photograph of Whitman, with two children, taken on his sixtieth birthday and AUTOGRAPHED BY HIM as follows,—*Harry and Kitty & Walt Whitman May 1879.*

909. WHITMAN (WALT). Complete Poems & Prose of Walt Whitman 1855 . . . 1888. Authenticated & Personal Book (handled by W. W.) . . . Portraits from Life . . . Autograph. *Portrait on title and other full-page portraits.* Royal 8vo, half cloth, marbled sides, white paper label on back strip, uncut. [Philadelphia: Ferguson Bros. & Co.] 1888 — *32⁵⁰*

> Edition limited to 600 copies, of which this is, No. One Hundred Twenty-Eight. UNIQUE COPY, BEING THE AUTHOR'S PRESENTATION COPY TO EDMUND CLARENCE STEDMAN, WITH AUTOGRAPH INSCRIPTION,—*The following book to Edmund C Stedman from his friend the author W W ("Bear forth folded my love—dear mariner for you I fold it here in every leaf")* Camden New Jersey, March 11 1889, written on fly-leaf. The author's autograph signature on the half-title of *Leaves of Grass;* and inserted is the original article, *My Book and I* by Whitman, with the name of the magazine from which it was extracted, *Lippincott's Magazine January 1887,* WRITTEN IN WHITMAN'S AUTOGRAPH at the head of the first page, and the original wrapper addressed to Mr. Stedman by Whitman pasted on the back of the last page, as it was originally mailed.
>
> Also there is inserted on the inside of cover a printed list of Walt Whitman Manuscripts in possession of T. H. Rome, 513 Lafayette Avenue, Brooklyn, N. Y., with a manuscript note at the foot of same; and an envelope pasted to back fly-leaf containing extracts from magazines and newspapers, of articles regarding Whitman and his works.
>
> On inside of back cover is an autograph note signed by Horace Traubel, to Mr. Gable, regarding the book, of which he says in part,—*We (Whitman and myself) worked over it together, he all the time ill, I all the time anxious, both of us all the time loving.* This volume came into Mr. Gable's possession directly from the Stedman collection.

910. WHITMAN (WALT). First Proofs with corrections in the AUTOGRAPH OF WALT WHITMAN and Second (Revised) Proofs of the Poems:— — *12⁵⁰*

FANCIES AT NAVESINK. First Proof, last half of poem only, with author's autograph corrections. 1p. 8vo. On the reverse is written in pencil, *Mr. Curtz, printer.* Second Proof, complete, with author's corrections incorporated. 1p. oblong folio. With footnote at bottom,—"*Navesink—a seaside mountain, lower entrance of New-York bay."

THE VOICE OF THE RAIN. First Proof, with author's autograph corrections and annotations. 1p. 12mo. With date, "June 1885," written in red ink in upper left-hand corner. Second Proof, correctly printed after author's revision. 1p. 12mo.

OF THAT BLITHE THROAT OF THINE. Second Proof, only, correctly printed after first revision. 1p. 8vo.

Together, 5 pieces.

> With about twenty-eight words and a number of punctuation corrections in pencil and ink in the AUTOGRAPH OF WHITMAN. The Poems were included in his works, 1888.
> ORIGINAL PROOF SHEETS in this state, i. e., with the autograph of the author, are VERY RARELY MET WITH.

911. WHITMAN (WALT). November Boughs. Imperial 8vo, original dark green beveled cloth, gilt lettered title on front cover and back strip, gilt top, uncut. Philadelphia: David McKay, 1888 — *12⁵⁰*

> FIRST EDITION. LARGE PAPER COPY, ONLY A FEW ISSUED IN THIS FORM. With autograph presentation inscription from Horace L. Traubel to H. Buxton Forman, July, 1896; and with Mr. Forman's bookplate. No portrait was issued with this edition.
>
> Laid in is an AUTOGRAPH LETTER SIGNED BY WHITMAN, RELATING TO THE BOOK, 1p. oblong 8vo. Camden, July 31, '88. To J. B. [John Burroughs]. An interesting letter, reading in part,—*Quite certainly I am weathering—to all appearance—this ab't. sixth whack of my war paralysis—(thanks mainly I opine to a sound strong body heredity from my dear father & mother)— . . . have finished (sent in all copy) my little Nov: Boughs—Horace Traubel is a noble faithful fellow.*
> VERY FINE COPY AND EXCEPTIONALLY RARE IN THIS FORM.

912. WHITMAN (WALT). November Boughs. *Frontispiece portrait.* 8vo, original maroon cloth, title in gilt on front cover and back strip, gilt top.

12⁻

Philadelphia: David McKay, 1888

FIRST EDITION. FINE COPY. WITH MANY OF THE LEAVES UNCUT, and ONE OF A FEW COPIES CONTAINING THE FRONTISPIECE PORTRAIT.

Made especially interesting by the insertion of a page of ORIGINAL MANUSCRIPT in Whitman's autograph entitled,—*A Sunny November Day,* and beginning,—*Nov. 8. 82—Forenoon—a slow ramble in the woods—pleasantly cool. The thick-strewn fallen leaves rustle as I walk, giving out wild fragrance. The breeze slightly murmurs overhead. All around tall pines and oaks, graceful, columnar, the oaks now half-denuded of their foliage—dazzling patches of sunshine, motley, breaking through—plenty of laurel and holly with their bright green flecking the silver and brown.*

913. WHITMAN (WALT). November Boughs. *Frontispiece portrait.* 8vo, limp maroon cloth, gilt lettered on front cover and back strip, uncut.

15⁻

Philadelphia: David McKay, 1888

FIRST EDITION. ONE OF A FEW COPIES BOUND UP IN LIMP CLOTH AND ENTIRELY UNCUT FOR PRESENTATION PURPOSES. WITH WHITMAN'S AUTOGRAPH INSCRIPTION, reading,—*J. H. Johnston from his friend the author Walt Whitman with love & memories—Jan: 6 1889.* With marginal note by the original owner, J. H. Johnston, on p. 32.

914. WHITMAN (WALT). Autograph Letter Signed, 1p. 4to, Camden, New Jersey, April 11, 1888. To Miss Helen E. Price. With addressed envelope. In pencil.

12⁵⁰

AN INTERESTING LETTER OF FRIENDSHIP, reading in part:
Yes I will sit to Warren Davis the painter—w'd like to have it over with in five or six sittings. . . .
I am still living here & comfortable & in good spirits enough but probably near the end of my rope—badly paralysed & do not go out at all except by being toted. . . .

915. WHITMAN (WALT). Autograph Letter Signed in full, 1p. oblong 8vo, Camden, New Jersey, Jan. 8, 1889. To a correspondent whom he addresses as "Tom"; [ALSO] *Photographic portrait* with his facsimile signature beneath, dated 1881. 8vo. Together, 2 pieces, matted as one in a black frame and glazed.

15⁻

This letter evidences Whitman's fondness for "vins fins" saying: *Tom, if you have it & you can, I wish you w'd fill my bottle again with that sherry. . . .*

916. WHITMAN (WALT). Autograph Letter Signed in full, 1p. oblong 12mo, Camden, [New Jersey], Oct. 31, 1889. To a correspondent whom he addresses as "Lou"; [ALSO] *Photographic portrait,* with his autograph signature in facsimile, and dated 1881. 8vo. Together, 2 pieces, matted as one in a brown frame and glazed.

12⁵⁰

A personal, though interesting letter, in which he imparts to his correspondent some minor incidents.

917. WHITMAN (WALT). Leaves of Grass with Sands at Seventy & A Backward Glance O'er Travel'd Roads. May 31, 1889. . . . Portraits from Life. Autograph. Special Ed'n. *Original photograph frontispiece and other portraits.* 12mo, limp black morocco, gilt lettered on front, gilt edges.

45⁻

[Philadelphia: Ferguson Bros & Co.] 1889

FINE COPY. VERY SCARCE. 300 copies only printed, with author's autograph signature on title-page.

PRESENTATION COPY from Horace L. Traubel, to Sarah R. Sheridan, July 25, 1898, with signed autograph inscription.

Laid in is an AUTOGRAPH POSTCARD SIGNED BY WHITMAN. Camden, N. Jersey, Feb. 7. 76. To Ben: Perley Poore (Editor of Poore's *Index*). Washington, D. C.; thanking him for a copy of the Congressional Directory.

918. WHITMAN (WALT). Autograph Letter Signed in full, 1p. small 4to, Camden, New Jersey, Oct. 9, 1890; [ALSO] *Fine photographic portrait* of Whitman, with a facsimile of his signature beneath, dated 1881. Together, 2 pieces, matted as one in a black frame and glazed. *12⁵⁰*

> A FINE LETTER which follows in part: *Y'r telegram rec'd & I send on the first piece (I am preparing two, one on the subject you named)—if it will do. The price is seventy five dollars ($75) and I reserve the right to print in future book.* . . .

919. WHITMAN (WALT). Autograph Letter Signed, 1p. small 4to, Camden, New Jersey, Sept. 20, 1890. To J. H. Johnston, Diamond Merchant, 150 Bowery Cor: Broome St: New York City. With addressed envelope. *15⁻*

> FINE LETTER written in purple indelible pencil in reference to Ingersoll's address, reading in part,—
> *Dear friend J. H. J.—have just heard by Horace Traubel that (thro' you) Col. Ingersoll favors the idea of a public meeting & address ab't me—(get the notion that he has been Solicited or even Persuaded Wh—I don't like at all—not warranted or authorised by me, at any rate—but let that pass)* . . .
> *Of course I don't know what Col. I's drift and vein may be, but I know it w'd be grand & something I sh'd be proud of—On the impulse of the moment I have gather'd these items enclosed & send to you to give all the note (with scraps enclosed all as it is) to Col. I with my respects, thanks & love.* . . .

920. WHITMAN (WALT). Leaves of Grass. Including Sands at Seventy. 1st Annex, Good-Bye my Fancy. 2d Annex, A Backward Glance o'er Travel'd Roads, *and Portrait from Life. Facsimile of author's signature on title.* 8vo, original brownish gray mat paper wrappers, yellow paper label on backbone, uncut. Philadelphia: David McKay, 1891-'2 *90⁻*

> EXCESSIVELY RARE EARLIEST ISSUE OF THIS IMPORTANT EDITION. One of 100 copies specially bound for presentation to the author's friends, with inscription in the autograph of Horace Traubel,—*To George M. Williamson from Walt Whitman Camden New Jersey Jan 7 1892.*
> Laid in is an autograph letter signed by Horace Traubel, 4pp. 8vo. Philadelphia, Feb. 25, '08. To Mr. Gable, regarding this copy and the edition of which it was a part. Mr. Traubel writes,—*The gray paper Leaves which you got at the Williamson sale is one of the hundred copies of the Leaves sent out by W. to his closer personal friends just before his death.* He continues by stating that it was Whitman's intention to autograph all of these books himself but that he was too ill and weak to do so and turned them over to Mr. Traubel, who wrote most of the presentation inscriptions, and adds,—*They were printed on the same paper as the common issue put on the market. They can be identified only by the inscriptions (W.'s or mine) & by the gray paper cover and yellow label. (By the way, the label was made by Curtz).* . . . *This was in a sense Walt's death-bed book.* . . .
> Laid in is a photograph of Whitman, with his AUTOGRAPH SIGNATURE and date, 1877.
> VERY FINE COPY IN PRACTICALLY PERFECT STATE OF PRESERVATION.

921. [WHITMAN (WALT).] Good-Bye My Fancy. 2d Annex co Leaves of Grass. Royal 8vo, stitched, uncut, last leaves stained. *17⁵⁰*
Philadelphia: David McKay, 1891

> FIRST EDITION. ONE OF A SMALL NUMBER OF LARGE PAPER COPIES PUBLISHED FOR PRESENTATION TO WHITMAN'S FRIENDS. This copy was presented unbound, presumably with the intention of having it put up in a finer binding than the other copies of this issue. With autograph presentation inscription,—*J. M. Stoddart from Walt Whitman with best respects, thanks & love—May 29 '91,* on title.
> Laid in is a slip containing an address written in the autograph of Horace Traubel, Whitman's friend and one of his literary executors, with a note below initialed by Mr. Gable, stating this fact and that it was given to him (Mr. Gable) Feb'y 19, 1908, while Mr. Traubel was on a visit to Altoona.

922. [WHITMAN (WALT).] Good-Bye My Fancy. 2d Annex to Leaves of Grass. *Frontispiece portrait.* Royal 8vo, original dark green beveled cloth, gilt lettered title on front cover and back strip, gilt top, uncut and unopened.

15ー Philadelphia: David McKay, 1891

FIRST EDITION. LARGE PAPER COPY, ONLY A FEW ISSUED IN THIS FORM. Unusually desirable, being unopened and almost as fresh as when issued.
Laid in is a photograph of Whitman, with his AUTOGRAPH SIGNATURE.

923. WHITMAN (WALT). Original Typewritten Manuscript entitled "Walt Whitman's Last—Good-Bye, my Fancy," and sub-titled "Concluding Annex to LEAVES OF GRASS," with signature and short note to proof-reader. Manuscript of about 300 words—of which the corrections (about FIFTY WORDS) and typographical marks are in the author's autograph in ink—written on one side of folio leaf; the note is on a small piece of an envelope.

32⁵⁰

A MOST IMPORTANT ITEM.
This manuscript, sub-titled "Concluding Annex to LEAVES OF GRASS," is said to be THE LAST COMPOSITION OF THE VENERABLE POET. It begins:
H. Heine's first principle of criticising a book was, What motive is the author trying to carry out, or express or accomplish? and the second, Has he achiev'd it?
The theory of my "Leaves of Grass" as a composition of verses has been from first to last, (if I am to give impromptu a hint of the spinal marrow of the business, and sign it with my name,) to thoroughly possess the mind, memory, cognizance of the author himself, with everything beforehand—a full armory of concrete actualities, observations, humanity, past poems, ballads, facts, technique, war and peace, politics, North and South, East and West, . . .—and above all America and the present— . . . Every page of my poetic or attempt at poetic utterance therefore smacks of the living physical identity, date, environment, individuality, probably beyond anything known, and in style often offensive to the conventions. . . . [Signed in full] *Walt Whitman*
Laid in is a portrait of the author—tinted lithograph, 4to, with facsimile of his signature.

924. WHITMAN (WALT). SYMONDS (JOHN ADDINGTON). Walt Whitman a Study. *Frontispiece portrait and 4 illustrations.* Imperial 8vo, original blue cloth, white paper label, uncut and unopened. London, 1893

13ー

FIRST EDITION. LARGE PAPER, 208 copies only printed on Arnold's Unbleached Handmade Paper, of which this is No. 68. FINE COPY, practically untouched.
Laid in is a memorandum IN THE AUTOGRAPH OF WALT WHITMAN, being a quotation from Charles Baudelaire, beginning,—*"The immoderate taste for beauty & art," says Charles Baudelaire, "leads men into monstrous excesses . . .,"* written in pencil and comprising about sixty words, and bearing autograph certification by Horace Traubel,—*a piece of Walt Whitman's scribble for Gable 1912* [Signed] *Traubel.*
Also laid in is an excerpt from a magazine or newspaper, containing full-length portrait of Whitman and his poem, *The Unknown Land.*

925. WHITMAN (WALT). When Lilies Last the Door-Yard Bloomed. PRINTED ON VELLUM. *Original watercolor drawing as frontispiece. Decorated capitals and tail-piece colored by hand by C. R. Ashbee.* 12mo, vellum, uncut.

22⁵⁰ [London] Essex House Press, 1900

SPECIAL EDITION, 135 copies only printed all ON VELLUM, of which this is, No. 86.
A beautiful little volume, with a charming original watercolor in symbolic design, delightful decorations to the initial letters.
From the Frank Maier collection, with bookplate.

926. WHITMAN (WALT). Song of Myself. *Portrait. Decorated border on title.* Square 8vo, full green morocco, sides with some of small gilt floral sprays within plain morocco border, gilt floral back, inside morocco border with gilt vine design, gilt top, uncut. Enclosed in Morris-paper folding-case, with unfinished calf lining. East Aurora, New York, 1904

15ー

Special issue of the Roycroft Press Edition, on Japan vellum paper; 100 copies only printed, this being, No. 70, numbered and autographed by Elbert Hubbard.

927. WHITMAN (WALT). Notes and Fragments: left by Walt Whitman and now edited by Dr. Richard Maurice Bucke, one of his Literary Executors. Imperial 8vo, dark blue pebbled cloth, gilt lettered title on front cover and back strip. *15*

[London, Ontario] Printed for Private Distribution Only, 1899

Limited to 225 copies, of which this is, No. One, signed by the editor.

UNIQUE COPY; containing autograph notes signed by Thomas B. Harned and Horace Traubel, who, together with Dr. Bucke, the editor, were Whitman's literary executors.

This was Mr. Harned's personal copy and bears his autograph signature,—*T. B. Harned July 1899*, at top of fly-leaf and has also his book-plate. Below the autograph signature is a written statement that at the above date, i. e., July 1899, they had only five copies of the book left unsold, and that it is now very scarce and much valued. Signed,—*Thomas B. Harned Literary Executor of Walt Whitman April 15, '17*.

Below this note and extending over the entire following page is an autograph note by Mr. Traubel regarding the book, in which he says,—*This was not a Whitman diary but a note book made out of note books and attached memoranda. I have his diaries —two rather bulky volumes—which so far (1917) I havn't published. . . .* Mr. Traubel has also written on the inside of front cover,—*This is Gable's book—1917*.

Laid in is an "At Home" card, with AUTOGRAPH SIGNATURE OF WALT WHITMAN, for April 14th, 1887, at the Westminster Hotel, N. Y.

928. WHITMAN (WALT). Catalogue of a Collection of Books, Letters and Manuscripts written by Walt Whitman. In the Library of George M. Williamson, Grand View on Hudson. *Portraits and some of the facsimiles in* TWO STATES, *one on Japan vellum paper and one on plain paper.* 4to, cloth, uncut. Enclosed in board slip-case. *11*

Jamaica, Queensborough, New York, 1903

Edition limited to 127 copies, of which 25 only were PRINTED ON JAPAN PAPER, this being No. 7 of the Japan paper copies. Contains excellent facsimiles of Whitman's manuscripts and title-pages of First Editions.

929. WHITMAN (WALT). BURROUGHS (JOHN). ORIGINAL MANUSCRIPT, signed by Burroughs, of his article, "Walt Whitman 30 May 1819–1892 March 25." Manuscript of about THREE THOUSAND WORDS, written in ink on 32 8vo sheets; AUTOGRAPH LETTER SIGNED by Burroughs, 2pp. 8vo. West Park, New York, June 9 [1905]. To Mr. Turner. With addressed envelope; [ALSO] AUTOGRAPH POSTCARD SIGNED by WALT WHITMAN. Niagara Falls, September 28 '80. To W. T. Harris, St. Louis, Missouri. Together, 4 pieces. Laid in full green levant morocco folding-case, gilt fillet borders, gilt lettered title and floral spray on front, white watered-silk lining, BY CURTIS WALTERS. *57 50*

VERY DESIRABLE MANUSCRIPT BY BURROUGHS, who was an intimate friend of Whitman, written probably shortly after Whitman's death.

The letter by Burroughs was written to Mr. Emory S. Turner of the Merwin-Clayton Sales Company, New York, regarding the manuscript which it accompanies. In this letter Mr. Burroughs says,—*I think the article on Whitman to which you refer appeared in The Critic. I think parts of it are incorporated in my Whitman book but am not sure.* He closes the letter with a personal and characteristic note,—*I have not felt a trout at the end of my line yet this year but hope to in a day or two.*

Laid in is a note from Mr. Turner to Mr. Gable regarding the manuscript and the letter.

The autograph postcard by Whitman adds a further interest and value to this group. Written from Niagara Falls on a Canadian postcard to a friend in St. Louis, it reads in part,—*Have finished my summer tour of St. Lawrence and the Thousand Islands, etc. . . . and am now on my way home to Camden, N. J. (stopping here a short time). I am unusually well and robust for a half paralytic. . . .*

930. WHITMAN (WALT). The Bibelot for May 1912. Contains three selections
from Leaves of Grass: Songs of the Open Road, Passage to India, and Song
of the Universal. 12mo, full peacock blue morocco, Jansenist, gilt inside
morocco borders, gilt top, original wrappers and advertisements bound in.
In board solander case, lined with silk.

Portland, Maine: Thomas B. Mosher, 1912

931. WHITMAN (WALT). Leaves of Grass. Facsimile Edition of the 1855 Text.
Engraved portraits. Printed on Japanese vellum paper. Imperial 8vo, white
vellum boards, the decorations reproduced from the original binding, uncut. Enclosed in board slip-case. Portland, Maine, 1919

FIRST ISSUE OF THE FACSIMILE EDITION, limited to 400 copies, this being No. 18
of 50 copies ON JAPAN VELLUM, numbered and signed by the publisher. A fine facsimile reprint of the original edition, published by Thomas Bird Mosher and William
Francis Gable, containing an Introduction by the publisher, engraved portrait of
Whitman as frontispiece and reprint of the original issue with the portrait on India
paper.
Laid in is a leaf of advertisement of Whitman's works with a NOTE IN HIS AUTO-
GRAPH and initialed by him, reading,—*Letter of July 25 rec'd. No copies of original
(1855) edition in my possession—Respectfully W. W.;* also an envelope addressed in
Whitman's autograph,—*Walt Whitman Care Major Hapgood Paymaster U S A cor
15th & F st Washington D C.,* with later presentation inscription and note,—*To Mr.
H. P. Main—with the Regards of Tho. Donaldson Feby 7 /97, "Referred to on Page 159
of Walt Whitman The Man,"* all in the autograph of Thomas Donaldson, the author
of the last-mentioned work.

932. WHITMAN (WALT). Leaves of Grass. Facsimile Edition of the 1855 Text.
Portrait on plain paper. Printed on Old Stratford paper. Imperial 8vo,
green cloth, stamped and lettered in facsimile of the original binding.
Enclosed in board slip-case. Portland, Maine, 1919

FIRST ISSUE OF THE FACSIMILE EDITION, limited to 400 copies, this being one of
250 on Old Stratford white wove paper. Identical with the above Mosher reprint,
except for the paper and binding and the addition of blue printed wrappers to the
facsimile reprint.
Laid in is an AUTOGRAPH POSTAL CARD, SIGNED BY WHITMAN. Camden, Oct: 26,
'82. To J. H. Johnston, Jeweler, 150 Bowery, New York City, saying that he had
been ill for ten days but not seriously so and that he expected to be about shortly.
Signed in full,—*Walt Whitman.*

933. WHITMAN (WALT). PENNELL (JOSEPH). ORIGINAL PENCIL SKETCH OF WALT
WHITMAN'S HOUSE, at 330 Michel Street, Camden, New Jersey. Made
June 6, 1919. Size, 7 by 5½ inches, with several sketches and annotations
in the margin, by Joseph Pennell.

A CHARACTERISTIC EXAMPLE OF THE BOLD AND FREE STYLE OF this famous etcher
and artist's drawing. Besides three groups of sketches appearing in the margin, are
the following annotations: *Sketch of Whitman House, 330 Michel Street Camden, N. J.,
Made 6, 6, 1919. Enquiring artist: Which is Whitman's House—Uninterested citizen:
Dunno one house from 'nother;* [ALSO] *I am told that at one time the present owner dealt
in parrots and used second hand automobiles.*
The drawing is signed "J. Pennell."

934. WHITMAN (WALT). SAUNDERS (HENRY S.—Compiler). A Whitman Controversy. Being Letters Published in Mercure de France 1913-1914.
With Introduction by Henry S. Saunders. 8vo, cloth. Toronto, 1921

PRIVATELY ISSUED, and limited to 35 copies, none of which were for sale. The
volume is mimeographed on one side of 48 leaves. The compiler states in his Preface,
—"I have interspersed a few notes throughout these letters, always in parenthesis,
and initialed." Signed, in ink,—*Henry S. Saunders.*

935

935. WHITMAN (WALT). Bronze plaque portrait of Walter Whitman, signed with monogram, "R. M. T." for "The Franklin Inn Club." Diameter, 4⅞ inches. [Philadelphia, 1919?]

936. WHITMAN (WALT). ORIGINAL AUTOGRAPH MANUSCRIPT of short poem, "The Dead Emperor." SIGNED. Manuscript of about 50 words, written in ink— with the exception of three words, *follow copy strictly*, which are in purple indelible pencil—on one side of oblong 8vo sheet. *20—*

EXCEEDINGLY BEAUTIFUL ORIGINAL MANUSCRIPT POEM in the form of a dirge, in clear and bold handwriting, signed in full, *Walt Whitman.* The complete manuscript follows:

follow copy strictly   *(personal*

THE DEAD EMPEROR.

To-day with bending head and eyes, thou too, Columbia,
Less for the mighty crown laid low in sorrow—less for the Emperor,
Thy true condolence breathest, sendest out, oe'r many a salt sea mile,
Mourning a good old man—a faithful shepherd, patriot.

937. WHITMAN (WALT). Autograph Letter Signed, 2pp. 8vo, 431 Stevens St., Cor. West, Camden, N. Jersey, May 2. To John Burroughs. With addressed envelope. *20—*

NOTEWORTHY LETTER; referring to Professor Edward Dowden of Dublin, who later edited Whitman's *Leaves of Grass* published in Glasgow, Scotland. The letter reads:

Dear John Burroughs, I send you a letter, &c. I rec'd from Dowden, as you are alluded to. I have written to Dowden, today, & sent it off,—so I suppose he will send you the books alluded to. Mine have arrived—Dowden advances, expands, or rather penetrates— the first two Chapters of his Shakspere [sic], which I have read thoroughly are very fine— (I have underlined passages on every page)—the Victor Hugo I have not yet read.—
. . . I am pretty strong yet, & go out,—but head, stomach & liver, all in a bad way, & seems as if nothing could bring them round.
Have rec'd a long & good letter from Rossetti which I will show you when you come. How are you getting along? How is 'Sula? . . . Walt

938. WHITMAN (WALT). ORIGINAL AUTOGRAPH MANUSCRIPT essay, "A Thought on Shakespeare." SIGNED. Manuscript of more than SEVEN HUNDRED WORDS, written in ink on one side of 6 small folio leaves. *1050—*

This AUTOGRAPH PROSE MANUSCRIPT is written with SCHOLARLY DICTION, and Whitman's similes are here drawn with a logic and versatility which is bound to charm the enthusiastic reader. There are a few corrections and additions and several words deleted, the ENTIRE MANUSCRIPT being in HIS AUTOGRAPH and signed in full at end,—*Walt Whitman.* The treatise commences:

A THOUGHT ON SHAKSPERE

The most distinctive poems—the most permanently rooted and with heartiest reason for being—the copious cycle of Arthurian legends, or the almost equally copious Charlemagne cycle, or the poems of the Cid, or Scandinavian Eddas, or Nibelungen, or Chaucer, or Spenser, or Ossian, or Inferno—probably had their rise in great historic peturbations, which they came in to sum up and confirm, indirectly embodying results to date. However precious to "culture" the grandest of those poems, it may be said, preserve and typify results offensive to the modern spirit, and long past away.
To state it briefly and taking the strongest examples, in Homer lives the ruthless military prowess of Greece, and of its special god-descended dynastic houses;—in Shakspere, the "dragon-rancors and stormy feudal splendor of medieval caste." . . . .
Poetry, largely considered, is an evolution, sending out improved and ever-expanded types —in one sense, the past, even the best of it, necessarily giving place, and, dying out. . . . Everywhere—their own lands included, (is there not something terrible in the tenacity with which the one book out of millions, holds its grip?) the Homeric and Virgilian works, the interminable ballad-romances of the middle ages, the utterances of Dante, Spenser, and others, are upheld by their cumulus-entrenchment in scholarship, and as precious, always welcome, unspeakably valuable reminiscences.
Even the one who at present reigns unquestioned—of Shakspere—for all he stands for so much in modern literature, he stands entirely for the mighty esthetic sceptres of the past, not for the spiritual and democratic, the sceptres of the future. . . .

Lots 939–950 omitted

THE RENOWNED COLLECTION OF THE LATE

WILLIAM F. GABLE

OF ALTOONA, PENNSYLVANIA

AUTOGRAPHS AND MANUSCRIPTS

SIGNED HOLOGRAPH MANUSCRIPTS, LETTERS AND DOCUMENTS BY
EMINENT AMERICAN, ENGLISH AND EUROPEAN WRITERS, SIGNERS
OF THE DECLARATION OF INDEPENDENCE, PRESIDENTS OF THE
UNITED STATES, OFFICERS IN THE REVOLUTIONARY AND
CIVIL WARS AND OTHER PERSONS OF DISTINCTION IN
PUBLIC AND PRIVATE LIFE

PART THREE

SOLD BY ORDER OF THE ADMINISTRATOR

ROBERT B. GABLE

AMERICAN ART ASSOCIATION, Inc.
MADISON AVENUE, 56TH TO 57TH STREET
ENTRANCE 30 EAST 57TH STREET, NEW YORK
Telephone: PLAZA 1270

Feb 13 & 14, 1924

By Emerson's Grave.

We stand by Emerson's
new-made grave without sadness —
— indeed a solemn joy and faith,
almost hauteur — our soul-benison
no mere
"Warrior rest, thy task is done,"
for one beyond all the warriors of the
world lies surely symbolled here.
A just man, poised on himself,
all-loving, all-enclosing, and sane
and clear as the sun. Nor does
it seem so much Emerson himself
we are here to honor — it is conscience,
simplicity, culture, humanity's attributes at their best, yet applicable
if need be to average affairs, and
eligible to all.

So used are we to suppose
a heroic death can only come from
out of battle or storm, or mighty personal
contest, or amid dramatic incidents
or danger. (Have we not been taught
so for ages by all the plays and poems?)

WALT WHITMAN
"By Emerson's Grave"—Original Mss.
[No. 620]

610. WHITMAN (WALT—American Poet). Autograph Letter Signed,—"*David Ferguson.*" 2pp. 8vo. Washington, April 29th, 1863. To Mrs. David Ferguson (the wife of a sick soldier in the Armory Square Hospital).

17 50

ENTIRELY IN WHITMAN'S AUTOGRAPH. Written in Armory Square Hospital for a sick soldier named David Ferguson, who was probably indisposed or unable to write. Reveals Whitman as an amanuensis performing an act of mercy during the Civil War, the letter reading in part:

Dear Wife, I am now to inform you that I have been now sick for two weeks—have been for the past week in Armory Square Hospital—have a pretty bad cold, the doctor does not call my disease by any particular name—I have considerable cough—but I think I shall be up all right before a great while, so you must not be uneasy—I have pretty good care taken of me here, & shall do well. . . I send you my love. I have this letter written by a friend who sometimes calls in to see me, & the other boys. Good bye for the present & God bless you & all. [Signed] *David Ferguson.*
The above letter is written by Walt Whitman, a visitor to the hospitals.

611. WHITMAN (WALT). Autograph Letter, 2pp. folio. Wash[ington], May 11, 1863. To [Moses Lane].

27 50

REMARKABLE CIVIL WAR AUTOGRAPH LETTER—WITH MENTION OF GENERALS HOOKER, LEE, DAVIS AND MCCLELLAN. Unsigned, but written by Whitman while a volunteer army nurse. COMMENTING ON THE BATTLES OF FREDERICKSBURG AND CHANCELLORSVILLE, the "Good Gray Poet" narrates his experiences in the hospital, the state of war, etc. The entire letter—while perfectly legible—bears appearances of having been written in haste while in a state of agitation, probably due to the turmoil resulting from the Battle of Chancellorsville, fought just one week prior to the date of Whitman's letter, which reads in part:

Never more heart-rending cases than these now coming up in one long bloody string from Chancellorsville and Fredericksburg battles. Six or seven hundred every day without intermission. We have already over 3000 arrived here in hospital from Hooker's late battles. I am at work somewhere among them every day or in the evening. It is not so exhausting as one might think—the endurance and spirit are supplied. My health, thank God, was never better. . . You there North must not be so disheartened about Hooker's return to this side of the Rappahannock. . . The blow struck at Lee. . .is in my judgment the heaviest and most staggering they have yet got from us, etc.

612. WHITMAN (WALT). Autograph Letter Signed,—"*Walt Whitman,*" 4pp. 4to. Brooklyn [N. Y.], October 15, 1865. To a friend and comrade, whom he calls Byron; [ALSO] *Portrait of Whitman* on 16mo leaflet, menu of a dinner given in his honor by his friends and admirers with 29-line verse to Whitman on last page, commencing,—"All hail to thee! Walt Whitman! Poet, Prophet, Priest!" 2 newspaper clippings about Whitman. Together, 4 pieces.

22 50

AN EXCEEDINGLY FINE LETTER OF WHITMAN AT THE AGE OF 36, WRITTEN FROM HIS MOTHER'S HOME, Portland Avenue near Myrtle, Brooklyn, N. Y., while on a leave of absence from the Attorney General's office in Washington, in which he refers to the bustle and noise of New York in the Sixties, speaks of his mother, and mentions his book, "Drum Taps." The letter reads in part,—

Byron I don't know certain whether I have written to you since I rec'd you last letter or not—but it came safe, & was glad to hear from you. Write soon, my dear comrade. . . Here is this place & New York, I go around quite a good deal—it is a great excitement to go around the busiest parts of New York, Broadway, & the wharves, & great ferries, the trucks & omnibuses etc. all jammed together, & such bustle & noise. . . [Etc.]

613. WHITMAN (WALT). ORIGINAL AUTOGRAPH MANUSCRIPT entitled,"Abstract of Charges, Affidavits, &c. presented by Hon. J. E. Cavanaugh, Delegate in Congress—against Judge Lyman E. Munson, Associate Justice U. S. Courts, Montana Territory; with Counter Statements, in behalf of Judge Munson." Including Autograph Letter Signed,—"*Walt Whitman, of A. G. office,*" 1p. 4to, Attorney General's Office, Washington, April 7, 1868, to Hon. O. H. Browning, Attorney General, *ad interim.* The abstract comprises 20pp. 4to. ENTIRELY IN WHITMAN'S AUTOGRAPH, the whole hinged together with several blank leaves, the last one of which is docketed,—"*Dec. 5, 1868. Recd of the Attorney General all of the papers relating to charges agst Judge L. E. Munson—*[Signed] *James M. Cavanaugh.*"

25

[*Continued*]

LENGTHY MANUSCRIPTS OF WHITMAN IN THE OFFICIAL CAPACITY OF GOVERN-MENT CLERK ARE OF GREAT RARITY. THE ABOVE MANUSCRIPT IS VERY LEGIBLE AND NEATLY WRITTEN. ITS SIMPLICITY AND TERSENESS OF STYLE is unlike some of his more extravagant literary compositions. Whitman's letter to Hon. O. H. Browning reads:

In obedience to your request, I have carefully examined the papers, presented by Hon. Mr. Cavanaugh, making grave charges against Judge Lyman E. Munson, Associate Justice, U. S. Courts of Montana Territory—& have prepared the following abridgement & abstract of said papers.

The principal charges made against Judge Munson were the accepting of bribes, extortion, etc., the first part of which is concluded with the following notation,— *The foregoing comprises an abridgement or brief of all the papers submitted in this case.* [Signed] *W.*

The above is followed by a second portion, with heading,—"*Subsequent Papers, handed in April 8, 1868.*" The third and last part, dated April 13, 1868, is marked,— "*In Behalf of Judge Munson—(handed in by Hon. Mr. Trumbull,)*" and is a denial of the foregoing charges.

The above is of added interest, in that it recalls the fact that it was while Whitman was in the employ of the government that he began scribbling portions of his poems on the backs of envelopes and on small pieces of paper.

614. WHITMAN (WALT). Autograph Letter Signed,—*Walt Whitman Solicitor's Office Treasury, Washington, D. C. U. S. America.* 6pp. 8vo. Washington, Jan. 18, 1872. To Prof. Edward Dowden, Dublin, Ireland. With addressed envelope, from which the postage stamp has been torn.   *40 —*

EXTREMELY FINE AND INTERESTING LETTER APOLOGETIC OF THE DEMOCRATIC SPIRIT OF HIS WRITINGS. ONE OF THE BEST WALT WHITMAN LETTERS OBTAINABLE.

Written shortly after his dismissal from a Government position at Washington, to Professor Dowden (a contributor to the "Westminster Review"), regarding literary criticisms concerning "Leaves of Grass" and "Democratic Vistas" and the opposition which these publications met with in the United States, stating,—

If you write again for publication about my books, or have opportunity to influence any forthcoming article on them, I think it would be a proper & even essential part of such article to include the fact that the books are hardly recognized at all by the orthodox literary & conventional authorities of the U. S.—that the opposition is bitter, & in a large majority—& that the author was actually turned out of a small government employment, & deprived of his means of support, by a Head of Department at Washington, solely on account of having written his poems.

I am in excellent health, & again & still work as clerk here in Washington.

Whitman then speaks of his friend, mentioning John Burroughs, Tennyson, Joaquin Miller and Ralph Waldo Emerson, whose philosophy he figuratively compares to a pot of tea, saying:

Emerson has just been this way, (Baltimore & Washington) lecturing. He maintains the same attitude—draws on the same themes—as twenty five years ago. It all seems to me quite attenuated—(the first drawing of a good pot of tea, you know—& Emerson's was the heavenly herb itself—is refreshing & welcome—but what must one say to a second, and even third or fourth, infusion?) I send you a newspaper report of his lecture here a night or two ago. It is a fair sample.

615. WHITMAN (WALT). AUTOGRAPH MANUSCRIPT POEM SIGNED of: "The Patrol at Barnegat." Manuscript of about ONE HUNDRED AND THIRTY FIVE WORDS, written in ink on one side of a 4to sheet and signed twice: "*Walt Whitman.*"   May, 1880   *47 ⁵⁰*

FIRST DRAFT OF THIS FINE POEM, written in blank verse, which commences:
Wild, wild the storm, and the sea high-running,
Steady the roar of the gale with incessant undertone muttering
Shouts of demoniac laughter fitfully piercing and pealing,
Waves, air, and midnight, their savagest trinity lashing. . .

There are a few pencil corrections in the autograph of the author.

616. WHITMAN (WALT). AUTOGRAPH MANUSCRIPT POEM OF: "A Clear Midnight." A Manuscript of about FORTY-FIVE WORDS written in ink on one side of a 12mo. sheet.   [1880]   *10 —*

A FINE POEM, with several corrections in the autograph of the author. It commences:
This is thy hour O Soul, thy free flight into the wordless,
Away from books, away from art, the day erased, the lesson done. . .

617. WHITMAN (WALT). AUTOGRAPH MANUSCRIPT OF "Autumn Nights," written on three sheets of tablet paper, dated Oct. 10, 11, 12, 1880, unsigned.

15

> AUTOBIOGRAPHICAL: *It is the Indian summer of the year—Is it not also the Indian summer of my life? I am now past sixty-one. The paralysis long numbing me has been lulled for two years—The esthetic beauty and moral nourishment of such October nights first led me to memorandize their scenes and impressions in notes originally jotted down as bases for a sonnet or a poem.* [followed by these words scorea througn:—] *Gradually I got into making them other times, and in the days—and do so now quite involuntarily.*
> *I watch departing Venus throwing out a sort of special light as if to say "I am not at my best and brightest just now from your point of view, neither am I by any means on my decay—I endure—everything endures—I shall be as lustrous as ever in due time—perhaps more lustrous!. . .* [Etc.]

618. WHITMAN (WALT). Autograph Letter Signed, 2pp. 8vo. 431 Stevens Street, Camden, New Jersey, June 17, '81. To John Burroughs, Esopus-on-Hudson, New York. With addressed envelope. *With portrait of Whitman, on Japan paper.*

52 50

> EXCEEDINGLY INTERESTING LETTER, REFERRING TO THE SUPPRESSED EDITION of "Leaves of Grass," and reading in part,—
> *I. . . return'd last evening from ten days down in the Jersey woods. . .*
> *I have just concluded a contract with J. R. Osgood & Co.: of Boston, for the publishing of my poems complete in one Volume, under the title of "Walt Whitman's Poems," (the old name "Leaves of Grass" running through the same as ever)—to be either a $2 book or a $2.50 one—if the former I to have 25 cts. royalty, if the latter 30 cts—The proposition for publication came from them—The bulk of the pieces will be the same as hitherto—only I shall secure now that consecutiveness & ensemble —I am always thinking of. Book will probably be out before winter. . .*
> Then Whitman speaks of having been to Boston and his plans for a summer trip to Boston and Canada, ending the communication thus,—*I will keep you posted, & will try to pay you a visit too—how is 'Sula? Write soon.* [Signed] *Walt Whitman.*

619. WHITMAN (WALT). Autograph Letter Signed, 2pp. large 8vo. Rand, Avery & Co., Printers. Boston, Sept. 24, 1881. To an unnamed person addressed as "Dear friend."

40

> BEAUTIFUL LETTER WRITTEN WHILE ON A TRIP, giving a vivid description of Ralph Waldo Emerson and his family. It commences,—
> *Yours rec'd—I am now back here finishing up—only staid a few days in Concord. . . Sunday, Emerson & his wife, son Edward & wife &c. gave me a dinner—two hours—everything just right every way—a dozen people there. (The family & relatives)—for my part I thought the old man in his smiling and alert quietude & withdrawness (he has a good color in his face & ate just as much dinner as anybody) more eloquent, grand, appropriate & impressive than ever. . .*
> *The book* [the suppressed edition of "Leaves of Grass"] *is done & will be in the market in a month or so—all about it has proceeded satisfactorily—& I have had my own way in everything. . . it will be a $2 book. . .*
> *Besides this general death-gloom of the nation* [President Garfield, who was shot by Guiteau in tne Washington Railroad Station, died September 19, 1881]*—have you heard of the sudden and dreadful death of our young friend Beatrice Gilchrist in performing some chemical experiment with ether?*
> Whitman then speaks of having met O. W. Holmes, Mr. James, Joaquin Miller and Longfellow.

620. WHITMAN (WALT). ORIGINAL AUTOGRAPH MANUSCRIPT SIGNED OF: "By Emerson's Grave." A Manuscript of about THREE HUNDRED AND FIFTY WORDS, written in ink on one side of 3 small folio sheets, signed at end: "*Walt Whitman.*" With envelope addressed in Whitman's autograph to *J. L. and J. B. Gilder, Critic Office, 30 Lafayette Place, New York City. April 29, 1882.* Each sheet and envelope tipped on a folio sheet of drawing paper; [ALSO] *Portrait of Whitman, engraved by Hollyer,* small folio. Together, 3 pieces.

150

> SUPERB WHITMAN MANUSCRIPT, with a few corrections in the Autograph of the author, also containing a four-line autograph note of instructions (written in red ink; the manuscript in black ink) for the proof-reader.
> From the William K. Bixby collection.

[See Frontispiece for Reproduction]

621. WHITMAN (WALT). Autograph Letter Signed, 1p. 4to. Camden [N. J.], Feb. 9 [1883]. To John Burroughs, Esopus-on-Hudson, New York. With addressed envelope. *Also portrait of Whitman.* — *12⁵⁰*

> FINE SPECIMEN. A letter of apology for having missed an interview with the naturalist, reading in part,—
> *McKay and Dr. Bucke are in treaty about the Dr.'s book, with the probability of Mc publishing it. To-day, afternoon feels like a precursor of Spring, so fresh & sunny— I am not busy at anything particular—(Seem to be like a skipper who has come into port at last & discharged cargo—& don't know what next.) Who did you see in New York? And exactly how are you? Write soon—& freely. Yours as always [Signed] Walt Whitman.*

622. WHITMAN (WALT). Autograph Signature, Camden, New Jersey, May 31, '84. Written in ink, *"Walt Whitman, Camden, New Jersey, May 31, '84–65th Birthday,"* [ALSO] *Bust portrait of Whitman, with his Autograph Signature. 8vo.* Together, 2 pieces, matted in a black frame and glazed. — *5*

> SPLENDID EXAMPLE of Whitman's writing written on his 65th birthday.

623. WHITMAN (WALT). Autograph Letter Signed, 2pp. 4to. Camden, Oct. 13, '87, ½ past 1 p. m. To an unnamed friend; [ALSO] *Bust Portrait of Whitman* taken in his declining years. Together, 2 pieces. — *17*

> INTERESTING PERSONAL LETTER, giving directions regarding the transfer of his clothes by express, in which he speaks of his declining health.
> *My dear friend, writes Whitman, I am having quite a good spell to-day (if it only lasts.)—I wish you, in conjunction with Peter Doyle, would go over to my room at Dr. Whites, & unlock the big trunk, (the one that is strapped) and take out*
> *My gray suit, coat, vest, & I think there are two pairs of pants, both alike.*
> *My black overcoat, quite heavy—it is the one in the trunk.*
> *Black felt hat, (there are two black hats, this is the lightest most flexible one—not the big fellow.)*
> *The pair of old buckskin gloves with sheepskin cuffs and do them up in a bundle— direct plainly to me, 431 Stevens St. . .* [Etc.]

624. WHITMAN (WALT). Autograph Letter Signed, 1p. oblong 12mo, [Camden, New Jersey]. May 10, '89. To Thos B. Harned. With addressed envelope. [ALSO] *Bust portrait of Whitman* with Autograph Signature *"Walt Whitman, 1881"* beneath. Together, 3 pieces, matted in a black frame and glazed. — *20*

> CHARACTERISTIC LETTER, reading,—*Tom if you will fill the brown bottle with Sherry for me & the small white bottle with cognac. My dear friend O'Connor is dead.*

625. WHITMAN (WALT). Autograph Letter Signed,—*"Walt Whitman,"* 1p. 4to. Camden [N. J.], July 20, '89. To *"Dear C. W. E."* Written in pencil. — *10*

> INTERESTING PERSONAL LETTER, written two years before his death; in which he speaks of his declining health and invalid condition, referring to his wheel chair. The letter begins:
> *Yr's rec'd & welcomed, as always—So you have flitted north on the Pacific Coast & settled in San Francisco. Good—no doubt—To use the N. Y. slang of low life I send you "good roots" for your new & future habitat—*
> *I am still holding out here—probably better than you might suppose—but bad enough— physically almost completely disabled.* [Etc.]
> Whitman then speaks of Dr. Maurice Bucke, John Burroughs and the death of William Douglas O'Connor—all authors and friends who wrote about the poet.

626. WHITMAN (WALT). ORIGINAL AUTOGRAPH MANUSCRIPT OF his prose article on the death of George Sand. Manuscript of about THREE HUNDRED WORDS, written in ink on one side of five 8vo leaves, with numerous autographic corrections, over twenty words having been deleted and crossed out by the author. *Portrait of Whitman* and several newspaper clippings regarding the death and burial of George Sand, some with autographic notations of Whitman thereon. Together, 3 pieces. — *50*

> WHITMAN'S BEAUTIFUL EULOGY ON THE DEATH OF THIS GREAT FRENCH WOMAN AND FAMOUS NOVELIST, GEORGE SAND. The manuscript commences,—
> *George Sand's rather the soul's tempest interior anguish restlessness love—the still, small, vital voice. Not without rich dramatic effects, & grandeur of personalities, on occasion—but preferring calm—like some fine landscape,—how still, yet how living!*

627. WHITMAN (WALT). ORIGINAL AUTOGRAPH MANUSCRIPT of his poem,—
"Thanks in old age." Manuscript of about ONE HUNDRED NINETY
WORDS, written in ink on one side of 2 narrow small folio leaves. A few
corrections and deletions in the author's autograph. *Portrait of Whitman.*
The whole neatly hinged to larger sheets of handmade paper. Beautifully
illuminated hand-lettered title-page; [ALSO] one 12mo. leaf of ORIGINAL
AUTOGRAPH MANUSCRIPT regarding Oriental Poetry, reading on the re-
verse,—"*Walt Whitman 1883* [4-line verse] *Leaves of Grass—page 350.*"
Together, 2 pieces.

105

"THANKS IN OLD AGE" IS A VERY FINE MANUSCRIPT OF ONE OF WHITMAN'S
BEAUTIFUL POEMS, which brings the reader into relation with the fundamental
human emotions of love and gratitude, written in the author's characteristic uncon-
ventional style, and reading in part,—
Thanks in old age—thanks ere I go,
For health, the midday sun, the impalpable air—for life, mere life.
For precious ever-lingering memories (of you, my mother dear—you, father—you,
   brother, sisters, friends.)
The poem is signed in full at the end, —"*Walt Whitman,*" and the portrait is a
striking likeness of "the Good Gray Poet" at the age of sixty-two.

THE RENOWNED COLLECTION OF THE LATE

WILLIAM F. GABLE

OF ALTOONA, PENNSYLVANIA

AUTOGRAPH MANUSCRIPTS
INSCRIBED COPIES
FIRST EDITIONS
LETTERS

OF

ALDRICH, MATTHEW ARNOLD, BRYANT, BURROUGHS, CLEMENS,
GEORGE AND ROBERT CRUIKSHANK, DARWIN, EMERSON,
EUGENE FIELD, RILEY, SWINBURNE, THOREAU,
BAYARD TAYLOR, WHITMAN, WILDE,
AND MANY OTHER NOTED

ENGLISH AND AMERICAN AUTHORS

PART FOUR

SOLD BY ORDER OF THE ADMINISTRATOR

ROBERT B. GABLE

March 10 & 11, 1924

AMERICAN ART ASSOCIATION, INC.

MADISON AVENUE, 56TH TO 57TH STREET

ENTRANCE 30 EAST 57TH STREET, NEW YORK

Telephone: PLAZA 1270

1104. WHITMAN (WALT). The United States Magazine and Democratic Review. New Series. Vols. IX, X, XI, XIII. From July 1841 to Dec. 1843. *Numerous portraits and illustrations.* 4 vols. 8vo, half calf, gilt, sprinkled edges.

New York, 1841–1843

Contains: Bervance, or, Father and Son; Death in the School-room—a fact; Wild Frank's Return; Child-ghost, a story of the last Loyalist; Last of the Sacred Army; and others by Walt Whitman. These volumes also contain contributions from Whittier, Bryant, Longfellow, Hawthorne, Lowell, Thoreau, and others.

1105. WHITMAN (WALT). Brother Jonathan. Vol. I, No. 5. January 29, 1842, containing, "Ambition—A Poem, by Walter Whitman." Royal 4to, original wrappers, uncut.

New York, 1842

ONE OF THE EARLIEST APPEARANCES OF WHITMAN'S WORK under his own name. EXCEEDINGLY RARE. Few pages spotted, as usual.

1106. WHITMAN (WALT). INGERSOLL (ROBERT G.). Liberty in Literature. Testimonial to Walt Whitman. New York [1890]; The Edinburgh Review, or Critical Journal. [Containing an article on Whitman.] London, 1908; BRENTON (J. J.—Editor). Voices from the Press. [Contains: "The Tomb Blossoms," by Whitman.] New York, 1850. *First vol. with portrait and original wrappers bound in.* Together, 3 vols. 8vo and 12mo, half calf, cloth and wrappers.

New York and London, 1850–1908

1107. WHITMAN (WALT). ORIGINAL AUTOGRAPH MANUSCRIPT of his poem—"Mannahatta" as published in "Leaves of Grass." Manuscript of about THREE HUNDRED SEVENTY-FIVE WORDS, written in ink on one side of 5 octavo leaves, having numerous corrections and alterations. Hinged in 4to mat.

A CHARMING POEM ON NEW YORK CITY—PROBABLY FROM WHITMAN'S BOYHOOD IMPRESSIONS OF THE GREAT METROPOLIS AND ITS HARBOR—commencing (reduced facsimile):—

Turning to the third page we read,—
> *The down-town streets, the jobbers' houses of business,—the houses of*
> *business of the ship-merchants, money-brokers, factors,*
> *Immigrants arriving, fifteen or twenty thousand in a week.*

And on the last page,—
> *The beautiful city. The city of hurried and sparkling waters.*
> *The city of spires and masts!*
> *The proud and turbulent city! The city nested in bays! My city! Etc.*

AN UNUSUALLY FINE AND CLEAN EXAMPLE OF MANUSCRIPT.

[See Reproduction]

1108. WHITMAN (WALT). Leaves of Grass. *Frontispiece portrait on plain paper.* Imperial 8vo, original green cloth, blind-stamped sides with rustic lettered title in gilt and triple gilt border on both front and back covers, gilt floral sprays and gilt lettered title on backbone, marbled end-papers, gilt edges, binding very slightly worn. Brooklyn, New York, 1855   *200*

FIRST ISSUE OF THE FIRST EDITION AND THAT MOST DESIRED BY COLLECTORS. In the green cloth binding with the rustic title, the gilt lines and marbled end-papers. Later issues lacked the gilt lines on the cover, had plain end-papers and plain edges. The later issues also contained some press notices of the book.
LAID IN, IS AN AUTOGRAPH LETTER SIGNED: "*Walt Whitman,*" 1p. oblong 12mo, Camden, Sept. 26, 1890. [To Wm. Sloane Kennedy.] Written in blue pencil. In this interesting letter, Whitman states that he is enclosing his preface note about O'Connor for the new book of the latter's tales. He also mentions Col. Ingersoll.
Accompanying the above are two cabinet photographs of Whitman.

1109. WHITMAN (WALT). Leaves of Grass. *Frontispiece portrait on plain paper.* Imperial 8vo, original green cloth, blind-stamped sides with rustic lettered title in gilt, gilt lettered title on backbone, canary end-papers.   *85*

Brooklyn, New York, 1855

FIRST EDITION. Second Issue. WITH ORIGINAL AUTOGRAPH SIGNATURE OF WALT WHITMAN BELOW FRONTISPIECE PORTRAIT.
LAID IN, IS AN AUTOGRAPH LETTER SIGNED: "*Walt Whitman,*" 1p. 4to, To an unnamed person, written in blue pencil. A fine businesslike letter in which Whitman speaks of a London Agency for photos.

1110. WHITMAN (WALT). Walt Whitman's Drum-Taps. 12mo, original brown cloth, title on gilt ground in circle on front cover and in blind on back, thin paper fly-leaves, plain edges. New-York, 1865   *35*

FIRST EDITION. This includes: "When Lilacs Last in the Door-Yard Bloom'd" and other pieces, with separate pagination. Whitman delayed the publication of Drum Taps, because of the death of President Lincoln, and only a few copies were bound at this time. It was not until a few weeks later that he added "When Lilacs Last in the Door-Yard Bloom'd;" "O Captain! My Captain;" and a few other poems.
THIS IS THE AUTHOR'S OWN COPY according to a certification pasted on end-leaf by Miss H. E. Price, a former owner. Pasted on the verso of the front cover is a one line extract from "Leaves of Grass" IN THE AUTHOR'S AUTOGRAPH, reading: *Angry cloth I see there leaping.*
On page 13 of the "Sequel," is a correction in the handwriting of Whitman where he changes the printed words "little spot," to "*drops of red,*" in the poem: "O Captain! My Captain!"

1111. WHITMAN (WALT). [O'CONNOR (WILLIAM DOUGLAS).] The Good Gray Poet. A Vindication. 8vo, wrappers, uncut and unopened. New York, 1866   *10*

FIRST EDITION OF THIS RARE PAMPHLET.
Laid in, is a small slip of paper IN THE AUTOGRAPH OF WHITMAN, signed: "*W. Whitman,*" which reads: *Please send me, (after reading first proof for corrections) two good proofs, one of which I will immediately read & return.*

1112. WHITMAN (WALT). BURROUGHS (JOHN). Notes on Walt Whitman, As Poet and Person. 12mo, cloth, uncut. Lacks end-papers. New York, 1867

30—

FIRST EDITION. RARE. JOHN BURROUGHS' FIRST PUBLICATION. WITH HIS SIGNATURE AFTER PREFACE.

LAID IN, IS AN AUTOGRAPH NOTE SIGNED: *"Walt Whitman."* 1p. oblong 16mo, no place, no date. To *"Dear M. P."* In this letter Whitman speaks of the publication of some pieces of his work, not specifying which, also naming the price as $10.00. At the bottom of the note above his signature appears the title: "New Poetry."

LAID IN, ALSO, IS AN AUTOGRAPH LETTER SIGNED: *"John Burroughs."* 1p. 12mo, West Park, N. Y., April 25, 1892. To Mr. Stoddard. A fine letter in which the famous naturalist says: *Horace Traubel writes me that you will look at an article of mine on Whitman. I enclose it herewith. The Forum took it and then withdrew it when the editor learned I was to have one in N. A. Review on a different phase of same subject.* . . .

1113. WHITMAN (WALT). AUTOGRAPH MANUSCRIPT PAPERS in the Case of General A. B. Dyer, 6pp. folio, ENTIRELY IN WHITMAN'S AUTOGRAPH. [Attorney General's Office, Washington, September, 1868]; Autograph Letter, not signed, 2pp. folio. [Washington, 1868.] Addressed "Sir." Together, 2 pieces, written in pencil.

35—

FINE WHITMAN MANUSCRIPT. OF HISTORIC, AS WELL AS OF LITERARY AND LEGAL INTEREST. THE CASE IS IN REFERENCE TO WHETHER OR NOT GENERAL DYER, CHIEF OF ORDNANCE, U. S. ARMY, IS LIABLE TO BE TRIED BY COURT MARTIAL; THE OFFENCE CHARGED IN THE REPORT OF A JOINT COMMITTEE OF CONGRESS BEING SECRET FRAUD AGAINST THE GOVERNMENT. Whitman's letter reads in part,—

The 88th article of War (2 Stat. 369) declares that no person shall be liable to be tried by general court martial for any offence committed more than two years before the issuing of the order for trial, "unless the person, by reason of having absented himself or some other manifest impediment, shall not have been amenable to justice within that period." The question submitted therefore, resolves itself into this, whether want of Knowledge of the offence by the government constitutes a "manifest impediment," . . . *The papers received with your previous communication of Sept. 25, 1868 touching on this subject, are herewith returned.*

THE PAPERS IN THE CASE ARE OF ABSORBING INTEREST, CONSISTING IN THE MAIN OF CITATIONS FROM ARTICLES OF WAR AND LEGAL OPINIONS BASED ON TRADITION AND PRECEDENT, and concluding thus,—

So that I conclude that under the "circumstances of the case" as set forth in the accompanying papers, Gen. D. is not now liable to be tried by Gen. court martial on the offences alleged against him.

1114. WHITMAN (WALT). Poems by Walt Whitman. Selected and Edited by William Michael Rossetti. *Frontispiece portrait of Whitman.* 16mo, original blue cloth, uncut. London: Hotten, 1868

15—

FIRST ISSUE OF THIS ENGLISH EDITION. Without the price mark 7/6 on back strip, which appears on the Second Issue. FINE COPY OF A VERY RARE EDITION.

LAID IN, IS AN AUTOGRAPH LETTER SIGNED: *"Walt Whitman."* 1p. 8vo, Camden, Nov. 15, no year. To *"Mrs. Johnston & dear Ida, & dear, dear Jack."* A personal letter in which he speaks of being afflicted with an *"obstinate dyspeptic affection."*

1115. WHITMAN (WALT). Poems by Walt Whitman. Selected and Edited by William Michael Rossetti. *Frontispiece portrait of Whitman.* 16mo, original blue cloth, uncut. London: Hotten, 1868

2⁵⁰

Second Issue of this English Edition, with the price mark 7/6 on back strip.

1116. WHITMAN (WALT). After All Not to Create Only. Recited by Walt Whitman, on invitation of Directors American Institute, on Opening of their 40th Annual Exhibition, New York, noon, September 7, 1871. 4to, sheets.
No place, 1871

10—

PAGE PROOFS, BROADSIDE FORM, PRINTED BY PEARSON, WASHINGTON, 1871. EXTREMELY RARE.

Laid in, is an Autograph Letter Signed: *"Walt Whitman."* 1p. 12mo, Camden, N. J., Sept. 12th, no year. To an unnamed person. A personal letter in which he sends his condolences for the death of the father of his correspondent. Accompanied by stamped addressed envelope.

1117. WHITMAN (WALT). After All, Not to Create Only. Recited by Walt Whitman. . . . New York, Sept. 7, 1871. 12mo, cloth, with title on gilt ground in circle on front cover.   Boston: Roberts Brothers, 1871   *10—*

> FIRST EDITION. FINE CLEAN COPY.
> LAID IN, IS AN AUTOGRAPH LETTER SIGNED: "*Walt*," to an unnamed person, 2pp. 12mo, Providence, R. I., October 22, 1868. A fine personal letter in which he narrates his plans and intentions.

1118. [WHITMAN (WALT).] Democratic Vistas. Memoranda. Narrow 8vo, green wrappers, uncut.   Washington, D. C., 1871   *10—*

> FIRST EDITION.
> LAID IN ARE TWO PAGES OF ORIGINAL PENCIL NOTES IN THE AUTHOR'S AUTOGRAPH (not signed) titled: "*Dem. Vistas,*" which commences: *Put in one (short) "splurge" to thank & celebrate the great geniuses, the Biblical bards & prophets both of the old & new testaments. . .*

1119. [WHITMAN (WALT).] Passage to India. Leaves of Grass. Narrow 8vo, half green calf, sprinkled edges.   Washington, D. C., 1871   *10—*

> FIRST EDITION. FINE COPY.
> LAID IN, IS AN AUTOGRAPH LETTER SIGNED: "*Walt*." 1p. 12mo, New York, Oct. 23, 1868. Presumably written to John Burroughs. In this letter Whitman states that he intends to spend a few days in New York and will then repair to his work.

1120. WHITMAN (WALT). BURROUGHS (JOHN). Notes on Walt Whitman, As Poet and Person. Second Edition. 12mo, cloth, uncut.   New York, 1871   *19—*

> This enlarged and revised edition contains supplementary notes dated 1871.
> With autograph note signed by the author on end-leaf in answer to a query, also appearing on end-leaf. Burroughs' note reads: *This is the 2d Edition with additions. John Burroughs.*
> LAID IN, IS AN AUTOGRAPH LETTER SIGNED: "*John Burroughs.*" 1p. 12mo, West Park, N. Y., Dec. 6, 1897. To an unnamed person. In this communication the naturalist thanks his correspondent for a copy of "Political Sermons," saying: *The tribute to Whitman is worthy, but I still feel the same about the imitations of him. . . .*

1121. [WHITMAN (WALT).] Leaves of Grass. 8vo, original smooth dark green cloth, gilt lettered title on back strip, uncut.
Washington [Electrotyped by Smith & McDougal, New York] 1872   *19—*

> FIRST ISSUE OF THIS EDITION, including: *Passage to India* with extra title-page and separate pagination, but without *After All, not to Create Only*, which was included in the later issues of this edition.
> AUTOGRAPH PRESENTATION COPY from Edmund Gosse to W. C. Monkhouse, with inscription in ink on fly-leaf.
> Laid in, is AN AUTOGRAPH MANUSCRIPT BY WHITMAN regarding improvement in the Devil's Character. 1p. 12mo. The manuscript commences: *If the devil were passing through my country and he applied to me for instruction on any truth . . . of this universe, I should wish to give it to him. He is less a devil knowing that 3 and 3 are 6 than if he didn't know it. . . .*

1122. [WHITMAN (WALT).] BUCHANAN (ROBERT). The Fleshly School of Poetry and Other Phenomena of the Day. 12mo, original wrappers.   London, 1872   *7—*

> FIRST EDITION. With notes on Walt Whitman.

1123. WHITMAN (WALT). Leaves of Grass. *With portraits.* 12mo, full green crushed levant morocco, Jansenist, inner morocco borders, gilt, gilt edges, BY THE EAGLE ART BINDERY.   Camden, 1876   *20—*

> AUTHOR'S EDITION. Bound in are two yellow wrappers, upon the first one is the following autograph presentation inscription: *To G. M. Williamson, from his friend, John Burroughs. Feb. 19, 1901.* Inlaid in one of the fly-leaves is AN AUTOGRAPH POSTCARD SIGNED: "*W. W.*" Camden, N. Jersey, Feb. 26, no year. Whitman speaks about the state of his health in this communication.

1124. [WHITMAN (WALT).] Leaves of Grass. *With portraits.* 12mo, half sheep, marbled board sides, colored leather label.   Camden, New Jersey, 1876   *14—*

> AUTHOR'S EDITION. WITH AUTOGRAPH SIGNATURE ON TITLE.
> Laid in, is an Autograph Letter Signed: "*Walt Whitman,*" 1p. 12mo, April 14, no date. To the Attorney Gen.'s Office, for Mr. French, Pardon Clerk. In this letter Mr. Whitman says: *Please unlock the case where my books & pamphlets are in Mr. French's room & send me by bearer 6 copies "Democratic Vistas" (a small book bound in green paper).* Accompanied by addressed envelope.

1125. [WHITMAN (WALT).] Two Rivulets. Including Democratic Vistas, Centennial Songs, and Passage to India. *Original photograph autographed, as frontispiece.* 12mo, half light sheep, marbled boards, colored leather label, broken. Not returnable.

Camden, New Jersey, 1876

AUTHOR'S EDITION. The photograph is autographed: *Walt Whitman born May 31 1819.* LAID IN, IS AN AUTOGRAPH LETTER SIGNED: *"Walt Whitman,"* 1p. 12mo, October 25, 1868. To Mr. & Mrs. Benedict. A personal letter in which he tells his correspondents the date he expects to be back in Washington.

1126. WHITMAN (WALT). Autograph Note Signed,—*"Walt Whitman,"* 1p. 8vo. Feb: 9 '80; GALLEY PROOF of "My 71st Year." Six-line verse, 1p. 12mo, with AUTOGRAPHIC ADDITION after third line, reading,—*"the War of '63 and '4,"* and marked at bottom,—*"Century Nov. '89;"* [ALSO] Galley Proof of "Fancies at Navesink." Poem of about 68 lines. Together, 3 pieces.

The note is a memorandum of going to Philadelphia to see his friend Col: Johnston, concluding with,—*The sun shining bright, & I feeling all right.* "Fancies at Navesink" contains a printed footnote reading,—*"*Navesink—a sea-side mountain, lower entrance of New-York bay."*

To proof reader— please read very carefully, follow punctuation &c. by copy.

The Dead Carlyle

Not for his merely literary merit, (though that was great)— not as "maker of books," but as launching into the self-complacent atmosphere of our days a rasping, questioning, dislocating agitation and shock, is the man's final value. It is time the English-speaking peoples had some true ideas about the verteber of genius, namely power. As if they must always have it cut and biased to the fashion, like a lady's cloak! Lacking . . . . needed . . . . in back . . . .

His mantle is unfallen. We certainly have no one left like him. I doubt if any nation of the world has.

Walt Whitman

[No. 1127]

106

1127. WHITMAN (WALT). ORIGINAL AUTOGRAPH MANUSCRIPT of his prose essay,—
"The Dead Carlyle." Manuscript of over FOUR HUNDRED WORDS, written
in ink on one side of 3 octavo leaves, signed at end,—"*Walt Whitman.*" **47**⁵⁰
With several autographic deletions, additions and corrections.

> INTERESTING MANUSCRIPT ON THE EMINENT SCOTTISH AUTHOR, commencing,—*Not for
> his merely literary merit, (though that was great)—not as "maker of books," but as launching
> into the self-complacent atmosphere of our days a rasping questioning and shock, is the man's
> final value. . . . [and concluding thus,—] His mantle is unfallen. We certainly have no one
> left like him. I doubt if any nation of the world has.*
> WHITMAN'S AUTOGRAPHIC DIRECTIONS TO PRINTER precede the essay,—*To proof reader—
> Please read very carefully copy, following punctuation &c.*

[See Reproduction]

1128. WHITMAN (WALT). Specimen Days & Collect. *Frontispiece portrait.* 8vo, **5**
three-quarter fawn calf, gilt, richly gilt back, gilt edges, BY MORRELL.
Glasgow: Wilson & McCormick, 1883

> BEAUTIFUL COPY OF THE FIRST ISSUE OF THIS EDITION.

1129. WHITMAN (WALT). Complete Poems & Prose of Walt Whitman. 1855 . . .
1888. Authenticated & Personal Book (handled by W. W.) . . . Portraits **20**
from Life. . . . Autograph. *Portrait on title and other full-page portraits.*
Royal 8vo, half green cloth, uncut.
[Philadelphia: Ferguson Bros. & Co.] 1888

> EDITION LIMITED to 600 copies, of which this is, No. 68. With facsimile autograph signa-
> ture of the author, Walt Whitman, on the half-title of *Leaves of Grass.*
> AUTOGRAPH PRESENTATION COPY from the author, with the following inscription in his
> autograph on end-leaf: *John H. Johnston, from his friend the author. Oct. 19 '89.*

1130. WHITMAN (WALT). November Boughs. *Frontispiece portrait.* 8vo, original **6**
maroon cloth, title in gilt on front cover and back strip, gilt top.
Philadelphia: David McKay, 1888

> FIRST EDITION. FINE COPY. WITH MANY OF THE LEAVES UNCUT, AND ONE OF A FEW
> COPIES CONTAINING THE FRONTISPIECE PORTRAIT.
> LAID IN, IS AN AUTOGRAPH POSTCARD SIGNED: "*W. W.*" Camden, Dec. 30, no year.
> A hurried communication stating that he is continuing well and that "*the Gilchrists*" have
> moved to another address.

1131. WHITMAN (WALT). Autograph Note Signed,—"*Walt Whitman,*" 1p. oblong **8**
8vo. No place or date. To Mr. Oldach. Mounted on cardboard.

> BRIEF NOTE TO BINDER REGARDING WHITMAN'S "NOVEMBER BOUGHS," reading,—*Mr.
> Oldach, give as he requests the "November Boughs" to Mr. David McKay* [publisher]*—&
> he will pay you the binding—except for 100 copies wh. I will pay you.*

1132. WHITMAN (WALT). November Boughs. *Frontispiece portrait.* 8vo, limp **30**
maroon cloth, title in gilt on front cover and back strip, uncut.
Philadelphia: David McKay, 1888

> FIRST EDITION. ONE OF A FEW COPIES BOUND UP IN LIMP CLOTH AND ENTIRELY UNCUT
> FOR PRESENTATION PURPOSES. WITH WHITMAN'S AUTOGRAPH INSCRIPTION, reading:
> *Richard J. Hinton from his friend the author Walt Whitman with love & old associations.
> Jan. 6, 1889.*
> With manuscript notations on last end-leaf by Horace Traubel mentioning "November
> Boughs," Walt Whitman meetings in New York, Hinton, Joel Benton, etc.

1133. WHITMAN (WALT). November Boughs. Royal 8vo, original dark green cloth, gilt lettered title on front cover and back strip, gilt top, uncut.

Philadelphia: David McKay, 1888

FIRST EDITION. LARGE PAPER COPY, ONLY A FEW ISSUED IN THIS FORM. No portrait was issued with this edition.

LAID IN, IS AN AUTOGRAPH POSTCARD SIGNED: "*Walt Whitman*," written to J. L. Gilder of the "Critic Office," in which he requests that two "Critics" be sent to him, also saying that he is busy with his book, the title of which he does not mention.

8 -

1134. WHITMAN (WALT). ORIGINAL AUTOGRAPH MANUSCRIPT of his prose essay,—"A Death-Bouquet—Fresh pick'd noontime early January 1890—By Walt Whitman." Manuscript of about FOUR HUNDRED WORDS, written in pencil (with the exception of title, which is in ink) on one side of 2 quarto leaves, pasted on cardboard sheet.

WRITTEN ABOUT TWO YEARS BEFORE WHITMAN'S DEATH. Interspersed with poetical quotations from different sources, including a verse from Whittier's "Burning Driftwood." Soliloquizing on the serenity of death, Whitman makes the following remark concerning HIS OWN EXPERIENCES AS VOLUNTEER ARMY NURSE IN THE CIVIL WAR,—*Of the many hundreds I myself saw die in the fields and hospitals during the Secession War the cases of mark'd suffering or agony in extremes were very rare.*

WHITMAN'S AUTOGRAPH DIRECTIONS TO PRINTER precede the essay,—*follow copy—send two good proofs to Walt Whitman Camden New Jersey;* his autograph signature thus appearing twice on the first page of the manuscript.

22 50

1135. WHITMAN (WALT). Camden's Compliment to Walt Whitman. Edited by Horace L. Traubel. *Frontispiece portrait.* 8vo, original cloth, gilt, gilt top, uncut.

Philadelphia, 1889

FIRST EDITION. WITH WHITMAN'S AUTOGRAPH SIGNATURE AND ADDRESS written in pencil on a slip pasted on end-leaf.

6 -

1136. WHITMAN (WALT). ORIGINAL AUTOGRAPH MANUSCRIPT of his Synoptic Autobiography, commencing,—"Walt Whitman, (from Holland and English immigration-stock, son of Walter Whitman, farmer and carpenter, and his wife, *nee* Louisa Van Velsor), was born May 31, 1819," etc. Over TWO HUNDRED FIFTY WORDS, written in ink on 1p. 4to.

VERY INTERESTING AUTOBIOGRAPHICAL SYNOPSIS OF WHITMAN'S CAREER FROM BOYHOOD UNTIL MAY, 1890, AT WHICH TIME HE WAS SEVENTY-ONE YEARS OF AGE (he died in March, 1892). He concludes with the statement,—*It remains to be said that W. W. is perceptibly of Quaker stamp, has been and is of buoyant spirits and robust physique, and yet lives (May, 1890) in Camden, New Jersey.*

20 -

1137. [WHITMAN (WALT).] Good-Bye My Fancy. 2d Annex to Leaves of Grass. *Frontispiece portrait.* 8vo, original maroon cloth, gilt lettered title on front cover and back strip, gilt top.

Philadelphia: David McKay, 1891

FIRST EDITION. FINE COPY.

LAID IN, IS AN AUTOGRAPH POSTCARD SIGNED: "W. W." New York, July 5, no year. To John Burroughs, the naturalist. It commences: *Still here—still quite well—sent you a paper yesterday with my "June" letter in—* . . .

5 -

1138. WHITMAN (WALT). Good-By My Fancy. 2d Annex to Leaves of Grass. 8vo, sewn, uncut.

Philadelphia, 1891

AUTOGRAPH PRESENTATION COPY with the following inscription written across the title by the author: *Geo. M. Williamson, from the author. Sept. 7, 1891.* WITH A SLIP OF PAPER ALSO BEARING THE AUTHOR'S PRESENTATION INSCRIPTION tipped on page of contents.

Laid in, is a fine original photo-portrait of Whitman. Also two Autograph Letters Signed: "*Traubel.*" To Mr. Wm. F. Gable. In the first, dated Feb. 22, 1908, Traubel mentions Whitman's "Good-Bye My Fancy and November Boughs." The second letter, Feb. 24, 1908, refers to the portrait.

12 50

1139. WHITMAN (WALT). Leaves of Grass. Including Sands at Seventy. 1st Annex, Good-Bye my Fancy. 2d Annex, A Backward Glance o'er Travel'd Roads, *and Portrait from Life. Facsimile of author's signature on title.* 8vo, original brownish gray mat paper wrappers, yellow paper label on backbone, uncut. **27.50**
Philadelphia: David McKay, 1891–'2

EXCESSIVELY RARE EARLIEST ISSUE OF THIS IMPORTANT EDITION, WHICH DID NOT EXCEED 50 COPIES.

AUTOGRAPH PRESENTATION COPY FROM WALT WHITMAN TO JULIUS CHAMBERS, with the following autograph inscription written in pencil on end-leaf by Horace L. Traubel, as follows: *For Julius Chambers sent over by Walt Whitman Jan 3, 1891 through Horace L. Traubel.*

Because of the illness of Whitman at this time and of his desire to see the edition, Mr. Traubel had a few copies quickly bound in wrappers for him, which the poet sent to intimate friends.

INSERTED BEFORE PAGE OF CONTENTS IS AN AUTOGRAPH LETTER SIGNED: "*Traubel.*" 1p. 12mo, Camden, Mar. 28, 1891. To Mr. Chambers. In this letter Mr. Traubel states that he is putting Mr. Chambers' name on the list of Whitman's pall-bearers.

Also laid in, is an Autograph Note Signed: "*Walt Whitman.*" 1p. oblong 12mo, Camden, April 9, 1888. To an unnamed person.

1140. WHITMAN (WALT). ORIGINAL AUTOGRAPH MANUSCRIPT of his poem,— "After the Supper and Talk." Twelve lines of verse, written in ink on 1p. 4to Signed at end,—"*Walt Whitman;*" [ALSO] Corrected proof of the foregoing, 1p. 12mo. With about nine words deleted and TWENTY WORDS ADDED IN WHITMAN'S AUTOGRAPH. Together, 2 pieces. **10-**

With WHITMAN'S AUTOGRAPH NOTATION,—*To precede some added Poems at end of a Volume,*" written below title. The manuscript commences,—
After the Supper and talk—after the day is done,
As a friend from friends his final withdrawal prolonging
Good-bye and Good-bye with emotional lips repeating,
(So hard for his hand to release those hands—no more will
    they meet.

1141. WHITMAN (WALT). Printed poem, "Salut au monde!" With autograph signature, "*Walt Whitman,*" at end. Six lines of verse, printed on 1p. oblong 12mo, green paper. **10-**

EXTREMELY RARE WHITMAN ITEM. A letter accompanying the verse states,—"*A very unusual Walt Whitman item, which I do not find indexed in any of his works. I do not know for what particular purpose it was written, but it bears his own autograph signature.*"

1142. WHITMAN (WALT). ORIGINAL AUTOGRAPH MANUSCRIPT of poem entitled,— "Younondio." Manuscript of about 40 words, written in ink on 1p. 4to. Signed at end,—"*Walt Whitman.*" With author's autographic corrections and deletions. **7.50**

FINE ORIGINAL MANUSCRIPT POEM, bearing Whitman's autographic notation at top of page,—*(printed in book first in "Critic.")*

1143. WHITMAN (WALT). Autograph Letter Signed,—"*Walt Whitman,*" 1p. 8vo. 431 Stevens St. [Camden, N. J.] Thursday afternoon ½ past 2, no year. To Mrs. Johnston. With envelope addressed to J. M. Stoddart, Philadelphia. **7.50**

INTERESTING LETTER OF FRIENDSHIP, reading in part,—*This is the queer little book, perhaps you may remember I spoke about, some weeks since. It is odd in form & may be without attractiveness at first—but somehow I think it real good & deep—(after you break the crust & get a little used to it.)*

1144. WHITMAN (WALT). A PAGE OF ORIGINAL AUTOGRAPH MANUSCRIPT from a poem. About SIXTY-SEVEN WORDS, written in ink on 1p. 4to, with two words corrected in pencil. Without signature, place or date, but marked as Page 11. **7.50**

THIS JOYOUS VERSE begins:
    A reborn race appears—a perfect World—all joy!
and ends with the line:
    Joy! joy! all over joy!

Lots 1145-1159 omitted

The STEPHEN H. WAKEMAN
Collection of Books of
NINETEENTH CENTURY
AMERICAN WRITERS

THE PROPERTY OF

Mrs. ALICE L. WAKEMAN

FIRST EDITIONS, INSCRIBED PRESENTATION AND
PERSONAL COPIES, ORIGINAL MANU-
SCRIPTS AND LETTERS

OF

NINE AMERICAN AUTHORS

AMERICAN ART ASSOCIATION, Inc.

THOREAU'S COPY OF WHITMAN'S "LEAVES OF GRASS"

1071. THOREAU'S COPY. [WHITMAN (WALT).] Leaves of Grass. *Frontispiece portrait on plain paper.* Imperial 8vo, original green cloth, blind-stamped sides with rustic lettered title in gilt and triple gilt border on both front and back covers, gilt floral sprays and gilt lettered title on backbone, *new* marbled end-papers. Portrait slightly foxed. Brooklyn, 1855

200.⁰⁰

HENRY D. THOREAU'S COPY OF THE FIRST ISSUE OF THE FIRST EDITION. Pasted at the foot of page 95, is an orange colored slip of paper, written in the autograph of Walt Whitman, which reads,—"*Concord, Mass. '81. Sept. 17. 11½ p.m.*"

Laid in the volume is a pencil Memorandum in the Autograph of Mr. Wakeman, signed with initials, also a Typewritten letter from Mr. Charles E. Goodspeed, both of which are relative to this particular volume. Mr. Wakeman's memorandum reads,—"*This copy of Leaves of Grass came to me from Mr. Sanborn through Mr. Goodspeed, as did most of my Thoreau treasures. I quote from his* [Mr. Goodspeed's] *letter* '*Some years ago, the binding of this book becoming loose Mr. Sanborn had it resewed. The vandal of a bookbinder inserted new end leaves. Mr. Sanborn was just able to save that part of one of them which had Thoreau's autograph.*'" Below this quotation from Mr. Goodspeed's letter is a note, in the autograph of Mr. Wakeman, which reads,—"*It also has in Sanborn's autograph 'F. B. Sanborn from Miss Thoreau. March 1873.'*"

Pasted on the front end-leaf of this volume is the original end-leaf to which Mr. Goodspeed refers in the sentence in his letter which reads,—"*Mr. Sanborn was just able to save that part of one of them which had Thoreau's autograph.*"

THE RENOWNED COLLECTION OF THE LATE

WILLIAM F. GABLE

OF ALTOONA, PENNSYLVANIA

ENGLISH & AMERICAN WRITERS
RARE HISTORICAL AMERICANA

INSCRIBED COPIES ~ ORIGINAL MANUSCRIPTS ~ LETTERS
OF FAMOUS AUTHORS ~ AUTOGRAPHS OF THE
"SIGNERS" ~ OF THE PRESIDENTS OF
THE UNITED STATES AND MANY
OTHERS DISTINGUISHED IN
THE FIELD OF LETTERS
OR IN PUBLIC LIFE

PART FIVE

SOLD BY ORDER OF THE ADMINISTRATOR
ROBERT B. GABLE

Nov. 24 & 25, 1924

AMERICAN ART ASSOCIATION, Inc.
MADISON AVENUE, 56TH TO 57TH STREET
ENTRANCE 30 EAST 57TH STREET, NEW YORK
Telephone: PLAZA 1270

1047. [WHITMAN (WALT).] Leaves of Grass. *Frontispiece portrait on
plain paper.* Imperial 8vo, original green cloth, blind-stamped
sides with rustic lettered title in gilt and triple gilt border on
both covers, gilt floral sprays and gilt lettered title on backbone,
marbled end-papers, gilt edges. Binding slightly defective at back.

215

Brooklyn, New York, 1855

THE GENUINE FIRST ISSUE OF THE FIRST EDITION AND THAT MOST DE-
SIRED BY COLLECTORS. Later issues lacked the gilt lines on the cover, had
plain end-papers and plain edges and the frontispiece portrait on India paper.
The later issues also contained some press notices of the book.
    Laid in is an Autograph Note Signed,—"*Walt Whitman,*" 1p. 8vo, Cam-
den, May 29. To "*My dear Bolger,*" in reference to printing an article
which evidently originally accompanied the note.

1048. WHITMAN (WALT). ORIGINAL MANUSCRIPT of a portion of his
"Hospital Notes." Dated Washington, October 13, 1863 and May
6, 1864. Manuscript of about THREE HUNDRED AND NINETY WORDS,
written in ink, on one side of three 8vo leaves, pasted on to larger
sheets. With numerous alterations and corrections by Whitman.

24

EXCEEDINGLY INTERESTING DIARY, OF HISTORICAL IMPORTANCE. Whitman was a volunteer army nurse during the Civil War, which fact renders
these notes more absorbing, being those of an actual eye witness. The name
of Gen. Kilpatrick, and General Meade's retreat are mentioned in it.

1049. WHITMAN (WALT). Autograph Letter Signed in full, 4pp. 12mo,
Brooklyn, July 11, 1864. To "Dear Comrade."

32 50

A SUPERB SPECIMEN, reading in part,—*I have rec'd. your letter of the 6th
as it has been sent on to me by Major Hapgood. My dear comrade, I have
been very sick . . . The Doctors say my sickness is from having too
deeply imbibed poison into my system from the hospitals. I had spells of
deathly faintness, and the disease also attacked my head and throat pretty
seriously.*

1050. WHITMAN (WALT). Autograph Letter Signed, "*Walt Whitman.*"
4pp. 4to, Attorney General's Office, Washington, August 26, 1865.
To "Dear friend."

47 50

VERY FINE WHITMAN LETTER, WRITTEN AT A MOST INTERESTING PERIOD,
WITH MENTION OF ANDREW JOHNSON. OF THE GREATEST HISTORICAL IN-
TEREST RELATING TO THE CIVIL WAR. The letter reads in part,—. . .
*Byron I am still here, and . . . am likely to remain employed . . . through
the fall . . . a great stream of Southerners come in here day after day, to
get pardoned—all the rich, and all the high officers of the rebel army
cannot do anything, cannot buy or sell, &c. until they have special pardons
—(that is hitting them where they live) . . . old and young, men & women
—come to this office to get them—sometimes the rooms are filled with a
curious gathering . . .
    Some 4 or 5000 pardons have been passed through here—but the President
hasn't signed more than 200—the rest are all blank yet—Andrew Johnson
seems disposed to be in no hurry about it—What I learn and know about
him (The President) I think he is a good man.
    . . . I have my meals sent up by the landlady—she gives me very good
grub . . . both rooms & board, ($32.50 a month)—I must close. I send
for my love & God bless you dearest comrade—Write soon, dear son, & give
me all particulars . . .*

1051. [WHITMAN (WALT).] Democratic Vistas. Memoranda. Narrow
12mo, original pale green wrappers, uncut and unopened.

19

Washington, D. C., 1871

FIRST EDITION. Fine Copy.
    Laid in is a portion of a manuscript IN WHITMAN'S AUTOGRAPH, written
in ink on a 12mo sheet, with the heading,—"*Pref. to Dem. Vistas.*"

1052. [WHITMAN (WALT).] Leaves of Grass. *Portrait frontispiece.* 8vo, *25~*
original green cloth, uncut.   Washington, D. C., 1872

EXTRA-ILLUSTRATED by the insertion of two portraits of Whitman. Laid
in and tipped in are numerous newspaper clippings containing articles relating to the author.

Also laid in is a portion of an AUTOGRAPH MANUSCRIPT BY WHITMAN, 1p.
4to, which contains the beginning of Whitman's essay on Emerson, headed,—
"*Emerson. Essays—1st series—copyrighted 1847.*"

1053. [WHITMAN (WALT).] Two Rivulets, Including Democratic Vistas, *15~*
Centennial Songs, and Passage to India. 12mo, half calf, leather
label. Binding slightly rubbed.   Camden, New Jerssey, 1876

AUTHOR'S EDITION. Tipped to stub, as frontispiece is a portrait of Whitman, upon which is his autograph inscription,—"*Walt Whitman born May
31, 1819.*"

Laid in is a post-card addressed in Whitman's hand to "*Pete Doyle, M St.
South—bet. 4½ & 6th, Washington, D. C.,*" written from Camden, March 17
[no year] and stating,—"*All going on about as usual. W. W.*"

1054. [WHITMAN (WALT).] Leaves of Grass. *With portraits.* 12mo, half *5~*
calf, leather label. Binding cracked at top.
                                        Camden, New Jersesy, 1876

AUTHOR'S EDITION. On the title-page is the inscription,—"*Whitman's
signature belonged in this place. Just before his death he undertook to sign
all these books, but did not go far before his strength gave out. H[orace]
T[raubel].*"

Laid in is a Proof of the title-page of the Author's Edition of "Leaves
of Grass," with the words, "With Portraits and Intercalations" at the bottom
of the page.

1055. [WHITMAN (WALT).] Leaves of Grass. *With portraits.* 12mo, half *27 50*
calf, leather label. Binding somewhat rubbed.
                                        Camden, New Jersey, 1876

AUTHOR'S EDITION, bearing the autograph signature,—"*Walt Whitman,*"
on the title-page.

On the fly-leaf preceding the title page, evidently in Dr. Bucke's autograph, appears the following inscription,—"*Mr. Ruskin has sent to Walt
Whitman for five complete sets of 'Leaves of Grass' and 'Two Rivulets'.
The distinguished art-critic observes in a letter that the reason those books
excite such hostile criticism is "They are deadly true—in the sense of rifles
—against all our deadliest sins." The Athenaeum March 20, 1880.*"

On the blank page preceding the advertisements at the end is a longer
inscription in the same autograph which states that Whitman is the guest
of Dr. Bucke in Canada, and that Dr. Bucke, in connection with the study
of Whitman which he is preparing, would like to receive communications
from persons personally acquainted with the poet.

Laid in is a post-card addressed in Whitman's hand to John Burroughs,
at Esopus-on-Hudson, N. Y., containing news of Whitman's health, and of
his recent removal to Mickle Street—all in Whitman's autograph, and signed,
—"*W. W.*"

1056. WHITMAN (WALT). Autograph Letter Signed, in full, 2pp. 8vo, *35~*
March 5, 1878. To JOHN BURROUGHS.

IMPORTANT LITERARY LETTER, reading in part,—*Yes, Johnston's taking
part in the lecture enterprise would be perfectly agreeable to me. The name
of the lecture would be The Death of Abraham Lincoln. (In my last letter
among the names proposed was S. S. Cox, M. C. I wish that name cancelled).*

1057. WHITMAN (WALT). Autograph Letter Signed,—"*Walt Whitman*," 2pp. 8vo. Camden, New Jersey, U. S. A., June 19, 1881. To "Dear Tom."

22.50

INTERESTING LETTER OF FRIENDSHIP, TELLING OF A TRIP TO THE JERSEY WOODS AND SEASHORE, and reading in part,—

I am still here & am well as usual—have just returned from some twelve days down in the Jersey woods, where I like to go this time of year (I believe I have told you about it)—Plenty of woods here in Jersey & plenty of seashore—& I like them both,—& I get a good deal of comfort out of them both . . . that was an awful affair on the river, & I tell you I looked over the lists of names the next two or three days with fear and trembling—I don't seem to remember Wm Hardy you mention—but I dare say I knew him among the men, poor fellow. [Etc.]

1058. WHITMAN (WALT). BROADSIDE. "The Voice of the Rain." Square 12mo, containing one printed stanza of 10 lines; [ALSO] Corrected Proof of Poem, with date June, 1885.

10

ORIGINAL ISSUE OF THIS BROADSIDE, not mentioned by Foley.

Accompanying the above is a bust portrait of Whitman by Gutekunst dated 1881. With the following statement in ink, probably written by Horace Traubel, reading,—*Made by Gutekunst 1881—copy given H. T. by W. W.*

1059. WHITMAN (WALT). November Boughs. Large 8vo, original green beveled cloth, gilt top, uncut. Philadelphia: David McKay, 1888

10

FIRST EDITION. LARGE PAPER COPY. ONLY A FEW ISSUED IN THIS FORM. On the fly-leaf is Thomas Harned's autographic inscription,—"*a first Edition. Thomas Harned, Literary Executor of Walt Whitman.*"

Laid in is a portion of an Autograph Manuscript (about 70 words) by Whitman, beginning,—"(*I had said before beginning*) *I will want my poems to be the poems of Joy.*" [etc.]

VERY FINE COPY AND EXCEPTIONALLY RARE IN THIS FORM.

1060. WHITMAN (WALT). Complete Poems and Prose, 1855 . . . 1888. Authenticated & Personal Book (handled by W. W.). *With portraits.* Large 8vo, half cloth, paper label on back, uncut, partly unopened. [Philadelphia: Ferguson Brothers & Company, 1888]

24

FIRST EDITION, with the autograph signature.—"*Walt Whitman,*" on title-page of "Leaves of Grass." Only 600 copies were printed.

Laid in is a portion of a manuscript (about 50 words) IN WHITMAN'S AUTOGRAPH, beginning.—"*In forming the book I have not been so anxious to compose technically fine or smart or melodious verses*" [etc.]

1061. [WHITMAN (WALT).] SYMONDS (J. A.). Walt Whitman. A Study. *Illustrated.* 8vo, cloth, uncut. London, 1893

15

LARGE PAPER. No. 30 of 208 copies printed on Handmade Paper. Laid in is a portion of a MANUSCRIPT BY WHITMAN, written on the inside of two envelopes torn open and pasted together, beginning. *I accept with joy (and only hope it is true) what Dr. Bucke gives for his enclosing summary of my pages, that the construction of them and every page of them [Leaves of Grass] is bedded upon so thorough and reverent a faith in God's schemes* [etc.]. With numerous changes and additions.

1062. WHITMAN (WALT). When Lilacs Last in the Dooryard Bloomed. *Original watercolor drawing as frontispiece. Decorated capitals and tailpiece COLORED BY HAND by C. R. Ashbee.* 12mo, vellum, uncut. [London] Essex House Press, 1900

32.50

SPECIAL EDITION of 135 copies only. PRINTED ON VELLUM THROUGHOUT. of which this is, No. 123.

Laid in is a portion of a manuscript (about 80 words). IN WHITMAN'S AUTOGRAPH. beginning.—"*The — Had been simmering inside for six or seven years—broke out during those times temporarily*" [etc.]

1063. WHITMAN (WALT). ORIGINAL AUTOGRAPH MANUSCRIPT OF *"An Old Man's Rejoinder."* Signed, *"Walt Whitman."* No date, with addressed envelope. To "Critic weekly paper." Manuscript of about ONE THOUSAND WORDS, written on the back of various old letters and opened envelopes of his, consisting of eight sheets ranging from 8vo. to 4to size, in red and black ink and in pencil. With numerous alterations and corrections in Whitman autograph.

35—

FINE MANUSCRIPT, written in Whitman's characteristic way.

1064. WHITMAN (WALT). ORIGINAL AUTOGRAPH MANUSCRIPT of his announcement of his Lecture on PRESIDENT LINCOLN. Consists of seven lines (about 31 words), entirely in Whitman's autograph, with instructions to the printer written at the top of the sheet, which is oblong 12mo size, reading,—*"Lead & put on 3d page if convenient."* [ALSO,] *engraved Portrait of Lincoln (14x11 inches) and a portrait of Walt Whitman (9½x7½ inches).* Together, 3 pieces neatly matted as one, in a mahogany frame.

50—

1065. WHITMAN (WALT). ORIGINAL AUTOGRAPH MANUSCRIPT, Signed (in the body of the Manuscript), *"Walt Whitman."* 1p. small 4to, with numerous corrections in ink by the author.

25—

A very interesting and characteristic piece. The poet, his own press-agent, pens the following "Personal" that his friends may know his whereabouts:

Walt Whitman still remains in St. Louis, Mo., his health quite infirm. When he gets out, there are two different ways he is fond of spending an hour. One is to go down and loaf on the East St. Louis bridge; the other is to visit a neighboring Kindergarten, where he is sure to be received tumultuously by the children, always telling them a story, "The Two Cats taking a Walk," or something of that kind.

1066. WHITMAN (WALT). ORIGINAL AUTOGRAPH MANUSCRIPT, Signed, *"Walt Whitman."* With title *"Father Taylor (and Oratory.)"* Manuscript of about SEVEN HUNDRED WORDS, written in ink, on one side of eleven 4to sheets, with proof corrections and alterations in the autograph of the author; [ALSO] ORIGINAL Carte de visite photograph with Autograph, *"Walt Whitman—born May 31, 1819—Xmas, 1864;"* Autograph Post Card, Signed *Walt Whitman* To Editor Century Magazine. Together, 3 pieces.

52 50

A SPLENDID TRIBUTE TO THE ORATORICAL SERMONS OF THIS MODEST ECCLESIASTIC—"Father Taylor."

1067. WHITMAN (WALT). ORIGINAL AUTOGRAPH MANUSCRIPT, Unsigned, with title, "National Literature." About SEVENTY WORDS, written on one side of oblong 8vo. sheet, mounted on larger leaf with corrections and alterations in ink and pencil in the autograph of the author.

10—

1068. WHITMAN (WALT). A page of ORIGINAL MANUSCRIPT from his prose work, "Democratic Vistas." About EIGHTY WORDS, written in pencil on 1p. 4to. Mounted on cardboard.

12 50

The manuscript page contains many author's autographic corrections and deletions.

1069. WHITMAN (WALT). A page of ORIGINAL MANUSCRIPT from "Poetry in America." Eleven lines, written in pencil, on 1p. square 12mo. Tipped to cardboard; TRAUBEL (HORACE). Autograph Note Signed. —"*Horace Traubel*," 1p. narrow folio. No place, 1909. To Mr. William F. Gable.

10

The manuscript. A REPRESENTATIVE WHITMAN SENTIMENT ON DEMOCRACY, reads.—*Democracy has been hurried on through Time by measureless invisible winds and tides resistless as the revolution of the globe, and as far-reaching and rapid. But in the highest walks of Poetry and Art, it has not yet had a single representative worthy of it upon the earth.* Presentation note of Mr. Traubel, Whitman's literary executor, accompanies the sentiment.

1070. WHITMAN (WALT). Autograph Letter Signed, 1p. 8vo, Aug. 8, no year. To Albert Rhodes.

15

NICE SPECIMEN, stating that he is glad to hear from Mr. Rhodes again. and would like him to come to visit him. He says, in conclusion.—*I am hauled up here like an old hulk, the voyaging done.—but the timbers may (or may not) hold together yet awhile—but maintain good heart and spirits most of the time.*

1071. WHITMAN'S COPY. FORMAN (H. BUXTON—Editor). The Poetical Works of Percy Bysshe Shelley. Second Edition, with the Notes of Mary Wollstonecraft Shelley. Vol. II. only. *Frontispiece.* 12mo, cloth uncut. London, 1886

22

WALT WHITMAN'S COPY. WITH HIS AUTOGRAPH SIGNATURE AND DATE ON TITLE-PAGE.—"*Walt Whitman. June 4, 1887.*" On the fly-leaf is an inscription.—"*To Mrs. Alma Calder Johnston from Walt Whitman Sept. 20, 1888;*" and below, on the same leaf is a 16-line Signed Autograph Inscription by Horace Traubel, pertaining to Whitman and Forman. Laid in, is an A.L.S. by Forman, 2pp. 12mo, June 19, 1885, with mention of two works "Sittron" and "Cosmo", and addressed to Messrs. J. Davy & Son.

116

THE RENOWNED COLLECTION OF THE LATE

WILLIAM F. GABLE

OF ALTOONA, PENNSYLVANIA

MANUSCRIPTS & PRINTED
WORKS BY THE WRITERS OF
BOOKS & THE MAKERS OF
HISTORY

AMERICAN ～ ENGLISH

RARE HISTORICAL AMERICANA ～ BRADFORD &
FRANKLIN IMPRINTS ～ DOCUMENTS & LETTERS BY
COLONIAL & STATE OFFICIALS, SIGNERS OF THE DEC-
LARATION, PRESIDENTS, GOVERNORS, GENERALS OF
THE REVOLUTIONARY AND CIVIL WAR PERIODS

Also

FINE FIRST EDITIONS ～ IN-
SCRIBED COPIES ～ AUTO-
GRAPH LETTERS, MSS. OF
AMERICAN & ENGLISH
AUTHORS

PART SIX

SOLD BY ORDER OF THE ADMINISTRATOR
ROBERT B. GABLE

Jan. 8-9, 1925

AMERICAN ART ASSOCIATION, Inc.

MADISON AVENUE, 56TH TO 57TH STREET

ENTRANCE 30 EAST 57TH STREET, NEW YORK

Telephone: PLAZA 1270

960. WHITMAN (WALT). Autograph Letter Signed:—"*Walt Whitman.*"
1p. 4to, Washington, June 9, 1865. To an unnamed person. *With portrait.* Together, 2 pieces.

22 50

> INTERESTING LETTER, with mention of his book "Drum Taps" and expressing appreciation for a book of "Homer" received, reading in part,—"*The Homer has come & is now lying before me. I thank you deeply. I am very well this summer, & go to the Hospitals daily & nightly . . . I enjoy my visits with a sad but profound joy & satisfaction—especially at night, when the light is nearly turned off; & I am soothing some suffering one . . . I send you . . . two copies of the little book Drum-Taps . . .*"

961. WHITMAN (WALT). . Autograph Letter Signed:—"*Walt Whitman.*"
1½pp. large 4to, Attorney General's Office, Washington, November 18, 1866. To BAYARD TAYLOR; *Three portraits of Whitman laid in.* Together, 4 pieces.

30 —

> FINE LETTER, from one great American poet to another, reading, in part,—"*I have received your letter of the 12th, . . . I wish to proffer* [sic] *you my friendship in return . . . Your book also came . . . I accept it as a kind & valuable gift . . . Permit me to send you in return, a copy of the new edition of Leaves of Grass . . .*"

962. WHITMAN (WALT). Autograph Letter Signed:—"*Walt Whitman,*"
4pp. 8vo. Washington, Wednesday afternoon, July 24, 1867. To an unnamed person in England addressed as "Dear friend." *Original photograph*, with autograph signature and date, 1884. Magazine excerpt,—"A Visit to Walt Whitman by Moncure D. Conway." Together, 3 pieces.

37 50

> Nicely written letter, SENDING A COPY OF HIS POEMS FOR REPUBLICATION IN ENGLAND, with an Introduction written by William O'Connor, author of "The Good Gray Poet, a Vindication."
>
> "*All is sent you,*" wrote Whitman, "*so that in case there comes any opening, you may have a proper copy, of latest date, prepared by me, to publish from. Of course I do not expect you, & would not permit you, to make yourself the job of running around & seeking after a publisher. Only please take charge of the copy—(I hereby clothe you with full power over it)—& should any good chance befall, it is what I would wish a London edition set up from . . . For occupation I hold a clerkship in the Attorney General's Office here, of pay sufficient, & duties entirely agreeable & consistent with my tastes.*" [Etc.]

963. WHITMAN (WALT). Poems. Selected and Edited by William Michael Rossetti. *Frontispiece portrait.* 12mo, original blue cloth, uncut, with 32 pages of advertisement at the end. Binding shaken, fly-leaf slightly foxed.

5 —

London: John Camden Hotten, Piccadilly, 1868

> FIRST EDITION. Laid in is a Government Post Card, mailed from Camden and addressed IN WHITMAN'S AUTOGRAPH to Sloane Kennedy, Belmont, Mass. The message, signed—"W. W.," is headed, "*Camden, Evn'g. May 28, '90,*" and refers chiefly to the state of Whitman's health.

964. WHITMAN (WALT). Autograph Letter Signed in full, 4pp. 8vo. September 2, 1868. To Byron Sutherland.

30 —

> A CHARMING PERSONAL LETTER, recalling their past friendship; Whitman's service under four Attorney Generals; favorable criticism of his work by Col. Hinton, and concluding,—"*Byron, I send you my love and friendship, dear soldier boy, and now that we have found each other again, let us try, as far as may be, to keep together.*"

965. WHITMAN (WALT). Autograph Letter Signed:—"*Walt Whitman.*" 2pp. 4to, Washington, March 9, 1868. To an unnamed person; *Engraved portrait of Whitman.* Together, 2 pieces.

25⁻

INTERESTING LETTER, with mention of Swinburne, suggests also, making use of the original plate of a portrait of Whitman made in 1855, should one be needed for a frontispiece for his volume of poetry. The letter reads in part,—"*I thank you for the copy of my poems sent by you . . . I consider it a beautiful volume. The portrait as given in it, is a marked blemish . . . if you wish to have a portrait, you might like to have the original plate of 1855 . . . from which you can print a frontispiece . . . I will thank you to convey to Mr. Swinburne my heartiest acknowledgements for the copy of William Blake (which has reached me,) & for his kind and generous mention of me in it . . .*"

966. [WHITMAN (WALT).] Democratic Vistas. Memoranda. Narrow 12mo, original pale green wrappers, uncut.

10⁻

Washington, D. C., 1871

FIRST EDITION. Laid in is a small envelope, mailed from Brooklyn, N. Y., on January 18 [no year], and addressed IN WHITMAN'S AUTOGRAPH as follows,—"*Walt Whitman, Attorney General's Office, Washington, D. C.*"

967. [WHITMAN (WALT).] Essays from "The Critic," by John Burroughs, Walt Whitman, and others. 12mo, original cloth, gilt top.

Boston, 1882

7⁻

FIRST EDITION. Contains "Death of Carlyle," and "Death of Longfellow," both by Walt Whitman, and an article on Whitman's "Leaves of Grass."

Laid in is an envelope addressed in Whitman's hand to John Burroughs in Washington, D. C. [Also] a short manuscript written in ink on a 12mo sheet in Whitman's Autograph, beginning,—"*If my ambition may dwell on the idea of arousing a poetry for that future nourished within itself,*" [etc.]

968. WHITMAN (WALT). Leaves of Grass. 1882; Camden's Compliment to Walt Whitman, May 31, 1889. Notes, Addresses, Letters, Telegrams. Edited by Horace L. Traubel. 1889. *Both with portraits.* Together, 2 vols. 12mo and 8vo, cloth, the latter uncut.

10⁻

Philadelphia, 1882-1889

LAID IN EACH VOLUME IS A MANUSCRIPT (ABOUT 100 WORDS) IN WHITMAN'S AUTOGRAPH.

969. WHITMAN (WALT). Autograph Letter Signed, 2pp. 8vo, August 4, 1884.

17⁵⁰

NICE SPECIMEN, consenting to write an article for the *Century* on the Hospitals and Hospital Nursing of the Secession War, as outlined by his correspondent.

970. WHITMAN (WALT). Autograph Letter Signed:—"*Walt Whitman.*" 1p. 4to, 328 Mickle Street, Camden. New Jersey, October 30/85. *With portrait.*

Letter to an unnamed person, acknowledging with thanks, a copy of "Bryant and his Friends," expressing uncertainty whether aforesaid thanks did not belong to General Wilson.

971. WHITMAN (WALT). Autograph Le..er Signed, 1p. 4to, "Camden, Jan. 17, '87." To "Editor, Picayune, newspaper, New Orleans, Louisiana." With addressed envelope; [ALSO] *Etched Portrait of Whitman*, with his Autograph Signature, in pencil, in the margin. Together, 2 pieces, matted and framed as one.

> The letter is regarding his article "New Orleans in 1848" which he had sent to the Editor of the "Picayune" and which the "Press" of Philadelphia would like to print in their columns, and asks that a proof of the article be sent on to the editor of the "Press."

20

972. WHITMAN (WALT). Autograph Letter Signed:—*"Walt Whitman,"* with one-line postscript unsigned. 1p. 4to, 328 Mickle Street, September 1/87.

> FINE SPECIMEN, regarding sitting for pictures.

15

973. WHITMAN (WALT). Autograph Letter Signed:—*"Walt Whitman."* 1p. 4to, Camden, New Jersey, September 17, '88. To Jacob Klein. With addressed envelope. Together, 2 pieces.

> Relates to Whitman sending an authentic volume of his "Leaves of Grass," by return mail to Mr. Klein for the price of $3.

11

974. WHITMAN (WALT). Autograph Letter Signed:—*"Walt Whitman."* 1p. 4to, Camden, New Jersey, "Dec. 18, A. M." With a 4-line postscript. To an unnamed person. *Portrait.* Together, 2 pieces.

> NICE LETTER, requesting the recipient to send him a work-basket for his sister, costing about $3½ or $4. In closing, Mr. Whitman sends *"my love to the little fellow & wish him (& all of you) Merry Christmas."*

975. WHITMAN (WALT). Fragment of ORIGINAL AUTOGRPH MANUSCRIPT of his Poem,—"As I wend to shores I know not." 1p. 4to, Unsigned, undated. Manuscript of about ONE HUNDRED AND THIRTY words, written in ink, with numerous corrections in the autograph of the author.

11

976. WHITMAN (WALT). ORIGINAL MANUSCRIPT Signed, *"Walt Whitman,"* of his poem, "A Voice from Death." Written in pencil, on one side of four 4to sheets, with instructions at head *"to printers and proof reader"* in ink. With numerous corrections in pencil by author. Manuscript of 6 stanzas, about 66 lines in all.

> VERY INTERESTING MANUSCRIPT, written on the Johnstown flood, and published in the *New York World*, of which Mr. Chambers was managing editor, at whose request Whitman wrote the poem.

32 50

977. WHITMAN (WALT). ORIGINAL AUTOGRAPH MANUSCRIPT, Unsigned, 1p. 8vo. Manuscript of about ONE HUNDRED AND TWENTY words, written in indelible pencil.

> FINE MANUSCRIPT, with references to Bryant, Emerson, Whittier, Longfellow, Bayard Taylor, Stoddard and others.

7 50

978. WHITMAN (WALT). AUTOGRAPH MANUSCRIPT with name in body of the MS., and 8 lines of printed proof with autograph corrections by Whitman. 1p. 4to. Written on a half sheet and the back of an opened envelope, pasted together. *With portrait on Japan paper.*

> VERY INTERESTING MANUSCRIPT, relating to his mother, Louisa Van Velsor, and others of his family.

10

979. WHITMAN (WALT). When Lilacs Last in the Dooryard Bloomed. *Original watercolor drawing as frontispiece. Decorated capitals and tailpiece* COLORED BY HAND *by C. R. Ashbee.* 12mo, vellum, uncut.   [London] Essex House Press, 1900

   SPECIAL EDITION of 135 copies only, printed on VELLUM throughout, of which this is, No. 133.

   Laid in, is a portion of a manuscript, evidently a diary memorandum (about 60 words), IN WHITMAN'S AUTOGRAPH, beginning,—"*Up at Esopus Ulster Co., N. Y. at J. B's,*" [etc.]

   17⁵⁰

980. WHITMAN (WALT). Autobiographia, or, The Story of a Life. New York, 1892; Leaves of Grass. Philadelphia, 1900; An American Primer. Edited by Horace Traubel. Boston, 1904; Catalogue of a Collection of Books, Letters and Manuscripts written by Walt Whitman, In the Library of George M. Williamson. Jamaica, N. Y., 1903; With Walt Whitman in Camden. By Horace Traubel. First 2 vols. New York, 1908; and other Whitmaniana. *Mainly illustrated.* Together, 9 vols. 16mo to royal 8vo, cloth, boards, and wrappers.   Various places, 1892-1920

   5⁻

981. WHITMAN (WALT). TRAUBEL (HORACE L.). "Walt Whitman at Date," and other articles on Whitman. From the New England Magazine. *Illustrated.* 8vo, plain wrappers, paper label, uncut. May, 1891; [Also] Autograph Manuscript of a Poem (about 40 words) by Whitman. No date; A.L.S. 6pp. 8vo, Detroit, Dec. 19, 1882. From Elisa Leggett to Walt Whitman; Portrait of Whitman on India paper; Newspaper clipping, with Autograph Notations by Whitman, dated June 15, 1878; and other Whitmaniana. Together, 11 pieces.

   8⁻

THE RENOWNED COLLECTION OF THE LATE

WILLIAM F. GABLE

OF ALTOONA, PENNSYLVANIA

AMERICAN · ENGLISH

RARE FIRST EDITIONS AND INSCRIBED VOLUMES
ORIGINAL MANUSCRIPTS AND AUTOGRAPHS
OF FAMOUS AUTHORS AND STATESMEN

Including

LETTERS OF GREAT HISTORICAL INTEREST,
AUTOGRAPHS OF PRESIDENTS OF THE U. S.
SIGNERS OF THE DECLARATION AND OTHER
CELEBRITIES OF COLONIAL AND LATER
TIMES, AS WELL AS THE GREAT AMERICAN
WRITERS OF THE NINETEENTH CENTURY

PART SEVEN

SOLD BY ORDER OF THE ADMINISTRATOR

ROBERT B. GABLE

March 3-4, 1925

AMERICAN ART ASSOCIATION · INC.

MADISON AVENUE 56TH TO 57TH STREET · NEW YORK

Telephone: PLAZA 1270

1049. WHITMAN (WALT). Franklin Evans; or, The Inebriate. A Tale of the
Times. By Walter Whitman. Royal 8vo, pamphlet, 31pp. stitched,
uncut. (Edges frayed; some fox marks.)   New York, 1842

32^{50}

FIRST EDITION. Whitman's first separately published work, which was never
reissued as a separate bound book. Published as the Extra to the *New World*,
New York, November, 1842, Number 34. Laid in is an Autograph Postal Card,
signed with initials, to John Burroughs. VERY INTERESTING CONTENTS.

[No. 1050]

1050. WHITMAN (WALT). Autograph Letter Signed, *"Walt."* 3pp. 8vo.
Brooklyn, Oct. 8, 1864.

30^{-}

INTERESTING PERSONAL AND LITERARY LETTER, reading in part,—*"My book*
[Drum Taps] is not yet printed. I still wish to stereotype it myself. I could
easily still put it in the hands of a proper publisher then, and make better terms
with him. . . . All the signs are that Gen. Grant is Going to Strike Forthwith,
perhaps risk all! One feels solemn who sees what depends. The military suc-
cess, though first class of war, is the least that depends. . . ."

[See Reproduction]

1051. WHITMAN (WALT). Autograph Letter Signed, *"Walt."* 3pp. 8vo,
New York City, August 25, 1866. To "Andy." With a 14-line postscript signed, *"Walter."*

19^{-}

NICE FRIENDLY LETTER, giving one an idea of "enjoying myself" in the early
sixties, comparing not unfavorably with the present "automania" age. The letter
reads in part,—*"My book is being printed—gets along rather slowly,—I ride out*
on Long Island & up New York, Central Park, &c. occasionally—the country is
beautiful now—I take a walk on Broadway almost every afternoon—then some-
times a sail on the river or bay—so you see I am enjoying myself in my way—
with three or four hours work every day reading my proofs, &c. . . ."
The closing sentence of the postscript reads,—*"'Be virtuous & you will be*
happy.'—From your Christian friend. . . ."

1052. WHITMAN (WALT). After All, Not to Create Only. Recited by Walt
Whitman on Invitation of Managers American Institute. . . . 12mo,
beveled green cloth boards, gilt top, uncut.

7^{-}

Boston: Roberts Brothers, 1871

First Regular Edition. Laid in is a small envelope addressed in Walt Whitman's Autograph as follows,—*"Walt Whitman, 431 Stevens Street, Camden, New*
Jersey," bearing postmark, *"Burlington, Vt., Jan. 30, 1884."*

123

1053. [WHITMAN WALT).] Democratic Vistas. Memorada. Narrow 12mo, original pale green wrappers, uncut. Laid in protecting cloth cover. Washington, D. C., 1871

14—

FIRST EDITION. Laid in is a portion of a manuscript IN WHITMAN'S AUTOGRAPH, written in ink on two small scraps of paper pasted together, beginning,—*"I accept with joy, (and only hope it is true) what Dr. Bucke gives as his enclosing summary of the Leaves"* [etc.].

1054. [WHITMAN (WALT).] Leaves of Grass. *With portraits.* 12mo, half calf, leather label. (Binding cracked, lacks a fly-leaf.) Camden, New Jersey, 1876

17 50

AUTHOR'S EDITION, bearing the autograph signature,—*"Walt Whitman,"* on the title-page.
Laid in is a post-card addressed to J. H. Johnston, 150 Bowery, N. Y. C., dated June 20 [1880] from Lake Huron, and containing news of Whitman's trip—the address and message being entirely in Whitman's Autograph, and signed, *"W. W."*

1055. [WHITMAN (WALT).] Two Rivulets, Including Democratic Vistas, Centennial Songs, and Passage to India. 12mo, three-quarter red levant morocco, gilt paneled back, gilt edges, BY RIVIERE. Camden, New Jersey, 1876

15—

AUTHOR'S EDITION. Tipped to stub, as frontispiece, is a portrait of Whitman, upon which is his autographic inscription,—*"Walt Whitman born May 31 1819."*
Laid in is a portion of Whitman's AUTOGRAPH MANUSCRIPT, reading as follows, *"Literature, it is certain, would be fuller of vigor and sanity, if authors were in the habit of composing in the forenoon—and never at night."*

1056. WHITMAN (WALT). Autograph Letter Signed, *"Walt Whitman,"* 2pp. 8vo, Camden, April 21, 1881. To Miss Helen E. Price. With addressed envelope and portrait. Together, 3 pieces.

25—

LONG AND DESIRABLE LETTER, reading in part,—
"All sorrowful, solemn, yet soothing thoughts come up in my mind at reminiscences of my dear friend, your dear mother. Have often thought of you all since '73, the last time I saw you so briefly, so sadly. [At the funeral of the poet's mother.] *. . . I have just returned from Boston, where I have been the past week; went on to read my annual 'Death of Abraham Lincoln' on the anniversary of that tragedy. I am pretty well for me—am still under the benumbing influences of paralysis, but thankful to be as well as I am."*

1057. WHITMAN (WALT). Autograph Letter Signed, *"Walt Whitman."* One page 4to, Philadelphia, January 16, '77. To JOHN BURROUGHS.

15—

FINE FRIENDLY LETTER, relating to a little visit of his in Philadelphia, reading in part,—*"I have a nice room here, with a stove and oak wood. Everything very comfortable and sunny—Most of all the spirit (which is so entirely lacking over there in Camden, and has been for more than three years) . . . I like your articles. . . ."*

1058. WHITMAN (WALT). Autograph Letter Signed, *"Walt Whitman,"* one page 4to. Camden, New Jersey, April 24, 1890. To J. M. Stoddart. With envelope addressed to J. M. Stoddart. Neatly hinged to larger cardboard sheet; GALLEY-PROOF of "To the Sun-Set Breeze." Sixteen-line verse, signed in autograph, *"Walt Whitman,"* one page oblong 8vo. Together, 3 pieces.

18—

SUBMITTING A MAGAZINE CONTRIBUTION and asking,—*"Can you use this in the magazine? It is intended to make one page full & square—& I shall require to see a proof beforehand. . . . The price is $60 & a dozen copies of the magazine number. I reserve the right of printing in future book. . . ."*
GOOD STEADY HANDWRITING, ALTHOUGH WRITTEN AT THE AGE OF 71.

1059. WHITMAN (WALT). November Boughs. *Frontispiece portrait.* 8vo, limp maroon cloth, gilt lettered on front cover and back strip, UNCUT AND UNOPENED.　　　　　　　　　　　　Philadelphia: David McKay, 1888

10—

FIRST EDITION. ONE OF A FEW COPIES BOUND UP IN LIMP CLOTH AND ENTIRELY UNCUT FOR PRESENTATION PURPOSES. Laid in, is an Autograph Memorandum, written in ink on an 8vo sheet and pasted on a cardboard, reading,—*"Walt Whitman, May 23, 1887. S. H. M. [Sidney Morse] is here (Camden, N. J.) Sculping W. W."*

1060. WHITMAN (WALT). Autograph Letter Signed. 2pp. 8vo. Dec. 29, 1883. To J. H. Johnston. With addressed envelope. Together, 2 pieces.

13—

CHARMING LITERARY LETTER, reading in part,—*"The little poem you speak of was sent to Harpers, accepted at once and paid for. When it will appear I know not."*

1061. WHITMAN (WALT). Autograph Letter Signed, in full, one page 4to. London, Ontario, Canada, no date. With portrait of Whitman. Together, 2 pieces.

12—

NICE SPECIMEN, regarding sending circular advertising his books to his addressee. He intends to stay at London until the middle of August, after which he will be at Camden, New Jersey, his permanent address.

1062. WHITMAN (WALT). Autograph Letter Signed, *"Walt Whitman."* One page 4to. No place, no date.

11—

Personal note to J. M. Stoddart, Editor *Lippincott's Magazine,* referring to some of his work.

1063. WHITMAN (WALT). Autograph Letter Signed, *"W. W."* 2pp. 4to. June 20th, no year. To John H. Johnston.

10—

LONG AND INTERESTING PERSONAL LETTER. Fine specimen.

1064. WHITMAN (WALT). ORIGINAL AUTOGRAPH MANUSCRIPT, unsigned, of his poem, *"You lingering sparse leaves of me."* Written in ink on one quarto page. Accompanied by fine proof portrait of Whitman, on Japanese vellum paper. Together, 2 pieces.

15—

1065. WHITMAN (WALT). ORIGINAL AUTOGRAPH MANUSCRIPT with title, *"A Word about Tennyson."* Manuscript of about SEVEN HUNDRED WORDS, written in ink on five sheets, different sizes. With numerous corrections by the author.

60—

A SPLENDID TRIBUTE TO ALFRED, LORD TENNYSON.

1066. WHITMAN (WALT). ORIGINAL AUTOGRAPH MANUSCRIPT, signed in full, of his poem, on the death of General Sheridan, entitled "Funeral Interpolations." Written in pencil on one quarto page, with numerous corrections, deletions and additions, entirely in Whitman's handwriting.

15—

1067. WHITMAN (WALT). ORIGINAL AUTOGRAPH MANUSCRIPT of his poem, "Thoughts." One page 8vo, Unsigned, and undated. Written on pink paper; [ALSO] Transcripts of other Whitman poems.

10—

These poems appear in the last portion of the third edition of "Leaves of Grass," in *"Thoughts,"* (six out of seven numbered poems, pages 408-411). This present manuscript is "Thoughts" No. 4 (pp. 410).

The printed text of the third edition accompanies each manuscript.

1068. WHITMAN (WALT). Newspaper clippings of his article entitled, "The Dead Emerson," THE FIRST PORTION BEING WRITTEN OUT IN WHITMAN'S HANDWRITING, and he has made a few corrections to the text of the article.

FINE WHITMAN ITEM, and of an important literary character.

1069. WHITMAN (WALT). When Lilacs Last in the Dooryard Bloomed. *Original watercolor drawing as frontispiece. Decorated capitals and tailpiece* COLORED BY HAND *by C. R. Ashbee*. 12mo, vellum, uncut.

[London] Essex House Press, 1900

SPECIAL EDITION of 135 copies only, PRINTED ON VELLUM THROUGHOUT, of which this is, No. 82.

Laid in is a manuscript (about 50 words) IN WHITMAN'S AUTOGRAPH, with the heading,—*"Literature,"* and beginning,—*"The tendency permitted to Literature, has always been & now is to magnify and intensify its own technism"* [etc.].

1070. WHITMAN (WALT). Autobiographia, or, The Story of a Life. *Frontispiece.* 1892; Voices from the Press; A Collection of Sketches, Essays, and Poems . . . [Contains contributions by Walt Whitman, Horace Greeley, Bayard Taylor, and others.] 1850; Together, 2 vols. 12mo and 8vo, cloth, the former uncut.   New York, 1850-1892

Laid in each volume is a manuscript (about 70 words in the first mentioned, and about 75 in the second) IN WHITMAN'S AUTOGRAPH.

1071. WHITMAN (WALT). Portion of an Autograph Letter (about 115 words), Camden, Dec. 5, 1890. To *"My dear J. M. S.";* [ALSO] WORTHINGTON (R.—Publisher). A. L. S., 2pp. 8vo, New York, Sept. 29th, 1879. To WALT WHITMAN. In reference to "Leaves of Grass;" A Rare Tintype of Whitman seated in the buggy presented to him by his friends; Picture of Whitman's birthplace in West Hills, L. I.; View of his Home at Camden, N. J.; and other Whitmaniana. Together, 8 pieces.

Lots 1072-1076 omitted

THE RENOWNED COLLECTION OF THE LATE

WILLIAM F. GABLE

OF ALTOONA, PENNSYLVANIA

AMERICAN · ENGLISH

FIRST EDITIONS. INSCRIBED VOLUMES
ORIGINAL MANUSCRIPTS. AUTOGRAPHS

Including

LETTERS OF HISTORICAL INTEREST, AUTO-
GRAPHS OF PRESIDENTS OF THE U.S., SIGNERS
OF THE DECLARATION AND OTHER CELEB-
RITIES, AS WELL AS THE GREAT AMERICAN
WRITERS OF THE NINETEENTH CENTURY

PART EIGHT

SOLD BY ORDER OF THE ADMINISTRATOR

ROBERT B. GABLE

TO BE SOLD ON THE AFTERNOON AND EVENING OF
THURSDAY, APRIL 16, 1925

AMERICAN ART ASSOCIATION · INC.
MADISON AVENUE 56TH TO 57TH STREET ⁄ NEW YORK
Telephone: PLAZA 1270

512. [WHITMAN (WALT).] Diary Notes of A Visit to Walt Whitman and Some of His Friends, in 1890. *Illustrated*. Manchester, 1898; Voices from the Press; A Collection of Sketches, Essays, and Poems . . . [Contains contributions by Walt Whitman, Horace Greeley, Bayard Taylor, and others.] New York, 1850. Together, 2 vols. 12mo and 8vo, cloth.

New York and Manchester, 1850–1898

Laid in each volume is a manuscript (about 250 words in the first mentioned, and about 40 words in the second) IN WHITMAN'S AUTOGRAPH.

12—

513. WHITMAN (WALT). Autograph Letter Signed, "*Walt Whitman.*" 4pp. 16mo, Brooklyn, Tuesday afternoon June 28,/64. To Charles W. Eldridge. With addressed envelope. Together, 2 pieces.

Interesting letter, written during the Civil War. Early specimens of such interest as the above are very scarce.

30—

514. WHITMAN (WALT). Autograph Letter Signed, "*Walt.*" 4pp. 8vo. Providence, October 20, 1868. To "*Dear Charley.*" With addressed envelope. Together, 2 pieces.

A CHARMING PERSONAL LETTER, regarding a personal about him which is to appear in the Sunday Morning Chronicle; the kindnesses extended to him by his friends in Providence, and concluding,—"*After all*, NEW ENGLAND FOR EVER! (*with perhaps just one or two little reservations*)."

21—

515. WHITMAN (WALT). Autograph Letter Signed: "*Walt Whitman.*" One page 4to, Washington, June 6, 1871. To Mrs. Botta. Accompanied by a cabinet size portrait of Whitman. Together, 2 pieces.

Whitman mentions his poem: "O Star of France."

13—

516. [WHITMAN (WALT).] Democratic Vistas. Memoranda. Narrow 12mo, half calf (binding slightly rubbed). Washington, D. C., 1871

FIRST EDITION. Laid in is a portion of a manuscript IN WHITMAN'S AUTOGRAPH, written in ink on an oblong 12mo sheet, beginning as follows,—"*Established poems have the very great advantage of chanting the already performed, the past*," [etc.] and containing numerous corrections.

15—

517. WHITMAN (WALT). Autograph Letter Signed, "*Walt Whitman.*" 2pp. 8vo, Camden, February 24, 1878. To John Burroughs. With addressed envelope. Together, 2 pieces.

Interesting letter, reading in part,—"*I am agreeable to the Lecture project, if it could be well put through. About the middle of April, the anniversary of the eve or night of Lincoln's murder, might be a good night.*"

45—

518. WHITMAN (WALT). AUTOGRAPH MANUSCRIPT (about 160 words) being biographical data, in connection with [probably] Elias Hicks. Written on verso of William F. Gable's A. L. S. One page 8vo, Reading, Penn., February 25th, 1880, requesting that Whitman favor him with an extract from one of his poems, autographed; [Also] KENNEDY (W. S.). Autograph Manuscript Signed with initials,—"*W. S. K.*," consisting of about 300 words, which were used later in his study of Whitman; 2 Portraits of Whitman; and other Whitmaniana. Together, 12 pieces.

SPLENDID COLLECTION, some of the pieces being very rare.

37⁵⁰

519. WHITMAN (WALT). Autograph Letter Signed, in full. One page 8vo. Sept. 19, 1881. To Mr. Clark.

NICE SPECIMEN, making an appointment to meet Mr. Clark at his office the next day.

9—

520. [WHITMAN (WALT).] WHITMAN (MARY—Sister of Walt). Autograph Letter Signed,—"*Mary.*" 3pp. 12mo, Greenport, L. I., Dec. 23 [1883]. To Walter Whitman. Delightful personal letter; Contents for a late edition of "Leaves of Grass," written in pencil in an unknown hand on 4 small 4to sheets, with a notation in ink in Whitman's Autograph; Three Original Photographs of the Walt Whitman Funeral—one of the house, and two of the services in the cemetery; and other Whitmaniana. Together, 10 pieces. *13 -*

521. WHITMAN (WALT). [BUCKE (R. M.).] Autograph Letter, 2pp. 4to London, Ont., 17 Aug. 1888. To Walt Whitman. In reference to new publications of Whitman's. With envelope addressed to Whitman; Autograph Manuscript (about 15 words) written by Whitman on back of small envelope, and tipped to folio sheet with some newspaper clippings bearing his autograph notations. Evidently suggestions for future writings; My Book and I. By Walt Whitman. An Article taken from *Lippincott's Magazine*, January 1887. With Whitman's Autograph Notations; and other Whitmaniana. Together, 7 pieces. *11 -*

522. WHITMAN (WALT). Three fine portraits of the Great Poet, each signed in full, enclosed in manila envelope, on which is written, in Whitman's handwriting: "*For Mrs. Louisa Whitman. Portraits of Walt Whitman, from W. W. himself, with love and remembrance. Oct. 1889.*" *32 50*
Charming mementos of The Good Gray Poet.

523. WHITMAN (WALT). Autograph Letter Signed, "*Walt Whitman.*" One page 8vo, Camden, Jan. 8 '91. To Mr. J. M. Stoddart. With addressed envelope; Medallion portrait of Mr. Stoddart laid in, all mounted on oblong folio sheet. Together, 3 pieces. *14 -*
INTERESTING LETTER, marked "*personal*" at heading, relating to the publishing of a monthly magazine for popular reading, with mention of Whitman's "*Leaves of Grass,*" and other works.

524. WHITMAN (WALT). Leaves of Grass. *Illustrated.* Philadelphia [1900]; At the Graveside of Walt Whitman: Harleigh, Camden, New Jersey, March 30th. And Sprigs of Lilac. Edited by Horace L. Traubel. 1892. Together, 2 vols. 8vo, cloth and wrappers, uncut, the latter unopened. *3 50*
Philadelphia, 1892–[1900]
The second mentioned is No. 396 of an edition of 750 copies.

525. WHITMAN (WALT). Leaves of Grass. Including a Fac-simile autobiography, variorum readings of the poems and a department of Gathered Leaves. [Two copies.] Philadelphia [1900]; Lafayette in Brooklyn. With an Introduction by John Burroughs. New York, 1905; Diary Notes of A Visit to Walt Whitman . . . By John Johnston, M.D. Manchester, 1898; A Plea for Shakespeare and Whitman. By William Timothy Call. Brooklyn, 1914; The Sunset of Bon Echo. [Publication of The Whitman Club of Bon Echo.] Edited by Flora Macdonald. Vol. 1. No. 6. April-May, 1920; BUCHANAN (ROBERT). White Rose and Red. A Love Story. [Dedicated to Walt Whitman.] Autograph Signature,—"*Robt. Buchanan,*" on title. Boston, 1873; Essai d'expansion d'une Esthétique. Contains "Walt Whitman et la Poésie contemporaine." [Two copies.] Havre, 1911. *Mainly illustrated.* Together, 9 vols., 16mo to 8vo, cloth, boards, and wrappers. *20 -*
Various places, 1873–1920
Laid in one volume of "Leaves of Grass" is a manuscript (about 100 words) IN WHITMAN'S AUTOGRAPH, autobiographic notes and draft of a poem.

526. WHITMAN (WALT). When Lilacs Last in the Dooryard Bloomed. *Original watercolor drawing as frontispiece. Decorated capitals and tail-piece* COLORED BY HAND *by C. R. Ashbee.* 12mo, vellum, uncut.

[London] Essex House Press, 1900

SPECIAL EDITION of 135 copies only, printed on VELLUM throughout, of which this is, No. 131.

Laid in is a manuscript (about 75 words) IN WHITMAN'S AUTOGRAPH, headed with titles,—"*Railroad poem, Poem of corn and meat (pork, beef, fish), Poem of Mines,*" [etc.] and followed by instructions concerning a Western Edition.

23—

527. WHITMAN (WALT). AUTOGRAPH MANUSCRIPT, Unsigned, entitled, "The Public Schools (to Come)," written in ink on 2pp. folio, with changes and interlineations.

FINE MANUSCRIPT BY THIS CELEBRATED AMERICAN POET.

16—

528. WHITMAN (WALT). ORIGINAL AUTOGRAPH MANUSCRIPT (unsigned), of his fine Poem entitled "*The Dead Tenor.*" Written on one quarto page. Together with printed transcript of the poem and portrait of Whitman at 61. Together, 3 pieces, matted as two.

11—

529. WHITMAN (WALT). Autograph Letter Signed, "*W. W.*" 2pp. 8vo. N. Y. City, March 13, no year. To JOHN BURROUGHS. With addressed envelope. Together, 2 pieces.

FINE ASSOCIATION PIECE, regarding a trip he contemplates taking with Burroughs, and asking Burroughs' permission to bring his boy Harry Stafford with him.

12—

530. WHITMAN (WALT). ORIGINAL AUTOGRAPH MANUSCRIPT POEM,—"*Abraham Lincoln—born Feb. 12, 1809.*" Unsigned and not dated. Two four-line stanzas, written in ink, on back of 4to sheet of one of his personal letters. With numerous alterations and corrections by the author.

Valuable as original data of this poem.

650—

531. WHITMAN (WALT). Autograph Letter Signed, "*Walt Whitman.*" 2pp. 8vo, Camden, New Jersey, July 11 (no year), with a seven-line postscript unsigned. To "*Dear John & Sula Burroughs.*" With addressed envelope; Portrait on Japanese vellum. Together, 3 pieces.

Friendly missive relating to his trip to New York, also to a letter of his in the Tribune of July 4th, some graham biscuits which he is sending by express to be soaked in milk as a hot weather diet; closing with the thoughtful inquiry, "*how is that baby?*"

18—

SALE NUMBER 2198
PUBLIC EXHIBITION FROM TUESDAY, NOVEMBER FIFTEENTH

1927

A FEW CHOICE
BOOKS & MANUSCRIPTS

CHIEFLY FROM

PRIVATE ENGLISH COLLECTIONS

TO BE SOLD BY AUCTION
AT UNRESERVED PUBLIC SALE
FRIDAY EVENING, NOVEMBER TWENTY-FIFTH
AT EIGHT-FIFTEEN

THE ANDERSON GALLERIES
⟦ MITCHELL KENNERLEY, President ⟧
489 PARK AVENUE AT FIFTY-NINTH STREET, NEW YORK
⟦REGENT 0250⟧

MANUSCRIPT OF THE INTRODUCTION
TO THE LONDON EDITION OF "LEAVES OF GRASS"

1900 136 **WHITMAN (WALT).** Autograph Manuscript of the Introduction to the London Edition of "Leaves of Grass." Written on 14 pp., 8vo.

A FINE MANUSCRIPT. In this Introduction, with an entire absence of vanity or self-consciousness, Whitman sets forth the salient points of "Leaves of Grass," and its message, with a brief description of himself in his 63rd year.

This MS. was given to Dr. Barrus by Thomas B. Harned, one of Whitman's literary executors. (*Dr. Clara Barrus*).

[SEE ILLUSTRATION]

137 **WHITMAN (WALT).** A pencilled fragment of Whitman's, written perhaps when he was working on his "Prayer of Columbus." *12⁵⁰* It is preceded by an asterisk, and is probably an interpolation which had got mislaid from its original text.

"It is in itself and with its preludes and surroundings one of those Tragedies which poems and plays cannot make more piteous and majestic, as in some grave tragedies indeed. See the tall figure of Columbus walk apart on those shores washed by the far Antilles' waves and hear—for who can doubt that his soul's expression took substantially such form—the prayer he utters." (*Dr. Clara Barrus*).

138 **WHITMAN (WALT).** A pathetic fragment of Whitman's composition in ink on old pink paper. The incoherence would suggest that it was written when mentally confused, disabled—perhaps after one of his early paralytic seizures. Given to Dr. *17⁵⁰* Barrus by Thomas B. Harned, one of Whitman's literary executors.

"Religion means degrees of realization, if any, of the fact which, the more clearness attained it too steadily becomes clearer,—the fact of our consciousness, undemonstrable as any consciousness, is except by itself, that enclosing this positive." There are a number of deletions and interpolations. (*Dr. Clara Barrus*).

139 **WHITMAN (WALT).** A fragment of MS. by Walt Whitman written on Stationery of the Attorney General's Office, Washington, D. C., August 22, 1865. *15*

ONE OF WHITMAN'S WAR MEMORANDA. It is headed: *"Copy to follow page 104 in my proof page.* SMALL MEMORANDA. *Thousands lost—here one or two preserved."* The memoranda concerns groups of Southerners waiting to see the Attorney General in reference to Pardons.

Whitman has also written directions to the printer, and the name of the compositor "George" appears at the top. (*Dr. Clara Barrus*).

140 **WHITMAN (WALT).** A. L. s., 1 p., 8vo. Camden, February 25, '87. Probably to Charles W. Eldridge, as it is written on the last page of a letter from him to Whitman. *35*

B

UNPUBLISHED. *"Am sitting here by the window in the little front room down stairs well wrapt up—for though bright & sunny it is a cold freezing day—have had my dinner (of rare stewed oysters, some toasted graham bread & a cup of tea—relished all)—am abt as usual—ups and downs . . . the worst is my enforced house-imprisonment . . . Spirits & heart though mainly gay, wh. is the best half of the battle. Love and comfort to you my friends—your wives & all—Write often if you can' (Monotony is now the word of my life),"* etc.

The letter from Eldridge to Whitman relates his being with William O'Connor at Dr. Channing's home in Pasadena in the hope of benefiting O'Connor's health. Whitman has written in red ink at the top of his letter: *"When read send to John Burroughs, West Park, Ulster County, New York."* (*Dr. Clara Barrus*).

Introduction to the London Edition.

America – that new world in so many respects besides its geography – has perhaps afforded nothing even in the astonishing products of the fields of its politics, its mechanical invention, material growth, & the like, more original, more autochthonic, than its late contribution in the field of literature, the Poem, or poetic writings, named Leaves of Grass, which in the following pages, we present to the British public.

141 WHITMAN (WALT). Autograph Post Card. Camden, N. J., August 30, 1887. To Charles W. Eldridge.

> "*Nothing specially new or different with me—yes, I am willing Grace should go on with the Calendar,*" etc. (*Dr. Clara Barrus*).

142 WHITMAN (WALT). Autograph Post Card. Camden, May 10, 1889. To John Burroughs.

> "*Our dear friend O'Connor died peacefully at 2 A.M. yesterday.*"

A message fraught with great pathos for those who kenew of the love between Whitman and O'Connor, the author of the pamphlet "The Good Gray Poet," and always an ardent champion of Whitman.

This card had been addressed by Whitman to Burroughs at "West Plains," and on its return to him had correctly addressed it. (*Dr. Clara Barrus*).

143 WHITMAN (WALT). A. L. s., 4 pp., 8vo. Camden, N. J., Monday afternoon, June 23, no year. To [Charles W. Eldridge.]

UNPUBLISHED. "*I have now been a week here, & am about the same—well enough to keep up and around, but with bad spells most every day. . . I keep pretty good spirits however. . . I am pleasantly situated here—have two nice rooms, second floor . . . they are the rooms in which my mother died, with all the accustomed furniture I have long been so used to see. . . I am glad to hear Nelly is feeling better . . . please hand her this letter to read—Nelly I still feel that I shall pull through, but O it is a weary, weary pull. . .*

I have amused myself with 'Kenelm Chillingly'—read it all—like it well—Bulwer is such a snob as almost redeems snobdom—the story is good, & the style a master's. Like Cervantes, Bulwer's old age productions are incomparably his best," etc. (*Dr. Clara Barrus*).

144 WHITMAN (WALT). A. L. s., 4 pp., 8vo. Camden, N. J., Monday forenoon, July 7, no year. [To Charles W. Eldridge.]

UNPUBLISHED. A FINE FRIENDLY LETTER. "*In my case there is no notable amendment & not much change. I have irregular spells of serious distress, pain, etc. in the head . . . my locomotion is about as bad as it was . . . Did you see Dr. Drinkard? & did he say any thing new about my sickness or symptoms? I have received a letter from John Burroughs to-day—he & his wife are evidently having real good healthy country times away there in the cool uplands of Delaware county—he is home. I am feeling comparatively comfortable to-day, & still hope for the best—but—*" etc. (*Dr. Clara Barrus*).

145 WHITMAN (WALT). A. L. s. in pencil, 2 pp., 4to. Broadway, N. Y., Friday afternoon, July 19, no year. [To C. W. Eldridge.] A little weak in folds.

UNPUBLISHED. "*I went leisurely up the Connecticut valley, by way of Springfield, through the best part of Massachusetts, Connecticut, and New Hampshire . . . by daylight . . . slowly up the White River valley, a captivating wild region by Vermont Central R.R., and so to Burlington, and about Lake Champlain where I spent a week, filling myself every day with the grandest ensembles of the Adirondacks always on one side, and the Green Mountains on the other, sailed after that down Champlain by day, stopt at Albany over night and down the Hudson by boat, through a succession of splendid and magnificent thunderstorms. . .*

Charley, who do you think I have been spending some three hours with to-day from 12 to 3—Joaquin Miller—He saw me yesterday towards dusk in 5th av. on a stage, and rushed out of the house and mounting the stage gave me his address, and made an appointment—he lives here, 34th st. in furnished rooms—I am much pleased with him—really pleased and satisfied—his presence, conversation, atmosphere, are infinitely more satisfying than his poetry—he is, however, mopish, ennuyed, a California Hamlet, unhappy every way—but a natural prince, maybe an illiterate one—but tender, sweet and magnetic," etc. (*Dr. Clara Barrus*).

Will of Walt Whitman —
Washington D.C.
May 15th, 1873

For the purpose of confirming and adding to my former Will,
written in 1872. & placed in charge of
my brother George W. Whitman, I hereby
again & further Will and bequeath,
All my property, namely,

Nine hundred & *fifty dollars,* deposited
by me, and now held in my name, by
book 101,398. of & in the Brooklyn
Savings Bank corner of Fulton &
Concord sts., Brooklyn New York, with
the interest accrued thereon. — Also

Five hundred and fifty dollars, deposited
by me, & now in my name by book
14,602. of & in the Freedman's Savings
and Trust Company, of 1507, Pennsylvania av. Washington, D.C., with
the interest accrued thereon — And also
any further sums deposited by me
in said Freedman's Savings Co. & credited on said book 14,602, with interest.
— Also.

The plates of my books "Leaves of Grass,"
"Passage to India" "Democratic Vistas"
& "As a strong Bird on Pinions Free"
— being some six hundred (or over) pages
of electrotyped or stereotyp'd plates —
— Also some three hundred and
fifty copies (cloth) of "As a Strong
Bird. &c" — all at S. W. Green's, 16
and 18 Jacob street, New York city.
— Also,

The Copies of my books & Money due from said copies,
or sales, at & by, M. Doolady,
98 Nassau st. N.Y. city.

Also, returns due, for my books, from
Samson Low & Co. booksellers,
London, England.

SLIGHTLY REDUCED FACSIMILE
OF THE FIRST PAGE OF WHITMAN'S WILL OF 1873

[NUMBER 147]

135

146 **WHITMAN (WALT).** A. L., 1 p., 4to. No place or date. [To Charles W. Eldridge.] With addressed envelope containing Whitman's rubber name and address stamp in lower corner. His health is improving, and he asks Eldridge to pay Godey with a money order he is sending him.

UNPUBLISHED. *"My condition continues favorable—& if I dared to hope this will last & improve in proportion—indicates recovery,"* etc.

This letter is only one of many Whitman wrote which refutes the charge which has been made that his debts set lightly upon him. John Burroughs said he was punctilious in paying what he owed. (*Dr. Clara Barrus*).

AUTOGRAPH WILL OF WALT WHITMAN

147 **WHITMAN (WALT).** Autograph Will of Walt Whitman, written on 3 pp., legal cap, and endorsed by Whitman for filing: "Will of Walt Whitman, May 16, 1873."

A MAGNIFICENT AND PRECIOUS WHITMAN DOCUMENT, written throughout without a single deletion and but one or two interpolations, in Whitman's exceedingly legible hand. The document commences: "WILL OF WALT WHITMAN—*Washington, D. C., May 15, 1873. For the purpose of confirming and adding to my former Will, written in 1872, & placed in charge of my brother George W. Whitman, I hereby again & further Will and bequeath ALL MY PROPERTY, namely:—"*

Then follow bequests of money in bank; the plates of "Leaves of Grass"; copies of his books; returns due from publishers and booksellers; salary, clothes; watches; and ALL HIS PERSONAL PROPERTY OF ANY DESCRIPTION WHATEVER to his Mother. Then follow requests to his mother to make special gifts to various relatives and others. THE WILL IS WITNESSED BY Harry J. Douglas and Palmer Tilton. (*Dr. Clara Barrus*).

[SEE ILLUSTRATION, PRECEDING PAGE]

148 **WHITMAN (WALT) AND BURROUGHS (JOHN).** Fragments of an early Manuscript by John Burroughs, on "Criticism," with emendations by Whitman. Written on 5 pp. 4to.

THIS IS PROBABLY A MANUSCRIPT OF THE WASHINGTON PERIOD, 1863-1873. The body of the manuscript is in the hand of Burroughs; the interpolations and corrections, including some deletions, and almost the entire last page are by Whitman. This latter portion, which appears to constitute the ending of the essay, reads: *"How a full-grown, original, American race of intellectual law-givers, of a type at present undreamed of, could redeem this condition, & ventilate with life-giving breezes, all the veins & arteries, & habilitate a real American literature! Few are they who can measure the unspeakable value, to man, of Literature. Yet over it all is Criticism."* (*Dr. Clara Barrus*).

BURROUGHS'S ESSAY ON WHITMAN
WITH EMENDATIONS BY WHITMAN HIMSELF

149 **WHITMAN (WALT) AND BURROUGHS (JOHN).** Original Autograph Manuscript by John Burroughs of "The Flight of the Eagle," (Whitman), WITH EMENDATIONS IN PEN AND PENCIL BY WALT WHITMAN. Written on 102 pp., 8vo.

A MANUSCRIPT OF GREAT LITERARY VALUE.

THIS ESSAY IS FOUND IN "Birds and Poets." It was first named "The Disowned Poet," the name finally chosen was decided upon by Whitman, this title among others being submitted to him by Burroughs.

THIS IS THE ORIGINAL MANUSCRIPT AS USED BY THE PRINTERS (their names appear on it in pencil, here and there) from which the printed essay, as it appears in Burroughs's "Birds and Poets" was set up.

THE EMENDATIONS BY WHITMAN CONSIST OF MANY PARAGRAPHS AND ONE ENTIRE PAGE, reading: *"Finally, as those men and women respect and love Walt Whitman best who have known him longest and closest personally, the same rule will apply to 'Leaves of Grass' and the later volume 'Two Rivulets.' It is indeed neither the first surface reading of those books, nor perhaps even the second or third, that will any more than prepare the student for the full assimilation of the poems. Like Nature, and like the sciences, they seem like endless suites of chambers opening and expanding more and more, and continually."* (*Dr. Clara Barrus*).

SALE NUMBER 2297
PUBLIC EXHIBITION FROM MONDAY, DECEMBER TENTH

RARE BOOKS, MANUSCRIPTS
& AUTOGRAPH LETTERS

INCLUDING THE

WALT WHITMAN COLLECTION

OF

BAYARD WYMAN

WASHINGTON, D. C.

SOLD BY HIS ORDER

TO BE SOLD BY AUCTION
AT UNRESERVED PUBLIC SALE
TUESDAY EVENING, DECEMBER EIGHTEENTH
AT EIGHT-FIFTEEN

THE ANDERSON GALLERIES

[MITCHELL KENNERLEY, President]

489 PARK AVENUE AT FIFTY-NINTH STREET, NEW YORK

1928

WITH TWENTY-FIVE UNPUBLISHED AUTOGRAPH LETTERS FROM FOURTEEN SOLDIERS WHO HAD BEEN NURSED BY WHITMAN IN THE HOSPITALS OF WASHINGTON OR ON THE FIELD

57 **WHITMAN (WALT).** The Wound Dresser. A Series of Letters written from the Hospitals in Washington during the War of the Rebellion. Edited by Richard M. Bucke. *Portrait.* Boston, 1898

180

12mo, original cloth, uncut.

FIRST EDITION. FIRST ISSUE. Accompanied by 25 autograph letters from 14 soldiers who had been nursed by Whitman in the hospitals of Washington or on the field. Five of these soldiers are mentioned in the above work. The letters are from John J. Barker, 2nd Tennessee Regiment; Livingston Brooks, 17th Pennsylvania; Erastus Haskell, 141st N. Y.; Lewis K. Brown, Maryland; Miss H. S. Cunningham in reply to Whitman's letter about Oscar Cunningham, 82nd Ohio; Fred Gray; Justus F. Boyd, A. S. Bush, E. D. Fox, W. A. Jellison, Lieut. A. J. Liebenau, Alfred L. Larr, W. H. McFarland, and Wm. E. Vandemark.

A SPLENDID COLLECTION OF UNPUBLISHED LETTERS throwing new light on the hospital work of the man they call *"Father"*, *"Uncle"*, *"Comrade"*. The Fred Gray letter is in answer to one from Whitman which was printed in "Uncollected Poetry and Prose" (edited by Emory Holloway) and is accompanied by a letter from Mr. Holloway, regretting that he did not have the Gray letter to publish in that work. Mr. Gray writes: *"My mother says she has read of your whereabouts & what you are doing from the news-papers—furthermore she states with unusual vehemence that she thought you a good & noble man. I state what my mother said merely as an illustration of what a great many others have remarked to me concerning you & your noble devotion to suffering man. . . ."* Another writes: *"The Relief association may be a very nice thing, but I can't see it, for I never get anything from them, yet you have given me more than all of the rest put together, so you are the relief association that I, as well as all the rest of the boys, like best."* All might to quoted, for they tell of suffering, of slow recovery, of return to the army or civil life, of never failing patriotism, and ALWAYS OF THE GREAT DEBT TO THE KINDNESS AND LOVE SHOWN BY WALT WHITMAN. *"Walt, it is useless for me to try to tell you how much I have missed you at night. When my supper was brought in there was still something wanting. That was your cheerful smiling face, and then too I missed your kiss of friendship and love as also your kind 'good night', or 'so long'."*

DRAFT OF WHITMAN'S PREFACE TO THE LECTURE ON LINCOLN

88 **WHITMAN (WALT).** Autograph Manuscript of the FIRST PREFACE to his Lecture on the Death of Abraham Lincoln, 1 p., folio, composed of portions of five old letters to Whitman pasted together. About March, 1880.

470

THE ORIGINAL ROUGH DRAFT showing many interlineations and differing in numerous instances from the Preface published in "Specimen Days and Collect." A SPLENDID EXAMPLE OF WHITMAN'S METHOD OF BUILDING A PROSE ARTICLE, WITH MANY OF THE FIRST WORDS THAT FLOWED FROM HIS PEN CROSSED OUT, AND STRONGER, BETTER WORDS AND PHRASES SUBSTITUTED. This preface was prepared for the second delivery of the Lincoln lecture, held in Association Hall, Philadelphia, April 15, 1880: *"How often since that dark and chilly Saturday—that dripping April day, now fifteen years bygone—my heart has entertained the dream, the wish, to give of Abraham Lincoln's death its own special thought and memorial. . . ."*

[SEE ILLUSTRATION]

138

How often since that dark and chilly
Saturday – that dripping April day now fifteen
years bygone – my heart has X entertain'd the
dream, the wish, to give of Abraham
Lincoln's death its own special thought
and memorial. Yet now the
sought-for opportunity offers, I find my notes
incompetent (why, for truly profound themes, is statement so idle? why does the right phrase never offer?)
and the fit, suitable tribute I dreamed of, unpresented
as ever. My speech here, is indeed less, because of
itself or any thing in it, because I feel a
desire apart from any talk to simply celebrate the day, the
martyrdom. It is for this my friends, I have called
you together. Oft as the rolling years bring back
again this hour, let it, be dwell upon. For
my own part I hope and intend, till my own dying day,
whenever the 14th or 15th of April comes, to annually
gather a few friends around me, and hold its tragic
reminiscence. It narrow or sectional reminiscence. It belongs to These States in
their entirely — not the North only but the South,
perhaps most tenderly and devoutly to the South,
of all, for there Lincoln's birth-stock. There
and thence his antecedent stamp. Why should I
not say that thence his manliest traits,
his universality – his canny easy ways and words,
upon the surface, his inflexible determination and
courage at heart. Have you never realized it,
my friends, that Lincoln, though grafted on the
West, is essentially, in personnel and character,
a Southern contribution?

REDUCED FACSIMILE
WHITMAN'S PREFACE FOR HIS LECTURE ON
THE DEATH OF LINCOLN

[NUMBER 88]

SALE NUMBER 2311
ON PUBLIC EXHIBITION FROM SUNDAY, JANUARY THIRTEENTH
⟦WEEK DAYS 9-6 P.M.—SUNDAYS 2-5 P.M.⟧

THE LIBRARY OF
JEROME KERN
NEW YORK CITY

⟦PART TWO⟧

J-Z

TO BE SOLD BY HIS ORDER
AT UNRESERVED PUBLIC SALE
MONDAY EVENING, TUESDAY AFTERNOON & EVENING
WEDNESDAY & THURSDAY EVENINGS
JANUARY TWENTY-FIRST, TWENTY-SECOND
TWENTY-THIRD, TWENTY-FOURTH
AT TWO O'CLOCK AND EIGHT-FIFTEEN

THE ANDERSON GALLERIES
⟦MITCHELL KENNERLEY, PRESIDENT⟧
489 PARK AVENUE AT FIFTY-NINTH STREET, NEW YORK
1929

"LEAVES OF GRASS" IN PERFECT ORIGINAL CONDITION

1437 WHITMAN (WALT). Leaves of Grass. *Engraved portrait.*
Brooklyn, New York, 1855

3,400

Small folio, original green cloth, gilt title and floral decorations on the back, gilt title, blind tooled decorations on the sides, gilt borders, gilt edges. In a morocco bound cloth slip case.

FIRST EDITION. FIRST ISSUE IN SUPERLATIVE CONDITION. On the title-page is the autograph of F. T. Palgrave, dated 1857, and in 1868 HE PRESENTED THIS COPY TO FREDERICK LOCKER, the inscription on the fly-leaf reading: *"F. Locker from F. T. Palgrave, June, 1868. This is the original first edition, printed by the hands of the Yankee Tupper himself.* Pasted on the inside front cover is the addressed portion of a wrapper to Frederick Locker in the hand of Whitman. Laid in are SIX IMPORTANT PIECES OF WHITMAN INTEREST OF CONSIDERABLE SCARCITY:

1. Cabinet portrait of Whitman, autographed by him.
2. Proof of an excerpt from the United States Review, entitled "Walt Whitman and his Poems." A lengthy article on "Leaves of Grass", hailing him as "An American bard at last."
3. Proof of an excerpt from the Brooklyn Daily Times, entitled "Walt Whitman, a Brooklyn Boy." In praise of "Leaves of Grass" just published.
4. Proof of an excerpt from the American Phrenological Journal, entitled "An English and an American Poet," quoting and commenting on Tennyson's Poems, 1855, and Whitman's "Leaves of Grass," 1855.
5. Printed letter to W. M. Rossetti, dated March 17, 1876, concerning his state of health and "Leaves of Grass."
6. Printed letter by W. M. Rossetti, dated May 20, 1876, in praise of Walt Whitman; urging the purchase of his "Leaves of Grass," and other books of poetry by him, for which Rossetti will be glad to accept orders, and forward the remittances to Whitman.

The three proofs just referred to had previously been pasted in a scrap book, and have become slightly torn at the top in removing them.

A RARE COLLECTION AND A MATCHLESS COPY. On the title-page is pasted the label of Whitman's one-time London agent Wm. Horsell, who presumably sold this copy to the editor of "The Golden Treasury."

1438 [WHITMAN (WALT).] Broadside Letter from Ralph Waldo Emerson to Walt Whitman, dated "Concord, Mass'tts, 21 July, 1855.

200

Small 4to (a large and a small hole at top). In a polished calf portfolio.

OF EXCESSIVE RARITY, OF WHICH BUT THREE COPIES APPEAR TO BE KNOWN. No COPY WAS FOUND AMONG WHITMAN'S PAPERS, according to Traubel. Mr. Wakeman, whose collection was sold in 1924, left a memorandum stating that "This is the rarest of all the Emerson items," and that but TWO examples were known. He did not know of the present copy.

THE LETTER RELATES TO "Leaves of Grass," of which he writes: "I am not blind to the worth of the wonderful gift of 'Leaves of Grass.' I find it the most extraordinary piece of wit and wisdom that America has contributed . . .," etc. This Broadside was evidently struck off by Whitman to send to friends. This copy was found between the leaves of the copy of "Leaves of Grass" which Whitman sent to Francis Palgrave. At the top is the line (which is somewhat damaged by the hole mentioned): "Copy for the convenience of private reading only."

IMPORTANT HISTORIC AND LITERARY COLLECTION

Including

WASHINGTON LETTERS AND OTHER RARE AMERICANA

and a Notable Group of

WHITMAN MSS. & FIRST EDITIONS

✔ ✔

The Property of

WILLIAM W. COHEN

of New York City

SOLD BY HIS ORDER

Unrestricted Public Sale
FEBRUARY 5, AFTERNOON & EVENING
FEBRUARY 6, EVENING

AMERICAN ART ASSOCIATION ✔ INC.

MADISON AVENUE 56TH TO 57TH STREET

NEW YORK CITY

1929

[SEE NO. 498]

"My dear Doctor, you ought to have been here at the fight. I said to your sister that together you and I could whip the world I believed!

"Now go at Once this very day to Chatto & Windus ... and ask for several copies of Whistler's pamphlet and you are not to give them away! but to make everybody else get them also at Chatto's ... You remember that I shoved Seymour Haden on ten years, well I rather fancy this will let old Ruskin down to the end of his Almanack with a run!"

WALT WHITMAN, A REMARKABLE COLLECTION OF
FIRST EDITIONS AND AUTOGRAPH MATERIAL
Numbers 496 to 612, Inclusive

496. WHITMAN (WALT). A Collection of Periodicals containing material by Walt Whitman, as below described. Together, 8 vols., 8vo, original printed wrappers. In half morocco slip-case, inner cloth wrapper.　　　　　　　　　　　　　　　New York, 1841–1870

35

FINE COLLECTION OF SCARCE MAGAZINES. The first five articles are in "The United States Magazine and Democratic Review," and the last three in "The American Review," "The Democratic Review," and "The Galaxy," respectively.

　　Death in the School-Room.　August, 1841; Wild Frank's Return.　November, 1841;
　　Bervance; or, Father & Son.　December, 1841; The Tomb Blossoms.　January, 1842;
　　The Child Ghost; a Story of the Last Loyalist.　May, 1842;
　　The Death of Wind-Foot.　June, 1845; A Dialogue.　November, 1845
　　A Warble for Lilac-Time.　May, 1870.

Of the above only the first and last mentioned were issued in the "Collected Works," so the remaining are obtainable in no other form.

497. [WHITMAN (WALT).] Voices from the Press: A Collection of Sketches, Essays and Poems, By Practical Printers, Edited by James J. Brenton. 8vo, original cloth sides, new back.　　　　　　　　　　　　　　　　　　　　　New York, 1850

5

This volume contains "The Tomb Blossoms," by Whitman on pp. 27 to 33. This is Whitman's first appearance in any book. The story had previously been published in the United States Magazine, January, 1842.

THE FIRST, SECOND, AND THIRD ISSUES OF "LEAVES OF GRASS"
Numbers 498 to 500, Inclusive

498. WHITMAN (WALT). Leaves of Grass. *With portrait frontispiece on plain paper.* 4to, ORIGINAL GREEN CLOTH, blind stamped floral sprays on covers, with gilt rustic lettered title, and triple gilt line borders on both front and back covers, gilt lettering and gilt conventional floral designs on back-strip, marbled end-papers, gilt edges. In green morocco slip-case.　　　　　　　　　　　　　　　Brooklyn, New York, 1855

3,450

SUPERB COPY OF THE RARE FIRST ISSUE OF THE FIRST EDITION. This is the issue most sought after by collectors, for it is the veritable FIRST STATE. Later issues lacked the gilt lines on the covers, had plain end-papers and plain edges, and the portrait was on India paper. They also had eight pages of reviews at the end. Contains Whitman's name in the copyright notice on the verso of the title-page, the misprint "abode" for "adobe" on page 23, thus including all the points of early issue.

[REPRODUCED ON OPPOSITE PAGE]

499. WHITMAN (WALT). Leaves of Grass. *With portrait on plain paper.* 4to, original green cloth, blind stamped floral sprays on covers, with rustic gilt lettering on front cover. In quarter green morocco folder.　　　　　　　　　　　Brooklyn, New York, 1855

375

FIRST EDITION, SECOND ISSUE. This copy has not the gilt bands on covers and gilt edges most the marbled end-papers of the first issue, but it bears all the other points of first issue. The portrait is on plain paper; it contains the error of "abode" for "adobe" on page 24; and it does not contain the eight leaves of reviews which Whitman inserted in all copies remaining unsold after the book had been sent out for review. AN UNUSUALLY FINE CLEAN COPY.

500. WHITMAN (WALT). Leaves of Grass. *With portrait on India paper.* 4to, original green cloth, with blind stamped floral sprays on covers, and rustic gilt lettering on front cover. In quarter green morocco folding-case. Brooklyn, New York, 1855 *750⁻*

FINE COPY OF THE FIRST EDITION, THIRD ISSUE. With the six leaves of Press Notices bound in the front of Vol.

Tipped in Vol. is an Autograph Letter Signed,—"*Walt Whitman.*" One page, square 12mo, Camden, December 27, 1873. To Messrs. Trubner & Company. This interesting letter concerns the royalties on the English Edition of "Leaves of Grass." It reads,—

"Please make out acct. of sales of my books, Leaves of Grass &c. for the closing year & remit me amount due, by mail here, by draft payable to my order."

501. WHITMAN (WALT). A Series of 9 Autograph Letters and one Telegram By Walt Whitman, and three pages of notes from the District Attorney's Office, as described below. Accompanied by a portrait of Whitman and one of James R. Osgood. The letters are mounted on 4to sheets, and the whole is bound in full green levant morocco, with inner gilt morocco borders, doublures and fly-leaves of white moire silk, gilt top; Also, Leaves of Grass. Third Edition [*sic*]. Boston, 1881–82. 12mo, original cloth. Together, 2 vols. *1,100⁻*

THIS REMARKABLE SERIES OF LETTERS CONCERNS THE SUPPRESSION OF "LEAVES OF GRASS." by District-Attorney Oliver Stevens, of Boston. When this work was first issued in Boston, complaint was made to the District Attorney by the Society for the Suppression of Vice. It is said that a certain woman whose name is unknown made out the complaint for the District Attorney, and this is the woman to whom Whitman refers in the following correspondence as the "vestal virgin."

This collection comprises,—

Autograph Notes of the District Attorney's Office. 3pp. 12mo. These notes are written in a feminine hand, evidently that of the "vestal virgin." They were sent to Walt Whitman, and they constitute a list of the passages to be expurgated from "Leaves of Grass."

Leaves of Grass. As described above. This edition was issued marked "Third Edition" on the title-page. The error was immediately discovered and only a few copies were sold before the change was made. The present copy is one of those few suppressed copies. It was sent to Whitman by the District Attorney shortly after the list of notes of passages objected to. It contains numerous marked passages, showing the lines that the District Attorney wanted omitted. Four of the passages are marked in blue pencil with a "W" by Walt Whitman, and these are the passages that he was willing to take out. The District Attorney threatened to bring suit against the Publishers to prevent the book's being sent through the mails. The outcome of the matter was that the book was withdrawn, and Whitman obtained the plates from the publisher.

Autograph Letter Signed,—"*Walt Whitman.*" One page 12mo, Camden, May 20, 1881. To Mr. Osgood.

INTERESTING LETTER arranging for the publication of the Boston edition of "Leaves of Grass." It reads in part,—"*I am fixing up the copy, which I will send on to you, in a few days . . . I am sole owner of the copyright.*"

Autograph Letter Signed,—"*Walt Whitman.*" 2pp. 8vo, Camden, May 29, 1881. To Mr. Osgood.

In this letter, Whitman discusses the details of publishing his work.

Autograph Letter Signed,—"*Walt Whitman.*" One page 8vo, Camden, June 1, 1881. To Mr. Osgood.

This letter states Whitman's terms, and the royalties that he expected from his book.

Autograph Letter Signed,—"*Walt Whitman.*" One page 8vo, Camden, March 7, 1882. To Mr. Osgood.

IMPORTANT LETTER concerning the suppression of "Leaves of Grass." It reads in part,— "*I am not afraid of the District Attorney's threat . . . under the circumstances i am willing to make a revision & cancellation in the pages alluded to—wouldn't be more than half a dozen anyhow.*" Whitman had not yet seen the long list of passages to which the District Attorney objected.

Autograph Letter Signed,—"*Walt Whitman.*" One page, 12mo, Camden, March 19, 1882. To Mr. Osgood.

In this letter Whitman requests further news of the case.

Autograph Letter Signed,—"*Walt Whitman.*" 3pp. 8vo, Camden, March 21, 1882. To Osgood and Company.

LONG AND INTERESTING LETTER about the suppression of "Leaves of Grass," and the publication of Dr. Bucke's Life of him. Whitman urges the publishers to accept Dr. Bucke's work, and to publish it in the same format and under the same terms as they had published "Leaves of Grass." The book was later refused, and appeared in 1883 in Philadelphia. Of the trouble with the District Attorney, Whitman writes, in part.—"*Hoping you are not alarmed at the District Attorney episode . . . I have about got into shape a volume comprising all my prose writings*

[*Continued*

Camden New Jersey
April 12 '82

Dear Sirs

Yours of 10th just
rec'd — If you desire to
cease to be the Publishers
of _Leaves of Grass_ unless I
make the excisions required
by the District Attorney —
if this is your settled decision —
I see indeed no other way
than "some reasonable ar-
rangement for turning the
plates over" to me —
— What is the am't of
royalty due me, according to
contract, from the sales altogether? & what is your
valuation of the plates?

Walt Whitman

[SEE NO. 501]

146

to be called (probably) *Specimen Days and Thoughts.* [Note at bottom of page]: *It at least will not be liable to any District Att'y episodes.*"

Autograph Letter Signed,—"*Walt Whitman.*" 2pp. 8vo, Camden, March 23, 1882. To Osgood and Company.

SUPERB LETTER REJECTING THE DISTRICT ATTORNEY'S LIST OF CORRECTIONS. It reads in part,—"*Yours of 21st rec'd, with the curious list, I suppose of course from the District Attorney's Office, of 'suggestions' lines and pages and pieces, &c. to be 'expunged.' The list whole & several is rejected by me & will not be thought of under any circumstances.*" Whitman then proposes to change certain passages, and to proceed with the publication and sale of the book, and adds,—"*If then any further move is made by the District Attorney and his backers . . . they will only burn their own fingers, & very badly.*"

Autograph Letter Signed,—"*W. W.*" One page 8vo, no place, no date. To Osgood and Company.

In this letter, Whitman suggests to his publisher that they make certain changes in "Leaves of Grass," and publish the book without any comment, so that to the casual reader there will appear no difference, and no undue comment will be made in the Press.

Autograph Letter Signed,—"*Walt Whitman.*" One page 8vo, Camden, April 12, 1882. To Osgood and Company.

FINE LETTER IN WHICH WHITMAN REMAINS STEADFAST IN HIS REFUSAL TO CAPITULATE TO THE DISTRICT ATTORNEY. It reads in part,—"*If you desire to cease to be the publishers of 'Leaves of Grass' unless I make the excisions required by the District Attorney, if this is your settled decision, I see indeed no other way than 'some reasonable arrangement for turning the plates over' to me.*"

Telegram sent by Whitman. Camden, April 5, 1882. To Osgood and Company. Written on telegram blank, as delivered to the recipients.

This telegram gives Whitman's final decision in the matter. It reads,—"*No I cannot consent to leave out the two pieces I am only willing to carry out my letter of March Twenty Third. Walt Whitman.*" [Vide infra.]

The present extraordinary collection was carefully preserved by Osgood and Company, and only dispersed at the sale of Mr. Osgood's Library in 1898. It is rare that the papers and letters of so famous and remarkable a controversy are preserved, complete and in perfect condition, for posterity. It is not too much to say that this is the most desirable Whitman item ever offered at public sale.

[SEE REPRODUCTION ON PRECEDING PAGE]

502. WHITMAN (WALT). Leaves of Grass. *With portrait frontispiece.* Thick 16mo, original green cloth, gilt lettering on front cover, both covers blind stamped, gilt leaves, and gilt lettered title with quotation on back-strip, sprinkled edges. In green morocco slip-case. Brooklyn, New York, 1856

RARE SECOND EDITION. With the quotation from Emerson on the back-strip, reading,—"*I greet you at the beginning of a great career. R. W. Emerson.*" With the leaf of Fowler and Wells' advertisements at the back. AN UNUSUALLY FINE AND WELL PRESERVED COPY.

503. WHITMAN (WALT). Leaves of Grass. *With engraved portrait frontispiece, with buff tinted background on plain paper.* 12mo, original orange cloth, heavily embossed. Boston: Thayer and Eldridge, 1860-61

GENUINE FIRST ISSUE OF THIS DATE, with the blind stamped butterfly on the back-strip, and the imprint of the printers on the verso of the title-page, beneath Walt Whitman's notice of copyright.

504. WHITMAN (WALT). Leaves of Grass. *With portrait frontispiece.* Thick 12mo, original wrappers bound in as fly-leaves, full green levant morocco (back faded). Boston: Thayer and Eldridge, 1860-61

THIRD EDITION. A few copies of this edition were sent to England, and bound in purple pebbled cloth. This is evidently one of those copies for it has the purple wrappers bound in as fly-leaves.

505. WHITMAN (WALT). Leaves of Grass. *With portrait frontispiece with buff tinted background.* 8vo, original grained cloth heavily embossed. Boston, 1860-61

Spurious Edition, without the imprint of the printers on the verso of the title-page.

506. WHITMAN (WALT). Leaves of Grass. 12mo, half morocco.   New York, 1867

25 FOURTH EDITION. Autograph presentation copy from R. Maurice Bucke to Mr. Forman. On the fly-leaf Mr. Forman has written: "Forty years ago, when Maurice Bucke gave me this book he & I were both outside students of Walt Whitman; and the collation of this edition with that of 1855 was one of his earliest bits of Whitman work. Most of the variations are in the writing of his brother Julius, who noted them under his instructions."
The variations referred to are on interleaves in the first part of the book. The H. B. Forman copy.

507. WHITMAN (WALT). Leaves of Grass. 12mo, original half morocco, sprinkled edges.
New York, 1867

7 50 FOURTH EDITION, including Drum Taps, and Songs before Parting.

508. WHITMAN (WALT). Leaves of Grass. 12mo, full green levant morocco, with gilt designs on covers. In full green morocco slip-case.   Washington, 1872

15 FINE EDITION. Includes, Passage to India, and After all not to Create only.

509. WHITMAN (WALT). Leaves of Grass. *With 2 portraits.* 8vo, half cream colored calf.
Camden, 1876

27 50 AUTHOR'S EDITION. This copy does not bear Whitman's signature on the title-page, as it was one of those which he kept for those who ordered directly from him. It was found in the poet's room when he died as is certified by the following autograph inscription of Thomas H. Harned, one of Whitman's literary executors,—"*To Dr. Slicer with regards of Thomas B. Harned. One of Walt Whitman's Literary Executors. This copy was found in the Author's room when he died.*"

510. WHITMAN (WALT). Leaves of Grass. *With 2 portraits.* 8vo, half cream colored calf (slightly rubbed; backbone torn at top).   Camden, 1876

35 AUTHOR'S EDITION, with the Autograph of Walt Whitman on the title-page.

511. WHITMAN (WALT). Leaves of Grass. *With 2 portraits.* 8vo, half cream colored calf (corners rubbed).   Camden, 1876

45 AUTHOR'S EDITION, WITH THE AUTOGRAPH SIGNATURE OF WALT WHITMAN ON THE TITLE-PAGE. Contains the intercalations printed in the text.
PRESENTATION COPY from Horace Traubel, with inscription on fly-leaf. Pasted inside the front cover is a portion of a sheet of paper, with the following autograph inscription by Whitman,—"*Leaves of Grass 1876 Edition. Autograph bound in Italian boards, perfect copy $5.*"

512. WHITMAN (WALT). Leaves of Grass. By Walt Whitman. Preface to the Original Edition, 1855. 12mo, original wrappers, uncut. In cloth wrappers.   London, 1881

27 50 FIRST SEPARATE EDITION OF THE PREFACE.

513. WHITMAN (WALT). Leaves of Grass. 12mo, brown cloth covers, with blue cloth back.
Boston: Osgood & Co., 1881–2

35 TRIAL COPY, printed on thicker paper than ordinary copies, with a special binding. Laid in is a check, signed by Whitman, April 26, 1884.

514. WHITMAN (WALT). Leaves of Grass. Third Edition [*sic*]. *With 2 portraits.* 12mo, original cloth.   Boston: Osgood & Co., 1881–2

80 FIRST ISSUE OF THE SUPPRESSED EDITION. Erroneously marked Third Edition on the title-page. Very few copies were so issued.

515. WHITMAN (WALT). Leaves of Grass. 12mo, original cloth.
Boston: Osgood & Co., 1881–2

110 SUPPRESSED EDITION. Inserted is an A. L. S. from Whitman [to David Bogue] dated Dec. 14, 1881: "*I wish you would have a little circular printed (or some special paragraph inserted in your regular list, & marked) announcing the new Osgood 1882 edition of Leaves of Grass with your place as the London agency & depository,—and send it to the names on the accompanying list—all special friends of the book.*"
There is also inserted the circular letter prepared by Bogue in compliance with Whitman's request.

148

516. WHITMAN (WALT). Leaves of Grass. *With 2 portraits.* 12mo, original cloth. 37⁵⁰

Boston: Osgood & Co., 1881–2

SUPPRESSED EDITION.

517. WHITMAN (WALT). Leaves of Grass. Philadelphia: Rees Welch, 1882; The Same. 20

Philadelphia: David McKay, 1882; The Same. Philadelphia, 1883; The Same. London, 1881. Second English Edition; The Same. Boston, 1900; The Same. *With illustrations.* Philadelphia, 1900. 2 copies. Together, 7 vols., 8vo, and 12mo, cloth.

Various places, 1881-1900

FINE COLLECTION of varying editions of "Leaves of Grass."

WITH TWO AUTOGRAPH LETTERS

518. WHITMAN (WALT). Leaves of Grass. The Poems of Walt Whitman [selected]. With 110

Introduction by Ernest Rhys. *Portrait.* 16mo, cloth, uncut, paper label.

London: Walter Scott, 1886

Laid in are TWO AUTOGRAPH LETTERS FROM WALT WHITMAN to ERNEST RHYS, WITH ORIGINAL ADDRESSED ENVELOPES, relating to the volumes Rhys was editing for the English trade; also, an A. L. S. and a post card from Rhys.

519. WHITMAN (WALT). Leaves of Grass with Sands at Seventy & A Backward Glance o'er 450

Travel'd Roads. *With numerous portraits.* 12mo, limp leather, with flap and inner pocket for papers, gilt edges. [Philadelphia, 1889]

FINE COPY OF THIS SPECIAL EDITION, limited to 300 copies. SCARCE, with the autograph of Walt Whitman on the title-page.

PRESENTATION COPY FROM THE AUTHOR TO HIS SISTER, with the autograph inscription on the fly-leaf, reading,—"*To My Sister Lou, from the author on his finishing his 70th year. May 31, 1891.*"

520. WHITMAN (WALT). Leaves of Grass. Including Sands at Seventy. . . . 1st Annex, 210

Good Bye My Fancy . . . 2d Annex, A Backward Glance O'er Travel'd Roads, and Portrait from Life. 8vo, original gray wrappers, with yellow paper label, entirely uncut. Philadelphia: David McKay, 1891–2

PRESENTATION COPY FROM TRAUBEL, with autograph inscription on fly-leaf, reading,—"*To H. Buxton Forman. Jan 7, 1892, sent by Walt Whitman from his sick bed. H. T. Camden.*" Walt Whitman was at this time very sick, and he had a few copies of this work bound up for presentation to his friends. They were larger than the ordinary copies, and entirely uncut, with yellow paper labels. Wells and Goldsmith in their Bibliography of Walt Whitman describe the wrappers as rough brown, but the present copy has gray wrappers.

Laid in is a Post Card in the Autograph of Whitman. Camden, September 27, 1891. To Mr. Forman. This interesting card concerns the publication of his books, and mentions his failing health. Also laid in is an Autograph Post Card from Horace Traubel. Camden, January 8, 1891. It reads in part,—"*Whitman in fatal condition. We watch him day by day with grave concern.*" The H. Buxton Forman copy, with bookplate.

IN ORIGINAL PRINTED WRAPPERS

521. WHITMAN (WALT). Leaves of Grass Imprints. American and European criticisms on 160

Leaves of Grass. 16mo, ORIGINAL PRINTED WRAPPERS (backbone slightly chipped). In quarter green morocco slip-case. Boston: Thayer and Eldridge, 1860

VERY RARE on account of its size and frail make-up. FINE CLEAN COPY, in the original wrappers as issued. This was a reprint of the criticisms of "Leaves of Grass" published in the Press. On the verso of the title-page, Emerson's letter to Whitman is printed in full.

[REPRODUCED ON OPPOSITE PAGE]

522. WHITMAN (WALT). Drum Taps. 12mo, original brown cloth, sprinkled edges. 130

New York, 1865

FIRST ISSUE OF THE FIRST EDITION, without the Sequel to Drum Taps. When Lincoln died, Whitman held up this issue and added the Sequel with a separate title-page and pagination. Only a few copies of the present first issue were published. VERY RARE.

Leaves of Grass

IMPRINTS.

American and European Criticisms

ON

"LEAVES OF GRASS."

BOSTON:
THAYER AND ELDRIDGE.
1860.

[SEE NO. 521]

523. WHITMAN (WALT). Drum Taps. 12mo, original cloth, sprinkled edges.

New York, 1865 *10*

FIRST EDITION. Second issue, with the sequel to Drum-Taps, and separate title.

524. WHITMAN (WALT). [O'CONNOR (W. D.).] The Good Gray Poet. A Vindication. *With portrait.* 8vo, original wrappers bound in, full blue levant morocco, gilt top, uncut. *25*

New York, 1866

FIRST EDITION OF THIS RARE PAMPHLET. O'Connor championed Whitman when he was dismissed from the Department of the Interior, for having written an indecent book, "Leaves of Grass."

525. [WHITMAN (WALT).] Notes on Walt Whitman, As Poet and Person. By John Burroughs. 12mo, cloth. New York, 1867 *35*

FIRST EDITION. AUTOGRAPH PRESENTATION COPY from the author with autograph inscription on the fly-leaf, reading *"James T. Fields. Regards of John Burroughs. June 13, 1867."*

526. WHITMAN (WALT). Autograph Letter Signed,—"*Walt Whitman,*" one page, 4to, Washington, August 31, 1867. To John Binckley. *30*

An application for a leave of absence. Underneath Whitman's letter, appears a note by Binckley, Acting Attorney General, granting the request. Very few items are extant relating to Whitman's days in the Attorney General's Office.

527. WHITMAN (WALT). Poems by Walt Whitman. Selected and Edited by William Michael Rossetti. *With portrait.* 12mo, original blue cloth. London, 1868 *17 50*

FIRST ENGLISH EDITION. The fine critical review of Whitman by the learned editor, occupying 64pp. of this volume, has never been reprinted.

528. WHITMAN (WALT). CARPENTER (GEORGE). Walt Whitman. New York, 1909; IRWIN (M. M.). Whitman: The Poet-Liberator of Woman. New York, 1905; BUCHANAN (ROBERT). David Gray, and Other Essays. London, 1868; STEVENSON (R. L.). The Essay on Walt Whitman. *Portrait.* [East Aurora] 1900; ELLIOT (C. N.). Walt Whitman as Man, Poet and Friend. Boston, 1915; and others similar. Together, 7 vols., 8vo, and 12mo, cloth and limp leather. Various places, 1868–1915 *5*

529. WHITMAN (WALT). Autograph Letter Signed,—"*Walt Whitman,*" 4pp., small 4to, Washington, September 28, 1869. To William O'Connor. With Autograph Addressed Envelope. Together, 2 pieces. *200*

FINE LETTER written to O'Connor, who was Whitman's first defender, and the author of the celebrated "Good Gray Poet." It is his explanation of a financial matter in which Whitman had been sued.

THE MANUSCRIPT OF "AFTER ALL NOT TO CREATE ONLY"

530. WHITMAN (WALT). ORIGINAL AUTOGRAPH MANUSCRIPT of "After All Not To Create Only." Written in ink on one side of 28 4to sheets, consisting of about 3,500 words. Bound in 4to volume, full Spanish calf, gilt top. *3,300*

SPLENDID MANUSCRIPT, containing numerous corrections and interlineations, revealing the care with which Whitman polished his poetry, and his power of self-criticism. Many lines, he has re-written and tipped down over the earlier version so that a comparison may be made between them.

On the first page is the following note regarding the history of the manuscript,—"*Afterwards called 'Song of the Exposition.' This Ms. given me by Walt Whitman January 2, 1885. W. S. Kennedy. Originally written & recited for the 40th Annual Exhibition of the American Institute, New York, noon, September 7th, 1871.*"

Another note says,—"*This Ms. was used in setting Roberts Bros. issue of the 'poem.'*"

531. WHITMAN (WALT). After all, Not to Create only. [Recited by Walt Whitman, on invitation of Directors American Institute, on Opening of their 40th Annual Exhibition, New York, noon, September 7, 1871.] Folio, stitched. In quarter green morocco slip-case, with inner cloth wrappers. [Washington: Pearson, 1871]

210

RARE FIRST ISSUE OF THE FIRST EDITION. PRINTED IN BROADSIDE FORM. According to the Bibliography of Walt Whitman by Wells and Goldsmith, this issue consisted of only a few copies. SIGNED AT THE END,—"*Walt Whitman.*" This edition was printed for him at the expense of the Institute, and the present copy was used by the poet while reciting it. It is printed in sermon style, large type, and was presented by Whitman to one of the Directors, and autographed for him on the spot.
THIS IS APPARENTLY THE ONLY COPY KNOWN TO BEAR THE AUTOGRAPH OF WHITMAN.

[REPRODUCED ON FOLLOWING PAGE]

532. WHITMAN (WALT). After all, Not to Create only. [Recited by Walt Whitman, in invitation of Directors American Institute, on Opening of their 40th Annual Exhibition, New York, noon, September 7, 1871.] Small folio, full green levant morocco, gilt top, each sheet tipped to stub. [Washington: Pearson, 1871]

110

RARE FIRST ISSUE OF THE FIRST EDITION. Accompanied by portrait of Whitman bound in as frontispiece. See note to preceding number.

533. WHITMAN (WALT). After all, Not to Create only. [Recited by Walt Whitman, in invitation of Directors American Institute, on Opening of their 40th Annual Exhibition, New York, noon, September 7, 1871.] Small folio, in sheets, printed on one side only. [Washington: Pearson, 1871]

145

RARE FIRST ISSUE OF THE FIRST EDITION. Vide infra. Probably not more than five copies of the present work are in existence. The three copies in the present collection, each differing in form, are among the rarest of Whitman items extant.

534. WHITMAN (WALT). After All, Not to Create Only. 12mo, original maroon limp cloth.
Boston, 1871

5

FIRST EDITION, SECOND ISSUE.

535. WHITMAN (WALT). After all, Not to Create Only. 12mo, original limp tan colored cloth. Boston, 1871

7 50

FIRST EDITION, SECOND ISSUE. The H. Buxton Forman copy.

536. WHITMAN (WALT). After All, Not To Create Only. 12mo, original green cloth, gilt top. Boston, 1871

5

FIRST EDITION, SECOND ISSUE. Of the second issue some copies were bound in cloth boards of various colors, and others in limp cloth of the same colors. Those in cloth are the more difficult to procure.

537. WHITMAN (WALT). Proof Issue of "Passage to India." Two large folio sheets containing all of the poem. [1871]

65

Those two sheets contain 15 stanzas, the same as were printed in the book, but the type is much larger, and this appears to have been a special proof, probably abandoned for the smaller type.

538. [WHITMAN (WALT).] Passage to India. Narrow 12mo, original green printed wrappers, uncut (slightly chipped). In quarter green morocco slip-case.
Washington, D. C., 1871

40

FIRST EDITION. With Leaves of Grass written in small type at head of title. Whitman's name does not appear on the title-page, but on the verso in the copyright notice. First issue with the title on front and advertisements on back wrappers. RARE.

152

Savagely struggled for, for life or death—fought over long,
'Mid cannon's thunder-crash, and many a curse, and groan and
      yell—and rifle-volleys cracking sharp,
And moving masses, as wild demons surging—and lives as noth-
      ing risk'd,
For thy mere remnant, grimed with dirt and smoke, and sopp'd
      in blood;
For sake of that, my beauty—and that thou might'st dally, as
      now, secure up there,
Many a good man have I seen go under.

14.

Now here, and these, and hence, in peace, all thine, O Flag!
And here, and hence, for thee, O universal Muse! and thou for
      them!
And here and hence, O Union, all the work and workmen thine!
The poets, women, sailors, soldiers, farmers, miners, students thine!
None separate from Thee—henceforth one only, we and Thou;
(For the blood of the children—what is it only the blood Mater-
      nal?
And lives and works—what are they all at last except the roads
      to Faith and Death?)

While we rehearse our measureless wealth, it is for thee, dear
      Mother!
We own it all and several to-day indissoluble in Thee;
—Think not our chant, our show, merely for products gross, or
      lucre—it is for Thee, the Soul, electric, spiritual!
Our farms, inventions, crops, we own in Thee! Cities and States
      in Thee!
Our freedom all in Thee! our very lives in Thee!

Walt Whitman.

[SEE NO. 531]

539. WHITMAN (WALT). Two Autograph Manuscripts, written in pencil, on two 12mo sheets, hinged on mounts.

20

These manuscripts are introductory notes to "Democratic Vistas" and "Memoranda for the War."

540. [WHITMAN (WALT).] Democratic Vistas. Memoranda. Narrow 8vo, original light green wrappers, entirely uncut (backbone slightly chipped). In quarter green morocco slip-case with inner cloth wrappers. Washington, D. C., 1871

180

FIRST EDITION. PRESENTATION COPY, with autograph inscription on the fly-leaf, reading,— "Mrs. Botta from the author."

541. WHITMAN (WALT). As a Strong Bird on Pinions Free, and Other Poems. Narrow 8vo, original green cloth. Washington, D. C., 1872

7 50

FIRST EDITION. FINE COPY. On the verso of the title-page Whitman's name appears in the copyright notice, below which is the name of the printer. With facsimile autograph of Whitman at the end of poem "Souvenirs of Democracy," and "Leaves of Grass" printed in small type at the head of title.

542. WHITMAN (WALT). Autograph Letter Signed,—"Walt," 2pp., 4to, no place, [April 1, 1873]. To his mother.

110

FINE PERSONAL LETTER. From the collection of his friend Dr. Bucke, as are the following three items, with the conjectured dates written on top of the letters by him. It reads in part,— "I have made a sort of commencement of my work today....I see in the papers this morning an awful shipwreck . . . a first-class steamship from England went down almost instantly, 700 people lost, largely women and children."

543. WHITMAN (WALT). Autograph Letter Signed,—"Walt," 2pp., 4to, no place, [April 4, 1873]. To his mother.

110

In this intimate letter, one obtains a better glimpse of the character of Walt Whitman than in his more serious and studied missives to his literary friends. It reads in part,—"At present my great hope is to get well, to get so I can walk & have some use of my limbs. I can write pretty well and my mind is clear, but I can not walk a block."

544. WHITMAN (WALT). Autograph Letter Signed,—"Walt," 2pp., 4to, no place, April 19, [1873]. To his mother.

120

In this letter, Whitman tells of the improvement of his health due to the treatment of his physician Dr. Drinkard.

545. WHITMAN (WALT). Autograph Letter Signed,—"Walt," 2pp., 4to, no place, May 11, [1873]. To his mother.

230

FINE PERSONAL LETTER, mentioning his friend Peter Doyle. It reads in part,—"Yesterday . . . I was out a good deal, walked some, a couple of blocks for the first time. Peter Doyle convoyed me. . . . You will see a piece in the paper about the Beecher and Tilton scandal, it is very coarse. I think Beecher a great humbug." Few of these letters to his mother are to be found, certainly none better than the present magnificent one.

PRESENTATION COPY OF A RARE ITEM

546. WHITMAN (WALT). Memoranda During The War. With 2 portraits. 12mo, original red-brown cloth, green end-papers, gilt edges.

Author's Publication: Camden, New Jersey, 1875–'76

675

RARE FIRST EDITION. Privately printed for presentation purposes. One of the few copies with leaf headed "Remembrance Copy," with space for inscription Inscribed,—"J. H. Johnston, his friend the Author." With the page of advertisements at the back. THIS IS PERHAPS THE SCARCEST OF ALL OF WHITMAN'S WORKS, as probably not more than 100 copies were issued.

547. WHITMAN (WALT). Two Rivulets Including Democratic Vistas, Centennial Songs, and Passage to India. 12mo, original half cream colored calf (rubbed).   Camden, 1876

> AUTHOR'S EDITION. Tipped on to stub in the front of Vol. is a portrait of Whitman, signed,—"*Walt Whitman born May 31, 1819.*" With autograph inscription on the fly-leaf, reading,—"*F. H. Babbitt from the author.*"

110

548. WHITMAN (WALT). Autograph Manuscript Signed,—"*Walt Whitman,*" one page, small 4to, Camden, March 16, 1880. Written in pencil.

> Manuscript of the poem entitled, "The Prairie States." It was published in March, 1880, on behalf of the Irish Famine Fund.

90

AN IMPORTANT WHITMAN MANUSCRIPT

549. WHITMAN (WALT). Original Autograph Manuscript of Portions of "Specimen Days and Collect." 14pp., 8vo, and small 4to. Accompanied by Proof Sheets with Autograph Corrections, and Letters to Whitman. With portrait photograph. Together, 5 pieces, tipped to 4to sheets, half brown morocco, gilt top. In cloth slip-case.

275

> This characteristic manuscript of Whitman is written on scraps of paper pasted together and on the backs of letters. What was apparently intended for a wrapper, bears the title, "*Specimen Days & Collect,*" in Whitman's Autograph. The other portions of the manuscript concern the hospitals of the Northern Army during the Civil War, in which Whitman served as nurse. The proof sheets bear many autograph corrections by Whitman. On the versos of the manuscripts, are several letters written to Whitman, requesting his autograph, or asking his opinions on literary matters. Accompanying this collection is an A. L. S. from William E. Vandermark, one of the soldiers for whom Whitman had cared. One page, 4to, Ulster County, N. Y. July 31, 1863. To Walt Whitman.

PRESENTED TO THE AUTHOR'S SISTER

550. WHITMAN (WALT). Specimen Days & Collect. *With 2 portraits.* 8vo, original yellow cloth, gilt top, uncut.   Philadelphia: Rees Welch & Co., 1882–83

410

> FIRST ISSUE OF THE FIRST EDITION, with the imprint of Welch & Co. PRESENTATION COPY, with autograph inscription on the fly-leaf, reading,—"*Mrs: Louisa O. Whitman from the author her brother Walt. October 5, 1882.*" One of a few copies of 8vo size bound up for presentation purposes.

551. WHITMAN (WALT). Specimen Days & Collect. 12mo, original cloth.
Philadelphia: Rees Welch & Co., 1882–83

20   FIRST ISSUE OF THE FIRST EDITION.

552. WHITMAN (WALT). Specimen Days & Collect. 12mo, full red levant morocco, gilt edges, BY TOUT. Original covers bound in.
Philadelphia: David McKay, 1882–'83

250

     With a tinted phototype portrait inserted, AUTOGRAPHED IN BLUE PENCIL BY WHITMAN. On pp. 315–316 Whitman has deleted "Two Letters" in indelible pencil, and had originally torn from this volume pp. 317 to the end. These have been neatly replaced. On p. 339 he had written "out/all to 374."
     THIS IS THE COPY PREPARED BY WALT WHITMAN AND SENT TO ERNEST RHYS FOR PUBLICATION IN ENGLAND. The addressed portion of the wrapper in which the volume was sent to Mr. Rhys, with Whitman's signature thereon, has been mounted and inserted.
     A 2pp. note by Mr. Forman relating to this volume and its association interest appears on one of the fly-leaves. The H. Buxton Forman copy, with bookplate.

553. WHITMAN (WALT). Specimen Days & Collect. *With portrait frontispiece.* 8vo, original cloth.
Glasgow, 1883

10   FIRST ENGLISH EDITION. FIRST ISSUE, with the name of the publishers gilt lettered on the back-strip. The H. Buxton Forman copy, with bookplate.

554. WHITMAN (WALT). Autograph Letter Signed. 3pp., 8vo, Germantown, August 28, 1883. To J. H. Johnston.

100

     "I have been out here . . . all this month at a very secluded place, good quarters, very quiet, on a visit to an old Quaker friend—his large family are all away at Newport—he is absent all day down town at business & I have the whole premises, house, horse and carriage when I want, large garden, good grub, library, etc., to myself," etc.

555. WHITMAN (WALT). Walt Whitman the Man. By Thomas Donaldson. *Illustrations.* New York, 1896; Diary Notes of A Visit to Walt Whitman. *Illustrations.* London, 1898; Liberty in Literature. By Robert Ingersoll. New York [1890]; Walt Whitman. By Dr. R. M. Bucke. *Illustrations.* Philadelphia, 1883; Walt Whitman's Poetry. By Edmond Holmes. London, 1902. A Life of Walt Whitman. *Illustrations.* London, 1905. Together, 6 vols., 8vo, cloth.
Various places, 1883–1905

10

556. WHITMAN (WALT). The Round Table Series. 6 parts in one vol., 8vo, half red morocco, gilt top, uncut.
Edinburgh, 1884

12 50

     The essay entitled Walt Whitman, Poet and Democrat is Part 4 of the series. It was written by John Robertson. LIMITED TO 100 NUMBERED COPIES.

557. WHITMAN (WALT). RHYS (ERNEST). Autograph Letter Signed,—"*Ernest Rhys,*" 2pp., 4to, London, April 28, 1887. To Walt Whitman.

10   INTERESTING LETTER, mentioning among others, Oscar Wilde, Herbert Gilchrist, Richard Jefferies, and others.

558. WHITMAN (WALT). Autograph Letter Signed,—"*Walt Whitman,*" one page, 4to, Camden, November 19, 1887. With Autograph Addressed Envelope. Together, 2 pieces

70

     UNUSUALLY FINE LETTER, AND IN SPLENDID CONDITION which is rare for a Whitman item It reads in part,—"*Everything is going on here much the same . . . and I sit here in the big chai by the window, (slowly waning I suppose). H. Gilchrist is back in London. . . . I am expectin Ernest Rhys here soon. Morse the sculptor is still here. Mr. Eakins, the portrait painter of Phila. is going to have a whack at me next week.*"

559. WHITMAN (WALT). November Boughs. Philadelphia, 1888; Leaves of Grass. Phila- *750*
delphia, 1891–2; Specimen Days in America. London, 1887; Lafayette in Brooklyn.
New York, 1904. Together, 4 vols., 8vo, and 12mo, cloth and boards.
Various places, 1887–1904

560. WHITMAN (WALT). Autobiographia: or, The Story of a Life. *Frontispiece.* New York, *5–*
1892; Democratic Vistas and Other Papers. London, 1888; Selected Poems. *Por-*
trait. New York, 1892; Gems from Walt Whitman. Philadelphia, 1889; Specimen
Days in America. London, 1887; Complete Prose Works. Philadelphia, 1892.
Together, 6 vols., 8vo, and 12mo, cloth. Various places, 1887–1892

561. WHITMAN (WALT). November Boughs. *With portrait.* Small 4to, limp maroon cloth,
entirely uncut. Philadelphia: David McKay, 1888
LARGE PAPER COPY OF THE FIRST EDITION. Only a few copies were issued in the present *400–*
format and binding for presentation purposes. With an autograph inscription on the fly-leaf,
reading,—"*Mrs. Louisa Whitman from her brother Walt, the author, with love. Oct: 1888.*"

LARGE PAPER—PRESENTATION COPY

562. WHITMAN (WALT). November Boughs. *With portrait.* Small 4to, limp maroon cloth,
entirely uncut. Philadelphia: David McKay, 1888 *460–*
PRESENTATION COPY OF THE LARGE PAPER ISSUE OF THE FIRST EDITION. Only a few copies
were issued in this format. With autograph inscription on the fly-leaf in the autograph of the
author, reading,—"*H. Buxton Forman from the author with affectionate wishes & best respects.*
May 22, 1890." Laid in the front of Vol. is the addressed portion of the wrapper in which the
book was sent to Mr. Forman, with Whitman's autograph.
Accompanying the above is an interesting post card from Whitman to Rhys, which reads in
part,—"*This is the 6th or 7th whack thro' the last fourteen years of my war, paralysis . . . I am still*
imprison'd to room & bed. I am finishing the little 'Nov: Boughs.' Walt Whitman." The H. Buxton Forman copy, with bookplate.

563. WHITMAN (WALT). November Boughs. *With portrait.* 8vo, original red cloth, gilt top.
Philadelphia, 1888 *1750*
FIRST EDITION, with the portrait frontispiece. RARE.

564. WHITMAN (WALT). Original Autograph Manuscript of the Additional Note to 'Poems
and Prose.' One page, oblong 4to. [Also] Proof of the 'Note at End' with Auto- *240–*
graph Corrections. Together, 2 pieces, pasted together.
SUPERB SPECIMEN OF WHITMAN'S PROSE. The additional note, all in his autograph, reads in
part,—
"*Seems to me I may dare to claim a deep native tap-root for the book too, in some sort. I came*
on the stage too late, for personally knowing much of even the lingering Revolutionary worthies, the
men of '76, yet, as a little boy I have been pressed tightly to the breast of Lafayette, (Brooklyn, 1825)
and have talked with old Aaron Burr, and also with those who knew Washington and his surround-
ings and with original Jeffersonians, and more than one very old soldier and sailor.
"*And in my own day and maturity my eyes have seen and heard Lincoln, Grant and Emerson,*
and my hands have been grasped by their hands."

565. WHITMAN (WALT). Complete Poems & Prose of Walt Whitman 1855–1888. Authenticated & Personal Book (handled by W. W.) . . . Portraits from Life . . . Auto- *170–*
graph. Imperial 8vo, marbled boards, half cloth, entirely uncut.
[Philadelphia, 1888]
PRESENTATION COPY FROM THE AUTHOR, with the following inscription in his autograph on
the fly-leaf,—"*H. Buxton Forman from the author with affectionate wishes & best respects, May*
22, 1890." This edition was limited to 600 numbered copies. Laid in the front of Vol. is an
A. L. S. of R. M. Bucke. 2pp. 8vo, London, Ontario, January 20, 1889. To Mr. Forman. This
letter contains an interesting criticism of the present volume. It is accompanied by a printed
transcript of the letter. The H. Buxton Forman copy, with bookplate.

566. [WHITMAN (WALT).] Complete Poems and Prose of Walt Whitman. 1855–1888. Authenticated & Personal Book (handled by W. W.) . . . Portraits from Life . . . Autograph. *With portrait.* Imperial 8vo, boards, half cloth, entirely uncut.

[Philadelphia, 1888]

340—

PRESENTATION COPY FROM THE AUTHOR TO HIS SISTER. With autograph inscription by Whitman on the fly-leaf, reading,—"*Lou Whitman from Walt. The first one given away, or looked at, even by himself, on its return from Publishers.*"

Tipped in the front of Vol. is an Autograph Letter Signed,—"*Walt Whitman.*" Written in pencil on one side of an oblong 8vo sheet. Camden, November 19, 1888. To Mrs. Louisa Whitman. Interesting letter mentioning his work "November Boughs," and adding, anent the present volume,—"*The big book (all my writings collected complete) will be done in about a fortnight. I shall send you one.*"

567. [WHITMAN (WALT).] Autograph Letter Signed,—"*R. M. Bucke,*" 4pp., 12mo, Mildenhall, Suffolk, June 9, 1889. To Walt Whitman. With Autograph Addressed Envelope.

5—

In this letter, Dr. Bucke who was Whitman's first authorized biographer, mentions Gilchrist, Edward Carpenter, and others of Whitman's literary friends.

568. WHITMAN (WALT). Autograph Letter Signed,—"*Walt Whitman,*" one page, 4to, Camden, March 7, 1889. To J. H. Johnston. With Autograph Addressed Envelope. Together, 2 pieces.

32 50

In this letter, Whitman speaks of his failing health. He also mentions Dr. Bucke and his meter invention.

569. WHITMAN (WALT). Camden's Compliments to Walt Whitman, May 31, 1889. Notes, Addresses, Letters, Telegrams. Edited by Horace L. Traubel. *With portrait frontispiece.* 8vo, original red cloth, gilt top, uncut. Philadelphia, 1889

7 50

FIRST EDITION. Presentation copy from Thomas B. Harned, one of Whitman's literary executors, with an inscription in his autograph on the fly-leaf.

570. WHITMAN (WALT). Autograph Corrected Proof Sheets of his article entitled,—"*Backward Glances over a traveled road,*" 7pp., 8vo. [circa 1890]

220—

A RETROSPECT OF "LEAVES OF GRASS," evidently written for a magazine, and containing a number of autograph corrections in the text. The title of the original article read, "My Book and I," which Whitman has here crossed off, and written, in ink, "Backward Glances over a traveled road." It is a philosophical survey, in the light of later years, of his famous "Leaves of Grass." He sums up,—

"*I look upon 'Leaves of Grass' now finished to the end of its opportunities and powers, as my definite carte visite to the coming generation of the New World.*"

571. WHITMAN (WALT). Good-Bye My Fancy. 2d Annex to Leaves of Grass. *With phototype portrait.* Royal 8vo, full red levant morocco, gilt top, uncut, BY TOUT.

Philadelphia: David McKay, 1891

130—

SPECIAL UNCUT COPY OF THE FIRST EDITION. Inserted is the addressed portion of the wrapper in which the volume was sent to Mr. Forman with the autograph of Whitman thereon. The portrait is signed,—"*Walt Whitman (Sculptor's profile, May 1891).*"

On the fly-leaf Mr. Forman has written,—"'*Good Bye My Fancy' was issued in red cloth boards, with much margin cut off. I obtained this uncut copy direct from Walt at the time of publication . . . The inscription under the portrait is written by him; it does not appear in ordinary copies.*" The H. Buxton Forman copy, with bookplate.

572. [WHITMAN (WALT).] Good-Bye My Fancy. 2d Annex to Leaves of Grass. *With portrait.* 8vo, maroon cloth, gilt top, uncut. Philadelphia, 1891

22 50

FIRST EDITION, one of a few copies issued with uncut fore and lower edges.

573. WHITMAN (WALT). Good-Bye My Fancy. 2d Annex to Leaves of Grass. *With portrait.* 8vo, maroon cloth, gilt top. Philadelphia, 1891

FIRST EDITION.

574. WHITMAN (WALT). Good-Bye and Hail Walt Whitman. Edited by Horace L. Traubel. Imperial 8vo, original gray wrappers, uncut. Philadelphia, 1892 *5⁻*
FIRST EDITION, printed throughout on heavy gray paper.

575. WHITMAN (WALT). CLARKE (WILLIAM). Walt Whitman. *Portrait.* London, 1892; TRIGGS (O. L.). Browning and Whitman. London, 1893; PLATT (ISAAC H.). Walt Whitman. *Portrait.* Boston, 1904; KENNEDY (W. S.). Reminiscences of Walt Whitman. Paisley, 1896; SAWYER (R. D.). Walt Whitman The Prophet Poet. Boston [1913]; and others similar. Together, 7 vols., 8vo, and 12mo, cloth and boards. Various places, 1892–1913 *25⁻*

576. WHITMAN (WALT). Walt Whitman: A Study. By John Addington Symonds. *With portraits.* Royal 8vo, cloth, paper label, entirely uncut. London, 1893
Edition limited to 208 numbered copies.

577. WHITMAN (WALT). In re Walt Whitman: Edited by His Literary Executors, Horace L. Traubel, Richard Maurice Bucke, Thomas B. Harned. 8vo, full grayish blue levant *10⁻* morocco, with elaborate gilt floral designs on covers, inner gilt morocco borders, gilt back, gilt edges. In board slip-case, with morocco edging. Philadelphia, 1893
Edition limited to 1000 numbered copies.

578. WHITMAN (WALT). Books about Whitman. TRIMBLE (W. H.). Walt Whitman and Leaves of Grass. London, 1905. First Edition; SYMONDS (JOHN ADDINGTON). Walt *12⁵⁰* Whitman: A Study. *With portrait and illustrations.* London, 1893. First Edition; BURROUGHS (JOHN). Notes on Walt Whitman as Poet and Person. New York, 1867; THOMSON (JAMES). Walt Whitman The Man and the Poet. London, 1910; Another copy; PERRY (BLISS). Walt Whitman: His Life and Work. *Illustrations.* Boston, 1906. First Edition. Together, 6 vols., 8vo, and 12mo, cloth and wrappers. Various places, 1893–1910

579. WHITMAN (WALT). The Wound Dresser. *Portrait.* Boston, 1898. First Edition; Criticism. An Essay. Newark, 1913; CARPENTER (EDWARD). Days with Walt Whit- *12⁵⁰* man. *Portrait.* London, 1906; HARTMAN (SADAKICHI). Conversations with Walt Whitman. New York, 1895. First Edition. In cloth wrappers; HUBBARD (ELBERT). Walt Whitman. New York, 1896. First Edition. In cloth wrappers. Together, 5 vols., 12mo, cloth, boards, and wrappers. Various places, 1895–1913

SUPERBLY EXTRA-ILLUSTRATED

580. WHITMAN (WALT). Walt Whitman The Man. By Thomas Donaldson. *With portrait.* One vol. extended to two vols. 8vo, full green levant morocco, gilt tops, BY PRATT. *175⁻* In green morocco slip-cases. New York, 1896
SUPERB EXTRA-ILLUSTRATED BIOGRAPHY OF WALT WHITMAN, FORMING THE FINEST ASSEM-BLAGE OF PICTORIAL, AUTOGRAPH, AND LITERARY MATTER EVER BROUGHT TOGETHER. Embel-lished with 77 portraits of Whitman, including several private photographs never published, 113 portraits of persons mentioned in the text, 22 views connected with the life of the poet, 124 smaller views, portraits, vignettes, and head and tail-pieces, 25 proof sheets of separate poems as issued by Whitman, and 77 Autograph Letters by well-known literary men. Each item is skilfully inlaid to size.
The twenty-five PROOFS of the Poems inserted in the above described volumes are from the Collection of J. H. Johnston, Whitman's life-long friend. The poet was accustomed to send a proof copy to Mr. Johnston, and it is doubtful if there are as many other examples now in existence.
Prof. Triggs, in Vol. X, of The Collected Works of Whitman, pages 129-134 gives a full account of Whitman's literary method.

[Continued

"He made his notes on scraps of paper, old envelopes, and in rudely constructed note-books. In composing he worked slowly and with much reflection and brooding. Many of the manuscripts of the first poems are mazes of pencilled corrections. After writing, the poem was commonly printed on proof-sheets at a Private Press and put away for revision. Even after incorporation in the general volume the poem suffered constant handling and re-shaping as the variorum readings prepared for this edition attest."

Prof. Triggs then prints a facsimile of one of these "proofs" which he styles "A Camden Proof."

LIST OF THE PROOFS, Numbered According to Prof. Triggs' List.

Of that Blithe Throat of Mine	No. 351
Thanks in Old Age	No. 363
A Twilight Song	No. 372
Old Chants	No. 396
On, On the Same, Ye Jocund Twain	No. 384
The Dead Tenor	No. 385
You Lingering Sparse Leaves of Me (2 copies)	No. 373
Going Somewhere	No. 359
Shakespeare-Bacon Cipher	No. 391
After the Supper and Talk	No. 380
Old Age Recitatives, Sail Out for Good, Eidolon Yacht!	No. 381
As One by One Withdraw the Lofty Actors (Death of General Grant)	No. 348
Fancies of Navesink—	
The Pilot in the Mist	No. 338
Had I the Choice	No. 339
Yon Tide with Ceaseless Swell	No. 340
Last of Ebb and Daylight Waning	No. 341
And Yet not You Alone	No. 342
Proudly the Flood Comes in	No. 343
By that Long Scan of Waves	No. 344
Then Last of All	No. 345
After Twenty Years	No. 370
As the Greek's Signal Flame (For Whittier's 80th Birthday, Dec. 17, 1887) Facs. of the MS. in Triggs' Edition. Vol. X, p. 134	No. 376
To the Year 1889 (To the Pending Year)	No. 390
Not Meagre Latent Boughs Alone	No. 374
Yonnondio	No. 357

The autograph material includes letters and notes of Horace Howard Furness, Oliver Wendell Holmes, George W. Childs, S. Weir Mitchell, Joseph Bennett, H. B. Lovering, and others.

581. WHITMAN (WALT). Calamus. A Series of Letters written during the Years 1868–1880 by Walt Whitman to a Young Friend (Peter Doyle). Edited, with an Introduction by Richard Maurice Bucke, M.D. one of Whitman's Literary Executors. *Illustrations on Japan paper.* 12mo, boards, cloth back, paper label, uncut.   Boston, 1897

60

FIRST EDITION. ONE OF 35 COPIES ON LARGE PAPER. Autograph presentation copy from R. M. Bucke to Mr. Forman. The H. Buxton Forman copy.

582. WHITMAN (WALT). Calamus: A Series of Letters written during the years 1868–1880 by Walt Whitman to a young friend (Peter Doyle). Edited with an Introduction by Richard Maurice Bucke. *With portraits on Japan paper.* 12mo, boards, uncut.   Boston, 1897

55

LARGE-PAPER EDITION, limited to 35 numbered copies, signed by Dr. Bucke.

583. WHITMAN (WALT). Calamus: A Series of Letters written during the years 1868–1880 by Walt Whitman to a young friend (Peter Doyle). Edited with an Introduction by Richard Maurice Bucke. *With illustrations on Japan paper.* 12mo, cloth.   Boston, 1897

10

FIRST EDITION.

584. WHITMAN (WALT). Walt Whitman (The Camden Sage) as Religious and Moral Teacher. A Study. By William Norman Guthrie. 8vo, full dark blue levant morocco, wide inner morocco borders, vellum doublures, gilt-tooled designs on covers, gilt top, uncut. In half morocco slip-case.   Cincinnati, 1897

12.50

Edition limited to 100 numbered copies.

585. WHITMAN (WALT). The Wound Dresser. A Series of Letters Written from the Hospitals in Washington during the War of the Rebellion. Edited by Richard Maurice Bucke. *Portraits*. 12mo, cloth, gilt top, uncut. Boston, 1898 *20⁻*

FIRST EDITION. Autograph presentation copy from R. M. Bucke to Mr. Forman, with addressed portion of the original wrapper in which the volume was sent, on the back of which Mr. Forman has written a note regarding the volume. The H. Buxton Forman copy, with bookplate.

586. WHITMAN (WALT). The Wound Dresser. A Series of Letters written from the Hospitals in Washington During the War of the Rebellion By Walt Whitman. Edited by Richard Maurice Bucke. *With portraits on Japan paper*. 8vo, buckram, uncut. *30⁻*
Boston, 1898

Edition limited to 60 copies, signed by Dr. Bucke.

587. WHITMAN (WALT). Notes and Fragments: left by Walt Whitman and now edited by Dr. Richard Maurice Bucke, one of his literary executors. 4to, cloth. *30⁻*
Printed for Private Distribution Only, 1899

EDITION limited to 225 numbered copies signed by Dr. Bucke. On the fly-leaf of this copy is a long autograph note by Thomas B. Harned explaining how Dr. Bucke came by the material contained in this volume.

588. WHITMAN (WALT). When Lilacs Last in the Door-Yard Bloomed. *With frontispiece, tail-piece, and numerous initial letters, all* COLORED BY HAND. 12mo, vellum boards. *17 ⁵⁰*
London: Essex House Press, 1900

Edition limited to 125 numbered copies, printed throughout on pure vellum.

589. WHITMAN (WALT). Cosmic Consciousness: A Study in the Evolution of the Human Mind. 4to, cloth, uncut. Philadelphia, 1901 *25⁻*

FIRST EDITION, signed by the author. In this work Dr. Bucke treats of Whitman's spiritual and moral ideas.

590. WHITMAN (WALT). Catalogue of a Collection of Books, Letters and Manuscripts written by Walt Whitman, in the Library of George M. Williamson. *With numerous portraits and facsimiles*. 4to, cloth. Jamaica, 1903 *27 ⁵⁰*

A full description of the Williamson Collection, the finest save for the present one now being offered at public sale.

591. WHITMAN (WALT). An American Primer. *With portrait and facsimiles*. 8vo, boards, half vellum, uncut. Boston, 1904

First Edition. Limited to 500 numbered copies.

10⁻

592. WHITMAN (WALT). Walt Whitman's Diary in Canada. *With portrait*. 8vo, boards, half vellum, uncut. Boston, 1904

FIRST EDITION. Limited to 500 copies.

593. WHITMAN (WALT). Memories of President Lincoln. 1906; The Book of Heavenly Death. 1905. Together, 2 vols. 12mo, boards. *12 ⁵⁰*
Portland: Thomas B. Mosher, 1905–1906

LIMITED EDITIONS printed throughout on Japan paper.

594. WHITMAN (WALT). TRAUBEL (HORACE). With Walt Whitman in Camden (March 28—
July 14, 1888). *With portraits mounted, and illustrations.* 8vo, cloth, gilt top, uncut.
Boston, 1906

10

FIRST EDITION. With autograph inscription on the inside of front cover, by the author,
reading,—"*Hells and Damns Edition fifty copies. This is number forty-eight. 1906.*" On the
fly-leaf is another inscription by the author, reading,—"*Walt Whitman said to me ' Be sure you
write about me honest; whatever you do, do not prettify me; include all the hells and damns,' Horace
Traubel.*"

1250

595. WHITMAN (WALT). A Little Book of Nature Thoughts. Selected by Anne Montgomerie
Traubel. 16mo, limp leather, gilt top, uncut.   Portland: Thomas B. Mosher, 1906

596. [WHITMAN (WALT).] BAZALGETTE (LEON). Walt Whitman. L'Homme et son oeuvre.
With portrait and facsimile. 8vo, original wrappers bound in, cloth, gilt top, uncut.
Paris, 1908

PRESENTATION COPY OF THE FIRST EDITION. With autograph inscription from the author
on the half-title to Isaac Hull Platt.
With bookplate of Isaac Hull Platt.

SPLENDIDLY EXTRA-ILLUSTRATED COPY
WITH AUTOGRAPH LETTERS OF WHITMAN

597. WHITMAN (WALT). Memories of President Lincoln. 4to, full blue levant morocco, gilt
top.   Portland: Thomas B. Mosher, 1912

190

EDITION LIMITED TO 300 COPIES, PRINTED ON HANDMADE PAPER. SUPERB COPY EXTRA-
ILLUSTRATED BY THE INSERTION OF 18 PORTRAITS AND 4 AUTOGRAPH LETTERS. The portraits
include one of Whitman, and eight of Lincoln, many finely engraved on India paper. The
letters comprise,—

WHITMAN (WALT). A. L. S., one page quarto. Camden, July 15, 1873. To the Postmaster,
Washington, D. C. A forceful and characteristic letter, giving instructions to have all
his mail sent to Camden.
BURROUGHS (JOHN). A. L. S., one page small quarto, West Park, N. Y., January 12th,
n. y., referring to Tennyson and his own photograph.
MOSHER (THOMAS B.). Two A. L. S., concerning his publications.
15 Portraits of Lincoln, by Hall, Brady, Gaspard, etc., many being India Proofs, including
early and rare engravings. Also a rare lithograph, "The Assassination of Lincoln."
2 Portraits of Whitman.
A Superb volume, which in its contents and extra-illustrations units the names of Lincoln
and Walt Whitman.

1750

598. WHITMAN (WALT). Walt Whitman's Anomaly. By W. C. Rivers. *With frontispiece.*
12mo, wrappers. In cloth wrapper.   London, 1913

599. WHITMAN (WALT). Walt Whitman: Yesterday and Today. 12mo, boards, fore and
lower edges, uncut.   Chicago: Brothers of the Book, 1916

FIRST EDITION, limited to 600 numbered copies.

600. WHITMAN (WALT). Original Autograph Manuscript of the poem "Proud Music of the
Sea Storm." 8pp., small folio. Accompanied by sheets of the poem as it appeared
in a magazine, mounted; Also, Portrait of Whitman, mounted. Together, 3 pieces,
bound in small folio volume, full green levant morocco, with elaborate gilt-tooled
designs on covers, inner gilt morocco borders, gilt back and top.

510

FINE MANUSCRIPT of this famous poem, with many corrections and interlineations by Whitman. The poem as printed, also contains corrections. This poem was printed in Leaves of Grass.

601. WHITMAN (WALT). Corrected Proof Sheet of "The Last of the Sacred Army" by Whitman, with a large number of corrections and deletions in Whitman's hand. *50*

602. WHITMAN (WALT). Autograph Manuscript, one page, small 4to. Headed "Names of Great Givers." Then follow the names of Peabody, Girard, Peter Cooper, Johns Hopkins, Isaac Williamson, Geo. W. Childs, Senator Stanford (deleted) and Ezra Cornell. *25*

603. WHITMAN (WALT). Autograph Manuscript, one page, 4to, hinged on mount. *30*

At the top Whitman has written in blue pencil, "W. W's Nov. Boughs." Then follows a list of Sir Walter Scott's Poetical works; evidently a list of those Whitman had read, as the page concludes: "(*all the poems were read by me, but the ballads over and over again*)."

604. WHITMAN (WALT). Autograph Manuscript of a Poem, entitled,—"*Now Precedent Songs, Farewell.*" One page, folio, comprising about 30 lines. Written in pencil and ink on pieces of paper joined together as is usual with Whitman's Mss. *100*

FINE MANUSCRIPT of this famous poem.

605. WHITMAN (WALT). Original Autograph Manuscript entitled,—"*Today.*" One page, 4to. Written in pencil (tear skilfully repaired). *50*

Above the poem is a note in Whitman's hand, reading,—"*sent April 21 to Herald.*"

A REMARKABLE COLLECTION

606. WHITMAN (WALT). A Collection of ORIGINAL AUTOGRAPH MANUSCRIPTS, Autograph Letters, Proof Sheets, Portraits, etc. Together, 32 pieces, each mounted on sheets tipped to stubs, full green levant morocco, with elaborate gilt borders on sides, surrounding gilt lettering on front cover, inner gilt morocco borders, gilt top. *750*

REMARKABLE COLLECTION OF MATERIAL BY AND RELATING TO WALT WHITMAN. Comprises—

1. Frontispiece: An original photograph of W. W. taken about 1885.
2. The Original Manuscript of "On, On the Same, Ye Jocund Twein!" One page, with many corrections, signed in full, "*Walt Whitman.*"
3. Proofsheet of the above, with numerous corrections by W. W.
4. Two proofsheets of the above, with the changes made.
5. The Original Manuscript of "Thanks in Old Age," one page.
6. Proofsheet of the above, with autograph notation: "published Nov. 25, '87."
7. Original Manuscript of "Halcyon Days" one page, showing many corrections.
8. Proofsheet of the above. One page.
9. Proofsheet of "The Dalliance of the Eagles." One page.
10. Proofsheets of "Fancies at Navesink," 3pp.
11. The Original Manuscript of "From Noon to Starry Night,—The Magic Trumpeter," Stanza 8, one page.
12. Autograph cheque for $450.00 to Thomas A. Wilson, signed, Camden, June 30, 1874.
13. Autograph Letter signed, of *John Burroughs*, dated Esopus, May 23, 1881, *addressed:* "*Dear Walt.*" 4pp. 8vo.
    A superb specimen of the correspondence of these life-long friends.
14. Proofsheets of "A Memorandum at a Venture," 3pp.
    As it appeared in The North American Review.
15. Proofsheet of an Open Letter by W. W., May 31, 1889, upon completing his 70th year.
16. Proofsheet of "Fables," by W. W. One page.
    This has not been reprinted in the Collected Works.
17. Proofsheet of "Ethiopia Saluting the Colors," one page.
18. Proofsheet of "Sparkles from the Wheel," one page.
19. Proofsheet of "Yon Lingering Sparse Leaves of Me," one page.
20. Proofsheet of "Bravo, Paris Exposition!" with corrections in the title and first line by W. W. One page.
21. Proofsheet of "Shakespere-Bacon Cipher," one page.
22. Proofsheet of "Old Age Recitatives," one page.
23. Proofsheet of "To the Sunset Breeze," one page.

[*Continued*

Do you know why what m~~n~~ does
to the soul? — Do you suppose that
the ~~melody~~ ~~mere melody of those instruments~~ the violencello, sad and sobbing
~~talk~~ ~~as~~ some human creature — the cornet, that
puts the call of day ~~light~~ and the laugh of
hope into voice, and spreads its utterance
around like a shower — the organ, presid-
over the rest, ~~refreshing and subduing them,~~ serious
and ~~large~~, from respect of whom all ~~all~~
keep still and know in that presence
their best ~~acts declarants~~ would be an
impertinence ~~— the~~ ~~Any that Me alive! and~~ the brass band whose
drums wake up the sleepers —
~~be~~ ~~ba~~ from their
bedrooms in the ~~flimsiest~~ and faint
~~yaspunk~~ in the ~~name of cowards~~ — Do
you suppose that in these, touched by the
~~greatest~~ players of the world, ~~give forth~~ ~~are the~~
the ~~primary~~ that move you? — No; there
is something else — ~~a thousand fathoms~~
something is in the Soul ~~which~~ and eludes
description. — No substantive or noun, no
~~one or phonograph~~
~~wording~~ or image, stands for ~~the~~ beautiful
mystery — ~~I'd to put off as the~~
from their
of ~~millions of degrees afar,~~
that is a region ~~I can only to~~
tell you of it ~~out us,~~ ~~one who~~ reaches his neck
at night and looks ~~after~~ the headland of the morning —
The Soul of Man has within itself
the vitality of all that is harmonious or pleasant.
~~To~~ it ~~come~~
of those secondary emanations ~~that~~ call
Beauty and Virtue, and such like,
~~life~~

24. Proofsheet of "A Twilight Song," one page.
25. Proofsheet of "Not Meagre, Latent Boughs Alone," one page.
26. Proofsheet of "After the Supper and Talk," one page.
27. Proofsheet of "The Voice of the Rain," one page.
28. Proofsheet of "Yonnondio," one page.
29. Thirteen engraved Portraits of Whitman at various periods of his life, views of his homes, etc., seven of these prints are finely hand colored.
30. Proofsheet of "Personal—The Foreign Reader at outset," an open letter, dated Camden, April, 1878. With several corrections in Whitman's autograph.
31. Autograph memoranda, dated Saturday, April 18th, about 20 lines in Whitman's hand, stating the effect of medicines upon his health, etc. A curious piece.
32. Autograph letter signed, Camden, October 22, no year. One page 12mo, regarding his books, etc.

607. WHITMAN (WALT). Autograph Jottings on Emerson. Written in ink and pencil on three slips of paper; Also, a wrapper with Whitman's notations on Emerson. To-gether, 2 pieces.   *55*

608. WHITMAN (WALT). Concluding portion of an Autograph Manuscript. One page, small 4to. Tipped on to larger sheet.   *20*
INTERESTING MANUSCRIPT on the future of Democracy.

609. WHITMAN (WALT). Original Autograph Manuscript on American Progress. One page, 4to. Tipped on to quarto sheet.   *80*
FINE MANUSCRIPT with many corrections. It begins,—"*Americans are charged with brag and vanity.*"

610. WHITMAN (WALT). Autograph Manuscript from "Goethe." One page, 4to. Written in pencil.   *25*
This manuscript consists of notes taken by Whitman from Lewe's Life of Goethe.

611. WHITMAN (WALT). A Collection of 17 Portraits of Walt Whitman, comprising original photographs, proofs, and reproductions, various sizes. With portraits of his father and mother. Together, 19 pieces.   *40*
Two of the portraits are autographed by Walt Whitman.

ESSAY ON THE SOUL—ORIGINAL MANUSCRIPT

612. WHITMAN (WALT). Original Autograph Manuscript on "An Essay on the Soul." 2½pp., folio, each sheet tipped to stub (lower margins strengthened). Accompanied by an engraved portrait of Whitman on Japan paper, Signed, in pencil, by the artist, —"*S. Hollyer.*" Bound in full red levant morocco, with gilt lettered cover, and gilt fillet borders on both covers, BY SANGORSKI AND SUTCLIFFE.   *530*
FINE MANUSCRIPT of this famous Essay by Walt Whitman. Contains numerous changes and interlineations, which show how carefully Whitman corrected even his prose writings.
[REPRODUCED ON OPPOSITE PAGE]

SALE NUMBER 3911
PUBLIC EXHIBITION FROM THURSDAY, APRIL 23

A HAWTHORNE COLLECTION
IMPORTANT LETTERS AND MANUSCRIPTS
INCLUDING A FOUR-PAGE LETTER
FROM HERMAN MELVILLE TO
MRS. NATHANIEL HAWTHORNE
CONCERNING "MOBY DICK"
THE PROPERTY OF A DESCENDANT OF HAWTHORNE

This materia
was displ
at Bowdoin C
Library (1930
as a loan
from Dr. Cly
Smyth, who
married H
one's daug

RARE FIRST EDITIONS · AUTOGRAPH LETTERS
MANUSCRIPTS · PRESENTATION COPIES OF
SAMUEL L. CLEMENS
[MARK TWAIN]

THE PROPERTY OF
IRVING S. UNDERHILL
BUFFALO, N. Y.

WHITMAN · BURROUGHS CORRESPONDENCE
OF AN INTIMATE CHARACTER

FIRST EDITIONS AND ASSOCIATION COPIES
MSS. AND DIARIES OF JOHN BURROUGHS

THE PROPERTY OF THE LATE
DR. CLARA BARRUS
BURROUGHS' LITERARY EXECUTOR

SOLD BY THEIR ORDER

UNRESTRICTED PUBLIC SALE
APRIL 29 AT 8:15

AMERICAN ART ASSOCIATION
ANDERSON GALLERIES · INC.
NEW YORK
1931

"LEAVES OF GRASS", 1855, INSCRIBED BY BURROUGHS

161 WHITMAN (WALT). Leaves of Grass. *Portrait.* Brooklyn, 1855 *500—*

Small folio, cloth (backstrip and corners worn).
FIRST EDITION. Second Issue, with blind fillets on the covers, yellow end-papers, portrait on India Paper, and eight pages of Press Notices. PRESENTATION COPY FROM DEWITT MILLER TO JOHN BURROUGHS AND FROM JOHN BURROUGHS TO DR. CLARA BARRUS. Inscribed on the end-papers: *"John Burroughs fr. his friend Dewitt Miller, The Orchard, New Rochelle, N. York, Sept. 1901"*, and then, IN BURROUGH'S HAND: *"To Clara Barrus, from her friend & comrade John Burroughs, July 4th, 1904"*. A VERY INTERESTING COPY, WITH UNUSUAL ASSO-CIATION INTEREST.

162 WHITMAN (WALT). Leaves of Grass. *Portrait.* Boston, 1860-61 *12⁵⁰*

12mo, cloth (signs of use and wear).
WORTHINGTON'S SPURIOUS ISSUE of the Thayer and Eldridge Issue. JOHN BUR-ROUGHS' COPY, with many pencilled notes in his hand, and a signed estimate of Whitman's taste. Laid down on the fly-leaves are clippings of reviews of Burroughs' book on Whitman, articles on Whitman, etc. Laid in is a fine A. L. s. by R. W. Clifton to Edward Dowden, relating to Whitman's poetry.

163 WHITMAN (WALT). Leaves of Grass. *Portrait.* Camden, 1876 *12⁵⁰*

12mo, original half calf (back damaged).
AUTHOR'S EDITION. Unsigned copy, with one portrait. The "intercalations" are printed in the book. Inscribed on the fly-leaf: *"Part of this book was set up by Whitman in a Camden printing office. He called it his 'Centennial Edition' and [it] was sold largely to those English friends who came to his rescue when he was 'poor, old, and paralyzed'. This copy was in his room when he died. To Clara Barrus, from Thomas B. Harned. Dec. 11 '04."*

164 WHITMAN (WALT). Two Rivulets. Camden, 1876 *20—*

12mo, original half calf.
AUTHOR'S EDITION. Unsigned copy, without the portrait. Inscribed on the fly-leaf: *"This book is one of the copies left by Whitman in his Mickle St. 'den' at the time of his death, and is presented to Clara Barrus by Thomas B. Harned, one of the author's literary executors."*

165 WHITMAN (WALT). Specimen Days & Collect.
Philadelphia, 1882-3 *22⁵⁰*

12mo, cloth (rubbed; one signature loose).
FIRST EDITION. FIRST ISSUE, with the imprint of Rees Welsh & Co. on the title-page and the backstrip. PRESENTATION COPY FROM BURROUGHS TO DR. BARRUS, inscribed on the fly-leaf: *"C. B. from J. B. October, 1901."* Beneath is written: *"Given to me by John Burroughs on the occasion of my second visit to Slabsides. Whitman had given it to him. Clara Barrus."*

166 WHITMAN (WALT). November Boughs, 1888 ❖ Good-Bye My Fancy. *Portrait*. 1891.   Philadelphia, 1888-91

Together 2 vols., 8vo., cloth, uncut.

FIRST EDITIONS. Each is inscribed on the fly-leaf: *"To Clara Barrus, M.D., Compliments of Thomas B. Harned."* Laid in is an envelope addressed to Charles W. Eldridge by Whitman.

167 WHITMAN (WALT). Leaves of Grass. *Portraits.*
                                             [Philadelphia, 1889]

75

12mo, limp morocco, gilt edges (rubbed).

THE RARE SPECIAL AUTOGRAPH EDITION, signed by Whitman on the title-page. One of 300 copies. Inscribed on the fly-leaf: *"Walt Whitman's 70th Birthday Book. This copy was in his 'den' at the time of his death. To Clara Barrus with sincere regards of Thomas B. Harned, one of the author's literary executors. Dec. 11, 1904."* There are many pencilled notes by Dr. Barrus.

THE RARE FIRST ISSUE OF
THE COMPLETE "LEAVES OF GRASS"
A SPLENDID ASSOCIATION COPY

168 WHITMAN (WALT). Leaves of Grass.   Philadelphia, 1891-2

120

8vo, original brown paper wrappers, uncut (backstrip missing; shaken).

THE SO-CALLED "DEATH-BED EDITION". ONE OF A VERY FEW COPIES HURRIEDLY BOUND IN COARSE WRAPPERS, AND PRESENTED BY WHITMAN TO FRIENDS. Whitman was very ill at this time. As he wanted to see the completed book, Traubel had a few copies hurriedly finished, and Whitman sent them to a few intimate friends. THIS WAS BURROUGHS' COPY, and has the names of visitors at Slabsides on the fly-leaf. Laid in is a card inscribed: *". . . This is the copy which John Burroughs had for years, at Slabsides but during the last 13 years of his life at Woodchuck Lodge. It is the copy he oftenest read from at the Lodge. Clara Barrus".* A SUPERB ASSOCIATION COPY OF ONE OF THE RAREST ISSUES OF "LEAVES OF GRASS", INTIMATELY LINKING THE PERSONALITIES OF WHITMAN AND BURROUGHS.

169 [WHITMAN (WALT).] Good-Bye and Hail Walt Whitman. At the Graveside of Walt Whitman: Harleigh, Camden, New Jersey, March 30th. And Sprigs of Lilac. Edited by Horace L. Traubel.   N.p., 1892

8vo, original wrappers, uncut.

FIRST EDITION. One of 750 copies, signed by the Editor. Presentation Copy from the Editor to John Burroughs, inscribed on the title-page: *"To John Burroughs, 'Love, exaltation, renewal', Camden, June 29, 1892. Traubel."* Laid in is a note by Dr. Barrus relating to Burroughs' contribution to this book.

170 **WHITMAN (WALT).** Letters written by Walt Whitman to His Mother, from 1866 to 1872. Together with Certain Papers Prepared from Material Now First Utilized. Edited by Thomas B. Harned. *75⁻*

New York, 1902

8vo, original wrappers (torn).

FIRST EDITION. ONE OF A FEW COPIES PRINTED TO SECURE COPYRIGHT. Inscribed on the front wrapper: "*A few copies printed to comply with the copyright laws. This is part of Vol. VIII of the definitive edition of Whitman. Thomas B. Harned.*" Beneath is Dr. Barrus' signature and the date "*Jan. 1905*".

171 **[WHITMAN (WALT).]** Notes and Fragments (Bucke). [London, Ontario] 1899. *One of 250 copies privately printed* ❖ Cosmic Consciousness (Bucke), Phila., 1901 ❖ Walt Whitman's Diary in Canada, 1904. *One of 500 copies* ❖ An American Primer (Whitman), 1904. *One of 500 copies* ❖ LaFayette in Brooklyn (Whitman), N. Y., 1905. *One of 250 copies* ❖ Complete Prose Works, 1901. V.p., 1899-1905

Together 6 vols., royal 8vo and 12mo, cloth and boards.

FIRST EDITIONS, with the exception of the last. All but two are Presentation Copies from Thos. B. Harned to Dr. Barrus; "Cosmic Consciousness" is a Presentation Copy from Elbert Hubbard to John Burroughs, re-presented by Burroughs to Dr. Barrus.

172 **[WHITMAN (WALT).]** With Walt Whitman in Canada (Traubel), 3 vols., 1908 ❖ In Re Walt Whitman (Traubel, Bucke, and Harned), 1893 ❖ Walt Whitman as Man, Poet, and Friend (Eliot) [1915].

V.p., 1893[-1915]

Together 5 vols., royal 8vo and 12mo, various bindings (Traubel's book lacks one plate).

The first two books are Presentation Copies from Thos. B. Harned to Dr. Barrus; the third is a Presentation Copy to Dr. Barrus from the author. There are many pencilled notations in Dr. Barrus' hand.

173 **[WHITMAN (WALT).]** Nathan the Wise. By Gotthold Ephraim Lessing. Translated by Ellen Frothingham. New York, 1868 *22⁵⁰*

12mo, cloth (shaken).

PRESENTATION COPY FROM WALT WHITMAN TO BURROUGHS, inscribed on the fly-leaf: "*John Burroughs from Walt Whitman, January, 1868.*" Beneath this is an inscription in Burroughs' hand: "*Clara Barrus, July 1904, From John Burroughs.*"

AN UNPUBLISHED CRITIQUE OF HIS OWN POETRY
BY WALT WHITMAN

174 **WHITMAN (WALT).** Autograph Manuscript, signed by Whitman with John Burroughs' name, 8 pp., 4to. Middletown, N. Y., Feb. 17, 1874. Accompanied by an A. N., 1 p., 8vo (conclusion missing), Camden, Feb. [2, 1874] Together 2 pieces.

160

A SUPERB MANUSCRIPT ENTITLED "IS WALT WHITMAN'S POETRY POETICAL?". Whitman wrote this thorough critique of his own work as a reply to an attack upon him in "The Nation", post-dating it Feb. 17th, at Middletown, where John Burroughs was then living. The covering letter to Burroughs suggests that the latter revise it and forward it to "The Nation" as his own. Thorough search of the files of "The Nation" and elsewhere shows that the article never appeared over Burroughs' signature, nor was it ever printed in Whitman's writings. In it Whitman defends himself with energy: "[His poetry] *is singularly emotional; probably no one has so daringly & freely carried 'manly attachment' into expression as this author. The 'rapture in being' and in the physical existence of things is also vehement, beyond example. Cheerfulness overarches all, like a sky. . . ."* A SPLENDID AND UNPUBLISHED ESTIMATE OF WHITMAN BY HIMSELF.

[SEE ILLUSTRATION]

175 **WHITMAN (WALT).** A. L. s. (*"Walt"*), 1 p., 8vo. Camden, June 5, [1874]. To John Burroughs.

12.50

A FINE LETTER OF CONDOLENCE ON THE DEATH OF BURROUGHS' NEPHEW: *"I will not write any of the usual condolences—Cha[u]ncy's malady & death seem to be of those events sometimes mocking with unaccountable sudden tragedies & cross-purposes all of us. . . ."*

WHITMAN AND EMERSON

176 **WHITMAN (WALT).** A. L. s. (initials), 3 pp., 8vo. Camden, April 1 [1875]. To John Burroughs.

170

A PENETRATING CRITICISM OF BURROUGHS' ESSAY ON EMERSON: *". . . Your pages produce a not agreeable notion of being written by one who has been largely grown & ripened & gristled by Emerson, but has at last become dissatisfied & finnicky about him, & would pitch into him but cannot—perhaps dare not. . . . My name might be brought in in one or two places as foil or suggestive comparison. . . . To my friends & circle; who know the relations and history between me & Emerson, the mere mention of the name . . . will be significant. . . ."*

177 **WHITMAN (WALT).** A. L. s., 4 pp., 12mo. N.p., June 17 [1876?]. To John Burroughs.

100

A FINE LETTER OF APPRECIATION OF BURROUGHS' FIRST ESSAY ON WHITMAN IN "THE GALAXY", 1866: *". . . Your late pieces show marked vitality—(struggling, almost chafing, underneath a continent, respectable form or exterior) & this is the best of them . . . not without one or two foibles, but the whole of the piece is glorious . . . the noblest piece of criticism on these things yet in America— as much nobler than the superb Emersonian pages on those subjects as lines & opinions with the blood of life . . . are nobler than the superbest marble-statue lines. . . ."* AN INTERESTING AND LENGTHY LETTER, closing with personal news.

Is Walt Whitman's Poetry Poetical?

To the Editor of the Nation: Middletown, N.Y. Feb. 17, 1874

As I suppose - or rather, know - that your paper is open to statements & views, even opposed to your own, if duly put, I would like to take up your review of that part devoted to analyzing Walt Whitman, & which appears to be the main part of the notice - of Mr. Miller's last volume of poems, and offer something on the other side. Your idea of the ad cap. tandum character of Whitman's verse is certainly the reverse of well founded; it is the almost universal testimony, that, at first harsh & offensive, it needs study, & more than one perusal, to give up its meaning, & confer pleasure. The author's theory has evidently been the Deep axiom, "it is reserved for first-rate poems never to immediately gratify." Whitman does not lack in sweets or graces, exercise, a stimulus, an inexhaustible suggestion, (An Italian critic complains that there is something cold & by a sort of harshness He nourishes, if at all, by removes & indirections, He is not sugar in cake, or ornament, or any special liquor or special cookery, for a banquet. He is not even, (at least apparently,) art, or beauty, or

REDUCED FACSIMILE OF FIRST PAGE

[NUMBER 174]

178 **WHITMAN (WALT).** A. L. s. (initials), 1 p., 4to. Camden, Jan. 24, '77. To John Burroughs.

32.50

Whitman approves of Burroughs' title "Birds and Poets": ". . . *a first-rate good name, appropriate, original & fresh. . . . 'Nature and Genius' is too Emersony altogether. I will think over the name of the piece devoted to me. . . . May-be I can think of a better name. . . .*" .

179 **WHITMAN (WALT).** A. L. s. (initials), 1 p., small 4to. Camden, Feb. 13 [1877]. To John Burroughs.

27.50

Whitman approves finally of "The Flight of the Eagle" as the title of Burroughs' essay on Whitman in "Birds and Poets", invites Burroughs to visit Anne Gilchrist, etc.

180 **WHITMAN (WALT).** A. L. s. (initials), 1 p., 8vo. Camden, Feb. 27 [1877]. To John Burroughs.

7.50

Suggesting alterations in "Birds and Poets". He likes the essays much, "*they are very living. The 'Beauty' chapter I think especially fine.*" He requests proofs of the chapter devoted to him ("The Flight of the Eagle").

181 **WHITMAN (WALT).** A. L. s. (initials), 1 p., 8vo. Kirkwood, May 17 [1877]. To John Burroughs.

40.—

A FINE LETTER OF APPRECIATION OF THE COMPLETED AND PUBLISHED "BIRDS AND POETS" "*. . . My impression of liking it . . . deepened & clinched. I especially much like . . . the chapter about me. There has certainly been nothing yet said that so makes the points (& eloquently makes them) I most want brought out & on record. . . .*"

WHITMAN PREPARES FOR HIS LECTURE ON LINCOLN

182 **WHITMAN (WALT).** A. L. s., 3 pp., 8vo and 12mo. Camden, March 11 [1878]. To John Burroughs.

130.—

"*. . . In composing the letter, let it be brief & don't mention the subject—or, if you do, just say indefinitely that it is about Abraham Lincoln. . . . I would like Gilder's name on the letter . . . about 8 or 10 names only—good ones only. . . . I would like Whitelaw Reid's name to cap the list—couldn't the World man Schuyler . . . come next. . . . Take Johnston into you councils, in any business & pecuniary arrangements he is very cute. . . .*" On a second sheet, Whitman has written "*Private. I care little—or rather nothing at all—about Bayard Taylor's or G. W. Curtis's name on the letter. Don't want them. . . .*"

183 **WHITMAN (WALT).** A. L. s. (initials), 2 pp., 4to. Camden, March 29 [1878]. To John Burroughs. *45*

POSTPONING THE LECTURE ON LINCOLN, BECAUSE OF ILL HEALTH: "*. . . I think it would be safer to fix the lecture night anywhere between the 10th & 20th May. . . . If convenient I should like to see the list of names & the draft of the letter before formally put out. . . .*" He writes at some length of his illness, concluding with references to Benton and the Gilchrists.

184 **WHITMAN (WALT).** A. L. s. (*"Walt"*), 2 pp., 16 mo. Camden, Dec. 12 [1878]. To John Burroughs. *55*

A TRANQUIL, NEWSY LETTER, enclosing various criticisms, a letter from Tennyson, referring to English orders for his books, etc.

WHITMAN'S WISHES AS TO A BIOGRAPHY

185 **WHITMAN (WALT).** A. L. s. (initials), 2 pp., 4to. Camden, Dec. 23-25 [1878]. To John Burroughs. *125*

AN IMPORTANT LETTER. "*. . . The* [Lincoln] *lecture is a fixed fact (to come) but I shall wait till I get good and ready. . . . Write me more fully about your proposed book . . . it is in the gestation of a book—the melting of the fluid metal, before the casting—that it receives that something to make its idiosyncrasy, identity. . . .*" Then, of Jeannette Gilder's proposed biography: "*I would like best to be told about in strings of continuous anecdotes, incidents, mots, thumbnail personal sketches, characteristic & true—such for instance as are in the 2nd edition of your old Wash'n Notes. . . .*"

186 **WHITMAN (WALT).** A. L. s. (*"Walt"*), 1 p., 4to. Camden, Jan. 25 [1879]. To John Burroughs. *65*

A FINE LETTER, BOLDLY WRITTEN. "*. . . To my notion Locusts and Wild Honey is the best . . . (the Speckled Trout piece suggested to me whether the fish couldn't afford a name for one of your books, for a change). . . .*"

187 **WHITMAN (WALT).** A. L. s. (*"Walt"*), 2 pp., 8vo. 1309 Fifth Avenue, N. Y., June 11 [1879]. To John Burroughs. *30*

"*. . . I send you the 'Tobacco Plant' with a piece of mine will interest you— (you'll see I have used one of your letters of last winter). . . . This has been a good visit for me—it sort of rehabilitates me for speaking & literary handling* [?]; *writing offhand more than I anticipated—half paralytic as I am. Henceforth I feel more at ease, more self confidence—which is always half the battle. . . .*"

188 **WHITMAN (WALT).** A. L. s., 2 pp., 12mo. Camden, Aug. 20 [1879]. To John Burroughs. *22.50*

A NEWSY LETTER, inquiring about the Delaware River trip ("A Summer Voyage on the Pepacton"), the Gilchrists, Mrs. Botta, his health (*"may be a trifle ruggeder"*), etc.

173

189 WHITMAN (WALT). A. L. s. (*"Walt"*), 1 p., 8vo. Camden, Aug. 29 [1879]. To John Burroughs. Accompanied by an Autograph Manuscript in pencil, 1 p., 4to.

55

"I have not been to any watering place—they are no company for me—the cities *magnificent for their complex play & oceans of eager human faces—but the country or sea for me in some sparse place, old barn & farm house—or bleak sea shore. . . . I have jotted off the enclosed & send you (of course use it or not). . . .* THE ENCLOSED MANUSCRIPT IS A SHORT BUT KEEN CRITIQUE OF HIS OWN POETRY, commencing: *"Whitman is not remarkable in details or minute finish. But in spirit, in reverence, in breadth, ensemble, and in his vistas, he stands unmatched. . . . His fields, his rocks, his trees, are not dead material but living companions",* etc., and concluding with a reference to J. A. Symonds' dictum: *" 'Walt Whitman is more thoroughly Greek than any man of modern times' ".* Some of this material was used by John Burroughs in "Pepacton", pp. 108-9.

A FINE LETTER, ENCLOSING A LETTER
BY ANNE GILCHRIST
AND A MAP OF HIS TRAVELS

190 WHITMAN (WALT). A. L. s., 2 pp., 8vo. St. Louis, Missouri, Nov. 23 [1879]. To John Burroughs. With two enclosures ❖ A. L. s. by Anne Gilchrist, 8 pp., 8vo. Haslemere, Oct. 6, 1879. To Walt Whitman ❖ Folding Map of the United States, 24 by 12 inches, issued by The Missouri Pacific Rail Road, on which Walt Whitman has drawn in blue and red crayon, the journeys he has made. (Somewhat torn in folds; backed with net.) Together 3 pieces.

120

Whitman's letter reads in part: *"I am still here—not yet (as an old Long Island aunt used to say) 'not yet out of my misery'. . . . I send you Mrs. Gilchrist's letter. . . . The rough map enclosed gives you some idea of my present jaunt, on the red line (the blue lines are old travels of mine). I have seen the December Scribner's—what you say of me in* Nature & the Poets *thoroughly delights, satisfies, & prides me. . . . Symonds, touching briefly but very commendably & mentioning my name, makes quite an extract from Dem: Vistas (summing up the general spirit of British literature as being markedly sombre & bilious). A. B. Alcott is expected here. . . . This is quite a place for the most top-loftical Hegelian transcendentalists, a small knot but smart. . . ."*

The letter from Mrs. Gilchrist which Whitman forwards for Burroughs' perusal is a long and characteristic one, full of news of the English circle, and admiration and affection for Whitman and his work. She writes largely of Tennyson, Edward Carpenter, the new edition of Blake, etc.

WHITMAN'S MAP OF HIS TRAVELS IS OF GREAT INTEREST. The blue line drawn by him traces his travels in New England and the Middle Atlantic States, the trip from Washington to Cincinnati, down the Mississippi to New Orleans, and back by St. Louis, Chicago, and the Great Lakes. A red line traces the journey to Denver and the mountains of Colorado.

191 WHITMAN (WALT). A. L. s., 2 pp., 8vo. St. Louis, Jan. 2, '80. To John Burroughs.

27 50

Thanking Burroughs for a present: *". . . Believe me I feel the gift & it comes just right too—John please forward the enclosed slip to unknown friend* [James T. Fields]. *The above* [referring to the engraving of the Mississippi Bridge on the letterhead] *is a fair picture of the great Mississippi Bridge, East St. Louis, where I have loafed many hours—only it sets up much higher than the print gives. I don't believe there can be a grander thing of the kind on earth. . . . Your letter was deeply interesting to me, made me see Emerson no doubt just as he is, the good, pure soul. . . ."*

192 WHITMAN (WALT). A. L. s., 2 pp., 8vo. Camden, Feb. 21 [1880]. To John Burroughs. *60—*

"*. . . I have not written out for print any notes of my jaunt yet. . . . Adding-ton Symonds has sent me a copy of the American edition of his 'Greek Poets'—Ruskin has sent to me [for] five sets of my books. . . . Dr. Bucke of London, Canada, is writing my life—I suppose he has sent you his printed circular, asking information, &c. What do you think of the project?*" He adds that he has given consent to Prof. Ritter for a musical setting of "Two Veterans".

WITH WHITMAN'S STATEMENT ON THE
SPURIOUS EDITION OF 1860-61

193 WHITMAN (WALT). A. L. s. ("*Walt*"), 1 p., 8vo. Camden, Nov. 26, '80. To John Burroughs. Accompanied by a letter-press copy of Whit-man's statement on Worthington's unauthorized reprinting of the Thayer and Eldridge Edition of 1860-61, 2 pp., 4to. Wherever the impression is faint, Whitman has gone over the words and letters in ink. *65—*

APPEALING FOR HELP IN STOPPING WORTHINGTON'S PIRACIES. "*. . . What could you do towards helping me in the matter stated by these two pages? Badly copied, but I can't write them out. I have sent duplicates to Watson Gilder & said I requested you to see him. . . . The locomotion business is worse . . . rendering me indeed at times practically helpless. . . . I thought Stedman's article fully as good as could be expected. . . .*" THE ACCOMPANYING DOCUMENT IS AN IMPORTANT AND COMPLETE STATEMENT OF THE DETAILS INVOLVED IN THE FAILURE OF THAYER AND ELDRIDGE, WORTHINGTON'S PURCHASE OF THE PLATES, UNSUCCESSFUL NEGOTIATIONS WITH WHITMAN AND WHITMAN'S SUBSEQUENT ATTEMPT TO COME TO TERMS, AND WORTHINGTON'S SURREPTITIOUS PRINTING OF THE VOLUME.

194 WHITMAN (WALT). A. L. s. (initials), 1 p., 8vo. [Camden] Dec. 7, '80. To John Burroughs. *55—*

FURTHER INFORMATION ABOUT WORTHINGTON: "*. . . Leavitt [the auctioneer] sold the plates (for Wentworth of Boston) in Sept. '79 for $200. Leavitt never saw or heard of any sheets—Worthington must have bo't the plates from Williams. . . . I thought I might as well let you know every new discovery—and shall continue to do so. . . .*" This information Whitman had obtained from Dr. Bucke.

195 WHITMAN (WALT). A. L. s. on card, 2 pp., 16mo. Camden [March 17, 1881]. To John Burroughs. Accompanied by proof of the poem "Patroling Barnegat", endorsed by Whitman: "*Harpers' April, '81*". *47^{50}*

"*Yours rec'd with the good 10—God bless you. . . . I go down three or four days at a time to my friends the Staffords, & get out in the woods a great deal. . . . Your letter don't contain the slip about the Emerson business you allude to—The just published Carlyle Reminiscences . . . don't confirm or add to my estimation of C—Much the contrary. . . .*"

WHITMAN VISITS THE DECLINING EMERSON AT CONCORD

196 WHITMAN (WALT). A. L. s., 2 pp., 8vo. Concord, Mass., Sept. 19, '81. To John Burroughs.

210—

A SUPERB LETTER ON EMERSON. At this time Whitman was visiting F. B. Sanborn and writes of his affection and hospitality, and of his visits with the aged Emerson: "... *Have had a curiously full and satisfactory time with Emerson —he came to see me Saturday evening early, Mrs. E. also, & staid two hours— yesterday I went there (by pressing invitation) to dinner & staid two hours— a wonderfully good two hours—the whole family were very cordial ... I took to them all—I cannot tell you how sweet and good (and all as it should be) Emerson look'd and behaved—he did not talk in the way of joining in any animated conversation, but pleasantly and hesitatingly & sparsely—fully enough —to me it seemed just as it should be. ...*" The letter concludes with a reference to the printing of Osgood's Edition of "Leaves of Grass", ultimately suppressed. A SUPERB LETTER OF GREAT ASSOCIATION INTEREST.

[SEE ILLUSTRATION]

197 WHITMAN (WALT). A. L. s. (initials), 1 p., 4to. Camden, March 29 [1882?]. To John Burroughs.

22⁵⁰

"I have run over the Carlyle proof & being in the mood have thought best to mark ... out certain passages. ... What you set out mainly to say & have to say seems to me very well said indeed, & I like the article. What you have to offer as the Carlyle-foil in defence of America I don't like so well. ... Unless one has got something outsmashing C himself—a battery-ram [sic] that batters his ram to the dust. ..."

198 WHITMAN (WALT). A. L. s., 2 pp., 8vo. Camden, Aug. 13 [1882]. To John Burroughs.

105—

A SPLENDID AND FULL LETTER TO BURROUGHS ON HIS RETURN FROM ENGLAND: "Welcome home again. ... *I commenced publishing L. of G. in June on my own hook, but found it vexatious from the start, & having quite vehement proposals from Rees Welsh ... I pass'd the use of the plates into his hands. ... Welsh's first edition (a cautious 1000) was ready about three weeks ago & was exhausted in a day—the second came in ab't five days ago & is now nearly gone— a third is ordered. ... I am throwing together a prose jumble, specimen Days (see slip enclosed)—nearly 200 pages already cast. ... O'C[onnor] & I correspond now quite often & just on the same terms as of yore. ...*"

199 WHITMAN (WALT). A. L. s. (initials) on a card, 1 p., 18mo. Camden, Aug. 27 [1882]. To John Burroughs.

25—

"... The type-setting of 'Specimen Days' will be all finished the coming week & the book out ten days afterwards—same sized vol: same sort of type, binding, general appearance &c. with L. of G.—same price. ... Does not what you saw of English society explain a good deal of Carlyle's cussedness?"

200 WHITMAN (WALT). A. L. s., 2 pp., 4to. Camden, June 23, '85. To John Burroughs.

55—

"Yours just received (with the 10—many thanks)—the kind invitation reiterated —&c. I am in pretty fair condition generally, but unable to walk or get around, except very small stretches, & with effort—somehow feel averse to leaving this shanty of mine—where I am probably getting along better than you think. Mrs. Gilchrist's essay has appeared in the Today. ... It is a noble paper. I have a little poem to appear in the Outing ["Fancies at Navesink"?] perhaps in the forthcoming number. ... I take the car to the ferry & get out on the river every pleasant day." John Burroughs has endorsed the letter: "... *Looks as if W. was not going to move. I shall try him again by and bye. J. B.*"

Concord Mass!
Sept: 19 '81

Dear John
      I keep on fairly
in health & strength —
have been out here a few
days the guest of Mr &
Mrs Ft B Sanborn — & everything most affectionate &
hospitable from them both
— & from others — Have had
a curiously full and satisfactory time with Emerson
— he *came* to see me Saturday even: early *Mrs E* & I staid two
hours — yesterday I went

[NUMBER 196]

201 WHITMAN (WALT). A. L. s. (initials), 2 pp., 4to. Camden, Dec. 21, '85. To John Burroughs.

52 50

A SPLENDID LETTER. "*. . . The death of Mrs. Gilchrist is indeed a gloomy fact. . . . seems to me mortality never enclosed a more beautiful spirit. . . . The walking power seems quite gone from me. I can hardly get from one room to another. . . . The 'free will offering' of the English through Rossetti has amounted in the past year to over $400. I am living on it. I get a miserable return of royalties from McKay . . . not $50 for both books, L. of G. and S. D. for the past year. John I like both the names in your note. I Cannot choose. If I can at all it is in favor of 'Spring Relish'. . . . As I close my bird is singing like a house afire & the sun is shining out—I wish you were here to spend the day with me.*"

202 WHITMAN (WALT). A. L. s., 2 pp., 4to. Camden, March 18, '86. To John Burroughs.

70 -

A LONG LETTER OF NEWS. He returns to Burroughs the three volumes of Emerson; he has been asked to review Rice's "Reminiscences of Lincoln", but what he has written seems unworthy the theme; he is writing on the Army Hospitals for the Century. "*. . . Beautiful here today and I am enjoying the sunshine, sitting here by the window looking out. Have read my Death of Abraham Lincoln paper twice this spring on applications ($25 and $30)—got along with it rather slowly but didn't break down. . . . Want to scoop up what I have (poems and prose) of the last MSS. since 1881 and 2, & put in probably 200 page book (or somewhat less) to be called perhaps November Boughs. I am getting along comfortably enough . . . my old horse has quite given out. We have a canary bird, dog, & parrot—all great friends of mine (& teachers). . . .*"

203 WHITMAN (WALT). A. L. s. (in pencil), 1 p., 4to. Camden, Oct. 26, '87. To John Burroughs.

15 -

"*I have just had my dinner (plain boiled beef, potatoes, & a roast apple—all relished well) & am now sitting here in my big chair in the little front room—cold and cloudy out, looks like winter. . . .*" He writes of O'Connor's paralysis, of an article in the "Pall Mall Gazette", of Bucke and Kennedy, and of Herbert Gilchrist's portrait, and concludes: "*I am much as usual—but the peg-letting-down goes on with accelerated pace. . . .*"

204 WHITMAN (WALT). A. L. s. (in pencil), 1 p., 4to. Camden, July 12, '88. To John Burroughs.

17 50

A FINE LETTER FROM THE AGING POET, outlining in some details the effects of his recent stroke. "*. . . It was probably the sixth or seventh whack of my war paralysis & a pretty severe one. The doctors looked glum—Bucke, I think, saved my life, as he happened to be here. . . . Every time lets me down a peg. . . . My head thicks somewhat today. . . . I am on to 90th page Nov. Boughs—it will only make 20 more.*"

205 WHITMAN (WALT). A. L. s., 1 p., 4to. Camden, Feb. 8, '89. To John Burroughs.

25 -

"*. . . I am sitting by the oak fire in my big chair, well protected as it is bitter cold. . . . The news from O'Connor is bad & worse . . . very dark in prospect. . . . Most probably I shall continue ab't the stage I am at present, maybe some time, but the future will eventuate itself, & it will of course be all right. . . . My books are all printed &c. (I have a big book, Complete Poems and Prose, for you.)*"

206 **[WHITMAN (WALT).]** L. s. by J. Hubley Ashton, 5 pp., 4to. Washington, June 13, 1902. To Charles W. Eldridge ❖ L. s. by Johnson Brigham, 5 pp., 4to. Des Moines, Nov. 14, 1910. To John Burroughs. Together 2 pieces.

14

TWO IMPORTANT LETTERS RELATING TO THE CIRCUMSTANCES IN WHICH WHITMAN WAS DISMISSED FROM THE DEPARTMENT OF THE INTERIOR. Ashton, Assistant Attorney-General of the United States at the time, writes in detail of Whitman's dismissal, of Harlan's obduracy and O'Connor's wrathful eloquence, and of the efforts made to reinstate Whitman in government employ. Brigham, defending Harlan, writes concerning a letter from the latter to DeWitt Miller about his reasons for dismissing Whitman. Charles W. Eldridge has stated Ashton's letter to be THE ONLY AUTHENTIC WRITTEN ACCOUNT OF THIS MUCH DISCUSSED EPISODE IN WHITMAN'S CAREER.

207 **WHITMAN (WALT).** Nine engraved and photographic portraits of Walt Whitman, from the earliest engraving ("Song of Myself") to one of the latest photographs. Beneath each picture is written an appropriate excerpt from "Leaves of Grass". In a long black frame, size: 54 by 14 inches.

THESE PORTRAITS WERE IN WHITMAN'S ROOM AT THE TIME OF HIS DEATH. They were presented to Dr. Barrus by Thomas B. Harned.

FIRST EDITIONS AND
SUPERB ASSOCIATION BOOKS

SELECTIONS FROM THE COLLECTION OF THE LATE

JAHU DEWITT MILLER

Sold by Order of the Supreme Court of the District of Columbia
George C. Ober, Jr., Administrator

THE WAYNE PAPERS

IMPORTANT AUTOGRAPH LETTERS AND DOCUMENTS
THE PERSONAL FILE OF GENERAL ANTHONY WAYNE

Sold by Order of the Daughter of the Late Wayne MacVeagh

ACKERMANN'S UNIVERSITY, COLLEGE, AND CATHEDRAL SERIES
PRESENTATION COPIES OF LONGFELLOW'S *EVANGELINE* AND *BALLADS*
GOLDSMITH'S *VICAR OF WAKEFIELD*
A SILVER TEASPOON WHICH BELONGED TO MARTHA WASHINGTON
OTHER IMPORTANT ITEMS
Sold in Settlement of a New England Estate

AND OTHER OUTSTANDING PROPERTIES

To be Dispersed at Public Sale on December 5 and 6
BY ORDER OF VARIOUS OWNERS

AMERICAN ART ASSOCIATION
ANDERSON GALLERIES · INC
1934

ONE OF THE FINEST COPIES THAT HAVE
APPEARED AT PUBLIC SALE

516. [WHITMAN (WALT).] Leaves of Grass. *Engraved frontispiece portrait.* Small folio, ORIGINAL GREEN CLOTH stamped in gilt and blind, gilt edges. Brooklyn, 1855

FIRST EDITION. FIRST ISSUE, in the correct binding with ornamental lettering and triple-line borders stamped in gilt on both sides, marbled end-papers, and without the 8 pp. of press notices.

With the exception of the inevitable slight foxing on the frontispiece and two or three pages, ONE OF THE FINEST COPIES THAT HAVE APPEARED AT PUBLIC SALE, WITH THE COVERS ALMOST AS FRESH AS ON THE DAY OF PUBLICATION.

WITH A FINE AUTOGRAPH LETTER
BY SENATOR HARLAN CONCERNING THE
REMOVAL OF WALT WHITMAN FROM A
CLERKSHIP IN THE INDIAN OFFICE

517. [WHITMAN (WALT).] Leaves of Grass. *With the frontispiece portrait on plain paper;* slightly foxed. Imp. 8vo, original green cloth stamped in gilt and in blind; new end-papers, minute tear in two places in back-strip. Brooklyn, 1855

FIRST EDITION. Second Issue, with fillet borders on the covers stamped in blind. This is one of the copies of this issue with the frontispiece in plain state; most copies have this plate on India paper. The 8 pp. of press notices are not present in this copy.

Inserted is an A. L. s. by James Harlan (Senator, and Secretary of the Interior), 2 pp., 4to, Mt. Pleasant, Iowa, July 18, 1894, to Dewitt Miller. A FINE LETTER, IN WHICH THE WRITER GIVES THE REASONS FOR THE REMOVAL OF WALT WHITMAN FROM A CLERKSHIP IN THE INDIAN OFFICE. The letter reads in part as follows:

"I am in receipt of your letter of 14th. inst. requesting me to give you the reasons for the removal of the late Mr. Walt Whitman, in 1865, from a Clerkship in the office of the Commissioner of Indian affairs, of the Department of the interior.

". . . I entered the Department of the Interior as its Chief, I found on its pay rolls a considerable number of useless incumbents who were seldom at their respective desks. Some of them were simply supernumerary, and some of them were worthless.

". . . It would not be possible for me now, after the lapse of about twenty nine years, to recall in detail the reasons reported to me by their respective heads of Bureaus, for their discontinuance in the public service, even if it were desirable and proper to recite them, after many of them like Whitman were passed over to the other side. It is, therefore deemed needful only to say in relation to his removal, that his Chief, Hon. Wm. P. Dole, Commissioner of Indian Affairs, who was officially answerable to me for the work in his Bureau, recommended it, on the ground that his services were not needed and no other reason was ever assigned by my authority . . ."

On the inner side of the back cover Mr. Miller has inscribed his name and place of residence.

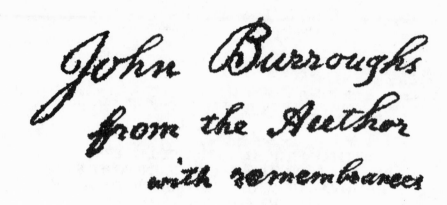

[NUMBER 518]

PRESENTATION COPY FROM THE AUTHOR TO
JOHN BURROUGHS, WITH AN AUTOGRAPH
INSCRIPTION BY BURROUGHS

518. [WHITMAN (WALT).] **Leaves of Grass.** *2 portraits.* 8vo, original half tan calf, cloth sides, leather labels, gilt edges.   Camden, 1876

AUTHOR'S EDITION, WITH A PRESENTATION INSCRIPTION BY WHITMAN AND WITH HIS SIGNATURE ON THE TITLE-PAGE. A PRESENTATION COPY OF GREAT IMPORTANCE, COMBINING THE NAMES OF WHITMAN AND JOHN BURROUGHS, WHITMAN'S INTIMATE FRIEND AND HIS FIRST BIOGRAPHER, AND INSCRIBED BY BOTH. The autograph PRESENTATION INSCRIPTION BY THE AUTHOR is displayed on the front end-paper and reads as follows: *"John Burroughs from the Author with remembrances".* The following leaf displays the AUTOGRAPH INSCRIPTION by the recipient: *"This volume has been in my possession since 1876 & is now exchanged with Dewitt Miller. John Burroughs. July 13, 1903."* Pasted down on the end-paper at the back is the portion addressed in Burroughs' hand of the wrapper in which the present volume was sent to Mr. Miller.

This copy contains the two portraits, and on the backstrip is the leather label reading "Centennial Ed'n-1876". This is also one of the few copies displaying the reading at the lower part of the title-page "With portraits and Intercalations". These intercalations are represented by short poems printed on small slips of paper and pasted down on pp. 207, 247, 359, and 369.

At the back is a leaf advertising a few of Whitman's writings. On the inner side of the back cover Mr. Miller has inscribed his name and place of residence.

[See illustration]

519. [———] Leaves of Grass. *2 portraits.* 12mo, half original sheep, marbled sides; rubbed, covers loose.   Camden, 1876

AUTHOR'S EDITION, with Whitman's signature on the title-page. PRESENTATION COPY FROM THE AUTHOR, with autograph inscription on the front end-paper: *"Wm. H. Kelly from the author."*

On the inner side of the back cover Mr. Miller has inscribed his name and place of residence.

182

PRESENTATION COPY OF THE AUTHOR'S EDITION

520. [WHITMAN (WALT).] Leaves of Grass. *2 portraits.* 8vo, original green cloth, gilt lettering on the backstrip, gilt top, uncut; covers somewhat worn.

Camden, 1882

AUTHOR'S EDITION, with Whitman's autograph on the title-page. PRESENTATION COPY FROM THE AUTHOR, with autograph inscription on the front end-paper: *"R Pearsall Smith from the author with love. Oct. 9, 1886"*.

Wells and Goldsmith write of this edition: "This is a scarce and almost unknown issue; it is doubtful if more than one hundred copies were printed. It appeared after the suppressions of the Boston edition and before the first Philadelphia edition . . . It is probable that Whitman had these made for a few friends while waiting for the first Philadelphia edition".

On the inner side of the back cover Mr. Miller has inscribed his name and place of residence.

AN APPARENTLY UNIQUE BROADSIDE

A Proof Copy, with Manuscript Corrections

521. WHITMAN (WALT). [Broadside.] *"Copy of Letter sent by Walt Whitman in response to invitation of 'Tertio-Millenial Anniversary Association' at Santa Fé, New Mexico"*. *"Camden New Jersey July 20 1883 . . ."* Folio, broadside. Enclosed in cloth folder.

AN APPARENTLY UNIQUE AND HITHERTO UNRECORDED PROOF OF AN UNKNOWN BROADSIDE BY WALT WHITMAN. THE HEADING AS TRANSCRIBED ABOVE, THE DATE LINE, THE PRELIMINARY SALUTATION, AND THE CLOSING WORDS AND SIGNATURE ARE ALL IN THE HAND OF THE AUTHOR.

This letter, expressing Whitman's inability to attend the celebration, is printed in the edition of his prose works published in 1914 at New York, appearing on pp. 388-9; but aside from this publication THE LETTER APPARENTLY IS ENTIRELY UNKNOWN EXCEPT BY THE PRESENT BROADSIDE.

Aside from the holograph material noted above, there are six corrections by Whitman in the printed portions. This is indeed A WHITMAN ITEM OF THE UTMOST IMPORTANCE AND RARITY.

[See illustration]

PRESENTATION COPY OF ONE OF A SMALL ISSUE
PRINTED FOR PRESENTATION PURPOSES ONLY

522. WHITMAN (WALT). November Boughs. *Frontispiece portrait.* 8vo, original limp maroon cloth, uncut; covers very slightly spotted.

Philadelphia, 1888

FIRST EDITION. ONE OF A FEW COPIES BOUND IN LIMP CLOTH, ENTIRELY UNCUT, FOR PRESENTATION PURPOSES. PRESENTATION COPY FROM THE AUTHOR, with autograph inscription on the front end-paper: *"from the author Walt Whitman Jan: 4 1889"*.

On the inner side of the back cover Mr. Miller has inscribed his name and place of residence.

183

Camden New Jersey July 20 1883

To Messrs: Griffin Martinez Prince, and other gentlemen at Santa Fé —

Dear Sirs:

Your kind invitation to visit you and deliver a poem for the 333d Anniversary of founding Santa Fe has reached me so late, that I have to decline, with sincere regret. But I will say a few words off-hand.

We Americans have yet to really learn our own antecedents, and sort them, to unify them. They will be found ampler than has been supposed, and in widely different sources. Thus far, impressed by New England writers and schoolmasters, we tacitly abandon ourselves to the notion that our United States have been fashioned from the British Islands only, and essentially form a second England only—which is a very great mistake. Many leading traits for our future National Personality, and some of the best ones, will certainly prove to have originated from other than British stock. As it is, the British and German, valuable as they are in the concrete, already threaten excess. Or rather, I should say, they have certainly reached that excess. To day, something outside of them, and to counterbalance them, is seriously needed.

The seething materialistic and business vortices of the United States, in their present devouring relations, controlling and belittling everything else, are, in my opinion, but a vast and indispensable stage in the New World's development, and are certainly to be followed by something entirely different—at least by immense modifications. Character, literature, a society worthy the name, are yet to be established, through a Nationality of noblest spiritual, heroic and democratic attributes—not one of which at present definitely exists—entirely different from the past, though unerringly founded on it. and to justify it.

To that composite American identity of the future, Spanish character will supply some of the most needed parts. No stock shows a grander historic retrospect—grander in religiousness and loyalty, or for patriotism, courage, decorum, gravity and honor. (It is time to dismiss utterly the illusion-compound, half raw-head-and-bloody-bones and half Mysteries-of-Udolpho, inherited from the English writers of the past two hundred years. It is time to realize—for it is certainly true—that there will not be found any more cruelty, tyranny, superstition, &c in the resumé of past Spanish history, than in the corresponding resumé of Anglo-Norman history. Nay, I thind there will not be found so much)

Then another point, relating to American ethnology, past and to come, I will here touch upon at a venture. As to our aboriginal or Indian population—the Aztec in the south, and many a tribe in the north and west—I know it seems to be agreed that they must gradually dwindle as time rolls on, and in a few generations more, leave only a reminiscence, a blank. But I am not at all clear about that. As America, from its many far-back sources and current supplies, develops, adapts, entwines, faithfully identifies its own—are we to see it cheerfully accepting and using all the contributions of foreign lands from the whole outside globe—and then rejecting the only ones distinctively its own—the autochthonic ones?

As to the Spanish stock of our Southwest, it is certain to me that we do not begin to appreciate the splendor and sterling value of its race element. Who knows but that element, like the course of some subterranean river, dipping invisibly for a hundred or two years, is now to emerge in broadest flow and permanent action?

If I might assume to do so, I would like to send you the most cordial, heartfelt respectful congratulations of your American fellow-countrymen here. You have more friends in the Northern and Atlantic regions than you suppose, and they are deeply interested in the development of the great Southwestern interior, and in what your festival would arouse to public attention.

Very respectfully &c.

Walt Whitman

[NUMBER 521]

184

PRESENTATION COPY TO E. C. STEDMAN

523. WHITMAN (WALT). November Boughs. *Frontispiece portrait.* Small 4to, original maroon limp cloth. Philadelphia, 1888

120—

R. H.

FIRST EDITION. PRESENTATION COPY OF THE RARE LARGE PAPER ISSUE TO E. C. STEDMAN, INSCRIBED BY THE AUTHOR AS FOLLOWS: *"E C Stedman from his friend the author W W Oct: '88".* A note on the last fly-leaf signed *"H. L. T*[raubell]." states that this copy is one bound in the rejected covers, later supplanted by the ordinary cloth binding. From the library of Edmund Charles Stedman, with bookplate.

524. —— Specimen Days & collect. 12mo, original yellow cloth. Philadelphia: David McKay, 1882-3

30—

FIRST EDITION. Second Issue, with the imprint of David McKay on the title-page and the backstrip. PRESENTATION COPY FROM THE AUTHOR, with autograph inscription on the front end-paper: *"Clayton Wesley Peirson from the author, Feb. 2, 1887. Walt Whitman".*

On the inner side of the back cover Mr. Miller has inscribed his name and place of residence.

CATALOGUE

OF

IMPORTANT LETTERS, MANUSCRIPTS AND BOOKS

BY OR RELATING TO

WALT WHITMAN

THE PROPERTY OF HIS INTIMATE FRIEND, BIOGRAPHER

AND LITERARY EXECUTOR

𝔗𝔥𝔢 𝔩𝔞𝔱𝔢 𝔇𝔯. 𝔕𝔦𝔠𝔥𝔞𝔯𝔡 𝔐𝔞𝔲𝔯𝔦𝔠𝔢 𝔅𝔲𝔯𝔨𝔢,

of London, Ontario

[SOLD BY ORDER OF H. L. BUCKE, ESQ.]

DAY OF SALE :

Monday, May 13th, 1935

SOTHEBY & CO.

I. WORKS BY WALT WHITMAN

[INCLUDING SIGNED OR PRESENTATION COPIES]

LOT 1

£3|10|–

WHITMAN (WALT) Complete Poems and Prose, *portraits, signature of the author on title to " Leaves of Grass ", half green cloth, uncut, unopened*   *large 8vo*   [1888]   KF

2   Whitman (Walt) A Collection of Nine early stories extracted from The United States Magazine and Democratic Review and bound together, *half black leather*   *8vo   New York*, 1841-45

2|15|–

Hollings

  ** The Collection includes : Death in the Schoolroom (Aug. 1841) ; Wild Frank's Return (Nov. 1841) ; Bervance : or, Father and Son (Dec. 1841) ; The Tomb-Blossoms (Jan. 1842) ; The Last of the Sacred Army (March 1842) ; The Child-Ghost ; a Story of the Last Loyalist (May 1842) ; The Angel of Tears (Sept. 1842) ; Revenge and Requital (July and Aug. 1845) ; A Dialogue (Nov. 1845).

2b

3   WHITMAN (WALT) Leaves of Grass Imprints. American and European Criticisms of " Leaves of Grass ", FIRST EDITION, *original wrappers*   16*mo*   *Boston : Thayer and Eldridge,* 1860

    ** " This was a reprint of criticisms of the first and second editions. Pages 7, 30 and 38 contain articles written by Walt Whitman anonymously to various papers. Dr. Bucke is the authority for this statement. The pamphlet was supplied gratuitously by the publishers as an advertisement . . . On account of its size and frail make-up it is now very rare ".—Wells and Goldsmith, *Bibliography of Whitman,* pp. 6-7.

    In this copy Dr. Bucke has marked the articles on pp. 7, 30 and 38 with blue pencil and the initials W.W.

£9
Wysseo
B.S.

4   Whitman (Walt) Leaves of Grass, *third edition, portrait, original cloth, bookplate of Dr. R. M. Bucke*
          12*mo*   *Boston, Thayer and Eldridge,* 1860-61

£1|5|=

5   WHITMAN (WALT) LEAVES OF GRASS. [Passage to India], *Washington, D.C.,* 1871 ; Democratic Vistas, FIRST EDITION, *ib.,* 1871, *bound in one vol. in green morocco, g. t., the original upper light green wrapper of both vol. (lower wrapper of one vol. only) preserved*
                                         12*mo*   1871

    ** SIGNED BY THE AUTHOR ON FLY-LEAF : " Walt Whitman. Camden. New Jersey. Oct : 31. 1890 ", bookplate of Dr. R. M. Bucke.

KF.

£4|10|=

6   WHITMAN (WALT) LEAVES OF GRASS, *second issue of the fifth edition, original green cloth*   12*mo*   *Washington, D.C.,* 1872

    ** PRESENTATION COPY FROM THE AUTHOR WITH INSCRIPTION BY HIM ON FLY-LEAF : " Dr. R. M. Bucke from the author. Sept : 7 1891 ", signature of the author " Walt Whitman " on title.

£10
Wysses

7   Whitman (Walt) Leaves of Grass, title, intercalations and portrait used by Walt Whitman to convert a very few left-over copies of the 1872 edition into a preliminary issue of the 1876 edition (these copies occur in a half calf binding mostly sent to friends), 3 *ll., unbound*   8*vo*   *Camden, New Jersey,* 1876

30|=.
Foyer

8 WHITMAN (WALT) COPY OF LEAVES OF GRASS. Set up, Cast, & printed Boston, Aug. 22—Sept. 19, 1881, at office of [Rand, Avery & Co., Printers, No. 117 Franklin St., Boston] 1881. Henry H. Clark, Superintendent Book Department. J. R. Osgood and Co. : 211 Tremont St. publishers of book. It is to be $2 retail & I am to have 25 cts a copy royalty. I was in Boston from Aug. 19 to Oct. Dan. Rogers the boy messenger. Boarding place, Mrs. Moffitt's Hotel, 8 Bullfinch place

* The above (except the words in square brackets, which are printed) is written by Walt Whitman on a sheet of paper accompanying a copy of *Leaves of Grass*, made up from sheets of previous editions with some passages added in the author's handwriting and very numerous corrections by him throughout. The list of Contents (15 leaves) is also in his handwriting. This formed the copy for the Boston edition of 1881-82.

Dr. R. M. Bucke, in his biography of Walt Whitman (1882), writes of this edition (p. 147):

> The next (seventh) edition of *Leaves of Grass* is that of James R. Osgood & Co., Boston, 1881-82 . . . . A few of the old [poems] are omitted (generally for the reason that what they contained was expressed elsewhere), in some instances two are run into one, and quite a number of new pieces added. The text throughout has been thoroughly revised, hundreds of slight alterations have been made, in many places words and lines omitted, and as frequently, in other places, words and lines added. The arrangement and the punctuation have been materially altered for the better, and the poems are so joined and blended by slight alterations in the text and by juxta-position, that *Leaves of Grass* now becomes a unit in a sense it had never been before. The original design of the author, formed twenty-six years before, has taken shape, and stands in this volume completed.

9 Whitman (Walt) Leaves of Grass. Preface to the original edition, 1855, *original wrappers (front wrapper slightly torn),* London : *Trübner and Co.,* 1881 ; Another copy, *foremargin of front wrapper and first 11 ll. defective (affecting text of wrapper and title), ib.,* 1881   *8vo* (2)

WHITMAN (WALT) LEAVES OF GRASS, *signature of author on title, original cloth*
     8vo Author's Edition, Camden, New Jersey, 1882
* " This is a scarce and almost unknown issue ; it is doubtful if more than one hundred copies were printed. It appeared after the suppression of the Boston edition and before the first Philadelphia Edition was issued by Rees, Welsh and Company. All copies were autographed, and it is probable that Whitman had these made for a few friends while waiting for the first Philadelphia Edition."—Wells and Goldsmith, *Bibliography of Walt Whitman,* p. 25.

WHITMAN (WALT) Leaves of Grass with Sands at Seventy, and a Backward Glance o'er Travel'd Roads, *special autograph edition, portraits, signature of the author on title, one of* 300 *copies printed, limp black leather, g. e.*   12mo *Philadelphia,* 1889

WHITMAN (WALT) LEAVES OF GRASS, *original brown wrappers, yellow paper label (back strip defective)*
8vo Philadelphia, David McKay, Publisher,
23 South Ninth Street,   1891-'2

*** PRESENTATION COPY FROM THE AUTHOR WITH INSCRIPTION BY HIM ON TITLE : " Dr. R. M. Bucke first copy completed L. of G. from the author with love Dec: 6 1891 ".

FIRST ISSUE. " Whitman was very ill at the time, and, wanting to see the edition, Horace Traubel had a few copies hurriedly bound in wrappers for him, and Whitman had them sent to intimate friends. This issue is extremely rare and did not exceed fifty copies ".—Wells and Goldsmith, *Bibliography of Walt Whitman*, pp. 34-5.

On the fly-leaf Dr. Bucke has transcribed a letter from Walt Whitman sent with this copy dated Camden N. J., Dec. 6 '91.

13 Whitman (Walt) Leaves of Grass, *wrappers (back defective and lower wrapper loose), Philadelphia*, 1891-'2 ; Grashalme, in answahl übersetzt von Karl Knortz und T. W. Rolleston, *half leather*, *Zürich*, 1889—Leaves of Grass, *wrappers*, 1897   8vo (3)

14 Whitman (Walt) Leaves of Grass, *original wrappers (back-strip defective), Philadelphia*, 1891-'2 ; Natuurleven, vertaald door Maurits Wagenvoort, *Haarlem*, 1898 ; Grashalme, in auswahl übersetzt von Karl Knortz und T. W. Rolleston, *wrappers*, *Zurich*, 1889 ; Leaves of Grass, *wrappers, Boston*, 1897
8vo (4)

15 WHITMAN (WALT) DRUM TAPS, FIRST EDITION, *original cloth*, FINE COPY, VERY RARE   12mo New-York, 1865

*** SIGNED BY THE AUTHOR ON FLY-LEAF : " Walt Whitman Camden New Jersey Nov: 4 1890 ".

THE FIRST ISSUE containing " Drum Taps " only. On the death of Lincoln, Whitman held up the edition and added " When Lilacs Last in the Dooryard Bloom'd " with separate title-page and pagination.

16 Whitman (Walt) Democratic Vistas. Memoranda, FIRST EDITION,
original light green wrappers, uncut
12mo *Washington, D.C.*, 1871

17 WHITMAN (WALT) Democratic Vistas, and other papers (Camelot
Series), *half brown morocco, g. t.* 8vo *London*, 1888

** PRESENTATION COPY FROM THE AUTHOR with inscription by him
on half-title : " Dr. R. M. Bucke from his friend the author
Walt Whitman to R M B ".

DEMOCRATIC VISTAS

18 Whitman (Walt) Passage to India. Leaves of Grass, FIRST EDITION,
original green wrappers (back slightly torn at top), uncut, unopened
12mo *Washington, D.C.*, 1871

19 WHITMAN (WALT) MEMORANDA DURING THE WAR, FIRST EDITION,
*2 portraits, has the " Remembrance Copy " leaf before title inscribed
by Walt Whitman : " [To] Wm. D. O'Connor [from] his friend
the author ", followed by a printed " Personal Note " (the words
in brackets also printed) ; on p. 47 line 14 the word " written "
is corrected by the author to " witless ", original cloth,* EXTREMELY
RARE
8vo *Author's Publication, Camden, New Jersey*, 1875-'76

** Inserted are two extracts from the *West Jersey Press* for 26th
Jan., 1876, and 15th March, 1876, relating to Walt Whitman,
reprinted in galley form :
" It is improbable that more than a hundred copies were
issued. The book is exceedingly rare."—Wells and Goldsmith,
Bibliography of Whitman, p. 19.

190

20 WHITMAN (WALT) TWO RIVULETS, FIRST EDITION, *original half leather binding (binding worn, back loose and defective)*
       12mo Author's Edition, Camden, New Jersey, 1876
** PRESENTATION COPY FROM THE AUTHOR with inscription by him on fly-leaf : " R. Maurice Bucke from the author with love. London Canada. Sept: 21 1880 ".
The portrait also signed by the author : " Walt Whitman born May 31. 1819 ".

£7/10/-
Quaritch

21 WHITMAN (WALT) SPECIMEN DAYS & COLLECT, FIRST EDITION (FIRST ISSUE), *original yellow cloth*
      8vo Philadelphia : Rees Welsh and Co., 1882-'83
** WITH INSCRIPTION BY THE AUTHOR ON FLY-LEAF : " Walt Whitman Camden New Jersey Oct: 31 1890 ". Bookplate of Dr. R. M. Bucke.

£17/10/-
Megaskis

22 Whitman (Walt) Elegiac Ode, the words from President Lincoln's Burial Hymn, by Walt Whitman, the music composed by C. Villiers Stanford, *red leather*   *large 8vo* [1884]
** Inscription on fly-leaf : " To Walt Whitman in remembrance of a pleasant visit to Camden from Donald MacAlister Cambridge England. Sept. 1887 ".

£1/10/-

23 Whitman (Walt) Proof sheets of " November Boughs ", *with portrait of Walt Whitman in his 70th year, in wrapper endorsed by Dr. Bucke : " Proof slips—sent me as struck off by W. W.— of November Boughs. R. M. B.", unbound*
** " November Boughs " was first published at Philadelphia in 1888.

£4/10/-
Ulysses

24 WHITMAN (WALT) GOOD-BYE MY FANCY, 2nd Annex to Leaves of Grass, FIRST EDITION, *portrait*, PRESENTATION COPY FROM THE AUTHOR *with inscription by him on fly-leaf : " R. M. Bucke from the author June 20 '91 ", original maroon cloth*
      8vo Philadelphia, D. McKay, 1891

£15
Ulysses

25 Whitman (Walt) Selected Poems, *portrait, original cloth*
     12mo New York, Charles L. Webster and Co., 1892
** Inscription on fly-leaf : " Presented to Dr. R. M. Bucke (in accordance with Walt Whitman's last wishes) by Charles L. Webster & Co. 5. April, 1892 ".

£2
Hollings

26 Whitman (Walt) Calamus. A series of letters written during the years 1868-1880 by Walt Whitman to a young friend (Peter Doyle) edited with an introduction by R. M. Bucke, M.D., one of Whitman's literary executors, *no. 1 of 35 large paper copies signed by the editor, boards, cloth back*   *8vo Boston,* 1897

£4
Ulysses

27 Whitman (Walt) The Wound Dresser. A series of Letters written from the Hospitals in Washington during the War of the Rebellion. Edited by R. M. Bucke, FIRST EDITION (FIRST ISSUE), *portraits, lower margin of several leaves damaged, original cloth*
     8vo Boston, Small, Maynard and Company, 1898

£2/5/-
Hollings

28 Whitman (Walt) Complete Prose Works, *original cloth, Philadelphia,*
    1892 ; Leaves of Grass, *wrappers, Philadelphia, n. d.* ; Poems,
    selected and edited by W. M. Rossetti, *cloth (binding torn),*
    1868 ; Selected Poems, Edited by Ernest Rhys, *presentation*
    copy from the editor to Dr. Bucke with inscription, cloth, 1886

                                                   8vo (4)

29 Whitman (Walt) Type-written Copies of 32 letters from Walt
    Whitman to Dr. Bucke, 1883-84, on 12 folio sheets

II. BOOKS RELATING TO WALT WHITMAN OR
WITH INSCRIPTIONS BY HIM

30 BUCKE (DR. R. M.) WALT WHITMAN   *8vo*   *Philadelphia*, 1883

✱✱ Two copies of the printed book mounted on folio sheets of blank paper to make a single text ready for corrections or additions.

£19

Ulysses

At the end is a MS. transcript of Chapter III of the printed version (pp. 175-190) on 21 folio sheets WITH NUMEROUS CORRECTIONS AND ADDITIONS BY WALT WHITMAN HIMSELF. For instance, the first 9 lines of the note at foot of p. 175 down to the words " sulkily adds " are in his hand. ALSO TWO LONG PASSAGES AT THE END OF CHAPTER III ARE WRITTEN BY WALT WHITMAN (1) From line 24 of page 187 " While no reader of *Leaves of Grass* ", etc., down to line 16 of the following page " as 'eligible' as any ? " (1 p. folio of manuscript) (2) From line 10 of p. 189 " I have been so occupied with the features portrayed ", etc., down to the end of the chapter on line 12 of the following page (1⅓ pp. folio of manuscript).

31 Bucke (R. M.) Walt Whitman, *portraits and plates, signature of Walt Whitman on fly-leaf, tear in one leaf (pp.* 135-6), *original cloth*   *8vo*   *Philadelphia*, 1883

£8

ulysses

32 Bucke (R. M.) Walt Whitman, to which is added English critics on Walt Whitman, edited by E. Dowden, *portrait and plates, bookplate of R. M. Bucke, cloth, Glasgow,* 1884—Kennedy (W. S.) Reminiscences of Walt Whitman, *cloth,* 1896—Burroughs (John) Notes on Walt Whitman as poet and person, *cloth, New York,* 1867—Guthrie (W. N.) Walt Whitman as religious and moral teacher, *wrappers, Cincinnati,* 1897   *8vo*   (4)

£7

Maggs

33 BUCKE (R. M.) A scrap-album of cuttings from newspapers and other periodicals collected by Dr. Bucke with upwards of 550 pieces (articles, lectures, poems, etc.) by or relating to Walt Whitman. Among them (p. 104) is a poem " *Patroling Barnegat* " by Walt Whitman, inscribed by Dr. Bucke " unpublished—private. Received from Walt June 3. 1880 ". On p. 517 is another single-sheet poem by Walt Whitman, " *Thanks in old age* " with inscription " pub'd Nov. 24 ". At p. 588 is a proof of an article by Walt Whitman on his friend W. D. O'Connor [d. 9 May 1889] with note " Reached me from W. W. 27th Sept. in letter dated 24th and 25th Sept. R. M. B.".

£21

Ulysses

3a

34 EPICTETUS. ENCHEIRIDION. Translated from the Greek by
T. W. H. Rolleston, *limp cloth wrappers*   8vo *London*, 1881

  ** WALT WHITMAN'S COPY with his signature on title and the note :
" E. is not (this trans : w'd say) in the interest of the ascetic
doctrines. Be bold—Be bold—Be bold—be not too bold ".

On the fly-leaf is another inscription by Whitman : " Walt
Whitman (sent me by my friend the translator T. W. H. Rolleston
from Dresden, Saxony) 1881 ".

Below is a later note by him : " March 1886—T. W. R. is now
in Ireland (Delgany, County Wicklow)—& edits the *Dublin
University Review* ".

And another, still later : " from 1881 to '88—Have had this
little vol. at hand or in my hand often all these years—have
read it over and over and over ".

On another fly-leaf is another long signed note by Walt Whitman
about his failing health, dated Nov. 7 '89.

Many marginal markings by Walt Whitman throughout.

35 Houghton (Lord) A selection from his Works (Moxon's Miniature
Poets), *half leather*   8vo *London*, 1868

  ** Presentation Copy from the author to Walt Whitman, with
inscription on half-title : " To Walt Whitman, with the respects
and regards of Richard Monckton Milnes Lord Houghton.
Philadelphia. Nov. 6th 1875 ".

36 Johnston (John) Diary Notes of a visit to Walt Whitman, *portraits
and plates, presentation copy to Dr. Bucke, cloth*, 1898—Donaldson
(T.) Walt Whitman the Man, *portrait and facsimiles, buckram,
New York*, 1896—Holmes (E.) Walt Whitman's Poetry. A
study and a selection, *cloth*, 1902 ; and others on Walt Whitman
8vo (14)

37 Mazzini (Joseph) Essays, edited by W. Clarke (Camelot series),
cloth   8vo *London*, 1887

  ** Walt Whitman's copy with note by Dr. Bucke on half-title :
" This little volume was sent to me Aug. '89 by Walt Whitman,
who had just been reading it—the marginal marking of passages
is (as far as I know) entirely by him. R. M. Bucke. London
Asylum. 21 Aug. '89 ".

38 Newspapers. Three old Newspapers kept by Walt Whitman.
The New-York Mercury for 18 March, 1754, *The Boston Gazette*
for 12 March, 1770, and the *American Mercury* for 18 April,
1799 ; *tears in folds*

39 Newspaper Cuttings. Two large scrap-books containing about
1,500 newspaper clippings relating to Walt Whitman from the
year 1854 to his death in 1892, *bound in half red leather*
folio (2)

40 Newspaper Cuttings. A Collection of cuttings from Newspapers
relating to Walt Whitman   1865-67

41 Pamphlets relating to Walt Whitman. A Collection of seven
published between 1883-96, two of them being presentation
copies to Walt Whitman with inscriptions   8vo (7)

£3/10/- Hollings

42 PHOTOGRAPHS. Five large and fine photographs of Walt Whitman
taken in September, 1887, *all signed and dated by the poet,
about 9in. by 7¼in.*

£15 Ulysses

[*See* FRONTISPIECE]

43 PHOTOGRAPHS. Six photographs of Walt Whitman, including one
signed " Walt Whitman Sept : 7 1891 " (7⅝*in.* by 6*in.*), one taken
in 1853 and 2 taken with Peter Doyle ; also 8 other photographs
or prints connected with Walt Whitman   (14)

£4 Shaw

44 PHOTOGRAPHS. An album containing 29 photographs or engravings
of Walt Whitman, 1855-1883 ; also phototypes of his father
and mother, preserved on sunk mounts, *half leather, g. e.,
bookplate of Dr. R. M. Bucke*   4to (13*in.* by 11*in.*)

£10 Ulysses

45 PHOTOGRAPHS. Four photographs of Walt Whitman, *all with
autograph inscriptions* (1) " Winter of 1863 Washington.
D.C.". (2) " Walt Whitman. Sarnia. June 23 1880 ". (3)
" Walt Whitman June 1 '87 ". (4) " Walt Whitman " (*no
place or year, but taken in extreme old age*)

£10/10/- Shaw.

46 PHOTOGRAPHS. A collection of 45 photographs and other portraits
of Walt Whitman

£4/4/- Reeve

47 Photographs, etc. A collection of 15 photographs or prints relating
to Walt Whitman. Photographs of Whitman's house in Camden,
New Jersey ; views of his tomb ; photograph of his brother
George (*circa* 1862) in uniform ; portraits of friends, etc. Also
a small collection of newspaper clippings relating to Walt
Whitman

£2/10/- Hollings

48 SADI. Flowers culled from the Gulistan, or Rose Garden, and
from The Bostan, or Pleasure Garden of Sadi, *several preliminary
leaves missing, title stained, half leather (wrappers bound in)*
16*mo London,* 1876

£5 Hollings

*** Walt Whitman's copy with his signature on title and inscription
by him on half-title : " Walt Whitman (from Thos. Dixon,
Sunderland, England. April '77)." On the same leaf is the
inscription (presumably by T. Dixon) " The Greetings of a
few kindred souls here to thee in 1877 ".

£2/10/- 49 Whitman (Walt) Walt Whitman Fellowship Papers. Years 1-5
(*no. 7 of fifth year wanting*), *unbound*   8vo 1894-99

50 Willard (Edward) Julius Caesar, an historical tragedy, *cloth*
8vo *Philadelphia,* 1890

£1. kt

*** Presentation copy with inscription on title (not autograph) :
" Walter Whitman, with compliments of the Author", and
signature : " Edward Willard " below.

III. AUTOGRAPH LETTERS, NOTES AND
MANUSCRIPTS BY WALT WHITMAN

51 WHITMAN (WALT) 1½ pp. folio and 1 p. 4to of autograph autobiographical matter giving an account of his life in New Orleans in 1848 with his brother Jefferson while engaged on the staff of " The Crescent " :

" . , . . For a few weeks after I commenced my duties at New Orleans, matters went on very pleasantly.—People seemed to treat me kindly . . . My health was most capital ; I frequently thought indeed that I felt better than ever before in my life . . . . Through some unaccountable means, however, both H. and M.C., after a while, exhibited a singular sort of coldness toward me . . . My own pride was touched, and I met their conduct by equal haughtiness on my part ", etc.

Also a portion of an autograph essay, 1 p. 4to, and a " Family Record ", 2 ll. 4to, with entries of the births and marriages of members of the Whitman family

52 WHITMAN (WALT) HIS SCRAP-BOOK, consisting of extracted articles from magazines WITH A LARGE NUMBER OF AUTOGRAPH MS. NOTES IN THE MARGINS OR ON INSERTED BLANK LEAVES

The MS. additions are chiefly critical notes on other authors, many of them long and of great interest. Among them are notes on Homer and Shakespeare, Dryden, Dr. Johnson, Oliver Goldsmith, Dr. Priestly, Keats, Richter, Francis Wright, etc.

In a long note on Goethe filling five pages he writes :

" Here is now (January 1856) my opinion of Goethe : He is the most profound reviewer of Life known.—To him life, things, the mind, death, people, are all studies, dissections, exhibitions. These he enters upon with unequalled coolness and depth of penetration. As a critic he stands apart from all men, and criticises them. He is the first great critic and the fountain of modern criticism. · Yet Goethe will never be well-beloved of his fellows. Perhaps he knows too much. I can fancy him not being well beloved of Nature for the same reason. A calm and mighty person whose anatomical considerations of the body are not enclosed by superior considerations makes the perfect surgeon and operator upon the body upon all occasions. So Goethe operates upon the world . . . his office is great . . . what indeed is greater ? ", etc.

Another long note begins :

" What are inextricable from the British poets are the ideas of royalty and aristocracy, the ideas of the radical division of those who serve from those who are served, and a continual recognition of the principles at the bases of monarchy and the societies and beliefs of caste ", etc.

And another :

" Homer and Shakespeare deserve all that has been bestowed upon them. They did what was to be done and did the work divinely. Homer poetized great wars, persons, events, throwing together in perfect proportion a perfect poem, noisy, muscular, manly, amative, an amusement, and excitement.

Shakespeare, the gentle, the sweet, musical, well-beloved Shakespeare, delineated characters ; they are better done by him than by any other poet at any time . . . Could there not be a poet of America doing no less than but different from either of them ? Stamping *this age*, and so all ages, in his poems ? ", etc.

53 WHITMAN (WALT) A LARGE COLLECTION OF LOOSE AUTOGRAPH
   NOTES · BY WALT WHITMAN, ideas for poems, fragments of
   poems, list of words to be used and other memoranda. Also a
   large collection of printed articles from magazines and newspapers cut out and preserved by Whitman with markings or
   marginal notes, *kept in five cardboard files*

£35

Wypoes

A specimen MS. note is a self-criticism by Whitman in file
numbered 5, dated Feb. 25th, '57 :

" Dined with Hector Tyndale. Asked H.T. where he thought I needed
particular attention to be directed for my improvement—where I could
especially be bettered in my poems—
He said—' In massiveness, breadth, large, sweeping effects without
regard to details,—as in the Cathedral at York (he said) I came away
with great impressions of its largeness, solidity and spaciousness, without
troubling myself with its parts '.
Asked F. le B. same question—viz. what I most lacked—He said—
' In *euphony*—Your poems seem to me to be full of the raw material of
poems, but crude and wanting finish and rhythm '.

Below is the note :

Put in my poems American things, idioms, materials, persons, groups,
minerals, vegetables, animals, etc.

In the same file is the following MS. note on Longfellow :

The Song of Hiawatha by H. W. Longfellow—A pleasing ripply poem—
the measure, the absence of ideas, the Indian process of thought, the
droning metre, the sleepy misty woody character, the traditions, pleased
me well enough.

With the same lot is another file containing a printed list
of subscribers to Walt Whitman's Buggy and Horse given him
Sept. 15, 1885, and other printed scraps

54 WHITMAN (WALT) WALT WHITMAN'S LECTURES, AN AUTOGRAPH
   ADVERTISEMENT IN POSTER FORM OF A PROPOSED SERIES OF
   LECTURES ON AMERICA WRITTEN ON A SHEET OF THICK PINK
   PAPER (6*in*. by 3⅝*in*.), *priced* 15 *cents and dated Brooklyn, New
   York*, 1858

WALT WHITMAN'S LECTURES :

£30

I desire to go by degrees through all these States, especially West and
South, and through Kanada : lecturing (my own way) henceforth my
employment, my means of earning my living—subject to the work
elsewhere alluded to that takes precedence . . .

AMERICA

A Programme, etc.

Some plan I seek, to have the vocal delivery of my Lectures free, but at
present a low price of admission, one dime—or my fee for reciting here
$10 (when any distance expences in addition).
Each Lecture will be printed with its recitation needing to be carefully
perused afterward to be understood.   I personally sell the printed copies.

On the back of the sheet Walt Whitman has written in a very
small crabbed hand a long note on *Leaves of Grass* and on his
lectures

55 WHITMAN (WALT) A. L. to his mother (not signed ; ? incomplete), 2 pp. 4to, written from the Attorney General's Office, Washington, without date (*the printed date* 186– *not filled in*) :

" . . . William O'Connor has returned, & has brought me news from you all, & about Jeff's offer to go to St. Louis. I don't know what to advise about it—but feel as if I was rather in favor of accepting the offer. Jeff must take it cool, & not get excited about it—after he has *decided* which to do, must go ahead for good, & not doubt his decision, or fear he has done wrong, etc. . . . Wm O'Connor was much pleased with his visit . . . he is a good fellow, & has been a good friend to me . . . I was down at the hospital Sunday afternoon . . . One soldier 12th Infantry was dying while I was there . . . I sat by him about half an hour . . . It was a fine afternoon, & very still in the ward—& off a block or so . . . they were ringing a chime of bells . . . playing a sort of tune, sounded loud & joyful—I sat and listened for a long while—the poor dying man kept looking at me with such a look "

Sold with the above are portions of 3 other holograph letters to his mother and several other scraps

56 WHITMAN (WALT) A. L. s. to his brother George, 4 pp. 8vo, July 12th, 1861. Giving details of his mother's health and of other members of the family

. . . " We are all very glad the 13th is coming home. There have been so many accounts of shameful negligence, or worse, in the commissariat of your reg't. that there must be *something* in it—notwithstanding you speak very lightly of the complaints in your letters. The *Eagle* of course makes the worst of it, every day, to stop men from enlisting.

All of us here think the rebellion as good as broke—no matter if the war does continue for months yet."

Small piece torn from corner and small hole in first leaf

57 WHITMAN (WALT) SIX LONG AND INTIMATE AUTOGRAPH LETTERS FROM WALT WHITMAN TO HIS FRIEND TOM SAWYER, A SOLDIER IN THE SECESSION WAR. He was a sergeant in Co. C. of the 11th Mass. Volunteers and had probably been in the army from the outbreak of the war. It seems that he was taken to Armory Square hospital about the end of '62 or beginning of '63 either sick or wounded, and his friendship with Whitman began there. One is dated from Washington 27 March, 1863, four have been given various dates in 1863 by Dr. Bucke, and the longest and most important (quoted in part last in the description below) is without date

In one (dated by Dr. Bucke 21 April, 1863) he writes :

As to me . . . . I manage to pay my way here in Washington [with] what I make writing letters for the New York papers etc. when I stopped here last January . . . I thought I would . . . see if I could not get some berth, clerkship or something—but I have not pushed strong enough . . . and I don't know as I could be satisfied with the life of a clerk . . . anyhow. So I have hung along here ever since. I guess I enjoy a kind of vagabond life any how. I go around some nights when the spirit moves me, sometimes to the gay places, just to see the sights. Tom I wish you was here—Somehow I dont find the comrade that suits me to a dot—and I wont have any other, not for good.

In one passage in a long letter without date he writes :

Tom, I sometimes feel as if I didnt want to live—life would have no charm for me, if this country should fail after all and be reduced to take a third rate position to be domineered over by England & France & the haughty nations of Europe etc, and we unable to help ourselves . . . This country I hope would spend her last drop of blood and last dollar rather than submit to such humiliation.

In another letter, also without date, he writes :

Dear comrade, you must not forget me. My love you have in life or death forever. I dont know how you feel about it, but it is the wish of my heart to have your friendship, and also that if you should come safe out of this war, we should come together again in some place where we could make our living, and be true comrades, and never be separated while life lasts—and take Lew Brown too, and never separate from him. Or if things are not so to be, if you get these lines, my dear darling comrade, and any thing should go wrong, so that we do not meet again here on earth, it seems to me (the way I feel now) that my soul could never be entirely happy, even in the world to come, without you, dear comrade. God bless you, Tom, and preserve you through the perils of the fight,

Sold with this lot are three letters from Thomas P. Sawyer, two to Walt Whitman and another

* A MOST IMPORTANT AND INTERESTING SERIES OF WHITMAN LETTERS.

57A WHITMAN (WALT) HOLOGRAPH ACCOUNT OF THE SCENE IN THE HOUSE OF REPRESENTATIVES at the adjournment of the 37th Congress on the 4 March 1863, MANUSCRIPT IN PENCIL, 13 ll. 12mo, *unbound* 1863

£20
ulysses

58 WHITMAN (WALT) AUTOGRAPH LETTER TO BETHUEL SMITH, a cavalryman in the Secession War, about 3 pp. 8vo (written on several sheets of paper), *dated by Dr. Bucke* " *Sept.* '63 ". Bethuel Smith was wounded on 11th June and was taken to Armory Square hospital, where he was nursed by Whitman

" . . . if you get this you must write to me, Thu. You need not mind ceremony between dear friends, for that I hope we are, Thuey, for all the difference in our ages . . . I am very well . . . & only need some employment, clerkship or something, at fair wages to make things go agreeable with me —no, there is one thing more I need & that is Thuey, for I believe I am quite a fool, I miss you so."

£11

Ulysses

ANOTHER A. L. TO THE SAME (in pencil), *without date*, written on 2 blank pages of a letter to him, *dated* 10 *Dec.* 1874, from Bethuel Smith's mother :

" . . . Years have passed away but friendship formed in . . . sickness . . . or with the wounded in hospital comes up again fresh and living as ever & as if it cannot pass away. Bethuel, dear comrade, how I should like to see you. I want to hear all about you . . . I worked in Washington after the war—had a stroke of paralysis now two years since, was getting better, then some serious troubles happened to me & I fell back again— I have left Brooklyn & Washington for good & am now laid up here—I am neither well enough to do any work nor sick enough to give up—go out some though lame & keep a pretty good heart hoping for better times."

With the above are sold 9 letters from Bethuel Smith to Walt Whitman (*mostly* 1863-4), 3 letters from Bethuel Smith's mother to Walt Whitman, and another

60 WHITMAN (WALT) A. L. s., 2 pp. 12mo, to his mother, *dated Friday 6th* [? *May*, 1864] :

" . . . there is an extra out here that Grant has advanced his army . . . to the region of the Chancellorsville battle of just a year ago & has either flanked Lee . . . or else that Lee has hurried back . . . to Richmond. Whether there is any thing in this story or not, I can't tell—the city is full of rumors . . . the Government is not in receipt of any information to-day—Grant has taken the reins entirely in his own hands—he is really dictator at present—we shall hear something important within two or three days—Grant is very secretive indeed—he bothers himself very little about sending news even to the President or Stanton—time only can develop his plans—I still think *he is going to take Richmond & soon.*"

£22
maggs

[See ILLUSTRATION]

2 o'clock p m Friday 6th
Mother just as I put this letter in
the mail, there is an extra out here that
Grant has advanced his army (or a portion of it) to the
region of the Chancellorsville battle
of just a year ago & has either
flanked Lee, as they call it, (got in on
his army between him & Richmond)
— or else that Lee has hurried back
or is hurrying back to Richmond —
— whether there is any thg in this
story or not, I can't tell — the city is

full of rumors & this may be one of
them — the government is not in receipt
of any information to-day — Grant has taken
the reins entirely in his own hands — he
is really dictator at present — we shall
hear something important within two or
three days — Grant is very secretive indeed
— he bothers himself very little about sending
news even to the President or Stanton —
— time only can develope his plans — I still
think he is going to take Richmond &
soon (but I may be mistaken, as I have
been in past) — well dearest mother keep up good courage
good bye for present — I wish you would &
write soon — Walt

LOT 60

200

61 WHITMAN (WALT) Two A. Ls. s. (without signature), written on
both sides of a 4to sheet. One, *dated 2 Oct.* [1868] is to " Dear
friend Harry Hurt " :

> . . . " Harry, you would much enjoy going round N.Y. with me, if it
> were possible, & then how much I should like having you with me.
> This great city, with all its crowds, & splendor, & Broadway fashion,
> & women, & amusements, & the river & bay, & shipping, & the
> many magnificent new buildings, & Central Park & 5th Avenue &
> the endless processions of private vehicles & the finest teams I ever saw
> for miles long of a fine afternoon—altogether they make up a show that I
> can richly spend a month in enjoying—for a change from my Washington
> life. I sometimes think I am the particular man who enjoys the show of
> all these things in N.Y. more than any other mortal—as if it was all got
> up just for me to observe and study " . . .

On the other side is another letter :

> Dear Lewy,
> I will write you just a line to let you know I have not forgotten you.
> I am here on leave, & shall stay nearly all this month. Duffy is here
> driving on Broadway & 5th Av. line. He has been up the Hudson river
> this summer driving hotel coach . . . Tell Johnny Miller there is still a
> sprinkling of the old Broadway drivers left. Balky Bill, Fred Kelly,
> Charley McLaughlin, Tom Riley, Prodigal, Sandy etc are still here. Frank
> McKinney & several other old drivers are with Adams Express "

£9

[*See* ILLUSTRATION]

62 WHITMAN (WALT) A personal Autograph Note on 2 scraps of paper
[1871] :

> " W.W. is now fifty-two years old. No worldly aim has engrossed his
> life. He is still unmarried. None of the usual ardor of business ambition,
> the acquisition of money, or the claims of society, pleasure, nor even the
> attractions of culture or art seem to have enslaved him. The thought
> of making this work* has spanned as it were the whole horizon of his life
> almost since boyhood."

£11/10/-

kf

* Presumably *Leaves of Grass*

63 WHITMAN (WALT) A long A. L. s. to his mother, 2 pp. 4to,
written in pencil, *from Washington* 28 *March* 1873, a month
after the stroke which ultimately caused his retirement
from the Government service and 2 months before his mother's
death in May of the same year :

> " . . . I think I am feeling better to-day, & more like myself . . . Charles
> Eldridge will be here in a few minutes, & bring the morning papers—
> he comes & sits a few minutes every morning before going to work . . .
> he & Peter Doyle hold out through every thing—most of the rest have
> got tired & stopt coming—(which is just as well). I go over to the office
> about 12 o: 1 most every day but only for a few minutes—have not resumed
> work there yet, but hope to Monday . . . it is so slow, so aggravating
> to be disabled . . . when one's mind & will are just as clear as ever ", etc.

£10

ulysses

64 WHITMAN (WALT) A SERIES OF 41 AUTOGRAPH POSTCARDS, SIGNED
WITH INITIALS TO PETER DOYLE, *all written from* 431 *Stevens St.,
Camden, New Jersey, dated with day of month but without year* ;
many with details of his health and spirits

> Camden. N. Jersey
> May 8. Noon.
> Every thing pretty much the same. Rather a bad week with me—
> no improvement—great distress in head & left side at intervals—cannot
> write much to-day—will do better next time.

£34

ulysses

Whitman's letters to Peter Doyle, one of his most intimate
friends, baggage-master on the Colonial and Federal express
from Washington to Boston, were published in 1897, with an
introduction by Dr. R. M. Bucke, under the title *Calamus.*
Whitman went to live at 431 Stevens Street in September, 1873.

65 WHITMAN (WALT) Autograph letter to William Stansberry, a
    Soldier in the Secession War, who was nursed by Whitman in
    Armory Square hospital in 1865, 3 pp. 8vo, *dated* 20 *May,*
    1874 :

> " Your letter of May 14 has come to hand today reminding me of your
> being in Armory Square Hospital & of my visits there, & meeting you in
> '65. Your letter strangely, deeply, touched me. It takes me back to
> the scenes of ten years ago, in the war, the hospitals of Washington &
> . . . the never-to-be-told sights of suffering & death . . . Dear Comrade, you
> do me good by your loving wishes & feelings to me in your letter . . .
> whether we shall ever meet each other is doubtful—probably we never
> will—but I feel that we should both be happy if we could be together—
> (I find there are some that it is just comfort enough to be together, almost
> without any thing else) . . . I remain about the same in my sickness. I
> sleep & eat pretty well—go about some, look stout & red (though looking
> now very old & gray, but that is nothing new)—weigh 185 now—am
> badly lamed in my left leg, & have bad spells, occasionally days, of feeble-
> ness, distress in head etc.
>   I think I shall get well yet, but may not : Have been laid up here a
> year doing nothing except a little writing . . . I am well situated here—
> but very lonesome—have no near friends (in the deepest sense) here at
> hand. My mother died here a year ago—a sorrow from which I have
> never entirely recovered & likely never shall—She was an unusually noble,
> cheerful woman, very proud-spirited & generous—am poor (yet with a
> little income & means just enough to pay my way with strict economy
> to be independent of want)."

Sold with the above are four letters from William Stansberry
to Walt Whitman, 1873-5, and another

66 WHITMAN (WALT) A VERY FINE COLLECTION OF 29 A.Ls. s. (GENER-
    ALLY SIGNED "WALT", OR WITH INITIALS) WRITTEN DURING
    THE YEARS 1876-1884 BY WALT WHITMAN TO HIS YOUNG FRIEND
    HARRY STAFFORD. The letters occupy about 54 pp. 8vo,
    4to, or folio, and are variously addressed (" Dear boy Harry ",
    " Dear Harry ", " Dear Comrade and Dear Son ", " Dear Hank ")

THIS REMARKABLE SERIES OF LETTERS IS ONLY COMPARABLE TO
THE AUTHOR'S FAMOUS LETTERS TO PETER DOYLE, WHICH WERE
PUBLISHED BY DR. BUCKE UNDER THE TITLE "CALAMUS"

IT IS IMPOSSIBLE WITHIN THE LIMITS OF A SALE CATALOGUE
TO GIVE AN ADEQUATE ACCOUNT OF THE EXCEPTIONAL INTEREST
OF THIS INTIMATE SERIES OF LETTERS

Camden, Feb. 23 [No year]

Dear boy Harry
> . . . . I have just rec'd yours of 26—a little wild & nervous & uncertain
> some parts, (but I am always glad to get any letters from you dear boy—
> Harry you certainly know well enough you have my best honorable
> loving friendship settled—Of the past I think only of the comforting
> soothing things of it all—I go back to the times at Timber Creek beginning
> most five years ago & the banks and spring & my hobbling down the old
> lane—& how I took a good turn there & commenced to get slowly but
> surely better, healthier stronger—Dear Hank I realise plainly that
> *if I had not known you*—if it hadn't been for you & our friendship & my
> going down there summers to the Creek with you—and living there with
> your folks & the kindness of your mother & cheering me up—I believe
> *I should not be a living man to-day*—I think & remember deeply these
> things & they comfort me—& *you my darling boy are the central figure of*
> *them all.* Of the occasional ridiculous little storms & squalls of the past
> I have quite discarded them from my memory—& I hope you will too—
> the other recollections overtop them altogether, & occupy the only per-
> manent place in my heart—as a manly loving friendship for you does also
> & will while life lasts " . . . .

Camden Dec. 1. [1880]

. . . . " A rascally publisher in New York named Worthington has been printing & selling a cheaper edition of my book for his own profit; no benefit to me at all—& it has been going on privately for a year . . . of course it is quite a hurt to me—will lead to a law suit, as I shall have to sue him & I hate getting into law—it is almost as bad to me to sue as to be sued " . . . .

In a letter written in 1881 he explains the theories worked out in *Leaves of Grass*

Camden, 11 Feb. [1881.]

. . . . Am a little surprised you take to L. of G. so quickly. I guess it is because the last five years has been *preparing & fixing the ground* more & more & more—& now that the seed is dropt in it sprouts quickly— my own feeling about my book is that it makes (tries to make) every fellow *see himself* & see that *he has got to work out his salvation himself*—has got to pull the oars & hold the plow or swing the axe *himself*—and that the real blessings of life are not the fictions generally supposed, but are real & are mostly within reach of all . . . I am still feeling under the weather . . . I am as weak as a cat & dull half-dizzy spells every day—I sent off two sets of books to-day . . . one set to a big lady in England. I enclose you a slip of a piece out to-morrow in the N.Y. *Critic* about the old man Carlyle, 85 years old, the grandest writer in England, just dead—they sent for me to write it ($10 worth) " . . . .

[*See* ILLUSTRATION]

In another letter also written in 1881 he defines his attitude to religion

431 Stevens Street Camden
Jan. 27 [1881].

. . . . " Take it easy about The minister & the Ingersoll business—the best answer you can make is to be quiet & good natured & even attentive *& not get mad worth a cent*—True religion (*the most beautiful thing in the whole world* & the best part of any man's or woman's or boy's character) consists in *what one does* square and kind & generous & honorable all days, *all the time*, & especially with his own folks & associates & with the poor & illiterate & in devout meditation & silent thoughts of God & death— & not at all in what he *says*, nor in Sunday or prayer meeting gas—my own opinion is that Ingersoll *talks* too much on his side—*a good life steady trying to do fair* & a sweet tolerant liberal disposition, shines like the sun, tastes like the fresh air of a May morning, blooms like a perfect little flower by the road-side—& all the talking and powowing *both sides* amounts to little or nothing " . . . .

In another letter he mentions Oscar Wilde, who visited him in 1882

Camden Jan. 25 '82

. . . . You say you wrote a *blue letter* but didn't send it to me—dear boy, the only way is to dash ahead and " whistle dull cares away "—after all its mostly in oneself one gets blue & not from outside—life is like the weather—you've got to take what comes, & you can make it all go pretty well if [you] only think so (& provide in reason for rain & snow). I wish it was so you could all your life come in & see me often for an hour or two— you see I think I understand you better than any one (& like you more too) —(you may not fancy so, but it *is* so)—& I believe, Hank, there are many things, confidences, questions, candid *says* you would like to have with me, you have never yet broached—me the same.

Have you read about Oscar Wilde? He has been to see me & spent an afternoon. He is a fine large handsome youngster. Had the good sense to take a great fancy to me ! . . . . (you say you know you are *a great fool*—dont you know every cute fellow secretly knows that about himself— I do)."

67   WHITMAN (Walt) A. L. s. to Peter Doyle, 1 p. 8vo

Kirkwood. New Jersey.
July 2 [1877]

Dear boy Pete

I still keep pretty well, & am again down here at the farm in the country, for a couple of weeks, & to stay over 4th of July . . . As I write this . . . it is a beautiful bright breezy forenoon—& I am going now down to the creek & spring to take a bath—it is about 90 rods distant, & I walk there & back—

Love, love, love
Your old Walt

I still make my headquarters in Camden.

£6

With this lot are sold transcripts of letters written by Walt Whitman to Peter Doyle in 1868 made in pencil by Dr. Bucke. 5011.

67A WHITMAN (WALT) A collection of Autograph Notes on a variety of topics, " Business ", the officials of Philadelphia, the Italian tragedian Modena, the Presidential Election of 1884, a visit to New York in 1878, etc., 26 *pieces*

£11
Ulysses

" Visit to N.Y. '78, July 3.   Visited the *Tribune* newspaper office to read ' proof '.   Up, up, up, in the elevator some eight or nine stories, to the top of the tall tower.   Then the most wonderful expanse & views !   A living map, indeed—all New York and Brooklyn, and all the waters and lands adjacent for twenty miles in every direction.   My thoughts of the beauty and amplitude of these bay & river surroundings confirmed.   Other thoughts also confirmed—that of a fitter name, for instance Mannahatta—" the place around which there are hurried and joyous waters continually "—(that's the sense of the old aboriginal word) . . . was treated with much courtesy by Whitelaw Reid, the Editor, who placed his cab at my disposal.   Had a pleasant evening drive through the Park—it being on my way home."

68   WHITMAN (Walt) Nine Autograph Postcards, signed with initials, to Harry Lamb Stafford, written during the years 1878-1884, from Camden and New York :

New York City. Aug. 5 [1881]

. . . . have been (a little) at Long Branch and Rockaway, but most of the time down on Long Island exploring the place where I was born (& the Whitmans etc for 250 years)—had a good time—am now here in New York—am going on to Boston very soon to print book . . .

Camden.   Saturday night.   Dec. 8 [1883.]

. . . . It is dark & rainy & foggy & miserable outside weather—but I have had a good supper & am sitting up here feeling jolly & thankful enough (yet a little lonesome). . . .

£10
Ulysses.

In his will dated 29 June, 1888, Walt Whitman left his gold watch to " Harry Stafford of Marlton, New Jersey "

69   WHITMAN (Walt) Strike and Tramp Questions of the eighteen-seventies.   A collection of cuttings and articles on these questions from magazines and newspapers, some with markings or notes by Walt Whitman, and a few Autograph Notes on scraps of paper, e.g. :

£6
Ulysses

" I find a large class of our talkers & writers, probably the largest class, always taking for granted that plenty of active manufactures, plenty of money and foreign markets, and a demand by the factories, stores etc for millions of employees, are the crowning result and triumph of a nation."

" In America the dangers are (or, shall I say, have been ?) from the existence of slavery & from the huge collection of ignorant & non-owning persons, generally immigrants, in the great cities."

70 WHITMAN (Walt) Two holograph Postcards to Peter Doyle, one
written from Canada, where he was staying with Dr. Bucke:

London. Ontario. Canada
July 24 [1880] p.m.

£5

Am all right again for me—was sick a bit three weeks—at times pretty
bad—was well taken care of here—*the best of friends* both Dr. and Mrs.
B (as *human* as I ever met, both)—Monday morning next I start on a long
Lake & St. Lawrence river trip, 900 miles (mostly by steamer, comfortable,
I reckon)—gone nearly three weeks, then back here—May write you from
Quebec—your papers come—W.W.

With this lot are 30 envelopes addressed by Walt Whitman
to Peter Doyle, 9 envelopes to Harry Lamb Stafford and 5
envelopes to Thomas Nicholson

71 WHITMAN (WALT) AUTOGRAPH NOTES (IN PENCIL) ON LONDON,
ONTARIO, CANADA, made during his stay there with Dr. Bucke
in 1880, 9 ll. :

£5/0/-

Ulysses

"London. 1880. Then about drinking habits. My observations
and goings around here pretty freely indoors and out, note so far a singular
scarcity of cases of intemperance ; I have seen no drunken man (nor
drunken woman)—have run across no besotted or low or filthy quarters
of the town either. I should say it was an unusually temperate city . . . .
By what I am told London would show finely to my eyes in September,
from the great annual fair, when there is a gathering of the farmers, and
their families, men and women, especially the young people—altogether
many thousands and the streets all alive with them for several days. On
this occasion one would get a direct view of the average people, the *humanity*
of this part of Canada (the main thing of every country). By what I
am told I am sure this average would please me much and would be very
high."

72 WHITMAN (WALT) DIARY IN CANADA. THE AUTOGRAPH MANU-
SCRIPT NOTES AND MEMORANDA MADE DURING HIS STAY IN
CANADA WITH DR. BUCKE IN 1880. WRITTEN MOSTLY IN PENCIL
ON 40 ll. OR SCRAPS OF PAPER

£16

Ulysses

** This diary was edited by W. S. Kennedy and published at
Boston in 1904. The manuscript is incomplete, the last entry
being under the date *Canada* 10-14 *July* [1880].

A printed copy of the diary up to that date in galley form
accompanies the lot.

72A WHITMAN (WALT) NOTES OF A TRIP ON THE ST. LAWRENCE AND
SAGUENAY RIVERS, JULY-AUGUST, 1880, HOLOGRAPH MANU-
SCRIPT in pencil on about 72 leaves or portions of leaves ; among
the places visited were Toronto, Kingston, Montreal, Quebec,
Tadousac, Chicoutimi, etc. :

Canada

£20

Ulysses

" A grand sane temperate land, the amplest & most beautiful . . . a
river & necklace of vast lakes, pure, sweet, eligible, supplied by the
chemistry of millions of square miles of gushing springs & melted
snows. No stream this for side frontiers—stream rather for the great
central current, the glorious mid-artery, of the great Free Pluribus
Unum of America—the solid Nationality of the present and the future,
the home of an improved grand race of men & women, not of some
select class only, but of larger, saner, better masses. I should say this
vast area was fitted to be their unsurpassed *habitat*, I know nothing finer—
the European democratic tourist, philanthropist, geographer or genuine
inquirer will make a fatal mistake who leaves these shores without understanding this—I know nothing finer, either from the point of view of the
sociologist, the traveller or the artist, than a month's devotion to even
the surface of Canada, over the line of the Great Lakes & the
St. Lawrence."

72B **WHITMAN (WALT)** Autograph Notes on birds and flowers, **14** *pieces* :

> " Canada July 18 '80.
>
> Swallow-Gambols. I spent a long time today watching the swallows—an hour this forenoon, and another hour, afternoon. There is a pleasant secluded close-cropt grassy lawn of a couple of acres or over, flat as a floor, & surrounded by a flowery and bushy hedge, just off the road adjoining the house—a favorite spot of mine. Over this open grassy area, immense numbers of swallows have been sailing, darting, circling and cutting large or small 8s and S's close to the ground, for hours to-day. It is evidently for fun altogether. I never saw anything prettier—this free swallow-dance. They kept it up, too, the greater part of the day."

£16.

WHITMAN (WALT) AUTOGRAPH NOTE ON " LEAVES OF GRASS ", on 2 pieces of paper :

> ' Leaves of Grass ' finished.
>
> " Boston, Oct. 22 '81. 8.30 a.m.—. . . Have been in Boston the last two months seeing the " materialization " of completed " Leaves of Grass "—first deciding on the kind of type, size of page, head-lines, consecutive arrangement of pieces etc. . . . I quite enjoyed the work and have felt the last few days as though I should like to shoulder a similar job once or twice every year . . . And so I have put those completed poems in permanent type form at last. And of the present prose volume—Are not all its items—(" ducks and drakes " as the boys term the little pebble flats they send at random to skip over the surface of the water, and sink in its depths)—is not the preceding collection mainly an attempt at specimen samples of the bases and arrieres of those same poems ? often unwitting to myself at the time."

£18
pensor

73A **WHITMAN (WALT)** A collection of Autograph Notes on various subjects, his life in Camden (written in 1884), a trip on the Mississippi and Missouri, notes for a projected poem in which each verse shall suggest a call, etc., 12 *pieces* :

> " Camden, Phila. April 8 '84.
>
> I have been living here in Camden now for nearly eleven years. Came on from Washington in the summer of '73, after my paralytic-stroke, and the death of my dear mother. Continued for three years in quite a bad way, not strength enough to walk any distance—stomach and head miserable. In '76 began to get better—went boarding down in the country and lay in the open air, as described in the preceding volume. From the fall of '76 to the present (April '84) I have been well enough to go around most of the time with occasional spells of sickness—one of which (over two months) I am just now recovering from."

£15

The above note is endorsed on the back : " [Apparently for a projected new 2 vol. ed. of his works.—W.S.K.] "

74 **WHITMAN (Walt)** A. L. s. to Dr. Bucke, 1 p. 8vo, 23 *Jun.*, 1892, written in blue pencil on yellow paper :

> " Am deadly weak yet—otherwise inclined to favorable . . . the plaster cast come safe to Dr. J. Bolton—Ralph Moore is dead—Tom Harned well—my doctors & attendants cont[inue ?] first rate—Horace ever faithful -- am propp'd up in bed."

£4/19/-
magg?

Horace must be Horace Traubel, who (with Tom Harned, also mentioned in this letter and Dr. Bucke) was one of Whitman's literary executors

75 **WHITMAN (Walt)** A. L. s. to Dr. Bucke, 1 p. 8vo, 27 *Jan.* [1892], written on yellow paper :

> " Feeble & weak & restless but not without favorable points—appetite holds out—eat two meals every day . . . McK. [David McKay, his publisher] was here—paid me $283 . . . to me the 1892 edn. [of Leaves of Grass] supersedes them all by far " . . . .

£4/15/-
ulysses

76 WHITMAN (Walt) A. L. s. to Dr. Bucke, 1 p. 8vo, 8 *Feb.*, 1892,
written in blue pencil :

" I keep on much the same—probably growing weaker . . . bad steady
pain in left side "

Written in the month before his death on the blank last page
of an A. L. s. from Hallam Tennyson thanking him on behalf
of his father for a copy of " Leaves of Grass "

77 WHITMAN (Walt) A. L. [to Tom Nicholson ?], *dated 4 Oct. [no year]*,
2 pp. 8vo, mentions " Leaves of Grass " :

" Did you see John Swinton's warm ¶ about my illustrious self in N.Y.
Times, 1st inst. ? John seems lately possest with L. of G. as with a demon.
I have found two or three others—a Mr. Norton of Boston is one. He is
an educated man, a Boston metaphysical thinker.—Give my best love to
John Burroughs, & lend him this note to read. J.B., dear friend, I wish
I could have you here if only just to take a ride with me for once up &
down Broadway, on top of a stage."

The letter is without signature and appears to be incomplete

78 WHITMAN (WALT) A LARGE COLLECTION OF AUTOGRAPH NOTES,
MEMORANDA AND PRELIMINARY STUDIES FOR *Leaves of Grass*,
etc., written in pen and pencil on scraps of paper. The notes
are very miscellaneous in character, suggestions for poems, notes
for future study, etc.

A poem in which is minutely described the whole particulars and ensemble of a first-rate healthy Human Body—if looked into and through,
as if it were transparent and of pure glass—and now reported in a poem—
Read the latest and best anatomical works
talk with physicians
study the anatomical plates
also casts & figures in the collections of design.

———

Poem illustrative of the *Woman* under the " new dispensation."
Collect all illustrative characters from history—the best mothers,
healthiest women, most loving women.
a woman is to be able to ride, swim, run, resist, advance, refuse, shoot,
defend herself, sail a boat, hunt, rebel, just as much as a man.
If the woman have not the quoted attributes in herself, the man cannot
have them afterward
The woman is to *be athletic* also.

———

POEM OF EXISTENCE.
We call one the past, and we call another the future
But both are alike the present
It is not the past, though we call it so, nor the
future, though we call it so
All the while it is the present only—
future and past are the present only.

———

In future " Leaves of Grass "
Be more severe with the final revision of the poem.
Nothing will do, not one word or sentence, that is not *perfectly* clear—
with positive purpose—harmony with the name, nature, drift of the poem.
Also *no ornaments especially no ornamental adjectives*, unless they have
come molten hot, and *imperiously prove themselves.*
No ornamental similes at all—not one
Perfect transparent clearness, sanity and health are wanted—*that*
is the *divine style*—O if it can be attained.

———

207

I am not content now with a mere majority . . . I must have the love of all men and all women.

If there be one left in any county who has no faith in me, I will travel to that county and go to that one.

————————

I subject all the teachings of the schools, and all dicta and authority, to the tests of myself.

And I encourage you to subject the same to the tests of yourself—and to subject me and my words to the strongest tests.

————————

Scantlings.

White, shaved, foreign, soft-fleshed, shrinking
Scant of muscle, scant of love power,
Scant of gnarl and knot, modest, sleek in costumes,
Averse from the wet of rain, from the fall of snow, from the grit of the
  stones and soil,
A pretty race, each one just like hundreds of the rest
Race of scantlings, from the strong growth of America.

————————

With the lot are a few MS. notes by Dr. Bucke and a few other anonymous MS. memoranda

The whole collection numbers upwards of 200 sheets and scraps

79 WHITMAN (WALT) HIS SCRAP BOOK. A thick 4to volume of cuttings from newspapers, extracts from books or magazines with many markings or notes by Walt Whitman. Also numerous MS. notes or memoranda written on sheets or scraps of paper and inserted. Many of these are short, consisting of two or three lines only, others are longer, sometimes covering several sheets ; one of his longer notes gives his view of England :

THE ENGLISH MASSES

(*Talk with Frank Leonard, " Yank ", etc—their travels through English towns with the American Circus*).

The large mass (nine tenths) of the English people, the peasantry, laborers, factory-operatives, miners, workers in the docks, on shipping, the poor, the old, the criminals, the numberless flunkies of one sort and another have some of the bull-dog attributes but are generally minus the best attributes of humanity. They are not a race of fine physique, or any spirituality or manly audacity, have no clarified faces, candor, freedom, agility, and quick wit.—They are short, have mean physiognomies (such as are in the caricatures in " Punch ")—fine-shaped men and women, city-bred, being very seldom met with in the city, and becoming less and less common in the country.—Bad blood, goitre, consumption, and the diseases that branch out from venerealism, gin-drinking, excessive toil, and poor diet, are to-day apparent, to greater or less degree, in two-thirds of the common people of Great England. They are wretchedly poor, own neither houses nor lands for themselves—have no homes—cannot look to have any homes—and are acquiring something fierce, morose, threatening in their physiognomy.—In their phrenology there is the most substantial basis of any race known—all that can make a solid nation and has made it.

Among the common classes in towns chastity is dwindling out. All drink, few are virtuous. In regard to intelligence, education, knowledge the masses of the people in comparison with the masses of the U.S. are at least two hundred years behind us.—With all these terrible things about the common people, what grand things must be said about England ! Power, wealth, materials, energy, individualism, are hers—and there is today but one nation greater than she is, and that is her own daughter."

The above is written on 3 sheets of official paper, dated 185—

Most of the printed and manuscript material here collected is of a " general knowledge " character, information on historical or geographical points, etc. *Bound in half calf*

80 WHITMAN (WALT) AUTOGRAPH NOTES, MAINLY IN PENCIL, ON HOMER, VIRGIL, DANTE, CHAUCER, SPENSER, SHAKESPEARE, SWEDENBORG, ROUSSEAU, SHELLEY and others, written on about 40 ll. or scraps of paper. Also a collection of printed articles extracted from magazines, etc., mainly on authors or literary subjects and with numerous marginal notes and markings by Whitman

£22

Ulysses

80A Whitman (Walt) Autograph Note on his parents :

£7 Ulysses

" All through young and middle age, I thought my heredity-stamp was mainly decidedly from my mother's side : but as I grow older, and latent traits come out, I see my dear father's also. As to loving and disinterested parents, no boy or man ever had more cause to bless and thank them than I."

80B WHITMAN (WALT) THE AMERICAN CONSTITUTION AND SLAVERY, LONG HOLOGRAPH MANUSCRIPT WRITTEN IN PENCIL, 22 *sheets of varying sizes*

£10 Ulysses

80C WHITMAN (WALT) THE SOCIAL CONTRACT, OR, PRINCIPLES OF RIGHT, HOLOGRAPH MANUSCRIPT, 11 ll. 4to   *n. d.*

£50 Ulysses

80D Whitman (Walt) Italian Singers in America, Autograph Note on 4 ll. :

£7 49.

Ulysses

" The best songstress ever in America was Alboni.—Her voice is a contralto of large compass, high and low—and probably sweeter tones never issued from human lips. The mere sound of that voice was pleasure enough . . . we used to go in the upper tiers of the theatre (the Broadway) on the nights of her performance, and remember seeing that part of the auditorium packed full of New York young men, mechanics, " roughs ", etc., entirely oblivious of all except Alboni, from the time the great songstress came on the stage . . . "

80E WHITMAN (WALT) Article on the " Wants " column in the daily newspaper, autograph manuscript, 14 ll. *written chiefly in green ink* :

£10

Ulysses

" . . . Happily, as to the latter class, in this country, work is not *yet* so hard to get, or employers *at present* so lordly, as to make it necessary for the carpenter or mason to run around and look to intermediate agencies for a situation. And among the commercial part of the community, there is a prejudice against filling even a subordinate clerkship through the means of the " want " column or Intelligence Office . . . "

80F Whitman (Walt) Autograph Draft of a Letter to a newspaper on the exchange of prisoners :

" Sir : whether it agrees with your own opinion or not I hope you will open your columns to this communication of mine seeking to stir up the government to a general exchange of prisoners . . . "

£7 10/-

On the back are some autograph pencil notes on prison and hospital life

Ulysses

On another sheet is an autograph note on the exchange question :

" It is generally belived in Washington that the President is in favor of a general exchange, but has been for the past year overruled by the head of the war department & others. The consequences are well known to all who mix much with the people & the soldiers. The administration has already established a name for bad faith which will tell for years to come . . . "

80G Whitman (Walt) Autograph Note (*imperfect*) on the appointment
 by Abraham Lincoln of a successor of Caleb Smith as Secretary
 of the Interior, 2 ll. 4to ; an Autograph Note in pencil on
 municipal legislation, 1 p. 4to ; other Autograph Notes, Drafts
 and other Documents ; also a collection of magazine articles
 made by Walt Whitman with marginal markings, etc.

(a small parcel)

80H WHITMAN (WALT) Autograph Drafts of Letters and Notes on the
 postal laws relating to book manuscripts, 6 sheets 4to

80I Whitman (Walt) Autograph Note on the genesis of *Leaves of Grass*,
 1 p. 4to :
 " The fifteen years from 1840 to 1855 may be considered as the gesta-
 tion-years or period of formation out of which *Leaves of Grass* rose.
 Not in the usual way of an author withdrawing, composing his work in a
 study, abstractedly addressing himself to the literary formulation, consulting authorities, and the like, but in the way of first merging oneself
 in all the living flood and practicality and fervency of that period . . .
 the scenes, sights & people of the great cities of New York and Brooklyn,
 with Broadway, the Bowery, South and West Streets, the shipping and
 ship-yards, & the incomparable water & bay life around New-York—
 Several extensive jaunts, too, through the States, one of them extending
 over a year, including all the western and Southern regions, New Orleans,
 Texas, the Mississipi and Missouri rivers, and some weeks over the Great
 Lakes and at Niagara."

81 WHITMAN (WALT) TWO PERSONAL AUTOGRAPH NOTES, possibly
 intended for use by Dr. Bucke in his biography, for which book
 Whitman himself seems to have supplied much material :
 " Of this maternal side, with its stock from the Netherlands—Dutch, it
 is not too much to say that both Walt Whitman's personality and his
 writings are largely to be assigned to that race-origin. A faithful and
 subtle investigation would here track home and far back many of the
 elements of " Leaves of Grass " . . . . the emotional, the liberty-loving, the
 social, the preponderating qualities of adhesiveness, immovable gravi-
 tation, simplicity, with a certain conservative protestantism, & other
 traits, are unmistakably from his motherhood and are pure Hollandic or
 Dutch."

 In the second note he details the conditions under which
 Leaves of Grass was composed

82 WHITMAN (WALT) AUTOGRAPH NOTES AND FRAGMENTS on various
 literary topics, the Nibelungenlied, Ossian, Shakespeare,
 Richard Burbage, etc. (16 *pieces*) :
 " America has been called proud and arrogant. It may be, but she does
 not show it in her literature. It is indirect and therefore more effective.
 Day by day and hour by hour, in tragedy and comedy, in picture and
 print, in every importation of art and letters, she submits to one steady
 blow of discrepancy . . . . "

83 WHITMAN (WALT) AUTOGRAPH NOTES AND FRAGMENTS ON HIS
 LECTURES, etc. (9 *pieces*) :
 " List of things recognised by my lectures."
 " I recognise in America the land of materials—the land of iron, wheat,
 beef, pork, fish and fruit.
 I recognise all the great inventions, machines, and improvements of
 to-day, the ten-cylinder press, printing thirty-thousand sheets an hour—
 the electric telegraph that binds continents and threads the bottom of
 seas—the track of railroads—the cheap newspaper."
 "—the idea that the common American mechanic, farmer, sailor, etc
 is just as eligible as any to the highest ideal of dignity, perfection and
 knowledge (I sometimes think an independent American working man
 is more eligible than any other) "

84 WHITMAN (WALT) AUTOGRAPH NOTES AND FRAGMENTS ON RELIGION (10 *pieces*) :

> " . . . the divine ideas of spirituality, of the immortal soul of the woman and the man, of another sphere of existence, of conscience and perfect justice and goodness, have been serenely preserved through millenia of years and with many traditions are here transmitted to us, to me, to you, whoever you are. I receive the great inheritance with welcome joy. I know life is in my own soul, not in the traditions, the phantoms— I know the traditions help me well—but how could I be developed even so far and talk with decision today without all those traditions?—I know, too, that I am the master and overseer of all religions—as you shall be—not their slave."

85 Whitman (Walt) Apparently a translation in the handwriting of Walt Whitman of a letter from Victor Hugo :

> To Arthur Monnanteuil
> Hauteville House
> 7th July, 1868.
>
> I accept your verses Mr. ———— You have drawn them from the true source of noble inspirations. Let us love forever, and propogate forever, la Liberté. Without wings, no bird. Without Liberty, no poet.
> Accept the assurance of all my sympathy,
> Victor Hugo.

On the fourth page Walt Whitman has written :

> If there be but one left, I shall be that one.

86 Whitman (Walt) Family Memoranda. MANUSCRIPT NOTES, CHIEFLY AUTOGRAPH, on family history and genealogy written on about 20 sheets, folio, 4to and 8vo, loose in 2 half calf covers

87 WHITMAN (WALT) ABOUT 40 LL. OR FRAGMENTS OF AUTOGRAPH MATTER in envelope endorsed : " Walt Whitman MSS. printed in Dr. R. M. Bucke's 'Notes and Fragments' of Walt Whitman (pp. 59-67) & sent to me by his son Edw. P. Bucke Nov. 24 1902.—W. S. Kennedy."

88 Whitman (Walt) Four MS. Notes by W. Whitman written on scraps of paper with some cuttings of printed articles by or relating to him. In an envelope endorsed : " Scraps of Walt Whitman's Manuscript etc received from Dr. R. M. Bucke's son by W. S. Kennedy November 24. 1902."

89 WHITMAN (WALT) NEW YORK 51ST REGIMENT. A COLLECTION OF AUTOGRAPH MS. NOTES AND MEMORANDA MADE BY WALT WHITMAN ON THIS REGIMENT DURING THE SECESSION WAR, including some long notes about his brother George, who was taken prisoner in 1864. Autograph notes on Brooklyn men in other regiments who took part in the war. Also some printed and manuscript matter (not autograph) on the history of the regiment

IV. AUTOGRAPH LETTERS TO WALT WHITMAN AND MANUSCRIPTS RELATING TO HIM

90 BUCKE (R. M.) HOLOGRAPH MANUSCRIPT OF THE ORIGINAL DRAFT OF HIS BOOK ON WALT WHITMAN. Some of the quoted passages are omitted or supplied in transcript or from a printed version. A transcript of *The Good Gray Poet* is included, but the articles, criticisms, etc. which had appeared previously and reprinted by Dr. Bucke in his book, are omitted; A TRANSCRIPT OF THE SAME BY ANOTHER HAND, REVISED BY WALT WHITMAN WITH NUMEROUS ALTERATIONS AND ADDITIONS BY HIM INCLUDING SOME ADDED HOLOGRAPH PASSAGES BY WHITMAN OF CONSIDERABLE LENGTH; The holograph MS. of the article written in the form of a letter to Dr. Bucke by William Douglas O'Connor (author of " The Good Gray Poet. A Vindication ") and printed in Dr. Bucke's " Life of Whitman ", pp. 73-98, at the beginning of the Appendix to Part I as a preface to " The Good Gray Poet " which is reprinted immediately after it; A Dialogue by Walter Whitman. A Transcript of an article published in the *Democratic Review* for Nov., 1845

91 Bucke (R. M.) A Collection of papers and documents relating to Walt Whitman made by Dr. Bucke including the holograph MS. of his lecture on Walt Whitman; Copies of some letters from Walt Whitman from 1860; Phrenological Description of W. Whitman (Age 29. Occupation Printer) by L. V. Fowler, N. York, July 16, 1849, manuscript, 6 ll., 4to; Several typed articles on Walt Whitman with corrections by Dr. Bucke; Walt Whitman's Genealogy, MS. in pencil by Dr. Bucke, 14 ll.; " Old Age's Lambent Peaks ", a poem by Walt Whitman, and 2 other poems by him printed on a galley slip (2 copies) and other papers   (*a parcel*)

92 Bucke (R. M.) Study of Faust and " Leaves of Grass ", a comparison, MANUSCRIPT, written by Dr. R. M. Bucke, 21 pp.

93 Bucke (R. M.) Walt Whitman. Man and Poet, MANUSCRIPT, written by Dr. R. M. Bucke, 15 ll.

94 Bucke (R. M.) A Lecture on Walt Whitman delivered at St. Thomas' about 1895, *partly type-written and partly printed*, 30 ll., *with MS. corrections by the author*

95 Bucke (R. M.) Walt Whitman. A Lecture delivered at Sarina, 9 March, 1900, *partly type-written and partly printed*, 65 ll., *with MS. corrections by the author*; Notes for a lecture on Walt Whitman by Dr. Bucke on loose sheets, 8vo and 4to; three pamphlets on Walt Whitman, etc.

96 DOYLE (PETER) A Collection of 8 A. L. s. from Peter Doyle to Walt Whitman, all written from Washington, Sept.-Oct. 1868 (or without year), *about* 18 pp. 8vo; Also A. L. s. from Henry Hurt

97 Farwell (Reuben) A series of 11 Letters written to Walt Whitman by Reuben Farwell, 1863-75, a soldier in the Secession War, four of them with endorsements by Walt Whitman. A letter to him from Fred H. M. Ready, and a typed copy of a fragmentary letter from Walt Whitman to Reuben Farwell

98 Heyde (Charles L.) A Collection of upwards of 60 Letters from Charles L. Heyde, husband of Hannah Whitman to his brother-in-law Walt Whitman, and a few to his mother-in-law written 1852-92

99 Heyde (Hannah, née Whitman) A Collection of 21 Letters from Hannah Whitman (Mrs. Charles Heyde) to her brother Walt, and 34 others from her to her mother 1853-92

100 Letters. A Collection of 30 Letters written to Walt Whitman in the late sixties (and after) mainly about Leaves of Grass, his work done in hospitals, etc. A few are from old friends, e.g. Geo. D. Cole (" Walt you know wat good times Petter (? Peter Doyle) and your selfe and me had together . . . how is old car no 29 my old car "). Several contain enthusiastic praise of Leaves of Grass, some are from unknown or anonymous correspondents. Among the collection is a letter written in pencil by Walt Whitman (1 p. 4to) to Miss Elmira Crossman on behalf of her brother, Captain H. F. Crossman, who was ill in hospital at the time. Also an Account in the autograph of Walt Whitman dated 13 August, 1867, for copies of Leaves of Grass supplied to French and Richardson

101 Letters. A collection of A. Ls. s. sent to Walt Whitman from friends and admirers during his summer in Canada in 1880. Among them are letters from Edward Carpenter (2), Mrs. Ann Gilchrist, Robert G. Ingersoll, John Burroughs, W. Hale White, Dr. R. M. Bucke, T. W. H. Rolleston, Harry Scovel, Frederick Locker (2), his sister Louisa (2), and others ; also a number of cuttings and printed articles, etc.

102 Letters. A collection of 80 Letters from H. Buxton Forman, T. B. Harned, P. K. Foley and Putnam's sons to Dr. R. M. Bucke, many relating to Walt Whitman   (80)

103 Letters. A collection of upwards of 40 Letters to Walt Whitman, his mother, and a few others, written between the years 1848-91. Those addressed to Walt Whitman include letters from his cousins Margaret L. Avery and Sarah Avery, 4 letters from his sister Louisa, his niece Hattie, and 3 from Jessie Whitman (" Dear Uncle Walt ")

104 O'Connor (W. D.) A long Autograph Article addressed to the Editor of the *Tribune* (45 ll. 4to) on the suppression of " Leaves of Grass " ; another on the same, entitled " Tobey or not Tobey ? " (49 ll. 4to) ; another entitled " Mr. Comstock as Cato the Censor " (17 ll. 4to) ; Manuscript copies of Walt Whitman's letters, 105 ll. folio ; and other manuscript and printed papers relating to Walt Whitman, cuttings from newspapers, etc.
(a parcel)

105　O'Connor (Mrs. W. D., *afterwards Mrs. Ellen M. Calder*) A series of 34 Letters written in the years 1881-97 to Dr. R. M. Bucke, with references to her Walt Whitman papers and her friendship with him

In a letter, *dated* 31 *Oct.*, 1881, she writes :

" . . . I thought I should have time to write up reminiscences of Walt for you . . . I will, however, put into shape for you, the one thought that always from the day I first read a line of Walt Whitman, pressed upon me, the certainty that none but a good and pure man would dare to write and publish what he did."

In another, *of* 29 *Dec.*, 1891, she writes :

" Can you steal a minute to tell me how you feel & think about Walt ? Can he possibly weather this storm or is it the end ? . . . If Walt can at all understand will you give him my love ? I know he has *thought* of me ; for on . . . the morning after Christmas he *came* to me. I *never* have seen him more plainly than I did then."

Mrs. Ellen M. O'Connor and her first husband W. D. O'Connor were both great friends of Whitman. See Emory Holloway's *Whitman*, p. 233, etc. W. D. O'Connor was the author of the vindication of Whitman published in 1866 under the title " The Good Gray Poet."

106　Price (Helen E.) A series of 7 Letters written 1872-3 by Miss Helen E. Price to Walt Whitman's mother. In a letter, *dated New Year*, 1873, she refers to some misunderstanding between Walt Whitman and herself :

" . . . Tell me about Walt too. I hope he is not angry with me any more. It almost broke my heart to think I had vexed him so much last summer, and to be thought forward and presuming by any of my friends grieved me so deeply, but Walt was always dear to me as you know, and always will be, no matter what his opinion may be of me . . . "

On Friday, 31 Jan., 1873, she writes :

" . . . I have just seen an account of Walt's illness in the papers and am so anxious to know the latest news . . . I know you will think it foolish of me but I feel as though I could hardly keep from starting right off to take care of him and I know I should if I was married and rich, but I do not suppose it would do for a young lady . . . Walt makes so many friends everywhere he goes that he is sure to be well taken care of. I do not feel any heart to write about any thing else . . . "

With this correspondence is also a letter from Mrs. Abby Price (mother of Helen Price) to Walt Whitman's mother

107　PRICE (HELEN E.) A series of 13 Letters written during the years 1881-97 to Dr. R. M. Bucke by Miss Helen E. Price, one of his most intimate New York friends, mainly relating to biographical material supplied by her to Dr. Bucke for his book on Walt Whitman published in 1883. The long notes she supplied (not preserved with these letters) were printed in that volume (pp. 26-32) with the following prefatory note :

The memoranda which follow were written for this volume in 1881 by a lady—Miss Helen E. Price, of Woodside, Long Island—whose acquaintance with Walt Whitman, and his frequent temporary residence in her parents' family, make her peculiarly competent to present a picture of the man in those periods of middle life (ib., p. 26)

In a letter, *dated* 27 *Sept.*, 1893, Miss Helen Price writes :

. . . The forthcoming " Century " will have an article as I see announced . . . . of Walt's letters to his mother . . . I was more than glad that the world should know as it has not yet done how altogether lovely and beautiful his character shows in all his relations to his family as a son and brother."

In another letter, *dated* 29 *Sept.*, 1895, she writes :

> " I think he (Walt) must have seemed even to those who knew him but slightly as the very sanest of men. I could even imagine that his presence alone might have brought healing and balm to unbalanced minds and diseased nerves, and yet I have seen him under the influence of strong excitement . . . But even on these occasions he was always and fully master of himself and I could not imagine him otherwise."

108 Rhys (Ernest) Two long A. Ls. s. from Ernest Rhys to Walt Whitman ; another from H. Garland ; four Letters from publishers to Dr. Bucke about Whitman's work, etc. (7)

109 Soldiers' Letters. A collection of about 60 Letters from soldiers to Walt Whitman, with autograph ticket inscribed " Soldiers Letters to me during the war." (Some since the war)

110 WHITMAN (GEORGE W.) A collection of 59 holograph Letters written by Walt Whitman's younger brother. George, mostly to his mother, from the army during the years 1861-65

** George Whitman (b. 1829) joined the army of the North in 1861 on the outbreak of the War of Secession. Wounded in Dec., 1862, and taken prisoner in 1864 he rose to the rank of Captain before the end of the war. Walt Whitman made his home for eleven years with George at Camden after his stroke in 1873.

Many of the letters are long and give many details of the fighting. Six of them are addressed to Walt Whitman himself. In a letter, *dated from the Camp of the 51st N.Y. Vols., Newport News, Va.,* 12 *Feb.* 1863, he writes :

> " Dear Walt
> Well here we are at Newport News, and glad enough to get out of the mud, in which the grand Army of the Potomac has lived . . . since we first joined it . . . Of course we know nothing at all about what they brought us here for . . . Anyhow I am glad to get out of the Potomac Army for it seems as if it would never be able to accomplish anything. And yet I believe it was as fine an Army (as far as their fighting qualities is concerned) as was ever seen "

111 WHITMAN (MRS. L.) An extensive collection of holograph Letters written to Walt Whitman by his mother, Mrs. L. Whitman (Louisa Van Velsor, 1795-1873), comprising 3 letters written to him in 1860 while he was away in Boston seeing to the publication of the 1860 edition of " Leaves of Grass " ; and a series of about 135 letters written to him at Washington during the years 1863-73, when he was engaged on hospital work during the Secession War and as a government clerk

** The collection includes a few letters written by or to other members of the family, one of them (a long letter from Mrs. Whitman to her daughter Hannah written in July, 1855) giving an account of the death of Walt Whitman's father.

With this lot are sold 7 ll. of pencil memoranda of biographical details of the Whitman family, compiled by Dr. R. M. Bucke from Mrs. Whitman's letters or other sources.

112 Whitman (Mrs. L.) Thirteen Letters to Walt Whitman from his mother, *all without date,* about 30 pp. 4to and 8vo

113 Whitman (Mattie) A series of 18 Letters to her mother and 5 to her brother, Walt Whitman, *written 1863-72, somewhat soiled and water-stained*

114 Whitman (Thomas Jefferson) An extensive Collection of about 80 Autograph Letters from Jeff. Whitman to his brother Walt, *written during the years* 1860-88, most of them dated from the Engineer's Office, Brooklyn Water Works or from St. Louis Water Works ; also a few Letters from Jeff. Whitman to his mother

115 Whitman (Walt) Notes and Fragments by Walt Whitman edited by R. M. Bucke, *second edition,* MANUSCRIPT AND TYPESCRIPT, 34 ll., 20 ll. written by Dr. Bucke and 14 ll. typewritten, with corrections and additions by Dr. Bucke, *unbound*   folio

*** Included with this lot are the originals of the 4 letters written by Jefferson Whitman during his visit to New Orleans in 1848 with his brother Walt Whitman which were printed in the volume. (1) Jeff's letter to his mother (incomplete) 29 *Feb.,* 1848, beginning " Our captain thought he would run the risk " ; (2) Jeff's letter to his father, 14 *March,* 1848 ; (3) His letter to his mother, 27 *March,* 1848 ; (4) His letter to his parents, 23 *April* (1848).

116 Whitman (Walt) Sunday Restrictions. Memorial in behalf of a freer municipal government and against Sunday Restrictions, by Walt Whitman, *copied from the " Brooklyn Star "* of 20 *Oct.,* 1854 *by W. E. Davenport,* MANUSCRIPT, 12 ll. 4to ; The Love of Eris. A Spirit Record. By Walt Whitman, *copied from the " Brooklyn Daily Eagle "* of 18 *Aug.,* 1846, *by W. E. Davenport,* MANUSCRIPT, 13 ll. 8vo ; Recollections of Walt Whitman, by Mrs. E. M. Calder, TYPESCRIPT, 14 ll. 4to

117 Whitman (Walt) A large collection of MS. Notes on Walt Whitman's last illness made by Dr. R. M. Bucke, Dr. Alexander McAlister, the attending physician, Dr. Longaker, and Mrs. Keller the Nurse, *from Dec.* 1891 *to his death on* 26 *March,* 1892 ; the fullest details of the progress of his illness are given day by day

END OF SALE

Sale No. 493

FIRST EDITIONS ⸗ AUTOGRAPH LETTERS
AND MANUSCRIPTS

OF OUTSTANDING IMPORTANCE

INCLUDING A REMARKABLE COLLECTION OF

LETTERS & MANUSCRIPTS BY

WALT WHITMAN

TOGETHER WITH HIS WILL, DATED MAY 15, 1873

Sold by Order of the
Various Owners

∽

To be Dispersed

WEDNESDAY AND THURSDAY EVENINGS

MARCH 25TH AND 26TH, 1936, AT 8:30 O'CLOCK

∽

Days of Exhibition

THURSDAY, MARCH 19TH, 1936, *from* 9 A. M. TO 6 P. M.
And daily thereafter until evening of sale
(**SUNDAY,** *from* 2 TO 5 P. M.)

∽

Sales Conducted by

E. HAROLD L. THOMPSON   ANTHONY N. BADE

Rains Galleries

A RARE COLLECTION OF FIRST CONTRIBUTIONS
BY WALT WHITMAN

232. WHITMAN (WALT). A Collection of Periodicals containing contributions by Walt Whitman, nearly all of which were printed LONG BEFORE THE APPEARANCE OF HIS FIRST BOOK.

DEATH IN THE SCHOOL ROOM, from the United States Magazine, Aug. 1841.

WILD FRANK'S RETURN, from the United States Magazine, Nov., 1841.

BERVANCE; or, FATHER AND SON, from the United States Magazine, Dec., 1841.

THE TOMB BLOSSOMS, from the United States Magazine, Jan., 1842.

THE CHILD GHOST; A STORY OF THE LAST LOYALIST, from the United States Magazine, May, 1842.

THE DEATH OF THE WIND-FOOT, from the American Review, June, 1845.

A DIALOGUE, from the Democratic Review, Nov., 1845.

A WARBLE FOR LILAC-TIME, from the Galaxy, May, 1870.

Together: 8 vols., 8vo, original printed wrappers as issued. Enclosed in a half black morocco slip-case with inner cloth wrapper.   New York, 1841-1870

A FINE COLLECTION OF THESE SCARCE MAGAZINES CONTAINING WHITMAN'S FIRST LITERARY ATTEMPTS. SELDOM OFFERED FOR SALE IN THIS ORIGINAL STATE.

A BEAUTIFUL COPY OF WHITMAN'S FIRST BOOK

233. WHITMAN (WALT). Franklin Evans; or, The Inebriate. A Tale of the Times. Small folio, unsewn. Enclosed in a half morocco slip-case.

New York, 1842

FIRST EDITION. WALT WHITMAN'S FIRST BOOK. SCARCE. This original temperance novel appeared in "The New World," edited by Park Benjamin, November, 1842. Whitman refers to it in the "Introductory" matter as "the account of a young man, who came to our great emporium to seek his fortune—and what befell him there."

234. ——. Voices from the Press. A Collection of Sketches, Essays and Poems. By Practical Printers. Edited by James J. Brenton. 8vo, original cloth, with a likeness of Benjamin Franklin in gilt on side, new back.   New York, 1850

WHITMAN'S FIRST APPEARANCE IN ANY COLLECTION. Containing "The Tomb Blossoms" on pages 27-33. The story had previously been published in the United States Magazine, January, 1842. PRESENTATION COPY from Benjamin Perley Poore, the well-known American journalist, whose contribution occurs on pages 219-235, inscribed in his autograph. AN EXTREMELY RARE WHITMAN ITEM.

PRESENTATION COPY TO HIS HOUSEKEEPER

235. WHITMAN (WALT). Leaves of Grass. *With 2 portraits.* 12mo, original half tan calf, leather labels, gilt edges (binding worn and hinges weak).

Camden, 1876

AUTHOR'S EDITION, WITH HIS SIGNATURE ON TITLE-PAGE. AUTOGRAPH PRESENTATION COPY FROM WHITMAN TO "MARY F. DAVIS FROM HER FRIEND THE AUTHOR."

This copy contains the two portraits, and is also one of the few copies with the "intercalations" referred to on the title-page. These occur on pages vi, 207, 247, 285, 359, and 369. At the back is a page of advertisements of Whitman's books. On the second fly-leaf is a presentation inscription from Mary Fenn Davis to Helen Campbell, dated July 17, 1886. There are numerous pencil scorings on the margins against many passages.

236. ——. Another Copy. *With 2 portraits.* 8vo, half cream colored calf, marbled boards, brown leather label. Camden, New Jersey, 1876

AUTHOR'S EDITION. With Waltman's autograph written in ink on the title-page. Fine clean copy from the well-known collection of Michael Sandys.

237. ——. Two Rivulets, including Democratic Vistas, Centennial Songs and Passage to India. *Frontispiece portrait.* 8vo, original half cream colored calf, marbled boards, brown leather label. Camden, New Jersey, 1876

FIRST EDITION. The frontispiece portrait of Whitman is signed in ink "*Walt Whitman born May 31, 1819.*"

238. ——. The Poetry of the Future. 8vo, sewn. Enclosed in a cloth case. [New York, 1881]

AN EXTREMELY RARE WHITMAN ITEM. On the first page the poet has written in ink "*Feb. '81.*" ONE OF A VERY FEW COPIES GIVEN TO THE POET FOR PRESENTATION PURPOSES WITH THE DATE IN INK IN WHITMAN'S AUTOGRAPH. An illuminating plea by the great American poet for original expression by the poets of America.

239. ——. Another Copy. On the first page Whitman has written "Feb: '81." 8vo, sewn. [New York, 1881]

240. ——. November Boughs. *Frontispiece portrait.* 8vo, red cloth, gilt top, uncut. Philadelphia, 1888

FIRST EDITION. With the rare frontispiece portrait. SCARCE IN THIS UNCUT STATE.

241. ——. Another Copy. 8vo, original cloth, gilt top, uncut. Philadelphia, 1888

FIRST EDITION. AUTOGRAPH PRESENTATION COPY from Horace Traubel to John Malone, with inscription on fly-leaf, dated July, 1896.

242. ——. Good-Bye My Fancy. 2d Annex to Leaves of Grass. *Portrait.* Tall 8vo, red cloth, gilt lettering, gilt top, uncut. Philadelphia, 1891

FIRST EDITION. One of a small number of large paper copies issued with uncut fore and lower edges.

THE RARE FIRST ISSUE OF THE COMPLETE "LEAVES OF GRASS"

243. WHITMAN (WALT). Leaves of Grass. 8vo, original gray paper wrappers (front wrapper loose, back wrapper wanting; back broken, and portion of paper label). In a half morocco slip-case. Philadelphia: McKay, 1891-'2

THE SO-CALLED "DEATH-BED EDITION." ONE OF A VERY FEW COPIES HURRIEDLY BOUND IN COARSE WRAPPERS AND PRESENTED BY WHITMAN TO FRIENDS. The present copy was presented to Mrs. Elizabeth Keller, and has the inscription inscribed by Traubel: "To Mrs. Elizabeth Keller from Walt Whitman, Jan. 1892." Whitman was very ill at this time, and as he wanted to see the completed book, Traubel had a few copies hurriedly finished, and Whitman sent them to a few friends.

UNIQUE MAP OF WALT WHITMAN'S TRAVELS, WITH THE ROUTES MARKED BY WHITMAN IN CRAYON

244. WHITMAN (WALT). A Folding Map of the United States, Issued by the Missouri Pacific Rail Road. 24 inches by 12 inches.

THIS MAP IS OF UNIQUE VALUE AS IT TRACES ALL OF WALT WHITMAN'S SOUTHERN AND WESTERN JOURNEYS IN HIS OWN HAND. His trip took him through Philadelphia, Harrisburg, Pittsburg, Columbus, Indianapolis, Terra Haute, St. Louis, Kansas City, Denver, where he took a detour into the Rockies, and on the return trip he followed the Achison Santa Fe line to Kansas City from where he retraced his original route. The 1879 trip is indicated in red; the previous journeys in blue. The blue lines tracing his former travels show his trip in New England and the Middle Atlantic States, the trip from Washington to Cincinnati, and another down the Mississippi to New Orleans and back by St. Louis, Chicago and the Great Lakes.

IN THE FALL OF 1879 WHITMAN TRAVELED AS FAR WEST AS THE ROCKY MOUNTAINS, TARRYING SOME TIME WITH HIS BROTHER JEFF IN ST. LOUIS, MISSOURI, WHENCE HE WROTE JOHN BURROUGHS THE FOLLOWING LETTER.

Together with an autograph letter signed "Walt Whitman." 2 pp., 8vo. With envelope addressed to "John Burroughs, Esopus on Hudson. Ulster County, New York," in Whitman's autograph.

Whitman describes his health and quarters, inquires about Burroughs' mother, and close friends, refers to the enclosed map, and thanks Burroughs, his staunch friend and champion, for his kind mention of him in an article on "Nature and the Poets" in Scribner's. He also mentions the favorable mention made of "DEMOCRATIC VISTAS" by John A. Symonds and remarks upon the unexpected arrival of A. B. Alcott, the father of Louisa May Alcott, and W. T. Harris, Commissioner of Public Education in Washington, and author of metaphysical books.

". . . I am still here—not yet (as an old aunt used to say) 'not yet out of my misery' . . . I send you Mrs. Gilchrist's letter which you needn't return—Gilder's which I enclose, I wish you to send back, some time. . . . The rough map enclosed gives you some idea of my present jaunt, on the red line (the blue lines are old travels of mine)— I have seen the December Scribner's. What you say of me in Nature and the Poets thoroughly delights, satisfies me and prides me. I saw in the Library a late London Fortnightly in which J. A. Symonds touching briefly but very commendingly and mentioning my name makes quite an extract from DEM: VISTAS (summing up the general spirit of British literature as being markedly sombre and bilious) . . ."

TWO UNIQUE AND FASCINATING WHITMAN ITEMS.

WALT WHITMAN'S WILL—MAY 15TH, 1873

245. WHITMAN (WALT). AUTOGRAPH WILL OF WALT WHITMAN, WRITTEN ON 3 PAGES, LEGAL CAP, AND ENDORSED BY WHITMAN FOR FILING: "WILL OF WALT WHITMAN, MAY 16, 1873." A MAGNIFICENT AND PRECIOUS WHITMAN DOCUMENT, WRITTEN IN INK THROUGHOUT IN WHITMAN'S EXCEEDINGLY LEGIBLE HAND ON THREE FULL PAGES OF LEGAL CAP, MENTIONING HIS FAMILY, HIS FRIENDS, AND GOING INTO GREAT DETAIL IN BEQUEATHING ALL HIS PERSONAL BELONGINGS, INCLUDING HIS ROYALTIES AND BOOKS. Enclosed in a full morocco folding case.

1873 WAS AN EVENTFUL YEAR IN WHITMAN'S LIFE. It was in that year that he had his first paralytic stroke which compelled him to leave his government job in Washington and come to live with his brother George in Camden, New Jersey. The other blow was the death of his mother, who died shortly after the execution of the will.

THIS MARVELOUS WHITMAN HOLOGRAPH BRINGS US PERHAPS CLOSER TO WALT WHITMAN, THE DEVOTED SON, BROTHER AND FRIEND, than any other document in existence. In it we find mention of everything that Walt Whitman owned in the world: the plates of his books "LEAVES OF GRASS," "PASSAGE TO INDIA." "DEMOCRATIC VISTA," and "AS A STRONG BIRD ON PINIONS FREE," being some 600 pages (or more) of electrotyped or stereotyped plates; 350 cloth copies of "AS A STRONG BIRD" at S. W. Green's, 17 Jacob Street, New York City, which he leaves to his mother in trust for his brother Edward. He expressed the wish that his mother (or brother if executor) pay $89 to Peter Doyle, his dearest friend, his silver watch, his hunting case and his love. Whitman's tenderness and solicitude for his brother Edward, a mental defective, were always in evidence. His savings and provisions kept this brother's present and future needs steadily in view.

"... The plates of my books, "LEAVES OF GRASS," "PASSAGE TO INDIA," "DEMOCRATIC VISTAS," and "AS A STRONG BIRD ON PINIONS FREE,"—being some six hundred (or over) pages of electrotyped or stereotyped plates—Also some three hundred and fifty copies (cloth) of AS A STRONG BIRD, &"—all at S. W. Green's, 17 and 18 Jacob Street, New York City,—Also

The Copies of my books and money due from said copies, or sales, at & by, M. Doolady, 98 Nassau St., N. Y. City.

Also, returns due, for my books, from Samson Low & Co. booksellers. London, England ...

... To My Mother, Louisa Whitman, in trust for my brother, Edward L. Whitman, to be used for his support & benefit, as to her may seem proper ...

... I wish Eighty Nine Dollars paid to Peter Doyle—that sum being due to him from me. I also will him my silver watch, Appleton-Tracy movement hunting-case. I wish it given to him, with my love.

I will my portrait in oil (by Charles Hine) to my brother George—also the old oil painting, portrait, with old frame. Also the portrait in oil, of mother, by Jacobs, small size.

I will my open-face silver watch to James Cornwell Whitman, son of my brother Andrew.

I will a good gold ring (one from my fingers) each to my brother George, brother Jeff, sister Mary, sister Hannah, and nephew James Cornwell Whitman—also, to each just named a good photograph portrait of me, such as may suit them—also a good bound copy of my poems, to each.

My gold watch is to go to my mother, to be disposed of or not, as she may think proper. (It is a good time piece, worth from 130 to $150.) If deceased, the proceeds to go to my brother Edward.

My portrait by Walter Libbey is to go to my brother Jeff ..."

UNQUESTIONABLY ONE OF THE MOST SPLENDID WALT WHITMAN DOCUMENTS IN EXISTENCE.

A WHITMAN AUTOGRAPH LETTER OF UNUSUAL CIVIL WAR INTEREST, IN WHICH THE GREAT POET DESCRIBES A FIELD HOSPITAL SCENE

246. WHITMAN (WALT). Original Draft of an Autograph Letter. 4 pp., 8vo. Written in a field hospital. 1865.

"... I am working quite actively.... I have been lately down to front a second time through the field hospitals—they are breaking them up and sending the bad cases up here, I suppose preparatory to some movement of course.... Many of the cases ... suffer fearfully. I am writing this in hospital as I am watching here to-night over a bad case.... With all their sadness, the wounded and sick get incredibly near to one. The new soldiers generally come in without a cent. I often given them little. Poor young men, they respond so affectionately to real kindness ...

I suppose you hear of Grant's plan to improve enormously the communication between here and the southwest by rail.... They say he has staked all on taking Richmond within three months ..."

A REMARKABLE WHITMAN MANUSCRIPT DESCRIBING A SCENE IN A FIELD HOSPITAL DURING THE CIVIL WAR WHERE HE NURSED THE SICK AND WOUNDED SOLDIERS. He also speaks of the generous contributions that have been sent and urges his friend to raise more funds. Whitman also mentions Grant and his plans to take Richmond with the aid of the Virginia Army and voices his faith in them.

IN AN UNPUBLISHED MANUSCRIPT WALT WHITMAN WRITES HIS OWN DEFENCE—"IS WALT WHITMAN'S POETRY POETICAL?"

247. **WHITMAN (WALT).** Autograph Manuscript Signed by Walt Whitman with John Burroughs' name: "Is Walt Whitman's Poetry Poetical?" 8 pp., 4to. Middletown, N. Y. Feb. 17, 1874. With an Autograph Letter 1 p., 8vo. Camden. Feb. [1874]. To John Burroughs, enclosing the manuscript.

EXTREMELY IMPORTANT UNPUBLISHED CRITIQUE OF HIS OWN POETRY BY WALT WHITMAN ENTITLED "IS WALT WHITMAN'S POETRY POETICAL?"

Walt Whitman wrote this long and thorough critique of his own work in reply to an attack upon him in "The Nation," post-dating it Feb. 17th at Middletown, where John Burroughs was then living. His covering letter to Burroughs suggests that Burroughs revise the manuscript and forward it to "The Nation" as his own. Thorough search of the files of "The Nation" and elsewhere shows that the article never appeared over the signature of John Burroughs, nor was it ever printed in Whitman's writings.

> "... Your ideas of the ad captandum [pleasing] character of Whitman's verse is quite certainly the reverse of well-founded; the almost universal testimony is that, at first harsh and offensive, "Leaves of Grass" needs study & more than one perusal, to give up its meaning & confer pleasure. The author's theory from the outset has evidently been based upon the deep axiom "it is reserved for first rate poems never immediately to gratify." Whitman does not lap in sweets or graces, but is eminently an exercise, a stimulus, an inexhaustable suggestion ..."

> "... He is never a garden with regular beds and walks and a marble fountain; but frequently the stretching landscape and distant sky, the rushing river, or briny sea— or perhaps the common and general road ..."

> "... The question remains, & must remain, for the future to settle, whether in him & and by him are not planted the hardy germs of a new & grander stock for poetry— certainly not less than the old, any more than our Science and Philosophy are—but necessitated by our vaster conditions of Democracy, and expressing them ..."

> "... The immortal Hebraic poems—Homer's, Virgil's, and Juvenal's compositions— Dante's, Shakespeare's and even Tennyson's—from the highest point of view, are all and each such characteristic yet generic growths. Walt Whitman's is the same in my opinion. The physiognomy of a race—of each race in the past—of our American race in the present—has the same old generic type, & yet is markedly different, and is characteristic only of itself."

AN UNPUBLISHED SPIRITED DEFENCE OF HIS PHILOSOPHY AND POETRY AND OF THE UTMOST IMPORTANCE TO THE STUDY AND THE UNDERSTANDING OF WALT WHITMAN AND HIS POETRY.

ORIGINAL AUTOGRAPH MANUSCRIPT OF WALT WHITMAN'S REMARKABLE POEM ON THE DEATH OF THE MARTYRED PRESIDENT GARFIELD, "THE SOBBING OF THE BELLS"

248. **WHITMAN (WALT).** Original Autograph Manuscript. 2 pp., 8vo, gauzed. "THE SOBBING OF THE BELLS." Written in ink in Whitman's characteristic hand. Bound in half brown morocco. September 19-20, 1881.

"THE SOBBING OF THE BELLS", WALT WHITMAN'S FAMOUS DIRGE OVER PRESIDENT GARFIELD, is dated: "MIDNIGHT, SEPT. 19-20, 1881". Upon its reverse side is the FIRST DRAFT OF THE POEM, carefully worked over and then crossed out, revealing the poet at work while still under the shock of the martyred president's tragic end.

> "*THE SOBBING OF THE BELLS*
>
> Midnight, Sept: 19-20, 1881
>
> The sobbing of the bells, the sudden death news everywhere
> The slumberers rouse—the rapport of the People,
> (Full well they know that message in the darkness,
> Full well return the sad reverberations,)
> The passionate toll and clang—city to city, joining, sounding, passing
> Those heart beats of a Nation in the night."

On the other side of the leaf in Whitman's Autograph is His First Conception of the Poem Corrected and then Crossed Out.

That Walt Whitman was profoundly stirred by the death of President Garfield so quickly following the attempted assassination of July 2nd is evident. This poem recalls Whitman's great "O Captain! My Captain!" written at the passing of President Lincoln 16 years earlier in a similar tragic manner—in that poem too are heard the ringing of the bells and the grief of a roused people.

"A CAROL-CLUSTER AT 69"

249. WHITMAN (WALT). Original Autograph Manuscript of "A Carol-Cluster at 69." 1 p., 4to.

A Fine and Characteristic Manuscript Poem by the Great Poet. Written in Whitman's Customary Indelible Pencil with Numerous Corrections and Additions in ink of the Introductory Lines of one of His Last Poems. An Exceedingly Interesting Specimen, being the Complete Original Draft with Numerous Corrections, Changes and Additions.

"A CAROL-CLUSTER AT 69

A Carol at sixty-nine! repetitions! rhapsodies divine!
Of ye, O God, Life, Nature, Freedom, Poetry,
Of ye, the lines in faith and joy, continuing, singing, on the same:
Of You, my Land—your rivers, prairies, States—of you, O mottled Flag!
Your aggregate retained—of north, south, east and west—their items all—none, none
    deserted;
Of me myself—the merry heart yet beating in my breast—the mind's hauteur—the
    body wreck'd, old, poor and paralyzed, of burning fires yet in the sluggish blood
Of undiminish'd Faith—of many a loving Friend."

Manuscript Poems of Walt Whitman are Extremely Rare.

"YOU TIDES WITH CEASELESS SWELL"

250. WHITMAN (WALT). Original Autograph Manuscript of "You Tides with Ceaseless Swell" from "Sands at Seventy." 1 p., 4to. Written in ink. With Numerous Changes and Corrections. Enclosed in a half morocco folding case.

"YOU TIDES WITH CEASELESS SWELL

You tides with ceaseless swell! you power that does this work!
You unseen force, centripetal, centrifugal, through space's spread!
Rapport of sun, moon, earth, and all the constellations!
What are the messages by you from distant stars to us? what Sirius'? what Capella's?
What central heart—and you the pulse—vivifies all? What boundless aggregate of all?
What subtle indirection and significance in you? what clue to all in you? what fluid
vast identity
Holding the universe with all its parts [entire] as one—as sailing in a ship?

A Fine Manuscript of a Poem in which Whitman Apostrophizes the Ocean in His Magnificent Poetic Style.

A BEAUTIFUL MANUSCRIPT POEM, WITH THE
FIRST UNPUBLISHED TITLE

251. WHITMAN (WALT). Original Autograph Manuscript of "By That Long Scan of Waves" from "Sands at Seventy," bearing the First Title of "With Every Heave and Roll." 1 p., 8vo. Written in ink. With Numerous Changes and Insertions.

Walt Whitman Scans the Ocean Waves and Muses over His Past Life. This First Version of this autobiographical poem is very important on account of its differences from the published version, especially in the rejected line

"(And yet may-be some hidden part to play, some object in the scheme's ensemble,
Hidden beneath or on the surface . . .)"

"WITH EVERY HEAVE AND ROLL

With every heaving wave, of ebb or flood called back
With every undulating crest and curl some light or shade, some retrospect,
Joys, travels, studies—silent panoramas—scenes ephemeral, mournful.
The long-past war, the battles, hospital sights, the wounded and dead:
Myself through every by-gone phase—my idle youth—my old age at hand.
My three-score years of life summ'd up . . ."

An Important Lyric from "Leaves of Grass" Portraying Whitman in a Reminiscent Mood and Revealing the Poet at Work.

"AS I WEND THE SHORES I KNOW NOT"

252. WHITMAN (WALT). Original Autograph Manuscript Poem "As I Wend The Shores I Know Not." 1 p., 4to. Written in ink. From "Sea Drift." Enclosed in a half morocco folding case.

"As I wend the shores I know not,
As I listen to the dirge—the voices of men and women wrecked,
As I inhale the impalpable breezes that set in upon me,
As the ocean so mysterious rolls toward me closer and closer,
At once I find the least thing that belongs to me, or that I see or touch, I know not;
I too but signify a little washed-up drift—A few sands and dead leaves to gather,
Gather—and merge myself as part of the leaves and drift.
O baffled, lost,
Bent to the very earth, here preceding what follows,
Terrified with myself that I have dared to open my mouth,
Aware now that amid all the blab whose echoes recoil upon me, I have not once had
the least idea who or what I am."

A Beautiful Manuscript of Verses Pulsating with Whitman's Poetic Sweep and Expressing in Beautiful Lines the Awe with which Nature Inspired Him.

253. ——. A. L. s., signed with initials. 1 p., 4to. Camden, May 24, '85. [To W. S. Kennedy]. (A few tears repaired).

About Kennedy's Manuscript "The Poet as a Craftsman".

"I would not put it OUT BY MYSELF. Such things never strike in so well in the abstract as in illustration of SOME DEFINITE PERSONAL CRITICAL CONCRETE THING. I suggest to you a criticism on TENNYSON AND WALT WHITMAN (or if you prefer on VICTOR HUGO, T. AND W. W.) where they should be worked in. What think you?"

254. ——. A. L. s. 2 pp., 4to. Camden, Dec. 2, '85. To W. S. Kennedy. (A few tears have been repaired).

"Your 'The Poet as a Craftsman' seems the best statement possible of the modern scientific American point of view—as it certainly is the highest & deepest (complimentary) statement of my theory and practice in L. of G." He follows with a list of well-known names he would like Kennedy to 'send copies to at his leisure.

255. ——. A. L. s., signed with initials. 1 p., 4to. June 20 ['86]. To W. S. Kennedy.

"I send you a note of Introduction to J. A. Symonds—whom I think most likely and valuable for the purpose you spoke of . . . Symonds has leisure, has long been a reader of L. of G. & I have heard has for some time been wanting to have something to say in print about it . . . I don't think well as requesting anything from Dowden," etc.

256. ——. A. L. s. 1 p., 4to. Camden, July 8, '86. To W. S. Kennedy.

A FINE LETTER IN WHICH WHITMAN EXPRESSES HIS WISHES CONCERNING THE USE OF HIS NAME IN BOOKS OR ARTICLES ABOUT HIM.

"I see in your letter, you have crossed out the 'Walt' in the name—I like best to have the FULL NAME always, if possible, instead of merely 'Whitman'. Give both words, & don't be afraid of the tautology," etc.

257. ——. A. L. s. 1 p., 4to. Camden, April 11, '87. [To W. S. Kennedy].

Written on the back of a letter from Ernest Rhys.

"I expect to go on to New York to speak my 'Death of Lincoln' piece Thursday after noon next—Probably the shake up will do me good . . . I don't make much reckoning of the N. Y. performance—the best is to be borne in mind (& warmly borne in mind) by a few dear N. Y. friends. Sunny & summery weather here & my canary is singing like a house a fire."

258. ——. A. L. s., signed with initials. 1 p., 8vo. Camden [Oct. 4, 1887]. To W. S. Kennedy].

He speaks of Bucke and O'Connor and supposes if "no news is good news" O'Connor must be on the mend. "I return Symond's letter herewith—the whole matter—this letter & the Fortnightly note—seems to me funny ('Perhaps there may be bairns, Kind sir, Perhaps there may be NOT"). Yes I like the little English Spec. Days, too. Keep y'r copy. I have a photo for you soon too—One from Cox's (N. Y.) I call it the laughing Philosopher."

259. ——. A. L. s., in pencil. 1 p., 4to. Camden, October 7, '88. [To W. S. Kennedy].

A FINE LETTER MENTIONING A HOST OF HIS FRIENDS.

"John Burroughs has been to see me, the dear good fellow. I was glad to have him & his talk did me good . . . I had a letter day before yesterday from O'Connor, he has great trouble with an affection of the eyes . . . I hear from Dr. Bucke every day or so—T. B. Harned was here an hour ago . . . Horace Traubel is faithful to the utmost . . . I forward with this mail a copy of November Boughs—McKay will be the publisher the coming week . . . What has become of the W W plaster bust?" etc.

260. ——. A. L. s., in pencil. 1 p., 4to. Camden, Dec. 18, '88. [To W. S. Kennedy].

"I have been thro' another very bad spell—ten days, two of them quite serious—but am somewhat better . . . my brain is flabby—my grip weak . . . My relations were never at all intimate with Lowell—there are a good many such . . . I have included all my stuff in 'Complete Vol.' a big book, authenticated by me now, rather cheaply bound, & I w'd like to send a package of four or five copies by Express to you." etc.

261. ——. A. L. s. 1 p., 4to. Camden, December 21, '88. [To W. S. Kennedy].

Written in pencil; another, also written in pencil, 1p., 4to. Camden, March 20, '89. Together 2 pieces.

"I have sent this evening five copies of the big book by express . . . there is no special hurry about delivering the books . . . The SATURDAY REVIEW (March 2) has a rather curious HOT & COLD I WOULD BUT DARE NOT sort of notice of Nov. B. & me in wh. O'Cs'and and Dr. B's names are toss'd ab't superficially & with attempted sarcasm," etc.

262. ——. A. L. s. 1 p., 4to. Camden, January 28, '89. [To W. S. Kennedy].

"I have sent M. Sarrazin a copy of the big book (like your copy) and also a package of slips & criticisms & notions &c abt. L of G. & self . . . Doctor makes a little fun of Howells's notice of NOV. BOUGHS in Feb. HARPER'S (the wonder is that it is so friendy and good), etc.

263. ——. A. L. s. 1 p., 4to. Camden, Feb. 1, '89. [Also] A. L. s., in pencil. 1 p., 4to. Camden, Feb. 11, '89. Together 2 pieces. [To W. S. Kennedy].

The second is more or less a continuation of the first, and relate to his condition, which is not so good at this time, and to Kennedy's condensed translation of Sarrazin. He writes also of Dr. Bucke and O'Connor, who is badly off.

264. ——. A. L. s., in pencil. 1 p., 4to. Camden, Monday, 7 A. M., '89 (June). [To W. S. Kennedy]. Written on the back of a letter to Whitman from R. M. Bucke.

"Am sitting here just ended my breakfast, an egg, some Graham bread & coffee—all wh. I relished—recd my morning mail & send you this fr. Dr. B—with my scribbling own back . . . Have written a little the last two weeks & sent off. Some accepted and paid some rejected . . . I want to get somewhere seaside or mountains," etc.

265. ——. A. L. s. 1 p., 4to. Camden, September 7, 1889. [To W. S. Kennedy]. A continuation of the letter the following day is in pencil, and is signed with initials.

" 'Poetes Anglaise' wh. I told you was out & I have had a copy (it has been out ever since and is out now)—it seems to be the MOST DETERMINED BLOW we have had happen to us, yet—Traubel's dinner book (as I call it) is not out printed yet, but will be very soon & I will send you one," etc.

ALMOST ENTIRELY ABOUT WHITTIER

266. WHITMAN (WALT). A. L. s., written in pencil. 1 p., 4to. Camden, Oct. 10, '89. [To W. S. Kennedy].

A Very Fine Letter Written Almost Entirely About Whittier.

"Whittier's poetry stands for MORALITY (not its ENSEMBLE or in any true philosophic or Hegelian sense but) as filter'd through the positive Puritanical & Quaker filters . . . Whittier is rather a grand figure—pretty lean and ascetic—no Greek—also not composite & universal enough (don't wish to be, don't try to be) for ideal Americanism . . . The sense of Mannahatta means THE PLACE AROUND WHICH THE HURRIED WATERS ARE CONTINUALLY COMING OR WHENCE THEY ARE GOING."

267. ——. A. L. s. 1 p., 4to. Camden, June 18, 1890. [To W. S. Kennedy]. Written in indelible pencil.

"Did I tell you my last piece (poem) was rejected by the Century (R. W. Gilder)—I have now been shut off by ALL the magazines here & the NINETEENTH CENTURY in England—& feel like closing house as poem writer—(you know a fellow doesn't make brooms or shoes if nobody will have 'em)—I shall put in order a last little 6 or 8 page annex (the second) of my Leaves of Grass & that will probably be the finish," etc.

268. ——. A. L. s. 1 p., small 4to. Camden, Aug. 4, '90. [To W. S. Kennedy]. Written in red ink on the inside portion of an envelope from Dr. Bucke.

"Have rec'd from Addington Symonds his two new vols. 'Essays Speculative & Suggestive'—one of the Essays 'Democratic Art, with reference to W.W.' of course the whole thing is scholarly & interesting & more—I have scribbled a brief piece anent of the Dem. Art essay & sent it to the Critic . . . but for a good while now all my pieces come back rejected (the Century, Harpers, the Eng. Nineteenth Century, the Cosmopolitan, etc., etc. all send my pieces back)," etc.

269. ——. A. L. s. 1 p., 4to. Camden, August 27, '90. [To W. S. Kennedy].
Written in indelible pencil.

13 —
T. E

"*Have just sold 50 copies folded in sheets (unbound) the big book (complete works)
$3. each—wh. quite sets me up . . . eyes giving out plainly—want to finish & turn out
this 2d annex while they serve, altho' I guess there is nothing to it . . . there, I believe
I have bubbled enough,*" etc.

270. ——. Four A. L. s., each 1 p., small 4to. Camden, Jan. 27, Nov. 1, Nov. 23,
and Dec. 23, 1890. [To W. S. Kennedy].

20 —
golds.

"*I believe I have a little poemet in forthcoming CENTURY . . . been kept indoors by
the bad weather . . . the old machine, the body & brain well shattered & gone (that
secession war experience was a WHACK or series of whacks irrecoverable) . . . Send
you herewith printed slip of 'Old Poets' . . . folks don't realize . . . what a wretched
physical shack (a western word) I really am—What was that of Epictetus ab't 'a spark
of soul dragging a poor corpse shell around'?*"

271. ——. A. L. s. 1 p., 4to. Camden, Aug. 29, 1890. [To W. S. Kennedy].

13 —
T. E

"*Enclosed I send what I have just scratched off about the Hollandisk piece . . . It is
quite a theme—quite significant—means a good deal to me and FOR ME—HOPE THE
MOOD will get hold of you one of these times soon . . . I sh'd suggest THE CRITIC
for the Hollandisk piece 'WALT WHITMAN'S DUTCH TRAITS is a good name—Of
course rambly and careless—like yr little Quaker piece,*" etc.

272. ——. Three A. L. s., one in pencil, small 4to. Camden, Oct. 29, 1890; Jan.
29 and Feb. 3, 1891. [To W. S. Kennedy].

20 —
golds.

"*The best report of the Ing's lecture was the Phil. Times . . . produced me $869.45 . . .
my piece 'Old Poets' (gossipy) is to be in Nov. N.A. review . . . the trial mulcted B 500
BUT THE GOVERNMENT HAS ASSUMED THE WHOLE THING—B seems to be
as wholly, morally, everyway scathless as I see it . . . We have just had a baking, O how
I wish I c'd send the dear fran one of our nice pumpkin pies—(a very little ginger no
other spice),* etc.

273. ——. A. L. s. 1 p., 4to. Camden, Nov. 12, '90. [To W. S. Kennedy]. Written in indelible pencil; also, another, unsigned, 1 p., 4to. Nov. 8, 1890. Together 2 pieces.

12 —
T. E

"*Did I tell you I had sent off an article 'National Literature' to the N. A. Rev? . . . I
am having bound up 100 more of the book complete works & 200 folded complete ready
in sheets (printed 600 & have got rid of 300) am licking the 2 & last annex into shape,*"
etc.

274. ——. A. L. s. 1 p., 4to. Camden, Dec. 29, '90. [To W. S. Kennedy].
Written in indelible pencil.

15 —
P forhun

"*J. M. Stoddart, Editor Lippincott's Magazine contemplates for the March number a
picture of & articles ab't (one or two from) W.W.—speaks of it as his Whitman
(proposed) number. If it suits, how w'd it do to send him that piece on Dutch points?
—if yes, send it on to him. I am in favor of it. I have just had an order (with the
money) f'm Melbourne Australia for four of the big books.*" etc.

275. ——. A. L. s. 1 p., 4to. Camden Night Jan. 20, '91. [To W. S. Kennedy].
Written on the back of a note from the North American Review, sending Whitman a proof of his article.

10 —
T. E

Whitman writes about the coming appearances of contributions in several magazines . . .
"*The Feb. N. A. Rev. (I suppose) will have a (funny) article by me headed 'American
Nat'l Literature. Is there any such thing or can there ever be?' Then the Youth's
Companion has accepted & handsomely paid for a wee little poem Ship Ahoy—so
you see the crank is grinding away even in old age,*" etc.

276. ——. Three A. L. s., and one unsigned piece. Various sizes, dated Feb. 11, July 7, and July 18, 1891. [To W. S. Kennedy]. Together 4 pieces.

"Send you a couple slips of the Dutch piece—it is the best thing of its kind yet . . . Ernest Rhys was married in London early last month . . . Dr. B. goes over in the Britannic . . . will go to see Tennyson—will see a cluster of g't L of G. friends . . . the birthday report is to be printed (article by Traubel) in Lippincott's August (of course I did not attempt a line of L of G.), etc.

277. ——. A. L. s. 1 p., 4to. Camden, Apr. 30, '91. [To W. S. Kennedy]. **Written on the back of a letter from Dr. Bucke.**

A GOOD LETTER, MENTIONING "GOOD-BYE," "LEAVES OF GRASS," AND "NOVEMBER BOUGHS."

"The proofs of little 'Good-Bye' are done (66) and the pages cast (if you like careless touches you'll be satisfied with it) 20pp: go into L of G. as concluding annex the rest is melanged prose 'as if haul'd in by some old fisherman's seine, & disburs'd at that' . . . It will after the first specific ed'n, be bound as latter part of 'November Boughs," etc.

278. ——. A. L. s., signed with initials. 1 p., small 4to. Camden, May 27, '91. [To W. S. Kennedy].

A CHARACTERISTIC LETTER, written on a sheet of yellow paper with Epictetus' definition of the living personality and body printed on it, which Whitman has accepted as applying to his own physical case: "a little spark of soul dragging a great lummux of corpse—body clumsily to and fro around."

Splendid short autograph word from Tennyson anent of birthday—have sent 'Good-Bye' to Garland—the preparatory all enclosing continual theory of L of G. is MYSELF, OPENING MYSELF first to the countless techniques, traditions, examples, items, knowledges &c.&c.&;"

279. ——. A Collection of 10 Autograph Postal Cards, signed "W. W." and "Walt Whitman," from August 11, 1886 to September 14, 1889. To W. S. Kennedy.

These and the following three lots constitute brief chats by Whitman, and relate to a variety of subjects and people, including references to his own writings and books, his condition of health, etc. A few excerpts follow:

"Book printing slowly proceeding—the sheets now in the bindery". "Shall send you the little Nov. Boughs soon". "Our friend (O'Connor) has no doubt been buried by this time—his death hour was peaceful". "R. W. Gilder seems to be a solid friend of L of G. and me. T.B.Ald. INCLINED but don't know".

280. ——. A similar collection, all but one signed in full, from Sept. 30, 1889 to April 30, 1890. 10 pieces.

"Still anchor'd in my big chair—inertia & paralysis—slowly hardening & defining deafness & (more slowly) blindness." "Sent out a little poemet (welcoming Brazilian republic) to McClure's & rec'd money for it. So Browning is dead." "Expect to give (and wish to) my Death of Abraham Lincoln memorandum April 15 in Phila."

281. ——. A similar collection, all but two signed in full, one signed "Walt W." and another "W. W." 12 pieces.

"Have just sold & sent to Eng'd my little p'k't-b'k L of G." I count Ing. as one of my noblest friends and upholders". "John Burroughs has been here to see me—he is well and hearty.' "The next N.A. Rev. is to have a piece by me on 'American National Literature!!! it is touched off with the most careless touch I probably ever allowed my pen." "Am sending of proofs of GOOD-BYE." "Send me word if 'SHIP AHOY' was printed in YOUTH'S COMPANION." "If you have not printed abt 'Good-Bye' keep it back for eight or ten days, as that will be preferable for reasons."

282. ——. A similar collection, all but two signed in full, from June 30, 1890 to October 12, 1890. 10 pieces.

"I want to send a copy of L of G. to Trans. editor or publisher . . . for courtesy in sending me paper." "Have a little piece in forthcoming CRITIC." "Fortunately have a placid, quiet, even solitary thread quite strong in the weft of my disposition." "Another letter from Symonds (I think there's something first class in him)." "Col. Ingersoll is to give a lecture ab't me I hear." "The Ingersoll lecture (Liberty & Literature) is to come off evn'g Oct. 21 . . . I shall go & show myself."

AN AMAZING COLLECTION OF WALT WHITMAN'S LETTERS, POSTAL CARDS, NEWSPAPER CLIPPINGS AND OTHER MATERIAL, BROUGHT TOGETHER IN A LARGE SCRAP BOOK BY WILLIAM SLOANE KENNEDY

283. WHITMAN (WALT). A LARGE SCRAP BOOK FORMED BY WILLIAM SLOANE KENNEDY, CONSISTING OF LETTERS AND POSTAL CARDS SENT TO HIM BY THE POET (96); LETTERS FROM WRITERS AND PUBLISHERS (12); COPIES OF LETTERS (18); MANUSCRIPTS BY WHITMAN (4); SCRAPS OF WHITMAN'S WRITING (11); ENVELOPES ADDRESSED (2); PRINTED BROADSIDES (4); PRINTED SCRAPS AND CRITICISMS (74); pasted in a folio scrap book, full canvas. With notations by Mr. Kennedy in many places, of comment and elucidation.

THIS IS INDEED, AN EXTRAORDINARY PRESERVATION OF THE CORRESPONDENCE BETWEEN THE POET AND ONE WHOM WHITMAN CONSIDERED ONE OF HIS SPECIAL FRIENDS, AS STATED BY HIM IN A MEMORANDUM FOUND BY TRAUBEL AMONG WHITMAN'S PAPERS AFTER HIS DEATH: *"W. S. Kennedy—A young college chap—accepts L of G. yet bolts at the sexual part—but I consider Kennedy as a real & ardent friend both of self & book."*

The correspondence commences Feb. 25, 1881 and concludes in this scrap book with May 8, 1889. The Letters and Cards are replete with references to his books, his lectures, his friends, and his health, AND MIGHT WELL BE CONSIDERED HIS AUTOBIOGRAPHY AS EXPRESSED IN HIS LETTERS, for the period covered . . . In the main they are signed in full—Walt Whitman," others are signed "W.W." as he sometimes did when space would not permit his full name.

THE BROADSIDES include: A PROOF of "The Dying Veteran"; "A Memorandum at a Venture"; "November Boughs", four poems from Lippincott's Magazine; "Of that blithe Throat of Thine"...."There is also a complete article by Whitman, excerpted from "Baldwin's Monthly" of "Some Diary Notes at Random."

THE NEWS AND OTHER CLIPPINGS AND EXCERPTS continue from April 1886 up to and including the Poet's Death and Funeral Obsequies.

On the first page of the Scrap Book Kennedy has written a long description of Whitman's "love-life" as he had the story from Horace Traubel, and concluded his narrative with the sentence: *"I think this is all romancing on Walt's part, to relieve himself of the charge of man-love.*

IT WOULD INDEED BE DIFFICULT TO GATHER ANOTHER SUCH COLLECTION OF THE MOST INTIMATE CHARACTER AS IS CONTAINED IN THIS SCRAP BOOK.

THE WHITMAN-PARTON DEBT CONTROVERSY

284. WHITMAN (WALT). A Collection of Manuscript Material, Letters, Articles, etc., relating to the controversy over the Whitman-Parton debt for $200 (or $250), said to have been contracted by Whitman in Brooklyn, in 1859 or thereabouts. Detailed as follows:

THIS SMALL AMOUNT OF MONEY, ASSERTED TO HAVE BEEN BORROWED BY WHITMAN FROM JAMES PARTON AND NOT REPAID, BECAME IN 1897 THE SUBJECT OF A HEATED AND ACRIMONIOUS CONTROVERSY, INVOLVING THE SECOND MRS. PARTON, HER NIECE ETHEL (who assumed the name of Parton), THOMAS WENTWORTH HIGGINSON, WILLIAM S. KENNEDY, AND OTHERS. THE PRESENT COLLECTION CONSISTS OF:

BUCKE (R. M.). L.s., 3pp., folio, typewritten, London, Ont., March 14, 1895. To Mr. Kennedy. *"You say that certain parties bring a charge against Whitman that he borrowed money and not only did not pay it but lied as to his ability so to do. Unless there is absolute evidence of this I think we should simply decline to believe it."* He then relates his own loan to Whitman of $200. which W. insisted on repaying about a year before his death, although Bucke had repeatedly told him it was a gift. THE LETTER IS A MOST INTERESTING ONE, RELATING MUCH OF THE INTIMATE LIFE OF WHITMAN, ETC. He says in part: *"I know little about Walt's children—do not know how many there were—believe there were several. He and their mother were not married. This is the whole story . . . I can imagine a perfect pure union without it (the marriage ceremony), and a very impure one under its sanction."*

Bucke then goes on to state his reasons for disbelieving the debt, as Whitman had no special need of money in 1859.

WHITMAN (G. W.). A. L. s. in pencil, Burlington, Iowa, March 26, 1895. To Dr. Bucke. *"I must say I was much surprised & pained to learn of the charges made against Walt . . . I will not believe them without strong proof of their truthfulness,"* etc.

PARTON (ETHEL). A. L. s., 6pp., 4to. Newburyport, Feb. 10, 1897. To Mr. Kennedy. She writes for Mrs Parton who is ill, in reply to a letter from Mr Kennedy, and gives in great detail the Parton side of the story of the debt. *"I am sorry to inform any one calling himself Walt Whitman's friend, that a story to the discredit of one he so warmly defends, is true: but true it unquestionable is. Nor is there any possibility of mistaken identity."* She then goes on in great detail about the transaction.

PARTON (ETHEL). A. L. s., 12pp., 8vo. Newburyport, Feb. 15, 1897. To Mr. Kennedy. This letter is in reply to one from Mr. Kennedy, and is to a great extent, a further explanation of the Parton side of the case. *"Neither Mrs. Parton nor I care to push this matter to publicity, I repeat. but neither can we refuse to support Colonel Higginson's assertion when called upon to do so, nor think his treatment of Whitman without warrant,"* etc. Camden.

TRAUBEL (HORACE). A. L. s., 2 pp., 8vo. March 8, 1897. To Mrs. Fairchild. *"Have just heard from the Partons and have replied to them in strong terms . . . When Higginson made the charge general he struck , , , a foul blow,"* etc.

PARTON (ETHEL). Typed and partly written in pencil L. s., 3pp., folio. Newburyport, March 19, 1897. To Mr. Kennedy. Mr. Kennedy had apparently written a pretty strong letter, evoking the present reply which is also possessed with considerable heat. *"I do not care whether what we bring is new or old, exculpatory, or damnatory, so long as it is the truth. Whitman is to me simply a formless literary monster and a poor sort of human being, and I am not concerned for his reputation in either capacity . . . his dozen or half dozen pages of genius will probably survive, while the many more of egotism, sensual savagery and other barbaric yawp will be mercifully forgotten,"* etc.

HARNED (THOMAS B.). Tpyed L. s., with a line here and there written in. Philadelphia, March 19, 1897. To Mr. Kennedy. *"You seem to have gotton yourself into a terrible stew over the alleged Parton matter . . . Bucke, Traubel, and myself are only the literary executors of Whitman and have absolutely nothing to do with the fiscal management of the estate. The present controversy arose because of a sweeping statement (contained in one sentence) made by Col. Higginson. This statement I hold is not only cowardly but unjustified. Even if the Parton episode be true it does not justify the broad statement made by Col. Higginson. Any man with a spark of honor would not relentlessly pursue a dead man,"* etc.

KENNEDY (WILLIAM S.). AUTOGRAPH MANUSCRIPT. "Did Walt Whitman Leave a Debt Unpaid? Parton vs. Whitman." 20pp., 8vo.

KENNEDY (WILLIAM S.). AUTOGRAPH MANUSCRIPT. "Some Cool After-thoughts on Whitman vs. Parton, 4pp., 8vo.

KENNEDY VS. HIGGINSON — RE W. W.

285. WHITMAN (WALT). A Collection consisting of an A. L. s. 3½ pp., 8vo. Cambridge, March 7, 1895, from Thomas Wentworth Higginson to Mr. William Sloane Kennedy; and an Autograph Manuscript of 14 pp., 4to and 8vo, entitled "Euphrasy and Rue for T. W. Higginson." At the top of the manuscript

Mr. Kennedy has written: "N. B. Not written for publication during the present generation . . . or the next. W. S. K."

A Most Interesting Pair of Manuscripts, which are accompanied by a news clipping of Higginson's article on the death of Whitman, which appeared in "The Evening Post," March 28, 1892.

In Higginson's letter he writes:

"I note what you say of Emerson & Whitman in POET-LORE & feel no impulse to controvert it. There is however no doubt that Emerson spoke to me at Newport (about 1870 I should say) of what he called the 'priapism' of Whitman, & this in a tone of decided annoyance. . . . As I know, we always differ about the MAN Whitman, & I may recapitulate the points wherein he never seemed to me a thoroughly wholesome or manly man (1) This 'priapism.' (2) the entire absence in his poetry of any personal love for any individual woman, its place being filled by the mere craving of sex for sex (3) his want of personal honesty in business matters,—(here he refers to the Parton episode)—(4) his not going with the army when we all looked to him as precisely the man to organize a regiment in Brooklyn, but selecting the minor and safe function of a nurse (5) his intense personal egotism, as shown by his building a costly tomb at a time when he was supposed to be a poor man and people were being asked to aid & support him," etc.

Kennedy's Rejoinder to this Letter is Most Forcefully Expressed in His Unpublished Manuscript "Euphrasy and Rue for T. W. Higginson." In this manuscript Kennedy minces no words and compares Higginson to Dr. Jekyll and Mr. Hyde.

"It is a very unedifying & painful spectacle to see a man of Thomas Wentworth Higginson's abilities & standing in society giving way for so many years as he has done to the worser passion of vindictiveness in his nature, in slandering while living, & hounding beyond the limits of the tomb the character & memory of America's greatest poet."

W. H. BALLOU'S INTERVIEW WITH WHITMAN

286. **WHITMAN (WALT).** Autograph Interview of W. H. Ballou with Walt Whitman. 4 pp., 4to. Pasted together in one long sheet.

This Reporter's Account is Headed "Mutilated by Walt himself. Verbatim et literatim report." It is very sketchy in make-up as a reporter's notes would naturally be, but here and there are complete quotations from Whitman himself. Here are a few such:

"I don't think America or the age realizes its own unparalled conditions and virtues. These are as near perfect as they can be in the vast aggregate of people."

"I fear not death. Socrates uttered the greatest truth when he said: 'No evil can befall a good man, whether he be alive or dead.'"

"I am an old bachelor who never had a love affair. Nature supplied the place of a bride with suffering to be nursed & scenes to be poetically clothed."

"I write three hours per day . . . not a teetotaler, only regret that I did not cultivate the use of tobacco & have a pipe as a companion & solace for my old age."

287. ——. The Gruesome Story of Walt Whitman's Brain After Autopsy, told in two (2) A. L. s. by Herbert T. Harned, of the Towne Scientific School, University of Pennsylvania, 3 pp., 4to and 8vo, Dec. 4, and Dec. 18, 1921; also, an Autograph Memo. in the hand of William S. Kennedy. Together 3 pieces.

288. ——. Proof of Four Poems from "November Boughs"; "You Lingering Sparse Leaves of Me"; "Going Somewhere"; "After the Supper and Talk"; Not Meagre, Latent Boughs Alone." 1 p., 8vo.

At the Top of the Proof Whitman has Written "Lippincott's Magazine. Nov. '87." Whitman had made one correction—a deletion of one word.

289. ——. Proof of a portion of Dr. Bucke's "Rough abstract and condensation of Sarrazin's "Walt Whitman," in "La Nouvelle Revue," 1st of May, 1888. One folio column. With 21 corrections by Whitman.

290. ——. PROOF of John Burroughs' Article on "Whitman's Self-Reliance," written for the Walt Whitman Fellowship Papers: No. 9, November, 1894. Folio galley-proof strip, corrected.

On the upper margins Horace Traubel has written a note to Mr. Kennedy, as follows:

> "Dear K—I thought you would like to see this. It goes to press tomorrow (23d) and I will send you early copies. I am hoping to see your and Jackson's 'talk' on Whitman & Tolstoi. Traubel. Nov. 22d, 1894."

291. ——. A Collection of 31 newspaper clippings about Whitman: Birthday celebrations, Articles on him and his Writings, Obituaries, etc. Two or three have scraps of Whitman's writing on them. 31 pieces.

292. ——. Report (to accompany bill H. R. 10707) from the Committee on Invalid Pensions to whom was referred the bill for the relief of Walt Whitman. 4 pp., 8vo. Washington, 1887; Incomplete excerpt from Outnam's Magazine of "The Carpenter," by W. D. O'Connor, with notations by Whitman in two places; 3 facsimile letters by Whitman. 5 pieces.

293. ——. ELDRIDGE (CHARLES W.). Portion of an A. L. 4 pp., 8vo. Los Angeles, March 5, 1888. To W. S. Kennedy.

AN INTERESTING LETTER ABOUT THE SPURIOUS EDITIONS OF THE "THAYER & ELDRIDGE" EDITION WHICH ARE BEING CIRCULATED IN CALIFORNIA. HE STATES HOW THE GENUINE EDITION MAY BE VERIFIED:

> "The stereotype plates, steel engraved portrait, and dies for cover are the same as used in the T & E edition, but on the back of the title-page immediately under the certificate of copyright IN THE GENUINE EDITION, appear the words 'Electrotyped at the Boston Stereotype Foundry' 'Printed by George C. Rand & Avery.' IN THE FRAUDULENT EDITION THESE WORDS ARE LACKING."

294. ——. RHYS (ERNEST). Four A. L. s., 8 pp. in all. Nov. 16, 1886 to Dec. 27, 1887. To W. S. Kennedy. About Walt Whitman, the difficulty of finding a publisher for his books; his finally obtaining the Wilson Bros. in Glasgow, etc. * A. L. s. of Fred W. Wilson, 1 p., Dec. 17, 1887. About publishing Whitman's book, and other letters from Dr. Bucke, Henry A. Beers, W. D. O'Connor, etc., about Whitman. Together 11 pieces.

295. ——. TRAUBEL (HORACE L.). Three A. L. s., 10 pp. in all. Dec. 10, 1897 to July 17, 1888. To W. S. Kennedy. About Whitman. In one of the letters he writes:

> "I have learned something in the Parton matter which will surprise and please you. Just now I have not time to go into any details. Suffice to say WALT PAID THE DEBT . . . I think I shall soon have the documents of confusion for T. W. H. & all the tribe of shouting blasphemers," etc.

296. ——. Pencil Sketch of the upper portion of Walt Whitman's face and head made by Sidney H. Morse in 1887. A notation by Mr. Kennedy states that it was scratched at the end of a letter to him.

297. ——. A Lock of Walt Whitman's Hair. Preserved in an envelope, with its contents written by Dr. J. Johnston: "From J. J. to J. W. W." November 16th, 1891. The J. W. W. mentioned is J. W. Wallace, who in joint authorship with Dr. Johnston wrote "Visits to Walt Whitman in 1890-91." A review of their book from the "London Times Literary Supplement" is included.

Lot 298 omitted

232

SALE NUMBER 4251
EXHIBITION DAILY FROM APRIL 11
WEEKDAYS 9 TO 6 · SUNDAY 2 TO 5

Manuscripts, Autograph Letters
First Editions and Portraits of

WALT WHITMAN

Formerly the Property of the Late
DR. RICHARD MAURICE BUCKE
London, Ontario, Canada

Purchased at Public Sale in London, England, by
THE ULYSSES BOOKSHOP, LTD.

Or by Private Treaty by
DR. JACOB SCHWARTZ
London, England

To be Dispersed at Public Sale
April 15 and 16, at 8:15 p.m.

By Order of Dr. Jacob Schwartz
Individually and as President of the
Ulysses Bookshop, Ltd., London, England

FOREWORD BY CHRISTOPHER MORLEY

AMERICAN ART ASSOCIATION
ANDERSON GALLERIES · INC
30 EAST 57TH STREET · NEW YORK
1936

BROOKLYN FREEMAN.

BY WALTER WHITMAN.

Vol. 1.—No. 1.—Price Two Cents.

BROOKLYN, SATURDAY, SEPTEMBER 9, 1848.

THE "FREEMAN."

Brooklyn, Saturday, Sept. 9.

FOR PRESIDENT,
MARTIN VAN BUREN.

FOR VICE PRESIDENT,
CHARLES F. ADAMS.

"The Brooklyn Freeman."

"The Daily Freeman."

"STRONG SENSUAL GERMS"

FROM BLUE ONTARIO'S SHORE might well be the title of this catalogue, for it analyzes the Whitman collection of the Canadian Dr. Bucke—last of Walt's executors and intimates. I call it a catalogue, for it is technically such, but to the seeing eye it is surely one of the most complete and exciting biographies of Whitman yet put together. More than Dr. Bucke's own book (which Walt mostly rewrote) and almost more than any commentary yet written, this extraordinary synopsis penetrates, tallies (as Walt would say), and concludes. No study of Whitman henceforward dare appear without reference to this material. From the carpentry days down to *Goodbye My Fancy* (loveliest of titles) here is the story. What souvenir could be pleasanter than Walt's memorandum listed here for 23½ days of carpenter work done in Brooklyn. $26.40 was the amount of his bill; if a day's work was 8 hours that would be 14 cents an hour. Suppose Walt had received 14 cents an hour for the time spent writing poetry: his friends would not have needed to buy a horse and buggy for him. I like the little flash we get of him (all my allusions here are to glimpses you'll find in this catalogue) sitting in the station at Mott Haven, to change cars on the way back to Mannahatta. He's been in Boston where they are punctuating his stuff and planning to make a real New England Author of him—and he's to get 25 cents royalty per volume. For a moment he believes he's going to be rich.

You can think of this as a catalogue if you like, but I call it BUCKE'S WHITMAN, edited by Schwartz and Hanaburgh. It was the learned and observant Dr. Jacob Schwartz of the Ulysses Bookshop who snapped up the whole Bucke collection when it appeared in London; and it is the devoted Mr. E. F. Hanaburgh of the American-Anderson who has compiled this raisonné, a whole winter's work. As with Walt on Blue Ontario's Shore, "they thrilled with the power's pulsations and the charm of their theme was upon them." Nor shall I forget the day when I met Dr. Schwartz in the back yard of a New York bookshop, he carrying a suitcase loaded with a few specimens of this incredible trove. There was Vol. I No. 1 of the *Brooklyn Freeman*, September 9, 1848—never before found. Edited by *Walter* Whitman. The printing office burned down immediately after the first issue, and this, Walt's own file copy, is probably the only survivor. There were innumerable notes — "strong sensual germs" — for the equally innumerable versions of the Leaves. One after another they came out of the suitcase, tidily salved in their rich morocco folders (how different from the shabby litter on Mickle Street). Here indeed was a voice speaking—and saying what the heart of any creator understands. "Do not go into criticisms or arguments at all". . . . "Make full-blooded, rich, flush, natural *Works*". . . . "Insert natural things, indestructibles, idioms, characteristics, rivers, States, persons". . . . "I am your voice—it was told in you—in me it begins to talk" . . . and then, in a blurted outcry that has the brevity of despair: "Make *The Works*."

No one who has a feeling for Walt will need to be told how much this catalogue suggests; to explore the full treasure will keep bickering disciples busy for years. Do you remember Stephen Vincent Benét's fine *Ode to Walt Whitman* a year ago?

> "Each disciple
> Jealously guards his own particular store
> Of acorns fallen from the oak's abundance. . . .
> You're still the giant lode we quarry
> For gold, fools' gold, and all the earthy metals. . . .
> He grows through the earth and is part of it
> Like the roots of new grass."

Somewhere in his memoranda Dr. Bucke mentions Walt's pleasure in singing in the bathtub. This was partly the exhilaration of novelty: I suspect it was only when visiting his more civilized friends—such as the Pearsall Smiths in Germantown or Dr. Bucke at the Ontario madhouse—that Walt had access to the luxuries of plumbing. (Even in 1918-19 when I used to go there often I don't remember any bathtub in the Mickle Street cottage.) And in a sense the best of Walt's writing represents humanity at large singing in its tub—a kind of frank booming improvisation—grave, innocent, and clean. (Occasionally a twirling gurgle when the suds go down the drain.) Walt was at his surest in those mild, confident, hair-and-soapsud moments. His distrust of argument, fear of intellectuals, was a wise timidity: his mind was not apt for the subtle clockwork of the wits. But among his wounded soldiers, stagecoach drivers, simple-minded Traubels and cosmic-consciousness Buckes, with anyone who didn't disconcert him by being clever, he brimmed his incomparable wisdom. Perhaps chief of the many rewards of this collection is its multiplied and clinching proof of Whitman as something more than the innocent bathroom reciter: as the patient reconsiderer of the word. In 1856 we see him noting:—

"In future 'Leaves of Grass'. Be more severe with the final version of the Poem . . . Also no ornaments especially no ornamental adjectives, unless they have come molten hot, and imperiously prove themselves . . ."

In 1857 he jots down:—

"The great Construction of the New Bible. Not to be diverted from the principal object—the main life work—the Three Hundred & Sixty-five—(it ought to be ready in 1859)."

And in 1868, in one of the many outlines for undelivered lectures:—

"First of all prepare for study by the following self-teaching exercises—Abstract yourself from this book,—realize where you are at present located,—the point you stand, that is now to you the centre of all. Look up, think of space stretching out . . ."

So, right down to the Death-Bed Edition (of which we have here Copy Number One) Walt continued his revision, his primitive Buddhism of preserving even the hair-clippings and toenails of his work.

Not for him Emerson's stoic confidence in Time as winnower, the sifter of the perfect five lines among five hundred. Walt intended to give Time all the help he could, and Dr. Bucke was his favorite cache. (He passed the Bucke to Posterity.) So here we find the most amazing collection of miscellaneous personalia. His early fables about dreams, death, and drink; memoranda of the voyage down the Ohio and Mississippi Rivers which first woke him to some vision of America; a few pious and tender memories of New Orleans ("I slide my hand for the brown melons of your breasts"); reading lists, scrapbooks, diaries of the War. The tragic panorama of the Whitman family is spread out as never before. The infinitely pathetic and illiterate letters of his poor old mother; brother George's correspondence from the battlefields; letters from brother-in-law Heyde in Vermont who made heavy weather of living with Hannah; letters from Mattie the wife of Jeff who went to run the waterworks in St. Louis. There are the postcards to Peter Doyle, the Diary in Canada, and the actual MS. copy, in full, from which the first complete Leaves was set up (the 1882). Mr. Hanaburgh, adopting a helpful scheme of arrangement, has set these things forth with brilliant care.

The lover of Walt knows how hard it is to be brief in rummaging such a haystack of curiosity. Here, better than I have even seen, is the chart and contour of the Walt Whitman Primer I have long hoped for. Here, if you are adept to read between lines, is Walt himself in all four dimensions—height and breadth and thickness (sometimes pretty thick), and durability. It is all very well to chuckle now and then (as one is bound) at his simplicities. (What could be more humorless than his comment, written into Dr. Bucke's MS., on his own sense of humor?) At his finest he actually did, like Emerson's Brahma, "clear the Sphinx's muddy eye," and "they reckon ill who leave him out." There was wisdom in those devotees who found in him something so important to the human heart that they cherished every scrap.

On the wall of the cabin where I write—it looks out into the woods

of Walt's own Paumanok—is a pencil scrawl on a rectangle of green
paper. It was written, I think, on a piece scissored from left-over
stock of the green wrappers and end-papers of the 1855 Leaves.
(There are several such pieces in this collection.) It says, in Walt's
hand:—

I do not expect to see myself in the present magazines, reviews,
schools, pulpits and legislatures—but presently I expect to see myself
in magazines, schools, and legislatures—or that my friends after me
will see me there.

March 1936

PREFATORY NOTE

THE part of Dr. Richard M. Bucke's Whitman material described in this catalogue is one of the largest collections of autograph manuscripts by an American author that has ever appeared at public sale in this country at one time. It is not in its bulk, however, that the importance of the collection lies, but in the fact that every scrap of paper comprising it is a link in the great chain of thought that finally established a new literature. An effort has been made to classify this material in such a way as to show the development of this new literature from its remote ancestry to the crowning achievement.

Dr. Bucke was a Whitman enthusiast of the highest type and, with certain reservations, allowed any earnest student of Whitman access to this material. To state, therefore, that any of this material except some of the family letters is unpublished, without consulting every work in the complete bibliographical list of Whitman material, would throw the descriptions open to doubt. Unquestionably there are a number of manuscripts in this collection which are unpublished, and some of these have been so described by virtue of failure to locate them after reasonable search. On the other hand, over half of the material printed in "Preparatory Reading and Thought", "Shorter Notes", "Meaning and Intention of 'Leaves of Grass'", "Rejected Lines", and "Variorum Readings" published in the complete works of Whitman is present in manuscript form in this collection.

While each of the manuscripts herein described may contain a complete idea, that idea may have been incorporated in a larger theme. In fact, Whitman's writing was so fragmentary—a line or two sometimes being added at a later date, and often many of these fragments pasted together to form a poem—that no assurance is given that any manuscript is absolutely complete unless it is so described.

The primary divisions of the catalogue, arranged under section headings such as "Building the Man" (p. 1), succeed each other in approximately chronological arrangement. The material within each of these divisions, however, is arranged by subject. The date given after the heading of each individual description is only approximate as determined by the paper, ink, pencil, and handwriting. The use of green or blue ink, for instance, usually indicates that the manuscript was written prior to 1855; the green, pink, or yellow papers that Whitman often employed were the wrappers or end-papers of the 1855 edition of "Leaves of Grass" and were chiefly used from 1856 to 1860; while manuscripts written in a large and bold hand in black ink were usually of the late period of the poet's life.

Unless another writer's name is given all manuscripts herein described are by Walt Whitman, and each manuscript is in ink unless described as being in pencil; collections, however, may be in either ink or pencil, or both. Many of the items are accompanied by typewritten transcripts, hand-drawn title-pages, and typewritten tables of contents, which are indicated simply by the words "with transcript and title" or the like, sometimes followed by a quotation of the title.

The bindings are all new, unless otherwise described, and are all by Sangorski & Sutcliffe. Each manuscript is carefully hinged or tipped in. Nearly all the items bound in cloth or part leather have the facsimile of Whitman's signature stamped in gilt on the side. On a few of the bindings and hand-drawn title-pages appear incorrect dates and statements.

The portraits in this collection are worthy of particular mention. Many of the items are accompanied by original photographs, reproductions, or engraved portraits of the poet. These form, as a whole, one of the largest collections in existence and include some hitherto unknown portraits and many signed and dated by Walt Whitman.

FIRST SESSION

Wednesday, April 15, 1936, at 8:15 p. m.

CATALOGUE NUMBERS 1 TO 162 INCLUSIVE

Building the Man

GENEALOGY AND BIOGRAPHY OF THE WHITMAN FAMILY AND ITS INFLUENCE ON THE POET

THE study of the heredity and biological development of the individual has today advanced to such a degree that certain theories have been so far confirmed as to establish a precedent for future laws; and in the time of Walt Whitman, Dr. Bucke, as head of the largest insane asylum in Canada, was probably the most advanced scientist in his theories of the influence of heredity on the individual. In the following fourteen items (Numbers 1-14) the heredity of Walt Whitman is traced so far as known, the analysis of the biological effect is made by Dr. Bucke, the phrenological report on Whitman is noted, and many biographical details of Whitman and his ancestors are given.

Whitman himself and W. S. Kennedy claimed that the Dutch ancestry predominated in Whitman, but a glance at the genealogical chart mentioned below will show that the English strain was actually predominant. But it is far more likely, as Kennedy hinted, considering the fact that Walt Whitman differed so greatly from the other members of his family so far as recorded, that the slight Welsh strain became dominant, and that the wild music of that nation reverberated through the pen of Whitman.

1. GENEALOGY AND BIOGRAPHY. 1850-1861. Autograph Manuscript, 2 pp., folio, about 525 words. With photograph signed *"Walt Whitman 1872"*, transcript and title; *"A Family Record"*. Small folio, half green polished morocco.

This manuscript contains on the recto the genealogy of the Whitman family, so far as it was known to Walt Whitman, with historical and biographical notes about some of the members. Most of this page was written about 1850, with a few annotations, such as the date of death of his great grandmother, inserted about 1861.

[Description concluded on following page]

On the verso is the record of Whitman's movements from 1823 to 1861, written about the latter date, though a biographical note at the bottom may have been written later.

"Sarah White, my great grandmother Whitman, lived to be 90 years old. She was a large, strong woman, chewed tobacco, opium &c.—petted her slaves, and had always a crowd of little niggers about her . . ."

2. GENEALOGY AND DIARY. 1849-1855. Autograph Manuscript, 2 pp., folio, about 450 words. With portrait, transcript of one page, and title: *"Genealogy of the Whitman Family. Also the concluding Portion of an Account of his return Journey to New Orleans"*. Small folio, half green levant morocco.

30

On the recto is a list of Whitman's immediate family written about 1852, and a biographical note about his relatives. On the verso is a page of Whitman's diary of his return journey from New Orleans in 1849, covering the boat trip on Lake Erie, Buffalo, Niagara, Albany, and the trip down the Hudson River.

3. WHITMAN FAMILY. 1883. Autograph Manuscript *"list of the immediate family"*, 1 p., oblong 8vo, about 40 words. Framed with portrait.

12 50

This list was sent to Dr. Bucke and was printed in his biography of Whitman. Naturally Whitman's own signature is included.

4. PATERNAL RELATIVES. 1862. Autograph Manuscript in pencil, 2 pp., 12mo, about 175 words. With portrait of Whitman's father, transcript, and title: *"Walt Whitman on His Grandfather, and Grand Uncles Isaac and Jacob, both Carpenters from whom Walter, his Father learnt the Trade: and Concerning His Father's early struggles in Life"*. 12mo, half white pigskin.

20

Of his father he writes: *"He was a first rate carpenter, did solid, substantial, conscientious work. I have heard mother say that he would sometimes lay awake all night planning out some unusually difficult plan in his building arrangements."*

5. MATERNAL RELATIVES. 1856-1864. Autograph Manuscript in pencil, 4 pp., 12mo, about 400 words. With portrait of Whitman's mother, transcript and title: *"Walt Whitman The History of His Maternal Progenitors"*. 12mo, half white pigskin.

Whitman here outlines the careers of his great grandparents Garret Van Velsor, a weaver, who married Mary Kossabone, and Capt. John Williams, who married Mary Woolley, all of whose sons followed the sea.

6. ANCESTORS. 1862-1873. Four Autograph Manuscripts, 3 in pencil, 4 pp., 16mo to 8vo, about 250 words. With transcripts, 2 clippings, and title: *"Walt Whitman Notes and Description of His Female Relatives"*. 8vo, cloth, undyed niger morocco back.

These manuscripts describe Hannah Brush, Whitman's paternal grandmother; and Sarah Mead, his maternal grandaunt, who lived to the age of ninety-six. The two clippings, one of which is annotated by Whitman, describe Mrs. Mead and report her account of seeing President Washington during his tour of Long Island.

7. WHITMANS IN THE REVOLUTION. 1861. Autograph Manuscript, 1 p., 8vo, about 160 words. With transcript and title: *"Memories of his Grandparents during the Revolution"*. 8vo, half red niger morocco.

Anecdotes of Kell Van Velsor, who rescued his horse from the British, and of the poet's grandmother Whitman.

8. HEREDITY. 1883. Autograph Manuscript, 1 p., 8vo, about 100 words. With transcript and title: *"Walt Whitman On His Parents"*. 8vo, half green niger morocco.

Apparently this note was written for "Specimen Days" but never used, for at the top Whitman wrote in pencil *"?Specimen Days"*.

"All through young and middle age, I thought my heredity-stamp was mainly decidedly from my mother's side: but as I grew older, and latent traits came out, I see my father's also . . ."

Written on the back of an A. L. s. by James M. Scovel, who writes:

"Dawn on us 'good Grey Poet' with the smiling light of thy countenance . . ."

9. BUCKE, DR. RICHARD M. Two Autograph Manuscript
Essays by Dr. Bucke: *"The Genesis of Walt Whitman"*, 13 pp.,
folio, about 2,800 words; and *"Walt Whitman, Man and Poet"*,
15 pp., 4to, about 3,100 words. The first bound in cloth, the
second in a cloth folder.

17⁵⁰

The first relates to the physical and mental qualities inherited by Walt Whitman and his brothers; the second to the influence of heredity on Walt
Whitman the poet.

Laid in is an autograph manuscript chart of Whitman's ancestors, by Dr.
Bucke.

10. THE OLD FOLKS AT HOME. 1850. Autograph Manuscript,
2 pp., folio, about 730 words. With a view of the birthplace of
the poet and title: *"A description of the Home Surroundings and
Characters of his Mother's Family . . . On Verso a similar
description of His Father's Family"*. Small folio, half blue
polished morocco.

45

A fascinating picture of early days on Long Island, gathered in part from his
mother, but with some reminiscences of his own.

*"Major Van Velsor was a good specimen of a hearty, solid, fat old gentleman,
on good terms with the world, and who liked his ease. For over forty years,
he drove a stage and market wagon from his farm to Brooklyn ferry . . . I
have been up and down with him many times . . ."*

*"The Whitmans were among the earliest settlers of that part of Long Island
. . . a stalwart, massive, heavy, long-lived race. They appear to have been
always of democratic and heretical tendencies . . ."*

Inserted is a clipping from "The Long-Islander": "Walt Whitman in Huntington", August 5, 1881, annotated by Whitman: *"is in Appendix to Dr.
Bucke's W. W."*

11. THE OLD HOME PLACE. 1850. Autograph Manuscript,
2 pp., folio, about 730 words. With title: *"Walt Whitman. A
Description of His Birthplace visited in company with His
Father"*. Small folio, half blue morocco.

27⁵⁰

West Hills and the surrounding country on the highest part of Long Island
always had a great influence upon Whitman and were lovingly described ir

many of his poems. At the time of the visit here recorded the old home place of the Whitman family was occupied by Walt Whitman's aunt and her family.

"West Hills is a romantic and beautiful spot; it is the most hilly and elevated part of Long Island. The 'high hill' affords an extensive and pleasant view.

"I went down to the old native place, it is indeed a fine situation, and it seemed familiar enough to me, for I remembered every part, just as well as though only a day had passed since the times when I used to scoot around there a youngster."

12. PHRENOLOGICAL DESCRIPTION. Manuscript *"Phrenological Description of W. (Age 29 Occupation Printer) Whitman by L. N. Fowler N. York July 16—1849."*, 6 pp., 4to, about 700 words. With autograph manuscript excerpts from the "Description" by Dr. Bucke, several clippings annotated by Whitman, and title. 4to, half green morocco.

The years 1848 to 1850 marked the turning point in Whitman's life when he emerged from erratic young manhood to thoughtful, aspiring, and awakened life; and probably this phrenological analysis was one of the contributing causes of the great change. Whitman thought that the "Description" was so true to his mind, physique, and character that he kept it at hand to the end of his life and often alluded to it in his writings.

Among the clippings, which are on longevity, personal magnetism, phrenology, etc., is one which Whitman entitled in manuscript *"The Physique of the Brain from a literary life."*

13. WHITMAN THE CARPENTER. 1852. Autograph Manuscript Memoranda, 1 p., folio, about 100 words and figures, written on an inside cover from one of Jefferson Whitman's writing books. Matted, ready to frame.

This appears to be the only manuscript carpentry account by Walt Whitman. Aside from the several computations for materials, labor, etc., it contains entries:

"July 31st 1852—Mr. Scofield owes W. W. for eleven days work".

"Aug. 21—made full week the past week (Scofield owes for 23½ days $26.42)".

246

14. LIFE AND WRITINGS. 1883. Autograph Manuscript *"Chronological forecast of Walt Whitman's life and the successive publications of Leaves of Grass &c."*, 6 pp., 4to and smaller, about 560 words. With a contemporary photograph signed *"Walt Whitman 1882"*, the printed text of the above manuscript from Bucke's biography of Whitman, and title. 4to, full green crushed levant morocco, blind and gilt tooled.

A VERY IMPORTANT, TYPICAL, AND COMPLETE WHITMAN MANUSCRIPT. This outline autobiography and list of Whitman's writings with comments was compiled for Dr. Bucke's biography of the poet. It is typical of Whitman's method of composition, being formed of numerous slips pasted together or on quarto sheets, with a separate manuscript title on a small slip.

On the back of one slip is a part of an autograph manuscript in pencil containing Whitman's description of crossing the Delaware in winter.

[See illustration]

285-

(brev: solid (mind the gps) 7(a
ital

1860 Third issue L. of G. - 456 pages.
12 mo., published by Thayer & Eldridge,
116 Washington street, Boston.
1862. W. W. leaves Brooklyn and New York permanently.
Goes down to the field of War — winters partly
in Army of the Potomac, camped along the
Rappahannock, Virginia. Begins his ministractions among the wounded
1863-'64 In the field and among the Army
Hospitals (See Specimen Days) page 20 to 81.
1865. At Washington city, as Government clerk.
1865-'66 (Prints New York (poem written during the war,
1865 — Drum-Taps, and Sequel to Drum-Taps. Washington
and other pieces
"President Lincoln's Funeral Hymn", 96 pages — 12 mo.
Washington
No publisher's name.

ital
1867 — a new edition Fourth L. of G. x 338 pages.
12 mo. The poems now begin the
order and classification they eventually
settled upon. This edition has Drum-
Taps and Songs before parting at the
end or part of the book. New York No publisher's
name.

[NUMBER 14]

The Gestation Years

FROM 1840 to 1850 Whitman wrote numerous stories and poems for magazines and newspapers, the stories taking the form of more or less morbid melodramas, the poems such as any educated youth of the period might write. Few Whitman manuscripts of this period are known, however, for the author thought so little of them that he either destroyed or used them to write other poems and prose on the backs. This period does, however, cover several important events in the formation of the poet, including his editorial work, his early political activities, and especially his trip to New Orleans.

15. WHITMAN'S OWN ACCOUNT OF THE GESTATION
37⁵⁰ YEARS. 1880. Autograph Manuscript, 1 p., 4to, about 145 words. With envelope inscribed by Whitman: *"Walt Whitman— the fifteen years from 1840 to 1855"*, transcript, and title. 4to, cloth, green morocco back.

Most of the facts related in this manuscript were used in "Specimen Days".

"The fifteen years from 1840 to 1855 may be considered as the gestation years, or period of formation, out of which rose Leaves of Grass. Not in the usual way of an author withdrawing, composing his work in a study, abstractly addressing himself to the literary formulation, consulting authorities, and the like, but in the way of first merging ones self in all the living flood and practicality and fervency of that period . . ."

16. "THIS SINGULAR YOUNG MAN". 1842. Complete Auto-
37⁵⁰ graph Manuscript, 2 pp., folio and 4to, about 310 words. With title. Small folio, undyed niger morocco back.

One of the very early melodramatic stories by Whitman, a rather morbid tale of a young man who had psychic visions of coming deaths in the community, particularly that of his sister.

17. THE BOY'S DREAM. 1844. Autograph Manuscript, 5 pp., 4to,
75— about 500 words. With transcript and title. Small 4to, half red niger morocco.

An early and beautiful complete story of a boy who *"fell asleep with the tears of foolish passion yet undried upon his cheeks.—And there he dreamed"* of all the coming years of pain and joy and success, and of his return to find his mother dead. *"Ah, happy that boy to wake and find it indeed but a dream"*. (See number 121.)

18. A RESCUE. 1846. Autograph Manuscript Fragment of a Story, 1 p., folio, about 300 words, in pencil. Framed with portrait.

17⁵⁰

Part of an early story about the rescue of an intoxicated young man on a winter night.

19. THE MISSISSIPPI RIVER. 1848. Autograph Manuscript Poems *"Like Earth O river, you offer us burial"* and *"Sailing down the Mississippi at Midnight"*, 2 pp., oblong 12mo, about 50 words, in ink and pencil. With title. 4to, cloth, orange niger morocco back.

70

These poems were doubtless written during Whitman's journey to New Orleans in 1848. The first consists of two stanzas in rhyme; and the second of one and one-half stanzas of the poem as it was published in "Collect".

20. NEW ORLEANS. Four A. L. s. by Jefferson Whitman, younger brother of Walt, with autograph additions by Walt Whitman, 14 pp., 4to, about 4,000 words. With title. 4to, cloth, green morocco back.

55

These four letters are of special importance in that they describe many of the events and scenes which so strongly contributed to the mental change that took place in Whitman between 1848 and 1850, and awakened within him that broad vision that created "Leaves of Grass".

Only the last leaf of the first letter is preserved, written about March 1, 1848, and describing the steamer trip down the Ohio and Mississippi rivers, and the arrival at New Orleans. The letter of March 14th tells of the work at the office of "The Crescent" newspaper, of which Walt Whitman was editor; describes New Orleans, its dirty boarding houses, and the walks of the two Whitmans about the city. Another letter of like character, dated March 27th, contains a long note by Walt Whitman concerning the payment of interest and with affectionate advice to his mother.

"My prospects in the money line are bright. O how I long for the day when we can have our quiet little farm, and be together again . . ."

The last letter, April 23rd, contains further accounts of their walks, but Jeff was not well and began to be homesick.

"Walter is very well indeed, he thinks this place agrees with him very much and he says he feels better than ever he did in New York . . . Walter is trying to save up all the money he can get, and allready he has quite a sum, as soon as he gets a thousand dollars he is comeing north . . ."

This letter also has a note at the end by Walt Whitman.

250

THE ONLY COPY LOCATED OF AN ISSUE
OF THE "BROOKLYN FREEMAN"

21. BROOKLYN FREEMAN. By Walter Whitman. Brooklyn, Saturday, September 9, 1848. Vol. 1—No. 1—Price Two Cents. 2 pp., folio. Framed between glass. In a box case.

APPARENTLY THIS IS THE ONLY COPY KNOWN OF ANY NUMBER OF THE "BROOKLYN FREEMAN".

Even before Whitman's journey to New Orleans it had been proposed to establish a "Free-Soil" newspaper in Brooklyn; and upon his return the "Brooklyn Freeman" made its appearance, under his editorship and backed by Judge Johnson. It was a hot political paper, supporting Van Buren for President on a platform to prevent the extension of slavery into new states, and as strongly opposing the whig ("Hunker") and democratic parties.

Aside from a long letter by Van Buren practically the whole of the paper was written by Whitman, including an announcement of the aims and purposes of the paper, the plan for its distribution, "Jefferson on the Non-Extension of Slavery". "How things have been managed in Kings County", "Our enmity to the South", "General Taylor's Principles", and others.

The night after the publication of this first number the printing plant was burned in one of the great fires of Brooklyn, but within two months Whitman had again started the paper and continued it with success until September 11, 1849.

[See frontispiece]

22. UNEMPLOYMENT IN NEW YORK. 1849. Autograph Manuscript *"Wants"*, 6 pp., folio, about 1,600 words. With transcript and title. Small folio, half green morocco.

This article on the unemployed English and Irish servant situation in New York apparently was written for the "Brooklyn Freeman" and the editorial "we" is used throughout. Here Whitman reviews the "want" columns of the newspapers and describes the employment agencies as he had seen them during his rambles about the city, mentioning particularly the Emigrant Aid Society.

23. SLAVERY AND DEMOCRACY. Autograph Manuscript of a Political Speech *"Slavery—the Slaveholders—the Constitution—the true America and Americans, the laboring persons"*, 20 pp., folio and smaller, about 3,000 words. With transcript and title. Small folio, full blue crushed levant morocco, gilt tooled on each side with a sword transfixing a wreath, symbolic of the period: shall slavery sever the Union?

This speech was probably written for the "Free-Soil" campaign of 1848 when Whitman started the "Brooklyn Freeman" and took an active part in the effort to elect Van Buren president. The speech was written to be delivered in Groton, probably New York, for Whitman directly addresses the people of that town near the end of the speech. This is the rough draft written on the same type of paper throughout, though on large and small sheets as usual. Some portions were left incomplete by the writer and perhaps a small portion is missing.

[Description concluded on opposite page]

A powerful speech upholding the constitution of the United States as it was first written.

"The meanest of liars is the American aristocratic liar with his paltering and stuttering denial of the plain intentions, purports, allotments and requirements of the Bargain his government debated for a dozen years and finally closed and practically agreed to by the enforcement of the Constitution . . . And I say the journeymen that built that mighty house [the constitution] were giants, and the architects that planned it were gods."

Whitman then denounces slavery and the slaveholders in unmeasured terms, opposes the extension of slavery into any newly formed state and the extradition of escaped slaves from the free states. Here too are found the democratic principles which he expounded throughout his life in poetry and prose.

"Real democracy and great riches are in some sort repugnant to one another . . . My own opinion is that no amount of riches which numbers can calculate will ever make up to any live man or live nation, for the deprivation of rational liberty and equality."

Building the Poet

PREPARATORY READING AND THOUGHT

THE following sixty-one items (Numbers 24-84) comprise the material studied by Whitman from 1845 to 1862, and consist largely of magazine excerpts and newspaper clippings, most of them annotated by Whitman with long or short critical observations, with any striking passage or quotation underlined. Interspersed are essays and opinions written by Whitman as a result of his reading. Many of these essays and notes were converted into poems, used in the lectures he outlined but never delivered and not published in his literary essays.

No author has left a more perfect record of his course of reading, and the thoughts that resulted in the greatest work of his life. Here one can trace, step by step, his aspirations and intentions, and how his daily life influenced his writings. Even before the great awakening of Whitman during the years 1848 to 1850 he had been endeavoring to analyze the literature of the world, and, with samples of poetry and prose by the great authors in his pocket, he would ramble to the hills and shores of Long Island, and leisurely reading and dreaming would absorb and criticise the works of his favorite authors. But with the advent of new spiritual emotions came a great surge toward knowledge of all literature, science, and art, which was continued with increasing fervor until the war period, and with more critical analysis to the time of his death.

This material is classified, in general, under ancient, French, German, English, and American literature, with natural history and miscellaneous subjects at the end.

24. BEGINNING OF LITERATURE. 1856. Autograph Manuscript in pencil, 1 p., 8vo, about 150 words, written around a newspaper clipping entitled "Greeks, Romans, and Hebrews". With transcript and title. Royal 8vo, cloth.

1 50

25. THE BIBLE. 1856. Autograph Manuscript Annotations in pencil on a magazine excerpt entitled "The Vanity and the Glory of Literature", about 60 words. 8vo, boards.

25

Apparently no book in the world had more influence upon Whitman than the Bible, and it is probable that when the great spiritual change came in the life of Whitman that he became obsessed with the idea that he was to write a new Bible for the people, a Bible that was to bring all nature to the people. To his adherents he succeeded in doing this; to the rest of the world he founded a new literature based upon his Bible of nature. Whitman's style more nearly approaches that of the Bible than any other literary production, and only last year Gay W. Allen demonstrated that hundreds of Whitman's poetical allusions were derived from the Bible. These annotations contain one of the most important of Whitman's comments on the Bible:

"The religion of the Bible, or rather of the New Testament, is a beautiful advanced stage in the neverending humanitarianism of the world—but as the Bible admits of exhaustion like the rest and is now exhausted it may be left to its fate on these terms: As long as it stands it is worthy of standing; these are perhaps the true terms of all religions."

26. THE BIBLE. 1857. Autograph Manuscript *"The Iliad, the Bible, the Eschylean tragedies (as Prometheus), the principal Shaksperean tragedies as the Hamlet—are not Complete"*, 2 pp., 8vo and 12mo, about 90 words. With transcript and title. 8vo, cloth, blue polished morocco back.

25

This manuscript, too, contains a hint of Whitman's intentions:

"The real owners and heirs of the Hebrew Bible, rejecting the New Testament and what it stands for still wait for the climax of the poem. Taking it altogether, it is wonderful how such a contradictory repertoire was brought together, and has held sway. Or is this diversity the very reason it has held together? Has there been something to touch, or approach every phase of human want, development, tenderness, fanaticism, &c.?"

27. HOMER AND SHAKESPEARE. 1856. Autograph Manuscript, 1 p., royal 8vo, about 170 words. With transcript and title: "Homer and Shakespeare. A Comparison". Royal 8vo, half green levant morocco.

35

"Homer poetized great wars, persons, events . . . Shakespeare, the gentle, the sweet musical, well-beloved Shakespeare, delineated characters . . .

"Could (shall) there not be a poet of America no less than they but different from, doing more than either of them? Stamping this age, and so all ages, in his poems? . . . Riveting the passing incidents, sentiment, persons, tendencies, visible things, landscapes, voyages, politics, Manhattan Island, the Yankee, the Californian, all American features and leading facts in poems? .. ".

28. PLUTARCH. 1856. Autograph Manuscript Biographical Notes
on Plutarch, 1 p., royal 8vo, about 160 words. With transcript
and title. Royal 8vo, boards.

15

Over the account of Plutarch Whitman has written in pencil:
*"Many trouble themselves about conforming to laws. A great poet is followed
by laws—they conform to him."*

29. DANTE'S INFERNO. 1859. Autograph Manuscript, 4 pp.,
small 4to, about 400 words, in pencil. With transcript and title:
"Notes on Dante's Inferno". Small 4to, full undyed niger morocco, gilt and blind tooled.

50

*"It signifies, in its way, that melancholy and imperious part of humanity, or
its elements, out of which the whole structure of the stern and vindictive
Jehovah theology has arisen—from the time of the primitive Jews down—
vengeance, gloating in the agony of sinners, bad men, enemies to be punished,
and the usual distinctions of good and evil."*

30. TASSO. 1854. Autograph Manuscript, 4 pp., 12mo, about 450
words, in pencil. With transcript and title. 12mo, half brown
levant morocco.

17 50

An account of the life, work, personal appearance, and character of Torquato
Tasso, with special mention of the critics who drove Tasso insane.

31. ANCIENT AND MEDIEVAL LITERATURE. 1846-1856.
Autograph Manuscript, 1 p., 8vo, about 140 words, with 4 maga-
zine excerpts containing numerous autograph manuscript notes.
Together 5 pieces, 8vo, boards or laid in board folders.

25

The manuscript contains notes on the central ideas of the Egyptian, Greek,
and Roman religions. A review of two works on early Roman history contains extensive marginal notes especially comparing Rome and America:
*"America now of all lands has the greatest practical energy. (But has it not
also the highest infusion of pure intellect?)."*
An excerpt dated 1846 on "Translators of Homer" contains this interesting
note:
*"The greatest poets can never be translators of the poetry of others—that is
in any other way than Shakespeare translated—which was by taking the poor
or tolerable stuff of others and making it incomparable".*
A magazine review of the "Literature of the Middle Ages" contains many
annotations, such as the following:
*"The English poet has reminiscences and continually extols them—the Ameri-
can poet has a future, and must extol it."*

32. ROUSSEAU. 1850. Autograph Manuscript Copy of a translation of an abstract from Rousseau's "Contrat Social", with
numerous original comments by Whitman, each signed *"orig.
W. W.",* 11 pp., 4to, about 2,100 words. With portrait of Whit-

140

man, transcript, table of contents, and title. 4to, full green niger morocco, gilt and blind tooled.

Though holding Rousseau, the man and most of his writings, more or less in contempt, Whitman was greatly influenced by "The Social Contract"; so much so that he copied this abstract from a translation, and made about ten short or extensive comments thereon. For instance, at the end of *"Chapter Sixth— The Sovereign Power"* he writes:

"Orig. W. W. (In short, the whole of this Contrat Social, goes to prove, (1760?-?70) that the true government, and of course the only one for men of sense, is that of a compact where laws are administered for justice, equal rights, and inherent liberty—as opposed to all the continental European, (especially French) ideas of Government".

And on *"Chapter Ninth"* he writes:

"Orig. W. W. (Where Rousseau is yet undeveloped is, in not realizing that the individual man or woman is the head and ideal, and the State, City, Government, or what not, is a servant, subordinate,—with nothing sacred about it . . .)".

33. ROUSSEAU. 1856. Autograph Manuscript *"J. J. Rousseau"*, 2 pp., 8vo, about 200 words. With transcript and title. 8vo, half red polished morocco.

22.50

A biographical sketch, with the comment:

"An American poet may read Rousseau, but shall never imitate him. He is a curious study, and will cause some contempt."

34. VOLTAIRE. 1856. Excerpt from Fowler's "Life Illustrated" of an article "Voltaire, A Fragment by Walt Whitman", with date of issue in autograph *"May 10, 1856"*, about 10 words, pasted on an 8vo sheet. In a board folder.

11-

35. FRENCH LITERATURE. 1855-7. 3 Autograph Manuscripts in pencil, 3 pp., 8vo and 12mo, about 250 words; and several annotated clippings. Together 4 pieces, boards or board folders.

20-

The first two manuscripts are notes on the lives of *"Diderot 1713-1784"* and *"Lafontaine"*, and apparently were used in writing the preceding article on Voltaire. The third manuscript is a critical comment on the classical tragedies of Corneille and Racine. The several clippings on "French Literature", "French Moralists", etc., contain numerous manuscript annotations by Whitman.

36. GOETHE. 1856. Autograph Manuscript Essay on Goethe, 4 pp., 8vo, about 450 words, in pencil. With transcript and title. Royal 8vo, full brown levant morocco, gilt and blind tooled.

52.50

Goethe had a great influence on the life and work of Whitman.

"Here is now (January 1856) my opinion of Goethe. He is the most profound reviewer of Life known. To him life, things, the mind, death, people, are all studies, dissections, exhibitions . . ."

37. GOETHE. 1858. Autograph Manuscript Essay on Goethe, 2 pp., 8vo, about 190 words, in pencil. With transcript and title. Royal 8vo, full red niger morocco, gilt and blind tooled.

37 50

This is a continuation of the preceding, written about 1858, and is quoted by Dr. Bucke as a continued essay.

"To the genius of America he is neither dear nor the reverse of dear. He passes with the general crowd upon whom the American glance descends with indifference. Our road is our own."

38. RICHTER. 1856. Autograph Manuscript Essay on the Life and Work of Jean Paul Richter, 2 pp., royal 8vo, about 250 words, in pencil. With transcript and title. Royal 8vo, cloth, green morocco back.

15

At the end is a short note on Carlyle's introduction of the German style into English literature.

39. FREDERICK SCHLEGEL. 1857. Autograph Manuscript Biographical Sketch with comments, 1 p., 8vo, about 170 words. With transcript and title. 8vo, half green niger morocco.

10

40. PARAPHRASE OF UHLAND'S VERSE. 1855. Autograph Manuscript Notes in pencil and ink on a Magazine excerpt of "The Prelude" by Wordsworth, and the translation of a poem by Uhland, about 75 words. 8vo, boards.

22 50

This is perhaps the only instance of Whitman's paraphrasing another man's poem. The translation from Uhland reads:

"Take now, boatman, take thy fee;
Thrice thy due I offer thee:
For with me two spirits crossed,—
Spirits of the loved and lost."

Whitman has written:

"Take O boatman thrice thy fee
Take—I give it willingly
For unwittingly to thee,
Spirits twain have crossed with me."

41. GERMAN AND NORTHERN EUROPEAN AUTHORS. 1858. Autograph Manuscripts on Schiller and Swedenborg, in pencil, 2 pp., royal 8vo, about 90 words; and an annotated excerpt on "Provençal and Scandinavian Poetry". Together 3 vols., royal 8vo, half morocco and boards.

15

This was all preparatory material for a lecture on "The Poets". On the sheet with the Schiller note is a list of other German authors, and accompanying the Swedenborg essay is a printed account of his life and work. The excerpt on Scandinavian poetry contains many critical and informative annotations by Whitman, one of which is *"for lecturing on 'the Poet'"*.

42. ENGLISH AUTHORS. 1856. Autograph Manuscript List of 82 English Authors from Chaucer to Dickens, with dates of birth and death, 2 pp., royal 8vo, about 200 words. With transcript and title. Royal 8vo, cloth, white pigskin back.

27 50

This and the following item were doubtless used in preparation of his lecture on "The Poets".

43. ENGLISH POETS. 1856. Autograph Manuscript, in pencil, 2 pp., royal 8vo, about 270 words. With transcript and title. Royal 8vo, cloth, green niger morocco back.

35

"What are inextricable from the British poets are the ideas of royalty and aristocracy . . . Of the leading British poets many who began with the rights of man, abjured their beginning and came out for kingcraft, priestcraft, obedience, and so forth,—Southey, Coleridge, and Wordsworth, did so."

44. CHAUCER. 1856. Autograph Manuscript Annotations on a Magazine Article on Chaucer dated 1849, 8vo, 22 pp., about 125 words in autograph. With title. Royal 8vo, half white pigskin.

10

These notes were later worked into a lecture on Chaucer.

45. EDMUND SPENSER. 1856. Autograph Manuscript Biographical and Critical Account of Edmund Spenser, 3 pp., 12mo, about 300 words. With transcript and title. 12mo, full undyed niger morocco, gilt and blind tooled.

35

"He is haunted by a morbid refinement of beauty—beauty three times washed and strained."

WHITMAN'S NOTES ON SHAKESPEARE

46. SHAKESPEARE. 1855-7. Autograph Manuscript, 9 pp., 8vo, about 1,200 words. With transcript and title: "Notes on Life and Work of William Shakespeare". 8vo, full black crushed levant morocco, gilt tooled with the arms of Shakespeare on each cover.

350

Apparently this is the longest manuscript devoted wholly to Shakespeare written by Whitman. Many of these notes were used in the "Collect" under the title "Poetry Today in America. Shakespeare—The Future". While the manuscript is devoted largely to biographical details it also contains many critical notes and comments. Shakespeare, Whitman writes:

"Bought and sold, bargained, was thrifty, borrowed money, loaned money, had lawsuits."

"Shakespeare put such things into his plays as would please the family pride of Kings and queens and of his patrons among the nobility . . . all these fed the aristocratic vanity of the young noblemen and gentlemen and feed them in England yet."

"Overcoloring. Many little things are too much overcolored in Shakespeare— far too much. . . . the sentiment is piled on, similes, comparisons, defiances, exaltations, immortalities, bestowed upon themes certainly not worthy the same,—thus losing proportion . . . Yet on great occasion the character and action are perfect. This is what saves Shakespeare . . ."

[See illustration]

Overcoloring.

Many little things are too much overcolored, in Shakespeare — far too much — The features of beloved women, the descriptions of brave actions, and hundreds more, are painted too intensely It is no answer to this, to say that a lover would so state the case about a woman he loved, or that a strong rich nature would be apt to describe incidents in that manner; and therefore Shakespeare is correct in so presenting them. — Immensely too much is unnaturally colored — the sentiment is piled on, similes, comparisons, defiances, exaltations, immortalities, are bestowed upon themes, certainly not worthy — thus losing proportion — the same, — Also most of the discursive speeches of the great and little characters are glaringly inappropriate, both words and sentiments such as could not have come from their mouths in real life and therefore should not in the plays. — Yet on great occasion the characters and action are perfect — This is what saves Shakespeare — Is he imitative of Homer? If so, where and how?

[NUMBER 46]

258

47. SHAKESPEARE. 1856. Autograph Manuscript, 1 p., royal 8vo, about 300 words. With transcript and title. Royal 8vo, half white pigskin.

70

"From the poet's thirty-seventh to about his forty-sixth year—his genius rose at once to its highest culmination . . . It was during this period that he most impressed upon his style that character which we now recognize as peculiarly Shakesperian, by crowding into his words a weight of thought until 'the language bent under it'. His versification becomes, like his diction, bolder, freer, careless of elegance, of regularity and even of melody, a sterner music, fitted for sterner themes."

48. SHAKESPEARE AND SPENSER. 1856. Autograph Manuscript, 1 p., royal 8vo, about 200 words. With transcript and title. Royal 8vo, half white pigskin.

70

Apparently only a part of this manuscript has been published, Dr. Bucke having deleted a paragraph, a part of which reads:

"The Sonnets. Shakespeare wrote his 'sugar'd sonnets' early—probably soon after his appearance in London—the beautiful young man so passionately treated and so subtly the thread of the sonnets, is without doubt, the Earl of Southampton who made Shakespeare the magnificent gift of a thousand pounds . . ."

49. MILTON AND THE BIBLE. 1853. Autograph Manuscript Notes on a Magazine Excerpt entitled "Christopher under Canvas", 1849, 4 pp., 8vo, about 310 words in autograph, in pencil. With transcript and title. 8vo, half white pigskin.

30

These notes are of great importance in the building of the literature of Walt Whitman. They appear to have been written in the advanced formative period, when the ideas and form of "Leaves of Grass" were taking shape, and show the influence of the construction of the Bible on Whitman's own work.

"The Paradise is (to us) nonsense, any how, because it takes themes entirely out of human cognisance and treats them as Homer treats his siege and opposing armies and their disputes . . . What is in the Bible had better not be paraphrased. The Bible is indescribably perfect—putting it in rhyme, would that improve it or not? Think of a writer going into the creative action of deity! The best poetry is simply that which has the perfectest beauty—beauty to the ear, beauty to the brain, beauty to the heart, beauty to the time & place. There cannot be a true poem unless it satisfies the various needs of beauty . . . The difference between perfect originality and second-hand originality is the difference between the Bible and Paradise Lost."

50. DRYDEN. 1856. Autograph Manuscript, 1 p., 8vo, about 40 words, in pencil. With title. Royal 8vo, half red niger morocco.

12.50

"Dryden seems to have been of vigorous make, sharp-tempered—used his poetical talent to make money, show up his enemies . . ."

51. SAMUEL JOHNSON. 1856. Autograph Manuscript, 1 p., royal 8vo, about 100 words, in pencil. With transcript and title. Royal 8vo, half brown levant morocco.

35

"Was always of coarse behavior,—wrote in a latinized style, not simple and with unlearned instincts, but pompous & full of polysyllables."

52. GOLDSMITH. 1851. Autograph Manuscript, 2 pp., 16mo, about 175 words, in pencil. With transcript and title. 16mo, cloth, green morocco back.

"As a writer and compiler, wonderfully ignorant."

20⁻

53. KEATS. 1856. Autograph Manuscript, 1 p., royal 8vo, about 100 words, in pencil. With transcript and title. Royal 8vo, half green polished morocco.

"Keats's poetry is ornamental, elaborated, rich in wrought imagery . . . Of life in the nineteenth century it has none, any more than statues have."

50⁻

54. SHELLEY AND KEATS. 1850-56. Autograph Manuscript Notes on Shelley, 1 p., 16mo, about 100 words, in pencil; with two clippings about and by Shelley, with manuscript annotations by Whitman; and a Magazine Review of Milnes' Life of Keats, with manuscript annotations by Whitman. Together 2 pieces, 8vo, boards and board folder.

The manuscript on Shelley is a sketch of his life and personal characteristics, and the Keats review contains a very significant manuscript note:

"The great poet absorbs the identity of others and the experience of others and they are definite in him or from him; but he presses them all through the powerful press of himself . . ."

35⁻

55. SIR HENRY TAYLOR. 1856. Autograph Manuscript Notes on a Magazine Review of Taylor's "Eve of Conquest", about 275 words, in pencil, 8vo, boards.

This review had a marked influence on Whitman, for on it he wrote: *"To be re-read and studied"*, also:

"The perfect poem is simple, healthy, natural—no griffins, angels, centaurs,—no hysterics or blue fire—no dyspepsia, no suicidal intentions."

15⁻

56. TENNYSON. 1855-7. Four Magazine Excerpts relating to Tennyson and his Works, with Autograph Manuscript Notes by Whitman, about 100 words. 4 vols., 8vo, boards.

The marginal notes include some choice comments:

"Tennyson is the imitation of Shakespeare, through a refined, educated, traveled, modern English dandy."

"The Poets are the divine mediums—through them come spirits and materials to all the people, men and women."

15⁻

57. DR. PRIESTLEY AND FRANCES WRIGHT. 1857. Two Autograph Manuscripts on *"Dr. Priestley. Conversation with Mr. Arnold, March 1, '57"*, and *"Frances Wright, Madame D'Arnsmont (talk with Mrs. Rose Feb. 9th, '57")*, 2 pp., royal 8vo, about 350 words, in pencil. 2 vols., royal 8vo, half morocco.

25

To the account of Dr. Priestley Whitman has added:
"(How these Unitarians and Universalists want to be respectable and orthodox, just as much as any of the old line people!)".

58. ENGLISH AUTHORS. 1855-7. Autograph Manuscript on Gerald Massey's Poems, 1 p., 8vo, about 70 words, in pencil; and 7 Magazine Excerpts on English Authors, all more or less annotated by Whitman. Together 8 pieces, 8vo, boards or board folders.

15

Including articles on Carlyle, Coleridge, Macpherson, Robert Southey (*"A good article"*), "Arnold's Lectures on Modern History", "The Strayed Reveller", and "New English Poets", *"the present school of poetry"*.

59. ENGLISH AUTHORS. 1855-7. A Collection of Excerpt Articles from Magazines on English Authors, all having autograph annotations and striking passages underlined by Whitman, about 75 words. 7 vols., 8vo, boards.

20

Including articles by or about Edmund Spenser, John Bunyan, Shakespeare, Waller and Marvell, Alexander Pope, E. B. Browning, and Scottish poetry.

60. EMERSON. 1852. Autograph Manuscript on the Character of Emerson's Writing, 2 pp., 8vo, about 220 words, in pencil. With an A. L. s. by Emerson concerning a lecture on *"The Spirit of the Times"* he was to give in England, also a portrait of Emerson, transcript, and title. 8vo, full green levant morocco, gilt and blind tooled.

115

Whitman was indebted to Emerson for the first marked appreciation of "Leaves of Grass", and Emerson had, with the exception of the Bible, more influence in forming the character and spirit of Whitman's great work than any other author. According to Dr. Bucke, who judged from the paper upon which it was written, this appreciation of Emerson was written in the early 'fifties. It is possible that the writing of this manuscript was the determining factor that produced "Leaves of Grass", for, according to Whitman, "Emerson brought me to the boil".

"He may be obscure, but he is certain . . . He pierces the crusts that envelope the secrets of life. He joins on equal terms the four great sages and original seers. He represents the freeman, America, the individual. He represents the gentleman. No teacher or poet of old times or modern times, has made a better report of manly and womanly qualities, heroism, chastity, temperance, friendship, fortitude . . .
"A few among men (soon perhaps to become many) will enter easily into Emerson's meanings; by those he will be well-beloved. The flippant writer, the orthodox critic, the numbers of good or indifferent imitators, will not comprehend him . . ."

61. EMERSON. 1852. Autograph Manuscript Notes on a Magazine
Review of Emerson's Poems, 1847, about 70 words, in pencil.
8vo, boards.

12⁵⁰

According to Dr. Bucke the preceding appreciation was written by Whitman
after reading this review and commenting upon it.

62. THOREAU AND INDIAN EPIC POETRY. Excerpt from
Thoreau's "Week on the Concord" about the laws of Menu, 6 pp.;
and a Magazine Excerpt "Indian Epic Poetry", both with autograph manuscript annotations by Whitman, about 120 words.
With title. Royal 8vo, half red niger morocco.

35—

"The style of a great poem must flow on 'unhasting and unresting'".

63. AMERICAN LITERATURE. Two Excerpts from Thoreau's
"Week on the Concord" on Chaucer and Ossian, and a part of
"American Literature" by Margaret Fuller, all with manuscript
annotations, about 60 words, and passages underlined by Whitman. Together 3 pieces, 12mo, boards or board folder.

22⁵⁰

64. AMERICAN LITERATURE etc. Two Autograph Manu-
scripts, on Longfellow's *"Hiawatha"* and *"Sculpture"*, 2 pp., 8vo,
about 215 words. Also several clippings and excerpts on Edgar
Allan Poe, Leland's "The Romantic in Literature and Art", and
"Phrenology", all with manuscript annotations by Whitman,
about 75 words; an excerpt from Thoreau's "Week on the Concord" on Anacreon; and several clippings about the wreck of the
"San Francisco" in 1854. Together 7 pieces, folio to 8vo, boards
or board folders.

40—

*"The Song of Hiawatha by H. W. Longfellow—A pleasing ripply poem—the
measure, the absence of ideas, the Indian process of thought, the droning
metre, the sleepy, misty, woody character, the traditions, pleased me much."*

AN ORIGINAL WHITMAN SCRAPBOOK

65. SCRAPBOOK. 1855-8. The foundation of this Scrapbook is
made up of Colton's "Geography and History" published about
1854, and Smith's "Atlas of Modern and Ancient Geography",
1855; interleaved with many sheets of yellow paper like the lining
of the second issue of the 1855 edition of "Leaves of Grass"; and
with hundreds of clippings, excerpts, whole newspapers, and
pamphlets pasted or laid in. Very thick 4to, half sheep, homemade ties; covers loose.

100—

WITH AUTOGRAPH NOTES, TITLES, AND WORDS THROUGHOUT. Here are gathered
together articles and notes on geography, science, travel, inventions, and
politics. Inside the front cover Whitman wrote a list of about a hundred of

the subjects, and notes at the end of the list *"In History & Geography of the world introduce everywhere lists of persons, the great persons of every age and land"*. This he has done.

Here are reports of scientific meetings, lectures, events, and phenomena; numerous descriptions of the opening of the west; travellers' accounts of the south, the Missouri River, Canada, South America, and other parts of the world. Asia was of special interest to Whitman, and many clippings relate to that continent.

After the publication of the first edition of "Leaves of Grass" Whitman began an intensive course of study to broaden his knowledge of science and literature. This was his textbook of geography and science, and from it he obtained the information so often incorporated in his poems and essays.

66. AUTHORS. 1852-8. Autograph Manuscript Lists of Authors, preceded by a manuscript note relating to his lists, 6 pp., 8vo and smaller, about 130 words. With about 25 magazine excerpts and numerous clippings, nearly all of which are annotated by Whitman, and with portrait and title. Royal 8vo, half blue polished morocco.

25

Some of the annotations are quite extensive. One, containing about forty words, reads in part as follows:

"This list of one week's issue of patents from the National Patent office at Washington illustrates America and American character about as much as any thing I know . . ."

67. CLIPPINGS. 1854-1886. A Collection of 23 newspaper clippings, mainly with autograph manuscript notes, headings, etc., about 70 words, including 7 by or relating to Whitman. 4to, cloth.

10

68. HISTORY AND SCIENCE. About 20 Magazine Excerpts and Newspaper Clippings with Autograph Manuscript Annotations, about 425 words. 2 pieces, 4to, boards and board folder.

15

Contains manuscript notes on keel-boats, physiognomy, ancient inscriptions, chronological eras, and many other subjects.

69. READING. 1856-8. Magazine Excerpts and Clippings with numerous Autograph Manuscript Notes, about 260 words. 4 vols., 8vo, boards.

15

On an article on egotism Whitman writes *"see above and* BEWARE"; a long note on light reading on the margin of "Thoughts on Reading" reads in part as follows:

"The thousands of common poets, romancers, essayists and attempters exist because some twenty or fifty geniuses at intervals led the way long before."

Other notes are about Asiatic literature, the Cossacks, progress, *"Heldenbuch"*, suggestions for a *"Poem among the Siamese"*, etc.

70. LITERATURE. 1854-7. Excerpts from Magazines with Autograph Manuscript Annotations, about 90 words, from a single
word to whole sentences, by Whitman. 9 vols., 8vo, boards or
board folders.

"Style is not to be shackled by sweeping rules."

17⁵⁰

71. POETIC METRES. 1855-6. Autograph Manuscript Studies of
Poetic Metres, about 400 words, with a part of an Autograph
Manuscript Poem on the verso of one leaf, about 80 words, 5 pp.,
8vo and 12mo. With titles. 2 vols., 8vo and 12mo, half morocco.

The poem is a part of the original manuscript of the "Song of Myself" as it
was sent to the printer of the first edition of "Leaves of Grass", but showing
two lines deleted from the published version.

"I am not to be denied—I compel;
I have stores plenty, and to spare;
And any thing I have I bestow."

37⁵⁰

72. THE ENGLISH MASSES. 1858. Autograph Manuscript, 3
pp., 8vo, about 300 words. With title. 8vo, half brown levant
morocco.

A vivid account of the common people of England as gathered from a *"Talk
with Frank Leonard, 'Yank', &c—their travels through English towns with
the American Circus".*

50

73. WONDERS OF THE EARTH. 1856-8. Two Autograph
Manuscripts, 2 pp., 8vo, about 225 words. 2 pieces, in board
folders.

The manuscripts begin as follows:

*"The most perfect wonders of the earth are not rare and distant, but present
with every person . . ."*
*"A New Way & The True Way of Treating in Books History, Geography,
Ethnology, Astronomy, &c. &c."*

20

74. WHALES AND FISH. 1856-8. Autograph Manuscripts *"The
Whale"*, about 165 words; and list of fish, about 215 words. 2
pp., 2 pieces, royal 8vo, boards and board folder.

Both pieces are illustrative of the careful preparatory study Whitman made
for his writings. The account of the whale was gathered from an old whale-
man, and through this information Whitman was able to detect an error in
his first edition of "Leaves of Grass" and correct it in, the edition of 1860.

25

75. METAPHYSICS AND TEMPERAMENT. 1853-5. Autograph Manuscripts, 2 pp., royal 8vo and 4to, about 475 words.
One with title and transcript. 2 vols., boards.

These two studies are of special interest, that on *"Insanity"* and *"Tempera-*

20

ment" because one of Whitman's brothers was insane, and that on metaphysics for its revelation of his attitude toward the learned:

"I waste no ink, nor my throat, on the ever deploying armies of professors, authors, lawyers, teachers, and what not. Of them we expect that they be very learned, and nothing more."

76. FOREIGN COUNTRIES. 1856-8. Autograph Manuscript Notes on Foreign Countries, 9 pp., 8vo and smaller, about 700 words. With title. Small folio, cloth, red niger morocco back.

These notes, most of which were used in Whitman's poems and essays, are on Tartary, the British in India, Russian serfs, Africa, Scythia and the derivation of the European races, Egypt and Assyria, and the *"Expedition of Savans to explore the sources of the Nile"*.

77. LITERARY AND OTHER NOTES. 1850-1882. A Collection of 13 Autograph Manuscript Notes, 13 pp., 4to and smaller, together about 600 words. With portrait and title. Small folio, half red niger morocco.

The collection consists of notes on the primitive poets, Milton (on the same sheet with a list of synonyms for "singer"), prehistoric literature (two), European and Asiatic nations, incidents in New York for "Specimen Days", and *"Of the Democratic Party '58—'59—'60"*. The last reads as follows:

"They think they are providing planks of platforms on which they shall stand—

Of those planks it would be but retributive justice to make them their coffins."

78. ANCIENT RACES. 1859. Autograph Manuscript Notes on Egypt, Assyria, and the Romans and Hebrews and their characteristics. 3 pp., 8vo and 12mo, about 275 words, in pencil. With transcript and title. 8vo, half undyed niger morocco.

79. UNNAMED LANDS. 1857. Autograph Manuscript, 1 p., 4to, about 180 words. With portrait and title: "On the intimate History of Past Ages". 4to, cloth, blue morocco back.

A part of the preliminary sketch in prose of "Unnamed Lands". The poem was first published in 1860.

80. "ITALIAN SINGERS IN AMERICA". 1858. Autograph Manuscript Essay, 3 pp., 4to, about 200 words. With a clipping on "Whitman & Alboni", transcript and title. Small 4to, half brown crushed levant morocco.

This is actually an article on Alboni, who inspired so many of Whitman's poems by her singing. The date of the manuscript is established by a reference to Piccolomini, then in New York. It is doubtful if the essay was published except possibly in a contemporary newspaper.

"The best songstress ever in America was Alboni. Her voice is a contralto of large compass, high and low—and probably sweeter tones never issued from human lips. The mere sound of that voice was pleasure enough. All persons

appreciated Alboni—the common crowd quite as well as the connoisseurs. We used to go in the upper tiers of the theatre (the Broadway) on the nights of her performance, and remember seeing that part of the auditorium packed full of New York young men, mechanics, 'roughs', &c., entirely oblivious of all except Alboni . . ."

81. RELIGION. 1854. Autograph Manuscript, 4 pp., folio, about 500 words; mounted. With transcript and title. Small folio, cloth, orange niger morocco back.

50—

This manuscript contains the substance of a lecture on religion. At the time it was written Whitman had the idea of promulgating his doctrines through lectures as well as by writing a book.

"I do not condemn either the Past or the Present—I know that they are and were what they could but be—Shall I denounce my own ancestry—the very ground under my feet that has been so long building."

"I know well enough the life is in my own soul, not in the traditions, the phantoms—I know the traditions help me well— . . . I know, too, that I am the master and overseer of all religions—and you shall be—Not their slave."

82. RELIGION. 1858. Autograph Manuscripts on Religion, 4 pp., small 4to to 12mo, about 210 words. With portrait, transcript, and title. 4to, cloth, morocco back.

30—

The first manuscript reads in part as follows:

"Founding a new American Religion (?No Religion). That which is comprehensive enough to include all the Doctrines & Sects—and give them all places and chances, each after its kind."

83. HUMANITY. 1856. Autograph Manuscript and Poem, 1 p., 8vo, about 90 words. Framed, with an etched portrait by Gilchrist.

12.50

"A main part of the greatness of a humanity is that it never at any time or under any circumstances arrives at its finality."

84. NOTES FOR LECTURES AND POEMS. 1854-61. Twelve Autograph Manuscript Notes, 12 pp., 8vo to 16mo, about 525 words. With portrait and title. Small folio, half green niger morocco.

70—

A highly interesting variety of notes illustrative of Whitman's preparatory work for poems and lectures. Included are notes on mathematics, ethnology, *"Four Kingdoms of Nature"*, *"Salt Works at Salina"*, *"The Air, the Sea, the Land"*, *"How many deeds of moment— . . . How many quiet lives entirely unfanfaronaded"*, lecture titles, singularity in literature and society, sublimity of nature, and a striking note on secessionists.

"The Union is proved solid by proofs that none can gainsay. Every state that permits her faction of secessionists to carry her out, shrivels and wilts at once. Her credit is the first thing that goes. A reign of terror is inaugurated. All trade, all business stops. . . . Incomes are not paid to widows, orphans, and old persons. The arm of the law ceases to lift itself, in any one's protection. The devils are unloosed . . .'"

Building "Leaves of Grass"

HE who can read and understand the preface to the first edition of "Leaves of Grass" can read and understand the poems of Whitman. In the following thirty-six lots (Numbers 85-120) are expressed the ideals and purposes used not only in the construction of the preface but of the poems as well; for so interchangeable were the poems and prose of Whitman that he often made one from the other by simply adding or omitting a word or two and altering the form. Here Whitman tells in his own words his meaning and intentions in "Leaves of Grass".

85. THE BUILDER. 1857. Autograph Manuscript, 2 pp., 8vo and 12mo, about 100 words. With transcript. 8vo, boards.

"Other poets have formed for themselves an ideal, apart from positive life, and disdainful of it—but for me, I ask nothing better or more divine than real life, here, now, yourself, your work, house-building, boating, or in any factory . . . Mine are not the songs of a story teller, or of a voluptuous person, or of an ennuyeed person,—but of an American constructor, looking with friendly eyes upon the earth and men and beholding the vista of the great mission of the States."

86. WHITMAN'S MOTTOES. Two Autograph Manuscripts, 2 pp., 16mo, about 70 words. Framed, with engraved portrait of Whitman bearing the autograph inscription *"Walt Whitman 1855"*.

The first of these manuscripts contains Whitman's motto during his construction of "Leaves of Grass".
"Make the WORKS—
Do not go into criticisms or arguments at all
Make full-blooded, rich, flush, natural WORKS—"
The second was Whitman's formula for his attitude in life:
"Boldness—Nonchalant ease & indifference . . . This is my way, my pleasure, my choice, my costume, friendship, answer, or what not."

[See reproduction of portrait on front cover]

87. SHAKESPEARE, SCOTT, AND WHITMAN. 1858. Autograph Manuscript, 1 p., 8vo, about 75 words, in pencil. Transcript and title. 8vo, half blue morocco.

"Shakespeare and Walter Scott are indeed limners and recorders . . . I will be also a master, after my own kind, making the poems of emotions, as they pass or stay—the poems of freedom, and the exposé of personality—singing, in high tones, Democracy and the New World of it through these States."

88. POET OF THE PEOPLE. 1856. Two Autograph Manuscript Notes, on 1 p., 8vo, about 90 words, in pencil. With transcript and title: "Walt Whitman on the Democracy of His Poetry". Royal 8vo, half green niger morocco.

25

These two notes contain the substance of the thirteenth paragraph of the 1855 preface.

"All others have adhered to the principle, and shown it, that the poet and savan form classes by themselves, above the people, and more refined than the people; I show that they are just as great when of the people . . ."

89. BOOK LEARNING. 1855. Autograph Manuscript, 1 p., royal 8vo, about 175 words, in pencil. With transcript and title. Royal 8vo, red niger morocco back.

30

The last part of this short essay was afterwards embodied in a poem.

"Book-learning is good, let none dispense with it, but a man may [be] of great excellence and effect with very little of it. Washington had but little. Andrew Jackson also. Fulton also. Frequently it stands in the way of real manliness and power . . . Let a man learn to run, leap, swim, wrestle, fight, to take good aim, to manage horses, to speak readily and clearly and without mannerism, to feel at home among common people . . ."

90. "LEAVES OF GRASS" SUBJECTIVE. 1856. Autograph Manuscript, 1 p., 8vo, about 210 words, in pencil. With transcript and title. Royal 8vo, half red niger morocco.

40

This manuscript consists of notes on Pythagoras and great masters, with the following note pasted on the sheet:

"Sept. '56. 'Leaves of Grass' must be called not objective, but altogether subjective—'I know' runs through them as a perpetual refrain."

91. RULES FOR COMPOSITION. 1853. Autograph Manuscript, 1 p., 4to, about 150 words, in pencil. With transcript and title. 4to, cloth, green morocco back.

40

Very early rules for the composition of "Leaves of Grass".

"Take no illustrations whatever from the ancients or classics . . . nor from the royal and aristocratic institutions and forms of Europe. Make no mention or allusion to them whatever, except as they relate to the new, present things —to our country—to American character or interests . . . Clearness, simplicity, no twistified or foggy sentences, at all . . ."

92. "LEAVES OF GRASS" A NEW BIBLE. 1857. Two Autograph Manuscripts, 2 pp., 24mo, about 60 words. Framed with engraved portrait.

35

These manuscripts present two of the great objectives before Whitman in 1857:

"The great Construction of the New Bible. Not to be diverted from the principal object—the main life work—the Three Hundred & Sixty-five—(it ought to be ready in 1859. (June '57)."

"Leading characteristics. To unite all sects, parties, States . . . To be one whom all look toward with attention, respect, love."

93. RULES FOR REVISION OF "LEAVES OF GRASS". 1856. Autograph Manuscript, 1 p., 8vo, about 85 words. With transcript. 8vo, boards.

80 —

"In future 'Leaves of Grass'. Be more severe with the final version of the Poem . . . Also no ornaments especially no ornamental adjectives, unless they have come molten hot, and imperiously prove themselves . . ."

94. AMERICAN MODELS. 1858. Autograph Manuscript, 1 p., 12mo, about 75 words. Framed with an engraved portrait of Whitman inscribed by the poet *"Walt Whitman in 1855"*.

27 50

"The best way to promulgate native American models and literature is to supply such forcible and superb specimens of the same that they will, by their own volition, move to the head of all and put foreign models in the second class."

95. MATERIALISM. 1858. Autograph Manuscript, 1 p., 4to, about 140 words, in pencil. 4to, boards.

15 —

Written on the back of wall-paper. Demonstrating *"that our immortality is located here upon earth—that we are immortal"*.

96. UNITY OF "LEAVES OF GRASS". 1858. Autograph Manuscript, 2 pp., 8vo, about 180 words, in pencil. With transcript and title. 8vo, cloth, blue morocco back.

45 —

"My Poems, when complete, should be A Unity, in the same sense that the earth is, or that the human body or that a perfect musical composition is . . . Poems—hasting, urging, resistless . . . Lessons—clear, alive, luminous, full of facts . . ."

97. "TRUE VISTA BEFORE". 1857. Autograph Manuscript, 1 p., 8vo, about 155 words, in pencil. With transcript and title. 8vo, cloth, brown levant morocco back.

25 —

"Friday, April 24, 1857. True vista before. The strong thought—impression or conviction that the straight, broad, open, well marked true vista before, or course of public teacher, 'wander speaker' . . . Not to direct eyes or thoughts to any of the usual avenues, as of official appointment, or to get such any way—to put all those aside for good.—But always to keep up living interest in public interests,—and always to hold the ear of the people."

98. THE POET. 1856. Autograph Manuscript, 1 p., 12mo, about 75 words. Framed, with portrait.

40 —

"Amid the vast and complicated edifice of human beings . . . he builds, as it were, an impregnable and lofty tower, a part of all with the rest and over-looking all—the citadel of the primary volitions, the soul, the ever-reserved right of a deathless Individuality—and these he occupies and dwells, and thence makes observations and issues verdicts."

99. THE AMERICAN POEM. 1854. Autograph Manuscript, 1 p., 8vo, about 130 words. With transcript and title. 8vo, cloth, green morocco back.

10—

Most of the ideas expressed in this manuscript were incorporated in the first two paragraphs of the preface of 1855.

"America (I to myself have said) demands at any rate one modern, native, all-surrounding song with face like hers turned to the future rather than the present or the past. It should nourish with joy the pride and completion of man in himself. What the mother, our continent, in reference to humanity, finally means . . . is INDIVIDUALITY *strong and superb, for broadest average use, for man and woman: and that most should such a poem in its own form express . . ."*

100. "AMERICA NEEDS HER OWN POEMS". 1855. Autograph Manuscript Notes, 2 pp., 12mo, about 140 words, in pencil. With transcript. Small 4to, boards.

35—

The recto of this manuscript contains the substance of the fourth paragraph of the preface of 1855, and the verso: *"Ought never to be forgotten in lectures".*

101. AMERICAN LITERATURE AND THE GREAT POET. 1855. Autograph Manuscript, 1 p., 4to, about 80 words. Framed with portrait.

32 50

An early draft of parts of the preface of 1855.

"American literature must become distinct from all others."

"The great poet submits only to himself. Is nature rude, free, irregular? If nature be so, I too will be so."

102. PROPERTY AND SOUL. 1853. Three Autograph Manuscripts, 3 pp., on 2 sheets 8vo, about 300 words, in pencil. With transcripts. 2 vols., small 4to boards.

42 50

Two of the manuscripts are early drafts of the ideas expressed in the third paragraph of the preface of 1855, one of which begins:

"The only way in which anything can really be owned, is by the infusion or inspiration of it in the soul".

On the verso of one of these manuscripts is the prose version of a part of section 46 in the "Song of Myself": *"Sit awhile wayfarer. I give you biscuits to eat and milk to drink".*

103. FUTURE OF AMERICA. 1856. Autograph Manuscript, 2 pp., royal 8vo, about 150 words, in pencil. In a board folder.

20—

"Produce great persons and the producers of great persons—all the rest surely follows. What has been but indicated in other continents, in America must receive its definite and numberless growth . . ."

On the verso is a working list of English authors with comments on a clipping.

270

104. MAN AN INTELLECTUAL ANIMAL. 1854. Autograph Manuscript, 1 p., folio, about 135 words, in pencil and ink. With transcript. Narrow small folio, boards.

22.50

"In other words, man is not only an animal like the others, but he alone has the quality of understanding and telling how divine a thing an animal is."

105. SHAMS. 1855. Autograph Manuscript, 1 p., 8vo, about 50 words. Framed with portrait.

30-

"It were unworthy a live man to pray or complain, no matter what should happen. Will he descend among those . . . whose virtues are lathered and shaved three times a week—to whine about sin and hell."

106. "THIS IS THE EARTH'S WORD". 1858. Autograph Manuscript, 1 p., 12mo, about 50 words. Framed with etched portrait.

12.50

107. PREFACE. 1856. Autograph Manuscript, 3 pp., 8vo, about 235 words, in pencil. With transcript and title. Royal 8vo, cloth, green morocco back.

50-

A part of the preface of 1855 rewritten in stronger terms for the preface of another edition.

"(Of the great poet) (Finally) For preface. It is not that he gives his country great poems; it is that he gives his country the spirit which makes the greatest poems and the greatest material for poems."

108. WHITMAN'S POEMS. 1858. Two Autograph Manuscripts, 2 pp., small 4to and 16mo, about 75 words. Framed with portrait.

30-

"No one will perfectly enjoy me who has not some of my own rudeness, sensuality and hauteur."

"Poems are to arouse the reason, suggest, give freedom, strength of muscle, candor, to any person that reads them—and assist that person to see the realities for himself".

109. CRITICISM OF "LEAVES OF GRASS". 1857. Autograph Manuscript, 1 p., 8vo, about 125 words, in pencil. With transcript. 8vo, boards.

20-

"Feb. 25th '57. Dine with Hector Tyndale. Asked H. T. where he thought I needed particular attention to be directed for my improvement—where I could especially be bettered in my poems. He said—'In massiveness, breadth, large sweeping effects, without regard to details' . . ."

"Put in my poems American things, idioms, materials, persons, groups, minerals, vegitables, animals, &c."

271

110. WHITMAN'S "BARBARIC YAWP". 1856. Autograph Manuscript, signed in text, 1 p., 12mo, about 80 words, in pencil. Framed with portrait.

20—

"On the other side is the 'barbaric yawp' of a very different poet—as different as a Collins steamship or a modern locomotive . . . is from the Lord Mayor of London's state barge".

111. THREAT TO TRANSLATORS. 1858. Autograph Manuscript, 1 p., 12mo, about 40 words. Framed with portrait.

15—

"Put a message in some poem . . . threatening whoever translates my poems . . . without translating every line."

112. CALIFORNIA VIGILANCE COMMITTEE. 1856. Autograph Manuscript, 4 pp., small 4to, about 450 words. With newspaper clipping laid in containing an account of the execution of two men by the California Vigilance Committee. 4to, boards.

50—

The recto of each sheet of this manuscript contains a list of about 225 words relating to the human body which Whitman incorporated in "I sing the Body Electric". On the verso is a note on the California Vigilance Committee written after reading the above clipping.

"The American people, ever sturdy, ever instinctively just, by right of Teutonic descent, have only to perceive any great wrong, and the work of redemption is begun from that hour. I heartily approve of the action of the California Vigilance Committee; it is worthy the promptness and just anger of the Anglo Saxon race . . ."

113. POEM OF MATERIALS. 1857. Autograph Manuscript outline of a poem, with part of a political speech on verso, 2 pp., 12mo, about 135 words. With transcript and title. 12mo, half green niger morocco.

25—

"The Poem (?One grand, eclipsing poem. Poem of Materials . . . words as solid as timbers, stone, iron, brick, glass, planks, &c . . ."

114. SONG OF THE BROADAXE. 1855. Autograph Manuscript, 1 p., folio, about 450 words, in pencil. With transcript and title. Small folio, cloth, brown levant morocco back.

45—

One of the best examples of Whitman's method of work. As Dr. Bucke has pointed out: "The idea of the poem came to him as a whole and instantaneously. He took the piece of paper and jotted down an outline which would serve to call up the image again to his mind. By the aid of the memorandum of the initial inspiration he wrote later the poem as he first conceived it. Words and phrases, the names of things and processes, had to be thought out and hunted up. In the outline he indicates also certain matters that he must investigate." (See Number 252.)

115. MAN AND NATURE. 1850-1860. Six Autograph Manuscripts, 7 pp., 8vo, about 510 words. With portrait and title. 4to, cloth, red morocco back.

45—

> The first manuscript is entitled *"Picture of the most flowing grandeur of a Man"*, and on the verso is a part of an early essay on the advance of mankind in America. A description of Whitman's early cartman friend Bloom follows, and then a choice simile:
>
> *"What we call Literature is but the moist wobbling cub, just born and its eyes not open yet in many days. You are a living man, and think; in that alone is a more heightless and fathomless wonder than all the productions of letters and arts in all the nations and periods of this earth."*
>
> Two manuscripts on the outdoor life of man form a prose draft of a portion of the "Song of Myself". The last is a note on time.

116. THE VOICE OF WALT WHITMAN. 1860-1890. Six Autograph Manuscripts containing three signatures in text, 8 pp., 8vo and 12mo, about 290 words. With portrait and title. 4to, cloth, blue morocco back.

45—

> The collection contains *"Voice of Walt Whitman to the mechanics and farmers of These States, and to each American Young Man, North, South, East and West"*, and on the verso an outline for a book for *"American Boys"*; a note on the *"spinal idea of Walt Whitman's poetry"*; an early draft of "When the Full-grown Poet Came" in "Good-Bye My Fancy"; a note on his reasons for *"this complete rupture with the customary rules and definitions"* in "Leaves of Grass", apparently written for a preface; a note on France; poem *"And there is the meteor-shower wondrous and dazzling"*, an early draft of a part of "Year of Meteors" in "Drum-Taps"; on the verso a note on whales.

117. POETIC SUGGESTIONS. 1854-1862. Nine Autograph Manuscripts, 9 pp., 8vo and smaller, about 290 words. With title. 4to, half brown levant morocco.

45—

> *"A poem in which is minutely described the whole particulars and ensemble of a first-rate healthy Human Body"*.
>
> *"Be careful to put in only what must be appropriate centuries hence"*.
>
> *"A volume—(dramatic machinery for localities, characters, &c) . . ."*
>
> *"Avoid all poetical similes . . ."*
>
> *"What shall the great poet be then? . . ."*
>
> *"The divinest blessings are the commonest . . ."*
>
> *"Make no quotations, and no reference to any other writers . . ."*
>
> *"Breath and Spray . . ."*
>
> *"Poemet, Leaf, Chant, Song . . ."*

118. POEMS TO BE WRITTEN. 1857-1880. Eleven Autograph
Manuscripts, 11 pp., 8vo and smaller, about 180 words. With portrait and title. 4to, cloth, green morocco back.

35—

> Lists of poems to be written, some with comments, and one elaborated:
>> *"The Body.*
>> *"Why what do you suppose is the Body?*
>> *Do you suppose this that has always existed—this meat, bread, fruit, that is*
>> *eaten, is the body? . . ."*
>
> Poems of language, insects, the different states, fruits and flowers, laughter,
> democracy of the future, visions at night, etc.

119. NOTES AND POEMS. 1854-1880. Twenty-seven Autograph
Manuscripts, 27 pp., 8vo and smaller, about 690 words. With
portrait and title. Small folio, half green niger morocco.

55—

> Contains a long note on *"Iron Works"*, and shorter notes on meteors, politics,
> violins, literary style, textbooks and common facts, Carlyle, Hans Sachs, the
> Neibelungen Leid, lectures, titles for poems, etc. There are six short poems,
> one reading as follows:
>> *"I last winter observed the Snow on a spree with the north west wind;*
>> *And it put me out of conceit of fences and imaginary lines."*
>
> Another:
>> *"What would it bring you to be elected and take your place in the Capitol?*
>> *I elect you to understand yourself; that is what all the offices in the republic*
>> *could not do."*

120. POEMS AND NOTES FOR POEMS. 1853-1880. Thirty
Autograph Manuscripts, 30 pp., 12mo and smaller, about 520
words. With title. Small folio, half blue polished morocco.

65—

> In this collection there are twelve fragments of poems, most of them early
> drafts of those published. The notes are mainly suggestions for his poems or
> for his prefaces.
>> *"Of this broad and majestic universe, all in the visible world, and much in*
>> *the greater world invisible, is owned by the Poet . . ."*
>> *"Lo, space, eternal, spiritual, hilarious,*
>> *Lo, the future free demesne, of what is at present called death."*

274

"Leaves of Grass"

THE POETIC INTERPRETATION OF AMERICA
THROUGH A PERSONALITY

THIS section presents in manuscript a portion of the first edifice constructed by Walt Whitman in 1855. Most of the forty-two items (Numbers 121-162) are early drafts of the poems that appeared in the first edition of "Leaves of Grass", but, as Mr. Furness points out, many a passage of beauty and strength was changed or omitted in the published work. Here are the first vivid poetic thoughts with which the author interpreted America through his own personality. Ever presenting the natural human being with all its physical and spiritual attributes, always upholding the natural laws as a sublime and beautiful religion, he broke the bonds of a stilted and hypocritical era of literature not only in America but throughout the world, sending forth a dazzling light that, unperceived at times, is still permeating all literary thought and action.

121. THE BOY'S DREAM. Autograph Manuscript Poem, 1 p., 4to, about 85 words; with part of an essay on *"Municipal legislation"* on verso, about 170 words, in pencil. 4to boards.

25—

This is a versification of the beginning of the very early prose story by Whitman entitled "The Boy's Dream". (See Number 17.)

122. "POEM OF EXISTENCE". 1854. Autograph Manuscript Poem, 1 p., folio, about 230 words. With title. 4to, half green niger morocco.

30—

A very early draft of ideas afterwards embodied in "Kosmos".

> *"Life communes only with life,*
> *Whatever it is that follows death."*

123. GREAT ARE THE MYTHS. 1854. Autograph Manuscript Poem, 1 p., small 4to, about 105 words; on the verso a part of an essay on *"The true friends of the Sabbath"*, about 130 words. With title. 4to, cloth, brown levant morocco back.

30—

This manuscript is apparently the earliest draft in verse of a portion of the preface of 1855, which was elaborated and published as a poem in the same edition. It was dropped from "Leaves of Grass" after 1876.

> *"Great are the myths—I too delight in them,*
> *. . .   . .*
>
> *Great are you—and great am I,*
> *We are just as good and bad as the oldest or youngest*
> *or any."*

"Song of Myself"

AROUND the "Song of Myself" was built the whole edifice of "Leaves of Grass", and the following eleven items (Numbers 124-134) are the earliest poetic interpretations of Whitman's central theme. The references to paragraphs are to the divisions in the "Complete Writings", New York, 1902.

124. "NIGHT OF THE SOUTH WINDS". Two Autograph Manuscript Poems, 2 pp., 4to, about 195 words, in pencil and ink. With portrait and title. 4to, cloth, orange morocco back.

135⁻

"Night of the South Winds", one of the most beautiful of Whitman's poems descriptive of the great outdoors, must have been one of those written while while he lay dreaming on the sands of Long Island on a summer evening. It is the theme of paragraph 21 in "Song of Myself".

> *"Night of south winds—night of the large few stars!*
> *Still slumberous night—mad, naked summer night!*
> *Smile, O voluptuous procreant earth!*
> *Earth of the nodding and liquid trees!*
> *Earth of the mountains, misty-topt!"*

On the verso is a poem which was deleted from paragraph 31 in "Song of Myself": *"The crowds naked in the bath."*

> *"A mouse is miracle enough to stagger billions of infidels!"*

125. "THE TESTS OF MYSELF". Autograph Manuscript Poem, 1 p., 8vo; also Autograph Manuscript, 1 p., small 4to. Together about 125 words. Framed with portrait.

37 ⁵⁰

The poem is a variorum rendering of a part of paragraph 2 in "Song of Myself".

> *"I subject all the teachings of the schools, and all dicta and authority, to the tests of myself."*

The manuscript declares that *"plenty of perfect-bodied, noble-sould men and women"* are more valuable than riches to America.

126. "TO BE AT ALL". Autograph Manuscript Poem, 1 p., small 4to, about 115 words; on the verso a list of words and thoughts to be used in poems, about 75 words, both in pencil.

40⁻

The theme of paragraph 27 in "Song of Myself".

> *"To be at all—what is better than that?*
> *I think if there were nothing more developed, the clam in its callous shell in the sand, were august enough."*

127. "MY HAND WILL NOT HURT WHAT IT HOLDS". Autograph Manuscript Poems, 2 pp., small 4to, about 195 words, in pencil and ink. With title. Small 4to, cloth, brown levant morocco back.

52 ⁵⁰

On the recto of the sheet is one of Whitman's strong sensual poems, a variant of paragraph 28 in "Song of Myself". On the verso is a stanza on *"The Suicide"*, a variant of paragraph 8; and another on death as the beginning of life, a variant of paragraph 49.

128. "TOUCH IS THE MIRACLE". Autograph Manuscript Poem, 1 p., small 4to, about 90 words; on verso a prose manuscript, about 105 words, both in pencil. With title. Small 4to, cloth, white pigskin back.

55

The poem contains the theme of paragraph 29 in "Song of Myself".

> *"It is no miracle now that we are to live on always.*
> *Touch is the miracle!"*

The prose manuscript describes Whitman's efforts to put his thoughts in writing.

> *"The greatest of thoughts and truths are never put in writing . . ."*

129. "I COULD LIVE WITH THE ANIMALS". Autograph Manuscript Poem, 1 p., 4to, about 125 words; prose manuscript on verso, on cleanliness of the human body, about 95 words in pencil. With title. 4to, cloth, brown levant morocco back.

60

The manuscript of the poem is the one from which it was printed in the first edition of "Leaves of Grass" and comprises the last part of paragraph 31 and first part of 32.

> *"I think I could turn and live awhile with the animals.*
>   . . .   .
>
> *They do not sweat and whine about their condition*
> *They do not lie awake in the dark and weep for their sins,*
> *They do not make me sick discussing their duty to God;*
> *Not one is dissatisfied . . ."*

130. THE SLAVE. Two Autograph Manuscript Poems, 3 pp., small 4to, about 260 words. With titles. 2 vols., 4to and small 4to, cloth, black morocco backs.

47 50

Two pages form a variant of paragraph 33 in "Song of Myself" wherein Whitman pictures himself as a Negro slave.

> *"I am a curse a negro thinks me;*
> *You cannot speak for yourself, negro;*
> *I lend him my own tongue;*
> *I dart like a snake from your mouth."*

On the verso of one sheet is a verse on the approach of a procession.

131. NATURE VERSUS BIBLES. Autograph Manuscript Poem, 2 pp., 4to, about 210 words; with prose manuscripts on verso of both sheets, about 350 words. With titles. 2 vols., 4to, cloth, morocco backs.

40—

Mr. Triggs states that this manuscript is an early version of paragraph 41 in "Song of Myself", but if so that paragraph was entirely rewritten.

"I know as well as you that Bibles are divine revelations,

  I say that each leaf of grass and each hair of my breast and beard is also a revelation just as divine.

    . . .   .

  I will take a sprig of parsley and a budding rose and go through the whole earth.

  You shall see I will not find one heretic against them.

  Can you say as much of all the lore of the priesthood?".

On the verso of one sheet is part of a prose essay on *"Little Smouchers"*, and on another descriptive notes, dated 1854, about three of Whitman's stage-driver friends.

132. THE BEGINNING AND THE END. Autograph Manuscript Poem, 1 p., small 4to, about 115 words. With title. 4to, cloth, brown levant morocco back.

50—

An early and stronger version of paragraph 44 in "Song of Myself".

"My spirit sped back to the times when the earth was burning mist,

  And peered aft and could see Concord beyond the aft, forming the mist,

  And brings word that Dilation or Pride is a father of Causes,

  And a mother of Causes is Goodness or Love—

  And they are the Parents yet, and witness and register their Amours eternally;

  And devise themselves to These States this hour.

  And my spirit travelled ahead and pierced the stern hem of life and went fearlessly through,

  And came back from the grave with serene face,

  And said, it is well, I am satisfied, I behold the causes yet.—"

133. GOD AND MAN. Autograph Manuscript Poem, 1 p., 4to; and Autograph Manuscript, 1 p., 4to. Together about 250 words. Both framed with portrait, inscribed *"Walt Whitman Sept: '87"*.

55—

The poem is an early draft of a part of paragraph 49 in "Song of Myself".

  "Mostly this we have of God: we have man.

  Lo, the sun:

  Its glory floods the moon,

  Which of a night shines in some turbid pool."

The manuscript is a prose draft of a part of "Song of Myself":

"Every hour of the day and night, and every acre of the earth and shore, and every point or patch of the sea and sky, is full of pictures".

134. "LIGHT AND AIR". Autograph Manuscript Poem, 1 p., 8vo, about 95 words. With title. 4to, cloth, orange morocco back.

25—

A variant form of paragraph 49 in "Song of Myself".

> *"Light and air!*
> *Nothing ugly can be disgorged,*
> *Nothing corrupt or dead set before them,*
> *But it surely becomes translated or enclothed*
> *Into supple youth or a dress of living richness . . ."*

———

135. "A NATION ANNOUNCING ITSELF". Two Autograph Manuscript Poems, 2 pp., small 4to, about 245 words. With title. 4to, cloth, blue morocco back.

42⁵⁰

The first is an early draft of part of the preface of 1855 in poetic form. It was published in the "Poem of Many in One" in 1856 and later incorporated in "By Blue Ontario's Shore".

> *"A nation announcing itself.*
> *I myself make the only growth by which I can be appreciated;*
> *I reject none, receive all, reproduce all in modern forms."*

On the verso is an early draft of a part of "Salut au Monde".

136. "I SEE WHO YOU ARE". Autograph Manuscript Poem, 1 p., 8vo, about 140 words, in pencil. With title. 4to, half blue polished morocco.

20—

An early draft of the first part of "A Song for Occupations".

> *"I see who you are if nobody else sees nor you either."*

137. PRIESTS. Autograph Manuscript Poem, 1 p., 8vo, about 75 words. With title. 4to, cloth, orange morocco back.

27⁵⁰

A suppressed and early rendering of the last part of "A Song for Occupations".

> *"Priests! until you can explain a paving stone do not try to explain God;*
> *Until your creeds can do as much as apples and hen's eggs let down your*
> *eyebrows a little."*

138. IN PATHS UNTRODDEN. 1859. Autograph Manuscript Poem, 1 p., 12mo, about 90 words. Framed with portrait, inscribed by the poet *"Walt Whitman & children of his friend J. H. Johnston New York 1879"*.

50—

This poem is a variorum reading of "In Paths Untrodden" in "Calamus".

> *"And now I care not to walk the earth unless a comrade walk by my side."*

139. MANHATTAN ISLAND. Autograph Manuscript Poem, 1 p., small 4to, about 90 words. With title. 4to, cloth, yellow morocco back.

30—

A part of the preface of 1855 expressed in a poem to be used at the beginning of another edition, and entitled *"Proem"*.

"These are the sights that I have absorbed in Manhattan island and in all These States."

140. A POET'S WANTS. Autograph Manuscript Poem, 1 p., 4to, about 155 words. With title. 4to, cloth, blue morocco back.

52 50

This poem is taken from the preface of 1855, merely changing the form and adding a few words.

"A little sum laid aside for burial money—a few clapboards around, and shingles overhead, on a lot of American soil owned—a few dollars to supply the year's plain clothing and food—and then away."

141. "YOU LUSTY AND GRACEFUL YOUTH". Autograph Manuscript Poem, 2 pp., 12mo, about 120 words in pencil. With title. 4to, cloth, orange morocco back.

25—

This is an early draft of "Youth, Day, Old Age and Night".

"You lusty and graceful youth! You are great;
You are not exclusively great in youth;
Your middle age shall be great with amplitude and steadiness and fullblooded strength."

On the verso is a draft of a verse for "Song of Myself".

142. THE GREAT LAWS. 1859-1864. Two Autograph Manuscript Poems, 2 pp., 8vo, about 80 words, in pencil and ink. With title. 4to, cloth, orange niger morocco back.

30—

"The Great Laws do not treasure chips, or stick for the odd cent;
I am of the same fashion—for I am their friend."

The poem in pencil on the verso is on the same subject but relates to his brother, Jess, then in an insane asylum.

"But I know for my consolation, of the great laws that emptied and broke my brother."

143. "REMEMBRANCES". Autograph Manuscript Poem, 1 p., 12mo, about 85 words; on the verso a list of rivers and cities of Europe, about 100 words, both in pencil. Small 4to boards.

15—

"Remembrances I plant American ground with,
Lessons to think I scatter as they come."

144. "AS OF FORMS". Autograph Manuscript Poem, 1 p., 8vo, about 105 words. With transcript and title. 8vo, cloth, brown levant morocco back.

17 50

An early draft of "Germs", first published in 1860.

"Things, faces, reminiscences, presences, conditions, thoughts—tally and make definite a divine indistinct spiritual delight in the soul."

145. A SONG OF JOYS. 1860. Autograph Manuscript Poem, 1 p., 16mo, about 50 words. Framed with portrait.

15—

An early draft of a part of "A Song of Joys".

"Perfect serenity of mind
To take with entire self-possession whatever comes".

146. "TO AN EXCLUSIVE". Autograph Manuscript Poem, 2 pp., 8vo, about 190 words. With portrait, transcript, and title. 8vo, cloth, brown levant morocco back.

62 50

Probably purposely omitted by Whitman from "Leaves of Grass" and apparently written after reading some violently adverse criticism of his poems, for he declares his determination:

"Rapacious! I take up your challenge!
I fight, whether I win or lose, and hereby pass the feud to them that succeed me."

147. "I AM NOT CONTENT NOW". Autograph Manuscript Poem, 1 p., 12mo, about 50 words. Framed with portrait.

25—

"I am not content now with a mere majority—I must have the love of all men and all women."

148. "SCANTLINGS". Autograph Manuscript Poem, 1 p., 12mo, about 60 words. Framed with portrait.

27 50

"White, shaved, foreign, soft-fleshed, shrinking . . .
. . .   .

A pretty race, each one just like hundreds of the rest,
A race of scantlings from the stony growth of America".

149. THE OAK TREE. Autograph Manuscript Poem, 1 p., small 4to, about 120 words. With title. 4to, cloth, orange morocco back.

25—

This contains most of the poem "I Saw in Louisiana a Live-Oak Growing", first published in "Calamus" in 1860. On the verso are manuscript suggestions for a poem on the approach of death.

150. A BROOKLYN SCENE. Autograph Manuscript Poem, 1 p., folio, about 150 words, in pencil. With title. Small folio, cloth, orange morocco back.

25—

"Shadows of men and houses, glistening.
A scene phantasmic spread off before me I see through the plate glass glistening."

151. THE HUMAN PROCESSION. Autograph Manuscript Poem, 1 p., small 4to, about 90 words. With title. Small 4to, cloth, brown levant morocco back.

32⁵⁰

> *"A procession without halt,—*
> *Apparent at times, and hid at times,*
> *Rising the rising ground, in relief against the clear sky, lost in the hollows*
> *stretched interminably over the plains.*
> *No eye that ever saw the starting, no eye that ever need wait for the ending."*

152. POETIC FRAGMENTS. Eight Autograph Manuscript Poems, 8 pp., small 4to and 12mo, about 485 words. With title. 4to, half green polished morocco.

75

The first two manuscripts are poetical forms of a part of the last paragraph of the preface of 1855.

> *"To this continent comes the offspring of the other continents."*

There are two variants of parts of the "Song of Myself", one on the slave and the other on the singers.

> *"A tenor strong and ascending, with glad notes of morning—with power and*
> *health."*

A poem on the growth of America is written on the back of a front wrapper bearing a part of the title of "Leaves of Grass". Another poetic interpretation of a part of the preface of 1855 relates to the libraries. Others read in part as follows:

> *"I do not flatter—I am not polite—but I adhere to you*
> *Baffled, exiled, ragged, gaunt."*

> *"Full of wickedness, I . . .*
> *Yet I look composedly upon Nature, drink day and night the joys of life,*
> *and await death with perfect equanimity."*

153. POETIC FRAGMENTS AND NOTES. Eight Autograph Manuscripts, 9 pp., small 4to and 12mo, about 240 words. With title. Small 4to, cloth, orange morocco back.

52⁵⁰

This collection begins with suggestions for a poem on the clean body; then follows *"You woman, mother of children"*; *"As the shores of the sea I live near are to me"*; *"The tough Scotch sailor"* used in "Salut au Monde", and on verso a poetic form of the preface of 1855 used in "By Blue Ontario's Shore"; *"The circus boy"*; *"How can there be immortality except through mortality?"*; *"After death"*; and *"As to you, if you have not yet learned to think"*.

154. WAIFS AND STRAYS. Seven Autograph Manuscript Poems, 7 pp., 8vo and 12mo, about 54 words. With title. 4to, half green polished morocco.

37⁵⁰

This interesting collection begins with two drafts of poems used in "Song of Myself", paragraphs 2 and 3: *"I call back blunderers"* and *"Do I not prove myself?"*. Then follow *"Ever the puzzles of birth and death"*; an early draft of a part of "The Sleepers"; *"Black Lucifer was not dead; or if he was I am his sorrowful, terrible heir"*; *"Remember if you are dying"*; *"I am become the poet of babes and little things"*; and *"The mystic roll from all America"* (the roll of the dead soldiers of the Civil War).

155. EXQUISITE EXAMPLES OF THE POETRY OF WALT WHITMAN. Fourteen Autograph Manuscript Poems, 14 pp., 8vo and smaller, about 430 words. With title. Small folio, half green polished morocco.

This is a collection of gems by Walt Whitman and contains fair examples of all his poetry. The first, eighth, and twelfth are variant forms of the "Song of Myself", and the first of these shows Whitman in the full strength of his poetic genius:

"Man, before the rage of whose passions the storms of Heaven are but a
*   breath;*
* Before whose caprices the lightning is slow and less fatal;*
* Man, microcosm of all Creation's wildness, terror, beauty and power,*
* And whose folly and wickedness are in nothing else existent."*

The second and third items are songs of the body and soul; the fourth, *"Have I refreshed and elevated you"*, is written on the back of a proof sheet of the 1856 edition of "Leaves of Grass"; the fifth relates to the great spiritual awakening of Whitman in 1850:

"I cannot be awake, for nothing looks to me as it did before,
* Or else I am awake for the first time, and all before has been a mean*
*   sleep."*

The sixth poem, on the industries of America, was probably written about 1880; and the seventh was probably written after reading of the wreck of the ship "California":

"Children and maidens—strong men, fighters from battle, wearied, wearied,
* Rocked in the twilight ripples, calmly they sleep in the ebbing tide,*
* To the ocean borne out, the hidden and measureless—ocean with room for*
*   all."*

The thirteenth is a variant of "To One Shortly to Die", and the last is a variant of "There was a Child Went Forth" in "Autumn Rivulets".

156. "LEAVES OF GRASS". 1855. Original Green and Original Pink Wrappers for the First Edition of "Leaves of Grass". 2 pieces, 4to. In a board folder.

These wrappers were printed to be used on the second issue of the First Edition of "Leaves of Grass". They are of the original width but have an inch cut from the top margin and measure 8 by 10 inches. They were used by Whitman for note paper.

After the death of Whitman his literary executors found among the poet's papers a copy of the edition of "Leaves of Grass" in the original green wrappers, upon which Whitman had written: "2d & fullest version of original edition 1855-56 (the 1st edition consisted of the Poems alone—some months afterwards the extracts &c. prefacing the text as here, were added—making this edition)." The history of the finding of Whitman's copy is given in "Walt Whitman's Workshop", by Clifton J. Furness.

10 — 157. —— Another set.

10 — 158. —— Another set.

7 5⁰ 159. —— Another set.

7 5⁰ 160. —— Another set.

5 — 161. —— Another set.

162. LEAVES OF GRASS IMPRINTS. American and European Criticisms on "Leaves of Grass". 16mo, original wrappers. In a
110 — half green morocco box case. Boston: Thayer and Eldridge, 1860

THE MOST IMPORTANT COPY OF THIS EXCEEDINGLY RARE FIRST EDITION. Dr. Bucke's copy, on the front cover of which he has enumerated the reviews in the work that were actually written by Whitman, as revealed to Dr. Bucke by the poet himself: "*Pp.* 7, 21, 30, 38". Three of these pages are marked "*W. W.*" by Dr. Bucke, and on p. 21 is marked the "New York Times'" account of Whitman's writing his own reviews.

Laid in is a newspaper review of "Leaves of Grass Imprints" clipped from the "Brooklyn City News", October 10, 1860, which was doubtless written by Whitman himself.

[END OF FIRST SESSION]

Big Brother to the Boys in
Blue and Gray

WITH the Civil War came the second great change in the life of Whitman, a moral and spiritual uplift brought about through his witnessing the sufferings of thousands of soldiers in the hospitals and tenderly administering to their wants. Though Walt Whitman was an ardent Union man, when he saw a wounded soldier before him it was only a suffering boy, regardless of the color of his uniform; and it seemed that the whole soul of Walt Whitman went out to each patient he helped, a soul of courage, cheer, and unlimited sympathy. They called him "father", "uncle", "brother"; and to the end of their lives, some but an hour and some many years later, they expressed a love and reverence for the man who had helped them in their darkest hour.

In this division has been placed the material relating to the war, whether written during that period or not. Most of the letters from the soldiers and their families are apparently UNPUBLISHED.

163. WALT TO GEORGE. A. L. s., 4 pp., 12mo, about 325 words; a few words torn from a corner. Brooklyn, July 12, 1861. In a board folder.

5⁄

George Whitman enlisted as a private in the 51st New York Volunteers, in the 13th division.

"We are all glad the 13th is coming home—mother especially. . . . All of us here think the rebellion as good as broke—no matter if the war does continue for months yet."

4th of March. 1863.

Well, here is the 4th of March, and two out of the four years of the Lincoln administration have gone by. And now there are two to follow. What will happen during those two years?

[NUMBER 164]

DESCRIPTIVE NOTES BY WHITMAN ON THE END OF THE THIRTY-SEVENTH CONGRESS

164. THE END OF THE 37TH CONGRESS. 1863. Autograph Manuscript *"Wednesday 4th March. Scene up to noon. Close of the 37th Congress—House"*. 16 pp., 16mo, about 700 words, one page in ink, the remainder in pencil. In a full green crushed levant morocco box case, gilt and blind tooled.

50—

A splendid example of Whitman's descriptive notes written at the scene of action. This is one of his famous "little livraisons, each composed of a sheet or two of paper, folded small to carry in the pocket, and fastened with a pin".

A significant note in ink, probably written early in the morning, precedes the account of the closing of Congress:

"4th of March. 1863. Well, here is the 4th of March, and two out of the four years of the Lincoln administration have gone by. And now there are two to follow. What will happen during those two years?"

"(11¼ A. M.) A member from New York has just been making a most excited little speech—at this moment the clerk is calling the ayes and noes—the members and many distinguished and undistinguished visitors are filling the floor, talking, walking, sauntering in twos or threes, or gathered together in little knots—the clapping of hands calling the pages—the fresh green of the carpets and desks—the strong good-tinted panel frames of the glass roof—the short decided voice of the Speaker—the continual (like soda-pop) burstings of members calling Mr. Speaker, Mr. Speaker—the incessant bustle, motion, surging hubbub of voices, undertoned but steady. . . ."

[See illustration]

165. RECORD OF THE 51ST NEW YORK VOLUNTEERS.
May, 1863. Autograph Manuscript Record of the 51st Regiment
in Kentucky copied by Walt Whitman from a letter from his
brother George, together with a manuscript list of the battles in
which the Regiment took part, 3 pp., 8vo, about 350 words. With
title. 8vo, cloth, blue polished morocco back.

The list of battles includes *"Roanoke, Newbern, Manassas Second, Chantilly,
South Mountain, Antietam, Sulpher Springs, Fredericksburg, Vicksburg,
Jackson (Miss.)."* [See Number 178.]

WHITMAN'S LETTERS TO TOM SAWYER, AND A
VIVID DESCRIPTION OF PRESIDENT LINCOLN

166. THE ELDER BROTHER OF THE WOUNDED. Six Rough
Draft A. L. by Walt Whitman, 16 pp., folio to 8vo, with Autograph Manuscripts on the back of two of the letters, 4 pp., 8vo,
April to November, 1863. To Sergeant Thomas P. Sawyer. With
three A. L. s. by Sergeant Sawyer, 9 pp., 8vo, including two to
Walt Whitman and one to Lewis R. Brown, another wounded
soldier. Together about 3,000 words. With transcript and title.
4to, full blue crushed levant morocco, gilt tooled with the arms of
the United States on each cover.

These letters express, to a greater degree than most others, the tender
brotherly love and sympathy of Walt Whitman to the wounded soldier in
general, and to Sergeant Sawyer an affection that was almost overpowering.
In his affections Whitman always maintained the exuberance of his boyhood,
and in that spirit these letters were drafted.

*"Tom I was at Armory last evening, saw Lewy Brown, sat with him a good
while, he was very cheerful, told me how he laid out to do when he got well
enough to go from the hospital, (which he expects soon) says he intends to
go home to Maryland—go to school and learn to write better, and learn a
little bookkeeping, &c.—so that he can be fit for some light employment. Lew
is so good, so affectionate . . . I saw Hiram but did not speak to him. He
lay pale and pretty sick, sound asleep. I could not help stopping before I
came away and looking at him—it was pitiful to see him so pale, sound
asleep. Poor Hiram—he is a good boy—he gets no better . . .*

*"I manage to pay my way here in Washington [with] what I make writing
for the New York papers, &c. . . . Even if we fail for a while elsewehere,
I believe this Union will conquer in the end, as sure as there's a God in
heaven. This country can't be broken up by Jeff Davis, and all his damned
crew. Tom I sometimes feel as if I didn't want to live—life would have no
charm for me, if this country should fail after all and be reduced to take a
third rate position, to be domineered over by England and France and the
haughty nations of Europe &c and we unable to help ourselves. But I have
no thought that will ever be, this country I hope would spend her last drop
of blood and last dollar rather than submit to such humiliation . . ."*

*"Tom you tell the boys of your company there is an old pirate up in Washing-
ton, with the white wool growing all down his neck—an old comrade who
thinks about you and them every day for all he don't know them, and will*

probably never see them, but thinks about them as comrades and younger brothers of his, just the same . . ."

In the next letter Whitman writes:

"Dear comrade you must not forget me for I never shall you. My love you have in life or death forever. I don't know how you feel about it, but it is the wish of my heart to have your friendship, and also if you should come safe out of this war, we should come together again in some place where we could make our living, and be true comrades and never be separated while life lasts,—and take Lew Brown too, and never separate from him . . . Good-bye my darling comrade, my dear darling brother, for so I will call you, and wish you to call me the same."

May 27, 1863. *"Well dear brother the great battle between Hooker and Lee came off, and what a battle it was—without any decisive results again, though at the cost of so many brave men's lives and limbs—it seems too dreadful, that such bloody conflicts without settling anything, should go on. The hospitals here are filled with the wounded, I think the worst cases and the plentiest of any fighting yet . . ."*

November, 1863. *"I am here in Brooklyn, spending a few weeks home at my mothers . . . Here in Brooklyn and New York where I was raised I have so many friends, I believe now I am here they will kill me with kindness, I go around too much, and I think it would be policy for me to go back to Washington. I have a brother here, very sick,—I have another brother in the 9th Army Corps, has been out 26 months. But the greatest patriot in the family is my old mother. She always wants to hear about the soldiers, and would give her last dime to any soldier that needed it . . ."*

PRESIDENT LINCOLN IN 1863

This three-page manuscript on President Lincoln was drafted in pencil on the back of one of the letters to Tom Sawyer and a part of the substance embodied in a letter to Mrs. Whitman on October 20, 1863.

"The President is generally moving at a slow trot. I see him very plainly, his dark brown face and the deep cut lines, and the eyes, &c., always to me with a deep latent sadness in the expression. He tells funny stories they say, it may be a foil to the powerful force of his. The sabres and accoutrements clank and the entirely unornamental cortege sweeps on. It excites no sensation only some curious stranger stops and looks.

"Sometimes I notice the President goes or comes in an open barouche. The cavalry always keeps close to accompany him with their naked sabres. Often I notice him as he goes evenings and sometimes in the mornings when he returns early, he turns off and halts at the large and handsome mansion of the Secretary of War in K Street and holds conference there. If in his barouche I can see from my window he does not alight, but sits there and I suppose the Secretary comes out to attend him. Sometimes one of his sons a boy of ten or twelve accompanies him riding at his right on a pony . . ."

On the back of the letter of November, 1863, Whitman has drafted an account of his hospital work, in the third person, probably for the "New York Times".

"We have alluded to his work being on his own personal independent system. But quietly he makes personal application for the soldiers himself of what he has, or receives, or purchases to the cases of the wounded or sick, each according to its special needs at the time. In this respect and truly he does sometimes transcendant good. The cases where aid of one sort or another is needed are to be counted by hundreds . . ."

[See illustration]

[21 April 1863]

Tom, I thought I would write you a few words, and take chances of its getting to you, although there is great excitement now about the Army of the Potomac, and they say about. There is nothing very special here in Washington — they seem to be shoving troops off from here now all the time, in small or large bodies — the convalescents are doing guard duty &c, so I suppose something is up. Hospitals. Tom, I was at Armory last evening, saw Lewy Brown, sat with him a good while, he was very cheerful, told me how he would do, when he got well enough to go from the hospital, says he intends to go to school, and learn to write better, and bookkeeping, &c — so that he can be fit for some light employment. Lew is so good, so affectionate — when I came away he reached up his face, and we gave each other a long kiss, half a minute long. We talked about you. I saw Horace Delay, pale and pretty sick, found asleep all the time, I too I could not help looking at him — it was pitiful — he is a good boy. Poor Horace — he gets no better. John Mahay does not get any better, in Ward E.

Tom, I do not know who you was most intimate with in the Hospital, or I would write you about them. As to me there is nothing new with me, or my affairs. I manage here in Washington to pay my way, & what I make writing letters for the New York papers, &c. When I stopped here last summer on my return from Falmouth. I thought I would stop a few days, and see if I could not get some berth, clerkship or something — but I have not pushed strong enough — and I so don't know as I could be satisfied with the life of a clerk in the departments. I guess I enjoy a kind of vagabond life anyhow, I go around some, nights when the spirit moves me, sometimes to the gay places, just to see the sights. Tom I wish you was here — somehow I don't find the comrade that suits me to a dot — and I won't have any other, not for good.

[NUMBER 166]

289

167. REUBEN FARWELL. A Collection of 11 A. L. s. by Reuben
Farwell, 32 pp., folio to 8vo, about 3,000 words. April 3, 1864,
to August 16, 1875. To Walt Whitman. With title. Small folio,
cloth, red polished morocco back.

5

The writer of these letters was "Little Mitch" alluded to in "Memoranda
During the War", a member of Company H, First Michigan Cavalry, who
had been befriended and cared for by Whitman in the Armory Hospital. His
letters show his love for the "wound dresser". One is typical, more especially
as it was written ten years after the war:

*"I have a wife & little girl 5 years old this month when we received your
Picture she kissed it and likes to show it to every one that comes in the
house. I felt proud of it myself. I will have to get a frame for it and hang
it up on the wall.*

*"Walt my dear old Friend how I would like to grasp your hand and give
you a kiss as I did in the days of yore. What a satisfaction it would be
to me . . ."*

168. ONE HOSPITAL PATIENT AND HIS FAMILY. Two
Rough Draft A. L. by Walt Whitman, 7 pp., folio to 12mo, about
600 words. September, 1863, and August, 1874. To Bethuel
Smith. Also an A. L. s. from Bethuel Smith to his mother, 9
A. L. s. to Walt Whitman, 1863-75, and 5 A. L. s. by Mrs. Maria
Smith, mother of Bethuel, to Walt Whitman, 1864-75; about 41
pp., 4to to 12mo, about 4,500 words. With transcript of the
Whitman letters, and title. Small narrow folio, half blue polished
morocco.

35

The letters by Walt Whitman are pictures of brotherly love and kindness to
a wounded Union cavalry boy to whom he brought a ray of sunshine in the
hospital.

*"I was very much disappointed when I went to Armory that evening to find
my dear comrade was gone so sudden . . . There is nothing new with me
here—I am very well in health and spirits, and only need some employment,
clerkship or something at fair wages to make things go agreeable with me—
no, there is one thing more I need and that is Thuey, for I believe I am quite
a fool, I miss you so . . . A good many wounded were brought here very
late Monday night 12 o'clock—some 70 to Armory Hospital—all cavalry . . .*

*"Thuey you went away without getting paid aint you broke? I can send you
a little, a few 10 ct bills . . ."*

Six letters from Bethuel, written between September 17, 1863, and February
28, 1864, tell of his recovery from his wounds, his appreciation for the ten
cent script, of rejoining his regiment and its movements. In August, 1864, he
was again wounded and then took his discharge from the army. A letter
from the mother of Bethuel in 1865 tells of his recovery, and adds:

"you have a Mother with you i would like to know of her welfare i think

she has one great blessing to comfort her in her age and that is having a kind hearted Son".

This correspondence dropped for nearly ten years, when Mrs. Smith wrote again, December 10, 1874, telling of the death of her husband and the welfare of Bethuel. Walt Whitman drafted his letter to Bethuel on the back of her letter:

"Years have passed away but I find there is something in the friendship formed amid sickness, or with the wounded in hospital. I find it comes up again as fresh and living as ever and remains as if it cannot pass away . . .

"I worked in Washington after the War—had a stroke of paralysis now two years since, was getting better, then some serious troubles happened to me and I fell back again—I have left Brooklyn and Washington for good—and am now laid up here—I am neither well enough to do any work, nor sick enough to give up—go out some though lame and keep a pretty good heart, hoping for better times . . ."

Walt Whitman sent his photograph to the Smiths, and on March 14, 1875, the mother wrote:

"we all see the picture and was very much pleased to see it Mary said that is the man that saved our brothers life to one of our neighbours".

And in another letter:

"It has always seemed to me that god sent you to save the life of our son that he might come home and see his parents once more even sick and wounded . . ."

169. MEMORIES OF HOSPITAL DAYS. Rough Draft A. L., 3 pp., 8vo, about 400 words. [Camden] May 20, 1874. To William Stansbury. With 4 A. L. s. by William Stansbury and 1 by his wife, 15 pp., folio and 8vo, Howard Lake, Minn., December 9, 1873, to July 21, 1875. Together 6 pieces, in a board folder.

25

William Stansbury writes:

"When I think of the kindness you shewn to me my heart is swelled with gratitude to you . . . in Armery Sq. you come in every evening I remember of your kissing me . . ."

To this letter Walt Whitman replied:

"Your letter of May 14 has come to hand to-day reminding me of your being in Armory Square Hospital and of my visits there, and meeting you, in '65. Your writing, or something it has started, extensively, deeply touches me. It takes me back to the scenes of ten years ago, in the war, the hospitals of Washington, the many wounded bro't up after the battles, and the never-to-be told sights of suffering and death. To think that the little gift and word of kindness, should be remembered by you so long—and that the Kiss I gave you amid those scenes, should be treasured up, and as it were sent back to me after many years!

"I am well situated here—but very lonesome—have no near friends (in the deepest sense) here at hand—My mother died here a year ago—a sorrow from which I have never entirely recovered, and likely never shall—she was an unusually noble, cheerful woman very proud spirited and generous— . . ."

Soldiers' Letters to me during the War (some since)

A COLLECTION OF LETTERS FROM THE WOUNDED SOLDIERS AIDED BY WHITMAN

170. THE WOUND DRESSER. A Collection of Letters from the wounded soldiers who were helped or befriended by Walt Whitman in the hospitals, and from their mothers, fathers, and relatives. 64 pieces, about 170 pp., folio to 12mo. With the original manuscript label with which Whitman docketed the collection: *"Soldier's Letters to me during the War (some since)"*. With title. 4to, cloth, green levant morocco back.

110

In this collection is embodied the wounded soldiers' opinion of Walt Whitman, their "father", "uncle", brother" and "comrade"; here too is expressed the love of fathers and mothers towards the man who acted as father and mother to the boys in blue and the boys in gray.

The collection is arranged alphabetically, with the name of each writer written in red by Dr. Bucke preceding the letter. Most of the letters bear the autograph docket by Whitman, and the collection includes two autograph notes by Whitman relating to the soldiers. Only a few typical quotations are given.

Caleb H. Babbitt. September 18, 1863. *"It does not seem as though I could ever repay you for your kindness towards me both while I was in the Hospital and since I came home'.*

L. K. Brown, August 10, 1863. *"The boys about the Hospital could ill spare you, if you are as good to them as you were to me. I shall never for get you for your kindness to me while I was suffering so mutch, and if you do not get your reward in this world you will in Heaven."*

Another letter by Brown, July 18, 1864. *"There is a many a soldier now that*

292

never thinks of you but with emotions of the greatest gratitude & I know that the soldiers that you have bin so kind to have a great big warm place in their heart for you. I never think of you but it makes my heart glad to think that I have been permited to know one so good."

E. D. Fox, July 14, 1864. *"You know I used to call you Father or 'Pa', and I still think of you as such for I am sure no Father could have cared for their own child better than you did me".*

Albert G. Knapp, April 2, 1876. *"I lay on a cot in 'Mother Whippy's' Ward at Judiciary Sqr. Hospt. in Washington sick nigh unto death when there came in one day, with charitable intent, a stalwart man of genial appearance & seemingly past the middle age since his hair & full beard were plentifully sprinkled with white. This man (whose frame, as I afterwards found, was no mean type of the generous heart within) came to my bed, sat down, & after some talk with me wrote a letter to my parents in Michigan . . . the name Walt Whitman is a household one in one family."*

[See illustration]

171. BATTLE OF THE WILDERNESS. Autograph Manuscript Account of the Battle of the Wilderness, by Whitman, as related by Hinds in January 1885 *"as he told them by the fire in S's* [Col. James M. Scovel's] *parlor"*, 1 p., 4to, about 150 words, in pencil. With title and transcript. 4to, cloth.

25—

"The scenes of May '64 as witness'd at Fredericksburg—that whole old town glutted, fill'd, probably 15 to 20,000 wounded broken, dead, dying soldiers sent northward from Grant's forces on their terrific promenade from the Rapidan down to Petersburg fighting the way not only day by day but mile by mile—sent up from the battles of the Wilderness . . ."

172. PRISONERS. 1865. Autograph Manuscript, 4 pp., small 4to, about 240 words, in pencil and ink. With transcript and title. Small 4to, half blue crushed levant morocco.

15—

The rectos of both sheets contain the draft of Whitman's appeal through the press for an exchange of prisoners. This appeal was made while he was trying to secure the exchange of his brother George, then in a Confederate prison:

"It is generally believed in Washington that the President is in favor of a general exchange, but has been for the past year overruled by the head of the War Department & others . . ."

On the verso of each sheet are pencil notes relating to an exchange of prisoners, prison life, and the Confederate wounded.

173. LINCOLN'S APPOINTMENT OF HARLAN. 1865. Autograph Manuscript *"A Glint inside of Abraham Lincoln's Appointment—one item of many"*, 2 pp., 4to, about 300 words; mounted. With transcript and title. 4to, half blue polished morocco.

50—

This manuscript contains most of the account of President Lincoln's appointment of James Harlan as Secretary of the Interior, as published in "November Boughs". It was Harlan who so disapproved of "Leaves of Grass" that he removed Whitman from his position as clerk in the department of the interior.

174. "LINCOLN AND WHITMAN". 1881. Autograph Manuscript, 1 p., folio, about 110 words. Framed between portraits of Lincoln and Whitman, the latter inscribed by the poet *"Walt Whitman London Canada Sept 22 1880"*.

15⁻

This manuscript was used by Dr. Bucke in his biography of Whitman. It is written in the third person, as though it were Dr. Bucke's account of an interview.

"He several times spoke of President Lincoln, whom he considered the most markedly national, western, native character the United States has yet produced. He never had any particular intimacy with Mr. Lincoln, but, (being a personal friend of John Hay, confidential secretary,) saw a good deal of L., was much at the White House, (1863 and '64) and knew the President's character behind the scenes . . ."

[See illustration]

175. "MARTIAL CONSTELLATION". 1864. Autograph Manuscript Poem, 1 p., 4to, about 120 words. On the verso is the autograph manuscript draft of a letter to the editor of the "New York Herald" seeking support for an exchange of prisoners, about 100 words. With title. 4to, cloth, blue polished morocco back.

15⁻

This poem was first published in "Drum-Taps", then in 1867 entitled "Flag of Stars! Thick-Sprinkled Bunting", and in 1871 "Thick-Sprinkled Bunting".

"Martial constellation! far sweeps your journey!
For the prize I see at issue is the world . . ."

¶ He occasionally several times often spoke of President Lincoln whom he considered the most markedly native national character the United States has yet produced. He never had any particular intimacy with Mr Lincoln, but (being a personal friend of John Hay, confidential secretary) saw a good deal of him (1863 and '64.) was much at the White House, and knew the Presidents real life character behind the scenes. In after years he desired to keep the anniversary of Mr Lincoln's death, by a public lecture he had prepared (see Specimen Days.) but he could get neither engagements audiences nor public interest. and after delivering this lecture in 1879, '80, and '81 to small gatherings. he stopped it.

note see page 95

note — small type   not'g

✗ at bottom of page

In one of the principal cities of the United States, the 15th anniversary of President Lincoln's death (April 15, 1880.) was commemorated by this public address. The next morning the discriminating editor of that paper relegated the Death of Abraham Lincoln, (as described and commented on by Walt Whitman,) to a half-supercilious notice of five or six lines — and fills two columns of his journal with a lecture, by a visiting English clergyman, on "the Evidential Value of the Acts of the Apostles"!

[NUMBER 174]

MEMORANDA

During the War.

BY WALT WHITMAN.

———

Author's Publication.
CAMDEN, NEW JERSEY
1875—'76.

[NUMBER 176]

THE MOST IMPORTANT PRESENTATION COPY OF
ONE OF WHITMAN'S RAREST BOOKS

"MEMORANDA DURING THE WAR" PRESENTED BY WHITMAN
TO THE AUTHOR OF "THE GOOD GRAY POET"

176. MEMORANDA DURING THE WAR. *2 portraits.* 12mo,
original dark red cloth, with presentation leaf and leaf of advertisements, gilt edges. In a half red niger morocco box case.
Author's Publication. Camden, New Jersey, 1875-'76
FIRST EDITION OF ONE OF WALT WHITMAN'S RAREST BOOKS. About 100 copies
were issued in separate form. AUTOGRAPH PRESENTATION COPY FROM THE

[Description concluded on page 58; see illustrations]

500—

296

Remembrance Copy.

TO *Mr D O'Connor*

From *his friend the author*

PERSONAL--NOTE.

Dear Friend :

I do not hesitate to briefly precede your Remembrance-Copy with some biographical facts of myself, I know you will like to have—also, to bind in, for your eye and thought, the little Portraits that follow*.

I was born May 31, 1819, in my father's farm-house, at West Hills, L. I., New York State. My parents' folks mostly farmers and sailors—on my father's side, of English—on my mother's, (Van Velsor s,) from Hollandic immigration.

We moved to Brooklyn while I was still a little one in frocks—and there in B. I grew up out of the frocks—then, as child and boy, went to the public schools—then to work in a printing office.†

When only sixteen or seventeen years old, and for two years afterward, I went to teaching country schools down in Queens and Suffolk counties, Long Island, and "boarded round." Then, returning to New York, worked as printer and writer, (with an occasional shy at "poetry.")

---

* The picture in shirt-sleeves was daguerreotyped from life, one hot day in August, 1855, by my friend Gabriel Harrison, in Fulton St., Brooklyn—and here drawn on steel by McRae—(was a very faithful and characteristic likeness at the time.) The head that follows was photographed from life, Washington, 1872, by Geo. C. Potter, here drawn on wood by W. J. Linton.

† There was. first and last, a large family of children ; (I was the second.) Besides those mentioned above, were my elder brother Jesse my dear sister Mary, my brother Andrew. and then my youngest brother Edward, (always badly crippled —as I now am of late years.)

[NUMBER 176]

AUTHOR TO WILLIAM D. O'CONNOR, AUTHOR OF "THE GOOD GRAY POET" AND WHITMAN'S MOST INTIMATE FRIEND DURING THE WAR PERIOD. On p. 47 a word is corrected in manuscript by the poet.

Tipped inside the front cover, apparently by either the author or O'Connor, are proofs of two articles by Whitman from the "West Jersey Press": "Walt Whitman's Actual American Position" and "Walt Whitman".

Laid in are three of Whitman's own clippings from "The New York Times" of February 26 and October 1, 1863, and December 11, 1864, entitled: "The Great Army of the Sick", "Letter from Washington" and "Our Wounded and Sick Soldiers". It was these articles that led O'Connor to write to Whitman "It fills me with infinite regret that there is not a book from you, embodying these rich and sad experiences. It would be sure of immortality. No history of our times would ever be written without it, if written with that wealth of living detail you could crowd into it. Indeed it would itself be a history". Thus it was O'Connor who inspired the writing of "Memoranda During the War". Doubtless this copy was the first of the small separate issue to be presented by the author, and was sent to the one who had helped and befriended him the most during his "wound dresser" days. Whitman himself said: "The O'Connor home was my home; they were beyond all others—William, Nelly—my understanders, my lovers. I was nearer to them than to any others—oh! much nearer".

Laid in is also a review of "Leaves of Grass" by William D. O'Connor, clipped from "The New York Times" of December 2, 1866; and an announcement of the forthcoming "Memoranda during the War" by Walt Whitman, clipped from the "Examiner", 1876.

THIS IS THE COPY THAT BRINGS INTO CLOSEST ASSOCIATION THE AUTHOR, THE FRIEND OF THE WAR DAYS WHO INSPIRED THE BOOK, AND THE REALISTIC YET SPIRITUAL RECORDS OF HOSPITAL WORK.

The Character of Walt Whitman Revealed in Letters from His Family

THE following six lots relate the intimate history of the Whitman family with many unrecorded details, especially in regard to the character of Walt Whitman. Practically all of the letters are UNPUBLISHED. At the end is Walt Whitman's autobiography, for Dr. Bucke's work was his in name only, Walt Whitman having supplied most of the information therein, and furthermore read every word and made thousands of corrections, deletions, and additions prior to its publication.

"TO HER, THE IDEAL WOMAN, PRACTICAL, SPIRITUAL, OF ALL OF EARTH, LIFE, LOVE, TO ME THE BEST"—WALT WHITMAN

177. MOTHER. A Series of 141 Autograph Letters from Mrs. Louisa Whitman, about 352 pp., folio to 12mo, about 70,000 words. 1860 to 1873. To her son, Walt Whitman. With portrait, under which is *Dearest Mother*, written by Walt Whitman; an

85—

A. L. s. *"Walt"*, 1 p., 8vo; transcript and titles. 2 vols., full brown crushed levant morocco, gilt tooled. With an extra copy of the transcript of the letters, 4to, cloth, niger morocco back. Together 3 vols.

A positive knowledge of the character of Walt Whitman is revealed in these letters, and a clear view obtained of a humane, careful, generous, diplomatic, ambitious and loving son; here too is revealed the source of Walt Whitman's buoyant nature, for no matter what suffering the mother endured, what sorrow came into her life, there was always a ray of sunshine penetrating the clouds and reflected in words of hope and cheer to her beloved son.

Tragedy followed the Whitman family. Jess, the eldest son, became insane and was sent to an asylum; Edward was weak-minded and helpless to the end of his days; Andrew died of tuberculosis, leaving a wife who became an outcast and sent her children to beg on the streets; Hannah made an unfortunate marriage; George, the soldier, was a generous but very practical character and not always in sympathy with the family; and Jeff, Walt's favorite brother and, with the exception of Walt, the finest character of all, lost his wife from tuberculosis shortly before the mother died.

These letters tell all the joys and sorrows of the mother, but they also tell of Walt as, strong and calm, ever cheerful, he endeavored to guide the Whitman family toward that perfect equanimity he himself had gained. Mother and son exchanged letters every week unless illness prevented, and the mother tipped the postman generously for prompt delivery. Each letter from Walt, no matter what his circumstances, contained from one to ten dollars, and often a little extra for a new dress, a sofa, a ton of coal, or back rent. The brothers and sisters too drew upon him to the extent of his resources; but money, as such, meant nothing to Walt and he passed it out as freely as the sunshine of the soul that emanated with every gift.

These mother's letters are terse, ungrammatical, and, as she grew older, somewhat critical of others; but to Walt they expressed the supreme mother love to a favorite son. Furthermore she took a lively interest in his work, asking for every magazine or newspaper in which he had a contribution, and often expressing her admiration. Politics, the news of the day, comment on mutual friends, and especially gossip of the family fill the major part of the letters.

The letters begin while Walt Whitman was in Boston in 1860 editing his new edition of "Leaves of Grass", and, with the exception of lapses of about three years when Walt was at home, were continued to the time of her death in 1873. She writes of the death of Andrew and the condition of his family, of the return of George from a Confederate prison, and on June 3, 1865:

"the english papers is very sypathetic for the honourable Jefferson davis poor mr Lincoln being murdered dont seem to be any thing to them compared with the American patriot as they call the great Jefferson davis."

In September, 1865, Mrs. Whitman made a visit to her daughter Hannah, in Burlington, Vermont, and tried her best to have Walt buy a small place there where mother and son could live in peace for the rest of their lives. On August 1, 1867, she declares that O'Connor's "The Good Gray Poet" is better than John Burroughs' book. In February, 1868, she comments on Walt's writing "Leaves of Grass" again, and on March 24th writes:

"the book for mary came friday and the galaxy to day with the ballad of sir ball i had forgotten all about the piece till i see it and then i had to think where i had heard of it and then it came to my mind what piece it was it is signed w i hope nobody will think you wrote it walt."

March 31, 1869. *"well walter i have the whisper of heavenly death it lays here on the table by my side i have read it over many times and have had one*

my dear beloved son dont be worried about me i hope i shall be all right again my nervous system is very much out of order i know i have brought in on by worrying but i cant seem to get over it my head feels bad sometimes my side is better if i could be with you dear walt i would be glad it wasent right for me to come here to live ~~here~~ as things has not been as i could wish but i hope i shall get a better appetite some Time as i have such trembling spells its all my nerves i know dont worry walter dear i hope your mother will get better if i could get away from here i would be glad george is good to me but he aint home much of his time

                   you must come on the 1 of the month

[NUMBER 177]

person ask me to let her take it home i said no i would rather not let it go out of my hands and am very glad i did so as you wish me to preserve it i felt as if i should preserve it for i liked it it was so solemn."

October 10, 1871. *"i dont know what i would doo walt if it wasent for you to think of me it seems as if all the other sons and daughters has their own to attend to which is perfectly natural. george and loo and Jeff insists on my breaking up housekeeping and they dident only insist but almost commanded me i told them i should remain here this winter if i lived. the none of them want edd Walter and they would soon get tired of paying his board and we aint much expense to any but you walter dear . . ."*

In 1872, however, Mrs. Whitman went to live with George in Camden, and in January Walt had his first paralytic stroke. On January 30, 1873, his mother writes:

"My dear darling walt i have just got your letter i am glad my dear walt you are as well as you are i know its bad enough to be confined in your room and unable to walk but i am glad to hear your friends is so kind i thought of peter i knew if it was in his power to be with you he would and cherefully doo everything that he could for you. i could wish you was here walter dear but as it cant be so i trust you will be restored to your usual health and you dear old mother . . ."

To the last Mrs. Whitman made plans to build a small house and live with

Walt, even going so far as to design the house, but her nervous system gave way, and then came the last letter:

"my dear beloved son dont be worried about me i hope i shall be all right again my nervous system is very much out of order i know i have brought it on by worrying but i cant seem to get over it my head feels bad sometimes my rheumatics is better if i could be with you dear walt i would be glad it wasent right for me to come here to live . . . dont worry walter dear i hope your mother will get better . . ."

[See illustration on opposite page]

LIFE AND DEATH IN THE CIVIL WAR

LETTERS FROM GEORGE WHITMAN TO HIS MOTHER
AND TO WALT WHITMAN

178. THE SOLDIER BROTHER. A Collection of 46 A. L. s. (some with initials) from George Whitman to his Mother, 8 A. L. s. to Walt Whitman, and an A. N. s. *"Walt"* to his Mother, 201 pp., folio to 12mo. June 28, 1861, to July 14, 1865. 4to, full blue crushed levant morocco, gilt tooled heart with red inlays on each cover.

55–

Far better than an orderly book and truer than most journals are these letter pictures of battles, sieges, marches, railroad and transport travels, condition of the people, camp scenes, plentitude and starvation, and all that was experienced in army life during the Civil War. They are the descriptions of a man who entered the ranks as a private at the beginning of the war and reached the rank of lieutenant colonel at its close, who was wounded and who suffered all the agonies and privations of a Confederate prison; and of a man who endured all with a calm serenity that ignored fear, a cheerfulness that disregarded conditions, and a manhood that made him not only the leader but the comrade of all under his command.

Through all the letters George Whitman expresses his intense love for his mother and family. He simply sends his money home with instructions to use it, and often actually implores that it should be used for the good of the family. The letters are never gloomy, and even in the darkest hours they sparkle with a ray of sunshine. Only a brief outline and a few short quotations are here presented as examples of the nature of the letters.

June 28, 1861, found George Whitman in Baltimore, with Confederate sympathizers firing into his camp. Beginning with 1862, he gives vivid descriptions of the battles of Roanoke Island and Newbern, a part of the latter account being written on captured Confederate note-paper:

"We marched right up under a terrible fire, formed in line of battle and went at them and fought them in splendid style for about 3 hours, when our boys drove them from their entrenchments and the day was ours".

On April 12, 1862, George wrote of his promotion to second lieutenant and on June 1st of being presented with a sword and belt by his company. July 12th he tells of a transport trip from Newbern to Hatteras on a ferryboat so crowded that many of the soldiers jumped overboard and were drowned. On September 15th came a full account of the part his regiment took in the second battle of Bull Run; and on the 22nd a nine-page account of the battle of Antietam.

"Near Antietam, Md. Sept. 30th 1862 . . . I see by the papers that Uncle Abe has issued a proclamation declaring the slaves free in all the States that

Danville Va. October 23ᵈ 1864

Dear Mother. I wrote you a line, from Libby Prison, a few days after I was taken prisoner, but think it doubtfull if you received it. I was taken, (along with almost our entire Regt—both Officers and men) on the 30ᵗʰ day of September, near the Weldon Rail Road, but am proud to think that we stood and fought untill we were entirely surrounded, Major Wright, Lieuts Pooley, Sims, and 9 other Officers of our Regt. are here; Capt. Walton and Lieut Butler was wounded, but I dont know how badly, I am verry well indeed, and in tip top spirits, am tough as a mule, and about as ugly, and can eat any amount of corn bread, so you see, dear Mother that I am all right, and my greatest trouble is that you will worry about me, but I beg of you not to fret, as I get along first rate. Please write to Lieut. Babcock of our Regt. and tell him to send my things home by Express. Much love to all. G. W. Whitman

[NUMBER 178]

are in rebellion on the first of next Jan. I dont know what effect it is going to have on the war, but one thing is certain, he has got to lick the South before he can free the niggers . . ."

On December 16, 1862, came the account of the first battle of Fredericksburg, where George was wounded and where Walt Whitman soon found him. George writes to his brother on January 13, 1863: "We have just come off pickett, everything along the river and in the camp is just the same as when you left."

About the first of March George obtained a furlough and after a visit home was sent to the western department. After the capture of Vicksburg he writes, on July 23, 1863:

"Our whole corps were encamped around here, before the surrender of Vicksburg, and we had dug miles of rifle Pitts, and would have had a big thing on Johnson, if we could have got him to come here and give us a fight. Vicksburg you recollect surrendered on the morning of July 4th, and on the afternoon of the same day, we started off to find Johnson . . ."

October 16, 1863. "I think just the meanest rebels that ever lived, are those that stay at home and oppose the draft, and blow about the violation of the Constitution, the liberties of the People, and all that sort of thing."

The stay in the west ended in the spring of 1864. The division arrived in Annapolis in the beginning of April after a harrowing railroad journey, and was at once prepared for the "Wilderness Campaign". That campaign and all the battles are described in detail insofar as Captain Whitman took part in them, and his regiment was at the offensive point in many of the battles. But good luck could not last forever, and on October 2, 1864, came the word from Petersburg, Va.:

"Here I am perfectly well and unhurt, but a prisoner. I was captured day before yesterday with Major Wright . . . and nearly the entire Regt. that was not killed or wounded. Lieut Butler was badly wounded. I am in tip top health and Spirits, and am as tough as a mule and shall get along first rate. Mother please dont worry and all will be right in time if you will not worry . . ."

Another message came from the prisoner on October 23, 1864.

On February 24, 1865, came the welcome letter to his mother from Officers Hospital at Annapolis:

"I arrived here yesterday from Hotel De Libby and if ever a poor devil was glad to get in a Christian Country it was me. I am perfectly well Mother although I am in the Hospital Buildings, and am not under Medical treatment . . ."

Laid in this volume, in an envelope endorsed by Dr. Bucke, is a tintype photograph of George Whitman in uniform, taken about 1862, and said to be unpublished and hitherto unknown. The A. N. s. *"Walt"* to his mother, inserted as a frontispiece to the volume, offers to start George in business as a house builder after the war. At the end of the volume is a clipping, endorsed by Walt Whitman, relating to the death of George's infant son.

[See illustration on opposite page]

179. AN INCOMPATIBLE FAMILY. A Collection of 68 A. L. s. from Charles L. Heyde to Walt Whitman and 7 to the Mother of Walt Whitman, 156 pp., folio to 12mo; together with 5 A. L. s. by Hannah Heyde, two of which are added to those of Mr. Heyde 15 pp., 4to to 12mo. Together about 35,000 words. Mainly Burlington, Vt., September 22, 1852, to February 27, 1892. Small folio, cloth, blue polished morocco back.

Charles L. Heyde married Hannah Whitman, sister of Walt Whitman. These letters present a picture of absolute incompatibility in married life, and one of the great torments in the Whitman family. On the one part a painter of rural scenery, temperamental, egotistical, educated, at times brutal, and apparently, from his handwriting, at times addicted to alcoholism or drugs. On the other part, Hannah, a real Whitman woman who loved her freedom and would not be browbeaten, whose letters express an undivided love for her family and an effort to live on friendly terms with her husband, but who was ill through many years of her married life.

No greater contrast could be found in epistolary correspondence than between some of the early letters of Mr. Heyde to Walt Whitman, when he stigmatized "Leaves of Grass" as *"irregular, disorderly, indifferent or defiant—the lower animal instincts—no accountability or moral sense or principle"*, and his high praise for "November Boughs" in 1888, when Walt and George Whitman were the only supports of his family.

These letters do, however, give an insight into the character of the poet and also into the drain on his resources, for never a letter was sent to Hannah that did not contain money, or to her husband that did not contain calm advice, plain and truthful but without rancour, that probably had more to do with holding the couple together throughout their lives than any other influence.

180. MATTIE WHITMAN. A Collection of 26 A. L. s. by Mattie
Whitman, wife of Jeff Whitman, 20 of which are to her mother-
in-law and 6 to Walt Whitman, together about 92 pp., 8vo and
12mo. Together about 7,000 words; all somewhat stained.
December 21, 1863, to November 15, 1872. 8vo, cloth.

15

These are the letters of a happy but frail mother and wife to the two people
she loved next to her husband and children. She, too, expresses her affection
for Walt Whitman and looks up to him as the head of the family.

Mattie gives a full account of the violent outbreaks of Jess Whitman which
finally led to his being placed in an asylum in 1864; and also of the conduct
of Nancy, widow of Andrew Whitman.

After their removal to St. Louis, where Jeff had charge of the water works,
Mattie contracted consumption, but in spite of her illness her letters were
always bright and cheerful.

181. HELEN E. PRICE. Seven A. L. s. by Miss Price and an A. L. s.
by her mother, 32 pp., 12mo, about 2,000 words. October 13,
1872, to March 27, 1873. All to Mrs. Whitman. With title.
12mo, cloth.

7⁵⁰

The Price family were intimate friends of the Whitmans in Brooklyn, and
these letters to Walt Whitman's mother express all the affection of a loving
daughter. They were all written during the last few months of Mrs. Whitman's life.

November 24, 1872. *"You know that I am one of your own girls. When Ma
came home that day and said that you were gone, I felt that I had lost my
other Mother."*

*"New Years 1873 . . . Tell me about Walt too. I hope he is not angry with
me any more. It almost broke my heart to think I had vexed him . . . but
Walt was always dear to me as you know, and always will be, no matter what
his opinion may be of me . . ."*

January 31, 1873. *"I have just seen an account of Walt's illness in the papers
. . . I feel as though I could hardly keep from starting right off to take care
of him and I know I should if I was married and rich . . . Walt makes so
many friends everywhere he goes that he is sure to be well taken care of . . ."*

February 9, 1873. *"I have just read over my letter and hope no man will get
hold of it."*

182. WHITMAN'S OWN "NOTES ON WALT WHITMAN AS
POET AND PERSON". Autograph Manuscript *"Current Criticism"*, 2 pp., 8vo, about 100 words. With portrait of John Bur-

35

roughs, transcript, and title. Also a copy of "Notes on Walt Whitman, As Poet and Person", by John Burroughs, N. Y., 1871. Together 2 vols., small 4to half brown levant morocco, and 12mo, cloth.

This manuscript is Whitman's review of Burroughs' work.

"It seems as if the debate over Walt Whitman and his Leaves of Grass were not only going to be kept up with more and more animation and earnestness every year, but that the discussion is bringing on an examination (and has so brought already), unwonted among us, of the very bases of the art of poetry . . ."

The copy of Burroughs' book is the Second Edition and contains Dr. Bucke's bookplate; laid in is a clipping containing O'Connor's review of Burroughs' biography of Whitman.

183. "WALT WHITMAN, A STUDY". The Original Autograph Manuscript of *"Walt Whitman, A Study by Richard Maurice Bucke"*, over 400 pp., folio and 4to, with about 1,400 words in the autograph of Walt Whitman. With an etched portrait of the poet by G. Waters, autographed *"Walt Whitman 1880"*; and an autograph manuscript by Walt Whitman mounted under the portrait: *"The disciples of a great master take on themselves the unnecessary duty, and often heroically perform it, of vindicating him"*. Thick small folio, half blue polished morocco.

THE ORIGINAL MANUSCRIPT OF DR. BUCKE'S BIOGRAPHY, which was submitted to the poet and contains his first revisions. Much of the text of this draft was deleted by Whitman and many notes added, though the great bulk of the changes were made in the fair copy which follows this item. Added notes by Whitman include:

"Generally the Coney Island beach, (a very different place then from what it is now-a-days,)".

"The love of women (to use the simple scripture phrase) has of course been and is, in a legitimate sense, one of man's elementary passions."

During the Civil War, when he heard his brother was wounded:

"Under these gloomy circumstances Walt Whitman, at an hour's notice, started for the field of defeat and death, down in Virginia."

The following note by Walt Whitman reveals the source of one of Dr. Bucke's "accidental letters":

"(one of hundreds that of course never dreamed of seeing print, recovered by me by a lucky accident)".

"He had a horror of ceaseless talkers or smart people, and of being questioned."

In this text is a manuscript copy of O'Connor's "The Good Gray Poet" with numerous autograph corrections by the author.

Walt Whitman's Autobiography

THE following eight lots (Numbers 184-191) comprise the manuscript fair copy of Dr. Richard M. Bucke's biography of Walt Whitman, which was sent to the poet for his inspection and revision, with thousands of autograph manuscript corrections and additions by Walt Whitman, and numerous deletions marked by him. This manuscript has been divided into the aforementioned eight sections, each being a chapter or appendix in the published work. Every word in this manuscript was carefully read by the poet, sometimes a whole page added in his handwriting, at times only a phrase, word, or even a punctuation mark added or changed; but there are so many of these emendations that if taken as a whole they would form a good sized autobiography. The source of Dr. Bucke's information was Walt Whitman, and to this information was added that of the poet's friends and enemies, the press, and all other sources Dr. Bucke could draw upon. But all passed through the editorial hands of Walt Whitman.

So complicated is the pagination of all these items that there is no assurance that the manuscripts are absolutely complete.

184. SECTION I. BIOGRAPHICAL AND GENEALOGICAL. Manuscript copy of the Introduction and Chapter I of Dr. Bucke's "Walt Whitman", 63 pp., folio, with about 1,000 words in the handwriting of Walt Whitman. With photograph of Whitman autographed *"Walt Whitman Sept: '87"*; autograph title by Whitman *"Dr. Bucke's Book copy—Sherman & Co: Printers March 1883"*; and title. Small folio, cloth, undyed niger morocco back.

This manuscript begins with a title written by Walt Whitman:

"Biographical Sketch—The poet in 1880—personal &c. His conversation. Appendix.—The Good Gray Poet, reprinted from the pamphlet of 1866—with an introductory letter (1883) written for this volume by William D. O'Connor."

One sheet of the genealogical chart is signed *"Walt Whitman"* and there are numerous corrections in his handwriting. A note in autograph in his biography reads:

"At home, through infancy and boyhood he was called 'Walt' to distinguish him from his father 'Walter', and the short name has always been used for him by his relatives and friends".

One page relating to his political activities is largely in autograph, and the description of writing "Leaves of Grass" is profusely annotated, one of the interlineations reading:

"Certainly no book was ever more directly written from living impulses and impromptu sights, and less in the abstract."

[Description concluded on page 68; see illustration]

306

25

¶ (I think too (twenty third year, or thereabout) along in his twenty-fifth or sixth year)

At one time he became quite a speaker at the Democratic mass-meetings. He spoke in New York city and down at country gatherings on Long Island. He was quite popular at Jamaica, and in Queens county. (He had been there a student at the Academy when a boy lad.)

run in

(in Brooklyn and New York 1840-55)

Though he took no strenuous personal part in the "politics" — in the city, state and national elections — he watched their progress carefully, sometimes aided in the nomination of candidates, generally voted at the municipal elections, and always at the Congressional and + Presidential ones. In the latter the votes of his younger years were cast for Van Buren, Polk, and for Hale, the "free soil" candidates and of later years Lincoln, Grant and Garfield.

as it is in fact.

¶ But Though all this practical tumultuous ^varied and generally outdoor was enjoyment to Walt Whitman, there had been there was in the years of his young maturity one supreme enjoyment, the Italian opera. And the climax of the opera to him was the singing of the famous contralto Albони. It was during the time of which I am now speaking, that she came to New York, (see note on future page) and he did not miss hearing her one single night ^run in

[NUMBER 184]

307

When Dr. Bucke remarks about the humor of the poet, Whitman writes:
"I believe it has been assumed by the critics that Mr. Whitman has not humor. There could not be a greater mistake".

In the reminiscences of Miss Helen Price, Whitman introduced a note:
"It was the society of my mother that was certainly Walt Whitman's greatest attraction to our house". And again in the same letter: *"It was in her friend-ship and in this woman's circle—a mother and two daughters that Mr. Whit-man passed not a few of his leisure hours, during all those years".* (See Number 181.)

There are many autograph interlineations in the descriptions of war and hospital days, in the account of Whitman's dismissal from his government position by James Harlan and the writing of "The Good Gray Poet"; also in the last four pages containing an account of his first stroke of paralysis.

185. "CHAPTER II. THE POET IN 1880—PERSONNEL" [*sic*]. Manuscript copy of Chapter II of Dr. Bucke's Biography of Walt Whitman, 14 pp., folio, with autograph manuscript interlineations by Walt Whitman, about 550 words. With portrait and title. Small folio, cloth, red niger morocco back.

30

Every paragraph in this chapter has numerous autograph alterations by the poet. These interlineations are quoted in italics.

"This chapter *has been mainly* written while Walt Whitman *visited at the house of* the writer *in Canada*, or while *he and I were* travelling together through the Provinces of Ontario or Quebec, or on *Lake Erie or* the St. Lawrence . . . *First, as to his personal appearance, noted at the time."*

"He had a way of singing, generally in an undertone, wherever he was or whatever he was doing when alone. You would hear him the first thing in the morning while he was taking his bath and dressing (*he would then perhaps sing out in full, ballads, or martial songs*)—and a large part of the time that he *sauntered outdoors during the day* he sang, usually tunes without words, *or a formless recitative.* Sometimes he would recite poetry, generally I think from Shakespeare *or* Homer, once in a while from Bryant *or others. His way of rendering poetry was peculiar but effective . . ."*

"As there are those who instinctively love him, so there are others *here and there*, who instinctively *dislike him. The furious assaults of the press during twenty-five years, the disgraceful action of Secretary Harlan in 1864, the continuous refusal of publishers to publish his poems, and of booksellers to sell them, the legal threats in 1881 of the Massachusetts Attorney General, voiced by Boston District Attorney Stevens, of Osgood & Co.,—persecution by the wretched Anthony Comstock and his pitiful 'Society for the Suppres-sion of Vice'—with the prevalent doubt and freezing coldness of the literary classes and organs, up to this hour, are fitting outcomes and illustrations of that other side."*

308

186. "CHAPTER III. CONVERSATION". Manuscript copy of Chapter III of Dr. Bucke's Biography of Walt Whitman, 15 pp., folio, with about 550 words in the poet's autograph. With portrait and title. Small folio, cloth, blue niger morocco back.

50

The manuscript additions are unusually extensive in this section, but only three are quoted. The last two were deleted in Dr. Bucke's printed biography.

"One little story was of an old Broadway driver, who, being interogated about a certain unpopular new-comer, answered with a grin, 'O he's one o' them pie-eaters from Connecticut'."

THE NEW LITERATURE

"He said one day that he considered the most distinguishing feature of his own poetry to be 'its modernness, the taking up in their own spirit of all that *specially* differentiates our era from others, *particularly* our democratic tendencies'. Another feature he said was its American nativity, that the whole of Leaves of Grass is autochthonous, the first utterance which puts into literature, with decision the native United States, not only in its practical, but in its social and political aspects. That this was done, not in an apologetic sense, but always as taking it for granted that our democratic society *is the centre and standard of all, especially the future—and that to produce it has been the principal reason for being of all the past.*"

"Though I know he is very fond of the best music and familiar with it, and has been so from his earliest years, and that the fondness has entered from the first into the spirit and letter of his poems, and colored them, I do not know whether or not he can be said to sing well."

187. "APPENDIX TO PART I". Manuscript copy of the Appendix to Part I of Dr. Bucke's Biography of Walt Whitman, 140 pp., folio and 4to, with the title-page and about 150 words in the autograph of Walt Whitman, and 20 pages in the autograph of William D. O'Connor. Small folio, cloth, brown levant morocco back.

25

This appendix contains William D. O'Connor's "The Good Gray Poet" and an introductory letter to "The Good Gray Poet" written especially for this work. At the end is a letterpress copy of O'Connor's comment on the suppression of "Leaves of Grass", with an autograph manuscript heading in red ink by Whitman: *"Copy for Dr. Bucke's Walt Whitman. Let this follow immediately after O'Connor's Good Gray Poet".*

WALT WHITMAN'S OWN HISTORY OF
"LEAVES OF GRASS"

188. HISTORY OF "LEAVES OF GRASS". Manuscript copy of Part II, Chapter I, of Dr. Bucke's Biography of Walt Whitman, 31 pp., folio, with about 500 words in the autograph of Walt Whitman. With portrait and title. Small folio, cloth, green niger morocco back.

70

This is certainly Walt Whitman's own history of "Leaves of Grass", for besides the extensive additions in his own handwriting are the far more important deletions of Dr. Bucke's account. Nearly the whole of the first page of the manuscript is suppressed in the printed version, and yet this suppressed portion concerns the all-important change in Whitman's life that took place about 1850.

"In the appendix to 'Specimen Days and Collect' we have enough of his earliest *composition* to enable us to judge of its quality. What strikes me as being the most remarkable thing about it is its enormous distance from the *work* that followed so soon upon it. Even the antecedent verse (except perhaps "Blood-Money") gives no intimation of the marvellous mental qualities that were soon to find a characteristic expression."

After thoroughly editing Dr. Bucke's account of Emerson's letter praising "Leaves of Grass", Whitman writes:

"It may be mentioned here that vastly as the two men, R. W. Emerson and Walt Whitman, differ in the outward show of their expression, there are competent scholars who accept both equally, and use them to complement each other."

"DRUM TAPS" AND LINCOLN

"In 1865 Walt Whitman published 'Drum Taps'—poems composed on battlefields, in hospitals, or on the march, among the sights and surroundings of the war, saturated with the spirit and mournful tragedies of that time,—including, in a supplement, 'When Lilacs last in the Door-yard bloom'd', commemorating the death of President Lincoln".

In 1881 and 1882 came the revision and suppression of "Leaves of Grass". On the verso of one leaf of this manuscript is a copy of the official letter by the district attorney suggesting a long list of suppressions to be made in "Leaves of Grass". To this list Dr. Bucke added a note, suppressed in the printed work: "It is beyond doubt that for all time to come these very passages will be selected by the most enlightened readers, of both sexes, as the surest proof of the stainless purity of the man who wrote this chastest of all books."

William D. O'Connor's article on the suppression of "Leaves of Grass" is pasted in as a part of the text, and as a preface to this article Walt Whitman wrote:

"There is an interior history of the persons, and their animus, behind the scenes, in Boston, who egged on Messrs. Marston and Stevens, which has not yet come to the light—but may, some day.

"After such plain narration of the facts, perhaps the keenest and most deserved comment upon this whole transaction (it was fitting that the one who attended to Hon. Mr. Harlan in 1865-'6, should also sum up the Marston-Stevens-Osgood affair in 1882,) is a letter by William D. O'Connor printed in the 'New York Tribune' of May 25, 1882, from which the following are extracts".

After the clipping Whitman writes:

"The Marston-Stevens-Osgood assault however, instead of bringing about the result intended (a suppression of 'Leaves of Grass',) immediately produced quite the contrary effect. The book was taken up by a Philadelphia house, Rees Welsh & Co., to whose miscellaneous business David McKay succeeded, and the latter is now publisher both of the completed poems and of the late prose work 'Specimen Days'. Of 'Leaves of Grass' the first Philadelphia edition, (without the omission of a line or word,) was ready latter part of September, 1882, and all sold in one day . . ."

[See illustration]

like thinking my tasks, and visiting New York to pay
you my respects

R W Emerson

This letter was eventually published,
(at first refused by Walt Whitman, but at
second pressing application he
consented) at the request of Chas A Dana
then managing editor of the "New York
Tribune." Though it could not arrest, it did good service in partially
offsetting the tide of adverse feeling and opinion which
set in against "Leaves of Grass." Walt Whitman
has since been severely censured for printing the letter
a so-called private communication of opinion, not
intended for the public. In answer to this, he
besides that there is no proof that the letter was meant to
be private, the editor of the "Tribune", who
was a personal friend of Walt Whitman
and Mr Emerson, would probably have been
a judge in such matters, and he sought it for the
columns of his paper, as legitimate and proper to both parties

¶ The next year, 1856, the second edition of Leaves of Grass
was published by Fowler and Wells, 308 Broadway N.Y.,
but the firm did not put its name on the title-page. The
volume is a small 16 mo. of 384 pages. The title page
contains the same as that of the first edition,
the only difference being that 1856 is substituted for 1855.
The same miniature engraving of the author, as that in the first
edition is used. The words Leaves of Grass are
the page heading throughout that part of the volume
which contains the poems and this gen. title, each
poem in this edition has a name, but in n. instances exactly
the same as it bears in later issues. The total
number of poems in this edition is thirty two. The twenty
new poems are (giving them as before the names they bear
in the edition dated 1840)

[NUMBER 188]

311

WITH WHOLE PAGES ADDED OR DELETED
BY WHITMAN

189. "CHAPTER II. ANALYSIS OF POEMS, &c." Manuscript copy of Part II, Chapter II, of Dr. Bucke's Biography of Walt Whitman, 33 pp., folio and 8vo, with about 600 words in the autograph of Walt Whitman. With portrait and title. Small folio, cloth, orange niger morocco back.

In this important section of the work Whitman has added or deleted whole pages. In the analysis of his poems he was exceedingly careful, and some of his comments on published criticisms had a sting. One critic writes:

"Elsewhere he speaks of the sick, sick dread of unreturned friendship, of the comrade's kiss, the arm round the neck—but he speaks to sticks and stones; the emotion does not exist in us, and the language of his evangel-poems appears simply disgusting."

To this Whitman replies:

"Yes 'disgusting' to fops and artificial scholars and prim gentlemen of the clubs, but sane, heroic, full-blooded natural men will find in it the deepest God-implanted voice of their hearts."

[See illustration]

$235\frac{1}{2}$

I would also say a few preparatory words about the newness Morris

¶ I might say here

To say only a preparatory word or two about the absence of ordinary rhyme, or tune in Walt Whitman's work. The question cannot be treated without a long statement and many premises. Readers used to the exquisite verbal melody of Tennyson and Longfellow may well wince at first at entering on Leaves of Grass. So does the invalid used to artificial warmth and softness indoors, or any well person, wince at the sea and gale and mountain steeps. But the rich, broad rugged rhythm and inimitable interior music of Leaves of Grass need not be argued for or defended to any real tone-artist. Here is the testimony on this point, take in below further from a lady a musician and art-writer Mrs. Fanny Raymond Ritter, wife of Music-Professor Ritter of Vassar College:

next is $235\frac{3}{4}$

It has already been told how, during the gestation of the poems, the author was saturated, for years, with the rendering, by the best vocalists and performers, of the best operas and oratorios.

[NUMBER 189]

313

190. "CHAPTER III. ANALYSIS CONTINUED". Manuscript copy of Part II, Chapter III, of Dr. Bucke's Biography of Walt Whitman, 19 pp., folio, with about 825 words in the autograph of Walt Whitman, and several notes in the autograph of Dr. Bucke. With photograph bearing the autograph *"Walt Whitman Sept: '87"*, printed version of this chapter and title. Small folio, half green niger morocco.

Nearly a half of this chapter is rewritten or changed, so many are the deletions and additions, including long marginal notes by Whitman and nearly a whole page inserted.

One note, written and then deleted by Whitman himself, is of importance, for he comments on America's imitation of old world authors.

"Are the United States really a success on any but lower grounds? Is there not, to their heart-action and blood-circulation to-day, a profound danger, a pervading lack of something without which their richest and amplest fruits will inevitably turn to ashes? It is in response to such inquiry—it is to supply such deficiency, (or rather to suggest the means of every man supplying it within himself and as part of himself)—that I consider the output of Walt Whitman's life and these poems to be so unspeakably important."

Another note reads:

"He alone illustrates the sublime reality and ideality of that verse of Genius, how God, after His entire Creation looked forth,'and pronounced it all good'."

On another margin is pasted a manuscript note by Whitman:

"The London 'Nineteenth Century' (December, 1882) in the course of an article on Walt Whitman, says 'he has a power of passionate expression, of strong and simple utterance of the deepest tones of grief, which is almost or altogether without its counterpart in the world'."

[See illustration]

261ᵗ (foot note — *all this leaf* small type nonpareil)

✻ The London "Times" (June. 1878.) in an article on the death of William Cullen Bryant takes for its main theme, this excessive *imitativeness* ⟨of American poets, literature⟩ and want of nativity —adding "Unless Walt Whitman is to be reckoned among the poets, American verse, from its earliest to its latest stages, seems an exotic, with an exuberance of gorgeous blossom, but no principle of reproduction." The same English journal *the same paper,* (March 25. 1882) in a long editorial on the death of Longfellow ⟨continues in a similar strain,⟩ ("we are not forgetting his 'Hiawatha' when we say that he might have written his best poems with as much local fitness in our own Cambridge as in its namesake across the Atlantic;") and sulkily adds : "

We are told that in Walt Whitman's rough, barbaric, untoned lines, full of questionable morality, and unfettered by rhyme, is the nucleus of the literature of the future. That may be so, and the Leaves of Grass may prove, as is predicted, the foundation of a real American literature, which will mirror the peculiarities of the life of that continent, and which will attempt to present no false ideal. Yet we shall be surprised if the new school, with its dead set towards ugliness, and its morbid turn for the bad sides of nature, will draw people wholly away from the stainless pages, rich in garnered wealth of fancy and allusions, and the sunny pictures, which are to be found in the books of the poet who has just died. "

[NUMBER 190]

WITH FOUR PAGES ALMOST ENTIRELY IN
WHITMAN'S AUTOGRAPH

191. "APPENDIX TO PART II." Autograph Manuscripts, Manuscript Copy, and Clippings forming the Appendix to Part II of Dr. Bucke's Biography of Walt Whitman, with over 1,200 words in the autograph of Walt Whitman, and several pages in the autograph of Dr. Bucke. 68 pp., folio and 4to. With photograph signed *"Walt Whitman* 1879", and title. Small folio, half orange niger morocco.

55⁻

The first four pages of this manuscript are nearly all in the handwriting of Walt Whitman, and one page is signed eight times in the text. Most of the clippings have titles and notes by Whitman.

The first of the clippings is Whitman's own review of the first edition of "Leaves of Grass" over which he has written *"From the Brooklyn 'Daily Times', Sept. 29, 1855"*; this, with many others in this volume, Whitman supplied to Dr. Bucke from his scrapbooks for this biography.

"Appendix to Part II. To recover what was distinctly said of any important past event or person at the time of his or its advent—what the wise ones had to say or predict—would it not indeed afford lessons of the deepest, sometimes of an unquestionably co[s]mic significance?"

[See illustration]

WITH A LOCK OF WHITMAN'S HAIR

192. PERSONAL APPEARANCE. 1881. Autograph Manuscript by Whitman, 1 p., folio, about 125 words. Framed with portrait signed by Whitman in 1872; and a lock of Whitman's hair, authenticated by Dr. Bucke: *"a piece of Walt Whitman's hair cut off by myself at Camden 20th July 1886 R. M. Bucke."*

25⁻

Written for Dr. Bucke's biography of Whitman.

"His large figure, his red face, his copious beard, his loose and free attire, his rolling and unusually ample collar, without neck-tie and always wide open at the throat, all meet, at times (and not so seldom either) with jeers and explosive laughter."

193. CHARACTER OF WALT WHITMAN. 1881. Autograph Manuscript by Whitman, signed in the text, 1 p., 4to, about 140 words. Framed with portrait, inscribed *"Walt Whitman, London Canada Sept 22—1880"*.

25⁻

Written for Dr. Bucke's biography of Walt Whitman.

"There are two natures in Walt Whitman. The one is of immense suavity, self-control, a mysticism like the occasional fits of Socrates, and a pervading Christ-like benevolence, tenderness, and sympathy."

all this Appendix (pages 278 to
346) in Brevier solid
— except where marked nonp.
or brev leaded

Appendix
to Part II

To recover what was distinctly said of
any important past event or person, at the time of
his or its advent — what the wise ones had
to say or predict, would it not indeed afford some
deep longer and suggestions of the deepest, sometimes of
unquestionable event, significance?

Judgements formed of men by their
contemporaries have a certain value apart from their
individual truth or falsity, for it was true at least
that such things were thought of the man.
Considered in this way, the opinions about Walt
Whitman have a value, and as I think a great value,
in the estimation of his character. Of
very few that ever lived have such extreme and
diverse opinions been held, and held with such persistency
and intensity of conviction. Few have been
more vehemently abused both in and out of print, and
certainly no man of modern times has been given any
thing like the rank that has been accorded to
Walt Whitman by certain of his contemporaries.

At any rate there is the refracted light — and
future ages may estimate no more powerful one — which
a majority of the criticisms of the XIX th Century Leaves of Grass now
the criticisers themselves and the society and
times whose impressions they utter

[NUMBER 191]

194. LIFE AND WORK. 1881. Autograph Manuscript by Whitman, signed in the text, 1 p., large folio, about 215 words. Framed with signed portrait, dated September 1887.

30

Written for Dr. Bucke's biography of Walt Whitman.

"Receiving the traditions of Washington from men who had seen and talked with that great chieftan . . . direct memories of . . . Jefferson, Adams, Paine and Hamilton, saturating as it were his early years—he brings on and connects all that receding time with the civil war of 1861-'65—with the persons and events of our own age—with Lincoln, Grant, Sherman, Lee . . ."

"Until a long period elapses few will know what the pages of Leaves of Grass bestow on America . . ."

195. THE POET OF DEMOCRACY. 1881. Autograph Manuscript by Whitman, signed in the text, 1 p., folio, about 238 words. Framed with portrait, inscribed *"Walt Whitman Sept: '87"*.

25

Written for Dr. Bucke's biography of Walt Whitman.

"Was it not time one should arise to show that a few selected warriors and heroes of the past, even the gods, have not monopolized and devoured (nay have hardly entered into) the grandeur of the Universe, or of life and action, or of poems? arise to 'shake out' for common readers, farmers, mechanics, laborers, 'carols stronger and haughtier than have ever yet been heard upon the earth'? Well did Thoreau, after reading and visiting Walt Whitman, hit the centre of the matter by exclaiming, 'He is Democracy'."

196. BUCKE, RICHARD M. Walt Whitman. *Portraits and illustrations.* 12mo, original cloth. In a half brown levant morocco box case. Philadelphia: David McKay, 1883

30

FIRST EDITION. THE AUTHOR'S OWN COPY, WITH HIS BOOKPLATE. WITH THE AUTOGRAPH OF WALT WHITMAN ON A FLY-LEAF.

Laid in is an autograph document by Walt Whitman, signed by David McKay, publisher of the above work:

"Philadelphia Dec. 5 1883 To prevent any mistakes it is distinctly understood, as far I am concerned, that the electrotype plates of a book, Walt Whitman 236 pages, now at Sherman's printing office, are the sole property of Dr. Richard M. Bucke, of London, Canada. David McKay".

Contemporary Opinion of Walt Whitman

PROBABLY THE LARGEST COLLECTION OF CLIPPINGS BY AND ABOUT THE POET

THE FIRST APPEARANCE IN PRINT OF MANY OF
HIS POEMS AND ESSAYS, TOGETHER WITH
CRITICAL REVIEWS, CONTROVERSIES
AND INTERVIEWS

197. SCRAPBOOKS Containing about 2,000 clippings from Magazines and Newspapers Published Throughout the Civilized World. Mounted in 3 vols., folio, half roan; covers worn. 1859 to 1896.

220—

DEITY OR FIEND. There was no half way between the viewpoints of the adherents of Whitman and those of his adversaries. To the former he was godlike in mind and body, and in his inspired interpretation of life and nature; to the latter he was all that was base and depraved, and his writings were either meaningless or vile and blasphemous.

However, through this vast mass of his own poems and essays with many parodies thereon, the biographical sketches, the criticisms by ardent admirers and fervid antagonists, the opinions of the most famous litterateurs and scientists throughout the civilized world, and last but not least the more mature opinions expressed in the obituaries in 1892, one fact predominates: Walt Whitman had founded a new literature, an American literature, be it good or bad. Critics, authors, scientists, all sought in vain for a parallel, searching the literature of the world from the Bible on down through Greek, Roman, English, German, and American authors, sometimes finding a slight similarity, especially to the Bible, but each acknowledging that the poetry of Walt Whitman was different from all, some judging it the worst and others considering it the most sublime of all.

These scrapbooks were made up by Dr. Bucke, the first two volumes containing some of Whitman's own clippings added to those gathered by Dr. Bucke; the third volume contains practically every obituary notice of Whitman published in the United States and Canada, with a few of European origin.

THE FIRST APPEARANCE IN PRINT OF MANY WHITMAN
POEMS AND ESSAYS

Of Whitman's own writings there are nearly a hundred poems and essays as they first appeared in newspapers and magazines, most of which were afterwards revised and published in "Leaves of Grass", "Specimen Days" and other works. A few were never republished. Nearly forty short poems were clipped from issues of "The New York Herald" between 1887 and May, 1888; "After All not to Create Only" was clipped from seven different publications in 1871; six numbers of "How I get around at 60, and take Notes" appeared in "The Critic" in 1881-2; a few of the others in the collection are "New Year's Day 1848", copied by the New York "Home Journal" from a lady's album; "A Carol of Harvest for 1867"; "The Broadway Pageant", 1869; "The Singer in Prison", 1869; "Only Crossing the Delaware", 1879; "Emerson's Books (the Shadow of them)", 1880; "By Emerson's Grave", 1882; "The Dead Tenor", 1884; "The Old Bowery", 1885; "A Thought on Shakespeare", 1886; "How I made a Book", 1886.

The reviews, favorable and unfavorable, cover all the works of Whitman from 1860 to his death, as well as the biographies and works about the poet by

W. D. O'Connor, John Burroughs, Dr. Bucke, T. W. Rolleston (a German critic), Robert G. Ingersoll, and others.

The large number of reports of personal interviews with "the good gray poet" and of reminiscences of his life and actions would make a volume that would probably portray the personal character of Whitman more truly than any work hitherto published. The accounts came from all classes; from boyhood friends, stage drivers, boatmen, patients in the hospitals, famous travellers, authors, and even critics.

The controversial articles are numerous, especially dating from the period after "Leaves of Grass" was suppressed in Massachusetts in 1882, with the reviewers leading the attack and strongly supported by the clergy. The defense, though small in number, included the powerful pens of Emerson, Rossetti, Swinburne (at first), the fiery O'Connor, and the never-ceasing Dr. Bucke.

The death of Whitman in 1892 again aroused the slumbering controversy, and in the weeks that followed nearly every hamlet, town, and city in the United States and Canada took sides for or against his work. The clergy and small-town newspapers were usually found denouncing Whitman in unmeasured terms; but the era of prudery was passing and truly literary men and women were beginning to think in terms of the future and to recognize that, whether they agreed with Whitman or not, he had founded a new literature.

NO BETTER PORTRAYAL OF THE CONTEMPORARY OPINION OF THE LIFE AND WORKS OF WALT WHITMAN CAN BE FOUND THAN IN THIS MASS OF CLIPPINGS FROM NEWSPAPERS OF ALL KINDS AND POLICIES.

The Second Preparatory Period

THE close of the Civil War found Whitman in a position where he could devote more time to writing and to study, and again came the old urge to prepare and deliver lectures. He outlined course after course of lectures and drafted a few, but, as before, it was easy to turn the lectures into poems or essays, and in most cases this was the final result. In this division (Numbers 198-208) are found outlines, lectures, suggestions, and poems preparatory to his mature work.

198. LECTURES. 1867. Autograph Manuscript *"List of things recognized by my lectures"*, 1 p., tall narrow folio, about 185 words. With portrait, transcript, and title. Folio, cloth, niger morocco back.

12⁵⁰

> "*I recognize . . . the idea that the common American mechanic, farmer, sailor, &c. is just as eligible as any to the highest ideal of dignity, perfection, and knowledge . . .*"

199. PREPARATION. 1868. Autograph Manuscript *"Outlines of lecture"*, 1 p., 4to, about 175 words, in pencil. With title. 4to, half blue niger morocco.

17⁵⁰

> "*First of all prepare for study by the following self-teaching exercises— Abstract yourself from this book,—realize where you are at present located,— the point you stand, that is now to you the centre of all. Look up, think of space stretching out . . .*"

200. DEMOCRACY. 1858-1872. Four Autograph Manuscripts, 4 pp., small 4to to 12mo, about 125 words. With title. Small 4to, cloth, niger morocco back.

12⁵⁰

Four suggestions for lectures on democracy.

"Come down strong on the literary, artistic, theologic and philanthropic coteries of these States . . ."

"I say this nation makes as great use of shallow Presidents as of it[s] brave and just Washington, or its wise Jefferson."

201. NOTES. 1858-1881. Twenty-two Autograph Manuscripts, 22 pp., 8vo and smaller, about 350 words. With an autograph title inserted: *"Glimpses of Walt Whitman from 1877 to '87 excerpted at the time"*, portrait and title. Small folio, half green niger morocco.

20

This collection contains three leaves from Whitman's notebooks relating to his *"New York Visit"*, June 13-25, 1878; his Canadian trip in 1880, and another in the same year containing miscellaneous notes, one about Charles Dickens. A note dated 1879 relates to the Mercantile Library in St. Louis, and others relate to the honesty of public officials in Washington, *"Kossuth in America in 1851"*; Victor Hugo, Modena the Italian tragedian, the beauty of human features, Boccaccio and Dante, *"The ruins in North America"*, the human voice, and others.

Whitman's Poetic Aspirations

IN the five following lots (Numbers 202-206) the ideas, some afterwards developed into poems and some too vast in scope for even Whitman to do more than suggest, outline the grandeur of his poetic vision, the minuteness of his poetic detail, and all the poetic aspirations of youth, manhood, and old age.

202. THE GREAT POET AND THE GREAT POEM. Five Autograph Manuscripts, 5 pp., small 4to to 24mo, about 110 words. With portrait and title. Small 4to, cloth, blue niger morocco back.

20

"The greatest poems may not be immediately fully understood by outsiders any more than astronomy or engineering may . . ."

"The Poetry of other lands lies in the past—what they have been. The Poetry of America lies in the future . . ."

"Health does not tell any more in the body, than it tells in literature. Which is the poem, or any book, that is not diseased?—(If perfect health appear in a poem, or any book, it propagates itself a great while). . . ."

203. POETIC SUGGESTIONS. 1858-1888. Fourteen Autograph Manuscripts, 14 pp., 4to and smaller, about 185 words. 4to, cloth, green niger morocco back.

20

Including: *"Theory of a cluster of Poems . . . Adam as a central figure and type"*; *"A poem which more familiarly addresses those who will, in future ages understand me . . ."*; *"Poem of Husband . . . Poem of Marriage"*; *"Religious Canticles"*; *"Secrets—Secreta"*; *"Companions"*; *"Poem of Young*

Men"; "Poem as in rapt and prophetic vision—intimating—the Future of America"; "Poem ante-dating, anticipating, prophecying"; "of Death—the song of Immortality and Ensemble"; and others.

204. POETIC VISION. 1858-1868. Fourteen Autograph Manuscripts, 14 pp., 4to and smaller, about 150 words. Portrait and title. 4to, cloth, green niger morocco back.

27⁵⁰

This collection contains complete outlines for poems, suggestions for poems, and examples in verse.

"The most Jubilant Triumphant Poem"; "Poem of a proud, daring joyous expression—for Manhattan island! Bully for you, Manhattan!"; "Poem of the Black person"; "Poem. There can be no greatest and sublimest character without having passed through sin"; "Poem of Poets";

*"National hymns, real American music,
The master's words, arrogant, fluent, final, severe."*

"Poem of the Devil counteractive of the common idea of Satan"; "Poem of Sadness . . . Sobs of the tempest, sobs of the voice"; "Drops of my Blood"; and others.

205. WHITMAN'S IDEAL WOMAN. 1858-1880. Thirteen Autograph Manuscripts, 13 pp., 4to and smaller, about 190 words. With portrait and title. 4to, cloth, green niger morocco back.

27⁵⁰

In this collection are eight manuscript outlines and suggestions for poems on Whitman's ideal woman and her attributes.

"Poem illustrative of the Woman under the 'new dispensation' . . . a woman is to be able to ride, swim, run, resist, advance, refuse, shoot, defend herself, sail a boat, hunt, rebel,—just as much as a man . . ."

"Mothers precede all"; "in Poems bring in the idea and term of Mother—the idea of the mother with numerous children—all, great and small, old and young, equal in her eyes—as the identity of America"; "In the Song of Kisses"; "Poem of Names"; "Manhattan, go in!"; "A City Walk";

"My two theses—animal & spiritual—became gradually fused in Leaves of Grass—runs through all the poems & gives color to the whole."

206. POEMS AND SUGGESTIONS. 1856-1870. Fifteen Autograph Manuscripts, 15 pp., 4to and smaller, about 220 words. With title. 4to, cloth, green niger morocco back.

25—

This collection contains poems, suggestions for poems, and lists of words to be used in poems. Among them is *"Shadows"*, a poem about Broadway; and the outline of a poem on suffering:

"That only when sex is properly treated, talked, avowed, accepted, will the woman be equal with the man . . ."

*"A breath to American air
Remembrance for a breed of full-sized young men and women."*

207. "THOUGHT OF THAT TO COME". 1861. Autograph Manuscript Poem, 1 p., 4to, about 75 words. Written on the back of a proof sheet of "Leaves of Grass", probably the edition of 1860. With title. 4to, cloth, white pigskin back.

10—

> "*Thought*
> *Of that to come—of experiences—of vast unknown matter and qualities lying*
> *inert—much doubtless more than known matter and qualities. . . ."*

208. "ALL THAT WE ARE". Autograph Manuscript Poem, 1 p., folio, about 175 words. With title. Small folio, cloth, undyed niger morocco back.

17⁵⁰—

> "*All that we are—the solid and liquid we are—we have advanced to,*
> *We have advanced from what was our cohesion and formation,*
> *We advance to just as much more, and just as much more.*
> *Time suffices, and the laws suffice."*

Maturity and Fame

IN the years from 1867 to 1880 "Leaves of Grass" assumed a well-rounded form, and though many subjects were yet to be treated and added, the outline was completed. These years brought fame to the author, especially in Europe, and new friends and enemies; but they also brought the third great change in Whitman's life: they brought physical suffering. Hospital days had overstrained the giant, and the occasional head-troubles which began during the war resulted in a paralytic stroke in January, 1873. This was followed by other slight strokes, and then the crushing blow caused by the death of his mother; and it was not until the latter part of 1879 that the poet recovered, to a certain extent, his mental and physical health. This period left a definite mark upon his writings; there was less intolerance, though he still maintained all of his early opinions, and he could even treat his critics with equanimity.

209. WALT TO HIS MOTHER. 1867. A. L., 2 pp., 4to, about 330 words. Washington, n.d. To his mother. In a board folder.

35—

An especially interesting rough draft or first leaf of a letter telling of O'Connor's report of his visit to Mrs. Whitman, advising Jeff about accepting an offer to take charge of the St. Louis waterworks, etc.

> "*Mother I send you the Harper's Weekly, with the picture of Abraham Lincoln & the Drummer Boy—I think it is tip top. . . . I was down at the hospital Sunday afternoon—the young man that had delirium tremens, that prayed so long, has got quite well—his prayers seemed to be answered,—at any rate, he is well & gone back to duty—while several others with the same complaint, are lying there not yet recovered."*

210. WASHINGTON FRIENDS. Rough draft A. L., 2 pp., 8vo, about 150 words. October 4 [1868]. To friends in the Attorney General's office. With transcript. 8vo, boards.

7 50

The letter alludes to the Grant-Colfax campaign, and continues:

"Did you see John Swinton's warm ¶ about my illustrious self in N. Y. Times, 1st inst.? John seems lately possest with L. of G. as with a demon. I have found two or three others—a Mr. Norton, of Boston—is one. He is an educated man, a Boston metaphysical thinker. Give my best love to John Burroughs . . ."

211. MANHATTAN ISLAND. Two rough draft A. L. on one sheet, 4to, about 525 words. [Brooklyn] October 2 [1868]. To Harry Hurt and Lewy [Brown], both soldiers whom Whitman had helped in the hospitals.

20

Feinberg

"Harry, you would much enjoy going round N. Y. with me, if it were possible, and then how much I should like having you with me. This great city, with all its crowds, and splendor, and Broadway fashion, and women, and amusement, and the river and bay, and shipping, and the magnificent new buildings, and Central Park and 5th Avenue, and the endless processions of private vehicles and the finest teams I ever saw, for miles long of a fine afternoon—altogether they make up a show that I can richly spend a month in enjoying—for a change from my Washington life. I sometimes think I am the particular man who enjoys the show of all these things in N. Y. more than any other mortal—as if it was all got up just for me to observe and study . . . I have marked the place about the Five Points. I went down there myself just for fun . . . I was there two hours—it was instructive but disgusting—I saw one of the handsomest white girls there I ever saw, only about 18—black and white are all intermingled."

"Dear Lewy . . . Tell Johnny Miller there is still a sprinkling of the old Broadway drivers left. Balking Bill, Fred Kelly, Charley McLaughlin, Tom Riley, Prodigal, Sandy, &c. &c. are still here . . ."

212. DEMOCRATIC VISTAS. Autograph Manuscript *"Opening of Preface to Dem. Vistas,"* 5 pp., 12mo and smaller, about 200 words, in pencil. Transcript and title. 12mo, cloth, green niger morocco back.

30

An early draft of a preface for "Democratic Vistas" never published as such, although portions of it were incorporated in the work.

"The central dominant facts and glories of America are always to be found in the mass or bulk of the People."

213. POSTAL RATES. Rough draft A. L., with an autograph manuscript list of references, 6 pp., 4to and small 4to, about 490 words. November 17 [about 1870]. To J. M. Edwards, postmaster at Washington. 4to, half blue niger morocco.

7 50

A request for a revised ruling from the postal department to reduce the rate on *"book manuscripts"*, defining the words and giving dictionary references.

214. DEMOCRATIC VISTAS. 12mo, original pale green wrappers, uncut; cover slightly spotted, small chips in backstrip. In a board folder. Washington, 1871

FIRST EDITION.

15

215. LEAVES OF GRASS. 1871. Autograph Manuscript, 9 pp., 12mo and smaller, about 700 words, in pencil and ink. With a preliminary autograph manuscript note in red pencil by William S. Kennedy, and with transcript and title. 12mo, cloth, green niger morocco back.

35

One of Whitman's own reviews of "Leaves of Grass", doubtless prepared for magazine or newspaper publication.

"No one of the themes generally considered fit for stock or motif for poetry is taken by W. W. for his foundation. No romantic occurence, nor legend, nor plot of mystery, nor sentimentalizing, nor historic personage or event, nor any woven tale of love, ambition, or jealousy is in his work.

"Yet the book is also saturated with active human life, the stir and hum of cities, the noise and show of trades, factories, ships, locomotives—fill page after page; with you move all the practical activity of our aroused land and time . . ."

216. PASSAGE TO INDIA. 12mo, original pale green wrappers, uncut and partially unopened. In a cloth box case.

Washington, 1871

25

FIRST EDITION. From the library of Dr. Richard M. Bucke, with bookplate.

217. PRESENTATION COPY. Leaves of Grass. 12mo, green cloth, uncut; one new end-paper. In a half morocco box case.

Washington, 1872

45

FIRST ISSUE of the 1872 edition. AUTOGRAPH PRESENTATION COPY, inscribed on the fly-leaf: *"Dr. R. M. Bucke from the Author Sept. 7, 1891"*.

218. WALT TO HIS MOTHER. A. L. s. *"Walt"*, 2 pp., 4to, about 340 words, in pencil. [Washington] March 28, 1873. To his mother. 4to, boards.

25

A splendid letter, written a month after his first paralytic stroke and two months before the death of his mother. It demonstrates Whitman's indomitable spirit in his first severe illness.

"The sun shines out bright & cheerful this morning—& in my east window I have a fine healthy rose bush—I see it has got two roses in bloom, & one just budding out . . .

"Still I feel I shall get as well as usual yet, dearest mother—and then I shall surely get—hire or buy or build a little place here, rooms enough to live in for you & Ed and me . . ."

219. PARALYSIS. Autograph Manuscript Memorandum, 1 p., 8vo, about 85 words. June 2, 1874. Giving Dr. Grier's diagnosis of Whitman's physical condition. With an A. L. s. by Dr. William G. Dunkard, July 24, 1873, containing his diagnosis of Whitman's condition; and three prescriptions by Dr. Grier. With transcript and title. 8vo, cloth, brown morocco back.

750

220. WALT WHITMAN TO PETER DOYLE. A Series of Forty-one A. N. s. *"W. W."* on postcards, about 950 words. Camden, January 15 to December 29, 1875. To Peter Doyle. 4to, half green niger morocco.

190

A fine series of short descriptive notes to his young friend Peter Doyle, the street-car conductor who had so tenderly cared for Whitman when he was first striken. These cards were written during the darkest period of Whitman's illness, when it was doubtful whether he would live another year. They describe his condition, the visits of John Burroughs and other friends, and above all his desire to see his friend Peter Doyle.

A PREFACE FOR "TWO RIVULETS"

221. "PREFACE TWO RIVULETS". 1876. Autograph Manuscript, 6 pp., 8vo and 12mo, about 630 words. With transcript and title. Royal 8vo, half blue polished morocco.

70

A preface for "Two Rivulets" not used for that work, though parts of it were incorporated in the preface to the two-volume centennial edition of Whitman's works.

"As ever, all tends to the future—to followings—and they to other followings . . . Of the chants of "Leaves of Grass" I have already, (anterior preface) alluded to their Religious genesis and foundation. Of that book, perhaps the mass is, in a sense, but the layer, the preparation, of indispensible deep soil, out of which and out of which only could come with hardy roots and springy stems the growth more definitely indicated in the present volume . . ."

[See illustration]

222. PREFACE TO "AFTER ALL, NOT TO CREATE ONLY". 1876. Autograph Manuscript, 2 pp., 8vo, about 140 words. With transcript and title. Royal 8vo, cloth, red niger morocco back.

25

Trent at Duke

A preface to "After all, not to Create only", or as it was afterwards called "The Song of the Exposition" which was written in 1871. This preface was published in the centennial edition of 1876.

"Ostensibly to inaugurate an Exposition of this kind on a minor scale—still more to depict the establishment of one of those grand permanent Cluster-Palaces from an Imaginative and Democratic point of view, and to idealize labor was the design of the following Poem . . . My book would indeed be marked by a lacuna if I did not chant this characteristic feature of the Modern, as distinguished from all previous ages . . ."

Eidólons

Preface Two Prefaces p. 12

After the
Waves in
unwilling the Vessel's
waves Wake

Preface.

— & they to other
(to followings) followings

& ever.

All tends to the future—

Is any Thing yet incomplete?
perverse? Time will see to it.
Indeed, what, even of the best,
would be justified by itself alone?
by the Present, alone? Few real.
ize how much they live in the fu.
ture, & how much the world does.
The whole edifice of Man or
State is planned & built for
what points beyond it,
for results of it, & escapes from
it.... Standing on the foundation
& superstructure of the Present,
the basis & bulk, only the Future
rising like pinnacles & gives sig.
nificance to all .... Whence the
sacred & universal law, intertwi.
ning all the rest & without

[NUMBER 221]

223. PREFACE OF 1876. Autograph Manuscript, 1 p., small 4to, about 120 words. Small 4to, boards.

7⁵⁰

"*And so I have put those completed poems in permanent type-form at last.*"

224. "WHITMAN'S POEMS SUMMED UP". 1876. Autograph Manuscript, 4 pp., 8vo and 12mo, about 420 words. With transcript and title. 8vo, half brown levant morocco.

22⁵⁰

"*Whitman's Poems summed up. 'Two Rivulets' joined with 'Leaves of Grass', may be summed up as the result of twenty years labor, & the attempt [to put] into a new unrhymed but rhythmical expression the events, & still more the spirit of those years with all their tremendous developments of war, peace, inventions, science—and the advent of America and republicanism. For such may be called the general aim of this author, although everything in both volumes revolves around the central human personality. The Body and the Soul are one, & in the latter the former is immortal . . .*"

225. "STRIKE & TRAMP QUESTION". 1876-9. Four Autograph Manuscripts and a Manuscript Title: "*Excerpts &c Strike & Tramp question*", with about 25 newspaper and magazine excerpts mainly annotated by Whitman, together about 165 words in manuscript. With portrait and title. Folio, cloth, orange niger morocco back.

17⁵⁰

These memoranda and notes were made in preparation for a lecture which was never completed, though a part was incorporated in the "Collect".

"*I shall only be too happy if these black prophecies & fears can be attributed (as of course they will be,) to my old age and sickness & a growling temper.*"

"*Read the revelations of Boss Tweed (Sept 15-20. '77) of the measureless, indescribable treachery, greediness, putridity of the municipal legis[lature]*".

On the back of one manuscript are directions by Whitman for binding "Two Rivulets".

226. NEW YORK. 1878. Autograph Manuscript, 1 p., 8vo, about 100 words. With transcript and title. 8vo, cloth, white pigskin back.

10—

Describing the view from the top of the Tribune building, where Whitman had gone to read proof.

"*My thoughts of the beauty and amplitude of these bay and river surroundings confirmed. Other thoughts also confirmed—that of a fitter name, for instance—Manahatta—'the place around which there are hurried and joyous waters, continually'—(that's the sense of the old aboriginal word) . . .*"

227. "ENGLISH SPARROWS". 1879. Autograph Manuscript, 3 pp., 12mo, about 200 words, in pencil. With transcript and title. 12mo, full undyed niger morocco, gilt and blind tooled.

20—

A complete sketch written at the home of his friends the Staffords.

"*An old extensive Ivy Vine . . . alive at this moment in its sunny exposure with the darting, flirting, twittering of scores, hundreds of English sparrows . . . Who knows but what there are beings of superior spheres looking on the busy, chattering activity and affectations of man, with the same critical top-loftical air? Echo—Who knows?*)"

228. "GORGEOUS FLOWERS". 1879-1884. Two Autograph Manuscripts, 2 pp., small 4to, about 100 words. With transcript and title. Small 4to, cloth, green niger morocco back.

12

> "*Aug: 9 '79— . . . great sun-flowers bend their tall and stately discs in full bloom in silent salute to the day-orb . . ."*
> "*Sunday Morning. Early May '84 . . . I mark the profuse pink-and-white of the wild honeysuckle, the creamy blossoming of the dog-wood. Delicate smells too—every thing most fragrant, early in the season—odors of the pine and oak and the flowering grape-vines . . ."*

229. CENTRAL PARK. 1879. Autograph Manuscript, 1 p., 4to, about 140 words, in ink and pencil. With a clipping describing Whitman's visit to New York in 1879, and with transcript and title. 4to, cloth, orange niger morocco back.

25

> "*All round this vast Pleasure Ground, has been built a costly, grim, forbidding stone fence, some parts 7 feet high, others lower capped with heavy bevelled rough marble—in my judgment a nuisance, the whole thing . . . The same error in Capitol Hill at Washington—exploiting the designs of ingrain carpets, with sprawling curves and meaningless lines."*

230. DIARY OF THE WESTERN TOUR. 1879. Autograph Manuscript Notes, 12 pp., 4to and smaller, about 500 words. With transcript and title. 4to, half green niger morocco.

35

With somewhat recovered health Whitman made a tour to the West from September to December, 1879, reaching as far as Denver and then turning south through Nevada, and East on the Arkansas river.

These notes relate to Missouri, Kansas, the Rocky Mountains, and nights and days on the Mississippi River. Many were afterwards embodied in "Specimen Days".

> "*How inexpressibly magnificent and ample it is! The Contrast—the alternation! After these easy, peaceful and fertile prairies of a thousand miles area covered in wheat, start of the grandest mountains of the globe, with many a savage cañon, and cloud piercing peaks by hundreds!—and spots of terror and sublimity Dante and Angelo never knew."*
> "*Spectacle of the men lying around in groups on the forward part of the lower deck at night—some asleep some conversing—glare of the fire upon them—some emigrants on their way 'up country'—young fellow and his stout German wife—gruffness of the mate to the boat hands . . ."*

231. "SPIRIT THAT FORM'D THIS SCENE". 1879. Autograph Manuscript Poem, 1 p., 4to, about 70 words. Framed with signed and dated portrait, 1879.

35

This is one of the most popular of Whitman's poems, and was "*Written in Platte Cañon, Colorado*". It is one of the poems in "From Noon to Starry Night".

> "*Spirit that form'd this scene,*
> *These tumbled rock-piles grim and red,*
> *These reckless heaven-ambitious peaks,*
> *These gorges, turbulent-clear streams, this naked freshness."*

329

The Edifice Completed

To Dr. Bucke was due the invigorating influence that pro-
longed the life of the "good gray poet", for in 1880 he took
Whitman to Canada, to new scenes and new people, and for the
rest of his life these scenes and people were pictured in prose and
poetry. This journey and the congenial talks with Dr. Bucke
also inspired the entire revision of Whitman's writings and their
consolidation into the final version of "Leaves of Grass", the
great pyramid of thought that was to permeate all literature, even
as the Bible and Shakespeare illuminated the pages of the world's
literature.

Invigorated by the northern wilds Whitman plunged into the
revision of "Leaves of Grass". One of the most prominent publishers of America was to bring out his next edition, Osgood &
Co. of Boston, publisher for many of the famous New England
authors. For months Whitman revised and rearranged his poems,
and then went to Boston to see his work through the press. Was
it the Boston of New England that influenced Whitman to revise
his picturesque punctuation? to submit to commas and semicolons
in place of the lively dash and exclamation point? There in the
printing office Whitman's whole system of punctuation and capi-
talization was altered, the text was revised, many deletions were
made, and much material was added.

Walt Whitman was to become rich, he was to receive twenty-five
cents royalty for every copy of "Leaves of Grass" that was sold.
About 2,000 copies were reported sold, and then came the crash.
Old New England intolerance would not stand for Whitman's
interpretation of both body and soul, and, rejecting the body,
suppressed "Leaves of Grass". It was a difficult position for
Whitman, who had dreamed of wealth, but, sacrificing his
royalties in exchange for the stereotype plates, he began publishing in Philadelphia. This was Whitman's last great fight, and he
won. "Leaves of Grass" became popular in America, as it had
always been in England, and his followers became legion.

232. DIARY IN CANADA. 1880. Autograph Manuscript, 41 pp.,
4to and smaller, about 1,300 words. June 18 to July 18, 1880.
With excerpt: "Interview with the Author of 'Leaves of Grass' ",

[Description concluded on page 92; see illustration]

[from Sarnia]

A moonlight excursion up
Lake Huron.

June 21, — ~~A moonlight~~
~~excursion up Lake Huron~~
We were to go at 8 p.m. but after
waiting forty minutes for a
music band, which, to my
secret satisfaction didn't come.
and the Hiawatha,
we went off without it.
Point Edward on the Canada
side and Fort Gratiot on the
Michigan. the crossing line
for the Grand Trunk RR and
looking well-alive with lights,
and the sight of shadowy-moving
cars, were quickly passed by our
steamer, pressing through
currents of rapids for a
mile there, very dashy and inspiriting —
and we were soon out on the

[NUMBER 232]

portrait autographed *"Walt Whitman London Sept 22 1880"*, transcript, and title. 4to, half blue polished morocco.

The original manuscript of the first sixteen pages of "Walt Whitman's Diary in Canada", edited by William S. Kennedy, Boston, 1904. It apparently contains all the published material, together with some variant readings and some unpublished notes.

"It is only here in large portions of Canada that wondrous second wind, the Indian summer, attains its amplitude and heavenly perfection—the temperature, the sunny haze, the mellow, rich, delicate, almost flavored air:

"'Enough to live—Enough to merely be'."

WHITMAN'S AUTOGRAPH MANUSCRIPT DIARY AND NOTES ON HIS CANADIAN TRIP

233. DIARY IN CANADA. Autograph Manuscript Diary and Notes, with manuscript title: *"St Lawrence & Saguenay trip July & Aug. 1880"*, 84 pp., 8vo and smaller. About 1,600 words. With three maps and two tables used by Walt Whitman on his trip; six views; portrait (spotted) autographed: *"Walt Whitman London Canada Sept 22 1880"*; transcript; and title. 8vo, half green niger morocco.

75

While containing practically all the material published in "Walt Whitman's Diary in Canada" from p. 16 to the end, as published in 1904, this manuscript also contains many notes omitted from that work, and furthermore contains fragments of prose and poetry on the verso of the leaves that have escaped notice. One picture of Quebec and the province which was omitted is of interest. It was probably written for an interviewer or was one of Whitman's self-advertisements:

"Walt Whitman is at Quebec, delighted with the queer old French city, making leisurely explorations among the old places, the churches, the hilly streets, the citidal, and the environs. He especially admires, all through the province, after passing the mouth of the Ottawa, the perpetual recurrence of pretty towns & villages. For two hundred miles the white clusters are continually repeated, or in groups, nestling in trees and orchards near the water, each with its glistening church spire or tower high in the middle of the town."

[See illustration]

234. CANADIAN LECTURE. 1880. Autograph Manuscript Notes for a Lecture in Canada which was never delivered. 5 pp., 12mo, about 160 words, in pencil. With transcript and title. 12mo, cloth, green niger morocco back.

15

A part of this manuscript was published in the "Extracts" in Kennedy's "Walt Whitman's Diary in Canada".

"Business—not the mere sordid, prodding muck-and-money-raking mania but an immense and noble attribute of man, the occupation of nations and individuals (without which is no happiness)—the progress of the masses—the tie and interchange of all the peoples of the earth."

Canada '80.

Aug 14 – I am writing this on the high balcony of the Asylum at Hamilton (Ontario Canada) – The city is spread in full view before me. (Is there not an escaped patient?) I see a great commotion, Dr W. and several attendants men & women, rushing down the cliff) –

a dark moist lowering forenoon. – balmy air though – wind South-west

Aug 14 – 5½ pm – Arrived back in London a couple of hours ago, all right. Am writing this in my room Dr B's house

[NUMBER 233]

235. "OTTAWA LECTURE". 1880. Autograph Manuscript Notes, 3 pp., 12mo, about 150 words. 8vo, boards.

10 Another lecture contemplated but never delivered.

"For thousands of years in the history of the masses of humanity, why does it seem as if that history was all dominated by one word War."

236. THE TEST OF CIVILIZATION. 1880. Autograph Manuscript, 1 p., 4to, about 80 words, with map of the route of his Canadian trip on verso, both in pencil. With portrait, transcript, and title. Small 4to, cloth.

5 Probably additional paragraphs for one of the preceding lectures.

"It is said, perhaps rather quizzically by my friends that I bring civilization, politics, the topography of a country and even the hydrography, to one final test, the capability of producing, favoring and maintaining a fine crop of children, a magnificent race of men and women."

237. LONDON, ONTARIO. 1880. Autograph Manuscript, 9 pp., 8vo, about 720 words, in pencil. With transcript and title. 8vo, cloth, orange niger morocco back.

15 An extensive description of London, the houses and people, the insane asylum directed by Dr. Bucke, Helmuth College, the produce, etc.

"Then about drinking habits. My observations and goings around here pretty freely indoors and out, note so far a singular scarcity of cases of intemperance; I have seen no drunken man (nor drunken woman)—have run across no besotted or low or filthy quarters of the town either . . . Here for a thousand people at the Insane Asylum, no alcohol-beverage is used—not a pint a week. The head physician, Dr. Bucke, never prescribes it . . ."

238. THE CALLS. 1880. Autograph Manuscript, 3 pp., 8vo, about 190 words. With transcript and title. Small 4to, half red niger morocco.

10 An outline for a poem.

"Poem (subject) ? for recitation something which in each verse shall comprise a call (local & native sea or land American wild) as the country girl (or boy) toward sun-down letting down the bars & calling the cows out of the lot Kush! Kush! Kush!"

One's Self I sing ——————————— 9

As I ponder'd in Silence ——————— "

In Cabin'd ships at Sea ——————— 10

To Foreign Lands ——————————— 11

To a Historian ————————————— "

To thee Old Cause ————————— "

Eidólons ————————————————— 12

For Him I sing ———————————— 14

When I read the Book ——————— "

Beginning my Studies ——————— "

Beginners ————————————————— 15

To the States ————————————— "

On Journeys through the States —— "

To a Certain Cantatrice ————— 16

Me Imperturbe ——————————— "

Savantism ——————————————— "

The Ship Starting ————————— "

I hear America Singing ————— 17

What Place is besieged? ———— "

Still though the One I Sing ——— "

Shut not your Doors ————————— "

21

THE "CONTENTS" OF "LEAVES OF GRASS"
IN WHITMAN'S AUTOGRAPH

[NUMBER 240]

The Final Revision of "Leaves of Grass"

THE following thirty-six lots (Numbers 239-274) contain the final revision of "Leaves of Grass" by the author, preceded by the poet's own account of the surroundings under which it was undertaken. The items are arranged in the order in which they appeared in the edition of 1881-2 published by James R. Osgood & Co. With the exception of four short poems the collection contains the complete text of that edition.

239. THE POET'S STUDY. Autograph Manuscript, 2 pp., 12mo, about 175 words, in pencil. With transcript and title. 12mo, full undyed niger morocco, gilt and blind tooled.

15

"May 13 to 26 '81. Down in the country mostly in the woods—enjoying the early summer, the bird music and the pure air. For interest and occupation, I busy myself three or four hours every day arranging, revising, cohering, here and there slightly rewriting (and sometimes cancelling,) a new edition of L of G complete in one volume. I do the main part of the work out in the wood.—I like to try my pieces by negligent, free, primative Nature, the skies, the sea-shore, the sunshine, the plentiful grass, or dead leaves (as now) under my feet, and the song of some cat-bird, wren, or russet thrush within hearing—like (as now) the half-shadowed tall-columned trees with green leaves and branches in relief against the sky. Such is the library, the study, where (seated on a big log) I have sifted out and given some finishing touches to this edition."

WITH WHITMAN'S INSTRUCTIONS TO THE PRINTERS

240. CONTENTS OF "LEAVES OF GRASS". Autograph Manuscript of the *"Contents"* of "Leaves of Grass", 15 pp., 8vo and 4to, about 1,100 words. With proof title-page marked *"this will do"*; Osgood's circular advertisement of the 1881-2 edition containing the contents; portrait autographed *"Walt Whitman born May 31 1819"*; and title. Small 4to, half undyed niger morocco.

100

On the first page are two autograph notes to the printer, and on the last is written:

"If convenient I wish some of the proof-readers would look carefully over the sheets of "Leaves of Grass" & revise this list of contents."

[See illustration on preceding page]

241. "INSCRIPTIONS". Autograph Manuscript Revisions in the first section of "Leaves of Grass" entitled "Inscriptions". 15 pp., 12mo, with about 130 words in autograph and hundreds of alterations in punctuation. With portrait, list of contents, and title. 12mo, half red niger morocco.

60

The printed text of the edition of 1876 was used for making the revisions for the edition of 1881-2. Besides the several directions to the printer, two titles have been changed, several lines deleted, and some lines added. Among the last are the following:

> "*Thou, Reader.*
> *"Thou, reader throbbest life and pride and love the same*
> *as I,*
> *Therefore for thee the following chants."*

242. "STARTING FROM PAUMANOK". Autograph Manuscript Revision of "Starting from Paumanok". 15 pp., 12mo, with about 60 words in autograph and hundreds of changes in punctuation. With portrait (spotted) signed *"Walt Whitman London Canada Sept 22 1880"*, and title. 12mo, half green niger morocco.

40—

WHITMAN'S AUTOGRAPH MANUSCRIPT REVISION OF "SONG OF MYSELF"

WITH A LOCK OF WHITMAN'S HAIR

243. "SONG OF MYSELF". Autograph Manuscript Revision of *"Song of Myself"*. 68 pp., 12mo, with about 300 words in autograph and thousands of changes in punctuation. With an engraved portrait of the poet on which he has written: *"I own this plate—to face p. 34 of MS"*; an autograph manuscript, about 250 words, in pencil, containing one of the earliest drafts of the beginning of "Song of Myself"; autograph manuscript on a slip: *"The Word is become Flesh"*; a clipping containing one of the first reviews of "Leaves of Grass", 1855; and, in a pocket in the back cover, a lock of Whitman's hair enclosed in a wrapper upon which Dr. Bucke has written *"W. W. hair"*. With title. 12mo, full brown crushed levant morocco, gilt tooled.

225—

A perfect ensemble of material relating to the foundation poem of "Leaves of Grass". To the running headline *"Myself"* which the poet has written on each page in many cases he added *"Whitman"*. The early version of the "Song of Myself" begins:

> *"I am your voice—It was tied in you—In me it begins to talk.*
> *I celebrate myself to celebrate every man and woman alive.*
> *And I say that the soul is not greater than the body,*
> *And I say that the body is not greater than the soul."*

[Description concluded on following page]

On the verso of this sheet is a prose explanation of his writings:

"I do not compose a grand opera with good instrumentation, and parts which you shall sing as I have written them, and whose performance will give fits to the dilletanti, for its elegance and measure . . ."

[See illustration on opposite page]

244. "CHILDREN OF ADAM". Autograph Manuscript Revision of "Children of Adam". 23 pp., 12mo, with about 100 words in autograph and hundreds of changes in punctuation. With portrait, table of contents, and title. 12mo, half green niger morocco.

45⁻

It was this section which caused the suppression of the Boston edition of "Leaves of Grass". Whitman absolutely refused to delete any parts or lines from the "Children of Adam", and though several of the most unrestrained lines were at first deleted in this revision they were restored with a *"stet"*.

245. "CALAMUS". Autograph Manuscript Revision of "Calamus". 24 pp., 12mo, with about 60 words in autograph and hundreds of changes in punctuation. With portrait autographed by Whitman in 1872, table of contents, and title. 12mo, half undyed niger morocco.

25⁻

246. "SALUT AU MONDE". Autograph Manuscript Revision of "Salut au Monde". 13 pp., 12mo, with about 100 words in autograph and hundreds of changes in punctuation. With a rare photograph by Sarony autographed *"Walt Whitman 1879"*, and title. 12mo, half red niger morocco.

40⁻

Some lines were added in manuscript and then deleted, such as:

"Pike's Peak, Mount Lincoln, the curious natural towers and red battlements, tipt by the sun,"

247. "SONG OF THE OPEN ROAD." Autograph Manuscript Revision of the "Song of the Open Road". 12 pp., 12mo, with about 75 words in autograph and hundreds of changes in punctuation. With portrait and title. 12mo, half green niger morocco.

30⁻

This poem contains several added lines and words, and occasional deletions.

248. CROSSING BROOKLYN FERRY. Autograph Manuscript Revision of "Crossing Brooklyn Ferry". 8 pp., 12mo, with about 70 words in autograph and many changes in punctuation. With portrait, view, and title. 12mo, half undyed niger morocco.

27⁵⁰

This famous poem contains two important deletions and a few additions. One of the additions is quoted in italics:

"Refusals, hates, postponements, meanness, laziness, none of these wanting, Was one with the rest, the days and haps of the rest."

34

Song of Myself

1

I CELEBRATE myself *and sing myself.*
And what I assume you shall assume,
For every atom belonging to me as good belongs to
    you.

I loafe and invite my Soul,
I lean and loafe at my ease observing a spear of sum-
    mer grass.

My tongue, every atom of my blood, form'd from this
    soil, this air,
Born here of parents born here from parents the same,
    and their parents the same,
I, *now* thirty years old in perfect health begin,
Hoping to cease not till death.

Creeds and schools in abeyance,
Retiring back a while sufficed at what they are, but
    never forgotten,
I harbor for good or bad—I permit to speak at every
    hazard,
Nature now without check with original energy.

2

Houses and rooms are full of perfumes—the shelves
    are crowded with perfumes,
I breathe the fragrance myself and know it and like it,
The distillation would intoxicate me also, but I shall
    not let it.

249. "SONG OF THE ANSWERER". Autograph Manuscript Revision of *"Song of the Answerer"*. 5 pp., 12mo, with about 40 words in autograph and numerous changes in punctuation. With portrait and title. 12mo, half undyed niger morocco.

20 —

Whitman here changed the title from "The Answerer" to *"Song of the Answerer"*.

250. "OUR OLD FEUILLAGE". Autograph Manuscript Revision of *"Our Old Feuillage"*. 6 pp., 12mo, with about 30 words in autograph and many changes in punctuation. With portrait and title. 12mo, half blue niger morocco.

15 —

Whitman tried three titles before settling on the above, formerly called "American Feuillage".

251. "A SONG OF JOYS". Autograph Manuscript Revision of *"Poem of Joys"*. 10 pp., 12mo, with about 65 words in autograph and many changes in punctuation. With portrait and title. 12mo, half undyed niger morocco.

25 —

Here an entire stanza is deleted, and an interesting line added:
"For not life's joys alone—the joy of death!"

252. SONG OF THE BROAD-AXE. Autograph Manuscript Revision of the "Song of the Broad-Axe". 12 pp., 12mo, with about 50 words in manuscript and many changes in punctuation. With portrait and title. 12mo, half red niger morocco.

37 50

Herein are placed the final touches of the poet to his typically American poem, of which the beginning is described in this catalogue (Number 114). While the punctuation has been changed throughout, only a few words have been added or deleted.

WHITMAN'S REVISION OF ONE OF
HIS GREAT POEMS

253. "AFTER ALL, NOT TO CREATE ONLY". Autograph Manuscript Revision of the "Song of the Exposition" or, as it was first named "After all, not to Create Only". 9 pp., 12mo, with about 150 words in autograph and hundreds of changes in punctuation. With a clipping from the "New York Evening Post" containing one of the first printings of the poem, and title.

80 —

There are many changes in this, one of Whitman's great poems, from the original as delivered. Verses are deleted and added, the poem first compressed and then extended. The first lines are new:
"(Ah, little recks the laborer,
How near his work is holding him to God,
The loving Laborer through space and time.)"

[See illustration]

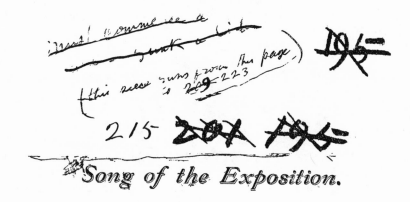

215

Song of the Exposition.

Ah. little recks the laborer,
How near his work is holding him
The Laborer

AFTER all/not to create only, or found only,
But to bring/perhaps from afar/what is already founded,
To give it our own identity, average, limitless, free/
To fill the gross/the torpid bulk/with vital religious fire/
Not to repel or destroy/so much as accept, fuse, rehabili-
tate/
To obey/as well as command/to follow/more than to lead/
These also are the lessons of our New World;
While how little the New/after all/how much the Old
Old World!

[NUMBER 253]

254. SONG OF THE REDWOOD-TREE. Autograph Manuscript Revision of the "Song of the Redwood-Tree". 4 pp., 12mo, with about 20 words in manuscript and many changes in punctuation. With portrait and title. 12mo, half red niger morocco.

12⁵⁰

Ed Naumley.

255. "A SONG FOR OCCUPATIONS". Autograph Manuscript Revision of "Carol of Occupations". 10 pp., 12mo, with about 55 words in autograph and many changes in punctuation. With title. 12mo, half green niger morocco.

17⁵⁰

256. "A SONG OF THE ROLLING EARTH". Autograph Manuscript Revision of *"A Song of the Rolling Earth"*. 7 pp., 12mo, with about 60 words in autograph and many changes in punctuation. With portrait and title. 12mo, half orange niger morocco.
This poem bears a new title and a new first line:
"A song of the rolling earth—and of words accordingly".

20⁻

Ed Naumley

257. "BIRDS OF PASSAGE". Autograph Manuscript Revision of *"Birds of Passage"*. 19 pp., 12mo, with about 130 words in autograph and many changes in punctuation. With portrait, table of contents, and title. 12mo, half undyed niger morocco.
The first two leaves of this section were Whitman's private proofs, struck off by the "New Republican Print" of Camden, with an autograph title. Some lines are deleted and some words added.

25⁻

342

258. "A BROADWAY PAGEANT". Autograph Revision of "A Broadway Pageant. 1860. Reception Japanese Embassy, June 1860". 5 pp., 12mo, with about 40 words in autograph and many changes in punctuation. With portrait and title. 12mo, half orange niger morocco.

10—

259. "SEA-DRIFT". Autograph Manuscript Revision of the first Poem in *"Sea-Drift"*, "Out of the Cradle endlessly Rocking". 8 pp., 12mo, with about 100 words in autograph and numerous changes in punctuation. With portrait and title. 12mo, half green niger morocco.

27⁵⁰

Published in "Passage to India". A poem that denoted Whitman's intense love and study of the sea. In this revision the poet adds a choice line at the end, describing the action of the sea as follows:
"Or like some old crone rocking the cradle, swathed in sweet garments, bending aside".

260. "SEA-DRIFT". Autograph Manuscript Revision of *"As I ebb'd with the ocean of life"*, *"To the Man-of War-Bird"*, "Tears", and the remainder of the poems in "Sea-Drift". 11 pp., 12mo, with about 70 words in autograph. With table of contents and title. 12mo, half green niger morocco.

30—

One of the two last poems in "Sea-Drift", entitled "Patrolling Barnegat" (a proof), and "After the Sea-Ship" (apparently also a proof), have been pasted in to add to this collection.

261. "BY THE ROAD SIDE". Autograph Manuscript Revision of *"By the Road's Side"*. 14 pp., 12mo, with about 90 words in autograph. With portrait, table of contents, and title. 12mo, half brown crushed levant morocco.

17⁵⁰

Added to this series of poems is a clipping from *"Cope's Tobacco Plant"*, the first printing of "The Dalliance of the Eagles", and proofs and clippings of three other poems.

343

262. "DRUM-TAPS". Autograph Manuscript Revision of *"Drum-Taps"*. 54 pp., 12mo, with about 200 words in autograph and thousands of changes in punctuation. Together with two autograph manuscripts totaling about 75 words, a photograph signed *"Walt Whitman* 1860", a clipping, table of contents, and title. 12mo, full blue crushed levant morocco, gilt tooled with the arms of the United States on front cover.

The final assembly and revision of Whitman's great war poems. Inserted is the poet's original manuscript suggestion for the poem that gave title to the work:

"Poem of the Drum—Cannot a poem be written that shall be alive with the stirring and beating of the drum?—Calling people up?—a reveille to ??—"

Another autograph manuscript is a review of "Drum-Taps" copied by the poet from the London "Nineteenth Century":

"It contains some of the most magnificent and spirit-stirring trumpet blasts, as well as some of the most deeply moving aspects of suffering and death ever expressed by poet."

At the end of the volume is mounted Whitman's account of "Life Among Fifty Thousand Sick Soldiers" clipped from the "Brooklyn Daily Eagle", docketed by Whitman *"Eagle March* 19, '63".

[See illustration]

Poem of the Drum

Cannot a poem be written that shall be alive with the stirring and beating of the drum? — Calling people up? — a reveille to ? ? —

foot note yous:

all this : nonp

✕ The London "Nineteenth Century" (December 1882,) says of "Drum Taps" it "Contains some of the most magnificent and spirit-stirring trumpet blasts, as well as some of the most deeply moving aspects of suffering and death ever expressed by poet.

[NUMBER 262]

WITH WHITMAN'S REVISIONS AND WITH
A LOCK OF HIS HAIR

263. "MEMORIES OF PRESIDENT LINCOLN". Autograph
Manuscript Revision of *"Memories of President Lincoln"*. 12
pp., 12mo, with about 70 words in autograph and many changes
in punctuation. Together with autograph manuscript: *"Write a
new burial service. A book of new things"*, mounted before the
text; a lock of Whitman's hair, authenticated in the handwriting
of Dr. Bucke, in a pocket at the end; a mounted clipping containing an account of Whitman's lecture on the death of Lincoln; a
photograph signed *"Walt Whitman 1860"*; and title. 12mo, full
black crushed levant morocco, gilt tooled with a laurel wreath on
front cover.

This section contains "When Lilacs last in the Dooryard Bloom'd", "O Captain! My Captain!", "Hush'd be the Camp To-Day", and "This Dust was once
the Man". The word changes are few but important, and the punctuation is
changed throughout.

No greater memorial to President Lincoln has ever been written than these
four poems, and Swinburne describes "When Lilacs last in the Dooryard
Bloom'd" as the "most sonorous nocturne ever chanted in the church of the
world".

[See illustration]

264. "BY BLUE ONTARIO'S SHORE". Autograph Manuscript
Revision of *"By Blue Ontario's Shore"*. 19 pp., 12mo, with about
95 words in autograph, many deletions, and numerous changes in
punctuation. With portrait and title.

"By Blue Ontario's Shore" is practically a poetical version of the preface of
1855.

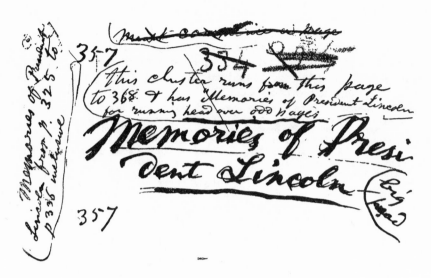

WHEN LILACS LAST IN THE DOOR-YARD BLOOM'D

1

WHEN lilacs last in the door-yard bloom'd,
And the great star early droop'd in the western sky in
the night,
I mourn'd—and yet shall mourn with ever-returning
spring.

Ever-returning spring, trinity sure to me you
bring,
Lilac blooming perennial, and drooping star in the
west,
And thought of him I love.

2

O powerful, western, fallen star!
O shades of night—O moody, tearful night!
O great star disappear'd—O the black murk that hides
the star!
O cruel hands that hold me powerless—O helpless soul
of me!
O harsh surrounding cloud that will not free my soul!

WITH AN ADDED PAGE AND MANY NEW LINES
AND TITLES IN WHITMAN'S AUTOGRAPH

265. "AUTUMN RIVULETS". Autograph Manuscript Revision of *'Two Rivulets'*. 53 pp., 12mo, with about 400 words in autograph and thousands of changes in punctuation. With table of contents and title. 12mo, undyed niger morocco sides with brown crushed levant morocco back.

60 —

This volume contains a whole page and many new lines and titles in holograph. The poem *"The Prairie States"* was written in pencil and pasted on the last leaf by Whitman, and two proof copies of poems were revised in manuscript and pasted in. The title *"Vocalism"* was substituted for "To Oratists"; *"Song of Prudence"* for "Manhattan's Streets I Sauntered, Pondering"; and new titles written in were *"The Return of the Heroes"* and *"Outlines for a tomb"*.

> *"The Prairie States.*
> *A newer garden of creation, no primal solitude,*
> *Dense, joyous, modern, populous millions, cities and*
>   *farms,*
> *With iron interlaced, composite, tied, many in one,*
> *By all the world contributed—freedom's and law's*
>   *and thrift's society,*
> *The crown and teeming paradise, so far, of Time's*
>   *accumulations,*
> *To justify the past."*

[See illustration]

266. "PROUD MUSIC OF THE STORM". Autograph Manuscript Revision of *"Proud Music of the Storm"*. 8 pp., 12mo, with about 35 words in autograph and many changes in punctuation. With portrait and title. 12mo, half undyed niger morocco.

15 —

267. "PASSAGE TO INDIA". Autograph Manuscript Revision of *"Passage to India"*. 11 pp., 12mo, with about 30 words in autograph and many changes in punctuation. With portrait and title. 12mo, half orange niger morocco.

27 50
Ca Hammony

268. PRAYER OF COLUMBUS. Autograph Manuscript Revision of the "Prayer of Columbus". 3 pp., 12mo, with about 10 words in autograph and many changes in punctuation. 12mo, half yellow niger morocco.

17 50
Einstein

The prose introduction was here deleted and did not appear in the Boston edition.

269. "THE SLEEPERS". Autograph Manuscript Revision of *"The Sleepers"*. 12 pp., 12mo, with about 40 words in autograph and many changes in punctuation. With portrait and title. 12mo, half black niger morocco.

20 —

a cluster

a cluster (runs from this page to p 488)

Autumn Rivulets

As consequent, &c.

As consequent from store of summer rains,
Or wayward rivulets in autumn flowing,
Or many a herb-lined brook's reticulations,
Or subterranean sea-rills making for the sea,
Songs of continued years I sing.

#

Life's ever-modern rapids first, soon
soon to blend
With the old streams of death.

#

Some threading Ohio's farm-fields or
the woods,
Some down Colorado's cañons from
sources of perpetual snow,
Some half-hid in Oregon, or away south-
ward in Texas.

[NUMBER 265]

349

270. "TO THINK OF TIME". Autograph Manuscript Revision of *"To Think of Time"*. 7 pp., 12mo, with about 70 words in autograph and many changes in punctuation. With portrait and title. 12mo, half undyed niger morocco.

15

There are several deletions in this poem, and the following verse is added:
> *"And I have dream'd that the purpose and essence of the*
> *known life, the transient,*
> *Is to form and decide identity for the unknown life,*
> *the permanent."*

271. "WHISPERS OF HEAVENLY DEATH". Autograph Manuscript Revision of *"Whispers of Heavenly Death"*. 14 pp., 12mo, with about 65 words in autograph and many changes in punctuation. With portrait, table of contents, and title. 12mo, half undyed niger morocco.

20

272. "THOU MOTHER WITH THY EQUAL BROOD". Autograph Manuscript Revision of "As a Strong Bird on Pinions Free". 8 pp., 12mo, with about 175 words in autograph and many changes in punctuation. With portrait and title. 12mo, half green polished morocco.

32 50

In this revision the title is changed and the following new introductory lines written:
> *"Thou Mother with thy equal brood,*
> *Thou varied chain of different States, yet one identity only,*
> *A special song before I go, I'd sing o'er all the rest,*
> *For thee, the future."*

"FROM NOON TO STARRY NIGHT"

273. "FROM NOON TO STARRY NIGHT". A new assembly of Poems under the title *"From Noon to Starry Night"* with Autograph Manuscript Revisions. 27 pp., 12mo, with about 165 words in autograph and hundreds of changes in punctuation. With table of contents and title. 12mo, half undyed niger morocco.

40

This is a new assembly of poems for the Boston edition, including some from "Leaves of Grass", together with a corrected proof of *"A Riddle Song"*, a poem excerpted from a newspaper with the manuscript title *"From Far Montana's Cañons June 25, 1878"* and extensive manuscript additions, another excerpt with the manuscript title *"What best I see in thee. To U. S. G*[rant]. *return'd from his world's tour"*, and others.

[See illustration]

From Noon to Starry Night

Thou orb aloft full-dazzling.

Thou orb aloft full-dazzling, thou hot October noon!
Flooding with sheeny light the gray beach sand,
Thou sibilant near sea, with vistas far, and foam,
And tawny streaks and shades, and spreading blue
Refuse losing the rest, O sun refulgent, my
My special word to thee.

Hear me, illustrious!
Thy lover me—for always I have loved thee,
Even as basking babe, then happy boy, alone by some wood edge, thy
    touching-distant beams enough,
Or man matured, or young or old—as now to thee I launch my invocation.

Thou canst not with thy dumbness me deceive,
I know before the fitting man all Nature yields,
Though answering not in words, the skies, trees, hear his voice—and thou,
    O sun,
As for thy throes, thy perturbations, sudden breaks and shafts of flame
    gigantic,
I understand them—I know those flames, those perturbations well.

Thou that with fructifying heat and light,
O'er myriad farms, o'er lands and waters, North and South,
O'er Mississippi's endless course, o'er Texas' grassy plains, Kanada's woods,
O'er all the globe that turns its face to thee, shining in space;
Thou that impartially enfoldest all—not only continents, seas,
Thou that to grapes and weeds and little wild flowers givest so liberally,
Shed, shed thyself on mine and me—mellow these lines
Fuse these here—with but a fleeting ray out of thy million millions,
Strike through this chant,

Nor only launch thy subtle dazzle and thy strength for these,
Prepare the later afternoon of me myself—prepare my lengthening
    shadows,
Prepare my starry nights.

[NUMBER 273]

351

274. "SONGS OF PARTING". Autograph Manuscript Revision of *"Songs of Parting"*, 18 pp., 12mo, about 135 words in autograph and hundreds of changes in punctuation. With portrait signed *"Walt Whitman June 1880"*, table of contents, and title. 12mo, half undyed niger morocco.

20

To the poem *"My Legacy"* Whitman has added in manuscript:

> *"Yet certain remembrances of the war for you, and*
> *   after you,*
> *And little souvenirs of camps and soldiers, with*
> *   my love,*
> *I bind together and bequeath in this bundle of songs."*

———

WHITMAN'S POEM ON THE DEATH OF PRESIDENT GARFIELD

275. "THE SOBBING OF THE BELLS". Autograph Manuscript Poem *"The Sobbing of the Bells. midnight Sept: 19-20 1881"*. 1 p., 8vo, about 65 words. Framed with photograph signed *"Walt Whitman 1879"*.

95

Apparently this is the first or one of the first drafts of the poem on the death of President Garfield, with the title written in pencil, and with short lines some of which were combined when the poem was first printed.

> *"The sobbing of the bells,*
> *The sudden death-news everywhere*
> *The slumberers rouse*
> *The rapport of the people*
>   . . . .
>
> *The passionate toll & clang,*
> *City to city joining, sounding, passing*
> *Those heart-beats of a nation in the night."*

[See illustration]

276. DEATH OF PRESIDENT GARFIELD. Autograph Manuscript Poem *"The Sobbing of the Bells—(Midnight Sept: 19-20 1881)"*. 1 p., 8vo, about 65 words. Framed with portrait signed *"Walt Whitman 1879"*.

35

A manuscript of the poem as it was sent to press. On the back of the frame is pasted the first printing of the poem, clipped from the "Boston Daily Globe". In this manuscript the first line reads:

> *"The sobbing of the bells, the sudden death-news every where".*

The Sobbing
of the Bells
midnight Sept. 19·20 1881

The sobbing of the bells,
The sudden death-news everywhere
The slumberers rouse
The rapport of the people
(Full well they know that
  message in the darkness,
Full well return, respond within
  their breasts, their brains, the
  sad reverberations.)
The passionate toll & clang,
City to city joining, sounding, passing
Those heart-beats of a nation
  in the night.

[NUMBER 275]

353

277. DEFENSE OF WALT WHITMAN. William D. O'Connor. A. L. s., 241 pp., 4to, about 12,000 words. Washington, February 22, 1882. To Dr. R. M. Bucke. With an autograph manuscript by Walt Whitman, 1 p., 4to, about 155 words. 4to, half green polished morocco.

65

The original manuscript of O'Connor's defense of Walt Whitman and a violent outburst against his critics. It was written specially for Dr. Bucke's biography of Whitman, whom O'Connor had named the "good gray poet". The autograph manuscript by Whitman reads in part as follows:

"William D. O'Connor's 'Good Gray Poet' of 1865-'6 and, after eighteen years, his letter now written (1883) in confirmation and re-statement of that pamphlet . . . are both in response to my solicitations, and will prove invaluable contributions to the future . . ."

278. SUPPRESSION OF "LEAVES OF GRASS". Two A. L. s. by William D. O'Connor, 94 pp., 4to, over 5,000 words. May and September, 1882. To the Editor of the "New York Tribune". With title. 4to, cloth, orange niger morocco back.

22.50
Feinberg

The original drafts of O'Connor's two letters on the suppression of "Leaves of Grass" in Massachusetts and on postmaster Tobey's refusal to allow printed selections from "Leaves of Grass" to pass through the mail. O'Connor was never mild in his letters, but these are vitriolic.

279. SUPPRESSION OF "LEAVES OF GRASS". 1882. A Collection of Letters and copies of Letters in the autograph of Dr. Bucke, William D. O'Connor, and others, relating to the history of the suppression of "Leaves of Grass". 25 pp., folio to 4to, about 1,800 words. Together with a collection of 15 excerpts from newspapers and magazines on the same subject. 2 pieces, folio and 4to, boards and board folder.

20

The collection includes O'Connor's investigation into the suppression of "Leaves of Grass", with copies of the various letters he wrote and received, Copies of the correspondence between Osgood & Co. and Walt Whitman, a clipping containing the district attorney's demand for the suppression of certain poems (docketed by Whitman), and others.

280. FIRST SEPARATE EDITION. This World, Vol. III, Nos. 24 and 26, June 17 and July 1, 1882. With supplement broadside in No. 24. 2 pieces, 8vo, sewn ❖ The Infidel Pulpit, Vol. I, Nos. 12 and 13, May 21 and 28, 1881. 2 pieces, 8vo, original wrappers. Together 4 pieces, in 2 cloth and board folding cases.

35

The broadside "Supplement to 'This World'" is the FIRST SEPARATE EDITION of Whitman's poem "To a Common Prostitute" which caused such a widespread controversy. The postmaster at Boston refused to allow it to be sent through the mail, and it was not until the postal authorities at Washington ordered it released that the issue was distributed. The issue of "This World" for July 1st contains a full account of the affair by the editor, George Chainey. "The Infidel Pulpit" contains "Lessons for To-Day from Walt Whitman" and "True Democracy", both by George Chainey.

281. "LEAVES OF GRASS FINISHED". Autograph Manuscript
"Leaves of Grass finished", 1 p., 4to, about 100 words. With
excerpts "'The Good Gray Poet' At Work on His New Edition"
and "Walt Whitman in Boston". With transcript and title. 4to,
half green niger morocco.

"Boston, Oct. 22, '81. 8.30 A. M. . . . Have been in Boston the last two months
seeing to the 'materialization' of completed 'Leaves of Grass' ".

282. PRINTING "LEAVES OF GRASS". Two Autograph Manuscripts, 2 pp., 4to and 12mo, with two excerpts containing autograph manuscript notes, together about 200 words. With portrait
and title. 4to, cloth, orange niger morocco back.

"Copy of 'Leaves of Grass' Set up, Cast, & printed Boston Aug: 22-Sept: 29
1881 . . . it is to be $2 retail—& I am to have 25 cts a copy royalty . . ."
"Nov 3 '81 I am writing this at Mott Haven station, waiting for the down-
ward cars—going back to Camden . . . Just read a most live and affectionate
criticism on the new L. of G. in last Sunday's Boston Herald, by Sylvan."

283. LEAVES OF GRASS: Preface to the Original Edition, 1855.
8vo, original wrappers, uncut; backstrip worn. In a board folder.

London: Trübner & Co., 1881

ONE OF 500 COPIES. Tipped in are four excerpts from an early printing of
this preface, with autograph manuscript additions by the author, about 100
words. Apparently these additions were made about 1860, but were never used.

284. "PURPOSE OF SPECIMEN DAYS". 1881. Autograph Manuscript, 2 pp., 12mo, about 180 words. With transcript and title.
12mo, half brown levant morocco.

This was written for Dr. Bucke's biography of Whitman.

"The purpose of 'Specimen Days' was to combine and weave in one pat-
tern . . . certain variegated record-threads of my personal experience, young
manhood in New York city and Brooklyn, with what I had seen of the Seces-
sion War . . . with a 'Collect' of various pieces, comments on my time and
spirit of the time especially as 'Democratic Vistas' . . ."

285. "SPECIMEN DAYS". Three Autograph Manuscript Notes for
"Specimen Days", 3 pp., 12mo, about 180 words. With transcript
and title. Small 4to, cloth, red niger morocco back.

"For there is Something in concrete Nature itself in all its parts—a quality
an identity, apart and superior to any appreciation of the same through realism
or mysticism (the very thought of which involves abstraction) or through
literature or art."

286. CRITICISM OF "LEAVES OF GRASS". Autograph Manuscript, 1 p., 12mo; on verso two stanzas from Tennyson's "Queen
of the May" copied by Whitman, together about 200 words, in
pencil and ink.

15

> This criticism of "Leaves of Grass" was sent to Dr. Bucke for his biography
> of Whitman.

> *"We have had man indoors and under artificial relations—man in war, man in*
> *love . . . but never before have we had man in the open air, his attitude*
> *adjusted to the seasons and as one might describe it, adjusted to the sun by*
> *day and the stars by night."*

The Last Phase

NATURALLY in this division there is not so much of manuscript material as of the final publication of the new literature of
the world, the publication of long forgotten pieces, some of them
suggested in the poet's early days of powerful thought and now
developed with the added judgment of old age. And then the final
scene, the poet sinking slowly to the eternity he longed to explore,
bright and cheerful to the end, and surrounded by his faithful
followers.

287. LIFE IN CAMDEN. Autograph Manuscript, 1 p., folio, about
110 words. With transcript and title. Small narrow folio, half
red niger morocco.

12 50

> Intended for a second volume of "Specimen Days".

> *"Camden—Phila April 8, '84—I have been living here in Camden now for*
> *nearly eleven years. Came on from Washington in the Summer of '73, after*
> *my paralytic stroke, and the death of my dear mother . . ."*

288. ORIGINAL PLASTER PORTRAIT OF WHITMAN BY
SIDNEY H. MORSE. Original Plaster Portrait of Walt Whitman, head to left, in high relief, signed "Sidney Morse Sculptor
1887", with a facsimile of Whitman's signature cut in the plaster
below the portrait. Size of head, 6 by 4½ inches, on plaster
plaque 9¼ by 8 inches. Framed.

55

> THIS IS THE ORIGINAL PLASTER PORTRAIT OF THE HEAD OF WHITMAN MADE
> ESPECIALLY FOR THE POET, which hung in his room until after his death, when
> it came into the possession of Dr. Bucke. In an envelope pasted on the back
> of the frame is a certificate by H. L. Bucke, October 5, 1935, certifying that
> this plaque was in the Bucke collection.

> In September 1888 Whitman wrote to S. H. Morse: "Your bust of me still
> holds out fully in my estimation. I consider it, (to me at any rate), the best
> and most characteristic, really artistic and satisfactory rendering of any—so
> tho't by me."—"In Re Walt Whitman".

289. "PRESIDENTIAL ELECTION". Autograph Manuscript, 1 p., folio; on verso, rough draft of a letter relating to the bankruptcy of the binders of "Leaves of Grass", together about 280 words, in pencil. With transcript and title. Small folio, cloth, green niger morocco back.

"Oct 31 '84—The political parties are trying—but mostly in vain—to get up some fervor of excitement on the pending election . . . But I like well the fact of all these National Elections—have written a little poem about it . . ."

15

290. MY BOOK AND I. 1887. Autograph Manuscript, 4 pp., 8vo and 12mo, about 250 words. With portrait, transcript, and title. Royal 8vo, half brown levant morocco.

20

Dr. Bucke states that this manuscript "seems to be a rejected passage from 'My Book and I', printed in "Lippincott's", January, 1887, and afterwards largely used in 'A Backward Glance'".

"Before—that nebula of thoughts and plans and misty hopes! the ardor—those toils and struggles of baffled, impeded articulation (most curious resume of all!)—those startings out, urging, cleaving, beating flights of wings, uncertain where you will soar, or bring up—or whether you will soar at all—to end perhaps in ignominious fall and failure . . . Afterwards—the way things work—the apparent terminations—the results so unexpected. Finally the looking back out of the still and pensive evening . . ."

291. NOVEMBER BOUGHS. A Set of Page Proofs of "November Boughs", 136 pp., 12mo. In a wrapper bearing autograph inscription by Dr. Bucke: *"Proof Slips—sent me as struck off by W. W. —of November Boughs. R. M. B."* With a review of the work docketed by Whitman *"Chicago News notice Feb 9 '81"*. In a half green niger morocco box case.

20

These sheets do not contain the title or preliminary pages, as they were not yet printed when Whitman sent the proofs to Dr. Bucke. It is doubtful if more than four or five such proofs were made. Certainly Horace Traubel, who helped Whitman with the work, had one, and perhaps Harned another; these, with the working copies, were probably all that were printed.

292. DEMOCRATIC VISTAS, and other Papers. 12mo, half brown polished morocco; rubbed. In a half brown levant morocco box case.   London: Walter Scott, 1888

35

One of the Camelot Series, edited by Ernest Rhys, and apparently one of the copies which the editor had specially bound to send to Whitman for presentation.

AUTOGRAPH PRESENTATION COPY, inscribed by the author: *"Dr: R. M. Bucke from his friend the author Walt Whitman to R. M. B."*

Laid in are two A. L. s. by Ernest Rhys to Whitman relating to the publication of his works in England, and giving all the Whitman news of that country.

293. TRIAL TITLES. Autograph Manuscript Trial Titles for "Sands at Seventy", 2 pp., 4to, about 60 words. In a board folder.

"Halcyon Days", "Carols at Candle-Light", "Annex Leaves", "Sands on the Shores of Seventy", and others.

15—

294. LEAVES OF GRASS with Sands at Seventy & A Backward Glance o'er Travel'd Roads. *Portraits.* 12mo, limp morocco; slightly rubbed.   [Philadelphia, 1889]

ONE OF 300 COPIES, with the autograph of the author on the title-page. Dr. Bucke's copy, with his bookplate.

25—

295. GOOD-BYE MY FANCY. 2d Annex to Leaves of Grass. *Portrait.* 8vo, original cloth, gilt top. In a half brown levant morocco box case.   Philadelphia, 1891

A FINE COPY OF THE FIRST EDITION. AUTOGRAPH PRESENTATION COPY FROM THE AUTHOR, inscribed on a fly-leaf "*R. M. Bucke from the author June 20' 91*".

Presentation copies of this book, the last work by Whitman actually issued during his lifetime, are exceedingly rare; and this copy, to one of his most intimate friends and literary executors, is of special interest.

60—

THE RAREST "LEAVES OF GRASS"

THE FIRST COMPLETED COPY OF THE "DEATH-BED EDITION"—
AUTOGRAPH PRESENTATION COPY TO DR. BUCKE

296. LEAVES OF GRASS. Including Sands at Seventy—1st Annex, Good-Bye my Fancy—2d Annex, A Backward Glance o'er Travel'd Roads, and *Portrait from Life.* 8vo, ORIGINAL BROWN WRAPPERS, yellow paper label; backstrip worn, label chipped. In a half black levant morocco box case.

Philadelphia: David McKay, 1891-2

THE FIRST COPY COMPLETED OF THE "DEATH-BED EDITION", PRESENTED BY THE AUTHOR TO ONE OF HIS MOST INTIMATE FRIENDS AND LITERARY EXECUTORS, with autograph inscription on the title: "*Dr. R. M. Bucke first copy completed ōf L. of G: f'm the author with love Dec: 6 1891*".

ONE OF THREE COPIES BOUND IN BROWN WRAPPERS. The story of the three copies bound in brown wrappers was told by Mrs. Anne Montgomerie Traubel, wife of Horace Traubel, in a letter to Mr. Oscar Lion: "There were three copies of the brown stone front . . . I used to be audacious. I remember the evening Horace came home with these volumes. He showed me two and asked me what I thought of them. 'They look like Philadelphia brown stone front houses'. He was displeased with that outspoken young lady and repeated the phrase to Whitman. 'Look respectable, eh?' he asked mildly. Later I saw them in the rough gray paper which I like very much."

On the first fly-leaf Dr. Bucke has copied Whitman's presentation letter:

"*Camden N. J. Dec: 6, 91. Send same time with this first copy (rude, flimsy cover, but good paper, print and stitching) of L. of G. at last complete—after 33 years of hackling at it, all times and moods of my life, fair weather and foul, all parts of the land, and peace and war, young and old . . .*"

375—

[See illustration]

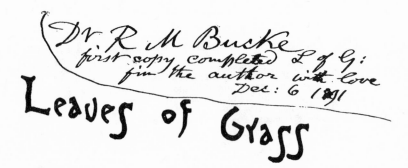

Dr R M Bucke
first copy completed L of G;
fim the author with love
Dec: 6 1891

Leaves of Grass

Including

SANDS AT SEVENTY... *1st Annex,*

GOOD-BYE MY FANCY... *2d Annex,*

A BACKWARD GLANCE O'ER TRAVEL'D ROADS,

and Portrait from Life.

COME, said my Soul,
Such verses for my Body let us write, (for we are one,)
That should I after death invisibly return,
Or, long, long hence, in other spheres,
There to some group of mates the chants resuming,
(Tallying Earth's soil, trees, winds, tumultuous waves,)
Ever with pleas'd smile I may keep on,
Ever and ever yet the verses owning—as, first, I here and now,
Signing for Soul and Body, set to them my name,

Walt Whitman

PHILADELPHIA
DAVID McKAY, PUBLISHER
23 SOUTH NINTH STREET
1891-'2

[NUMBER 296]

THE "DEATH-BED EDITION"

WITH ONE OF THE LAST LETTERS WRITTEN BY WALT WHITMAN

297. LEAVES OF GRASS. Portrait. 8vo, original gray wrappers, paper label, uncut; part of label missing. In a cloth box case.

Philadelphia, 1891-2

THE FAMOUS "DEATH-BED EDITION" IN GRAY WRAPPERS, of which not more than fifty copies were made. Whitman was very ill and expected to die at any moment, but he wanted to see his last edition of "Leaves of Grass". Horace Traubel had a few copies bound in wrappers which Whitman sent to his most intimate friends. (See the preceding description.)

APPARENTLY THE LAST LETTER WRITTEN BY WHITMAN MENTIONING "LEAVES OF GRASS". Laid in is an A. L. s. "W. W.", 1 p., 4to, about 60 words, with original envelope addressed by the poet to Dr. Bucke. So far as located Whitman wrote only six letters after this, one short note to Dr. Bucke and five personal notes to his sister Hannah, and in none of these did he mention "Leaves of Grass". The "McK" mentioned in the letter was David McKay, publisher of the "Death-Bed Edition". One of the advertising slips mentioned is enclosed with the letter.

"Jan 27 [1892] noon Feeble & weak & restless but not without favorable points —appetite holds out—eat two meals every day— . . . McK was here—paid me $283— I enc two adv't slips—to me the 1892 edn supersedes them all by far— adv. intended for N. Y. Trib—God bless you W. W."

[See illustration]

298. LEAVES OF GRASS. *Portrait.* 8vo, original gray wrappers, paper label, uncut; part of label missing, small chip in one cover. In a cloth box case.

Philadelphia, 1891-2

THE "DEATH-BED EDITION". With several passages marked in pencil by Dr. Bucke. Laid in are manuscript quotations from the work, and a list of pages containing *"Great lines"* by Dr. Bucke.

299. PROOFS AND INTERCALATIONS. 1874-1891. A Collection of Proofs, Galley Proofs, and Intercalation Slips, containing Prose Articles and Poems by Walt Whitman. 29 pieces, small folio to 16mo. In 29 board folders.

A SPLENDID COLLECTION OF THESE EXCEEDINGLY RARE WHITMAN BROADSIDES. While living in Camden it was Whitman's custom to have his poems put in type at a printing establishment, the proof returned and corrected, and the revised copy again printed. At times these slips were inserted in his published works as "Intercalations"; in the Centennial Edition of "Leaves of Grass", for example, some copies had the words "With Portraits and Intercalations" at the foot of the title-page. It was also Whitman's custom to demand a proof from any publisher who accepted his writings. This collection contains various proofs, galley proofs, and intercalations, comprising:

Death of a Fireman. From the New Republic, Camden, N. J. Nov. 14th, '74.

Walt Whitman's Actual American Position. From the West Jersey Press, Jan. 26th, 1876 (2 copies).

[Description concluded on page 122]

360

Jan 27 noon
Feeble & weak & restless
but not without favorable points—
—appetite holds out — eat two meals
every day — bowel movement
every day (rather strange after
such a long interregnum)
— McK was here — paid me $283
— I enc' two adv't slips — to me
the 1892 ed'n supersedes them
all by far — adv. intended for
N Y Tribe — God bless you W W

[NUMBER 297]

Walt Whitman. From the West Jersey Press March 15th, 1876. (A reply to Robert Buchanan.)

Personal. U. S. America: Camden, N. Jersey, April, 1876. To the Foreign Reader, at outset.

Walt Whitman. The true reminiscence of his writings. From the "West Jersey Press", May 24th, 1876.

Remembrance Copy. (Used in "Memoranda During the War"; see Number 171.)

Patrolling Barnegat. With a note by Dr. Bucke on margins: *"Unpublished— private. Received from Walt June 3, 1880".*

Sunday with the Insane. (Galley proof, 1880, with three words deleted.)

Summer Days in Canada. (Galley proof, with newspaper clippings of the same letter, 1880.)

The Dead Carlyle. (Docketed in autograph by Whitman *"Boston Literary World Feb: 12—1881—".*)

Death of Carlyle. (Galley proof, with excerpt of the article from "The Critic", 1881.)

A Memorandum at a Venture. From the North American Review. (In four sheets, dated by Dr. Bucke *"June 1882".*)

—— Another copy, in one sheet.

With Husky-Haughty Lips, O Sea! (Autograph note by Dr. Bucke: *"Given me by W. W. Nov. 1883 before it was published . . ."*)

Your kind invitation to visit you and deliver a poem for the 333d Anniversary of Founding Santa Fé . . . (Written in 1883. 2 copies, one bearing a note by Dr. Bucke.)

The Dead Tenor. From the Critic—New York, Nov. 8, '84.

Thanks in Old Age. (At the top Whitman wrote *"pub'd Nov. 24"* [1887].)

Old Age's Lambent Peaks. A Carol Closing Sixty-nine. To get the Final Lilt of Songs. (Three poems on one sheet, 1888; 2 copies.)

Preface (by Whitman to "Tales" by William D. O'Connor, with autograph note by Dr. Bucke at bottom, 1889).

A Backward Glance on My Own Road. (Galley proofs, 1890. With signed envelope addressed to Dr. Bucke.)

Shakespeare for America. From "Poet-Lore" September 15, 1890.

Philadelphia, Oct. 21st, 1890. Col. Ingersoll's Lecture—"Liberty and Literature". Walt Whitman, when call'd for, rose and said . . .

Have We a National Literature? From the North American Review, March, 1891. (Galley proofs, in four sheets.)

Halcyon Days. (Corrected.)

To the Sun-set Breeze.

Of that Blithe Throat of Thine. (Docketed by Whitman: *"From January Harpers".*)

300. WHITMAN CONTRIBUTORS. 1885-6. Four Circulars containing lists of Contributors to Funds collected for Walt Whitman. 4 pieces, 8vo and 4to, and numerous clippings. In 4 board folders.

15⁻

The material includes:

"Private. Walt Whitman's Buggy and Horse. Sept. 15. 1885." 4 pp., 8vo. A statement of receipts and disbursements of funds for a buggy and horse for Walt Whitman, with a newspaper account of the presentation.

"September 1885. Walt Whitman. A Subscription list is being formed in England . . . Mr. Herbert H. Gilchrist, Honorary Secretary . . . Mr. W. M. Rossetti, Treasurer". Facsimile. 2 leaves, one blank.

Facsimile of a letter from Walt Whitman, dated May 30, 1886, with printed subscription list on second leaf, signed in autograph "*Herbert H. Gilchrist Hon: Sec:*", with some names and amounts written in by Mr. Gilchrist.

Another copy, on which Whitman has written "*to W. M. Rossetti (facsimile-print)*", with several clippings from English papers about raising funds for Walt Whitman.

301. CALAMUS. A Series of Letters written during the years 1868-1880 by Walt Whitman to a young Friend (Peter Doyle). Edited with an introduction by Richard M. Bucke. *Portraits and illustrations on Japan paper.* 12mo, boards, cloth back, uncut.

25—

Boston, 1897

One of 35 copies on large paper. This is Number 1, signed by Dr. Bucke and originally retained by him.

302. LEAVES OF GRASS. Grashalme: Gedichte, In Auswahl übersetzt von Karl Knortz und T. W. Rolleston, Zurich, 1889 ❖ Walt Whitman: Naturleven, Vertaald door Maurits Wagenvoort, Haarlem, 1898. 2 vols., 12mo, original wrappers, uncut. In 2 board folders.

15—

The First German and First Dutch Editions of "Leaves of Grass". Laid in the first is an A. N. s. by Walt Whitman on a postcard to Rolleston, one of the translators.

303. WHITMAN AND LINCOLN. 1880-1887. Material relating to Whitman's Lectures on Lincoln. 5 pieces, 8vo and smaller. In a board folder.

17 50

This material includes an account of Whitman's lecture on Lincoln clipped from "The American Register", May 1, 1880, with nine words in autograph; programme of the lecture April 15, 1886, containing the poem "O Captain! My Captain!"; an excerpt from the "Philadelphia Press" April 16, 1886, containing a report of the lecture; broadside announcement of the lecture at Unity Church, April 5, 1887; and an admission ticket to the lecture at Madison Square Theatre, New York, April 14, 1887.

304. CONTRIBUTIONS BY WALT WHITMAN. Contributions to Magazines, etc. 11 pieces, folio and 4to. In a cloth box case.

27 50

"The Child's Champion" in "The New World", November 20, 1841, one of Whitman's earliest contributions; "Dirge for Two Veterans" with music by F. L. Ritter, 1880; "The Dalliance of the Eagles", in "Cope's Tobacco Plant", November, 1880; articles on Poe, Burns, Shakespeare, Tennyson, his own work, and a poem "Yonnondio", in six numbers of "The Critic", 1882-90; "The Human Voice" in "Munyon's Illustrated World", October, 1890; "Ship Ahoy" in "The Youth's Companion", March 12, 1891.

305. CONTRIBUTIONS BY WALT WHITMAN. 1850-1892. A Collection of Contributions by Whitman to various Magazines and Newspapers. 12 pieces, folio to 4to. In 8 board folders.

30—

The collection includes: The Indians of Long Island, about 1850; *"Three Young Men's Deaths"* in "Cope's Tobacco Plant", April, 1879, with the title in autograph; "Emerson's Books, (the Shadows of them.)" in "The Literary World", May 22, 1880; *"Bumble Bees and Bird Music"* in "The American", title in autograph; *"Bible as Poetry"* in "The Critic", February 3, 1883, title in autograph; "An Indian Bureau Reminiscence" and "Some Diary Notes at Random" in "Baldwin's Monthly", February, 1884, and December, 1885; "Walt Whitman's Life", in "Munyon's Illustrated World", April, 1890; three numbers of "Once a Week" containing "A Thought of Columbus", July 2, 1892; facsimile of the same, July 9, 1892; and "Walt Whitman's Last Poem" by Horace Traubel, July 16, 1892, with manuscript changes by the author.

306. CONTRIBUTIONS BY WALT WHITMAN. 1867-1891. Magazines containing Poems and Prose by Walt Whitman. 21 pieces, 8vo, original wrappers. In a cloth box case.

15—

In this collection are four numbers of "The Galaxy", six of the "North American Review", four "Lippincott's", two "Harper's", No. 1 of the "Broadway Magazine" containing "Whispers of Heavenly Death", No. 2 of the "Kansas Magazine" containing "The Mystic Trumpeter", and a number of "To-Day".

These contain essays on Burns, "Have We a National Literature?", "The Poetry of the Future" and others; poems "A Carol of Harvest for 1867"; "O Star of France", autographed *"Walt's Poem"*; "Patrolling Barnegat"; "November Boughs", and others.

307. WHITMAN'S LAST DAYS AND HIS WILL. Manuscript Account of Whitman's last Illness, 159 pp., folio and smaller. December 23, 1891, to March 26, 1892. 4to, half blue niger morocco. With a Manuscript Copy of Whitman's Will, made by Dr. Bucke on April 1, 1892, 6 pp. 4to, cloth, black niger morocco back. Together 2 vols.

70—

The account of Whitman's last illness contains the medical reports made by the nurse, Mrs. Elizabeth Keller, and the three physicians, Dr. Longaker, Dr. Alexander McAlister, and Dr. Bucke. Many of Dr. Bucke's notes are personal, and one is of great importance since it alludes to Whitman's children. *"23 Dec. . . . In the Evening—I asked him if he did not want to say something to me about that Southern matter. He said 'my children?' I said 'yes'. He said 'well I guess not'. I said Harned thinks someone ought to know the main facts in case of any trouble arising hereafter—he said 'in money matters you mean?' I said 'yes'. 'Oh' he said 'there will be no trouble of that kind' and went on to say that the people were of good family and would of themselves never come forward and claim connection."*

308. BUCKE, DR. RICHARD M. A Collection of Autograph Manuscripts, Typescripts and Proofs by Dr. Bucke about Walt Whitman. 7 pieces, folio to 8vo, cloth, boards or board folders.

15

The collection includes the autograph manuscript of *"Walt Whitman—a Lecture"*, 40 pp., folio and smaller; and corrected typescript of the same, with additions in manuscript, 1900.

Autograph Manuscripts of *"Walt Whitman's Genealogy"* and *"Jean François Millet and Walt Whitman a curious parallel"*, together 23 pp., 4to and folio, in one volume.

Autograph manuscript *"Study of Faust and Leaves of Grass"*, 22 pp., 4to.

Corrected typescript of three Lectures *"Memories of Walt Whitman. No. 2"*, *"Walt Whitman. Man and Poet"* (2 copies), and *"Portraits of Walt Whitman"*. With corrected page proof of the first, 1894.

Corrected typescript of another lecture on Whitman.

309. WHITMAN'S FRIENDS. A Collection of Monographs on Walt Whitman and Reviews of his Works. 14 pieces, 8vo. In six cloth or board folders.

55

The collection includes seven reviews of "Drum Taps" by John Burroughs and others, 1865, one docketed by Whitman.

WILLIAM D. O'CONNOR. "The Good Gray Poet". 8vo, original wrappers. N. Y., 1866.

ANNE GILCHRIST. "A Woman's Estimate of Walt Whitman" in "The Radical", 1870.

—— "A Confession of Faith" in "To-Day", 1885.

A review of the "Life of Anne Gilchrist" in "The Atlantic Monthly", 1887.

GABRIEL SARRAZIN. "Poètes modernes de l'Amérique: Walt Whitman" in "La Nouvelle Revue", 1888. Autograph presentation copy from the author to Walt Whitman with manuscript corrections by the author. Laid in are two broadside translations from Sarrazin in an envelope addressed by Whitman.

310. ABOUT WALT WHITMAN. A Collection of Contributions relating to Walt Whitman. 7 pieces, small folio to 8vo. In five cloth or board cases.

15

R. L. STEVENSON. "The Gospel according to Walt Whitman" in "The New Quarterly Magazine", London, 1878.

JOHN ROBERTSON. "Walt Whitman Poet and Democrat" in "The Round Table Series", Edinburgh, 1884.

SWINBURNE CONTROVERSY. Three numbers of "The Fortnightly Review", 1887, containing articles by A. C. Swinburne, John A. Symonds and Roden Noel.

WALTER HAMILTON, EDITOR. Parodies of Walt Whitman. London, 1888.

A review of "November Boughs" by Hamlin Garland, 1888. With A. L. s. by Garland, to Walt Whitman.

311. DR. JOHN JOHNSTON. Notes of Visit to Walt Whitman, 12mo, wrappers, Boston, 1890 ❖ Diary Notes of a Visit to Walt Whitman, 12mo, cloth, Manchester, 1898. Together 2 vols.

Both are autograph presentation copies from the author to Dr. Bucke. The first was printed for private circulation. Laid in are four photographs of Whitman's home in Camden taken by Dr. Johnston and signed by him, and his own signed photograph.

55

312. ABOUT WALT WHITMAN. 1866-1890. A Collection of Monographs and Contributions relating to Walt Whitman. 14 pieces, folio to 12mo. In 13 board folders.

WILLIAM D. O'CONNOR. "The Good Gray Poet". 8vo, original wrappers. N. Y., 1866.

—— "'C.' On Walt Whitman" in "The Round Table", 1867.

MARY E. WAGER-FISHER. "Poet's Homes. Walt Whitman" in "Wide Awake", 1878.

THE REV. JOHN P. HOPPS, Editor. "A Study of Walt Whitman's Genius and Poetry" in two numbers of "The Truthseeker". London, 1880.

H. B. COTTERILL AND T. W. ROLLESTON. "Ueber Wordsworth und Walt Whitman". Dresden, 1883. AUTOGRAPH PRESENTATION COPY from T. W. Rolleston, with autograph manuscript notes by Dr. Bucke.

EDWARD DOWDEN. Review of Dr. Bucke's "Walt Whitman" in "The Academy", 1883.

—— "English Critics on Walt Whitman", 1889. With manuscript note by Whitman *"Supplementary to Dr. Bucke's W. W."*

WILLIAM S. KENNEDY. "The Poet as a Craftsman". N. Y., 1886.

KARL KNORTZ. Walt Whitman. Vortrag. N. Y., 1886. Autograph presentation copy from the author to Dr. Bucke.

ELIZABETH P. GOULD. "Walt Whitman among the Soldiers" in "The Critic", N. Y., 1887. With autograph note by Walt Whitman *"W. W. Among the Soldiers"*.

FRANCIS H. WILLIAMS. "The Poetry of Walt Whitman" in "The American", 1888. On the first page Whitman wrote: *"Article 'The Poetry of Walt Whitman'"*.

THOMAS T. GREG. "Walt Whitman: Man and Poet". Warrington, 1888. With presentation A. L. s. by the author to Walt Whitman.

ROBERT G. INGERSOLL. "Testimonial to Walt Whitman" in "The Truthseeker", N. Y., 1890.

313. CONTRIBUTIONS ABOUT WALT WHITMAN. A Series of 24 Magazines containing Contributions about Walt Whitman, published in England from July 4, 1868, to 1897. 24 pieces, royal 8vo. In a cloth box case.

15

314. CONTRIBUTIONS ABOUT WALT WHITMAN. A Series of 22 Magazines published in England from 1868 to 1892. Folio and 4to. In a cloth box case.

10

315. THE DEATH OF WHITMAN. A Series of 13 Magazines published in England containing contributions relating to the poet's death in 1892. Folio and 4to. In a cloth box case.

12<u>50</u>

316. CONTRIBUTIONS ABOUT WALT WHITMAN. A Series of 8 Periodicals published in foreign languages containing articles about Walt Whitman, 1868 to 1890. Folio to 8vo. In a cloth box case.

14—

317. CONTRIBUTIONS ABOUT WALT WHITMAN. A Series of 44 American Magazines containing contributions by and about Walt Whitman, 1871 to 1892. Royal 8vo. In a cloth box case.

15—

318. CONTRIBUTIONS ABOUT WALT WHITMAN. A Series of 26 American Magazines containing contributions about Walt Whitman, 1892 to 1896. Royal 8vo. In a cloth box case.

10—

319. CONTRIBUTIONS ABOUT WALT WHITMAN. A Series of 22 American Magazines containing contributions about Walt Whitman, 1892 to 1894. 4to. In a cloth box case.

17<u>50</u>

320. CONTRIBUTIONS ABOUT WALT WHITMAN. A Series of 72 American Periodicals containing contributions about Walt Whitman, 1860 to 1892. Folio and smaller. In a cloth box case.

20—

[END OF SALE]

 # 13,489<u>50</u>

SALE NUMBER 4289

FREE PUBLIC EXHIBITION

From Saturday, January 9, to Time of Sale
Weekdays 9 to 6 · Sunday 2 to 5

PUBLIC SALE

Wednesday, January 13, at 8:15 p.m.
Thursday, January 14, at 2 and 8:15 p.m.

EXHIBITION & SALE AT THE

AMERICAN ART ASSOCIATION
ANDERSON GALLERIES · INC

30 EAST 57TH STREET · NEW YORK

✦ ✦ ✦

Sales Conducted by

HIRAM H. PARKE · OTTO BERNET · H. E. RUSSELL, JR

1937

The Genesis and Development of "Leaves of Grass"

In the following collections can be traced the development of "Leaves of Grass" from its conception to the finished work, and the environment that inspired the work. Little of this material was published until after the death of the author, and some has never been published. In 1902 Whitman's literary executors published "The Complete Writings of Walt Whitman", and the references are to the New York edition in ten volumes, the first three containing "Leaves of Grass" and the remainder the prose works. In some cases reference is also made to the first edition of 1855.

THE GENESIS OF "LEAVES OF GRASS"

WITH AN UNPUBLISHED TABLE OF CONTENTS
TO THE FIRST EDITION

559. WHITMAN, WALT. A Collection of rough draft AUTOGRAPH MANUSCRIPTS. 15 pp., 4to and 8vo. About 2,250 words. [1850-5.]

THE ORIGINAL ROUGH DRAFTS OR PRELIMINARY FORMS OF A PORTION OF THE MATERIAL USED IN THE FIRST EDITION OF "LEAVES OF GRASS", TOGETHER WITH SOME OF THE POEMS WHITMAN REJECTED FOR THAT EDITION. Although the ideas promulgated in his great work had been shaping themselves in his mind for a number of years, it was not until 1853 that the definite purpose to publish those ideas became the one object of Whitman's life. He then abandoned all other occupations and began to write and rewrite the poems in the "Song of Myself".

The "Song of Myself" is "Leaves of Grass" in epitome, the scientific, philosophic, and religious basis of the whole structure. This collection contains the earliest forms of five of these "Songs", forms which were not published in any edition of "Leaves of Grass", and which remained unknown until after the death of their author, when they were published by his executors. The references in the following descriptions are to the First Edition of "Leaves of Grass" (Brooklyn, 1855) and, in brackets, to the "Complete Writings of Walt Whitman".

THE EARLY DRAFTS OF THE "SONG OF MYSELF"

The genesis of the ideas expressed on pp. 20 and 28 of the 1855 edition [Works III: 102-9] are found on three pages of manuscript in connected form:

"All tends to the soul,
As materials so the soul,
As procreation, so the soul—if procreation is impure, all is impure.

[Description continued on page 218; see illustration]

As procreation, so the soul if procreation
is impure all if impure
As, the body, flesh, graft, growth, brain,
prune this graft so the soul—
All tends to the soul As materials so the soul
As procreation so the soul — if procreation
What is impure, the soul all is impure

All it tends to the soul, and to that
which follows what is called
death concurs with the body
As the shadow follows the shape
of the body so the soul
and has the shape of the body,
and comes not unless of the body,
so the soul concurs with the
body, and comes not unless of the body,
As materials are, so the soul,
As experiences, thefts childhood,
maturity, suffering so the soul,
As craft, lies, thefts, adulteries,
sarcasm, greed, denial, avarice,
hatred, gluttony, so the soul,
As the types set up by the
printer and faithfully returned their impression,
whatever they are, mean and
are, so you a man's life
and a woman's life is borne out and internally
returned in their soul

[NUMBER 559]

370

As the shadow concurs with the body and comes not unless of the body, so
the soul concurs with the body and comes not unless of the body . . ."

"I am the poet of Reality,
And I say the stars are not echoes,
And I say that space is no apparition . . .

   . . .   .

"Hurrah for Positive Science!
Bring honey-clover and branches of lilac!

   . . .   .

"And to shake my friendly right hand, governors and millionaires shall stand
all day waiting their turns. . . ."

Song on the sense of touch, a preliminary draft of a part of page 32 [Works, III: 112-3], with many interlineations and changes:

"You villian touch! What are you doing?
Unloose me, the breath is leaving my throat;
Open your floodgates! You are too much for me. . . ."

The same theme is pursued on another page of manuscript [Works, III: 113].

"There can be nothing small or useless in the universe;
The insignificant is as big as the noble;
What is less than touch?

   . . .   .

"We do not doubt the mystery of life;
We do not doubt the east and the west;
We do not doubt sight."

WHITMAN'S ORIGINAL TABLE OF CONTENTS AND
ESTIMATE OF THE NUMBER OF WORDS AND PAGES
IN THE FIRST EDITION OF "LEAVES OF GRASS"

On the verso of one of the preceding leaves Whitman has written a table of contents for the First Edition of "Leaves of Grass", and opposite each entry the number of pages of manuscript. Over the sheet are scattered various computations to estimate the number of printed pages required, and several notes, such as: "1200 *letters in page of Shakespere's poems.* 1600 *letters in one of my closely written MS pages like page 2".*

In the upper corner is the very significant note in ink: *"left with Andrew 5 pages MS."* This alludes to Andrew Rome, one of the printers of the First Edition of "Leaves of Grass". It has been stated by biographers that Whitman set up "most" of the type for his work, but it is natural to assume from this note that Andrew Rome also set a portion. THIS PAGE APPARENTLY IS UNPUBLISHED.

In accordance with the strict limitations he had planned for "Leaves of Grass" Whitman rejected many of the poems he had written, and the three items which follow were not only rejected for the first edition, but were never published during his lifetime. The first was rejected because it was not descriptive of America, and the second was against his principle of criticising his fellow-men.

[Works, III: 260:]
"Advance shapes like his shape—the king of Egypt's shape,
Shapes that tally Sosostris—gigantic in structure, wholesome, clean-eyed. . . ."

[Description concluded on opposite page]

371

[Works, III: 261:]
"*I see an aristocrat;*
 I see a smoucher grabbing the good dishes exclusively to himself and grin-
   ning at the starvation of others as if it were funny,
 I gaze on the greedy hog; he snorts as he roots in the delicate greenhouse.
 How those niggers smell!
 Must that hod-boy occupy the same stage with me?
 Doth the dirt doze and forget itself?
 And let tomatoes ripen for busters and night walkers,
 And do no better for me—
 Who am a regular gentleman or lady,
 With a stoop and a silver door-plate and a pew in church? . . ."
[Works, III: 283:]
"*The Triumphant Poem*
 Poem of approaching death for a young man.
 Poem of approaching death
"*O for joy! O come at last! O strength! O perfect content! . . ."*

THE FIRST SKETCH IN PROSE OF "UNNAMED LANDS"

On the verso of two of the preceding leaves is a large part of the preliminary prose sketch of the poem "Unnamed Lands" (first printed in 1860) [Prose Works, VI: 49-50]: "*The best and most important part of history cannot be told. It eludes being examined or printed. It is above even dates and reliable information. . . ."*

On the verso of two other leaves are, apparently, portions of editorials written for the "Freeman" a newspaper edited by Whitman in 1850-1.

Here, then, are the beginnings of "Leaves of Grass", the transient, ephemeral thoughts upon which was built a new literature for America; and here, too, on the verso of one of the leaves, may be found Whitman's own description of the force that urged him on [Works, III: 265]:

"*The retrospective ecstacy is upon me, now my spirit burns volcanic;*
 The earth recedes ashamed before my prophetical crisis."

PROGRESS AND PRINCIPLES OF "LEAVES OF GRASS"

560. WHITMAN, WALT. A Collection of ORIGINAL MANUSCRIPTS by Walt Whitman. 9 pieces, 11 pp., folio to 12mo. About 1,150 words. [1855-88.]

A COLLECTION RELATING TO THE PRINCIPLES OF "LEAVES OF GRASS", TOGETHER WITH REVISIONS AND NEW POEMS WRITTEN AFTER THE FIRST EDITION WAS PUBLISHED.

After the 1855 edition of "Leaves of Grass" was published Whitman immediately began to write new poems and to revise the old. He broke up the whole of the prose preface, rewriting much of it in verse which was published from time to time in later editions. One portion of the preface, in this collection, was rewritten in verse but not published during his lifetime. It is an almost word-for-word transcript from the preface, p. X of the edition of 1855, but placed in the "Writings" among the "Rejected Lines and Passages" [Works,

III: 271]. This poem is written on the back of a part of the green front wrapper of the First Edition [see Number 574].

"...   ...   .

A little sum laid aside for burial money,
A few clapboards around, and shingles overhead, on a lot of American soil
owned,
A few dollars to supply the year's plain clothing and food,
And then away!"

Another portion of the preface of the First Edition, p. IV, was transcribed into verse and published in the second edition as the "Poem of Many in One", and later in "By Blue Ontario's Shore". The manuscript version in this collection, however, was not published until after Whitman's death [Works, III: 214].

"Its crimes, lies, defections, slavery, are you and me,
Its Congress is you and me—the officers, capitols, armies, ships, are you
and me,
Its inventions, science, schools, are you and me."

Still another transcription of the preface into verse, pp. V and VI of the first edition, is found on the verso of the preceding leaf, and APPARENTLY IS UNPUBLISHED.

"Sanity and ensemble characterize the great master,
Innocence and nakedness are resumed,
Theories of the special depart as dreams,
Nothing happens, or ever has happened, or ever can happen, but the vital
laws are enough . . ."

A prose draft for a poem, written about 1858, on two sheets of paper pasted together. [Works, VI: 138.]

"Did you ever think, for a moment, how so many young men, full of the stuff
to make the noblest heroes of the earth, really live—really pass their lives,
year after year, and so till death?—Constant toil—ever alert to keep the wolf
back from the door—no development—no rational pleasure . . . unaware of
any amusement except these preposterous theatres, and of a Sunday these
screams from those equally preposterous pulpits."

On the verso of one of the preceding leaves is part of a poem:

"Whose happiest days were those, far away in woods and on hills, he and
another, wandering hand in hand, they twain apart from other men, for
days and days . . ."

On another sheet is the final draft of most of "A Note Yet—The United States To-day" published in "November Boughs". [Prose Works, III: 270-271.]

Another rejected poem of twelve lines [Works, III: 281] begins:

"See—there is Epicurus—see the old philosoph in a porch teaching".

From time to time Whitman jotted down notes on the thoughts and principles he wanted to express in his poems, together with some warnings. Many of these were collected in his "Writings" under the title "Meaning and Intention of 'Leaves of Grass' ".

[Prose Works, VI: 10:]
"Poet! beware lest your poems are made in the spirit that comes from the
study of pictures of things—and not from the spirit that comes from the con-
tact with real things themselves".

[Prose Works, VI: 19:]
"Tell the American people their faults—the departments of their character
where they are most liable to break down . . ."

[Prose Works, VI: 4:]
"Poem of my adherence to the good old cause . . . Poem of the People—

represent the People, so copious, so simple, so fierce, so frivolous".
[Prose Works, VI: 5:]
"All through writings preserve the equilibrium of the truth that the material world, and all its laws, are as grand and superb as the spiritual world and all its laws . . ."

THE DEVELOPMENT OF "LEAVES OF GRASS"

561. WHITMAN, WALT. A Collection of AUTOGRAPH MANUSCRIPT NOTES, Outlines, Ideas, and Theories used by Whitman in the development of the preface and several of the poems of "Leaves of Grass", 12 pieces, 13 pp., 8vo. About 1,150 words.

50⁓
a

AN ESPECIALLY INTERESTING COLLECTION OF NOTES, some of which were more fully developed in the final paragraphs of the introduction to the First Edition of "Leaves of Grass". One idea is expressed in three different forms on three separate sheets, one form being in verse. This idea was finally developed in "After all, not to Create Only" [Works, III: 227].

"Walt Whitman's law,
  For the new and strong artists of America,
  For the fresh brood of teachers, perfect literats, the diverse savans and the coming musicians.
  There shall be no subject but it shall be treated with reference to the ensemble of the world,—and no coward or copyist shall be ever more allowed . . ."

Another sheet begins as follows:

"A New Doctrine—leading feature.—There is in the soul an instinctive test of the sense and actuality of any thing—of any statement of fact or morals . . . First however, prepare the body, it must be healthy, mature, clean . . ."
[Prose Works, VI: 38.]

On one sheet is an outline of the attributes of man as expressed by Walt Whitman throughout his works:

"A cluster of poems . . . expressing the idea and sentiment of Happiness, Extatic life, Serene Calm, Infantum, Juvenatum, Maturity—a young mans moods.
"Middle-age—Strong, well-fibred, bearded, athletic, full of love, full of pride and joy.
"Old Age—Natural Happiness, Love, Friendship."

Other sheets contain outlines for a *"Poem of Fables"*, Plato and Aristotle on Athletics, Art and Science; notes on *"The origination and continuance of metre"* [Prose Works, VI: 36], the works of Virgil, etc.

WHITMAN IN THE CIVIL WAR

562. WHITMAN, WALT. A Collection of AUTOGRAPH MANU-SCRIPTS and Notes written during the Civil War, together with numerous letters from his hospital patients, or relating to them. About 4,350 words. Together 25 pieces.

105⁓
a

IMPORTANT WAR MEMORANDA, AND NOTES AND LETTERS RELATING TO THE WOUNDED SOLDIERS. During a part of the war Whitman held clerkships in Washington and in his leisure hours visited and helped the sick and wounded soldiers in the hospitals; he also found time to visit some of the battlefields, sometimes during the fray. One manuscript is entitled *"Incidents for (Soldier in the Ranks)"* a poem apparently never published, and some of the notes were not published until after his death. [Works, III: 289.]

"Describe a group of men coming off the field after a heavy battle, the grime, the sweat, some half naked, the torn and dusty cloths, their own mothers would not recognize them.

"The moon rises silently over the battlefield but red as blood coming above the smoke—you look over the field, you see little lights moving around, stopping and moving around again, they are searching for the wounded, they are bringing off the dead. . . ."

On an envelope Whitman has written: *"characteristic soldier's letter written after the battle of Gettysburgh (6th July 1863) by H. Winstanley of Brooklyn 14th . . . I saw him in hospital, asked him about the 14th—he handed me this letter".* Inside the envelope is the original letter reporting the casualties in company I, which had twelve men left after the battle.

Two memoranda tell of the killing of the color-bearer of the 14th regiment at Bull Run and of an inquiry by the mother of Frank Lester, a captive at Spottsylvania.

"About 12 last night I saw the government dispatch announcing Gen. Sherman's capture of Savannah . . .

"November Boughs" [Prose Works, III: 218:]

"Immense numbers (several thousands) of these Pardons have been passed upon favorably: the Pardon Warrants (like great deeds) have been issued from the State Department, on the requisition of this office. But for some reason or other, they nearly all yet lie awaiting the President's signature. He seems to be in no hurry about it, but lets them wait . . ."

WHITMAN'S WORK FOR THE WOUNDED SOLDIERS. On March 24, 1867, a woman wrote to her brother, then an officer who was in Post Hospital with pneumonia. Whitman wrote a reply for the officer, the original pencil draft of which accompanies the sister's letter. A patient writes as follows:

"New York, July 22, 1869. You will remember the writer of this letter. he is only one of the many whom you befriended during our struggle for the right, one of Uncle Sam's boys, whose cause you made yours in poetry, charity and words of cheer, for the hale and hearty as well as the wounded and jaded soldier. I wont forget Walt Whitman. . . . I was reading 'Drum Taps' last night. No man can depict army life so vividly that had not spent his time among the boys . . . H. B. Thompson."

Mr. and Mrs. J. B. Pratt write in 1870: *"Permit me to write to you though a stranger by sight though a much respected friend of myself and wife for the many great kindnesses shown to us by attending to and writing to us about our son Alfred when in the great Army hospittal at Washington . . ."* With other similar letters.

BROADWAY BEFORE AND AFTER LINCOLN'S DEATH

563. WHITMAN, WALT. AUTOGRAPH MANUSCRIPT NOTES, 8 pp., 24mo, in pencil and ink. About 250 words. [New York, April 15, 1865.]

35⁓
a⁄

THE ORIGINAL MANUSCRIPT NOTES WRITTEN BY WALT WHITMAN AS HE WALKED UP BROADWAY THE AFTERNOON FOLLOWING THE ASSASSINATION OF PRESIDENT LINCOLN.

"between 4 and 5 in the afternoon I crossed the river from Brooklyn & took a walk up Broadway. The scene was solemn & most eloquent. I had so often seen Broadway on great gala days, tumultuous overwhelming shows of pride

& oceanic profusion of ornamentation & deck'd with rich colors, jubilant show crowds, & the music of a hundred bands with marchers & opera airs—or at night with processions bearing countless torches & transparencies & gay lanterns covering the houses.

"The stores were shut, & no business transacted, no pleasure vehicles, & hardly a cart—only the rumbling base of the heavy Broadway stages incessantly rolling . . . In this death the tragedy of the last five years has risen to its climax—the blood of Abraham Lincoln was permitted by the ? [sic] Spiral windings of black & white around the columns—the mighty crowd at 6 o'clock winding their way home—the crowds around the buletin boards.

"When a great event happens, or some signal solemn thing spreads out among the people it is curious to go forth and wander awhile in the public ways."

ORIGINAL MANUSCRIPT NOTES AND CLIPPINGS FOR A HISTORY OF THE BROOKLYN REGIMENTS DURING THE CIVIL WAR

564. WHITMAN, WALT. A Collection of AUTOGRAPH MANUSCRIPT NOTES, about 77 pp., 4to to 24mo. About 5,700 words. With annotated proof sheets and numerous clippings.

APPARENTLY UNPUBLISHED NOTES for a history of the Brooklyn regiments or for biographical sketches and records of the Brooklyn soldiers during the Civil War.

Naturally Whitman's greatest interest was in the 51st New York Volunteers, for his brother George became a major in that regiment, and though most of the material relates to it there are several pages of notes relating to soldiers of the 14th and 139th New York Volunteers, who also came from Brooklyn.

The collection centres upon galley proofs of a history of the "Fifty-first New York City Veterans" written by Walt Whitman for the "New York Daily Times" and published October 29, 1864. There are several copies of these galleys, and on two of them Whitman has written extensive pencil notes relating to the later history of the regiment and men.

The manuscript notes all relate to the same subject. One is apparently a part of a rough draft letter submitting his article to "The Times":

"I think the 51st New York Veterans lately captured almost entire while bravely fighting deserves some such mention. The statements in the abstract I send are all facts. You will see I have avoided anything·like puffing, but given an abstract only."

A full page is devoted to abuse of Governor Seymour for appointing outside officers to the regiment instead of promoting its own officers.

"The Governor, (Seymour) then made still another appointment of an outsider to the Lieutenant Colonelcy of the 51st, but he also declined for the same reason. A remark was made by a person present at the interview I speak of that this trick of taking advantage of the misfortune & absence by accident of war, of the veteran officers of the 51st regiment to foist outsiders over their heads & prevent the well-earned promotion of those in regular line, was a trick worthy of the New York ward politicians."

A typical note is that on John Faron:

"He was chief engineer of the Tecumseh down sick in the hospital, though very feeble when he heard of the impending fight, he rose from his sick bed &

*join'd his vessel, he said it would hurt him more to have her go in a fight &
he lying away idle than anything that happened aboard—he did his duty—was
aboard doing it when the Tecumseh went down & was lost with the rest, &
his body doubtless lies in that iron wreck at the bottom of the Gulf."*

In one of Whitman's little manuscript notebooks in this collection are several
interesting entries, including one of special importance:

*"The way to bring in the severest wipe to the bevy of American 'poets' is to
draw a strong picture of the splendor, variety, amplitude, &c of America, with
her noble heroic masses of young and other men,—also fill up the picture with
her great distances, the unparalleled romance & heroism of this war, with all
its peculiar & unprecedented points (locale)—& then scornfully add (or make
precede)—as if the silly little trembling & tepid sentimental warm water, that
is called the works of the American poets has any reference here or any foot-
hold in our future."*

*"At Spotsylvania threw up a good line of breastworks with tin cups, plates,
spoons, &c.—officers with their swords, men with their cups, &c.—scratching
very hard, every one at work—this was in the morning, after marching all
night—latter part of afternoon had to skedaddle by crawling off flat on their
bellies."*

Another booklet contains the following lines:

*"Many a loving soldier's arms about this neck have cross'd & clung,
Many a loving soldier's kiss been press'd & dwelt upon these lips."*

WHITMAN TEACHES A NEW AMERICAN
LITERATURE

565. WHITMAN, WALT. Original rough draft AUTOGRAPH MANU-
SCRIPT, in pencil, 3 pp., tall 8vo. About 850 words.

WALT WHITMAN'S PROPHECY OF THE AMERICAN LITERATURE OF THE FUTURE,
EMBODYING HIS OWN IDEALS AND THE FRAMEWORK OF THE LITERARY SCHOOL
STARTED BY HIMSELF. [Prose Works, VI: 39-42.]

*"Understand that you can have in your writing no qualities which you do not
honestly entertain in yourself. Understand that you cannot keep out of your
writing the indication of the evil or shallowness you entertain in yourself . . .*

*"Come, now, I will give the first lesson for a young man, for newer and
greater literati. Absorb no longer, mon ami, from the text books, go not for
some years to the labors of the recitation room, or desk, or on the accepted
track of tourists. Ascend to your own country. Go to the west and south. Go
among men, in the spirit of men. Go to the swimming bath, the gymnasium,
the new buildings where the working carpenters and masons are . . . Become
. . . one who does not condemn civilization and refinement but grows through
them to be superior to them . . ."*

WALT WHITMAN DISCLAIMS ORIGINALITY IN
"LEAVES OF GRASS"
AN ORIGINAL AUTOGRAPH MANUSCRIPT ON THE
IDEALS OF HIS WORK

566. WHITMAN, WALT. ORIGINAL AUTOGRAPH MANUSCRIPT of *"Philosophy of Leaves of Grass"*, 3 pp., about 400 words, 8vo. [Camden, 1776.]

ONE OF WHITMAN'S FINEST ANALYSES OF "LEAVES OF GRASS". Whitman's never-ending opinion that he had a definite message to give to the world often led him to review his own works for the public through the press or through his friends. He even supplied much of the material used by John Burroughs in his "Notes on Walt Whitman", and sent reviews of his works to friends in England. This is the rough draft of such a review. [Prose Works VI: 12-4.]

"Walt Whitman's philosophy—or perhaps metaphysics, to give it a more definite name—as evinced in his poems, and running through them, sometimes quite palpable in his verses, but far oftener latent, & like the unseen roots or sap of a tree, is not the least of his peculiarities—one must not say originalities, for Whitman himself disclaims originality, at least in the superficial sense. His notion explicitly is that there is nothing actually new only an accumulation or fruitage or carrying out of the old, or its adaptation to the modern & to their new occasions & requirements.

"He evidently thinks that behind all the faculties of the human being, as the sight, the other senses, & even the emotions & the intellect, stands the real power, the mystical identity, the I or Me or You.

"Yet there is certainly something in Walt Whitman's works which has never been ventured before—something which never could have been ventured until now (on the arrival & successful proof of America)—something which, even yet, many leading critics refuse to admit as a legitimate theme for verse . . .

"The idea of the books is Democracy. That is carried, far beyond Politics, into the regions of Taste, the standards of Manners and Beauty, & even into Philosophy and Theology.

"In one way or another, now strongly odorous, now at second or third or fourth remove, now a silent background (as in the poems of the Hospitals and the Dead in Drum Taps) this determined resolution or idea pervades the whole of both books . . ."

WHITMAN ADVISES A FRIEND NOT TO
READ HIS BOOKS

567. WHITMAN, WALT. Rough Draft AUTOGRAPH MANUSCRIPT, 1 p., 4to, with many interlineations and corrections. About 250 words.

A FINE MANUSCRIPT ON HIS "LEAVES OF GRASS" apparently written as an interpolation in one of his own reviews of his works, as the whole page is enclosed in brackets. [Prose Works, VI: 33-4.]

" 'Don't read my books', I heard Walt Whitman good-naturedly yet emphatically say one day to an intelligent but conventional questioner whom he personally liked: 'You want something good in the usual sense, a plot, a love-story, something based on the accepted principles, and on etiquette & prece-

dents. I have written no such books. I have attempted to construct a poem on the open principles of Nature, as comprehended not only in the material worlds of astronomy, the earth and sea, but as in all the movements of history & civilization, wars, the shows of cities, and in man with all his attributes, animal, intellectual & spiritual. The whole drift of my books is to form a race yet unknown, athletic characters, men and women for the United States to come. I do not write to amuse or furnish poetry, so-called; and will surely repel at first those who have been used to the jingle of rhymes. Every page of my books emanates Democracy, absolute, unintermitted, without the slightest compromise, and the sense of the New World in its future, a thoroughly revolutionary formation, to be exhibited less in politics, and more in theology, literature and manners . . .'"

LITERARY AND DESCRIPTIVE PREPARATORY
NOTES FOR "LEAVES OF GRASS"

568. WHITMAN, WALT. A Collection of ORIGINAL MANUSCRIPT NOTES, 23 pp., 8vo and 12mo. About 1,050 words.

This collection is illustrative of Whitman's careful preparatory reading for, and search for accuracy in statements that were finally embodied in "Leaves of Grass". In the 1855 and 1856 editions, for instance, Whitman wrote "Where the she whale swims with her calves", but after an interview with an old whaler Whitman wrote one of these pages of notes, and in the 1860 edition changed the line to read "Where the she whale swims with her calf". [Prose Works, VI: 137.]

None of these notes were published until after the death of Whitman, when they were incorporated in the "Complete Writings".

[Prose Works, VII: 15:]

"Spenser's single object through the vast amplitude and variety of his 'Fairie Queene' is 'to fashion a gentleman of noble person in virtuous, brave, and gentle discipline.'"

Ten pages of biographical and critical notes are devoted to Cervantes and Don Quixote.

[Prose Works, VI: 64-9:]

"Don Quixote. The object, besides writing a good and amusing story, was to foil the fanaticism for romances of Chivalry, of the Amadis de Gaul type, which then generally prevailed in Spain. (The esoteric meaning discovered by modern critics is mostly bosh)."

Notes written in 1857 give a description of China from the personal observations of a friend.

[Prose Works, VI: 60-2:]

"Talk with Elias Pierson, who was in China, in the rebel army, in Canton, and all through the country: A religious building . . . The 'josh' . . . Slavery . . . Personal size and attributes . . . Chinese Army . . . Climate . . . Executions . . . Pekin . . . Lascars . . ."

Other travel notes are on *"Brutish Human beings—Wild men—the 'Koboo'"* [Prose Works, VI: 54]; and *"Valley of the lower Rio Bravo"*, an extract from Emery's report.

A suggestion for a poem [Works, III: 289-90]:

"Make a demand for the ideal . . .
"Thy true development, in thy unloosen'd soaring spirit!"

569. WHITMAN, WALT. A Collection of Magazine Reviews of the Works of English and other Authors, with MANUSCRIPT ANNOTATIONS by Whitman, 5 pieces, about 135 pp.; together with 13 pp. of autograph manuscript comments and criticisms.

50—

Goodspeed

A SPLENDID COLLECTION OF MATERIAL ILLUSTRATING WHITMAN'S LITERARY DEVELOPMENT PRIOR TO AND IMMEDIATELY FOLLOWING THE PUBLICATION OF "LEAVES OF GRASS". Most of the comments on English authors were written about 1852, with subsequent annotations made from 1857 to 1859. [Nearly all are in Prose Works VI.]

The material on Leigh Hunt's "What is Poetry" contains a biographical note and the comment *"a good essay"*; while the most striking passages, in Whitman's estimation, are outlined. A review of the "Life and Correspondence of Robert Southey" is noted as *"This is a very finely done criticism"*; at the end is a note on Robert Burns: *"Burns was faithful to lowly things, customs, idioms, Scotland, the lasses, the peasant, and to his own robust nature . . ."*

Elaborate notes on a review of Keats' "Hyperion" explain much that Whitman was endeavoring to incorporate in his own poems: *"The originality must be of the spirit and show itself in new combinations and new meanings and discovering greatness and harmony where there was before thought no greatness . . ."* He describes Lessing as *"the R. W. Emerson of his age . . . paved the way for Goethe and Schiller"*.

On a review of Wordsworth Whitman has pasted one of the lyrics of Spring upon which he comments; *"Wordsworth, it seems, is the originator of this kind of poems—followed here by Bryant, and others"*, and again: *"yet with all this glorification of Wordsworth read the personal traits of him, with sayings, looks, foibles, &c.—as given by those who knew him."*

A literary review of Chaucer contains over a page of manuscript biographical notes and many marginal comments. Replying to an assertion that Shakespeare translated Chaucer Whitman writes: *"As to Shakespeare's translations—they are the translation of so much beef and bread into vital human body and soul"*; and he sums up Chaucer: *"Chaucer was plainly a strong, wholesome man, with large perceptive organs, friendly, amative, of independent spirit,—possessed of the true English tastes, rude, fond of women, fond of eating and drinking, not to be gulled by priestcraft or kingcraft."*

The manuscript pages of comments (about 2,000 words) on various authors, such as Ossian, Niebuhr, Alexander Smith, Bayard Taylor, and others, are interspersed with ideas and ideals to be used in Whitman's own poems.

"Most poets finish single specimens of characters.—I will never finish single specimens; I will shower them by exhaustless laws, as nature does, extricating not only themselves but successive productions out of themselves, sweeter and fresher continually." [Prose Works VI: 87.]

"The secret is here: Perfections are only understood and responded to by perfections. This rule runs through all, and applies to mediocrity, crime, and all the rest; each is understood only by the like of itself. Any degree of development in the soul is only responded to by the similar degree in other souls. One religion wonders at another. A nation wonders how another can be what it is, can like what it likes, and dislike what it dislikes. A man wonders at another man's folly . . ."

570. WHITMAN, WALT. A Collection of AUTOGRAPH MANUSCRIPT
Business Letters, Editorial "Puffs", Letters to Walt Whitman
about "Leaves of Grass", Articles about Whitman, etc. Together
forty-two pieces, 4to and smaller. About 10,000 words.

This collection is of special importance as illustrating Whitman's salesmanship
methods and the effects of "Leaves of Grass" upon the public. It contains
one of Whitman's famous "puffs" written to attract attention to his work
[Prose Works, VI: 35-6, see also Numbers 566 and 567]:

*"We suppose it will excite the mirth of many of our readers to be told that a
man has arisen, who has deliberately and insultingly ignored all the other, the
cultured classes as they are called, and set himself to work to write 'America's
first distinctive Poem', on the platform of these same New York Roughs,
firemen, the ouvrier class, masons and carpenters, stage-drivers, the Dry Dock
boys, and so forth; and that furthermore he either is not aware of the existence of the polite social models, and the imported literary laws, or else he
don't value them two cents for his purposes."*

There is a rough draft letter, 1867, to an agent for "Leaves of Grass", and an
autograph statement of French and Richardson's account for thirty-seven
copies of his work. On July 20, 1883, Whitman writes to a friend thanking
him for corrections in "Leaves of Grass", and on the back of the same sheet
is the statement of a principle he observed throughout all his writings:

*"I know some of my best friends will be angry with me; but in my opinion
(as in a question of science, or diagnosing a disease) what is best in the
matter, if you state it at all, is to state the exact truth."*

Proof sheets of the beginning and end of "A Backward Glance o'er Travel'd
Roads", with corrections and a note by Whitman: *"Send this set of proofs
back to me by Horace Traubel".*

The letters to Whitman, some of them anonymous, express an intense appreciation of "Leaves of Grass" and affection for the poet.

*"I am no poet, but I can thank you for expanding my soul, and showing me
beauties where I silently felt they must be, for teaching me to love all and
everything, to feel in sympathy and harmony with every atom of God's beautiful universe."*

*"I have been reading Leaves of Grass again and now that I know the Author
I better understand them and bless you for your brave words for woman-
hood."*

Other material includes several of the announcement cards of Whitman's lecture on Lincoln at Madison Square Theatre, with an admission ticket; manuscript copies of two contributions by Whitman to Brooklyn newspapers in
1846 and 1854; a copy of "Scenes and Sonnets. By Alfred Ford", on which
Whitman has written *"Balloon Corespondent of the Daily Graphic"*, with three
balloon letters laid in; etc.

381

571. —— AUTOGRAPH MANUSCRIPT Account of Whitman's Paternal
Grandmother, her Family and Home, 4 pp., 4to. October 17,
1860, with a pencil note at the end dated 1884. About 350 words.

AN INTERESTING SKETCH OF WALT WHITMAN'S GRANDMOTHER AND THE WHIT-
MAN HOME.

*"Hannah Brush (my grandmother Whitman, my father's mother) and her
sister were orphans, brought up by their Aunt Vashti Platt . . . Mother has
told me that Grandmother Whitman, when she was a girl, living with her aunt
in the farmhouse, has counted as many as sixteen little 'niggers' in the kitchen
eating their meal of samp and milk . . .*

*"I remember very well the old house of the Whitmans at West Hills—the one
used for two or three generations previous to my father, and which my father
was born in. When I was a boy, I used to go into it. I remember the great
heavy timbers, low ceilings, upper chambers, &c.—and the kitchen, &c. It had
on one side a beautiful grove of black-walnuts, locust, &c. and in the rear a
small peach orchard. All was in great neglect, however . . . [1884—It is still
standing—used as a granary, coach-house, &c.]."*

WALT AND GEORGE WHITMAN

572. WHITMAN, WALT. A Collection of 7 AUTOGRAPH MANU-
SCRIPTS by Walt Whitman; an A. N. s. by George Whitman; and
2 other A. L. s. About 2,500 words. With 2 contemporary newspapers and 4 clippings. Together 16 pieces.

WALT WHITMAN'S ORIGINAL NARRATIVE OF HIS EFFORTS TO RELEASE HIS
BROTHER FROM A REBEL PRISON. George Whitman had served throughout the
Civil War, rising from a private to captain and acting lieutenant-colonel of
the 51st New York Volunteers, when his regiment was surrounded and captured at the battle of Poplar Grove Church, September 30, 1864. His family
had not heard from him since the official return of prisoners on October 3rd.
Walt Whitman writes as follows:

*"Monday Night. December 26, 1864. I am writing this in the front basement
in Portland Avenue, Brooklyn, at home . . . George's trunk came by express
to-day, early in forenoon, from City Point, Virginia. Lt. Babcock of the 51st
was kind enough to search it out there & send it home. It stood some hours
before we felt inclined to open it. Towards evening mother & Eddy looked
over the things. One could not help feeling depressed . . . I am aware of the
condition of the union prisoners south, through seeing them when brought up
& from lately talking with a friend just returned from taking part in the exchange at Savannah & Charleston by which we have received 12,000 of our
sick. Their situation, as of all our men in prison, is indescribably horrible.
Hard, ghastly starvation is the rule . . ."*

On February 19th, 1865, came a welcome letter from Capt. William Cook, an
exchanged prisoner, enclosing the following autograph note from George
Whitman:

George W. Whitman Capt. 51st Regt. N. Y. Vols. Prisoner of war at Dan-

ville Va. in tip top health and spirits. Mothers Address, Mrs. Louisa Whitman, Portland Ave near Myrtle Ave, Brooklyn, N. Y."

Then Walt Whitman writes:

"Brooklyn, Jan. 19 & 20, 1865. We have just heard from George after a blank of four months. He is in the Confederate Military Prison at Danville, Va. (or rather was on Nov 27, for his letter has been nearly two months getting here). When captured, he & the other officers were taken to Libby Prison in Richmond, from there to Salisbury, N. C. & from there to Danville, where they are kept (on corn meal, a little bacon, &c.) in a tobacco warehouse . . . We first received one of those significant slips of paper (of which I have seen so many bushels, one time and another, brought up by exchanged prisoners, dingy, soiled, half legible records of death, home addresses of prisoners, &c.) written by his own hand with mother's name on . . ."

Walt Whitman at once went to Washington to use every effort to obtain his brother's exchange, and on February 17th writes as follows:

"I heard to-day from Head-quarters of the Armies, at City Point, by official letter from Lt. Gen'l Grant's military secretary. He writes that the Lt. Gen'l has directed a special exchange for George & also for Lt. Pooley. This is an addition to the order already given by Maj-Gen. Hitchcock, the U. S. Commissioner of Exchange & promised to be acted upon by Col. Mulford personally . . . We have sent both from Brooklyn & City Point boxes of provisions & cloths, but it is probable they have not reached him . . ."

A letter by J. W. Mason tells of forwarding the box by a flag of truce. Again Whitman writes:

"Feb. 25, 26, 27, & 28. These four days have put me through all the changes of hope & dismay about getting George exchanged. I had been thinking for a fortnight that he was at last as good as within our lines . . . But Sunday night I heard to my consternation, that although all the Danville prisoners had indeed come up, . . . neither George nor any other 51st officer had come . . .

"The Gen'l does not undertake to explain why George & the other 51st officers, (for this time I included all in my request) did not come up, but he does not think it is because the secession authorities wish to hold on to them, nor because (as I also inquired on that point) they wish to punish them for trying to break out of the military prison . . ."

Early in March Captain Whitman was exchanged and, after a furlough to recuperate, rejoined his regiment in April. On May 9th Walt Whitman writes:

"Col. Wright (I met him in Pennsylvania avenue) told me to-day quite a good deal about George—spoke of the universal opinion of the regiment, officers & men, of his coolness, self-possession, good-natured, very little of talker, never talking about himself, quiet but dangerous when roused . . ."

"July 27, 1865. This morning the 51st packed everything up, obedient to orders received last night, & moved from Camp Augur, across the long bridge, through Washington, to the Baltimore depot, whence they departed about 7 p.m. for New York. I was down among them, saw George, Sam'l Pooley, & all the officers & men . . ."

The newspapers contain an account of the record and services of Captain Whitman, and the clippings an account of the capture of his regiment.

573. WHITMAN, WALT. A Collection of Proofs of Poems and Articles, with some Broadside Publications. Together 33 pieces, folio to 16mo.

50

a

A SPLENDID COLLECTION OF WHITMAN'S BROADSIDE POEMS, PROSE ARTICLES, AND ADVERTISEMENTS. After a poem was written it was often printed on proof sheets and put away for revision, and all poems and articles published in newspapers and magazines were carefully read in proof by the author. From two to six proofs were usually made, and Whitman often sent these duplicates to his friends. THEIR EPHEMERAL CHARACTER AND LIMITED NUMBER MAKE THESE PROOFS OF EXTREME RARITY. Professor Triggs, in the "Collected Works of Walt Whitman", styles the following as "Camden Proofs", printed at a private press, and they are here numbered according to the Trigg list.

"A Carol Closing Sixty-nine." No. 323.
"Ah, not this Granite Dead and Cold." [Washington's Monument.] No. 350.
"To Get the Final Lilt of Songs." No. 353.
"Going Somewhere." No. 359.
"Thanks in Old Age." No. 363.
"Twilight." No. 372.
"As the Greek's Signal Flame. For Whittier's 80th birth-day, December 17, 1887." No. 376.
"Shakespere-Bacon's Cipher." No. 391.

PUBLISHER'S PROOFS:

"Death of Carlyle" [1881], with manuscript address to W. D. O'Connor, 2 photographs of Carlyle, one signed; and a photograph of Mrs. Carlyle.
"The Soldiers, &c. From an Occasional Correspondent. Washington, February, 1865."
"The Bible as Poetry." ["Critic", Feb. 3, 1883.]
"A Thought on Shakespeare." ["Critic", August 14, 1886.]
"A Memorandum at a Venture." From the "North American Review." [A reprint of Whitman's defense of "Children of Adam".] 14 copies.

OTHER BROADSIDES:

Leaflet Literature. Published by Angela T. Heywood. Princeton, Mass. [1882.] On the suppression of "Leaves of Grass" in Boston.
—— Another copy, Nov. 5, 1882. An Open Letter to Walt Whitman. 3 copies.
The Word—Extra. Censorship of the Press. Princeton, Mass.
The Book for Fall! [Advertising "Specimen Days and Collect".] 2 copies. With two wrappers addressed by Whitman to Dr. Bucke.

ORIGINAL WRAPPERS FOR THE FIRST EDITION OF "LEAVES OF GRASS"

574. WHITMAN, WALT. 2 GREEN front wrappers and 5 complete PINK wrappers for the First Edition of "Leaves of Grass", 1855. Together 7 pieces.

11

These wrappers were used on the second issue of the First Edition of "Leaves of Grass". They are of the original width but have had an inch cut from the top margin and measure 8 by 10 inches. They were used by Whitman for note paper [see Number 560].

A SUPERB SET, BOUND IN FULL LEVANT MOROCCO
WITH DOUBLURES

575. WHITMAN, WALT. The Complete Writings of Walt Whitman. Issued under the editorial supervision of his Literary Executors, Richard Maurice Bucke, Thomas B. Harned, and Horace L. Traubel. With additional bibliographical and critical material prepared by Oscar Lovell Triggs. *Illustrations*, FRONTISPIECES IN COLOR. 10 vols., 8vo full blue levant morocco, gilt tooled backs, gilt tooled borders on sides, with four onlays of white morocco, doublures of red morocco, fly-leaves of red watered silk, gilt tops, uncut.

New York: G. P. Putnam's Sons, 1902

PAUMANOK EDITION. ONE OF 300 SETS.

JEFF AND WALT WHITMAN

576. WHITMAN, THOMAS JEFFERSON. A Collection of 95 A. L. s., about 400 pp., 4to and 8vo. April 3, 1860, to July 14, 1888. To his brother Walt and to his mother.

A COLLECTION ESPECIALLY VALUABLE for the clear insight it gives into the family life of the Whitmans and Walt's relations thereto. Jeff, as he was always called by the family, was the youngest and favorite brother of Walt, and the nearest in sympathy both mentally and physically. They were devoted to each other and kept up a regular correspondence from the time Walt left home in 1860 to within two years of the death of Jeff in 1890.

Jeff wrote interesting letters with all the gossip of the family and neighborhood, now mingled with strong expressions, and then with sympathy and pity. When the first letter was written Walt was in Boston seeing the third edition of "Leaves of Grass" through the press, and Jeff writes:

"I quite long for it to make its appearance, what jolly times we will have reading the notices of it wont we, you must expect the 'Yam Yam Yam' writer to give you a dig as often as possible but I dont suppose you will mind it any more than you did in the days of your editorship of the B. Eagle."

The war letters are of special importance, for Jeff, then engineer of the Brooklyn Water Works, acted as agent for Walt to collect money to aid the patients in the hospitals, and in almost every letter sent sums ranging from fifteen cents to $50.00 until long after the war. Hearing that his brother, Capt. George Whitman, was wounded, Walt went to Washington to find and to help him. On January 1, 1863 Jeff writes urging Walt to have George resign his commission and return home:

"Just think for a moment of the number of suckers that are gaining all the

real benefits of the war (if that is not wicked to say) and think of George and thousands of others running all the risk while they are drawing all the pay."
February 6, 1863. *"Walt, you must be doing more real good than the whole sanitary Commission put together."*

On the back of a letter by George Whitman, dated April 2, 1863, Jeff writes: *"We think that we shall call you 'The B. Water Works Soldiers Aid Society' with power."*

May 27, 1863. *"I cannot agree with you Walt in relation to the President. I think that he is not a man for the times, not big enough. He dont seem to have even force enough to stop bickerings between his own Cabinet and Generals nor force enough to do as he thinks best."*

During the summer of 1863 Jeff wrote long descriptions of the New York draft riots.

July 19, 1863. *"I guess the only wonderfully frightened men were Opdike and Seymour, if we perhaps except the Copperhead dem.'s that incited the rioters on and then deserted them . . . There are now more than 400 rioters that have paid their lives for their plunder. The papers are not allowed to publish this."*

Towards the end of 1863 a younger brother, Andrew, died from tuberculosis; the eldest brother, Jess, became violently insane; and another brother, Edward, an imbecile. Walt Whitman was able to be at home for only a short time and all the care of the household fell upon Jeff. In the fall of 1864 Capt. George Whitman was taken prisoner [see Number 572], and Jeff sent him boxes of food and clothing.

In July, 1865, Walt was dismissed from his position in the Indian Bureau by Secretary Harlan because of his authorship of "Leaves of Grass", and on July 16, 1865, Jeff writes as follows:

"When I came to the statement that Harlan was a parson of course his conduct was to be expected. From that class you can never get anything but lying and meanness. I hope you do not allow it to have any effect on you, you must not. The poor mean-minded man. If Christ came to earth again and did'nt behave different from what he did when he was here he would have a mighty poor show with Harlan would'nt he?"

After the war many of Jeff's letters were to his mother until her death in 1873, for he had moved to St. Louis where he had charge of the water works. As the two brothers grew older their affection seemed to grow stronger, and to the end Jeff's cheery letters encouraged and helped Walt.

George Campbell Smith, Jr.

PUBLIC SALE

Tuesday, November 23, at 8:15 p.m.
Wednesday, November 24, at 2 and 8:15 p.m.

EXHIBITION & SALE AT THE

AMERICAN ART ASSOCIATION
ANDERSON GALLERIES·INC

30 EAST 57TH STREET · NEW YORK

Sales Conducted by

HIRAM H. PARKE · OTTO BERNET · H. E. RUSSELL, JR

1937

COPY OF "LEAVES OF GRASS" PREPARED AND ANNOTATED BY WALT WHITMAN FOR THE FIRST ENGLISH EDITION EDITED BY WILLIAM MICHAEL ROSSETTI

561. WHITMAN, WALT. Copy of "Leaves of Grass" prepared by Walt Whitman from two dissected copies of the New York 1867 edition, with some pages from "Drum-Taps", New York, 1865, to supply the text for the first English edition of Whitman's "Poems", 1868, edited by William Michael Rossetti, with pagination and occasional corrections and annotations in the handwriting of Walt Whitman, comprising about 500 leaves, 12mo, each separate and unsewn. Laid in a half green levant morocco slip case.

THE COPY SENT BY WALT WHITMAN TO WILLIAM MICHAEL ROSSETTI FOR THE PUBLICATION OF THE FIRST ENGLISH EDITION OF WHITMAN'S "POEMS", issued in 1868.

A COPY OF TRIPLE ASSOCIATION INTEREST, for Rossetti, in turn, gave it to Anne Gilchrist, one of Whitman's dearest friends and admirers (author of "A Woman's Estimate of Walt Whitman" and "A Confession of Faith"), from whose estate it was privately purchased. Laid in is a note in the handwriting of Anne Gilchrist, reading *"Unbound Copy of Leaves of Grass Annotated by Walt Whitman for the London edition of his poems."*

THIS COPY CONTAINS ABOUT 180 WORDS IN WHITMAN'S AUTOGRAPH, in addition to the pagination, punctuation, cut-outs, and insertions, all done by Whitman himself. The verso of each sheet is crossed out, also by the author.

SALE NUMBER 59

FREE PUBLIC EXHIBITION

From Thursday, October 27, to Time of Sale

Weekdays 9 to 5:30 · Sunday 2 to 5

George C. Smith, Jr.

PUBLIC SALE

Wednesday and Thursday

November 2 and 3 at 8:15 p. m.

EXHIBITION & SALE AT THE

PARKE-BERNET GALLERIES · INC

742 FIFTH AVENUE · NEW YORK

Northwest Corner of 57th Street

Sales Conducted by

HIRAM H. PARKE · OTTO BERNET · H. E. RUSSELL, Jr

1938

not the losers

Dec. 7th

That Walt Whitman, of whom I wrote to you, is the most interesting fact to me at present. I have just read his 2d edition (which he gave me) and it has done me more good than any reading for a long time. Perhaps I remember best the poem of Walt Whitman on America & the Sun Down Poem. There are 2 or 3 pieces in the book which are disagreeable to say the least, simply sensual. He does not celebrate love at all — it is as if the beasts spoke. I think that men have not been ashamed of themselves

[NUMBER 228]

A REMARKABLE LETTER MAINLY ABOUT
"LEAVES OF GRASS"

228. THOREAU, HENRY D. A. L. s. (initials), 9 pp. 4to. Concord, December 6, 1856. To H. G. O. Blake, about 1,500 words. In a half morocco slip case.

250
ypil

A REMARKABLY LENGTHY LETTER, FULLY ONE-HALF RELATING TO WALT WHITMAN AND TO "LEAVES OF GRASS", reading in part as follows:

"That Walt Whitman, of whom I wrote to you, is the most interesting fact to me at present. I have just rec'd his 2nd edition ["Leaves of Grass"] (which he gave me) and it has done me more good than any reading for a long time. Perhaps I remember best the poem of Walt Whitman on America and the Sun Down Poem. There are 2 or 3 pieces in the book which are disagreeable to say the least, simply sensual . . . I have found his poem exhilirating [sic] encouraging . . . One woman told me that no woman could read it—as if a man could read what a woman could not . . . On the whole it sounds to me very brave & American . . . I do not believe that all the sermons so called that have been preached in 'this' land put together are equal to it for preaching . . ."

[See illustration]

The A. Edward Newton Collection
PART THREE: N-Z

FREE PUBLIC EXHIBITION

Daily from Saturday, October 25, to Time of Sale
Weekdays 9 to 5.30
Sunday, October 26, from 2 to 5

PUBLIC SALE

Wednesday, October 29 at 8.15 p.m.
Thursday, October 30 at 2 and 8.15 p.m.

EXHIBITION & SALE AT THE
PARKE-BERNET GALLERIES · INC

30 EAST 57 STREET · NEW YORK

[SALE NUMBER 306]

Sales Conducted by
HIRAM H. PARKE · OTTO BERNET
HARRY E. RUSSELL, JR · LOUIS J. MARION

1941

»529« WHITMAN, WALT · A.D.s., 2 pp., small 4to, about 450 words. Camden, New Jersey, November 26, 1880. To an unnamed correspondent. Laid in a half morocco small folio volume.

250

A VERY FINE DOCUMENT, respecting the unauthorized publication of *Leaves of Grass* by Richard Worthington, reading in part as follows:

"R Worthington 770 Broadway New York about a year ago bo't at auction the electrotype plates (456 pages) of the 1860-1 edition of my book *Leaves of Grass*—plates originally made by a young firm *Thayer & Eldridge* under my supervision there and then in Boston (in the Spring of 1860), on an agreement running five years. A small edition was printed and issued at the time, but in six months or thereabout Thayer & Eldridge failed and these plates were stored away and nothing further done till about a year ago (latter part of 1879) they were put up in N Y City by Leavitt auctioneer, & bought in by said Worthington. (Leavitt before putting them up wrote to me offering the plates for sale. I wrote back that said plates were worthless, being superseded by a larger & different edition—that I could not use them the 1860 ones myself, nor would I allow them to be used by anyone else—I being the sole owner of the copyright.

"However it seems Leavitt did auction them & Worthington bo't them . . . I had supposed the whole thing dropt, & nothing done, but within a week past, I learn that Worthing has been slyly printing and selling the Volume of *Leaves of Grass* from those plates (must have commenced early in 1880) and is now printing and selling it . . ."

✦ *On the front end-leaf of the volume Mr. Newton has written: "This important bibliographical document is more clearly written than any other Whitman manuscript I have seen. I used frequently to see Walt come into Porter & Coates, where I was employed, to see how 'Leaves of Grass' was selling. A. Edward Newton. March 25, 1926." Beneath the inscription Mr. Newton has inscribed: "I Gave G. W. $4.00 for this item! (1919)." The above document is quoted in full in A Magnificent Farce.*

[See illustration]

(Canada at the time) I wrote to ~~Washington referr~~ to his previous offer, then destined by me and asking whether he still had the plates & was disposed to make the same offer; to which I rec'd no answer. I wrote a second time; and again no answer.

I had supposed the whole thing dropt & nothing done, but within a week past, I learn that Worthington has been slyly printing and selling the Volume of _Leaves of Grass_ from those plates (must have commenced early in 1880) and is now printing and selling it. On Nov. 22, 1880, I found the book (printed from those plates, at Porter & Coates' store, cor. 9th & Chestnut Sts. Philadelphia. P & C told me they procured it from Worthington, & had been so procuring it off & on, for nearly a year.

First I want Worthington effectually stopt from issuing the books. Second I want my royalty for all he has sold, (though I have no idea of ever getting a cent.) Third I want W. taken hold of, if possible, on criminal proceeding.

I am the sole owner of the copyright—& I think my copyright papers are all complete— —I publish & sell the book myself—it is my sole means of living—what Worthington has done has already been a serious detriment to me. —Mr. Eldridge, (of the Boston firm alluded to) is accessible in Washington DC—will corroborate first parts of the foregoing—(is my friend)

Walt Whitman 431 Stevens street
Camden New Jersey

A FINE DOCUMENT BY WALT WHITMAN

[Number 529]

SALE NUMBER 524

RARE FIRST EDITIONS
AUTOGRAPH LETTERS AND
MANUSCRIPTS

The Distinguished Library of

HOWARD J. SACHS

Stamford, Conn.

PUBLIC AUCTION SALE BY HIS ORDER

FEBRUARY 1 AT 8:15 P.M.

PARKE-BERNET GALLERIES · INC

30 EAST 57 STREET · NEW YORK 22

1944

FROM THE AUTHOR OF "LEAVES OF GRASS"
TO THE AUTHOR OF "DRACULA"

118. WHITMAN, WALT. A.L.s. *"Walt Whitman."* 1 p., 4to, Camden, N. Jersey, [431 Stevens St.], March 6, 1876. To Bram Stoker. With stamped, addressed envelope bearing upon its face: *"Abraham Stoker,* 119 *Lower Baggot Street, Dublin, Ireland"*, in Whitman's hand. In a morocco-backed cloth slip case.

An interesting letter to the author of *Dracula*. Reads in part as follows: " '*Bram Stoker,* "*My dear young man, your letters have been most welcome to me—welcome to me as Person & then as Author. I don't know which most. You did well to write to me so unconventionally too. . . . Edward Dowden's letter containing among others your subscription for a copy of my new edition has just been rec'd. I shall send the books very soon. . . . My physique is entirely shatter'd—doubtless permanently from paralysis & other ailments . . .*"

Bram Stoker and Prof. Dowden weathered all the storm that arose over the works of Whitman, and in the depth of his admiration Stoker wrote to Whitman eliciting the above reply.

INSCRIBED BY WALT WHITMAN AND OSCAR WILDE

119. WHITMAN, WALT. Leaves of Grass. *Frontispiece portrait on plain paper; slight foxing,* and slightly offset from title-page. Small folio, original green cloth, stamped in gilt and blind, gilt edges; inner hinges cracked and a few other small cover defects, a few small tears in the front end-leaf, and a small piece torn from a blank corner of one leaf. In a cloth slip case.

London, 1855

FIRST EDITION. FIRST ISSUE. In the correct binding with ornamental lettering and triple line borders stamped in gilt on both sides, and without the leaves of press notices. This copy has brown end-papers, and judging from the age of the paper, and the author's inscription (see below), this might have been Whitman's own copy bound with the present end-papers at his request.

A SUPERB ASSOCIATION VOLUME LINKING THE NAMES OF WALT WHITMAN, AND OSCAR WILDE. INSCRIBED BY THE FORMER on the front fly-leaf: *"The days in Boston on my visit—April* 13th-19th *1881—the good times with you dear Boyle & my other dear new friends—the affectionate kindnesses—talks, &c. Walt Whitman."*

BENEATH WHITMAN'S INSCRIPTION, OSCAR WILDE HAS INSCRIBED: *"The spirit who living blamelessly yet dared to kiss the smitten mouth of his own century. Oscar Wilde".* From the library of the American Author, John Boyle O'Reilly, with his autograph signature, and date *"Sept.* 1877" inscribed above Whitman's inscription, and also on the recto of the frontispiece portrait. With a signed portrait of Whitman pasted down on the front end-leaf. The tissue guard is not present in this copy.

APPARENTLY THE SECOND COPY OF THIS ISSUE TO APPEAR AT PUBLIC SALE IN AMERICA BEARING AN AUTOGRAPH INSCRIPTION BY THE AUTHOR.

[See illustration]

John Boyle O'Reilly—
sept 1877.

The days in Boston on
my visit—April 13th-19th 1881—
—the good times with you dear Boyle
& my other dear new friends,—the
affectionate kindnesses—talks &c.
Walt Whitman

The spirit who living blameless
but dared to kiss the
smitten mouth of his
own century!

Oscar Wilde

[NUMBER 119]

Sale No. 969

LIBRARY

OF THE LATE

Thomas Bird Mosher

PORTLAND · MAINE

AND EXAMPLES OF HIS OWN

PUBLICATIONS, MANY PRINTED ON VELLUM

Sold by Order of His Son

H. H. MOSHER

Grand Rapids, Michigan

PART ONE

Public Auction Sale

May 10 and 11 at 2 p. m.

PARKE-BERNET GALLERIES · INC

NEW YORK

1948

468. WHITMAN, WALT. After All, Not to Create Only. (Recited by Walt Whitman, on invitation of Directors American Institute, on Opening of their 40th Annual Exhibition, New York, noon, September 7, 1871.) Folio sheets, printed on one side only. [Washington: Pearson, 1871]

RARE FIRST ISSUE OF THE FIRST EDITION. PRINTED IN BROADSIDE FORM, WITH THE FOLLOWING PRINTED AT THE TOP OF THE FIRST SHEET "(PROOFS—OFFICE AMERICAN INSTITUTE, NEW YORK)". According to the Bibliography of Walt Whitman by Wells and Goldsmith, this issue consisted of only a few copies. This edition was printed for Whitman at the expense of the Institute.

Accompanying the above is an A. N. s. by Horace Traubel, 1 p., 4to, Boston, Oct. 1905, reading: *"These sheets of After All Not to Create Only were given to me long ago by Walt Whitman & now I pass them along to my dear friend Tom Mosher with my love. Horace Traubel."*

WITH AUTOGRAPH REVISIONS

471. WHITMAN, WALT. A new assembly of poems for *Whispers of Heavenly Death,* with Autograph Manuscript revisions. Comprises 19 poems, of which 18 are printed and one written ENTIRELY IN WHITMAN'S AUTOGRAPH. These printed poems have been excerpted from an edition of his works and pasted down on 12mo sheets. Stitched together with a title-page in Whitman's autograph reading *"Whispers of Heavenly Death".*

THESE POEMS WERE ASSEMBLED FOR AN EDITION OF "LEAVES OF GRASS," published after 1870. Below the manuscript title-page which is in Whitman's autograph, is the following note in ink by Horace Traubel: *Given by Walt Whitman to me* (1889) *and given by me to Thomas Mosher (Camden,* 1906). *Horace Traubel".*

In the poem "Assurances" the author has added one line in his autograph. The first verse of the poem "Yet, Yet, ye downcast hours" is written entirely in Whitman's autograph, and he has deleted some words in the first and second lines of the second verse. The poem "Joy! Shipmate! Joy!" (To My Soul) is written ENTIRELY IN THE AUTOGRAPH OF THE AUTHOR, and is entirely revised from the first published version as it appeared in "Passage to India" published in 1870. In the poem "As Nearing Departure" he has added three words to the first line, and to the first line of the second verse he had added a word, and in the second line of the third verse he has crossed out the pronoun "we" and substituted "I".

[See frontispiece]

---

473. WHITMAN, WALT. Memoranda During the War. 12mo, unstitched sheets, uncut and partly unopened; some discoloration of paper on which title-page is printed, and small break in fore-margin of last page.

Camden, 1876-76

FIRST EDITION. ONE OF WHITMAN'S RAREST BOOKS. ABOUT 100 COPIES WERE ISSUED IN SEPARATE FORM. The present copy does not have the leaf with heading "Remembrance Copy", and does not have the two portraits issued with the work.

On the top margin of the title-page Horace Traubel has written, in ink, *"Given by Walt Whitman to Horace Traubel* (1891) *and given by Horace Traubel to Thomas Mosher.* 1905".

474. [WHITMAN, WALT.] Leaves of Grass. *2 portraits*. 12mo, original half cream-colored calf, brown leather label on backstrip; leaf of advertisement at end; backstrip discolored. Camden, 1876

AUTHOR'S EDITION. This copy has the wording *"With Portraits from life"* printed below "Author's Edition" on the title-page. Some copies have the words "With portraits and Intercalations"; the intercalations being short poems printed on small slips of paper pasted to the blank portions of pp. 207, 247, 359 and 369, as listed in the bibliography of Walt Whitman by the late Alfred Goldsmith. In the present copy the intercalations are printed in and are listed in the "Contents". Mr. W. S. Kennedy in his *Fight of a Book for the World* (1926) states that there were two issues of this volume, the first issue having the reading "With Portraits from Life" as in the present copy.

Inscribed by Horace Traubel on the front end-papers, in ink, as follows: *"W. W. himself did some typographical work on this 1876 edn. in the office of the New Republican, Camden, New Jersey. H. T."* and on the integral part of the end-leaf *"This, too, for Thomas Mosher & for the best of reasons. Traubel. July,* 1904. *This volume is incomplete. W. W's autograph belongs on the title-page".*

———   ———   ———

482. WHITMAN, WALT. November Boughs. Royal 8vo, green cloth, gilt top, other edges uncut. Philadelphia, 1888

LARGE PAPER ISSUE OF THE FIRST EDITION. ONLY A SMALL NUMBER OF COPIES WERE ISSUED IN THIS FORMAT. With the following in the autograph of Horace Traubel on the front end-leaf: *"Sent to Thomas Mosher by Horace Traubel. July* 1904. *This copy of N. B. is from an edition made by W. W. for his personal friends & none put upon the market. H. T."*

Joy! Shipmate! Joy!
(To my own Soul.)

Joy — shipmate! joy!
For now the long, long anchorage
    we leave!
Our ship is clear at last — she
    leaps!
She swiftly courses from the
    shore — Joy! shipmate!
    joy!
Soon, soon we breathe the
    breezes — soon, soon we sail the sea!
The sea of Freedom, Time, and
    Space — the all-expanding
    sea.

WALT WHITMAN AUTOGRAPH POEM: NUMBER 471

SALE NUMBER 1060

FREE PUBLIC EXHIBITION

From Tuesday, April 19, to Date of Sale
Weekdays from 9:30 to 5 ⸱ Closed Sunday

PUBLIC AUCTION SALE

Tuesday and Wednesday Evenings
April 26 and 27 at 8 p. m.

EXHIBITION AND SALE AT THE

PARKE-BERNET GALLERIES · INC

30 EAST 57 STREET · NEW YORK 22
PLAZA 3-7573

Belonging to

FRANK CAPRA

Beverly Hills, Calif

Sales Conducted by
H. H. PARKE
L. J. MARION · A. N. BADE
H. E. RUSSELL, JR. *and* A. NISBET

1949

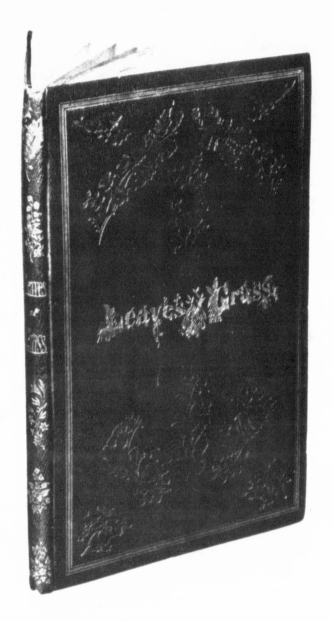

[NUMBER 366]

A SUPERB INSCRIBED COPY OF "LEAVES OF GRASS"

1,500-

366. [WHITMAN, WALT.] Leaves of Grass. *Frontispiece portrait on plain paper.* Small folio, ORIGINAL GREEN CLOTH, stamped in gilt and blind, gilt edges. In a full green morocco solander case. Brooklyn, 1855

FIRST EDITION, FIRST ISSUE, in the correct binding, with ornamental triple-line borders stamped in gold on both sides, portrait on plain paper, marbled end-papers, and without the eight pages of press notices.

ONE OF THE FINEST IF NOT THE FINEST COPY THAT HAS BEEN OFFERED AT PUBLIC SALE, with the covers and text in crisp state. The frontispiece, which is usually found more or less foxed, is, with the exception of a few faint fox-marks, as fresh as on the day of issue.

BESIDES ITS SPLENDID CONDITION THIS COPY HAS THE ADDITIONAL IMPORTANCE OF BEING SIGNED BY THE AUTHOR in ink on the title-page, as follows: "*Walt Whitman August 3, 1884.*" IT IS BELIEVED TO BE ONE OF THREE KNOWN INSCRIBED COPIES.

With the Robert J. Hammershlag bookplate.

[See illustration on the preceding page]

PRESENTATION COPY TO LORD TENNYSON

750-

367. WHITMAN, WALT. Leaves of Grass, 12mo, original green cloth, entirely uncut. In a cloth slip case. Washington, 1872

PRESENTATION COPY FROM WHITMAN TO ALFRED, LORD, TENNYSON. Inscribed on front end-leaf in Whitman's autograph: "*Alfred Tennyson from Walt Whitman, with his love*". A SUPERB COPY.

[See illustration]

Lot 368 omitted

402

PARKE-BERNET GALLERIES · INC
New York · 1953

★ ★ ★

Property of ALEXANDER SELLERS, *Media, Pa.*
C. S. HUTTER, JR., *Keswick, Va.*
And Other Owners

Public Auction Sale
Tuesday and Wednesday,
May 12 and 13 at 1:45 p. m.

BELIEVED TO BE THE ONLY SURVIVING PAGE OF MANUSCRIPT
OF "THE LEAVES OF GRASS," 1855

1,500

59A. WHITMAN. W. AUTOGRAPH MANUSCRIPT of a portion of *"The Leaves of Grass"*, unsigned, written on 1 p., small folio, consisting of about 200 words; torn in fold. In a full levant folding case, with silk protecting cover. (*N. Y. Collector*)

A MOST IMPORTANT MANUSCRIPT, BELIEVED TO BE THE ONLY SURVIVING PAGE OF THE MANUSCRIPT OF THE ORIGINAL EDITION (1855), and differing in some respects from the subsequent editions of the work.

Regarding the manuscript of *The Leaves of Grass*, Mr. Horace Traubel in his work *With Walt Whitman in Camden* (Vol. I, p. 92), states "We spoke about the first edition of the Leaves. It is tragic—the fate of these books. None of them were sold—practically none—perhaps one of two, perhaps not even that many. We had only one object—to get rid of the books—to get them out some way even if they had to be given away. You have asked me questions about the manuscript of the first edition. It was burned. Rome kept it several years, but one day by accident, it got away from us entirely—was used to kindle the fire or to feed the ragman".

On the verso are three columns of words in pencil in Whitman's hand, indicating that this may have been intended for a thesaurus compilation or a dictionary for Whitman's use.

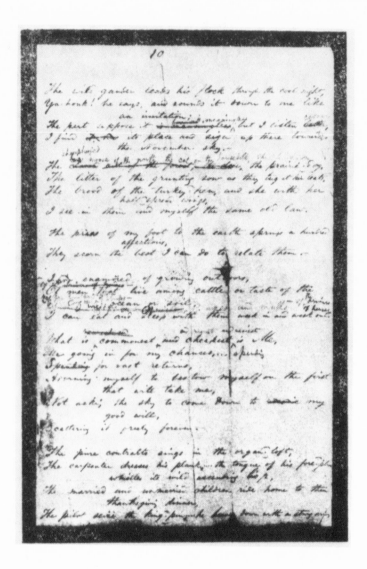

404

SWANN
Auction Galleries

Books - Autographs - Prints - Literary Properties

PUBLIC AUCTION SALE

THURSDAY, MARCH 21st, 1957, AT 2 P. M.

Exhibition from March 18th to Time of Sale

AMERICAN MANUSCRIPT ACCOUNT BOOKS
ART AND ILLUSTRATED BOOKS
FINE FIRST EDITIONS
MUSIC   *   SPORTING
BINDINGS   *   CURIOSA
AMERICANA AND THE WEST

WHITMANIANA

Collected by J. H. and Bertha Johnston,
including books, letters, and ephemera

SALE No 462

471 FOURTH AVENUE   NEW YORK CITY 16
Phone: MUrray Hill 4 - 6183

THE JOHN H. AND BERTHA JOHNSTON
COLLECTION OF WHITMANIANA

The following extensive collection of books, pamphlets, autograph letters, and ephemeral material, all relating to Walt Whitman, come from the collection of John H. and Bertha Johnston, who were intimate friends of Whitman, Traubel, Bucke, and other members of the Whitman circle.

The collection is rich in memorabilia about Whitman, autograph letters concerning him, photographs, and other ephemeral pieces. A COLLECTION OF UNUSUAL INTEREST, AS IT COMES FROM THE LIBRARY OF AN INTIMATE FRIEND OF WHITMAN HIMSELF.

---

244 (WHITMAN, WALT). Abbie Nott, and Other Knots, by "Katinka." Frontispiece. 12mo, original cloth; ends of backstrip frayed, foxed.
Philadelphia, (1856)
Attributed to Whitman, partly on the basis of the three-line motto in the volume — "certainly the first instance in which Leaves of Grass was drawn upon for a book motto." — Winterich.

245 (WHITMAN, WALT). Leaves of 'Grass Imprints: American and European Criticisms on "Leaves of Grass." 16mo, 64 pages, original printed wrappers.
Boston: Thayer and Eldridge, 1860
FIRST EDITION — ONE OF THE RAREST OF WHITMAN EPHEMERA, issued gratuitously "as a circular to all persons disposed to commence the study of the Poems." Three of the lengthier reviews are by Whitman himself. Backstrip frayed.

246 WHITMAN, WALT. Poems. Selected and edited by W. M. Rossetti. Portrait. 16mo, cloth.
London, 1868
FIRST ENGLISH EDITION. FIRST ISSUE, with no price on backstrip. Ads at both beginning and end, the first leaf of those at the front being missing. Loose in binding.

247 WHITMAN, WALT. After All, Not to Create Only. 12mo, 24 pages, gilt-decorated green cloth. FIRST PUBLISHED EDITION.
Boston, 1871

248 (WHITMAN, WALT). Leaves of Grass. Thick 12mo, blue cloth.
Washington, 1872
FIRST EDITION TO INCLUDE "PASSAGE TO INDIA." Includes, at end, the 14-page "After All, Not to Create Only." Backstrip torn and loose.

TWO-PAGE LETTER TO PETER DOYLE

249 WHITMAN, WALT. Splendid Autograph Letter, signed "Walt" to "Dear Pete," 2 pages, 12mo.
Camden, May 22, 3¼ P. M., (1874)
A FINE, CHARACTERISTIC LETTER, chiefly about his poor health. Quoted in full in "Calamus," page 153.

PRESENTATION COPY OF THE CAMDEN 1876 EDITION

250 (WHITMAN, WALT). Two Rivulets, including Democratic Vistas, Centennial Songs, and Passage to India. Mounted photographic portrait. 12mo, original ¾ calf; all edges gilt.
Camden: Author's Edition, 1876
SIGNED BY WHITMAN ON THE PHOTOGRAPH — "Walt Whitman, born May 31, 1819." Worn copy; several leaves loose, a few margins frayed.
PRESENTATION COPY, inscribed in Whitman's hand, on flyleaves at beginning and at end — "Mrs. Amelia F. Johnston, from the author." With a photograph of Mrs. Johnston laid in.

251 WHITMAN, WALT. Leaves of Grass. Portrait. 8vo, cloth; inner hinges broken. Glasgow, 1884

WHITMAN'S OWN COPY OF "GRASHALME"

252 WHITMAN, WALT. Grashalme: Gedichte. In Auswahl uebersetzt von Karl Knortz und T. W. Rolleston. 12mo, 180 pages, printed wrappers; unopened.
Zurich, 1889
FIRST EDITION of this German version of portions of "Leaves of Grass." Wrappers torn and loose.
Inscribed — "For J. H. Johnston, from Horace Traubel. 1913. COPY HANDLED BY WALT WHITMAN, taken from his effects."

253 WHITMAN, WALT. Grashalme: Gedichte. In Auswahl uebersetzt von Karl Knortz und T. W. Rolleston. 12mo, 181 pages, printed wrappers.
Zurich, 1889
FIRST EDITION. Wrappers loose; entire volume split.
Inscribed — "To Miss Bertha Johnston, 1892, from H. L. T. [Traubel]. THIS VOLUME WAS HANDLED BY WALT WHITMAN."

254 WHITMAN, WALT. Calamus: a Series of Letters written during the Years 1868-80 to a Young Friend (Peter Doyle). Edited by Richard Maurice Bucke. Frontispiece. 12mo, coth. Boston, 1897
FIRST EDITION; with a signed inscription to John H. Johnston from the publisher, Laurens Maynard, June 25, 1897.

255 WHITMAN, WALT. Selections from the Prose and Poetry. Edited by O. L. Triggs. Portrait. Small 8vo, buckram; top edge gilt. Boston, 1898
FIRST EDITION. With a signed inscription to J. H. Johnston from Laurens Maynard, the publisher, 1898.

256 WHITMAN, WALT. Complete Writings. SALESMAN'S DUMMY COPY OF THE PAUMANOK EDITION, consisting of specimen pages, fine photogravure plates (some hand-colored), and descriptive text. Tall 8vo, flexible brown morocco. New York: Putnam, (1902)
INSCRIBED BY THE PUBLISHERS, to J. H. Johnston, 1902.

257 WHITMAN, WALT. Complete Writings. SALESMAN'S DUMMY COPY of the Camden Edition, consisting of specimen pages, numerous photogravure plates, and descriptive text. Tall 8vo, flexible black morocco.
New York: Putnam, (1902)
WITH AN AUTOGRAPH INSCRIPTION FROM THE PUBLISHERS, to J. H. Johnston, 1902. Inside back cover exhibits samples of the vellum and green morocco backstrips.

258 WHITMAN, WALT. The Book of Heavenly Death. Compiled from Leaves of Grass by Horace Traubel. Portrait. Small square 4to, boards; end of backstrip frayed; uncut. ONE OF 500 COPIES. Portland: T. B. Mosher, 1905

259 WHITMAN, WALT. Foglie di Erba .... versione di Luigi Gamberale. Portrait. Small 8vo, 1+570 pages, printed wrappers, frayed and split.
Milano: Remo Sandron, circa 1907

260 WHITMAN, WALT. The Gathering of the Forces: Editorials, etc., written as Editor of the Brooklyn Daily Eagle in 1846 and 1847. Edited by Cleveland Rodgers and John Black. Photogravure plates. 2 volumes. Large 8vo, boards, rubbed, leather labels; uncut. LIMITED LETTERPRESS EDITION.
New York, 1920

261 WHITMAN, WALT. Walt Whitman's Workshap: a Collection of Unpublished Manuscripts. Edited by Clifton J. Furness. Illustrated. 4to, ½ cloth; uncut, dust jacket. Cambridge: Harvard U. Press, 1928
FIRST EDITION; one of 750 copies. Laid in are two typed letters signed by Furness, regarding Whitman and Mrs. Gilchrist, etc.

262 WHITMAN, WALT. New York Dissected: a Sheaf of Recently Discovered Newspaper Articles. Introduction and Notes by Emory Holloway and Ralph Adimari. Illustrated. 8vo, buckram. New York, 1936

263 WHITMAN, WALT. Poems from "Leaves of Grass." Translated [into Yiddish] by Louis Miller. Illustrated. 12mo, cloth; dust jacket. (New York, 1940)

264 WHITMAN RELIC. The last desk-blotter used by Whitman, 4½ x 12 inches. SELF-AUTHENTICATED BY THE PRESENCE OF NUMEROUS REVERSED SIGNATURES OF WHITMAN, AS THEY WERE BLOTTED FROM LETTERS OR PAPERS HE SIGNED.

Inscribed in pencil — "To Calder, out of the collection of Horace Traubel, May 30, 1892."

265 WHITMAN RELICS. Group of 5 books and strands of hair from Whitman's head.

A UNIQUE COLLECTION, from the Johnston Whitman memorabilia. One lock is in envelope reading "Walt Whitman's Hair, cut from his head by Alma Calder Johnston in 1881"; another is in envelope noting "cut from his head at 1309 Fifth Ave., July 1878."

266 WHITMANIANA. (Binns, Henry Bryan). Moods & Outdoor Verses, by Richard Askham. Small 12mo, buckram; top edge gilt, others uncut. London, 1902

FIRST EDITION. Tipped in is a crowded Autograph Postcard Signed by Binns, presenting this pseudonymous volume.

267 ——. Binns, Henry Bryan. The Great Companions. 12mo, boards; dust jacket. London, 1908

FIRST EDITION. Poems in the style of Whitman, by his biographer.

268 ——. Born, Helena. Whitman's Ideal Democracy, and Other Writings. Edited by Helen Tufts. Mounted portrait. Square 12mo, boards; uncut. ONE OF 500 NUMBERED COPIES. Boston, 1902

269 ——. Brooks, Van Wyck. The Times of Melville and Whitman. Thick 8vo, cloth. FIRST EDITION. (New York), 1947

270 ——. Bucke, Richard Maurice. Man's Moral Nature, an Essay. 12mo, cloth. New York, 1879

FIRST EDITION. Dedicated to Whitman, "the man who inspired it .... the man who has the most exalted moral stature." Pasted inside cover is the original wrapping cover, addressed from Bucke to Miss Johnston.

271 ——. Bucke, Richard Maurice. Walt Whitman. Illustrated. 12mo, cloth; top edge gilt. Philadelphia, 1883

FIRST EDITION. "This is an important biography. WHITMAN NOT ONLY CAREFULLY EDITED THE BOOK, BUT WROTE THE FIRST TWENTY-FOUR PAGES." — Wells & Goldsmith.

272 ——. Bucke, Richard Maurice. Cosmic Consciousness: a Study in the Evolution of the Human Mind. 4to, cloth; inner hinge torn. Philadelphia, 1901

FIRST EDITION, limited to 500 numbered copies printed from type, and SIGNED BY THE AUTHOR. Laid in is a photograph, taken and inscribed by Charles V. Elliot, showing Bucke at the summerhouse at Asylum Lake, 1899.

273 ——. Bucke, Richard Maurice. Was Walt Whitman Mad? 1895 * The Origin of Insanity. 1892 * R. M. Bucke, a Sketch, by James H. Coyne. 1906 * and a group of 8 original photographs of Bucke, some with his family.

The pamphlets are all extracts or offprints, unbound.

A MAGNIFICENT SERIES OF FIFTY LETTERS
TO J. H. JOHNSTON ON WALT WHITMAN

274 —. **Bucke, Richard Maurice.** Splendid collection of 50 lengthy and highly interesting Autograph Letters Signed, to J. H. Johnston. 4to.

London, Ontario, 1887-1901

FILLED WITH REMARKS ON WHITMAN, THE SIGNIFICANCE OF HIS WORK, HIS PERSONALITY, etc., etc. A very few of the letters are typed; some refer to Ignatius Donnelly's work on the Bacon-Shakespeare cipher, and other matters.

275 —. **Burroughs, John.** Notes on Walt Whitman, as Poet and Person. Second Edition. 12mo, cloth; inner hinge weak. New York, 1871

276 —. **Burroughs, John.** Fine group of 8 Autograph Letters Signed, all to Mr. Johnston. Together, 13 pages, 12mo. 1878-1912

Also, two Typed Letters Signed by Burroughs, and several letters by Clara Barrus.

277 —. **Carpenter, Edward.** Days with Walt Whitman. 3 portraits. 12mo, cloth. New York, 1906

278 —. **(Carpenter, Edward).** Towards Democracy. 16mo, 519 pages, leatherette; India-paper issue. London, 1912

INSCRIBED — "To J. H. Johnston, in remembrance of his friendly visit to Millthorpe, 31 July 1912, from Ed. Carpenter." Also, laid in, Autograph Postcard Signed by Carpenter, wishing Johnston bon voyage, and enclosing the book.

279 —. **Carpenter, Edward.** Group of 3 Autograph Letters and 1 Autograph Postcard Signed, all to Mr. Johnston. Together, 6 pages. 12mo and 16mo. SEVERAL REFERENCES TO WHITMAN. Millthorpe, 1912

280 —. **Clarke, William.** Walt Whitman. Portrait. 16mo, cloth. FIRST EDITION. London, 1892

281 —. **Davenport, William E.** Poetical Sermons: a Thank Offering of Song. Small 12mo, cloth. Brooklyn, 1896

FIRST EDITION; inscribed "With the author's greetings. W. E. Davenport." Many of the poems are directly in the style of Whitman; some refer to him.

282 —. **Donaldson, Sam'l.** Poems on Facts and Fancies, Practical Points, Common Observations, etc. 12mo, cloth. FIRST EDITION. Philadelphia, 1885

FROM WHITMAN'S LIBRARY, with a crowded 2-page note written and signed by J. H. Johnston, 1885, noting that he had been helping Whitman on July 14, 1885, when Donaldson appeared, asking Whitman to give his opinion of the book. The poet "didn't want the book unless he could do as he liked with it .... I asked Walt to send it to me in a few days, which he did July 31st...."

283 —. **Donaldson, Thomas.** Walt Whitman the Man. Illustrated. 12mo, buckram; top edge gilt, others uncut . New York, 1896

FIRST EDITION. Inscribed — "Mr. J. H. Johnston, with compliments and regards of The Publisher. Nov. 17th/96."

284 —. **Elliot, Charles N., Editor.** Walt Whitman as Man, Poet and Friend: Autograph Pages from Many Pens. Square 8vo, ¾ suede (rubbed); top edge gilt. Boston, (1915)

ONE OF 500 NUMBERED COPIES. Facsimiles of writings by Bucke, Burroughs, Dowden, Peter Doyle, Garland, Howells, Theodore Roosevelt, W. M. Rossetti, Traubel, and others. Laid in are two lengthy letters signed by Elliot, Seattle.

285 — . **Elliot, Charles N.** Group of 8 lengthy Typed Letters Signed and 2 Autograph Letters Signed, all to J. H. Johnston, and all entirely regarding Whitman. 4to. Portland, Oregon, 1912-16

286 ——. **Freedman, Florence B.** Walt Whitman Looks at the Schools. 12mo, cloth. FIRST EDITION. New York, 1950

287 ——. **Furness, Clifton J.** Group of 4 Autograph Letters and 5 Typed Letters Signed, all to Bertha Johnston. Together, 13 full pages, 4to. Boston, 1928-30
ENTIRELY CONCERNED WITH HIS WHITMAN RESEARCHES, his book "Walt Whitman's Workshop," and related matters.

288 ——. **Harned, Thomas B.** Whitman and Physique. Tall 8vo, (12 pages), sewed; unopened. Philadelphia, May 1899
Issued as Whitman Fellowship Papers, Fifth Year, Number 8. Pages 43-54.

289 ——. **(Hartmann), Sadakichi.** Conversations with Walt Whitman. 12mo, 51 pages, pictorial wrappers; uncut. FIRST EDITION. New York, 1895

290 ——. **Heywood, Ezra H.** An Open Letter to Walt Whitman. BROADSIDE, 12 x 6¾ inches. Princeton, Mass., circa 1882
RARE AND CURIOUS WORK, issued by Angela T. Heywod at the Word Office, and headed "Leaflet Literature." Heywood, who had been jailed for publishing "Cupid's Yokes," here gives a report of "the latest raid on Leaves of Grass, for which I was arrested by Anthony Comstock."

291 ——. **Holmes, Edmond.** Walt Whitman's Poetry: a Study & a Selection. Small square 4to, buckram. uncut. FIRST EDITION. London, 1902

292 ——. **In Re Walt Whitman:** Edited by Horace L. Traubel, Richard Maurice Bucke, Thomas B. Harned. Tall 8vo, 452 pages, cloth; top edge gilt, others uncut. Philadelphia, 1893
FIRST EDITION; one of 1000 numbered copies. Inner hinge cracked.

293 ——. **Ingram, William.** Group of 4 Autograph Letters Signed, to Bertha Johnston. Together, 8 pages, 12mo. Philadelphia, January-April 1892
ALL CONCERNING HIS VISITS TO WHITMAN, in his last illness.
"I went over today to see Walt .... he had eggs, toast & coffee for breakfast"; "I found him bolstered up in bed; he held on to my hand hard for some time"; "I thought I saw a change for the worse; he don't talk to the nurses now only by signs." Another letter encloses "ivy leaves lying on Walt's casket.' '

294 ——. **Ingram, William.** Group of 7 Autograph Letters Signed, to Bertha Johnston. Together, 22 pages, 12mo. Also includes 3 photographs of Ingram.
Telford, Bucks County, etc. 1891-95

295 — . **Johnston, John, M.D.** Group of 9 Autograph Letters Signed, all to J. H. Johnston, including many references to Whitman. Together, 32 pages, 12mo. 1892-1909

296 ——. **Kennedy, William Sloane.** Reminiscences of Walt Whitman, with Extracts from his Letters and Remarks on his Writings. 12mo, two-toned cloth; top edge gilt, others uncut. FIRST EDITION. Paisley, 1896

297 ——. **Kennedy, William Sloane.** The Fight of a Book for the World: a Companion Volume to Leaves of Grass. 12mo, cloth.
West Yarmouth, Mass., 1926

298 ——. **Le Gallienne, Richard.** Group of 3 Autograph Letters Signed, to Mr. Johnston. Together, 6 pages, 12mo.　　　　　　　　　　　　New York, 1898

Two refer to portraits of Whitman, Johnston's Whitman collection, etc.
Accompanied by a handsome cabinet photograph of Le Gallienne (1898), and a copy of the Whitman Fellowship Dinner menu of 1898, with a signed sentiment by Le Gallienne.

299 ——. **Lloyd, J. William.** Dawn-Thought on the Reconciliation * Life's Beautiful Battle. Together, 2 volumes. 12mo, cloth.
　　　　　　　　　　　　　　　　　　　Westfield, N. J., (1904; 1910)

EACH VOLUME INSCRIBED BY LLOYD TO J. H. JOHNSTON. Each volume has a quotation from Whitman on the title.

300 ——. **Maynard, Laurens.** Splendid group of 15 lengthy Autograph Letters Signed, all to J. H. Johnston, and all referring to Whitman. Together, 29 pages, 4to and 8vo.　　　　　　　　　　　　　　　　　　Boston, 1896-98

ALL CONNECTED WITH TEXTUAL AND OTHER PROBLEMS OF WHITMAN PUB-LICATION — Maynard's firm (Small, Maynard) published an edition of "Leaves of Grass" in 1897.

301 ——. **Memorabilia.** Group of 15 printed, autograph, and typed poems, records of celebrations, etc. 4to and smaller; loose.　　　　　　　　　Vd.

Whitman Birthday Celebrations at Bolton, 1907, 1908, and 1911 * Hawkins. Poem for Whitman Day, 1910 * poems by Robertus Love, Sam Walter Foss, Bertha Johnston, and others * and similar pieces. SOME HAVE SIGNED INSCRIPTIONS.

302 ——. **Overton, Grant.** The Answerer. 12mo, cloth. FIRST EDITION.
　　　　　　　　　　　　　　　　　　　　　　　New York, 1921

303 ——. **Perry, Bliss.** Walt Whitman: His Life and Work. Illustrated. 12mo, cloth; top edge gilt, others uncut.　　　　　　　　　　　London, 1906

304 ——. **Photographs of Whitman.** Group of 14 photographs, and reproductions of photographs, of Whitman. Also, photograph of Whitman's Dog and Mary Davis; original wash-drawing of Whitman's birthplace; and a plaster bas-relief of the Whitman tablet (cracked and repaired).

305 —. **Platt, Isaac Hull.** Walt Whitman. Portrait. 24mo, cloth.　Boston, 1907

INSCRIBED — "Presented to his friend John H. Johnston, by the perpetrator. Hull Platt. Jan. 1911."

306 ——. **Platt, Isaac Hull.** Group of 9 Autograph Letters Signed, to J. H. Johnston, many quite lengthy, and all referring to Whitman. 8vo and 12mo. Also included is a signed photograph of Platt.　　　　　　　　　　1901-12

307 ——. **Proctor, Thomas.** Some Personal Recollections and Impressions of Walt Whitman. Pages 29-39 IN: Journal of Hygiene and Herald of Health, for February 1898, offered entire. 8vo, printed wrappers.　　New York, 1898

308 ——. **Robertson, John.** Walt Whitman, Poet and Democrat. 52 pages IN: The Round Table Series, edited by H. B. Baildon, offered complete. 8vo, pictorial cloth; top edge gilt.　　　　　　　　　　　Edinburgh, 1887

309 ——. **Sawyer, Roland D.** Walt Whitman, the Prophet-Poet. 12mo, 76 pages, ½ cloth; dust jacket FIRST EDITION.　　　　　　　Boston, (1913)

310 ——. **Shephard, Esther.** Walt Whitman's Pose. Thick 8vo, coth; dust jacket.
FIRST EDITION.   New York, (1938)

311 ——. **Silver, Rollo G.** Thirty-One Letters of Walt Whitman. 8vo, (22 pages),
printed wrappers.   Np, 1937
   Offprint from "American Literature." With a signed inscription by Silver, to Bertha
Johnston, and a letter to her regarding the pamphlet. Accompanied by two uninscribed
copies. Together, 3 items.

312 ——. **Thomson, James.** Walt Whitman, the Man and the Poet. Introduction
by Bertram Dobell. 12mo, cloth; uncut. FIRST EDITION.   London, 1910

313 ——. **Titherington, Richard H.** The Good Gray Poet. Pages 138-146, and
numerous text illustrations, IN: Munsey's Magazine for November 1895, offered
complete. 8vo, cloth.   New York, 1895
   Front cover notes this as the "Edition De Luxe.'

314 ——. **Traubel, Anne M.** (Mrs. Horace Traubel). Fine Autograph Letter
Signed, to Mr. Johnston: 2 pages, 8vo.   Philadelphia, January 26, 1892
   "You will be saddened to hear that Walt's physician, Dr. Longaker, feels that WALT'S
DAYS ARE UNDOUBTEDLY NUMBERED. Despite his cherriness and improved appetite
he is subtly losing ground. The nurse says she can see that within the past week he has lost
flesh .... Walt said to Horace on Sunday night,' I am low, very low, away down, and feel
that I am losing ground.' I stopped in to see him this afternoon .... he was passing through
a terrible spell...."

LENGTHY COLLECTION OF LETTERS BY MRS. TRAUBEL

315 ——. **Traubel, Anne M.** Magnificent collection of 65 lengthy Autograph
Letters Signed, to Bertha Johnston. Together, about 250 pages, 4to and 8vo.
                                                   Philadelphia, chiefly 1938-46
   INCLUDING A VAST QUANTITY OF IMPORTANT MATTER ON WHITMAN, with
remarks on his publications, his personal life, Traubel, Bucke, Whitman memorials, etc., etc., etc.

316 ——. **Traubel, Horace, Editor.** At the Graveside of Walt Whitman: Harleigh,
Camden, New Jersey, March 30th, and Sprigs of Life. 4to, printed wrappers;
uncut.   (Philadelphia), 1892
   LARGE-PAPER ISSUE. Cover title — "Good-Bye and Hail Walt Whitman."
WITH AN AUTOGRAPH INSCRIPTION BY TRAUBEL, 1892.

317 ——. **Traubel, Horace.** Give All to Love. Tall 8vo, 8 leaves, self-wrappers.
                                                            Philadelphia, 1902
   At head of title — "Collect: Two: Philadelphia, The Conservator." INSCRIBED — "To
J. H. Johnston, Horace Traubel."

318 ——. **Traubel, Horace.** Chants Communal. 12mo, ½ cloth; uncut.
                                                                 Boston, 1904
   FIRST EDITION. Tipped in is a card inscribed by the author, to J. H. Johnston.

319 ——. **Traubel, Horace.** With Walt Whitman in Camden (March 28-July 14,
1888). Illustrated. Large 8vo, 473 pages, cloth; top edge gilt.   Boston, 1906
   INSCRIBED — "Bertha Johnston. This copy of his 'Diary' is out of Horace's personal
collection and goes to you with life-long memories and reaffirmed faith. Anne M. Traubel,
Sept. 8th, 1931."

320 ——. **Traubel, Horace.** With Walt Whitman in Camden. (July 16-October 31, 1888). Illustrated. Thick large 8vo, 570 pages, cloth, back and top gilt.

New York, 1915

Laid in, Autograph Letter signed by Anne [Traubel], referring to the work.

321 ——. **Traubel, Horace.** With Walt Whitman in Camden (March 28-July 14, 1888) (November 1, 1888-January 20, 1889). Illustrated. Large 8vo, 590 pages, cloth; top edge gilt. FIRST EDITION. New York, 1914

INSCRIBED — "For John H. Johnston, one of the principal inhabitants of the Whitman world whose love Walt cherished & whom Walt loved & also now in these later days .... still my own dear comrade brother, Horace Traubel. Camden, July 24, 1914."

322. ——. **Traubel, Horace.** Chants Communal. 12mo, printed wrappers; uncut.

New York, 1914

INSCRIBED — "For John H. Johnston, 1914, Camden, Horace Traubel."

323 ——. **Traubel, Horace.** Collects. 12mo, printed wrappers; uncut.

New York, 1914

FIRST EDITION; issued as Volume 2, Number 1, of The Glebe.
INSCRIBED — "For John H. Johnston in Camden, July 23, 1914. Horace Traubel."

324 ——. **Traubel, Horace.** Optimos. Second Printing. Portrait. 12mo, buckram.

New York, 1919

WRITTEN DURING WALT'S LAST ILLNESS

325 ——. **Traubel, Horace.** Fine group of 4 Autograph Postcards Signed, all to Mr. Johnston. Camden, February-March 1892

Feb. 18 — "Walt reads some letters. Takes a little interest in letters or papers. Could continue in this stage a long while. Sleeps — sleeps — sleeps...."

Feb. 22 — "No change in Waltt's condition. He has gone off into the silences...."

Feb. 23 — "No change. It is sadly discouraging. He suffers from abject feebleness."

March 23 — "Walt not better, indeed has spent a sad & miserable day."

326 ——. **Traubel, Horace.** Remarkable group of about 35 Autograph Letters Signed, many very lengthy, all to J. H. and Bertha Johnston, filled with references to Whitman, lecture activities, etc. 4to and 8vo, loose.

Camden, 1890-1912

327 ——. **Triggs, Oscar Lovell.** Walt Whitman: a Character Study. Tall 8vo, (16 pages), sewed; unopened. Philadelphia, April 1899

Issued as Whitman Fellowship Papers, Fifth Year, Number 3. Pages 7-22.

328 ——. **Walling, William E.** Whitman and Traubel. 12mo, cloth.

New York, 1916

FIRST EDITION; with a signed inscription to Bertha Johnston from Anne M. Traubel

329 ——. **Walt Whitman Fellowship.** Group of about 30 of its Papers, etc., chiefly 1890's * Walt Whitman Foundation Bulletin. 10 numbers, and related material * Walt Whitman Society of America. Several items. 4to and smaller; loose.

330 ——. **Williams, Francis H.** Walt Whitman as Deliverer. Tall 8vo, (20 pages), sewed. Philadelphia, August 1894

Issued as Whitman Fellowship Papers, No. 4. Pages 11-30.

331 ——. **Autograph Collection.** Huge collection of several hundred Letters and Autograph Letters Signed, all to J. H. and Bertha Johnston, from W. D. Howells, R. G. Ingersoll, J. W. Wallace, W. S. Kennedy, Harned, Donaldson, Jessie Whitman, Harriet Sprague, Joseph Auslander, Mencken, Will Carleton, Christopher Morley, Bliss Perry, Theodore Tilton, Elbert Hubbard, Martha L. Davis, Hamlin Garland, Amelia E. Barr, Charlotte P. Gilman, and scores of others, chiefly referring to Whitman. 4to and smaller; loose.

A MAGNIFICENT AND EXTENSIVE COLLECTION, well worth careful examination. Also included are numerous photographs (many of them signed), pamphlets, newspaper clippings, and other ephemeral material.

332 ——. Group of 15 books and pamphlets of Whitman interest. 8vo and 12mo, cloth and wrappers. Vp, vd.

Burroughs. Whitman, a Study * Karsner. Horace Traubel * Whitman Exhibition, Detroit. Public Library, 1945 * several magazine articles concerning Whitman * and others.

333 ——. Group of typed and manuscript articles, letters, etc., regarding Whitman. 4to and smaller; loose.

Recollection of Whitman, by Chandos Fuller * Whitman, I Would Converse With You, by Sol Margulies * Walt Whitman, a Paper before the Bolton Literary Society, March 11, 1892, by J. Johnston, M.D. * Some Personal Recollections & Impressions of Whitman, by Thomas Proctor * lengthy letter by the Quaker William Taylor of Los Angeles * and others.

414

S<small>ALE</small> N<small>UMBER</small> 1882

William J. K. Vanston

PUBLIC AUCTION SALE

Tuesday and Wednesday Afternoons
February 24 and 25, at 1:30 *p. m.* promptly

EXHIBITION AND SALE AT THE

PARKE-BERNET GALLERIES·INC

980 M<small>ADISON</small> A<small>VENUE</small> • 76<small>TH</small>-77<small>TH</small> S<small>TREET</small>

N<small>EW</small> Y<small>ORK</small> 21

TR<small>AFALGAR</small> 9-8300

↗   ↗   ↗

1959

MANUSCRIPT AND CORRECTED PROOF OF
A "LEAF OF GRASS"

1,950- 602. WHITMAN, WALT. A Riddle Song. Autograph manuscript, 2 pp., 4to; with proof, 1 p., 4to, corrected in the author's hand; and envelope, inscribed and signed. Together 3 pieces, tipped in to 1 vol., folio, half green morocco. [Camden, 1880]

R<small>OUGH AND HEAVILY CORRECTED DRAFT OF A POEM COLLECTED IN</small> "F<small>ROM NOON TO STARRY</small> <small>NIGHT,</small>" <small>WITH PROOF, PRESENTED TO WHITMAN'S BIOGRAPHER AND FRIEND DR. R. M. BUCKE.</small> The manuscript is written on the inside of wrappers from "A Passage to India" cut into strips and formed into two pages by pasting to two sheets of coarse paper. The proof is corrected to conform textually with the draft, with small exceptions, in its "final" form. The punctuation of both varies from the current printings.

The inscribed envelope reads: "*Rough draft in MS & first proof of Riddle-Song Published* *1880 Walt Whitman Camden NJ May 26, '80* [line] *for my friend Dr R M Bucke W W*." It was in this year that Whitman visited Dr. Bucke in Canada.

[A] Riddle Song.
By Walt Whitman

That which eludes this verse, and any verse,
Unheard by sharpest ear, unform'd in clearest eye, or
       cunningest mind,
Nor form nor fame, nor happiness, nor wealth
And yet the pulse of every heart and life
       throughout the world incessantly,
Which you and I, and all, pursuing ever, ever miss;
Open but still a secret, the real of the real, an
costless illusion,
Vouchsafed to each, yet never man the owner,
Which poets vainly seek to chant — historians
       to tell in prose,
Which sculptor never chisel'd yet, nor painter,
Which vocalist never sung, nor orator nor
       actor ever utter'd,
Invoking here and now, I challenge for
       my song.

       [blank line]

Indifferently in public, private haunts — in solitude,
Behind the mountains and the wood, recluse,
Companion of the city's crowded streets, through the assemblage,
It and its radiations, constantly glide.

[NUMBER 602]

416

Sale Number 1997

American and Foreign
Autographs

Of Great Historical Significance
Over Six Centuries

BY EMINENT STATESMEN · AUTHORS · SCIENTISTS
DOCTORS · PHILOSOPHERS AND MUSICIANS

Collected by the Late
DR. MAX THOREK

CHICAGO · ILLINOIS

Sold by Order of the Executors of His Estate

Public Auction
Tuesday · November 15 at 1:45 and 8 p. m.
Wednesday · November 16 at 1:45

PARKE-BERNET GALLERIES · INC
New York · 1960

417

INAUGURATION OF THE THOMAS PAINE BUST

2,900~

626. WHITMAN. WALT. *American Poet.* A.Ms. on the Inauguration of the Thomas Paine Bust. Written in ink on 6 pp., 8vo, about 730 words. With two portraits of the poet, one signed, and a portrait of Paine; the portrait stained. Bound in a full brown levant 8vo volume, gilt top.

A FINE REVIEW OF PAINE'S CHARACTER. On the final page Whitman has written: *"For the inauguration of the Thos. Paine bust written out in the woods Kirkwood (White Horse) N. J., Oct. 2, '76. W. W."* With a number of autograph corrections by the author. Accompanying the above: "A Vindication of Thomas Paine" . . . By R. G. Ingersoll. Boston. 1877 ✣ "Paine, The Religious and Political Reformer. An Address." By B. F. Underwood, N. Y., n.d. Each 12mo, half cloth.

[See illustration on facing overleaf]

350~

627. WHITMAN. WALT. A.L.s., one page, oblong 4to. Brooklyn, 29 December 1864. Headed *"Private note to Editor."* 53 words of text.

A note transmitting a *"communication which I hope you will publish for sake of the soldiers dying & suffering in Southern prisons"* and asking for editorial comment on the same subject.

PRAISES A SCULPTURED BUST OF HIMSELF AND MENTIONS "LEAVES OF GRASS" "NOVEMBER BOUGHS" and "SPECIMEN DAYS"

450~

628. WHITMAN. WALT. A.L.s. One p., 4to, *"Camden, Wednesday P.M., Sept. 19. '88."* To *"Dear S.H.M."* (Sidney H. Morse, sculptor.) Written in pencil. With etched portrait by S. Hollyer. & signed by him; fold across print.

A FINE LITERARY LETTER TO MORSE THE SCULPTOR WHO MADE A BUST PORTRAIT OF WHITMAN. *"Am surviving yet & in good spirits (sort) after the past nearly four months. Am still imprisoned here in my sick room. . . . November Boughs is all done, printed & press'd & waits the binding . . . then I am to have a Complete W W in one large vol. . . . L of G, Spec. Days, & Nov. B. - all & several condensed in one . . . Your bust of me still holds out fully in my estimation. I consider it (to me at any rate) the best & most characteristic really artistic & satisfactory rendering of any—so tho't by me. The bust of Elias Hicks pleases & satisfied me first rate. . . ."*

225~

629. WHITMAN. WALT. A.N.s. on postal card. Camden. 6 February. 1891. To [William] Sloane Kennedy, an intimate friend and author of biographical and critical works on Whitman.

A sixty-three word budget of general news, mentioning his own ill health and the fact that work of his has been rejected by a major New York publisher.

Lots 630-631 omitted

419

CATALOGUE

OF

NINETEENTH CENTURY AND MODERN FIRST EDITIONS PRESENTATION COPIES AUTOGRAPH LETTERS AND LITERARY MANUSCRIPTS

INCLUDING

AUDEN's *Poems*, 1928, CONAN DOYLE's *The coming of the fairies*, 1922, PRESENTATION COPY AND HEMINGWAY's *A farewell to arms*, 1929, PRESENTATION COPY; FIRST EDITIONS AND PRESENTATION COPIES OF ALDINGTON, BEARDSLEY, BECKETT, BEERBOHM, CHURCHILL, NORMAN DOUGLAS, ELIOT, GRAVES, JOYCE, D. H. LAWRENCE, T. E. LAWRENCE, WYNDHAM LEWIS, HENRY MILLER, ORWELL, POUND, PRIESTLEY, SIEGFRIED SASSOON, GERTRUDE STEIN, DYLAN THOMAS, EDGAR WALLACE, THOMAS WOLFE AND YEATS; A PAINTING BY D. H. LAWRENCE AND A PORTRAIT OF JAMES JOYCE

IMPORTANT LETTERS AND MANUSCRIPTS OF WILLIAM MORRIS, DANTE GABRIEL ROSSETTI, RUSKIN, SIEGFRIED SASSOON AND OTHERS, FORMERLY THE PROPERTY OF SIR SYDNEY COCKERELL; A JOURNAL AND COMMONPLACE BOOK OF EDGAR WALLACE; A COLLECTION OF MATERIAL RELATING TO IVOR NOVELLO; IMPORTANT HITHERTO UNKNOWN LETTERS OF WALT WHITMAN

LETTERS AND MANUSCRIPTS OF ALDINGTON, BADEN-POWELL, BALDWIN, BEERBOHM, ARNOLD BENNETT, RUPERT BROOKE, BROWNING, SIR FRANCIS BURTON, ROY CAMPBELL, CHESTERTON, CHURCHILL, WILKIE COLLINS, CONRAD, MARIE CORELLI, DE LA MARE, DICKENS, CONAN DOYLE, ALLISON DRUMMOND, DURELL, ELIOT, GRAVES, GRAHAM GREENE, HARDY, MAURICE HEWLETT, HENRY JAMES, KIPLING, T. E. LAWRENCE, MEREDITH, HENRY MILLER, SHAW, STEVENSON, SWINBURNE, DYLAN THOMAS, WILDE, WISE AND YEATS

WHICH WILL BE SOLD BY AUCTION BY

SOTHEBY & CO.

P. C. WILSON, C.B.E.   A. J. B. KIDDELL   C. GRONAU   P. M. H. POLLEN   G. D. LLEWELLYN   R. P. T. CAME
M. J. WEBB LORD JOHN KERR THE EARL OF WESTMORLAND, K.C.V.O. J. L. MARION (U.S.A.) P. M. R. POUNCEY
M. J. STRAUSS   D. J. NASH   T. E. NORTON (U.S.A.)   A. T. EELES   P. D. THOMSON   D. ELLIS-JONES
R. J. DE LA M. THOMPSON   D. E. JOHNS   E. J. LANDRIGAN III (U.S.A.)   A. J. STAIR (U.S.A.)   M. D. RITCHIE
A. M. KAGAN (U.S.A.)   A. HOLLOWAY   D. J. CROWTHER   SIR PHILIP HAY, K.C.V.O., T.D.   C. H. HILDESLEY
G. HUGHES-HARTMAN   E. L. CAVE (U.S.A.)   V. ABDY   J. M. STOCK   J. BOWES-LYON

Associates:

A. R. A. HOBSON   JOHN CARTER, C.B.E.   N. MACLAREN   H. A. FEISENBERGER   J. F. HAYWARD
P. J. CROFT   A. MAYOR   C. C. H. FENTON

AFFILIATED COMPANY: SOTHEBY, PARKE-BERNET INC., NEW YORK

Auctioneers of Literary Property and Works illustrative of the Fine Arts

AT THEIR LARGE GALLERIES, 34-35 NEW BOND STREET, W1A 2AA

Telephone: 01-493 8080

DAYS OF SALE:

MONDAY, 17TH JULY, 1972   LOTS   1-320

AT TEN-THIRTY A.M. PRECISELY

TUESDAY, 18TH JULY, 1972   LOTS 321-579

AT ELEVEN O'CLOCK PRECISELY

(*daughter of the late Maurice Buxton Forman*)

The material catalogued below (lots 522 to 536) has remained hitherto unknown to Whitman scholars. None of the letters appear in the recent edition of Whitman's *Correspondence*, 5 vol., ed. Edwin Haviland Miller (with a solitary exception where a partial text is printed from an incomplete transcript, see lot 526): the existence of some of these letters has, however, been inferred from other sources, and in these cases the letters figure, as indicated below, in the Check List of Whitman's Lost Letters included in the *Correspondence*.

522 WHITMAN (WALT) THE AUTOGRAPH DRAFT OF HIS POEM "THE OX TAMER" ("In a faraway northern county, in the placid pastoral region") WITH REVISIONS AND DELETIONS (the basic text and some revisions in ink, other revisions in both pencil and blue crayon) the words "(printed 1876)" subsequently added by Whitman below title, *written on four irregular-sized sheets of paper pasted end to end to form a long slip, signed at end* (*in blue crayon*), WITH ENVELOPE INSCRIBED BY WHITMAN (in ink) "Rough draft in MS. of *Ox-Tamer* (Published in *Two Rivulets* in 1876) Walt Whitman May 1880"

£ 1,000—

*** "The Ox Tamer" was first published in the New York *Daily Graphic*, *Dec.* 1874, but is thought to have been originally composed as early as 1860 (see *Leaves of Grass*, ed. H. W. Blodgett and J. Bradley, 1965, p. 397). The present draft contains significant variants from the text which eventually reached print, some of which indicate that the poem was actually composed during the Civil War 1861-5 (thus the poet refers at one point to "these sights and sounds of war")

523 WHITMAN (WALT, A.L.s., *3 pages, 8vo, Brooklyn, N.Y.,* 26 *March* 1872, to H. Buxton Forman, DISCUSSING THE PROPOSAL TO PUBLISH A COMPREHENSIVE ENGLISH EDITION OF "LEAVES OF GRASS", *the letter containing a newspaper cutting* (*pasted in by Whitman*) *from the New York Tribune of the same day about International Copyright, also an enclosed printed leaflet advertising Whitman's books*

£ 480

... I should like to make one or two suggestions before the book is begun. A preface or introduction mainly of statistical nature (about the book & myself) including a brief syllabus of the plan & idea of "Leaves of Grass" from its own point of view—would be judicious—but I dont think favorably of a literary criticism for preface ...

524 WHITMAN (WALT) A.L.s., *2 pages, 8vo, Camden, New Jersey, Oct.* 23 [*postmark:* 1878], to Dr. Richard Maurice Bucke, returning a letter (not now present) from Buxton Forman and explaining "have nothing decisive to say at present *for myself* about New English edition," expressing his desire to come and see his correspondent "& be with you all truly", reporting on his health, and mentioning "a long & kind letter" he had received from Tennyson, " . . . As I scribble this (noon) the greatest gale I ever knew seems to be just subsiding—Our town streets are strewed with wrecks, roofs, timbers, trees &c," *subscribed* "*Love to you & yours Walt Whitman,*" *with the original envelope* (*stamped and postmarked*)

£ 450

525 WHITMAN (WALT) SERIES OF 5 A.Ls.s. AND 10 AUTOGRAPH POSTCARDS, 2 *February* 1887-17 *January* 1888, TO ERNEST RHYS, concerning the English editions of Whitman's "Specimen Days" and "Democratic Vistas" which Rhys was preparing for publication and CONTAINING THE AUTOGRAPH MANUSCRIPTS OF WHITMAN'S PREFACE AND ADDITIONAL NOTE FOR "SPECIMEN DAYS" AND OF HIS PREFACE FOR "DEMOCRATIC VISTAS" (all three specially written for the English editions of these two works), *two of the letters written in blue pencil, all else written in ink, with the five original envelopes*

* The Preface for "Specimen Days" fills one page, large 4to, signed, a few revisions in the text and annotated at the top by Whitman with a note about printing (sent with the letter of 8 *March* 1887); the Additional Note for "Specimen Days" occupies three pages, large 4to, a few revisions in text, note by Whitman about printing at top of first page (sent with the letter of 15 *March* 1887); the Preface for "Democratic Vistas" occupies three pages, 8vo, signed, some revisions in text and some annotations in blue pencil for the printer (sent with the letter of 11 *September* 1887).

The fifteen communications in the present lot constitute the bulk of Whitman's letters to Rhys during 1887: this material has remained hitherto unknown, though three other letters to Rhys falling within the same period are printed in the *Correspondence*, vol. 4, 1969, and five of the present letters (two of them actually on postcards) are recorded in the Checklist of Whitman's Lost Letters, op. cit., p. 425.

526 WHITMAN (WALT) Two A.Ls.s., 22 *January*-11 *May* 1890 (the first in pencil), *original envelopes*, and one autograph postcard s., 18 *November* 1890, to Ernest Rhys, reporting on the writer's health and spirits (" . . . fairly buoyant spirits &c.—but surely slowly ebbing . . . "), commenting on the state of society in America (" . . . generally busy enough all over her vast demesnes (*intestinal agitation* I call it)—talking, plodding, *making money*, every one trying to get on— perhaps to get toward the top . . . "), AND SENDING VARIOUS PRINTED SLIPS (STILL PRESENT) OF FOUR DIFFERENT POEMS, EACH ANNOTATED IN WHITMAN'S HAND, viz: *Thou who hast slept all night upon the storm* with autograph note by Whitman about "The terrible gale & destruction here this morning . . . "; *A Twilight Song*, two copies, both annotated by Whitman and one signed by him (the other having his name in print); *Old Age's Ship & Crafty Death's*, annotated in pencil; *For Queen Victoria's Birthday*, two copies, both annotated in ink with a request to print in a newspaper of 24 May: *also* four cuttings from different English papers containing printings of the latter poem, a small collection of portraits and engravings including two portraits of Whitman signed by him in blue crayon (one an engraving, the other a photograph dated by him 1887), *with the original wrapper addressed to Rhys by Whitman and marked "printed photographs"* [*postmark:* Camden, N.J. 27 *Feb.* 1887], and 4 A.Ls.s. to H. Buxton Forman from Ernest Rhys, 1889-90, mentioning Whitman

* An incomplete text of the first of these letters is printed from a transcript in the *Correspondence*, vol. 5, 1969 (no. 2179): the letter of 11 May is recorded there in the Checklist of Whitman's Lost Letters, p. 331.

527 WHITMAN (WALT) A.L.s., *1 page, 4to, Camden, New Jersey,* 22 *May* 1890, to H. Buxton Forman, sending news of himself, *with the original envelope*

... I am feeling pretty well at present, but have had a bad winter—have had *the grip* & a second attack—was out yesterday four or five miles, to the bay shore & linger'd some time by the water side—eat & sleep middling well—in good spirits ... shall probably get out this fine afternoon in wheel chair ... Love to you & best wishes & remembrances to British friends.

** This letter is recorded in the Checklist of Whitman's Lost Letters in the *Correspondence,* vol. 5, 1969, p. 331. Included is an autograph note by Forman, 1 p., 8vo, written for the English press and reporting on the contents of the present letter ("the latest news of Walt Whitman"), together with the printed proof and a cutting (from *The Athenaeum*) of Forman's report.

£ 300-

528 WHITMAN (WALT) Autograph Postcard s., *328 Mickle Street, Camden, New Jersey,* 16 *June* '90, to H. Buxton Forman, answering an enquiry about *Specimen Days* etc. and sending news of his health ("I am keeping on fairly—have been out in wheel chair to the river side (Delaware) to-day ... "), *together with* autograph note by Forman, 1 *page,* 8vo, being a report on Whitman's health written for the press and quoting the present postcard ("writing to our correspondent on the 16th of June, nearly a month later than the date of our last bulletin, he says ..."); Buxton Forman's retained copy (signed) of his letter to Whitman, 4 *pages,* 8vo, 26 *Sept.* 1888, about George Eliot's opinion of *Leaves of Grass* and her gratitude to Forman in 1871 for "pressing on her attention its scope, meaning, and original force"; letter to Forman from Josiah Child of Kegan Paul, 30 *Oct.* 1891, describing his copy of *Specimen Days* (4)

£ 120-

529 WHITMAN (WALT) Three A.Ls.s., *4 pages,* 18-29 *October* 1891, to H. Buxton Forman, concerning a proposal from Heinemann, Balestier & Lovell for the publication of an authorised edition of Whitman's works—a proposal which Whitman wishes to place "wholly & absolutely" in Forman's hands to negotiate terms etc. ("If you can do this for me, I will not make a parade of thanks here ... "), explaining Whitman's own attitude to the project (" ... one great point with me in this opportunity is to give an absolutely correct & authentic text & typography—wh: is already beginning to be vitiated here & abroad"), also sending news of his health (" ... only waning slowly, doubtless surely ... "), *two original envelopes; together with* the A.L.s. to Whitman from Joseph B. Gilder, 13 *Oct.,* 1891, broaching the subject of the proposed edition (forwarded by Whitman to Forman with his letter of 18 Oct.), 2 typed Ls.s. to Forman from the publishers, 29 *Oct.*- 26 *Nov.* 1891, rough pencil draft of letter by Forman, and a few related magazine cuttings

** The letters to Forman of 18 and 19 *October* contained in this lot are recorded in the Checklist of Whitman's Lost Letters in the *Correspondence,* vol. 5, 1969, p. 332.

£ 950-

423

530 WHITMAN (WALT) A lock of his hair, contained in a folded sheet of the yellow letterpaper with the printed heading (quotation from Epictetus) he was using in the last year of his life, INSCRIBED IN HIS HAND on the outer panel of the folded sheet "A lock of hair WW 73ᵈ year" and signed by him on the inside "Walt Whitman / America—Oct: 29 1891", *the folded packet tied with a blue ribbon: also* another sheet of Whitman's yellow letterpaper SIGNED AND DATED BY HIM FOUR TIMES, viz. "Walt Whitman / Oct: 29 '91—America" (once) and "Walt Whitman / America—Oct: 29 1891" (three times)

£ 65—

531 WHITMAN (WALT) Collection of printed slips, cuttings from American newspapers and magazines and a few offprints: all containing articles by or referring to Whitman and sent by him to H. Buxton Forman, c. 1876-91, many of the cuttings marked by Whitman in blue pencil against relevant passages and some briefly annotated by him, the collection including:—two copies (each on two slips printed one side only) of his article *A Backward Glance on My Own Road* (both annotated in his hand "Critic—New York Jan. 5 '84"); extract containing his article *My Book and I* (annotated by him in blue pencil "Lippincott's Magazine January 1887"); offprint from the North American Review of his article *The Poetry of the Future* (note by him "Feb: '81"); cutting from the *Philadelphia Press, 3 Nov.* 1891, describing Sir Edwin Arnold's visit to Whitman ("A Poet's Greeting to a Poet") annotated by Whitman in blue pencil "fishy fishy"; another cutting referring to Edward Emerson's "full account of his father's opinion of Walt Whitman" which Whitman has corrected to "*foul* account," *together with* 20 wrappers or envelopes (stamped and postmarked) addressed to Buxton Forman by Whitman (evidently the wrappers in which much of this material was sent)

£ 220—

532 WHITMAN (WALT) Good-By my Fancy. [second and final "Annex" to *Leaves of Grass*], PRE-PUBLICATION ISSUE IN THE FORM OF ROUGH PRINTED SLIPS, comprising the Preface (on two slips) and the sequence of poems on six large oblong slips (containing two or three "pages" to a slip), *all the slips printed on one side only*   [1891]

£ 480—

533 BUCKE (RICHARD MAURICE, *friend and disciple of Walt Whitman*) Four A.Ls.s., *11 pages, 4to, 9 January* 1884-12 *November* 1885, *London* (*Ontario*) to H. Buxton Forman, about Walt Whitman and the bibliography of *Leaves of Grass*, also discussing Forman's edition of Keats, sending news of himself and his family, etc., *with one envelope*

£ 160—

... What W.W. says p. 346 of 2ᵈ ed. is distinctly untrue, and this is a poser to me well as I fancy I know W.W. how the devil he can or ever could tell a plain lie like this ... Of course Walt does not pretend (or ever did) to his friends that the 1ˢᵗ Ed. sold, we have often talked about it and the last time we did so he said that scarcely a single copy sold and he was wishing that he had a lot of those copies now that he gave away and threw away in '55 & '56 ...

424

534 GILCHRIST (HERBERT, *artist friend of Walt Whitman*) Original pen drawing of Walt Whitman at Timber Creek ("a favourite haunt") "Drawn from nature in the summer of 1878", *explanatory autograph caption signed by the artist; on the back of the sheet a half-length pen sketch of Whitman, on card (size of sheet: approx: 100mm. by 164mm.)*

£120

535 TRAUBEL (HORACE, *friend and companion of Walt Whitman*) Five A.Ls.s., *25 pages, 8vo and 4to, 24 May* 1889 *and* 3 *January*-24 *September* 1891, to H. Buxton Forman: the first written on both sides of the integral leaf of the printed leaflet announcing the *Whitman Testimonial* (planned for Whitman's approaching seventieth birthday), Traubel's letter appealing for some personal expression from Forman "touching the man & the season that we may include in a pamphlet, commemorating the day", the other letters reporting on Whitman's behaviour and progress during his last illness, discussing his portraits etc., *with the original envelopes*: also related cuttings sent to Forman by Traubel (including cuttings from three different issues of the *Camden Post, 1-7 Aug.* 1891, concerning Whitman), a copy of the printed leaf containing Whitman's letter to W. M. Rossetti of 17 *March* 1876, and a photograph of Whitman's tomb inscribed to Forman by Traubel in 1897

£150

24 May 1889 . . . Knowing your past connection with Walt Whitman—your brave espousal of his cause (which you have made your own)—I doubt not you will feel the spur of the moment to utter some fervent latest word of greeting & well-wishing. There should be & can be no hesitation on the part of the friends of this noble & great man to sweeten & uphold his last days; & when we reflect that every word now uttered in his honor is a word going in him to the right spot—to the solacing of his old age & illness—no man who wishes him well can hesitate to speak . . .

4 Jan 1891. . . . I write this almost at W.'s bedside—I hear him moaning & breathing in the next room. He has shaken off the bronchial affliction which was the first demonstration of his illness but is left in utter weakness & without a peg to hang a hope upon. Day by day he seems to suffer deeper inroads: a bit sapped here, a bit there, by subtle ways which count for much—yes, for everything in the long run . . . Walt very frankly expresses his anxiety to die—to shake off this burden, which increases & is heavier with each day.

24 March 1891 . . . having introduced a doctor there at last, I am in hope that he will be made more comfortable if not more strong. There is no doubt he has taken a great drop this winter. . . . Walt is averse to doctors. It was up-hill work to convince him of his necessity . . .

536 FORMAN (H. BUXTON) The Autograph Manuscript of his obituary essay on Walt Whitman, with occasional revisions and deletions, *22 leaves, 8vo, written on one side only (beginning* "One of the most remarkable men of the present century has just passed away . . ."): *together with* two variant galley proofs of the essay (one with slight corrections), and THREE COPIES OF THE FACSIMILE OF WHITMAN'S LETTER TO DR. JOHNSTON OF 6 FEB. 1892 (executed at Whitman's request for distribution to his friends) and two copies of the printed leaflet concerning the facsimile

£160

APPENDIX

Notes on Whitman Collections and Collectors

By CHARLES E. FEINBERG

I

IT IS MOST FITTING that the Library of Congress should be the first library to commemorate the centennial of the publication of *Leaves of Grass*, by Walt Whitman, the national poet of democracy in America.

I truly feel that this exhibition in the Library of Congress as an expression of the acceptance of his work is the answer Whitman most desired when he wrote: "The proof of a poet shall be sternly deferr'd till his country absorbs him as affectionately as he has absorb'd it."

Walt Whitman was familiar with the city of Washington and the library here. In one of his unpublished manuscript notebooks Whitman writes of his first visit: "February 11th, 1863, Wednesday—went also into the Congressional Library—a splendid view from the high colonnade in front of it." [1]* In another manuscript note, dated December 20, 1865, Whitman writes: "Send copy Drum Taps to Congressional Library," and on the back of the note he has docketed, "Mem of sending Drum Taps—to Congressional Library." [2]

Walt Whitman's 10 years in Washington began with his arrival December 17, 1862, with a letter of introduction from the Mayor of Brooklyn, Martin Kalbfleisch, [3] and letters from others to assist him in finding his wounded brother George. The letter that helped him secure the pass was written by Moses Lane to Capt. James J. Dana, Washington, who in turn wrote a few words to Lt. Col. W. E. Dosten, Provost Marshal. [4] Colonel Dosten referred the request to General Heintzelman, who issued the pass allowing Walt Whitman to go to Falmouth, where his brother George was in the hospital.

---

*All numbered references in the text refer to items in the Feinberg Collection with the following exceptions:

8, 9	The Trent Collection of Duke University Library.
11, 16, 24	The Van Sinderen Collection of Yale University Library.
15, 32	The Oscar Lion Collection of the New York Public Library.
28	The Berg Collection of the New York Public Library.
31, 34	Miss Gertrude Traubel.

Whitman, commissioned as a volunteer by the Christian Commission, returned to Washington and stayed on to help nurse the sick and wounded. The commission, dated January 20, 1863, reads: "The Commission is given to Walt Whitman of Brooklyn, N. Y. His services (as a delegate) will be rendered without remuneration . . . His work will be that of . . . visiting the sick and wounded, to instruct, comfort and cheer them . . ." The document [5] is signed by George H. Stuart, Chairman, Christian Commission. Though the existence of the commission has been questioned, this document is tangible proof of its reality.

Whitman had friends who became collectors of his writings, while other Whitman collectors became his friends. The collectors may not have been gifted with the creative sense; or, if they had it, they may have lacked the ability to translate that sense into the work of a Whitman. However, through the preservation of the manuscripts, letters, books, and other material, they did much to enhance and ennoble the illumination of Whitman's great creativity.

Whitman himself formed the foundations of such collections by building the most extensive of them. He hopefully believed he would continue to be read, by people in foreign countries as well as by Americans, and that his writings would acquire a degree of literary importance. He preserved much of his early poetry and prose in addition to his correspondence. Fortunately for collectors and literary historians, this early habit continued throughout his life. He kept drafts of letters, bills regarding publication matters, memoranda of events in his literary and personal life, and notebooks of ideas for future poetry and prose writings. He also brought into existence a wealth of additional material for collectors to find. This he did by presenting manuscripts to many of his friends (even duplicate manuscripts, for he usually wrote a second copy to be sent to the printer); by his habit of having his poems set in type and correcting from printed proofs; by keeping editions of his books unbound, and then binding them in small batches as they were sold, occasionally binding a specially requested poem along with a printed plate left over from another edition. He gave away many manuscript items to friends and admirers. He liked to feel that a little bit of himself was included when he sent a manuscript along with a letter, a book, or a newspaper. Such material was especially directed to those who he felt would best serve as collectors of Whitmaniana, men such as John Burroughs, Dr. Richard Maurice Bucke, Thomas Donaldson, George M. Williamson, H. Buxton Forman, Edmund C. Stedman, Thomas B. Harned, and Horace Traubel.

Because of the large and diverse amount of material available, today's collector of Whitman is privileged, through his interests, in effect to know Whitman, a man whose life and times were so much different from our own, and yet a man who becomes as well known as one's own friend.

Many of Whitman's friends saved his letters because of their personal interest, as well as because they discerned their literary importance. Through his letters you know Whitman as a struggling, creative individual; you come to know his habits, his likes and dislikes, his mode of living. You come to know his strength and his weakness; his friends and early admirers; the people of other nations who encouraged his work and who with words of great praise and admiration made known his name now engraved on new literary horizons. Today Walt Whitman lives throughout the world, because there were a dedicated few who bridged the period from Whitman's day to our own, and these few would not let perish the greatness of the man. Whitman's acceptance came not only from Americans, but also from English, French, Danish, and other peoples, whose cultural perceptions were more advanced than those of the rough and ready pioneering American people and who found in Whitman's poems the voice of the United States— the voice of Democracy—the voice of the New World.

II

John Burroughs, naturalist and author, when he came to Washington in 1863, sought Whitman and found him among the group of friends which included William O'Connor, Edmund C. Stedman, and Charles Eldridge (Whitman's former publisher). Burroughs, who often accompanied Whitman on his visits through the hospitals, was the author of the first book written on the poet, *Notes on Walt Whitman, as Poet and Person*, in which he mentions first reading *Leaves of Grass* in 1861. Through his intimate friendship with Whitman, he became one of the first to collect the poet's books and to preserve his letters and manuscripts. The early notebooks, kept by Burroughs for the years 1863–68, contain the record of his first meeting with Walt and the development of their friendship. One complete notebook is devoted to a sustained estimate of Whitman as poet and man: in it, quite deliberately and with a sense of its importance, Burroughs sets down the record of the first two years of friendship and the evolution of his own opinion of *Leaves of Grass*. In his last notebook, for 1919–21, he wrote his final comments on Whitman. Earlier he had written: "To tell me that Whitman is not a large, fine, fresh, magnetic personality, making you love him, and want always to be with him, is to tell me that my whole life is a deception, and all the impression of my perceptives a fraud."

In his Walt Whitman collection were many editions of *Leaves of Grass*. Prominent among these were a first edition and a brown paper wrapper copy of the "Deathbed Edition." His collection of William O'Connor's letters about Whitman and the fight against suppression of *Leaves of Grass* covers the period of the withdrawal of the 1881 Osgood edition. The collection, rich in the quality of its manuscript material, includes: "Is

Walt Whitman's Poetry Poetical?" written in 1874. It is a splendid estimate of Whitman by himself. Burroughs' collection of Whitman letters, and his own letters about Whitman, cover the period of their 30 years of intimate friendship.

III

Dr. Richard Maurice Bucke, physician and author of London, Ontario, wrote his first letter [6] to Whitman on December 19, 1870:

Dear Sir; Will you please send to the enclosed address, two copies of Leaves of Grass, one copy of Passage to India and one copy of Democratic Vistas. Enclosed you will find $7.25—$6.75 for the books and fifty cents for postage. I do not know exactly what this last item will be but I fancy fifty cents will be enough to pay for it. I am an old reader of your works, and a very great admirer of them. About two years ago I borrowed a copy of the 1855 edition of Leaves of Grass and I have a great ambition to own a copy of this edition myself; would it be possible to get one? Before getting that, the only thing I had ever seen of yours was Rossetti's selection. Lately I have got a copy of the 1867 edition of Leaves of Grass, and I have compared the Walt Whitman in that with the same poem in the 1855 edition, and I must say that I like the earlier edition best. I have an idea that I shall be in Washington in the course of 1871; if I am, it would give me much pleasure to see you, if you would not object. I am afraid, however, that, like other celebrities, you have more people call upon you than you care about seeing; in that case I should not wish to annoy you. At all events believe me

    Faithfully yours,

                          R. M. BUCKE.

This letter led to an enduring friendship and a correspondence of hundreds of letters from Bucke to Whitman over the ensuing 22 years; one result was a collection of Whitman books, letters, manuscripts, and portraits. Since the sale of the Bucke Collection by auction in 1935, many Whitman collectors have been trying to bring some of the items together again. A large part of the collection came to Bucke because he was one of Whitman's three literary executors. He collected every edition of Whitman's writings and tried to get every paper and magazine, both in English and foreign languages, that printed a Whitman poem or a critical commentary on his work. He asked Whitman for proof-sheets, scraps of manuscripts, and whole manuscripts. The catalog of the Bucke Collection is a solid basis for a good Whitman bibliography. Among the many rare and unique items was the only known copy of the first issue of the *Brooklyn Freeman* for Saturday, September 9, 1848, which Whitman edited. This copy is now in the Trent Collection of Duke University. Interestingly, the original manuscript prospectus for this newspaper, dated July 11, 1848, names the paper *The Banner of Freedom* and lists a number of subscribers and the amounts subscribed—from $10 to $100. It has a paragraph of endorsement written by Whitman and signed by (Judge) S. E. Johnson.

This manuscript item has, however, been separated from the newspaper and is in another collection. [7]

Among the hundred manuscript items in the Bucke Collection were poems and notes for the first several editions of *Leaves of Grass* and a Whitman manuscript on Lincoln which was written on a number of pieces of paper pasted together. Many collectors of Whitman manuscripts are familiar with his method of pasting together and writing on the backs of envelopes and letters written to him. Whitman at one time said to Traubel: "You don't know, Horace, what a good investment that stove has been: I take a few of the autograph fellows, poke them in, put logs on top of them, apply a match: then the fire is here. It is a great resource in trouble!" He didn't always put the letters asking for autographs in the fire. Many a letter requesting Whitman's autograph, as well as other letters and bills, ended by having the other side of the paper used as a part of a manuscript poem or prose—thereby acquiring an unexpected touch of immortality. Other important items are the original manuscript of *Walt Whitman*, which was written by Bucke and bears autograph corrections and revisions by Whitman, [8] and the first completed copy of the last edition of *Leaves of Grass*, inscribed by Walt Whitman to Dr. Bucke: "F'm the author with love—Dec. 6—1891." [9] The friendship, started in 1870, remained unbroken until the poet's death.

IV

Thomas Donaldson, onetime agent of the Indian Bureau, for many years with the Smithsonian Institution, later of Philadelphia, and author of the book, *Walt Whitman, the Man*, had built up a very fine collection of Americana. He had Washington's autograph military order book, a contemporary manuscript copy of the thirteenth amendment to the Constitution, and original historical documents and manuscripts of Washington, Lincoln, Jackson, Sheridan, Grant, Garfield, Sherman, and Walt Whitman.

Donaldson had known Whitman in 1876, and after many years of friendship he let Whitman know he was writing a book about him. From time to time Whitman would give him letters and manuscripts and occasionally present him with an inscribed copy of one of his books. At one time Donaldson had expected to be among Whitman's literary executors. His Whitman collection of manuscripts was notable, and many are now choice possessions of other collectors and libraries. The Whitman manuscript of *Pictures*, from the Donaldson Collection, is now in the Van Sinderen Collection at Yale University. The manuscript *War Diary*, is in the Pierpont Morgan Library. A letter from Whitman to Tennyson and the reply from Tennyson are in the T. E. Hanley Collection. Other important manuscripts from Donaldson's collection are the 36-page article, "Carlyle, From

American Points of View," rejected by *The North American Review*, May 20, 1882; an article on Lincoln; an article on Aaron Burr (now in a private collection); Whitman's article on Ralph Waldo Emerson, partly written and partly printed, with his autograph postal card offering it to the Philadelphia *Sunday Press*, April 28, 1882 (it was refused); and the article, "By Emerson's Grave," published in *The Critic* (New York), May 6, 1882, possibly a rewritten version of Donaldson's manuscript article by Whitman on Emerson, as Emerson died April 27, 1882. Another manuscript from Donaldson Collection, *Of That Blithe Throat of Thine*,[10] was recently shown at a Whitman exhibition held in the American Library in London and arranged by the United States Information Service. The Donaldson Collection included proof-sheets of *November Boughs*, inscribed by Whitman, and his copy of Voltaire's *Philosophical Dictionary*, with Whitman's autograph on the title page;[11] the poet's pass to go to and to return from the fortifications at Alexandria in 1864; and a Bible which Whitman inscribed to Donaldson, April 1890. Also included were three letters from Mrs. Elisa Seaman Leggett of Detroit to Whitman; Mrs. Leggett, about the time she wrote these letters, sent her grandson Percy Ives, who was then an art student with Thomas Eakins in Philadelphia, to visit Whitman, who recorded these visits in his Commonplace book;[12] letters written by Percy Ives to his grandmother, with sketches of Walt Whitman, are in the Leggett family papers of the Burton Historical Collection at the Detroit Public Library.

V

George M. Williamson, linen importer and book collector of New York, wrote Walt Whitman on September 27, 1888, proposing to buy manuscripts. Whitman told Horace Traubel:

There's nobody I'd rather sell manuscripts to but I'd rather sell them to nobody . . . Williamson has been a good friend—he has shown his love in the most practical ways. Tell him for me that he's a buster: tell him he shall have a set of the sheets untrimmed [13] and welcome . . .

At a later date in answer to another letter [14] Whitman said:

I would like to humor Williamson but don't see how I can do it. He will have to content his 'happy owner' soul with patience: I can give him no hope. That whole mania for collecting things strikes me as an evidence of disease—sometimes of disease in an acute form. And indeed, that is what makes a remarkable matter more remarkable—that a man such as we know Williamson to be should care a damn whether he was the happy owner of a manuscript—any manuscript—or not. Well, give him my love: that is real: and if he is satisfied to be the happy owner of my love he owns it—tell him so—and welcome.

Williamson was a discriminating collector. The introduction to the auction catalog for his collection tells of his special interest in books associated in a personal way with their authors or with those who owned them. In his collection were George Washington's copy of *Don Quixote* in four volumes, with Washington's autograph on each title page; Longfellow presentation copies; and Hawthorne's copy of *The Scarlet Letter*, with annotations in his autograph.

When *November Boughs* was published, Whitman sent Williamson an inscribed copy of the book, as well as the manuscript and the corrected proof-sheets. This was only one of many choice Whitman items that Williamson listed in the fine catalog he printed for private distribution. His collection of Whitman material began chronologically with the pamphlet *Franklin Evans*, which was published as an extra to *The New World* in 1842. He had a copy of all the different editions of the *Leaves*, including the scarce paper-bound 1871 edition and a gray paper-covered "Deathbed Edition,"[15] copy sent to him at Whitman's request and inscribed by Horace Traubel. He also had a fine copy of *Memoranda During the War* inscribed to: "John Swinton—from his friend the author."

For his catalog Williamson had facsimiles made of a few of his outstanding manuscripts, among them Whitman's draft for a poster advertising *Drum Taps;* [16] a page manuscript, *To Make a Personal Item,*[17] originally sent to John Swinton; the first page of a 20-page manuscript, *As a Strong Bird on Pinions Free;* the first draft of *The Patrol at Barnegat;* [18] and the Bible Walt had inscribed to Thomas Donaldson, April 1890. There was also a facsimile of Whitman's one-page manuscript *Of Emerson,*[19] which had been inserted in a pink paper wrapper, first edition copy of *Leaves of Grass;* when this copy of the *Leaves* was sold in 1908, the manuscript page was neither included with the book nor listed separately. Subsequently this copy of the *Leaves* was in the Frank Maier Collection, and later in the William F. Gable Collection.

Since there has always been a question of how many copies of this first edition were printed, it might not be out of place to discuss the matter at this point. A holograph statement [20] sent by Charles Jenkins (Bookbinder, 389 Hudson Avenue, Brooklyn) to Whitman, although seemingly a piece of trivia, was saved by a collector and is now important, for it established the exact number of copies of the first edition of *Leaves of Grass* and gives the various forms and quantities of each issue. Jenkins billed Whitman for the binding of 200 copies in June 1855; he charged 32 cents a copy for this, and finding that he had lost money at that price on the first 200 copies, he had the binding of subsequent copies done by another bindery, Davies and Hands, who charged 58 cents a copy. Thus they bound an additional 183 copies in July, 46 of them in boards. Although Frank B. Sanborn, in writing of the Emerson copy of *Leaves of Grass*, describes it as "bound in paper," it may have been a copy of this paper-board bound issue. Unfortunately, this copy, now at the University of Michigan, has been rebound, so we cannot check this. In December another 169 copies were bound in cloth, but at a cheaper price because of the omission of gold leaf. At this time 150 copies were bound in paper at 2 cents each. Ninety-three additional copies were bound in cloth in January 1856. Thus a total of 795 copies of the first edition were printed and bound.

Despite the comparatively large number of copies bound in boards and paper wrappers, no copy in boards is known to exist, and only three copies in paper wrappers have survived, including the Houghton copy now in the Library of Congress, and Whitman's own copy (from the second issue), which belonged for a while to Horace Traubel and is now in the Oscar Lion Collection of the New York Public Library.

VI

Not all who collected Whitman material during his lifetime knew him personally. H. Buxton Forman, 30 years old, was one of the younger literary generation when he first wrote to Walt Whitman in February 1872:

I have been a long time trying to persuade one or another of our publishers to print a complete English edition of your works—verbatim, without any retrenchments; and I have gone so far as to offer my poor services in justifying as far as criticism can justify poetry, those portions which they take exception to, or fear to print. Supposing I ultimately succeeded, would a verbatim reprint of the latest edition, with an introductory essay, have your approval?

And again in 1876:

As a faithful student of your books, I have made it my business to obtain every edition I could, and all portraits and notable accounts and criticisms. But there is one edition in particular which I have never been able to see even,—that mentioned by Rossetti as having been issued in 1856. Can you tell me whether there is or is not an edition between that one set up by yourself in 1855 and that of Thayer and Eldridge dated 1860–61? If there is, can you give me any particulars that will help me towards buying it? I live in hopes of publishing some day a good English edition of your works; and my enquiries about editions are not mere bibliomania. I find they vary considerably; and my experience is that the careful collation of various versions of a poet's work is often a key as well as an incitement to the right understanding of his spirit and intent. I am at present engaged on an edition of Shelley which will be the handsomest in form, and the most extensive in matter (I hope), yet published; and that takes up most of my time.

The edition of Shelley that Buxton Forman was editing was published as *The Works of Shelley*. Already the author of *Our Living Poets*, he later wrote books on Elizabeth Barrett Browning, William Morris, and others. His library reflected his interest in Keats and Shelley manuscripts, letters and manuscripts of Elizabeth Barrett Browning and Robert Browning, Charles Lamb, Christina and Dante Rossetti, and Swinburne.

An important item in his collection was a 28-page manuscript, homemade notebook of Whitman's, who wrote some of these notes to remind himself to go back to different hospital wards and get from soldiers the details of their battles. Forman wrote bibliographical notes on the fly leaves of many of his Whitman books. In the copy of the second edition, which he finally acquired, he wrote:

This 2nd edition of Leaves of Grass, which is far rarer than the 1st edition & contains a quantity of new poems, was issued in a green cloth cover, with the edges cut, as usual in the state. The present copy was found by R. M. Bucke, folded ready for binding, & is the only uncut copy he or I ever saw or heard of.

Another item, with a two-page descriptive note by Forman, was a copy of *Leaves of Grass Imprints* with an autograph presentation inscription: "H. B. Forman, Walt Whitman."

Whitman books collected by Forman are now scattered in many libraries and private collections. His copy of the first edition of *Leaves of Grass* and a number of other editions are now in the New York Public Library. His 1882 "Author's Edition" and the 1889 "Pocketbook Edition" are at Yale. Proof sheets of *After All, Not To Create Only* [21] are in a private library, and many other libraries have Whitman books and manuscripts containing Forman's autograph or bookplate.

On the occasion of Whitman's 70th birthday in 1889 Buxton Forman wrote: [22]

For Whitman, so long as there is life, there must be happiness. . . . I think, then, that for the poet whose seventieth birthday was celebrated on the 31st of May, the word poet needs enlargement so as to include somewhat of the meaning of the word prophet. Whitman, of all living men, deserves best to be called the prophet of the world's hope; for of all he is the most absolute in his optimism, the most unwavering in his faith in the ultimate perfection of the great scheme of nature . . . and whatever else *Leaves of Grass* may be, I have long held it to be the most original book which the world has yet produced . . .

Forman was one of the many friends Walt Whitman had in England, a friendship started in 1872. He continued to add books and manuscripts to his Whitman collection after the author's death.

VII

Edmund Clarence Stedman was a poet, critic, and editor on whom Whittier bestowed the title: "Poet and friend of Poets." Stedman's collection of books, letters, and manuscripts of American and English contemporary writers indicates his interests. His book *Poets of America* was based to a large extent on the material he had in his own collection. Later he edited the 11-volume edition of *A Library of American Literature*, again using many manuscripts of poems, letters, and portraits he had previously acquired.

Stedman first met Walt Whitman in Washington in 1863, in the company of John Burroughs, William O'Connor, Charles Eldridge, and others. In an early letter to Stedman, June 17, 1875, Whitman writes, "I am leisurely preparing a volume. (Two Rivulets) . . . all sorts of things, prose and poetry. Won't be out for five or six months." When *Two Rivulets* was published in 1876, Walt sent him a copy, along with a matching presentation copy of the *Leaves of Grass with Portraits and Intercalations* in the "Centennial Edition," inscribed: "E. C. Stedman from the author with his friendship and thanks." Stedman's collection included an 1855 first edition of *Leaves of Grass*, a copy of *Passage to India*, and other material. Stedman's letter [23] to Walt on his receiving an inscribed presentation copy of *November Boughs* is worth quoting:

OCT. 25, '88.

Dear Walt, Your seasons outlast mine. Your book, always to be handed down and transferred by my clan, reached me on my fifty-fifth birthday, and made me wonder that your November Boughs still hang so rich with color while my October Leaves are already pale and wilted. I am very grateful for your remembrance, and touched by it withal. In many respects this collection (so strikingly and fittingly put up) is one of the most significant—as it is the most various—of your enduring works. Rest tranquil, as you ever are, in the ripeness of your harvest and fame—well assured that, whether your pilgrimage is still to be long or brief, you "shall not wholly die." I am always more and more your reader, and

Your attached friend,

EDMUND C. STEDMAN.

This copy of *November Boughs* and a number of other Whitman items were sold in 1911 and were later in the Whitman collection brought together by William F. Gable.

An interesting group of manuscripts in Stedman's collection was the first rough draft of Whitman's *Song of the Universal*, delivered at Tuft's College, June 17, 1874; a second draft of the poem; the third draft; and the final completed version. [24] The earlier drafts show Whitman's method of developing his ideas, finally crystallizing them in the finished draft.

A copy of Stedman's own book, *Poets of America*, which included a chapter on Whitman, was inscribed on April 14, 1887: "To Walt Whitman with love and sincere admiration of Edmund C. Stedman." [25]

In a letter [26] of September 8, 1888, Stedman writes to Horace Traubel:

My son has sent to me the final proof sheets of the passages which I selected from Walt's poetry for the Library of American Literature. Will you kindly show these to him, and then return them to me . . .

The problem was to give a really characteristic and sympathetic representation within the utmost space that could be allotted. (You see there

438

are 149 other authors in the same vol.—the space for each averaging only 3½ pages. I have given Walt twelve.)

So I begin with the American note—the New World; then the cosmic and radical, following with human heroism, evolution, &c. &c. Then, for pure lyric splendor and sustained flight, the long passage from Out of the Cradle. Next, my favorites, for imagination—vitality—feeling, among his complete short poems: The Frigate-bird, Ethiopian, O Captain, Old Ireland, Platte Canon, &c.; then through the Vast Rondure, to broader life and immortality. Thus I suggest, at least, an epitome of Whitman's course in thought and song, from port to destination.

My love and constant honor to the grand old bard of whom the last tidings that reached me were satisfying.

Sincerely yours,   EDMUND C. STEDMAN.

In the 11 volumes of his *Library of American Literature*, [27] which Stedman presented to Walt, Whitman has with his blue pencil corrected one of his own poems. After Whitman's death, Anne Montgomerie Traubel received the set.

The presentation copy of the *Complete Poems and Prose*, with the inscription by Walt Whitman—"The following book to Edmund C. Stedman from his friend the author W. W. (Bear forth folded my love—dear mariner, for you I fold it here in every leaf.) Camden, New Jersey, March 11, 1889"—became a part of the Stedman Collection. Stedman's last book from Whitman was a copy of the Deathbed Edition [28] in gray paper covers, with a pencilled note by Horace Traubel that he was sending it to Stedman by Walt Whitman's wish, Jan. 3, 1892. On the poet's death, Stedman wrote the following poem, which was read at the funeral:

> Good-bye, Walt!
> Good-bye from all you loved of Earth—
> Rock, tree, dumb creature, man and woman—
> To you their comrade human.
> The last assault
> Ends now, and now in some great world has birth
> A minstrel, whose strong soul finds broader wings.
> More brave imaginings.
> Stars crown the hill-top where your dust shall lie,
> Even as we say good-bye,
> Good-bye, old Walt!

This was a sincere tribute written by an old friend and collector.

VIII

Thomas B. Harned, prominent Camden lawyer, was a close family friend of Walt Whitman for many years. Whitman named him as one of his three literary executors, and a large part of Harned's Whitman collection of books, letters, and manuscripts, now in the Library of Congress, is described in detail in the following catalog.

IX

Horace Traubel, the most intimate friend of Walt Whitman in his later years, at the age of 15 met Whitman when he first came to Camden in 1873. For many years Traubel kept notes in which he recorded daily conversations with Whitman. Whitman would give Traubel some old letters and discuss the circumstances of their receipt. He presented Traubel with the letter [29] Ralph Waldo Emerson wrote him after reading *Leaves of Grass*, in which he wrote: "I greet you at the beginning of a great career." At times Whitman would dig up some old proof sheets and tell Traubel of different rejections by magazine and newspaper editors.

Through the years Traubel accumulated more detailed knowledge of Whitman's literary and personal life than any other friend. Largely on the basis of this knowledge he wrote "Walt Whitman: Poet and Philosopher and Man," which *Lippincott's Magazine* published in March 1891. The original manuscript [30] was corrected by Walt Whitman, and the article is indicative of the intimacy of the two.

Another product of this relationship has been *With Walt Whitman in Camden* of which four volumes have been published to date. The original notes were written by Traubel within a few minutes after he left Whitman each day. There are additional notes [31] written by Traubel, now being transcribed, which will eventually bring the published volumes up to the time of Whitman's death. Almost every book or book article written on Walt Whitman since the first volume was published in 1906, and there have been hundreds, have quoted from the conversations and letters in *With Walt Whitman in Camden*.

On the death of Whitman, Horace Traubel became the third of the literary executors named in the poet's will, the others being Dr. Bucke and Thomas B. Harned. Before this Traubel already had a large number of letters written to Whitman, which the poet had given him for his collection, as well as Walt's famous "Blue Book" [32] copy of the third edition of 1860–61. These letters formed a source collection for the authoritative notes written for future publication. The additional letters and manuscripts and books which came to Horace Traubel after the poet's death enhanced the collection he already had. He acquired two autograph volumes of Whitman's commonplace books; one beginning January 1876 and ending May 30, 1889; the other starting with May 31, 1889, and ending in December 1891.

Traubel also acquired a manuscript notebook dating from about 1854, another dating from 1856; several notebooks written during Whitman's hospital period of 1863–64; and a small book labelled "Words". [33] This last work had been bound by Whitman by cutting out all the pages of a book and retaining the stubs to allow sheets of paper, fragments, and clippings to be tipped in; the sheets of paper used are various, some left-over green wrappers from the first edition of *Leaves of Grass*, some yellow end-papers left from the second issue of *Leaves of Grass*, some unused stationery of the city of Williamsburgh, etc., including many other paper fragments of various colors; the covers were pierced to permit two pieces of cord to tie front and back covers together. Whitman saved all manuscript notes, clippings, words, and phrases on grammar and language with the intention of writing an American dictionary. Many other items of Traubel's Whitman collection are now in different libraries and private collections. One gap in his collection was the second edition of 1856, [34] which he finally acquired in 1902.

Horace Traubel was the literary executor most active in the continued publication matters concerning the writings of Walt Whitman and he usually acted for all three executors. During the 30 years of existence of his own periodical, *The Conservator*, he printed numerous articles about Whitman. For many years he hoped to print a facsimile edition of the unique "Blue Book" copy of the 1860–61 edition showing the corrections and revisions made by Whitman in different colored pencils, in preparation for later editions. The project of reproducing this copy could not be completed. Traubel was concerned not only with collecting Walt Whitman; he wanted also to share his knowledge and his enthusiasm for Whitman with everyone who would read or listen.

X

To a large extent these available scattered Whitman items stimulated great interest in many collectors during Whitman's lifetime and after his death. His books and letters were scattered throughout Europe and England; pertinent items were known in the United States from Maine to California and in Canada.

Whitman himself gave most of his books a degree of importance to collectors. Many copies are autographed "Walt Whitman" on the title page; others have a signed photograph; and he inscribed copies of different editions to friends and buyers of his books.

Whitman planned to autograph the title page of his final edition of *Leaves of Grass*. The title page was to read *Portraits from Life—And Autograph*. The following paragraph was to be included at the bottom of the title-page: "*Author's small Ed'n . . . (Less than 200 pub'd) . . . revised, authenticated, completed . . . cumulus of 36 y'rs (f'm 1855 to date) . . . the present vol. personally handled by W. W. . . . price $5.00 Camden, N. J. 1892.*"

The make-up copy [35] was made ready, Whitman signed the title page and added the paragraph he desired, but his last illness forced him to drop the words "and autograph" and the paragraph he had wanted for the title

page. Death prevented the further printing of another Whitman autographed item that could be collected by friends, collectors and admirers.

His manuscripts, letters, postcards, and books continue to be game in a
happy hunting ground for the collectors of Walt Whitman—National Poet
of America—whose *Leaves of Grass* is sure to be read long after its first
hundred years.

"Notes on Whitman Collections and Collectors," by Charles E. Feinberg, was originally
published in *Walt Whitman A Catalogue Based Upon the Collections of The Library of
Congress*, Washington, D.C.: The Library of Congress, 1955, pp. V-XVIII.

Appendix

The following is a selective list of the important auction catalogues consulted but not included in the compilation.

1898

22-23 February 1898. Stan. V. Henkels. (Sale 805)

31 March-1 April 1898. Bangs & Co.

1902

1-2 December 1902. Bangs & Co.

1904

21 January 1904. The Anderson Auction Company. Hon. William E. Robinson. (Sale 260)

1905

20-21-22 March 1905. The Anderson Auction Company. Bishop John Fletcher Hurst. (Sale 371)

19 May 1905. The Anderson Auction Company. Evert Jansen Wendell. (Sale 391)

1909

22-23 November 1909. The Anderson Auction Company. Frank Maier. (Sale 784)

7-8 December 1909. The Anderson Auction Company. Louis I. Haber. (Sale 789)

1911

15-16 February 1911. The Anderson Auction Company. Judge Jacob Klein. (Sale 895)

7-8-9-10 March 1911. The Anderson Auction Company. (Sale 896)

2 June 1911. The Merwin-Clayton Sales Company. (Sale 402)

1912

26 February 1912. Stan. V. Henkels. (Sale 1049)

1913

17-18-19-20-21 March 1913. The Anderson Galleries. Mrs. May C. Smith and Edwin Davis French.

13-14-15-16 October 1913. The Anderson Galleries. William Nelson. (Sale 1005)

1914

23-24-25 November 1914. The Anderson Galleries. Robert Louis
Stevenson.

1915

10-11 May 1915. The Anderson Galleries. (Sale 1160)

1916

11 March 1916. Stan. V. Henkels. (Sale 1163)

29-30-31 March 1916. The Anderson Galleries. (Sale 1214)

24 May 1916. Stan. V. Henkels. Eustace Conway. (Sale 1168)

3 November 1916. Stan. V. Henkels. (Sale 1177)

1917

25-26 January 1917. The Anderson Galleries. (Sale 1270)

1 May 1917. The Walpole Galleries. (Sale 51)

1920

26-27-28 April 1920. The Anderson Galleries. H. Buxton Forman.
(Sale 1493)

4-5-6-7 October 1920. The Anderson Galleries. H. Buxton
Forman. (Sale 1516)

1921

4 March 1921. The American Art Association. Charles Romm.

9-10-11 May 1921. The Anderson Galleries. William Brewster.
(Sale 1583)

1922

18 January 1922. The Anderson Galleries. Edgar Saltus. (Sale
1622)

4-5 December 1922. The Anderson Galleries. (Sale 1691)

1924

17-18-19-20 March 1924. The Anderson Galleries. John Quinn.
(Sale 1820)

30 April-1-2 May 1924. American Art Association. Herbert L.
Rothchild.

10-11 November 1924. The Anderson Galleries. William Harris
Arnold. (Sale 1873)

1-2 December 1924. American Art Association.

1925

20-21 January 1925. American Art Association. Florence Sturdivant.

1926

23-24 March 1926. The Anderson Galleries. Oliver Henry Perkins. (Sale 2047)

16-17 November 1926. American Art Association.

1927

14-15-16 February 1927. American Art Association. Major W. Van R. Whitall.

1928

3-4 December 1928. The Anderson Galleries. (Sale 2298)

1929

13-14 February 1929. The Anderson Galleries. Thomas L. Raymond. (Sale 2320)

1930

20-21 January 1930. Plaza Art Galleries.

25-26 February 1930. American Art Association Anderson Galleries. (Sale 3823)

2-3 December 1930. American Art Association Anderson Galleries. Frederick W. Lehmann. (Sale 3871)

1932

19-20-21 April 1932. American Art Association Anderson Galleries. Frank Irving Fletcher. (Sale 3966)

1933

6-7 December 1933. American Art Association Anderson Galleries. (Sale 4069)

15 December 1933. American Art Association Anderson Galleries. (Sale 4072)

1934

4-5 January 1934. American Art Association Anderson Galleries. (Sale 4073)

25-26 January 1934. American Art Association Anderson Galleries. Mrs. Henry D. Hughes. (Sale 4082)

4-5 April 1934. American Art Association Anderson Galleries. (Sale 4098)

1935

18 January 1935. American Art Association Anderson Galleries. Robert J. Hammershlag. (Sale 4147)

24-25 April 1935. American Art Association Anderson Galleries. (Sale 4175)

13-14 November 1935. American Art Association Anderson Galleries. (Sale 4201)

1936

14-15 January 1936. American Art Association Anderson Galleries. Abel Cary Thomas. (Sale 4221)

18-19 March 1936. American Art Association Anderson Galleries. (Sale 4242)

22-23 April 1936. American Art Association Anderson Galleries. (Sale 4253)

30 April 1936. American Art Association Anderson Galleries. J. Percy Sabin. (Sale 4255)

24-25 November 1936. American Art Association Anderson Galleries. Mrs. Milton E. Getz. (Sale 4279)

1937

13-14 April 1937. Rains Galleries.

11-12 November 1937. American Art Association Anderson Galleries. (Sale 4346)

1938

3 March 1938. Parke-Bernet Galleries. Morris L. Parrish. (Sale 13)

12-13 December 1938. American Art Association Anderson Galleries. (Sale 4422)

1939

18-19 October 1939. Parke-Bernet Galleries. (Sale 130)

1940

7-8 February 1940. Parke-Bernet Galleries. (Sale 171)

1942

28-29 October 1942. Parke-Bernet Galleries. (Sale 398)

446

1944

20 January 1944. Swann Auction Galleries. Titus C. Geesey. (Sale 70)

1946

4-5 November 1946. Parke-Bernet Galleries. (Sale 802)

1947

12-13 May 1947. Parke-Bernet Galleries. (Sale 871)

6-7 November 1947. Swann Auction Galleries. Alfred F. Goldsmith. (Sale 190)

1948

11-12 October 1948. Parke-Bernet Galleries. (Sale 990)

1949

9-10 November 1949. Kende Galleries. Arthur Pforzheimer.

1950

30-31 October-1 November 1950. Parke-Bernet Galleries. Oliver R. Barrett. (Sale 1190)

1951

4-5 April 1951. Swann Auction Galleries. M. Robert Dorn. (Sale 285)

3-4 December 1951. Parke-Bernet Galleries. Edward Hubert Litchfield. (Sale 1292)

1952

29-30 January 1952. Parke-Bernet Galleries. (Sale 1309)

1953

3 December 1953. Swann Auction Galleries. (Sale 367)

1954

7-8 December 1954. Parke-Bernet Galleries. (Sale 1556)

1955

1-2 March 1955. Parke-Bernet Galleries. (Sale 1574)

1-2 November 1955. Parke-Bernet Galleries. Henry S. Borneman. (Sale 1620)

22 November 1955. Parke-Bernet Galleries. (Sale 1626)

1960

    13-14 January 1960. Swann Galleries. (Sale 537)

1963

    12 November 1963. Sotheby & Co. The American Academy of Arts and Letters.

    3 December 1963. Parke-Bernet Galleries. Gen. Culver C. Sniffen. (Sale 2235)

1968

    25 January 1968. Swann Galleries. (Sale 750)

INDEX

452

Whitman, Walt (continued)

Whitman, Walt
Manuscripts (continued)

Whitman, Walt
Works (continued)

468